FANNY BURNEY

Fanny Burney

A Biography

CLAIRE HARMAN

HarperCollins*Publishers*

HarperCollins*Publishers*
77–85 Fulham Palace Road,
Hammersmith, London W6 8JB
www.**fire**and**water**.com

Published by HarperCollins*Publishers* 2000

Copyright © Claire Harman 2000

1 3 5 7 9 8 6 4 2

The author asserts the moral right to
be identified as the author of this work

A catalogue record for this book
is available from the British Library

I S B N 0 00 255690 1

Set in PostScript Linotype Minion by
Rowland Phototypesetting Ltd, Bury St Edmunds, Suffolk

Printed and bound in Great Britain by
Omnia Books Limited, Glasgow

To my mother and my father

CONTENTS

ILLUSTRATIONS

Fanny Burney at the age of thirty, painted at Chesington Hall by her cousin Edward Francesco Burney in the summer of 1782. *(From the Collection at Parham Park, West Sussex)*

Dr Charles Burney, by Sir Joshua Reynolds (1781). *(By courtesy of The National Portrait Gallery, London)*

Fanny's mother, Esther Sleepe Burney. *(Collection of Paula Peyraud)*

Mrs Elizabeth Allen of King's Lynn, by an unknown artist. *(Collection of Professor Lars Troide)*

The Burneys' house at the corner of St Martin's Street and Long's Close (1811). *(By courtesy of The National Portrait Gallery, London)*

A view looking north into the observatory at the top of the house. *(By courtesy of The National Portrait Gallery, London)*

Samuel Crisp, by Edward Francesco Burney (1782). *(By courtesy of The National Portrait Gallery, London)*

David Garrick in 1769. *(From the Collection at Parham Park, West Sussex)*

Drury Lane Theatre in 1775. (Mary Evans Picture Library)

Fanny's younger brother Charles, painted by Daniel Gardner. *(By courtesy of The National Portrait Gallery, London)*

Fanny's sister Susan.

A miniature of Fanny Burney painted by John Bogle in 1783. *(Collectoin of Paula Peyraud)*

Hetty Burney with her cousin Charles Rousseau Burney (later her husband) and uncle Richard Burney, the dancing-master. *(Collection of J.R.G. Comyn/By courtesy of The National Portrait Gallery, London)*

A masquerade at Mrs Corneley's in Soho Square. *(By courtesy of The National Portrait Gallery, London)*

Dr Burney in Charles Lorraine Smith's 'A Sunday Concert' (1782). *(The Trustees of the British Museum)*

Joshua Reynolds's portrait of Hester Thrale and her daughter Queeney, painted in the late 1770s. *(Gift of Lord Beaverbrook, The Beaverbrook Art Gallery, Fredericton, N.B., Canada)*

Samuel Johnson, by Thomas Trotter (1782). *(Henry W. and Albert A. Berg Collection, The New York Public Library, Astor, Lenox and Tilden Foundations)*

The burning of Newgate Prison during the Gordon Riots of June 1780. *(From Old and New London by Walter Thornbury, London, 1897)*

James Burney, by Joseph Nollekens. *(Henry W. and Albert A. Berg Collection, The New York Public Library, Astor, Lenox and Tilden Foundations)*

John Webber's reconstruction of *The Death of Captain Cook*. *(Image Library, State Library of New South Wales)*

Queen Charlotte, by William Beechey. *(The Royal Collection © 2000, Her Majesty Queen Elizabeth II)*

The Royal Terrace at Windsor Castle in 1783. *(The Royal Collection © 2000, Her Majesty Queen Elizabeth II)*

James Gillray's caricature of George III and Queen Charlotte, 'Temperance enjoying a Frugal Meal'. *(The Trustees of The British Museum)*

'The Trial of Warren Hastings in Westminster Hall', engraving by R. Pollard after E. Dayes. *(Hulton Getty)*

Mary Delany, by John Opie. *(By courtesy of The National Portrait Gallery, London)*

Frederica Locke, by Dowman.

Norbury Park soon after its completion in the 1770s.

Alexandre Piochard d'Arblay, a pencil drawing thought to be by William Locke junior (c.1792–3). *(By courtesy of The National Portrait Gallery, London)*

Germaine de Staël, by Gérard. *(Château de Coppet, Switzerland/AKG, London)*

Monsieur d'Arblay's sketch plan of the interior of Camilla Cottage. *(Henry W. and Albert A. Berg Collection, The New York Public Library, Astor, Lenox and Tilden Foundations)*

Alexander d'Arblay. *(By courtesy of The National Portrait Gallery, London)*

Carl and Horace Vernet's portrait of d'Arblay. *(From the Collection at Parham Park, West Sussex)*

Dr Burney in old age, by John Nixon. *(Christies Images)*

Charlotte Broome. *(By courtesy of The National Portrait Gallery, London)*

Fanny's favourite niece and executrix Charlotte Barrett. *(Henry W. and Albert A. Berg Collection, The New York Public Library, Astor, Lenox and Tilden Foundations)*

Portrait of Frances Burney, by an unknown artist. *(Private collection/by courtesy of The National Portrait Gallery, London)*

BURNEY FAMILY TREE

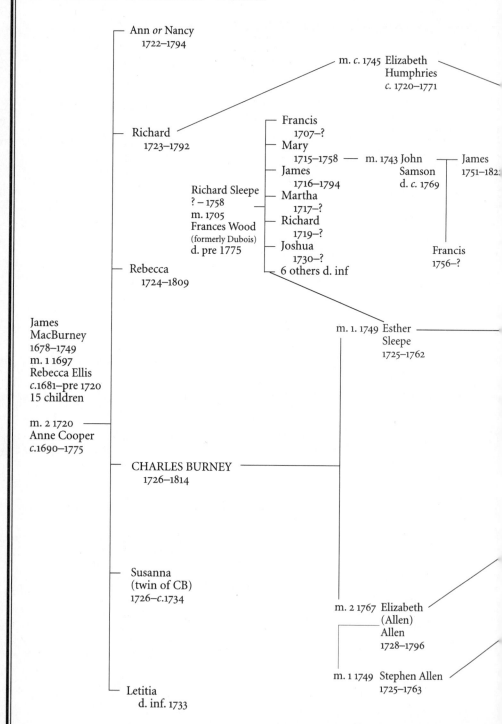

Ann *or* Nancy
1722–1794

Richard
1723–1792

m. *c.* 1745 Elizabeth
Humphries
c. 1720–1771

Francis
1707–?

Mary
1715–1758 —— m. 1743 John
Samson
d. *c.* 1769

James
1751–182:

James
1716–1794

Martha
1717–?

Richard
1719–?

Richard Sleepe
? – 1758
m. 1705
Frances Wood
(formerly Dubois)
d. pre 1775

Joshua
1730–?

6 others d. inf

Francis
1756–?

Rebecca
1724–1809

James
MacBurney
1678–1749
m. 1 1697
Rebecca Ellis
*c.*1681–pre 1720
15 children

m. 2 1720
Anne Cooper
*c.*1690–1775

m. 1. 1749 Esther
Sleepe
1725–1762

CHARLES BURNEY
1726–1814

Susanna
(twin of CB)
1726–*c.*1734

m. 2 1767 Elizabeth
(Allen)
Allen
1728–1796

m. 1 1749 Stephen Allen
1725–1763

Letitia
d. inf. 1733

James
d.inf.1747
Charles Rousseau
1747–1819
Anne *or* Nancy
1749–1819
Richard Gustavus
1751–1790
James Adolphus
1753–1798
Elizabeth Warren
('Blue')
1755–1832
Rebecca
1758–1835
Edward Francesco
1760–1848
Thomas Frederick
1765–1785

m. 1770 Ether Burney
(see below)
m. 1781 Revd John Hawkins
post 1735–1804

m. 1788 William Sandford
1759–1823

Hannah Maria
1772–1856
Richard Allen
1773–1836
Charles Crisp
1774–1791
Frances
1776–1828
Sophia Elizabeth
1777–1856
Henry
1781–d.inf.
Cecilia Charlotte Esther
1788–1821
Amelia Maria
1792–1868

Catherine
1786–1793
Martin Charles
1788–1852
Sarah
1796–*post* 1868

Ether (Hetty)
1749–1832
James
1750–1821
Charles
1751–1752
FRANCES
1752–1840
Charles
1753?–1754
Susanna Elizabeth
1755–1800
Charles
1757–1817
Henry Edward
d. inf. 1760
Charlotte Ann
1761–1838

m. 1770 Charles R. Burney
(see above)
m. 1785 Sarah Payne
1758–1832

m. 1793 Alexandre-Jean-
Baptiste Piochard
d'Arblay
1754–1818
m. 1782 Molesworth Phillips
1755–1832
m. 1783 Sarah Rose
1759–1821
m. 1 1786 Clement Francis
*c.*1744–1792
m. 2 1798 Ralph Broome
1742–1805
m.   1787 Jane Ross
1772–1842

Alexander Charles
Louis Piochard
1794–1837
Frances
1782–1860
Charles Norbury
1785–1814
John William James
1791–1832
Charles Parr
1785–1864
Charlotte
1786–1870
Marianne
1790–1832
Clement Robert
1792–1829
Ralph (Dolph)
1801–1817

Richard Thomas
1768–1808
Sarah Harriet
1772–1844

Richard
1790–1845
Henry
1792–1845
Caroline Jane
1802–1871
Thomas
1806–1846
?12 others, including
5 d. inf.

Maria Allen
1751–1820
Stephen Allen
1755–1847
Elizabeth Allen
1761–*c.*1826

m. 1772 Martin Folkes Rishton
*c.*1747–1820
m. 1772 Susanna Sharpin
1755–1816
m. 1 1777 Samuel Meeke
d. *c.*1796
m. 2 (BY 1797) ____ Bruce

Stephen
*c.*1775–1855
Edward
1777–1815
Elizabeth Mary
1779–1801
9 others

ACKNOWLEDGEMENTS

I would like to thank the following for their assistance with my research: the Librarians and staff of the British Library, the London Library, the New York Public Library, the Bodleian Library, the Guildhall Library, the Library of Westminster Abbey, the Corporation of London Record Office, the Public Record Office, the London Metropolitan Archives, City of Westminster Archives Centre and Surrey History Centre. Tina Fisk and other members of staff of the Heinz Archive of the National Portrait Gallery were particularly helpful in the location and identification of pictures, as was Susanna Kerr of the Scottish National Portrait Gallery.

I am indebted to Professor Lars Troide of the Burney Project at McGill University for his hospitality and interest in my research, Mrs Wendy Chapman of Norbury Park, Mickleham, Sonja Rewhorn of Juniper Hall Field Studies Centre, Mr Archie Stirling, Rosemary Rendell of the Catholic Records Society and John Martin Robinson of the Georgian Group. I would also like to thank John and Cynthia Comyn not only for permission to reproduce the portrait of Hetty Burney, Charles Rousseau Burney and Richard Burney in their possession but for their hospitality and generous access to their collection of Burney papers.

I discussed many of the ideas in this book with Scott Ashley, whose unflagging interest in the project was immensely encouraging. I would like to thank him and also Annie Bartlett, Sandie Byrne, Lorna Clark, Lyndall Gordon, Georgina Hammick, Roger Lonsdale, Patrick McGuinness, Jaqueline Pearson, Donald Scragg, Kathryn Sutherland and Neil Waddell for their assistance in various ways.

During a computing crisis, Lynne Munro of the Oxford University Computing Centre and John Birtill rescued a large amount of text from virtual death. I am very grateful to them both, and to Charles Schmidt, who helped transcribe parts of obsolete Amstradiana.

At HarperCollins, I would like to thank my editors Richard Johnson and Robert Lacey and picture researcher Cathie Arrington.

ACKNOWLEDGEMENTS

During the writing of this book I was the recipient of a Wingate Scholarship and a grant from the Royal Literary Fund, and would like to record my gratitude to the trustees of both.

PREFACE

Dr Johnson: Ay, never mind what she says. Don't you know she is a writer of romances?
Sir Joshua Reynolds: She may write romances and speak truth.[1]

By dint of outliving her parents, five siblings, husband and child, the novelist Fanny Burney (then Madame d'Arblay) became the caretaker of a vast quantity of family papers in her later years. Her father's archive alone seemed at one point to be taking over her life, for, as she discovered when she began to sort through his literary remains in the 1820s, he seemed to have 'kept, unaccountably, All his Letters, however uninteresting, ceremonious, momentary, or unmeaning'. She destroyed quantities of these papers and edited the remaining ones ruthlessly using scissors and heavy black ink; a process she applied to her own archive in the last decade of her life and which was continued after her death by her niece and literary executrix Charlotte Barrett, who pasted over more than a thousand passages in Madame d'Arblay's diary, and cut out or deleted many others.

Millions of words remain, nevertheless, in tens of thousands of family letters, diaries, memoirs, drafts, notebooks, manuscripts and Fanny Burney's famous journal covering the period from 1768 until shortly before her death in 1840. The historical and literary importance of the Burney papers was recognised early on. Fanny Burney was one of the best-known and most highly respected novelists of her generation, whose 'uncommonly fine compositions'[2] had been admired by writers as diverse as Jane Austen and Lord Byron. She had also led a long and eventful life which brought her into contact with some of the most famous men and women of her time; David Garrick, Samuel Johnson, Hester Thrale, Joshua Reynolds, Richard Sheridan, Edmund Burke, Warren Hastings, Madame de Staël, Talleyrand, Châteaubriand, Napoleon. She was a member of the

Royal Household during the period of George III's 'madness' in 1788 and a refugee in Brussels during the Battle of Waterloo: she had been an intimate of Dr Johnson in the 1780s, yet lived long enough to meet Sir Walter Scott. When the *Diary and Letters of Madame d'Arblay* were published in seven volumes between 1842 and 1846, she began a new posthumous career as the leading journalist of the Georgian age.

The first edition of the *Diary and Letters* was a re-editing, with some deletions, of Burney's own selection, bequeathed to Charlotte Barrett in 1839 'with full and free permission . . . to keep or destroy',[3] though Burney must have calculated that the loyal and scholarly 'Charlottina' was unlikely to destroy much. The diaries have been in print ever since, in one form or another. Some editions, like Christopher Lloyd's,[4] were short and sweet, presenting Fanny Burney as a sentimental Regency 'miss'; others, like Austen Dobson's of 1904, attempted to put the work in its historical context. Annie Raine Ellis's 1889 edition of the *Early Diary* (using material not touched by Mrs Barrett, who began her selection with the publication of *Evelina* in 1778) was remarkable for its thoroughness and completeness: she included everything she could read of the mauled manuscripts (cut away and pasted over by several generations of the author's heirs) and included excerpts from Susan and Charlotte Burney's papers as well.

Ellis's approach prefigured that of modern scholars, who have laboured to recover every obliteration by means of the latest x-ray and photographic technology. The Burney Project at McGill University is dedicated to this task, which has been going on for some thirty years and is not yet within sight of an end. Joyce Hemlow, the great Burney scholar and biographer, brought out the first of what she expected to be a ten-volume edition of Fanny Burney's *Journals and Letters* in 1972. In the event, she oversaw the publication of twelve volumes between that date and 1984 and the present team (under Professor Lars Troide) has published three of a projected further ten volumes of the *Early Journals and Letters*. Recently there have also been scholarly editions of Fanny Burney's plays (all but one unperformed in her lifetime), Sarah Harriet Burney's letters, Charles Burney's letters and fragmentary manuscript memoirs, and there are plans to publish the letters of Susan Burney and possibly of Charlotte Burney too. By the time the Burney Project has exhausted its rich mine of material, we will know more about this logomaniac tribe and their associates than any other eighteenth-century family.

The very length and thoroughness of Fanny Burney's journals and letters enforce their standing as a trustworthy record, but while they provide almost unrivalled documentation of fact, they also represent a huge input of authorial control over the interpretation of her life. Basically, a writer who seems to leave no stone unturned is not inviting interpretation at all. 'Mystery provokes Enquiry', as Burney herself warned her cousin Rebecca Sandford[5] when she was arguing to keep intact the text of her forthcoming *Memoirs of Doctor Burney* – a book which, as we shall see, provides countless examples of the manipulation and invention of biographical fact. Burney's nephew Richard was anxious about the book exposing the family's humble origins, or, more specifically, *his* humble origins, since he had omitted to tell either his wife of twenty years or the College of Arms (when he was applying for armorial bearings in 1807) of his grandmother's 'undignified Birth', not to mention – if he knew of it – his own mother's illegitimacy. Fanny's refusal to withdraw the *Memoirs* might seem to cast her in the role of fearless truth-teller on this occasion, but her motive was far more to avoid provoking Enquiry than to dispel 'mystery' *per se*. Her version of her father's life may not have been the whole truth, but it was *full*: everything seemed to be accounted for. As a way of controlling information about the family it was highly effective; as proof of Fanny's veracity it left much to be desired.

The *Memoirs* have consistently been viewed as an aberration, both of style and technique, an embarrassing filial rhapsody written by a woman in her dotage. Biographers look to Burney's diaries (especially the early ones) as much purer sources of information: 'we never turn from the Memoirs to the Diary without a sense of relief', Thomas Macaulay wrote in his well-known essay on Madame d'Arblay; 'the difference is as great as the difference between the atmosphere of a perfumer's shop, fetid with lavender water and jasmine soap, and the air of a heath on a fine morning in May'.[6] But since *Memoirs of Doctor Burney* was essentially Madame d'Arblay's autobiography, based on and superseding her journals, they cannot be dismissed quite so readily. Nor does Macaulay's delight in the heathy freshness of the *Diary* acknowledge the artificiality of the form which we take to show Fanny Burney at her most open and truthful. Burney began her diary in March 1768, aged fifteen, with a famous address to Nobody, surely one of the most self-conscious, attention-grabbing pieces of supposedly confidential writing ever composed:

> To have some account of my thoughts, manners, acquaintance & actions, when the Hour arrives in which time is more nimble than memory, is the reason which induces me to keep a Journal: a Journal in which I must confess my *every* thought, must open my whole Heart! But a thing of this kind ought to be addressed to somebody – I must imagion myself to be talking – talking to the most intimate of friends – to one in whom I should take delight in confiding, & remorse in concealment: but who must this friend be? – to make choice of one to whom I can but *half* rely, would be to frustrate entirely the intention of my plan. . . . To whom, then, *must* I dedicate my wonderful, surprising & interesting adventures? – to *whom* dare I reveal my private opinion of my nearest Relations? the secret thoughts of my dearest friends? my own hopes, fears, reflections & dislikes? – Nobody!
>
> To Nobody, then, will I write my Journal! since To Nobody can I be wholly unreserved – to Nobody can I reveal every thought, every wish of my Heart, with the most unlimited confidence, the most unremitting sincerity to the end of my Life![7]

Behind the elaborate joke of this is the admission that the whole enterprise is unsound, that there is, literally, *nobody* with whom the diarist can be completely unguarded.

On matters of 'unlimited confidence' and 'unremitting sincerity' Burney was, like all diary-writers, on shaky ground. Matters of fact, on the other hand, she felt to be her forte. Fanny Burney was blessed with a phenomenal memory and could repeat back quantities of conversation on one hearing, as if, as her father joked, 'you carry Bird Lime in your Brains – for every Thing that lights there, sticks'.[8] This knack seems to have had an affinity with her sister Hetty's prodigious ability to transcribe or play back pieces of music (Hetty amazed the composer Sacchini in 1773 by playing from memory the overture to his new opera *Il Cid*, which had not yet been published).[9] When Fanny memorised speech, the sound of the words was pivotal: 'my memory was not more stored with the very words than my voice with the intonations of all that had passed', she said when recalling part of the trial of Warren Hastings.[10] On another occasion she wrote of a friend's speech-mannerisms, 'I think, if possible, his Language looks more absurd upon Paper even than it sounds in conversation, from the perpetual recurrence of the same words', which suggests that she was transcribing from memory word for word. This wasn't the only way Fanny Burney recorded speech – sometimes she remembered the argument and reconstructed the wording more loosely (I have included an interesting example of this process at work in her recollection of Warren Hastings' trial in the Appendix) – nor was her diary always freshly written, however spontaneous it sounds. She came to rely on 'writing up' her journal – sometimes at a distance of weeks or months – using notes she had jotted down on erasable ivory tablets. There was some element of hindsight at work in almost all her autobiographical writing.

Fanny Burney's phenomenal powers of memory may well have made her overconfident about her own rightness, which she extended from being reliable in matters of fact to being correct in interpretation. Even in her own lifetime, some people thought Fanny Burney too much of a novelist to be taken seriously as a historian or biographer, and when in her later years she published *Memoirs of Doctor Burney*, the critic John Wilson Croker thought her 'recollections' betrayed 'consummate art – or a confusion of ideas which has had the same effect'.[11] More damningly, several readers who had personal knowledge of people and events mentioned in the *Memoirs* objected very strongly to Fanny's version. Her stepbrother Stephen Allen leapt to the defence of his mother, the second Mrs Charles Burney (who, as we shall see, came off extremely badly in the *Memoirs*), and Mrs Delany's ex-servant, Anne Agnew, felt the portrait of her former mistress so faulty that the author 'must fancy she was writing a novel and therefore could embellish her story in any way she liked'.[12] In the light of these criticisms, the affectionate joke that Samuel Johnson made about Fanny back in the 1780s rings a little hollow: '[N]ever mind what she says. Don't you know she is a writer of romances?'[13]

Ironically, Madame d'Arblay prided herself on her 'reverence for truth';[14] indeed she seems to have been obsessed with it. 'I can use no softer term than Defamation for the least attack upon my veracity', she wrote defiantly during the row with Stephen Allen following the publication of the *Memoirs*. Joyce Hemlow, the author of the first scholarly biography of Fanny Burney in 1958, defended her subject's veracity rather weakly on the grounds that:

While she did not always tell the full truth about some of the family difficulties, sins, and errors, she did not tell un-truths. As a biography, therefore the *Memoirs* is limited by the point of view and selection of material, but within its limits it is authoritative, and more authoritative than anything else written on Dr Burney, or likely to be written. It is based on knowledge that no other biographer can hope to have.[15]

This was surely exactly the response Fanny wanted to provoke: no one could 'know more' about her father than she did, and any sins of omission she may have committed by suppression of certain facts were in the cause of filial piety and family privacy, and therefore excusable. Unsurprisingly, biographers of Charles Burney have taken a less charitable view of Fanny's tampering with the evidence. Roger Lonsdale claims, very plausibly, that the effect is sometimes 'to destroy the true nature of [Charles] Burney's personality',[16] and concludes that Fanny was 'consciously dishonest' at times, to the effect that she 'cannot be trusted'.[17]

It seems likely that the experience of going through her father's papers in the last twenty years of her life made Madame d'Arblay acutely aware of the problem of how to control her own posterity. She was shocked to find how much the self-portrait that emerged of her father differed from her own view of him and decided to 'set the record straight'. This led to a general overhaul of her own 'record' too. Fanny's account in the *Memoirs* of her first meeting with Dr Johnson and Mrs Thrale on 20 March 1777, originally described in a letter to her elderly mentor Samuel Crisp, provides one of innumerable examples of how she rewrote biographical evidence to suit her own purposes better. In the *Memoirs*, the letter she quotes as offering 'genuine detail' of the occasion is an elaborate augmentation of the original. It is fascinating not just as an example of hindsight and score-settling (particularly in the material relating to Mrs Thrale) but of Fanny exercising an assumed right to shape her material; you can see in it both a novelist's anxiety to convey character and a memoirist's concern not to look foolish in his private and peremptory judgements. This particular letter was a prime candidate for careful polishing up, affording Fanny the opportunity to set in stone her 'first impressions' of the great man. Much of what she adds in her later version is decorative. Johnson arrived at the Burneys' house in St Martin's Street later than the other guests (Mrs Thrale, Miss Thrale, their cousin Miss

Owen and the writer William Seward), disturbing the performance of a duet by Fanny's sisters Hetty and Susan. Johnson was no music-lover, and was even more short-sighted than Fanny or her father. Instead of sitting and listening to the duet, he drew his chair up to the harpsichord and '*poked his Nose* over the keys', as Fanny related in her original letter, expanding her description by several paragraphs in the *Memoirs* to include an account of her sisters' discomfort at his behaviour and William Seward's amusement at it. At other points in the *Memoirs* version, a few cracks begin to show. Not only does Fanny add a great deal more detail about Johnson's uncouth appearance – 'He is, indeed, very ill-favoured' – but queerly apologises for noticing it at all, apparently addressing Crisp thus:

> But you always charge me to write without reserve or reservation, and so I obey as usual. Else, I should be ashamed to acknowledge having remarked such exterior blemishes in so exalted a character.[18]

The description of Mrs Thrale – with whom Fanny later had a famous friendship and an even more famous quarrel – is brief in the original 1777 letter:

> Mrs Thrale is a very pretty woman still, – she is extremely lively and chatty, – has no supercilious or pedantic airs, & is really gay and agreeable.[19]

In the letter quoted in the *Memoirs* this becomes a whole paragraph, with the superlative removed from 'pretty' and the following qualification added: 'though she has some defect in the mouth that looks like a cut, or scar'. Giving with one hand in the revamp ('she is full of sport, remarkably gay, and excessively agreeable'), Fanny is all too ready to take away with the other:

> I liked her in every thing except her entrance into the room, which was rather florid and flourishing, as who should say, 'It's I! – no less a person than Mrs. Thrale!' However, all that ostentation wore out in the course of the visit, which lasted the whole morning; and you could not have helped liking her, she is so very entertaining – though not simple enough, I believe, for quite winning your heart.

The last part of that sentence points up a bizarre aspect of Fanny's rewrite: its ostentatious address to Samuel Crisp. Like almost everyone else mentioned in the original letter, Crisp was long dead by the time Fanny produced her new, longer version, but if anything, she invokes his goodwill and solicits his approval more in the false letter than in the real one. The futility of introducing such material is rather striking. Other sentimental tributes include an interpolation after the mention of the duet played by Hetty and Susan. Not only does Fanny adjust her elder sister's name to the familiar 'your Hettina' (and use the opportunity to insert a jibe against the Thrale party's lack of musical appreciation), she adds a convoluted and archly-worded eulogy to her father and Crisp: 'But every knowledge is not given to every body – except to two gentle wights of my acquaintance; the one commonly hight il Padre, and the other il Dadda. Do you know of any such sort of people, Sir?' Crisp's answer, had he lived to read this, would have been a firm *No*, since Fanny never addressed him in her real letters in quite such gushingly intimate terms (though it is possible of course that she *spoke* like this).

Making up 'private correspondence' specifically for publication is a fairly unusual way of asserting one's authority as a truthful historian. It gives some idea of the lengths to which Fanny Burney would go to create a strong enough impression of what she considered to be the truth. Perhaps it comes as no surprise that none of the best-known stories about her life bears close inspection; each is riddled with contradictory statements, inconsistencies, evidence of editing or elaboration. In the light of this, the extensiveness of the Burney papers begins to look less like a gift to a biographer than an intolerable burden. One begins to long for lacunae like those Cassandra Austen so thoughtfully provided for posterity when she burned her sister Jane's private papers. And as the Burney archive continues to grow with the recovering of more and more formerly obliterated material, the problem becomes even more complicated. It is fairly obvious in most cases why particular passages in the family papers were suppressed – dullness, scandal, a hasty judgement, a literary blemish – but the reasons why others were rejected remain obscure, or worse, seem trivial. Trivial erasures are the most disturbing of all: the subjectivity of the whole procedure comes sharply before us.

Should we worry about Madame d'Arblay's second and third thoughts? Are they not as likely to get us near the truth as her original statements did, for all her claims to being able to act like an eighteenth-century form of tape-recorder? As one pores over the details of her life, finding inconsistencies in the record, what is a biographer to make of this strangely creative autobiographer? Is she an inveterate liar, or an inveterate writer? I hope to demonstrate in this interpretation of her life that the layers of autobiographical information left by 'a writer of romances' may not be equally trustworthy, but can be equally significant. Fanny Burney understood intuitively that remembering things is a cumulative process, even a collective process, which the act of putting into words helps to arrest. Things didn't 'happen' to Burney until she had put them into words. She then, typically, went on to find more words, and more again. By unpicking the layers of that record we may hope to see more clearly how her anxious and active imagination worked.

A NOTE ON NOMENCLATURE

Names and problems of identity are centrally important in all Fanny Burney's novels, which makes it rather ironic that the name of the author herself has become a contentious issue. None of her novels revealed her name on the title page – her first novel did not even sport the conventional tag 'By a Lady', and the subsequent ones were attributed to 'the author of Evelina', etc. *Memoirs of Doctor Burney* 'by his Daughter, Madame d'Arblay', was the only work she signed in her lifetime. Her diaries, published posthumously, were attributed to 'Madame d'Arblay' until the publication in 1889 of the *Early Diary*, which introduced her baptismal name 'Frances Burney'. 'Fanny Burney', the name by which she was known familiarly until her marriage in 1793 and to the world through Johnsoniana, was adopted in the title of Austin Dobson's 1903 biography and was used extensively by critics and biographers during the twentieth century, including the eminent Burney scholar, biographer and editor Joyce Hemlow. This is the name under which the Burney Project is publishing her *Journals and Letters* and *Early Journals and Letters* even though a number of critics, notably and most eloquently Margaret Anne Doody, have been arguing since the 1980s that the diminutive is a patronising form which should no longer be tolerated. 'It makes the author sound the harmless, childish, priggish girl-woman that many critics want her to be', Doody has written. 'Let her have an adult full name'.[20]

But which 'adult full name'? It comes in many forms, making the search for material in catalogues and indexes peculiarly time-consuming. She is variously listed under A [Arblay], B [Burney] and D [d'Arblay], sometimes, as in the London Library, under all three. As preparations are made to raise a memorial to the author in Westminster Abbey, an ardent debate is taking place among members of the Burney Society on both sides of the Atlantic as to which name will appear, with the threat of an absurd compromise: 'Frances (Fanny) Burney d'Arblay'.[21] Bibliographical convention would dictate the use of her name at death, Frances d'Arblay, but no one seems happy with that; it is unfamiliar. Similarly, though 'Frances Burney' is used on the title pages of several modern reprints of her novels, 'correctness' rarely extends as far as the cover, where the author is most often still known as 'Fanny Burney', presumably because it is more recognisable to the reading public.

I have decided to use the latter style (interspersed with her married name in the later part of her life), despite the danger of appearing overfamiliar. In a work of criticism, I feel that the more formal 'Burney' or 'Frances Burney' would be correct throughout; in a biography, that deals with a subject from earliest childhood, the informal name is often more appropriate. I have also used familiar versions of some names within the Burney family which are subject to confusion through multiple use; to distinguish between Fanny's mother and sister I have called the first Esther and second Hetty, and have used the familiar shortening of Susanna Burney's name to Susan and Frederica Locke's to Fredy on the grounds that they were Fanny Burney's intimates. Her father is called Charles Burney (Dr Burney after 1769), her brother Charles Burney Junior (although he too gained a doctorate in 1808). Her husband is referred to as d'Arblay or M. d'Arblay, and their son, who was given the anglicised form of his father's Christian name, as Alex.

❧ 1 ❧

A Low Race of Mortals

'The Burneys are I believe a very low Race of Mortals', wrote Dr Johnson's confidante Hester Thrale in February 1779 of her daughter's music master and his family. The remark was scribbled in the margin of her journal as a gloss on her opinion that Dr Burney's second daughter, Fanny, was 'not a Woman of Fashion'.[1] This was such an obvious thing to say about twenty-six-year-old Fanny Burney that it hardly bore mentioning, unless from mild spite. The Burneys were indeed not 'people of Fashion'; they were representative of the coming class, the intelligentsia; self-made, self-educated, self-conscious people in uneasy amity with their wealthy and well-born patrons. No doubt those patrons found it obliquely threatening that a 'low race' could produce so many high achievers: in 1779 Dr Burney, author, composer and teacher, was halfway through publishing his ground-breaking *General History of Music*; Fanny had shot to fame the previous year with her first novel, *Evelina*; another of the Burney daughters was a famous harpsichordist; and one of the sons had circumnavigated the world with Captain Cook. The Burneys, and people like them, had every reason to think they were being admired rather than sneered at.

There had been no patrimony, titles or property to smooth Dr Burney's path in life; he had achieved his position through a combination of natural genius and unstinting hard work, his eye forever on the main chance, his 'spare person' worn to a ravelling. Mrs Thrale claimed not to understand the devotion Burney inspired in his children – ''tis very seldom that a person's own family will give him Credit for Talents which bring in no money to make them fine or considerable',[2] she wrote in her diary; but what was 'no money' to Mrs Thrale was riches to the Burneys, just as their reception among the 'Great folks' – at her own house, Streatham Park, for instance – was more than enough to make them feel 'considerable'. Fanny Burney's pride in the insignificant-looking man who had effected these miracles was boundless, and she saw no absurdity in describing her father as the powerful 'trunk' of the Burney tree.[3] Charles Burney had so successfully overcome his humble background that he really did seem to have sprung up from nowhere and to have started his family history afresh.

One of the Doctor's other harpsichord pupils in 1779 (they were all young ladies 'of Fashion') had told Mrs Thrale that 'these Burney's are Irish people I'm sure; Mac Burneys they used to be called'.[4] Where the girl picked up this information one can hardly imagine, unless through class instinct; the Doctor did not advertise his changed name. Charles MacBurney, as he was first known, was born in Shrewsbury in 1726, the twin to a sister called Susanna and the youngest son of his father's second family. His grandfather, James, who was of Scottish or Irish descent (accounts differ), had had an estate in Shropshire and a house in Whitehall in the late seventeenth century, but by the time of Charles's birth the family money had all but disappeared. The story goes that the grandfather MacBurney was so disgusted by his son James running off with a young actress, Rebecca Ellis, that he disinherited him. The old gentleman rather perversely followed up this gesture of affronted rectitude by marrying his own cook and starting a second family, of whom the eldest son, Joseph, inherited most of the property. This son frittered his inheritance away, was imprisoned for debt and supported himself later by becoming a dancing-master; but despite his fall from grace and wealth, he seemed happy with his lot (or so Charles Burney, his half-nephew, thought when they met in the 1750s), and that branch of the family was noted for its cheerfulness and striking good looks.

The outcast older brother James and his teenaged bride Rebecca had their first child in 1699 and went on to have fourteen more over the next twenty years, of whom at least nine survived. James had been expensively educated at Westminster School and had had some training in portrait painting under Michael Dahl, a fashionable Swedish portraitist who had painted the Swedish royal family as well as Queen Anne and members of the English aristocracy. James's character was not, however, one to capitalise on these advantages, being 'volatile, & improvident'.[5] He was more concerned with keeping up his reputation as a convivial dinner-guest and bon-viveur (an activity which presumably got him away from his home full of babies) than with establishing himself in any one place or profession long enough to make anything of his talents as a painter, dancer, copyist or fiddler. As one of his children recorded later, the inevitable consequence of his fecklessness was that 'his family was left to lament, that his talent for pleasantry, & love of sociability, overcame his prudential care, either for himself or them'.[6]

Poor Rebecca MacBurney, the mother of fifteen children and still only in her thirties, died, it is assumed, some time before 1720. That was the date at which James made his second marriage, to Ann Cooper of Shrewsbury, the daughter of a herald painter. A painting said to be of Ann Cooper shows a very handsome and assured young woman. She is reputed to have had a small fortune and to have turned down an offer of marriage from the poet William Wycherley;* both these things make it the more mysterious that she accepted the proposal of James MacBurney, unemployed forty-two-year-old father of nine. But MacBurney's charm was legendary, and perhaps Ann's age made a difference – she was about thirty at the time. They had six children, four of whom, Ann, Richard, Rebecca and Charles, lived to great ages. The youngest child died in infancy and Charles's twin, Susanna, at the age of about seven.

How much of a wrench the death of his twin was to the little Charles Burney is hard to tell, since he was ejected from the family at the age of three and sent with his older brother Richard to live with a woman called Ball in Condover, four miles outside Shrewsbury. He was left in the care of Nurse Ball nine years – his whole childhood – a fact which shocked his daughter Fanny when she discovered it almost ninety years later. Fanny was particularly appalled by the mother's behaviour, which she thought 'nearly unnatural',[7] and she destroyed what evidence there was of the 'niggardly unfeelingness' and neglect she felt her father had suffered. By editing the episode out of her father's papers, Fanny hoped to conceal 'a species of Family degradation' from public view; but no member of the public could have been more upset by it than she. She had known her grandmother Burney all her childhood, when the widow was living in Covent Garden with her two unmarried daughters. It must

---

* According to the 'Worcester Memoirs'. Wycherley died in 1716, aged about seventy-six, and Ann Cooper was born in 1690, but although it sounds an unlikely courtship, Wycherley in fact married a woman even younger than Ann a fortnight before his death.

have seemed astonishing that this same grandmother, so much part of the family background, had, for whatever reason, opted out of caring for her own sons all those years before. Fanny's novels are full of orphaned or abandoned children laid open to peril through lack of parental care; in them, bad parents are punished or vilified and made to repent, but Ann Burney seemed to have committed the cardinal sin of unfeeling and got off scot-free.

Charles Burney himself did not seem embittered by the long separation from his parents, although his intense affection for his own children (especially when they were little) and his apparent desire to establish a solid, admirable and outstanding Burney dynasty within one generation may have been reactions against it. The splitting up of the MacBurney family in the late 1720s was probably necessitated by lack of money. James went back to London temporarily to take up work as an actor at the new Goodman's Fields Theatre at about this time; perhaps he and his wife felt that the boys would be better off out of the way, getting some education at Condover village school. The fact that Ann Burney's later relations with her sons were detached could of course have been the effect as much as the cause of her not bringing them up herself, but Fanny seems not to have considered the kind of harsh compromises that might have to be made when a couple with five children of their own (and nine older semi-dependants) find themselves close to destitution. The threat of poverty is the most potent danger that faces the heroines of Fanny Burney's novels; all other evils stem from it. But it is also something that never really overcomes any of them. Poverty brings out the best in her heroines: they act with dignity, expand their sensitivities, and support themselves by plain sewing, teaching, governessing or becoming ladies' companions. The charting of a gentlewoman's descent into wage-earning carries a sort of illicit thrill for author and reader alike (one can say quite clearly a sexual thrill, because of the unspoken threat of prostitution, the obvious last-ditch job-opportunity for women), but *class* always ultimately protects Burney's heroines from crossing the line into 'degradation'.

In the 1740s, the MacBurneys were struggling to cross that line in the other direction. The family name was changed, soon after Charles's birth, from MacBurney (or 'Mackburny' as the twins were christened) to plain Burney. This was probably done to facilitate James's revived stage career, for as the scholar Roger Lonsdale points out, Charles Burney himself suggested the reason for another actor's name-change from McLaughlin to Macklin might have been 'to get rid not only of its Paddy appearance but of its harshness'.[8] The new name had an added significance for Charles: it marked a fresh start. Burney's later success, riding under the banner of an (as he thought) untraceable family name, became a source of profound pride to himself and his children, so important to Fanny that her stated reason for destroying most of her father's early memoirs was to protect 'the Name of Burney', even if it was only a few decades old and had started life as a professional convenience.

Charles Burney was assimilated back into his re-christened family when they moved to Chester in 1739. He had led what seems a truly happy, country-boy's life at Condover with Nurse Ball, and left her with an 'agony of grief'.[9] But the city offered obvious advantages, and at the Free School in Chester he began the musical training, as choirboy and then organist, which was to shape his life. The cathedral organist suffered from gout, and recruited the fourteen-year-old Burney as an assistant while the boy was still hardly able to read music. His success was such, both as a singer and player, that his half-brother James, who was organist of St Mary's Church in Shrewsbury, asked to have him as an assistant. Charles 'ran away' back to his native town for a couple of years, despite his parents' disapproval, but by 1744 was back in Chester, on the persuasion of his father 'who I believe, loved me very affectionately', as Charles wrote later.[10]

However fragmented their family life was at times, James MacBurney's strong paternal love and good nature held the clan together, and there were evenings of great gaiety in the household. Charles Burney inspired similar affection among his own children, recalling after one family party in later years,

> we were as merry, & laughed as loud as the Burneys always do, when they get together and open their hearts; tell their old stories, & have no fear of being *Quizzed* by interlopers. It was so in my poor dear old father's time, & my boyish days – when my brother Thomas from London – or James from Shrewsbury came on a visit to Chester, we used, young & old, Male & female, to sit up all night – not to drink, but to laugh *à gorge deployée*.[11]

5

Charles Burney's important career break came the same year (1744), when the composer Thomas Arne was passing through Chester on his way from Dublin to take up the post of composer at the Drury Lane Theatre. Arne got to hear of the diligent and talented young musician, who was already composing as well as able to play the violin, harpsichord and organ, and suggested to James Burney that the boy ought to be apprenticed to 'an eminent Master in London'. On a subsequent meeting, Arne said that he himself would take Charles for £100 down, with no further liabilities, and at a third attempt said he would take him for nothing, realising he was still getting a good deal. Delighted and grateful, the Burneys of course agreed, though Charles was to look back on the bargain with mixed feelings.

Once in London, Arne got as much out of his apprentice as possible, making him transcribe quantities of music, teach junior pupils, run errands, play in the Drury Lane band and sometimes sing in the chorus there, any payment always going straight into the master's pocket. Arne himself was passing the peak of his fame; the revival of his *Masque of Alfred* in 1745, containing the popular patriotic song 'Rule, Britannia!', was not successful, but his close connections with the capital's best musicians and actors were very valuable to young Burney, who lived with the curmudgeonly composer and his wife in Great Queen Street and attended parties with them at the house of Arne's sister, the actress Susannah Cibber. The charismatic David Garrick, who was to become a close friend of Burney, was the star of this coterie, which included Drury Lane and Covent Garden's other leading men and ladies James Quin, Peg Woffington and Kitty Clive. Burney met literary men too, through his friendship with 'the Scottish Orpheus' James Oswald, James Thomson, Tobias Smollett and Christopher Smart among them. His career as an arch-networker among London's bohemians was off to an excellent start.

As time went on, Burney became disillusioned with his apprenticeship to Arne. He was a hard worker, but his master's regime did not reward his zeal. In fact, he came to think that Arne was deliberately holding him back. He felt he was wasted and wasting almost 'into a consumption' as an amanuensis, a chore which he hated (but which, years later, he was happy to impose on his own daughters). Arne was immoral, unfriendly and unprincipled, and after two years Burney's loyalty to him had evaporated. When Fulke Greville, direct descendant of the Elizabethan poet, and 'then generally looked up to as the finest gentleman in town',[12] expressed a desire to take Burney into his employ – not as an apprentice, of course, but as a gentleman's companion and music-maker – an escape route opened. It was not possible to leave Arne immediately, but Burney began to be patronised by Greville, invited to his grand country seat, Wilbury House in Wiltshire, and taken about when Greville was in town.

Greville's style of life was lavish, 'even princely', as Fanny Burney learned from her father; he spent a great deal of time at the races or gambling clubs, at country houses or city mansions, with his outriders and entourage always on show, and two French-horn players hanging around waiting to perform 'marches and warlike movements'[13] during mealtimes. Charles Burney's position in this splendid circus was a privileged one, based as much on his affability and intelligence as on his undoubted musical skills.* Burney was treated with respect and entrusted with Greville's confidences, taking an active part in his master's dramatic elopement with the beautiful heiress and poet Frances Macartney in 1748. It was a marriage to which no one actually objected, so the secrecy was unnecessary, but it was typical of Greville that he turned his nuptials into something of an amusement, and his twenty-two-year-old companion, enjoined to give the bride away, was only too happy to act as accomplice.

Though Burney was sampling high life through his increasing involvement with Greville – who finally bought the young musician out of his articles in 1748 for a down payment to Arne of three hundred pounds – he had developed his own social circle independent of either master. He had made the acquaintance of a gentleman called William Thompson, and spent three months of 1745 at Thompson's home in Elsham, Lincolnshire, in 'one continued series of mirth, amusement & festivity'. Miss Molly Carter, with whom he was still corresponding in the year of her death, 1812, was one of the 'young ladies of the neighbourhood' with whom Burney was probably in love. She was 'very young, intelligent and handsome', as he recorded in his memoirs;[15] adding meaningly, '[I] never passed my time more pleasantly in my life'. In London, he attached himself to the household of his brother Richard, who was earning a living as a dancing-master in Hatton Garden. Both young men had fond

---

* Margaret Anne Doody's suggestion that a homosexual attraction between Greville and Burney 'does not seem impossible'[14] seems to me too far-fetched to be helpful in this connection.

memories of their uninhibited village upbringing, and probably tried to reproduce something of its freedom and jollity in the regular private dances held in Richard's house. Writing in 1806, Burney recalled 'the familiar manner in which the sexes treated each other in the hops I had seen in my early youth, in a village, where those *ballets* were literally *Country dances*, not *Contre-danse*, as the French pretend'.[16] Perhaps the same 'familiar manner' animated the Hatton Garden parties too. Certainly it was at one of them that Charles Burney met Esther Sleepe, an attractive young woman of about twenty-three. He had 'an ardent passion for her person [. . .] from the first moment I saw her to the last',[17] and Esther seems to have reciprocated his strong feelings. By the autumn of 1748 he had got her pregnant.

Esther Sleepe was an intelligent and accomplished young woman, a professional musician (at the time when she met Burney she was, unusually for her sex, a freeman of the Company of Musicians) of respectable but humble background.* Her father appears to have been Richard

---

* Esther Sleepe's parentage and date of birth are difficult to ascertain, and scholars disagree over them. She is either the 'Esther ye Daugh' of Mr Sleepe by – his Wife' born 19 May 1723 and baptised on 9 June at St Vedast, Foster Lane (Joyce Hemlow's choice), or the Hester, daughter of Richard and Frances Sleepe baptised at St Michael le Quern on 1 August 1725 (the choice of the editors of Dr Burney's memoirs). Professor Hemlow bases her decision on the information given by Esther's great-grandson, Richard Allen Burney, in his application to the College of Arms in 1807, where he names her father as 'James Sleepe of Foster Lane'. The *Memoir* editors cite the passage by Dr Burney that describes his first wife thus: 'the daughter of old Sleepe, the head of the City waits and furnisher of bands for municipal festivities, and Mrs Sleepe, the daughter of a M. Dubois, who kept a Fan Shop in Cheapside'. This encourages the identification of Esther's father as Richard Sleepe, a freeman of the Company of Musicians (as was she) and leader of the City waits (the Lord Mayor's band), who died in 1758. He married a Frances Wood in 1705, whom the *Memoir* editors reasonably assume was the daughter of the M. Dubois mentioned in Dr Burney's account, with her surname anglicised, as were those of many exiled Huguenots.[18]

The two 'Mr Sleepe's could, of course, have been one and the same person (there is no mention of the name 'James' except in the 1807 document), or they could have been brothers. It also strikes me as a strong possibility that the two registered births – of 'Esther Sleepe' (1723) and 'Hester Sleepe' (1725) respectively – were those of sisters, and that the second girl was given, as was very often the case, the name of a sibling who had died in infancy. The likelihood of 'Mr Sleepe' and 'Richard Sleepe' being the same man and Esther and Hester sisters is increased by the fact that after the Great Fire of 1666, the parish of St Michael le Quern was amalgamated with that of its neighbour, St Vedast, Foster Lane (both churches having been destroyed, and only St Vedast rebuilt – by Wren). The two girl babies were therefore baptised at the same font, two years apart, and not at two different churches, as scholars have hitherto assumed. This would favour the identification of Esther as the daughter of Richard Sleepe, d.1758, and Frances Wood (Dubois), d. before 1776, who was baptised on 1 August 1725, which I take to be correct.[19]

Professor Hemlow's alternative identification is further weakened by the uncertain reliability of

Sleepe, a jobbing musician and leader of the Lord Mayor's band, which performed at civic functions, parades and other occasions which required 'City musick', such as the laying of the foundation stone of the Mansion House.[20] Esther's mother was the daughter of a M. Dubois, probably Pierre Dubois, of an immigrant Huguenot family who kept 'a Fan Shop in Cheapside' at 43, The Poultry. The type of shop indicates some connection with musical instrument-making, since Parisian instrument-makers had no guild of their own in London at the time and 'often became members of the company of Fan-makers'.[21] No doubt it was through music-making that Richard Sleepe and Frances Dubois (who had anglicised her name to Wood) met. They were married in 1705.

In *Memoirs of Doctor Burney*, Fanny Burney gives portraits of her mother and maternal grandmother which are so idealised as to be positively irritating. Her maternal grandfather, however, comes off very badly. 'Old Sleepe' was, she roundly asserts, 'wanting in goodness, probity and conduct', leaving his daughter 'nothing to boast from parental dignity, parental opulence, nor – strange, and stranger yet to tell – parental worth'.[22] He lived until 1758, by which time he must have been at least in his seventies, and yet he does not feature in any of Fanny Burney's personal reminiscences, nor in those of her father, and he did not have anything to do with his daughter's marriage to Charles Burney in 1749. Taken with Fanny's dark hints about his reprobate nature, Sleepe's absenteeism suggests either that he had abandoned his wife and family, which was numerous, or perhaps spent time in prison. Thirteen children of the couple are recorded in the baptismal registers of three separate city parishes;* considering the extent of Blitz damage to parish records in the City, this has to be taken as a minimum number. At least six of the children must have died in infancy, because of the re-use of their Christian names; the seven possible survivors range in age from a brother eighteen

Richard Allen Burney's information. Known in the family as a snob (an accusation which seems borne out by his desire to acquire a coat of arms), Richard Allen Burney was trying to present his genealogy to the College of Arms in the best possible light. As I discuss elsewhere (see Preface), he may not have known of his own mother's illegitimacy; or if he did, he concealed it from the College. His apparent knowledge of a 'James Sleepe of Foster Lane' may have been handed down in the family (though it is odd that it disagrees with Dr Burney's version), or perhaps extrapolated, for purposes of establishing some presentable facts, from the very records which Professor Hemlow used to corroborate his evidence.

* St Ann's Blackfriars, Christ Church Greyfriars, and St Vedast and St Michael le Quern.

years older than Esther to another brother five years her junior. The only siblings of hers known to survive into the latter half of the century were a sister called Mary, born in 1715, and a brother called James, born the following year, who was maintained as a poor relation and part-time handyman by the Burneys, much-loved but referred to as if slightly simple.

Another factor that suggests that Richard Sleepe may have absconded from family life is that Esther is said to have been brought up in her maternal grandfather's household, the 'Fan Shop in Cheapside'. French was the language spoken most often there; the little girl, we read in the *Memoirs*, did not learn that language so much as 'imbibe' it.[23] Esther's grandfather Dubois was a Huguenot whose family had come to London in the great Protestant exodus following the revocation of the Edict of Nantes in 1685, but his daughter Frances, very oddly, had been brought up as a Roman Catholic and continued to practise that religion devoutly all her life. In the *Memoirs*, Fanny Burney can only account for her grandmother's religion by guessing that it was a matter of 'maternal education',[24] but if so, Frances Dubois Sleepe practised Catholicism in isolation and did not seek to pass it down to further generations.

Her influence and example were probably all the stronger for this, and, as we shall see, Charles Burney later feared Fanny might succumb to Roman Catholicism. The child of a mixed marriage in an age of bigotry, grandmother Sleepe represented a kind of ecumenical ideal: in her granddaughter's opinion, 'the inborn religion of her mind [. . .] counteracted all that was hostile to her fellow-creatures, in the doctrine of the religion of her ancestors'. She had, in Fanny's words, a nature 'so free from stain, so elementally white, that it would scarcely seem an hyperbole to denominate her an angel upon earth'.[25] Little wonder that pious Fanny tried to copy such a paragon. 'If praying for the Dead make a Roman Catholic', she wrote to her sister many years later, 'I have been one all my life'.[26] Esther Sleepe, too, believed in the power of prayer and in communion with the dead. Fanny was at pains to point out that her mother 'adhered steadily and piously through life' to the Anglican faith, but the truth is that they had both inherited a religious intensity and a degree of superstitiousness from their admired and beloved relative: they were both proud English Protestants, but said their prayers, as it were, with a pronounced French Catholic accent.*

Charles Burney's fondness for his mother-in-law, whom he loved 'as sincerely as if she had been his mother-in-blood',[30] clearly owes something to the failure of warmth from his actual 'mother-in-blood', but also reflects gratitude for Mrs Sleepe's support of her daughter through the shameful illegitimate pregnancy and beyond. Burney neither abandoned his mistress nor felt free to marry her in 1748, because of his arrangement with Greville, which had been in operation less than a year and had two more years to run. Not only would there be legal penalties applicable (in theory) if he married before 1751, but in a wider sense, Burney's hopes of promotion in life depended on staying with Greville, to whom he felt he owed a debt of gratitude for buying him out of the articles with Arne. The prospect of waiting two years to marry must have been hard for Esther and her mother to bear; the pregnancy became daily more obvious, and Burney increasingly anxious about how to broach the subject with his patron.

The Grevilles themselves had their first child, a daughter called Frances (later the famous beauty Mrs Crewe, a friend and patron of Charles Burney) in November 1748, and by the next spring were ready to depart on an elaborate foreign tour, intended to last 'some years'. They expected Burney to accompany them, and it seems, for a time at least, he felt he would have to go. He had a miniature portrait of Esther painted by the well-known artist Gervase Spencer 'just before our marriage' (though it is unlikely that Esther would have sat to any artist in the last months of her pregnancy or during the four weeks after the birth), ostensibly to take with him on the trip. Perhaps he thought she would see the expenditure of about three pounds on this memento as a gesture of commitment. It was an uncomfortable juncture; she could not have been anything other than alarmed at the prospect of her baby's father leaving the country for so long, and in such grand company.

---

* The date at which Fanny's maternal grandmother died is uncertain, and the paucity of references to her in Charles Burney's memoirs and Fanny's early diaries slightly puzzling. She was alive in 1764, when Charles Burney wrote to his daughter from Paris to 'tell your grandmothers' he had arrived safely, and dead by May 1775, when Fanny recalls in her diary how deeply she mourned for her.[27] The reference to 'writing a Letter to my Grand mama Sleepe' in July 1768[28] may be misleading, since the word 'Sleepe' has been recovered from Madame d'Arblay's emendations to her manuscript, and is possibly a simple error. Fanny was in correspondence with her other grandmother, Ann Burney (who died in October 1775), in August 1768.[29]

Boldness was not one of Charles Burney's virtues. He dithered child-ishly about how to get out of the projected Italian tour, dropping hints to the Grevilles that he was in love, and looking gloomy. His child, a girl they named Esther, was born on 24 May 1749. Burney always doted on children, and perhaps the sight of his first-born and his vulnerable, patient mistress had a catalysing effect. He knew he couldn't really leave them, and to introduce the subject in conversation with the Grevilles, he showed them the portrait of his sweetheart (not mentioning the baby, of course). There are indications that the aristocratic young couple found his melancholic behaviour a bit of a joke. Their light-hearted dismissal of his problem when it finally got an airing was to ask why he didn't marry her. 'May I?' Burney asked, delighted at getting permission so easily. He and Esther were married the very next day, at St George's Chapel, Hyde Park Corner, a popular venue for shotgun nuptials.

The critic Margaret Anne Doody has pointed out how significant this incident is in terms of Burney's later example to his children, all of whom preferred devious or passive means of problem-solving to direct action. The idea of gaining permission and not offending one's superiors became ingrained in the family ethos; as Doody says: 'Charles was to inculcate in his children the pervasive dread of offending someone whose permission should be asked, and he indicates some unwitting enjoyment of being the person who had power to give or withhold permission from his children, the only group to whom he could give it and to whom he need not apply for it.'[31] This 'pervasive dread' was felt most sharply and most destructively by his second daughter, Fanny. Even when she was sixty-two years old, Fanny did not dare address her father 'contrary to orders' as he lay dying: '[t]he long habits of obedience of olden times robbed me of any courage for trying so dangerous an experiment'.[32]

When the Grevilles went off to Italy in the summer of 1749, Burney was left to fend for himself and his young family. He had not lost Greville's goodwill, but the patronage had gone, and from the splendours of Wil-bury House Burney had to adjust to life as organist of St Dionis's Back-church in Fenchurch Street. He had taken over payment of the rent on Mrs Sleepe's fan shop at Easter 1749, and may have been living there with Esther as man and wife some time before their wedding in June. His father died around the same time, and it was perhaps as early as this year that his mother and sisters Ann and Rebecca came from Shropshire to live over the shop at Gregg's Coffee House in York Street,* run by a kinswoman, Elizabeth Gregg. Female dependants became, from this period onwards, a given of Charles Burney's life. He was earning a tiny salary of £30 per annum from St Dionis's and had to supplement it with odd jobs of teaching and composing (his first published song was to words by his friend the poet Christopher Smart).

One of his pupils was the Italian opera singer Giulia Frasi, at whose house and at the Cibbers' Burney used to meet George Friedric Handel. Burney revered Handel's music and, starstruck, had shadowed the great man round Chester once in his youth. On closer acquaintance, some of the glamour necessarily faded. Handel was short-tempered and extremely impatient of mistakes, bawling at Burney for singing a wrong note in one of Frasi's lessons, as Burney recalled in his memoirs:

> [. . .] unfortunately, something went wrong, and HANDEL, with his usual impetuosity, grew violent: a circumstance very terrific to a young musician. – At length, however, recovering from my fright, I ventured to say, that I fancied there was a mistake in the writing; which, upon examining, HANDEL discovered to be the case: and then, instantly, with the greatest good humour and humility, said, 'I pec your barton – I am a very odd tog: – maishter Schmitt is to plame.'33

Burney was to meet a great many famous men on his way to becoming one himself, and had stories about most of them. Like his father before him, he knew the value of a good stock of anecdotes and told them well – comic voices included. He intuited that the ability to converse, to tell stories and (perhaps most importantly for his later connection with Dr Johnson) to *listen* was going to be his surest way to earn and keep a place in the influential company he craved. Fanny Burney thought her father's written reminiscences did no justice to his anecdotal powers, or the charm and wit of his conversation, that they constituted 'little more than Copying the minutes of engagements from his Pocket Books'.34 She was clearly disappointed that he hadn't left anything more solid for posterity to marvel at, but for Charles Burney the primary function of

---

* Now part of Tavistock Street, Covent Garden.

his stories (which drip with dropped names) was to make an immediate impression on a live audience.

With his patrons abroad and his responsibilities multiplying, the better life that Burney wanted for himself and his family seemed to be receding from his grasp in the early 1750s. Esther had given birth to two more children, James in June 1750 and Charles the year after. In order to keep the household going Burney pushed himself to do extra teaching, as well as playing in the theatre band almost every evening and composing. His rewriting of Arne's *Masque of Alfred* had its first performance in February 1751 at Drury Lane, a momentous occasion for the twenty-four-year-old musician, but one he couldn't attend because of a prior engagement at a subscription concert. 'I fear my performance there was not meliorated by my anxiety for the fate of my Offspring at Drury Lane', he wrote:

> I hardly staid to play the final Chord of the last piece on the Organ, ere I flew out of the concert-room into a Hackney coach, in hopes of hearing some of my stuff performed (if suffered to go on) before it was finished; but neither the coachman nor his horses being in so great a hurry as myself, before I reached Temple bar, I took my leave of them, & 'ran like a Lamp-lighter', the rest of the way to the Theatre; and in a most violent perspiration, clambered into the Shilling Gallery, where scarcely I cd obtain admission, the rest of the House being extremely crowded, wch did not diminish the sudorific state of my person. I entered luckily, at the close of an Air of Spirit, sung by Beard, which was much applauded – This was such a cordial to my anxiety & agitated spirits, as none but a diffident and timid author, like myself, can have the least conception.[35]

The impatience with the hackney coach, the muck sweat, the obscurity of the Shilling Gallery and the sense of eavesdropping on his own work's first performance all seem to typify the urgency, anxiety and effort with which Burney strove to establish himself in the world. His work habits became almost manic; he pushed himself to the point of collapse, and then sank into protracted illnesses. In the winter before the debut of *Alfred*, he spent thirteen weeks in bed, a disastrously long time for a breadwinner, and certain to have agitated his restless mind. He was a small, very thin man, whose constitution was in fact as strong as an ox but who looked as if he might turn consumptive with every passing chill.

In this, as well as in frame and feature, his second daughter was to resemble him closely.

The illness of 1751 must have alarmed Burney considerably. A short convalescence in Islington (then a balmy village) made him begin to credit his doctor's insistence that he seek a permanent change of air. Reluctantly, he began to think of leaving the capital. When the offer of the post of organist at St Margaret's Church in Lynn Regis, Norfolk, came up, combining sea air, light duties, a much larger salary and, since 1750, a regular coach service to London (splendidly horsed and armed to the teeth with muskets and bludgeons), it would have been folly to refuse. Burney moved there alone in September 1751 'to feel his way, & know the humours of the place'.[36]

Lynn Regis (now known as King's Lynn) was a thriving mercantile centre in the mid-eighteenth century, with valuable wine, beer and coal trade and corn exports worth more than a quarter of a million pounds a year. It supplied six counties with goods, and sent river freight as far inland as Cambridge. The wealthy aldermen of Lynn were keen to improve the cultural life of the town and to acquire a good music-teacher for their daughters; to this end they had increased the organist's salary by subscription to £100 a year in order to attract Burney (clearly some influential friend or friends had a hand in setting this up), and were prepared to raise the pay even further when they feared they might lose him.

Burney at first resented his provincial exile: the organ in St Margaret's was 'Execrably bad' and the audiences as unresponsive as 'Stocks & Trees',[37] but over the months his attitude changed. He began to be patronised by some of the 'great folks' of north Norfolk – the Townshends at Raynham, the Cokes at Holkham Hall, the Earl of Buckinghamshire at Blickling, Lord Orford (Horace Walpole's nephew) at Houghton – and his spirits rose. All these grandees had large estates, beautiful grounds, art collections and libraries. Burney found that in Norfolk there might be, if anything, even more influential patrons at his disposal than in London, and that the burghers of Lynn were prepared to treat him as the ultimate authority on his subject. Soon he was writing to Esther in encouraging tones. Pregnant for the fourth time, she and the three children joined him in the spring of 1752, and it was probably at their first address in Lynn, Chapel Street, that their daughter Frances was born on 13 June. The new baby was baptised on 7 July in St Nicholas's, the fishermen's chapel just a few yards away, with Frances Greville, returned from the Continent, named as godmother.

The choice of Mrs Greville helped re-establish Charles Burney's connection with his former patrons, but it also had a literary significance, since Mrs Greville was not just a formidable intellectual but an accomplished poet, whose 'Prayer for Indifference' – published in 1759 – became one of the most famous poems of its day. The Burneys must have expected something substantial to come of the connection, for Fanny's sharp judgements of her godmother both personally – she thought Mrs Greville 'pedantic, sarcastic and supercilious'[38] – and as a godparent – 'she does not do her duty and answer for me'[39] – betray more than pique.

The modest provincial household into which Mrs Greville's namesake, Frances, was born was bent on intellectual improvement; Charles and Esther Burney had set themselves a course of reading in the evenings which included 'history, voyages, poetry, and science, as far as Chambers's Dicty, the French Encyclopédie, & the Philosophical transactions'.[40] Not many young couples went to the expense of subscribing to the first edition of Diderot's *Encyclopédie*, and not many Lynn housewives would have relished reading it of an evening, but Esther Burney was an earnest autodidact, 'greatly above the generality of Lynn ladies',[41] whose card-playing evenings bored her, and whom she was soon making excuses to avoid. Esther was a city girl, born and bred, and was probably keener even than her husband to get back to London. He had his teaching and the great houses to visit; she had four young children to look after in an unfamiliar provincial community. As their daughter was to observe later: 'That men, when equally removed from the busy turmoils of cities, or the meditative studies of retirement, to such circumscribed spheres, should manifest more vigour of mind, may not always be owing to possessing it; but rather to their escaping, through the calls of business, that inertness which casts the females upon themselves'.[42]

Esther found two like-minded women in Lynn during her nine years' residence there, Elizabeth Allen and Dolly Young, with whom she formed a sort of miniature literary salon. They met regularly at the house of the richest, most beautiful and most voluble of the three, Mrs Allen, a corn merchant's wife, who had a 'passionate fondness for reading' and 'spirits the most vivacious and entertaining'.[43] Dolly Young was nearer to Esther in temperament; studious and sensitive, she became Esther's particular friend, and a sort of aunt to the children, several of whom, including Fanny, she helped deliver. Unlike her two married friends, Dolly Young was not at all beautiful; her face had 'various unhappy defects' and her body was 'extremely deformed'[44] (almost certainly through smallpox) – an odd companion for Mrs Allen, who was widely regarded as the town's great beauty. Charles Burney admired all three: 'I thought no three such females could be found on our Island', he wrote later, noting with approval, 'They read everything they cd procure'.[45]

Only a few months after baby Frances was born, her year-old brother Charles died and was buried on the north side of St Nicholas's. Esther was soon pregnant again, but this child, also named Charles, did not survive infancy. Her sixth child, a daughter christened Susanna Elizabeth, was born in January 1755, a frail baby who was lucky to escape the smallpox outbreak that lasted in Lynn from 1754 to 1756. There were so many deaths during this period that St Margaret's churchyard was closed due to overcrowding, and the hours of burial had to be extended from 8 a.m. to 9 p.m. each day to cope with the demand. Typhus outbreaks were also common in Lynn, and Charles Burney must sometimes have wondered if the 'change of air' for which he had left London was going to cure him or kill him.

By the mid-1750s the Burneys had moved to a house on the High Street, near to stately old St Margaret's Church and in sight of the masts of the ships docked on the Great Ouse. It was a just a few minutes' walk to the foreshore, where the children could watch the traffic on the river. The waterfront was full of warehouses with watergates to let small boats in at high tide, and the quays were always busy, with coal and wine and beer being loaded, or the fishing fleet bringing cod and herring in. Salters and curers', shipbuilders', sail and ropemakers' premises lined the docks, with their noise and smell of industry. Once a year, in July or August, the whaling fleet came in from its far journey to Greenland, the decks laden with monstrous Leviathan bones. The bells of St Margaret's would peal in celebration and the town enjoy a general holiday, for Lynn was proud of its mercantile nature, never mind the reek from the blubber houses as the rendering process got under way, or the stench of the Purfleet drain at low tide.

Fanny Burney, like her mother, was essentially a city-lover, and spent most of her adult life living right in the middle of London or Paris. Her childhood in Lynn was happy because she was constantly in the company of her 'very domestic' mother[46] (who nursed the children herself) and adored father, but country-town life does not seem to have appealed to her imaginatively, and she avoided writing about it. Spa-towns, seaside towns, rural retreats and, most of all, London, appear in her novels time and again, but workaday places like Lynn get short shrift. 'I am sick of the ceremony & fuss of these fall lall people!' she wrote when visiting Lynn Regis as a young woman. 'So much dressing – chit chat – complimentary nonsense. In short, a Country Town is my detestation. All the conversation is scandal, all the Attention, Dress, and *almost* all the Heart, folly, envy, & censoriousness. A City or a village are the only places which, I think, can be comfortable, for a Country Town has but the bad qualities, without one of the good ones, of both'.[47]

The Burneys' was a self-contained and self-sufficient household. Charles Burney had stools placed in the organ loft of St Margaret's for his family, from which they could look down on the rest of the town during services. Esther did not mix much with the local women and educated her children at home, except for James, who had a couple of years at the grammar school on grounds of his gender. Hetty was the child who showed greatest promise, both intellectually and musically. Even as a small girl, it was clear she had the makings of a first-class harpsichordist, and attention was lavished on her by both parents. Fanny, who showed no special ability at anything and no inclination to learn to read, was left to develop in her own time. There was always a baby to play with: another son christened Charles was born in December 1757, when Fanny was five and Susan almost three. An eighth child was born in late 1758 or early 1759, and christened Henry, but he died in 1760. Fanny had been too young to remember the death of the second baby Charles, but was turning eight when Henry died.[48] It must have affected her sadly; she was known as a 'feeling' child, of the most delicate sensibilities towards all living creatures.

Fanny Burney's intense admiration for her father had its roots in these early years in Lynn. In such a community, a talented, energetic and ambitious man like Charles Burney was treated with enormous respect. He persuaded the corporation to have St Margaret's 'execrable' organ cleaned, and when it fell apart in the process, got them to have a brand new one built, on which he performed dazzlingly various pieces of exciting contemporary music, such as Handel's *Coronation Anthem*. Charles Burney's playing in church, Charles Burney's subscription concerts and Charles Burney's evening parties were the best by far (there was no competition) in a town Fanny described as culturally in 'the dark ages'.[49]

But however popular he was in Lynn, Charles Burney never intended to stay there very long, and the children must have got used to their parents talking about London as if it were their real home. Burney made a couple of attempts to leave during the 1750s, but his obligations (and some strategic salary hikes) kept him in place. His noble patrons made him feel valued and full of potential; Lord Orford was particularly generous, and allowed the musician the run of his library at Houghton. Burney would get the key from the housekeeper and wander around when the master was absent, no doubt fostering fantasies of one day possessing such a library and such a lifestyle himself. Early on in his Norfolk days, Burney had bought a mare called Peggy on which to travel the long distances from Lynn to his aristocratic and county clients, and typically he made use of the time spent on horseback (she was obviously a very trustworthy animal) teaching himself Italian from the classic authors, with a home-made Italian dictionary in his pocket. He bore all the marks of a man in training for something greater. His mind was turning to literary schemes, and perhaps it was as early as in these years that Burney first conceived his plan to write a history of music, something monumental in the style of Diderot's *Encyclopédie* or Samuel Johnson's new *Dictionary of the English Language*, to which he was also a subscriber. He kept himself in touch with the musical and intellectual life of London by going to town every winter. He hardly needed the urgent advice of his friend Samuel Crisp, whom he had met through the Grevilles:

is not settling at Lynn, planting your youth, genius, hopes, fortunes, &c., against a north wall? [. . .] In all professions, do you not see every thing that has the least pretence to genius, fly up to the capital – the centre of riches, luxury, taste, pride, extravagance, – all that ingenuity is to fatten upon? Take, then, your spare person, your pretty mate, and your brats, to that propitious mart, and, 'Seize the glorious, golden opportunity,' while yet you have youth, spirits, and vigour to give fair play to your abilities, for placing them and yourself in a proper point of view.[50]

By 1760, Burney felt he had fulfilled his obligations to the 'foggy aldermen' of Lynn Regis. He decided to move his growing family back to London, ostensibly to further their chances in life, but more immediately to further his own. James, an easy-going boy who had not shone at school, was not to accompany them. It was agreed that he should join the navy, and he was signed up as Captain's Servant on board the *Princess Amelia*. This was a recognised way for poorer boys to get some rudimentary officers' training, but it was also an abrupt and dangerous introduction to adult life for a ten-year-old, and one wonders why his parents submitted him to it. Perhaps their ignorance of seafaring was as great as their backgrounds suggest. The *Princess Amelia* was a man-of-war, a huge floating artillery, with eighty cannon and 750 men on board, a far cry from the fishing boats and merchantmen James might have watched sailing up the Great Ouse. The Seven Years' War was at its height, and the *Princess Amelia* was on active service: the year James joined the crew, it formed part of Hawke's squadron in the Bay of Biscay and was almost blown up by French fireships in the Basque Roads the following year. News from the war took a long time to reach England, and the Burneys would have had little idea of the danger their son was in until it was well past. James's career would keep him out of family life all through his formative years, and, not surprisingly, his own later behaviour as a family man was eccentric, to say the least. The violent contrasts between home life and the sea must have made the former seem vaguely surreal to him; he didn't let one impinge on the other, and it is doubtful that his family ever understood the privations or excitements of his day-to-day existence.

The Burney family made their momentous move to London in September or early October 1760, to a house on Poland Street in Soho, a significantly better address than Charles Burney's last one in the City. Soho, which had been very sparsely inhabited up to the sixteenth century but heavily developed by speculators after the Great Fire, was new and fashionable. The elegant squares and streets that spread their gridwork across the fields, the former military yard and around the old windmill* contained rows of houses quite different from the 'Cottages . . . Shedds or meane

---

* Which was demolished by the 1690s, but is still commemorated in the name of Great Windmill Street, off Shaftesbury Avenue.

habitacons' that had straggled there as recently as 1650.[51] Poland Street had been begun in 1689 and named, topically, in honour of John Sobieski's intervention against the Turks at the siege of Vienna. It wasn't one of the best addresses in the area – Leicester Fields, Golden Square and King's (later Soho) Square had far more aristocratic associations – but it was a very respectable one for an ambitious music-teacher. Soho was full of middle-class families providing services to the rich: Huguenot craftsmen and jewellers, German instrument-makers, gun-makers, portrait-painters, wine merchants, watchmakers, architects and medical men. Next door to the Burneys was a hair-merchant who made wigs for the legal profession, a specialised business with dignified associations. The children of the two households played together in the little paved yards behind the properties.

By the time Fanny Burney was writing the *Memoirs* in the late 1820s, she was aware that her readers might be unimpressed by the family's former address, 'which was not then, as it is now, a sort of street that, like the rest of its neighbourhood, appears to be left in the lurch'.[52] She stressed how genteel Poland Street had been in the 1760s, when the Burneys had lords, knights and even a disinherited Scottish Earl for neighbours, and exotic visitors such as a Red Indian Cherokee chief who was staying in a building almost opposite number 50 and whom the Burney children watched come and go with awed delight.

The contrast with Lynn was dramatic, the scope for entertainment and amazement seemingly endless. Though there were still fields and allotments a stone's throw away in the undeveloped land to the north of Oxford Road (now Oxford Street), London was full of shows and spectacles guaranteed to impress young children straight from the provinces. The theatre at Drury Lane was well known to them through their father's long association there with Arne and his friendship with Garrick; they also knew the rival theatre at Covent Garden and the splendid opera house in the Haymarket, which had room for three thousand spectators (about a third of the population of Lynn Regis). London was filling up with teahouses, coffee houses, strange miniature spas, assembly rooms, puppet shows and curiosity museums to cater for the leisure hours of the rapidly expanding metropolitan population.

The Burney children were too young to attend the famous pleasure gardens at Vauxhall and Ranelagh, Bagnigge Wells or Marylebone, but they could admire the fashion-conscious crowds strutting and posing in

Pall Mall and St James's Park, or the guests, magnificently dressed for masquerades and balls, arriving by carriage or chair outside Mrs Corneley's assembly rooms in Soho Square. When Fanny was writing her novel *Evelina* a decade and a half later, the remembered excitement of her own arrival in London made all the difference to her treatment of a familiar fictional device. The first impressions of a fresh-faced country heroine had been used by Defoe, Richardson, Fielding, even Cleland (unlikely though it is that Fanny Burney ever read *Fanny Hill*), to provide a sardonic commentary on the London social scene, but Burney knew it from life as well as from fiction. Evelina's breathless letters to her guardian, Mr Villars, catch the childish beguilement of the author herself experiencing the bustling, brightly-coloured, noisy, smelly and dangerous life of the capital for the first time when she arrived there in 1760, an open-minded, open-eyed and open-mouthed eight-year-old.

Charles Burney admitted that a great deal of his success as a music teacher on his return to London in 1760 derived from 'the powers of my little girl', eleven-year-old Hetty. Musical child prodigies were fashionable, and even before the family's move to London, Hetty had performed on the harpsichord at the Little Theatre in the Haymarket[53] and attracted the praise of the king's brother by her mastery of 'some of the most wild and difficult lessons of Scarlatti'.[54] Burney wrote showy exercises for her and for his brother Richard's eldest son, Charles Rousseau Burney, a precociously talented violinist and keyboard player. The next generation of musical *Wunderkinder* to hit London would be Maria Anna and Wolfgang Amadeus Mozart in 1764, but for the time being the Burneys held the laurels. The proud Charles published a volume of harpsichord lessons to cash in on the method he had used to teach these two celebrated young performers, and was overcome with requests for new pupils, especially from among the 'great folks' in whose drawing rooms and music rooms his ingratiating charm went down particularly well.

Compared with her high-achieving older sister, her lively brother James and 'angelic' little Susan, Fanny must have seemed dull. She did play the harpsichord, but unsurprisingly chose not to be heard doing so in a household full of virtuosi, restricting herself to 'thrumming' occasionally on the keyboard when she thought she was alone. Hetty not only got intensive music tuition from her father; she was also her mother's 'chief attention'.[55] Together mother and eldest daughter were reading all of

Pope's works and the *Aeneid* in translation, heavy fare by the standards of the day for female education, while at eight, Fanny couldn't even make out the letters of the alphabet. Susan was more advanced than Fanny, though three years younger. The struggle to teach Fanny to read had been going on some time. In Lynn, she had been 'taught' by her older brother, who teased her by holding the book she was meant to be reading from upside-down. The letters were so incomprehensible to her that she didn't notice any difference either way, but the real pathos of this story is in the fact that she had been relegated to the tutorship of James at all.

Though her father was to say that his second daughter 'was wholly unnoticed in the nursery for any talents, or quickness of study',[56] he admits that in her 'childish sports' she was unusually inventive. When she was with her siblings or playmates she displayed a marked talent for mimicry and spontaneous invention, repeating scenes they had seen together at the theatre (where the Burneys often had the use of Mrs Garrick's box) and happy, before an uncritical audience, to 'take the actors off, and compose speeches for their characters'.[57] In a memorandum book for 1806 Fanny included the reminiscence of one of her childhood acquaintances, a Miss Betty Folcher: 'You were so merry, so gay, so droll, & had such imagination in making plays, always something new, something of your own contrivance'.[58] In front of adults, though, the young girl clammed up. When a family friend dubbed Fanny 'the little dunce', her mother stood up for her, saying she 'had no fear about Fanny'; but privately Esther and Charles had begun to worry about their third child's 'backwardness'.[59] 'Today', the psychoanalyst Kathryn Kris has noted in a study of Fanny's case, 'such visual perceptive difficulty, in sharp contrast to auditory fluency, would be recognised as a form of dyslexia'.[60]

When Fanny did eventually learn to read it happened, according to her father, 'all at once [. . .] as if by intuition, nor did any of the family ever know how the talent was acquired'.[61] The miraculous style of this turnaround sounds suspicious, and one is tempted to see it as a symptom of Charles Burney's curious inattentiveness to the details of his children's lives. If the children did not display conspicuous 'talent or quickness of parts', he was unlikely to notice them, being, in Thomas Babington Macaulay's opinion, 'as bad a father as a very honest, affectionate, and sweet-tempered man can well be'.[62] Fanny wrote later of the 'conscious intellectual disgrace' she had felt about her illiteracy, indicating the degree of shame she experienced as well as the harshness with which she was apt to judge herself. Like many dyslexic people, she had developed complex and often arduous methods to get round the problem, and had learned a great deal of poetry, especially that of Pope, by committing Hetty's overheard lessons to memory.* Her powers of recalling things, and of making up what she could not recall, were indeed very strong, although her parents didn't seem to realise it. But the shame was strong, too. Later in life she habitually denied having any talents at all: if she wasn't perfect in a subject, she would say she had no knowledge of it. On the question of her struggle into literacy, it is likely that she learned to read gradually, certainly with difficulty and mostly on her own, but waited to reveal her learning until it was substantial enough to impress her father.

Fanny claimed to have begun writing her own compositions as soon as she could read, using a scrawling form of handwriting, like 'scrambling pot-hooks',[63] that was 'illegible, save to herself'.[64] This too sounds odd, more like the sort of scribble-writing most pre-literate children experiment with than the real thing. The earliest surviving examples of Fanny's handwriting are remarkably neat and eminently legible. The 'pot-hooks' claim of a private, unreadable hand also suggests a childish stratagem to deflect the kind of jeering criticism she had experienced from her brother. It is worth bearing in mind that Fanny's eyesight was poor, and that her short sight can only have hindered her progress with letters. Though apparently reading and writing by the age of ten, it is likely that she was still relying heavily on her memory and composing, as she had done for years, mostly in her head.

Charles Burney was often absent from the house because of his long teaching hours, both at Mrs Sheeles's school in Queen Square, where he had an annual salary of £100, and at the many private houses he attended. He loved his family strongly and sentimentally, and if, as Macaulay rather acidly put it, 'it never seems to have occurred to him that a parent has other duties to perform to children than that of fondling them',[65] there are worse things he could have done. The affection he inspired in his family, and in Fanny particularly, was deep and sincere, and was often remarked on with envy by outsiders. He was a volatile man, highly strung and sometimes manically energetic. Family life was a balm to him, a

---

* Pope remained her favourite poet, with Shakespeare, for life.

source of entertainment and relaxation, and the more sensitive of the children must have intuited that it was important not to disturb this state of things. The girls strove all their lives to please and placate him, and the boys, oppressed by the struggle to be sources of pride to their father, each dropped out in rather spectacular ways.

Charles Burney had more than his usual preoccupations of work and money and self-advancement to deal with at this time. Not long after the move to Poland Street, Esther's health began to decline. She was pregnant for the ninth time in twelve years, and had developed a cough which was thought to be consumptive. In the summer of 1761 she was ordered to Bath and Bristol Hotwells, leaving her husband tied to his teaching at Queen Square until the end of the term. At first, there seemed to be some improvement as a result of the curative waters, but back in London Esther grew weaker. The baby, Charlotte Ann, was born on 3 November and put out to nurse. All through 1762 Esther's condition deteriorated, and she died on 29 September, after a week or more of 'a most violent bilious complaint, wch terminated, after extreme torture, in an inflammation of the bowels'.[66] Of the children, only Hetty was at home to witness this dreadful calamity. Fanny, Susan and Charles had been sent to Mrs Sheeles' 'to be out of the way',[67] and James, who had been discharged from duty on the *Magnanime* at his father's request eleven days earlier, does not seem to have got home in time.

Mrs Sheeles said later that of the many children she had known, none had displayed so much grief over anything as Fanny Burney did at the death of her mother. She 'would take no Comfort – & was almost killed with Crying'.[68] Fanny must have been dreading the blow for some time, for in a letter to her father many years later she described how one of the girls at the school (where the little Burneys seem to have been parked fairly often) had complained of her sullenness 'when I had been dejected by some hints of the illness of my dear mother'.[69] When the 'hints' became sad reality, despite weeks, perhaps months, of desperate praying, Fanny was inconsolable. Stuck in Queen Square among strangers, she had not even been able to say goodbye to her mother, and must have heard with a pang of the melancholy deathbed intimacies with which Hetty had been honoured.

Charles Burney was prostrated by the death of his wife, catapulted into an impenetrable world of private grief:

I shut myself up inadmissable & invisible [to] all but relations, without a thought on anything else till after the funeral, and then for a fortnight did nothing but meditate on my misery. I wrote elegyac Verses on her Virtues & Perfection. [...] It was painful to me to see any one who knew & admired her as all my acquaintance did. But having my mind occupied by business was a useful dissipation of my sorrow; as it forced me to a temporary inattention to myself and the irreparable loss I had sustained.[70]

The younger Burneys, aged ten, seven and four, were not brought home immediately, but had to suffer the exposure of their bereavement among the rich young ladies boarded in Queen Square, one of whom, Lucy Fox-Strangways (the older sister of the girl who had complained about her dullness), compassionately took Fanny under her wing, 'called me her *Child*, & took the office of *School Mother* upon her for me'.[71] When they did go back to Poland Street, the children were neglected by their grief-stricken father. None of them, as Fanny wrote sadly, was 'of an age to be companionable',[72] and he was writing to his old friend Dolly Young in desperate terms: 'From an ambitious, active, enterprizing Being, I am become a torpid drone, a listless, desponding wretch!'[73] Fanny found this letter (she claimed) when going through her father's posthumous papers: it was 'so ill-written and so blotted by his tears, that he must have felt himself obliged to re-write it for the post'.[74] It contains a long and highly emotional account of Esther's death and his subsequent distress. Perhaps Charles Burney thought better of sending it, or, as Fanny claimed to think, wept so much writing the letter that in order to send it, he had to make a fair copy.

The tears, conversely, might have been those of tender-hearted Dolly Young herself, who died in 1805 and might well have left this memorial of former times to her former friend. But it is odd that the document seems to have been unknown to Fanny when she was weeding her father's papers in the 1820s and wrote to Hetty complaining how little material she had found 'relative to our dear & lovely own Mother; [...] from whatsoever Cause, he is here laconic almost to silence. 3 or 4 lines include all the history of his admiration & its effects'.[75] Roger Lonsdale has pointed out the inaccuracy of this statement – at least two pages of Dr Burney's surviving memoirs deal with his first wife – but Fanny's hyperbole indicates her disappointment at her father's omission. The letter to Dolly

Young only exists in Fanny's printed version of 1832, but would seem to answer all the shortcomings she noted in Charles Burney's memoirs, and bears witness to the perfect union which she believed her parents' marriage to have been. She quotes the whole of it (131 lines rather than '3 or 4 lines'), with the prefatory remark that 'a more touching description of happiness in conjugal life, or of wretchedness in its dissolution, is rarely, perhaps, with equal simplicity of truth, to be found upon record.'[76] Could she possibly have made this letter up, from the accounts of her mother's death which she had heard her father and Hetty relate, in order to fill what she felt was a yawning gulf in the record? Could this long and gushing tribute to Esther, suspiciously materialising in her father's archive and then disappearing again, have been another of Fanny's attempts at impressionistic truth?

According to the letter, the dying Esther had attempted to comfort her eldest daughter by assuring her that they would meet again in the next world:

> She told poor Hetty how sweet it would be if she could see her constantly from whence she was going, and begged she would invariably suppose that that would be the case. What a lesson to leave a daughter! – She exhorted her to remember how much her example might influence the poor younger ones; and bid her write little letters, and fancies, to her in the other world, to say how they all went on; adding, that she felt she should surely know something of them.[77]

The role that was being passed on to Hetty was a heavy one; Charles Burney, in 'an unrestrained agony of grief' at his wife's bedside, was incapable of giving consolation to anyone. Esther's concern for Hetty and 'the poor younger ones', and her businesslike last day full of instructions and advice to her husband (including her recommendation to him that he marry Dolly Young), indicate how much Charles needed 'mothering' too. Mothering their father was what all the Burney daughters ended up doing to a greater or lesser extent all their lives – none more assiduously than Fanny.

But at the time, what must have affected the children most strongly in their mother's dying words was the comforting assurance that she would be looking down on them 'from whence she was going', and the fantastical suggestion that she would be able to receive letters after she was dead. It was a fancy that had been given wide currency by Mrs Elizabeth Rowe's bestselling book *Friendship in Death: Twenty letters from the Dead to the Living*, published in 1729 and kept more or less constantly in print until the late nineteenth century, a book which Fanny had certainly read* and which is highly likely to have been introduced into the household by her mother. Mrs Rowe's book discouraged excessive mourning (which is of course, strictly speaking, an impiety): 'If you could conceive my Happiness instead of the mournful Solemnity with which you interr'd me', she imagines a two-year-old boy writing to his bereaved mother, 'you would have celebrated my Funeral Rites with Songs, and Festivals'.[78] Esther Burney no doubt wanted to blunt her children's grief in the same way, with the assurance of an afterlife that is suggested by her advice to Hetty to 'write little letters [. . .] to her in the other world'. But to Fanny, this must have made her unliterary status seem even more of a deprivation than ever, not simply 'conscious intellectual disgrace' but a barrier to communion with her dead parent. The 'angelic' mother on her 'sublime' deathbed had emphasised the value she set on literariness not just by quoting from favourite works (including parts of Gray's 'Elegy') and suggesting poetry-writing as a form of therapy to her husband, but by endorsing the death-defying, almost magical properties of the written word.

After the death of his wife, Charles Burney threw himself into his teaching and often left the children to their own devices. The girls never had a governess; Hetty, who was busy at the harpsichord much of the time, was expected to undertake that function more or less. (It was no accident that both Fanny and Susan became extremely discriminating and appreciative listeners to music.) A succession of housekeepers must have been employed, but none stayed long enough or impressed herself on the children strongly enough to have been kept in the family records, apart from 'an old Welsh woman' whose accent amused Mr Burney.[79] It was a melancholy and lonely time for Fanny, who went to bed every night praying 'for my dear Mamma, & that I might be good enough to join her'.[80]

---

* It appears in her third novel, *Camilla*, when one of the characters, overheard reciting from it, is thought to be reading an illicit love-letter.

The children had always been close, but they drew closer, Fanny and Susan especially. Two anecdotes about them in their father's fragmentary memoirs illustrate both his pleasure in their childish charms and the girls' characteristics of sense and sensibility respectively. The story about Susan, the tender-hearted darling of the family, dates from before Esther's death. At the age of five, she was so overcome by the acting in a performance of the melodrama *Jane Shore* that she cried out from the box to the apparently starving heroine of the piece, 'Ma'am, will you have my ollange?' which, her father recalls, 'the audience applauded much more than the artificial complaints of the actress'.[81] The story about Fanny illustrates her 'natural simplicity and probity', which in Charles Burney's view had 'wanted no teaching'. She and her sisters were playing with the wigmaker's children next door:

> [T]he door of the wig magazine being left open, they each of them put on one of those dignified ornaments of the head, and danced and jumped about in a thousand antics, laughing till they screamed at their own ridiculous figures. Unfortunately, in their vagaries, one of the flaxen wigs, said by the proprietor to be worth upwards of ten guineas – in those days a price enormous – fell into a tub of water, placed for the shrubs in the little garden, and lost all its gorgon buckle, and was declared by the owner to be totally spoilt. He was extremely angry, and chid very severely his own children; when my little daughter, the old lady, then ten years of age, advancing to him, as I was informed, with great gravity and composure, sedately says; 'What signifies talking so much about an accident? The wig is wet, to be sure; and the wig was a good wig, to be sure; but its of no use to speak of it any more; because what's done can't be undone'.[82]

This story is made to sound comical in the *Memoirs*,* and the thought of the little girls running round in judges' and advocates' wigs, screaming with laughter – until the accident, and probably then still sniggering – is a charming one. But it has a melancholy undertow. *What's done can't be undone.* If the statement of Fanny's age is accurate, the incident took place

---

* I have used the *Memoirs* version rather than the slightly different one in Dr Burney's fragmentary memoirs, which does not, for instance, include the detail of the tub of water being there for the shrubs. The story did, after all, happen to Fanny; Charles Burney only knew it second-hand.

in the year when Esther was dying or dead. The coining of such a fatalistic apothegm by a ten-year-old ('the wig is wet' became family shorthand for any situation that had got beyond their control) suggests an unusual degree of reflectiveness. It must have served to remind the wigmaker quite sharply that the ruination of a hair-piece was a relatively paltry loss.

Fanny was referred to in that story as 'the old lady', a nickname which settled on her 'from the time she had reached her eleventh year'. In a passage from the *Memoirs* apparently 'Copied from a Memorandum-book of Dr. Burney's',* she has her father recall:

> in company, or before strangers, [Fanny] was silent, backward, timid, even to sheepishness: and, from her shyness, had such profound gravity and composure of features, that those of my friends who came often to my house, and entered into the different humours of the children, never called Fanny by any other name, from the time she had reached her eleventh year, than The Old Lady.[83]

Fanny would not have left this in the record if she had not thought it to her credit. Behaving like an old lady, decorously, soberly and with 'gravity and composure of features', was for her the only proper way. 'From the time she had reached her eleventh year' clearly aligns the onset of 'profound gravity' with her mother's death, after which it may have seemed to Fanny irreverent and inappropriate to be gay in public – in her novels, only the heartless characters 'get over' a death. People often described Fanny Burney as 'shy', but 'reserved' seems a much more accurate word. From her diaries and letters, which exist from her sixteenth year, we know that, privately, she was sharp, witty, devastatingly observant, judgemental, romantic and prone to 'fits' of irrepressible high spirits. Her sobersides public persona was clearly a form of camouflage, developed through the long habit of not wanting to have attention drawn to herself, with the criticism she imagined would inevitably follow of her looks, her melancholy, her 'backwardness', her lack of polish. To be *re*served was also to be *pre*served.

---

* But actually a reworking of his memoirs, or a piece of autobiography written in the third person – compare the fragment in *Memoirs of Doctor Charles Burney*, pp.141–2, with the 'same' passage in Fanny's *Memoirs* vol. 2, pp.168–71.

❦ 2 ❦

A Romantick Girl

In the two years following his wife's death, Charles Burney was too preoccupied with work and his own sorrows to realise how badly his household was being run; but the concern of his friends became clear. David Garrick and his wife Eva, whom Burney had known since the 1740s, began to take a special interest in the young family and found excuses to be kind to them. When the Garricks were going abroad in the winter of 1763, they asked the Burney children to take care of their spaniel, Phill, and on their return insisted the dog stay on at Poland Street permanently, claiming he preferred it. They also gave the Burneys free run of Mrs Garrick's private box at Drury Lane, and Fanny and her siblings saw the great 'Roscius' perform there as often as they could, accompanied by a chaperone (not, one notices, by their father himself). In the early 1770s Fanny recorded seeing Garrick in some of his most famous roles, King Lear, Macbeth, Richard III ('sublimely horrible!'[1]), Bayes in George Buckingham's *The Rehearsal* and Abel Drugger in Jonson's *The Alchemist*:

> Never could I have imagined such a metamorphose as I saw! the extreme meanness – the vulgarity – the low wit – the vacancy of Countenance – the appearance of *unlicked Nature* in all his motions.[2]

Garrick, who loved children and had none of his own, called in at Poland Street whether he expected the master of the house to be present or not. The children idolised him, and he couldn't resist the pleasure of entertaining them with 'an endless variety of comic badinage, – now exhibited in lofty bombast; now in ludicrous obsequiousness; now by a sarcasm skilfully implying a compliment; now by a compliment archly conveying a sarcasm':[3]

31

he used to take off the old puppet-show *Punch*, placing himself against a wall, seeming to speak through a comb, & to be moved by wires. Nobody talked such pretty nonsense, as our great Roscius, to children and lap-dogs.[4]

Charles Burney became a frequent guest at the Garricks' house by the Thames at Hampton, being taken down there on Saturdays when Garrick was not acting, and delivered home on Monday mornings. He was often absent for long periods, or sealed in his study when at home. On such occasions the children were left with each other and the servants.

Burney's thoughts were running on remarriage, but not to Dolly Young, despite Esther's deathbed instructions and the children's strong predilections. Dolly was the obvious choice as a second *mother*, but not as second wife; her 'peculiarly unfortunate personal defects' were clearly too much of an obstacle for Charles Burney. His eye was on Esther's other close friend from Lynn, the handsome and spirited Mrs Allen, who had been widowed in 1763, only months after Burney's own loss. Elizabeth Allen was thirty-eight and had three young children: Maria, aged twelve, Stephen, eight, and Bessy, who was only two. Her husband Stephen had left them a fortune of £40,000 from his business as a corn merchant: £5000 went directly to his wife (with a supplementary income of £100 per year until she remarried), and Allen's two properties in Lynn were entailed on the children until their majorities (bringing in rent meanwhile to support them).[5] By any reckoning, Elizabeth Allen was a wealthy woman, added to which she was clever and beautiful and familiar to the family from their happy days in Lynn and her friendship with Esther. Charles Burney must have found the prospect of an alliance with her almost irresistible.

In the fragments of his manuscript memoirs, Burney recalls how he pursued the attractive widow, who had kept in touch by letter and saw him regularly when she came to London every winter. He began to feel 'very seriously impassioned', and clearly believed he stood a good chance of success, but his advances were premature. The unambiguous verses he was writing to her offended rather than seduced 'The Witch':

> Her image by night & by day
> Still haunts me, both sleeping & waking,
> Steals my peace & spirits away
> And my heart keeps incessantly aching.[6]

32

Mrs Allen found this poem presumptuous, and refused to see the music master for over a year. He had to retreat with his tail between his legs, admitting later that, 'After this rebuff I had very little hopes that our acquaintance wd ever be renewed'.[7]

With the failure of his attempt to restart some kind of home life, Burney began to wonder what to do with his children. He decided to send two of the girls to France to be educated on the cheap by boarding with a respectable Protestant woman in Paris, where they would pick up what they could of the language and culture. The two he chose were not the eldest girls, Esther and Fanny, but Esther and Susan. Burney's anxiety about finding a suitably Protestant governess was such that he was prepared to pay over the odds: 'I thought it best', he wrote in his memoirs, 'whatever might be the expence, to avoid putting them in the way to be prejudiced in favour of any religion except our own, as it might distract their minds, &, if opposed, render them miserable for the rest of their lives.'[8] Was this a reasonable fear on his children's behalfs? Were they really made of such flammable stuff as to be 'rendered miserable for the rest of their lives' by a change of ideology? Fanny, certainly, *became* such a person, fiercely clinging to what she knew, but she, more than any other of the Burney children, had spent a lifetime trying to anticipate her father's wishes.

There was another consideration in Charles Burney's decision not to send Fanny abroad – her 'backwardness'. Although Fanny had managed to learn to read and write, Susan was the quicker and more advanced student, and her education a more worthwhile use of funds. Burney was clearly thinking in terms of efficiency. He knew he couldn't subsidise his children indefinitely (especially now that he had been spurned by the rich widow), and he sought to launch his family at the earliest opportunity 'to shift for themselves as I had done'.[9] Young Charles, aged only six in the summer of 1764, would cost money to educate (he went to Charterhouse in 1768 and on to Cambridge); James, fortunately, was already established in his naval career – he had joined the *Niger* as Captain's Servant in 1763 and was made a midshipman as soon as he turned sixteen three years later. For the girls, however, 'shifting for themselves' could only mean marrying as well as they could, and for Fanny, the 'dunce', staying at home and acting as secretary-cum-housekeeper to her father was probably thought (by him, at any rate) more than sufficient preparation.

Charles Burney returned from depositing Hetty and Susan in Paris in the summer of 1764 in a mood of renewed optimism. He had bought a great many books and indulged one of his favourite pastimes, introducing himself to famous men (in this case the philosopher David Hume, then secretary to the English Ambassador). Burney's ambitions were still unfocused. He couldn't work out how to insert himself into the literary world except through the theatre, where his friendship with Garrick – who consistently encouraged his work as a composer for the stage – gave him a foothold. A nice opportunity opened up in 1765 when Garrick suggested that Burney should translate Jean-Jacques Rousseau's operetta *Le Devin du village* for production at Drury Lane. Burney happened to have made an English version of this piece some years before, and its transition to the stage was swift, though not as successful as the translator probably hoped. The first night of *The Cunning-Man*, in November 1766, was watched from Mrs Garrick's box by the Burney children Hetty (who had stayed in Paris only a year), Fanny, Charles and possibly even little Charlotte, all sitting forward to monitor the audience's reactions to their beloved father's debut as a writer. They themselves were being watched from the orchestra by Garrick, who seems to have been more interested by the spectacle in the box than the one on the stage, and described to Charles Burney later,

> the innocent confidence of success with which [the children] all openly bent forward, to look exultingly at the audience, when a loud clapping followed the overture: and their smiles, or nods; or chuckling and laughter, according to their more or less advanced years, during the unmingled approbation that was bestowed upon about half the piece – contrasted with, first the amazement, next, the indignation; and lastly, the disappointment, that were brought forth by the beginning buzz of hissing, and followed by the shrill horrors of the catcall: and then the return – joyous, but no longer dauntless! – of hope when again the applause prevailed.[10]

The possibility of hissing and catcalls had clearly not crossed the children's minds. It was a rude awakening to the fact that though their father seemed a demi-god at home, he had yet to prove himself to the rest of the world. The children were not ignorant of theatre audiences' rough manners. Noisy commentary, free criticism, missile-hurling and occasional fisticuffs were part and parcel of a night out at either of London's licensed playhouses. The attention of the crowd was hard to attract and, once gained, fickle and demanding, and though the segregation of the crowd into gallery, pit and boxes afforded some protection to members of the audience from each other, no part of it felt any obligation to respect what was going on on the stage. Fanny Burney satirised the situation memorably in the Drury Lane episode in *Evelina*, where the fop Lovel says of theatre-going, 'one merely comes to meet one's friends, and shew that one's alive. [. . .] I confess I seldom listen to the players: one has so much to do, in looking about, and finding out one's acquaintance, that, really, one has no time to mind the stage [. . .] pray – what was the play tonight?'[11] The onus was on the manager and players, but most of all on the author, to entertain an essentially indifferent rabble. The unharmonious 'buzz of hissing' and 'shrill horrors of the catcall' that greeted their musician father's first literary performance was, to the Burney children, a startling demonstration of that audience's power.

With hindsight, Fanny Burney was in no doubt that her father's ultimate aim in life had been to achieve fame as an author, and that *The Cunning-Man* marked a turning point for him. Her remarks in the *Memoirs* about the vocation they shared are revealing:

> it was now that, vaguely, yet powerfully, he first fell into that stream of ideas, or visions, that seemed to hail him to that class indefinable, from its mingled elevation and abjectness, which, by joining the publicity of the press to the secret intercourse of the mind with the pen, insensibly allures its adventurous votaries to make the world at large the judge of their abilities, or their deficiencies – namely, the class of authors.[12]

Fanny was writing this (in the 1820s) at the end of her own long career as a writer, which makes her persistent anxieties about the 'mingled elevation and abjectness' of authorship all the more interesting. When her own first book came to be published she was impressed, with traumatic intensity, by the fact that the author's initial 'intercourse of the mind with the pen' (secretive and confidential) led to the total exposure of him or herself to an unknowably large and critical audience. As a novelist, Fanny Burney became both audience and performer, watching and anatomising the world around her which then, in the form of her readers, was free to read and anatomise *her*.

The example of the careless crowd at Drury Lane hissing her father's work is likely to have intensified her fears of the judgemental 'world at large', but also demonstrated the mutually exploitative nature of the compact between artist and audience and the complexity of the traffic between doing, looking, speaking, writing and reading. The passage in the *Memoirs* about the first performance of *The Cunning-Man* both describes and demonstrates this. It records Garrick's observations, but was actually written up by Fanny, one of the children he was observing, when she was composing her father's *Memoirs* sixty years later. The passage seems to be a recollection by Garrick of watching the Burney children watching the audience that was watching their father's translation of Rousseau's operetta. It is actually a recollection by the elderly Madame d'Arblay of what her father reported that Garrick had acted out for him after the performance. The 'incident' when unpicked is seen to be not one but many, the different parts relating to each other in casual or even chaotic ways. Madame d'Arblay's objective as a biographer and autobiographer was to obfuscate such complexities. Consciously or not, she was aware that observation and recollection are dynamic processes that can be arrested by the act of writing. Writing things down became her way of taking possession of the past and attempting to impose on it shape and meaning.

In the same year that Hetty and Susan went away to Paris, Charles Burney accidentally met and renewed his friendship with Samuel Crisp, his old acquaintance from Wilbury days. This was to be of great significance to Fanny, for Crisp became, after her father, the most respected and influential person in her early life. Crisp had first met Burney in 1747, when he was forty and the young musician only twenty-one. He was in an enviable position – handsome, highly cultured, uncumbered by wife or family and possessed of a private income. He spent his life in the improvement of his mind and the refinement of his taste: he read a great deal, travelled, listened to music, studied paintings and sculpture and was regarded as a true connoisseur of the arts by his friends, many of whom were aristocratic and most, like him, rich. Charles Burney was grateful for a really well-informed mentor who could educate him in 'almost every species of improvement' and for whom 'the love of music [. . .] amounted to passion'.[13] Thomas Arne had made the profession of music seem like drudgery; Crisp was the first person to show Charles that it could aspire to the highest aesthetic ideals.

Crisp, a collector of musical instruments and *objets d'art*, had brought back from one of his visits to Italy the first large pianoforte, or 'harpsichord with hammers',[14] that was ever constructed. Burney had ample opportunity to play this remarkable instrument and appreciate the 'magnificent and new effect' of the sound it produced when Crisp sold it to Fulke Greville. Crisp could play several musical instruments and had a tenor voice which Charles Burney thought better than that of many professional singers. But he never took part in the Burneys' later musical evenings, preferring to keep his accomplishments to himself. He was a true dilettante, in Fanny's words in the *Memoirs*, 'a scholar of the highest order; a critic of the clearest acumen; possessing, with equal delicacy of discrimination, a taste for literature and for the arts'.[15]

Unfortunately, there was one area where Crisp's clear acumen and delicate discrimination failed him, and where he was not content with the status of gifted amateur. He was convinced that he was a dramatic poet, and by 1754 had finished his *magnum opus*, a tragedy in verse called *Virginia* (based on the story in Livy, retold by Chaucer in *The Physician's Tale*) which he had been writing for at least five years. He offered it to his friend David Garrick for production at Drury Lane, and season after season expected it to be put on, but Garrick prevaricated. Sure of his play's merits, Crisp decided to put pressure on Garrick through his influential friends. He got the Earl of Coventry to give a copy of it to the Prime Minister, Pitt the Elder, who said it was 'excellent'[16] and persuaded the Earl's wife, Lady Coventry, to take the manuscript back to Garrick personally. This was 'a machinery such as none could long resist', as Lord Macaulay wrote of the incident.[17] Lady Coventry (*née* Gunning) was one of the famous beauties of the day, idolised like a latter-day film star; she and her sister were followed by crowds of admirers, seven hundred of whom, reportedly, once waited outside an inn just to catch sight of them.[18] When she came bearing *Virginia*, Garrick had to concede to the power of Crisp's manoeuvring. He agreed to put the play on in the spring of 1754, although he insisted on cutting some scenes, by which, as even the author was prepared to admit, it was 'rendered much more Dramatic than it was at first'.[19] Garrick took the role of Virginius himself, with Mrs Cibber as his daughter, the tragic heroine; but despite their best efforts, the play lasted only ten nights – not a disaster, by any means, but a sharp disappointment to Crisp, who thought he had given birth to a classic.

Crisp spent the next year revising *Virginia*, and took mortal offence when Garrick, unsurprisingly, expressed no interest in a revival. Crisp complained of Garrick's ill-will, his friends' lack of enthusiasm, the fickleness of the public – anything but admit that there might be something wrong with the work. 'The fatal delusion that he was a great dramatist, had taken firm possession of his mind', Macaulay wrote. 'He lost his temper and spirits, and became a cynic and hater of mankind.'[20] Crisp came to regret that he had ever allowed Garrick to alter a line of *Virginia*, and thirty years later was still smarting from the play's failure, convinced that he had only missed out on literary glory through other people's errors of judgement. Sending the surviving segments of the play to Fanny Burney after Crisp's death, his sister, Sophia Gast, gave her own version of the affair: 'The then manager [Garrick] would not suffer the too much approved, and greatly admired performance, to be acted as in its pristine state, but insisted on many alterations'. Garrick's motivation was clear to Mrs Gast: simple jealousy. Fanny Burney, who had known both Garrick and Crisp very well, and was loyal to the memory of both, scored the word through.[21]

Crisp left England for Italy in 1755, not intending to return. However, after a few years' self-imposed exile he came back to live a life of retirement 'in one of the wildest tracts of Surrey'.[22] This was the hamlet of Chesington,* about two miles north-west of Epsom (now a heavily-developed suburb just inside the London orbital motorway), where he took up residence as a long-term paying guest in a decaying country house belonging to one of his bachelor acquaintances, Christopher Hamilton.

Chesington Hall was falling into ruin when Christopher Hamilton took it over from the Hatton family in 1746. Fanny Burney calls him the 'hereditary owner', but she could have been wrong about this,† as she

---

* The modern spelling is 'Chessington'.
† The County History says that Hamilton paid for the property, but records in the Surrey History Centre state that he was 'only son and heir' of Rebecca Hatton of Chesington. Mrs Hatton was, presumably, widow or sister of Thomas Hatton, owner of Chesington Hall until his death in 1746. The different surname of Rebecca's children indicates that they were the issue of an earlier marriage.

was about 'the long dignity' of the house's name, which Hamilton himself had made up in the 1740s.[23] Fanny tended to romanticise everything about Chesington, the 'long-loved rural abode [where] the Burneys and happiness seemed to make a stand',[24] and it is easy to see how the Tudor house, with its old wood, old windows and curious passageways, would have appealed to an imaginative child. It was built of brick around 1520 and had retained most of its early features, including a long gallery on the first floor, tapestries, canopied beds, carved cupboards and a chimney-piece 'cut in diamonds, squares and round nobs, surmounting another of blue and white tiles'.[25] The windowpanes were 'hardly so wide as their clumsy frames', and were 'stuck in some angle close to the ceiling of a lofty slip of a room', or looked out from the attics onto 'long ridges of lead that entwined the motley spiral roofs of the multitude of separate cells'. A crumbling Elizabethan 'cell' was just what Samuel Crisp was looking for, and he was glad to adopt what Fanny later described as 'some pic-nic plan'[26] with Hamilton, joining a number of other waning gentlemen at Chesington Hall 'who had quitted the world, and who in this Chateau met only at meals, at Tea, and afterwards at a game of cards'.[27]

Crisp's retirement was not complete, and he came up to town every spring to visit the latest exhibitions and attend plays, concerts and the opera. It was on one of these trips that he re-met Charles Burney and quickly re-established their friendship. They had been out of touch during the period of the *Virginia* episode, when Burney had finally taken his friend's advice and moved back to London from King's Lynn – the period, too, during which Esther had died. The sight of the young music-master, as thin and overworked as ever, heroically trying to maintain his household in Poland Street, must have touched Crisp deeply. Burney was the only one of his friends to whom he divulged the secret of how to find Chesington Hall, and it soon became a refuge where the musician could retire to work, or simply stroll among the box-walks or the fruit trees, or admire a good view of Epsom from the summer-house on the 'Mount'.

On the death of Christopher Hamilton, Chesington Hall passed to his sister Sarah, who, guided by Crisp's advice, let half the house and most of the surrounding land to a farmer named Woodhatch, retaining the other part as 'a competant establishment for receiving a certain number of boarders'.[28]* Crisp became, in effect, the head of a household that consisted of himself, Mrs Hamilton,† her good-natured niece Kitty Cooke, and a shifting cast of lodgers. The Burneys were always welcome, and over the years Chesington Hall became a second home, especially when any of them needed a convalescent 'change of air'. Crisp took great interest in all the children, but was particularly fond of Fanny, who returned his affection abundantly. She was an adolescent who sometimes behaved like an 'old lady'; he an old gentleman who like to indulge youthful high spirits. Genial, cultivated and attentive, Crisp became a kind of ideal grandfather to the Burney children, a second 'Daddy' – the pet name he was more than happy to adopt.

In the year during which Hetty and Susan were away in Paris, Fanny had the house on Poland Street to herself for long stretches of time. She was twelve years old, had free access to her father's growing library, and was keen to improve herself. She studied conscientiously, made notes, copied extracts and kept a *catalogue raisonné*, possibly in competition with her two sisters abroad. A long manuscript translation from the French of Fontanelle's 'Entretien sur la pluralité des mondes' has survived[30] which may have been made during these years: it indicates the seriousness of Fanny's studies, her ambition and also her characteristic self-consciousness – underneath the title appear the words 'Murdered into English by Frances Burney'.

Her reading, as suggested by entries in her early diaries,[31] was heavily

---

* Chesington Hall was pulled down in 1833–4 and rebuilt on the old foundations. It was this short-lived Victorian building (demolished a century later and now covered over by a residential estate) which Constance Hill and her sister Ellen visited when writing *Juniper Hall* (published in 1904). Neither Ellen Hill's picture of the Hall in that book (p.147) nor an older amateur drawing in the archives of the Surrey History Centre gives much idea of the house as it was in Crisp's day, but the records of leases and releases do. They itemise the rooms reserved by Sarah Hamilton after the property was divided: 'on the ground floor, the Hall and the Brown and Best Parlours next the Garden with the closets therein, the small beer cellar, the under ground cellar communicating with the small beer cellar, and those rooms up a pair of stairs called the Best Chamber, the Brown Room, the Paper Room, the Wrought Room and the Green Room; the rooms up two pair of stairs (except the first room which communicates with the Back Stairs wherein the farmer's men usually lie), Stable, Coachhouse, the Brewhouse with the Apple Chamber over it, the Pidgeon House, the Great Garden adjoining the sd. messuage and Brewhouse, the Necessary in the Garden, the Lower Garden adjoining the Necessary, the Pound Meadow, the Walk to the Church with trees on both sides of it and the fruit thereof, the use of the Pump and all other Courts, yards, ways and passages in and about the sd. messuage'.[29]

† Like many spinsters of mature years, Sarah Hamilton had adopted the title 'Mrs'.

weighted towards works of moral instruction, sermons, standard histories, poetry and the 'female conduct books' which were deemed an essential part of a young woman's mental baggage. One of the most popular and influential of the conduct-book writers was James Fordyce, whose *Sermons to Young Women* Fanny knew well.* Fordyce asserted the authority of his sex with confidence: 'Men [. . .] are in general better judges than women, of the deportment of women',[32] while its moral inferiority was also acknowledged: 'The world, I know not how, overlooks in our sex a thousand irregularities, which it never forgives in yours'.[33] The disturbing sexual power of women could only, in Fordyce's view, be put to proper use as an inducement to and reward for good male behaviour. A roomful of riotous men, he asserted, could be 'checked all at once into decency' by the accidental entrance of a virtuous woman.[34] Restraint was the key to proper female conduct: wit, in women, 'is commonly looked upon with a suspicious eye', and 'war, commerce, politics, exercises of strength & dexterity, abstract philosophy & all the abstruser sciences, are most properly the province of men'.[35] This left little for women to do (besides entering rooms virtuously) other than going astray, the irreparable personal disaster which opened the way to widespread social disintegration.

Because Fanny had no one with whom to discuss her reading or to guide it, and because her veneration for the written word was intense, the messages of authors such as Fordyce impressed her very strongly, reinforcing an already anxious and conservative nature. Their severity appealed to the neglected child, whose 'straightforward morality', in her father's opinion, had 'wanted no teaching'.[36] At this impressionable age, and unguided, she assumed a set of standards which proved a constant agitation to her natural morality. She assented to the conventional view, as articulated by Fordyce, of the superior authority of the male sex, although her common sense and sense of justice often told her otherwise. For example, reading the *Iliad*, aged sixteen, she found herself 'provoked [. . .] for the honour of the sex':

Venus tempts Hellen with every delusion in favour of her Darling, – in vain – Riches – power – honour – Love – all in vain – the enraged Deity

---

* And which Jane Austen knew well too – it is the book Mr Collins insists on reading aloud to the Bennet girls in *Pride and Prejudice*.

41

threatens to deprive her of her own beauty, & render her to the level with the most common of her sex – blushing & trembling – Hellen immediately yields her Hand.

Thus has Homer proved his opinion of our poor sex – that the Love of Beauty is our most prevailing passion. It really grieves me to think that there certainly must be reason for the insignificant opinion the greatest men have of Women – At least I *fear* there must. – But I don't in fact *believe* it – thank God![37]

The poet – not just a man, but a truly '*great man*' – had to be right: but wasn't. 'Fear' and 'belief' contradicted one another, and the only way Fanny could resolve the problem was by sticking to the evidence of her own experience. She lost no opportunity in her books to expose the disadvantages under which her own sex laboured, but did so, characteristically, through realistic representation of women rather than by direct criticism of men. Modern readers can't help interpreting her works as feminist, but Fanny Burney herself would have been shocked and distressed to have been associated with anything so subversive. In the fight between duty and justice, duty was always going to win. A person such as her father, who embodied her primary duty, thus became an idealised figure, incapable of doing wrong – even though she knew he did act wrongly sometimes. It was a paradox that affected her profoundly, creating tensions in her writing which provide much of her works' interest, but which ultimately may have inhibited her from becoming a great artist.

Fanny Burney's attitude to novels and novel-writing reflects the same anxieties. She never completely outgrew her poor opinion of the form, derived from the views of old-fashioned moralists such as Fordyce (who thought that novels 'carry on their very forehead the mark of the beast'). She projected onto her father the same strict tastes. Novels were not banned in the liberal Burney household; as well as Richardson and Fielding, Fanny had read Sterne (although she pityingly called him 'poor Sterne') and many other works which Fordyce would have abominated. The house was full of reading-matter quite apart from the mostly musical and classical texts in Charles Burney's library, and lack of supervision meant that while Fanny read much more demanding books than most 'educated' young ladies would have encountered, she also read a great deal more 'low-grade' literature, and knew many risqué works, such as Swift's 'The Lady's Dressing Room', well enough to parody them.[38] The sort of literature she enjoyed and the sort of literature she felt 'allowed' to write were not the same thing at all.

When she tried to amalgamate entertainment with moral instruction in her own work, the results were patchy. In *Evelina*, which was published anonymously, the attempt was successful because Burney felt free to make her heroine mildly fallible, and open to moral improvement; in the later books, when she had to own authorship, her heroines represented pure virtue under attack – a very much less dramatic or entertaining formula. Clearly, the only way Fanny Burney could justify to herself her own persistent interest in writing fiction (and her last novel, *The Wanderer*, though her least satisfactory, is probably the most ambitious) was by stressing its moral purpose. 'If many turn aside from all but mere entertainment presented under this form', she wrote in the dedication to *The Wanderer*, 'many, also, may, unconsciously, be allured by it into reading the severest truths, who would not even open any work of a graver denomination'.[39]

Fanny's juvenilia seems to have been mostly of a 'grave denomination': 'Elegies, Odes, Plays, Songs, Stories, Farces, – nay, Tragedies and Epic Poems, every scrap of white paper that could be seized upon without question or notice'.[40] It was an obsessive, absorbing pleasure which she kept secret, convinced 'that what she scribbled, if seen, would but expose her to ridicule'.[41] Her 'writing passion'[42] was partly a response to loneliness, partly, as is evident from the astonishing diversity of the forms she tried, a form of interaction with the authors she read and admired. The extent of that interaction was very unusual. As an old woman, Fanny described to her younger sister Charlotte how she got by heart one of William Mason's poems by 'repeating it, in the dead of sleepless Nights, so often, so collectedly, so *all to myself*, that I believe I must have caught every possible meaning of the Poet, not only in every sentiment, but in the appropriation of every word, so as to be able to pronounce as I conceive him to have thought, [. . .] entering into the Poem as if it had been the production of my own brain'.[43] This describes something more akin to a form of ecstatic spiritual communion than to what we normally understand by *reading*. Her use of the word 'appropriation' seems particularly apt.

In her early teenage years, Fanny had plenty of time in which to indulge her 'writing passion', and a safe place, her 'bureau', in which to lock her works away. This was not a piece of furniture, but a closet in the Poland Street bedroom, the only part of the house which was inviolably hers. Even as a forty-year-old, Fanny was expected to share a bedroom with her half-sister, and it is unlikely that she ever had a room of her own before her marriage, except at Mrs Thrale's in the late 1770s and at court in the late 1780s. It is clear from the early diaries that as an adolescent Fanny stayed up at night writing or reading until the candle ran out, with her sisters asleep nearby.[44] There was nothing casual about these secretive literary pursuits 'in the dead of sleepless Nights'. By Fanny's mid-teens, the stack of compositions in the 'bureau' included at least one full-length novel.

On her return from Paris,* eleven-year-old Susan was struck by the differences between her two elder sisters, one of whom had enjoyed the same opportunities for travel and education as herself, the other of whom had stayed at home:

> The characteristics of Hetty seem to be wit, generosity, and openness of heart; – Fanny's, – sense, sensibility, and bashfulness, and even a degree of prudery. Her understanding is superior, but her diffidence gives her a bashfulness before company with whom she is not intimate, which is a disadvantage to her. My eldest sister shines in conversation, because, though very modest, she is totally free from any *mauvaise honte*: were Fanny equally so, I am persuaded she would shine no less.[46]

Observers who were less well-disposed than Susan might easily have dismissed Fanny as affected or dull. The superior intellect was not on public display (now or ever), while the bashfulness and 'degree of prudery' were marked. By the age of fourteen Fanny had adopted patterns of behaviour – all stemming from vigilant self-appraisal – that she would never be able to break completely.

But there was another side to Fanny's character, of 'wildness' 'frisky-

---

* 1766 is the likely date: Susan's miscellaneous writings show she was in London by the spring of 1767.[45]

ness' and invention, which Susan's company brought out. Only Susan was shown the precious writings, and 'the stolen moments of their secret readings' together were, in retrospect, 'the happiest of their adolescent lives'.[47] Among the pieces Susan read was Fanny's manuscript novel, 'Caroline Evelyn', a sad tale of abandonment and ill-usage, which ended with the young heroine dying in childbirth. Like the 'Elegies, Odes, [. . .] Tragedies and Epic Poems' Fanny had been writing, it reflected the melancholy that had settled on her after her mother's death. But with Susan re-established at home, such mournful ruminations had become obsolete. In that year,* Mr Crisp had been amused and surprised to see Fanny dancing a wild jig on the lawn at Chesington Hall, 'with Your Cap on the Ground, & your long hair streaming down your Back, one shoe off, & throwing about your head like a mad thing'.[50] This was a far cry from the bashful, mumbling behaviour Fanny usually displayed in public. '[T]here is a nameless Grace & Charm in giving a loose to that Wildness & friskyness sometimes', Crisp told her years later, acknowledging how much of this element there was in his young friend's character, however seldom anyone outside the family circle got to see it.

Change was in the air in the Burney household. Unknown to his children, Charles Burney was once again courting Mrs Allen. The opportunity to renew acquaintance with the beautiful widow had come in 1765 when she placed her elder daughter, lively fourteen-year-old Maria, at school in London and rented a house in Great Russell Street as a winter base. Charles Burney was appointed to teach Maria music, and arranged for the lessons to take place at teatime, in order that 'when he was liberated from the daughter, he might be engaged with the mother'.[51] Chastened by his earlier failure, Burney adopted a gentler line of courtship over the next eighteen months or so, accompanying Mrs Allen to the opera and to concerts, both of which she loved, and sending her his prose version of Dante's *Inferno* instead of poems like 'The Witch'. In truth, there was nothing for Mrs Allen to gain materially from a remarriage: she would lose the £100 annual income under her first husband's will and gain a low-earning husband with six children and a chaotic

---

* The date – 1766–7 – is conjectural, based on Crisp's estimate in 1779 that the incident took place 'about a Dozen Years ago'[48] and Fanny's statement in 1771 that she had not been to Chesington 'for almost five years'.[49]

workload. Nevertheless, Burney kept up the campaign, contriving meetings when the widow's 'imperious' mother was absent. He was clearly in love, as well as very keen to find a second mother for his family and a supporter (financially and morally) for his work. By the spring of 1767, his patience was in sight of paying off: 'my beloved Mrs Allen [. . .] began to be weaned from her fears', he wrote, 'by affection and consta[nt] importunity; and I flattered myself I was gaining ground'.[52]

When Elizabeth Allen returned to Lynn for the summer in April 1767, Burney bombarded her with letters, sent under cover to Dolly Young or in a feigned hand to avoid the vigilant mother's eye. Like his daughter Fanny, he seemed to relish a conspiracy: 'our correspondence had all the Air of mystery and intrigue; in that we seemed 2 young lovers under age trying to out-wit our parents and guardians'.[53] Unfortunately, Elizabeth's mother could not be outwitted forever, and her objections to the match were strong. Charles decided to try another approach through her son Edmund, and to this end arranged a trip to Bristol Hotwells, taking 'my 2d daughter Fanny' along with him.

This was Fanny's first, and possibly only, visit to Bristol, and lasted only three days, but the impression made on the fifteen-year-old must have been extremely vivid, for she set a large part of her first published novel there. She had no idea of the real purpose of her father's visit – to her it was a delightful privilege to be his sole companion, a pleasure possibly enhanced by the melancholy association of the Hotwells with her mother's last illness. Any special marks of attention from her father must have been flattering, and one can imagine that Burney was in a particularly animated mood at the thought of gaining consent to his nuptials. He was also, presumably, keen to give Fanny a treat of some kind, knowing that if his plans went ahead, there would no longer be any question of her going abroad to school.

Burney took Fanny with him again, with one of her sisters (probably Susan), when he went to Lynn in June 1767 for a wild courtship holiday. It was the first time Fanny had been back to her native town since the family moved to London in 1760, and it was of course another place deeply associated with her mother. They stayed at Mrs Allen's dower-house opposite St Margaret's for a month, during which time Burney and Mrs Allen visited 'almost every place and thing that is curious in Norfolk, making love chemin faisant'[54] (the way Burney did everything).

Dolly Young acted as chaperone on this tour, but was possibly not very strict, nor always in attendance. Who else, after all, was there to attend to the girls while Burney was 'making love', if not Dolly?

By the end of their romantic holiday, the couple had come to an agreement. They were to marry, but secretly; only their closest friends, Dolly Young and Samuel Crisp, were to know about it. The ceremony took place on 2 October at St James's Church, Westminster. Charles must have found some excuse of work to account for his three-day absence on honeymoon at a farmhouse near Chesington Hall – arranged by Crisp – after which he and his new wife returned to their separate houses in town as if nothing had happened. Several reasons for this strange deception suggest themselves. Old Mrs Allen, Elizabeth's mother,* viewed Burney as a fortune-hunter, and continued to disapprove of the match. Perhaps Elizabeth's brother Edmund also disapproved, since he took no part in the wedding. As it was, the bride was given away by her banker, Richard Fuller. Since the couple did not wait to gain the Allen family's consent, either they had given up trying to win it as hopeless, or they had become lovers and wanted the cover of legitimacy (albeit secret) in case Elizabeth became pregnant. Charles Burney had, after all, got Esther pregnant before they were married, a fact that Elizabeth, as an intimate of both parties, would very probably have known.

The banker was a symbolic presence at the ceremony that October morning, since the disparity of wealth between the couple had threatened the match, and was still being argued over by the bride's son and the groom's daughter sixty-six years later. Mrs Allen had, at what date is unclear, invested a large part of her £5000 in the English Factory in Russia, which subsequently failed. In an overtly self-justifying letter to Dolly Young,[55] Charles Burney claimed that his second wife's money was *almost all gone* before the Russian bankruptcy, which itself was 'many months before our marriage'. If this had been the case, his wife must have frittered away a fortune in the four years of her widowhood and come to the new marriage dependent on *him*. But by remarking 'I never touched a penny from the wreck in Russia', Burney acknowledges that something was salvaged from it; Stephen Allen, Elizabeth's son, claimed

---

* 'Allen' was Elizabeth's maiden name as well as her first married name.

this sum was as much as £1000 (again, the date at which it was recovered is unknown). Allen also reckoned that his mother was in possession of at least £600 at the time of her marriage, and was owed £900 by a family friend, James Simpson.* With her properties and the rent from them added, the whole amount his mother brought to her second marriage was 'not actuated at less than £4000'.[56]

Fanny's rather jaundiced impression, expressed in her correspondence following the publication of her *Memoirs of Doctor Burney*, was that if the second Mrs Burney was wealthy at the time of her marriage, she did not spend the money on anyone but herself. Her father had, understandably, seen it more as a matter of pride to himself than blame to his wife that he continued to support his family by force of sheer hard work 'without encroaching on the income of my wife'.[57] The notion that Elizabeth's money made no difference to the household is disingenuous, however. The Burneys' standard of living rose considerably (including the grand acquisition of their own coach), and Charles Burney, whether because of his reduced workload or increased well-being (or both), suddenly saw his career taking off in previously unthought-of ways. Within two years of his remarriage he had taken his doctorate at Oxford, written his first book, and was preparing for an extensive research tour on the Continent. Elizabeth was the enabling factor in all this.

The dispute in the 1830s between Stephen Allen and Fanny Burney confined itself to the matter of Elizabeth Allen Burney's money, but there was a great deal more for a son to object to in Fanny's *Memoirs* than the insinuation that his mother was 'destitute of any provision when she consented to a second marriage'.[58] Fanny's version of the growth of affection between Mrs Allen and her father clearly reflected her own difficulties in coming to terms with it, but it is almost breathtakingly unfair and inaccurate if we are to believe Dr Burney's own account (and there is no reason why we should not) in the fragmentary memoirs on which Fanny herself purported to be basing her book.

In Fanny's account, the affair was initiated by Mrs Allen ('very handsome, but no longer in her bloom'[59]) on her arrival in London with Maria. She was widowed, but not, Fanny suggests, very severely, unlike

---

* Why she should have loaned such an enormous sum, apparently without interest, for a period of thirty years, is a mystery.

Charles Burney, whose 'superior grief' was 'as deep as it was acute'.[60] Her father's degree of grieving was a problem for Fanny, who was disturbed by the thought that he might have 'got over' Esther's death. She makes his profound bereavement not only the cause of 'feeling admiration' in Mrs Allen, who 'saw him with daily increasing interest',[61] but a way of clearing her father of any complicity in the affair: 'insensibly he became solaced, while involuntarily she grew grateful, upon observing her rising influence over his spirits'. Pages of Fanny's chapter on 'Mrs Stephen Allen' are taken up with eulogies of her own dead mother, put into the mind, if not the mouth, of Charles Burney:

> If, by any exertion of which mortal man is capable, or any suffering which mortal man can sustain, Mr. Burney could have called back his vanished Esther to his ecstatic consciousness, labour, even to decrepitude, endurance even to torture, he would have borne, would have sought, would have blessed, for the most transient sight of her adored form.[62]

In an attempt to rebut the idea that her father's willingness to remarry might undermine the 'pristine connubial tenderness' of his first vows, Fanny came up with an ingenious interpretation of his behaviour, extremely unflattering to her stepmother:

> The secret breast, alive to memory though deprived of sympathy, may still internally adhere to its own choice and fondness; notwithstanding the various and imperious calls of current existence may urge a second alliance: and urge it, from feelings and from affections as clear of inconstancy as of hypocrisy; urge it, from the best of motives, that of accommodating ourselves to our lot, with all its piercing privations; since our lot is dependent upon causes we have no means to either evade or fathom; and as remote from our direction as our wishes.[63]

In other words, Charles Burney remarried, but stayed secretly, 'internally' faithful to 'the angel whom [he] had lost'. He 'recoiled from such an anodyne as demanded new vows to a new object', but couldn't help inflaming Mrs Allen all the more with the pathos of his vulnerability and 'noble disinterestedness' in her fortune when it was 'completely lost' in the Russian bankruptcy.[64] So much for the 'not less than £4000' Stephen

Allen spoke of. So much, also, for any hint of Charles Burney's 'very impassioned' feelings for Mrs Allen, his 'constant importunity' and pursuit of her to a hasty, secret marriage against her family's wishes and her own best interests materially. If Fanny had got one thing right, it was that Elizabeth Allen must have felt unusually 'impassioned' about her new husband in return.

Fanny was writing her account, it must be remembered, more than sixty years later, and the intensity she ascribes to Charles Burney's bereavement reflects her own intense losses by that date. But if the gulf of years makes it hard for her to untangle her own motives and feelings, it adds interest to the details which she considers significant with hindsight. There is no record of when the news of their father's marriage was broken to the Burney children. Charles Burney simply relates that he and his new wife 'kept our union as secret as possible for a time, inhabiting different houses'.[65] Fanny goes further, relating that though the secret was 'faithfully preserved, for a certain time, by scrupulous discretion in the parties, and watchful circumspection in the witnesses' (Crisp and Miss Young), something happened to force the hand of the clandestine couple:

> as usual also, error and accident were soon at work to develop the transaction; and the loss of a letter, through some carelessness of conveyance, revealed suddenly but irrevocably the state of the connection.
>
> This circumstance, however, though, at the time, cruelly distressing, served ultimately but to hasten their own views; as the discovery was necessarily followed by the personal union for which their hands had been joined.[66]

What the miscarried letter contained is of less importance than at which address it was 'lost', Burney's or his wife's, and by whom 'found'. 'Some carelessness of conveyance' – such a throwaway phrase – would have had to involve, in this case, either somebody wrongly opening a letter addressed to someone else, or reading a letter already opened by the addressee. The children had probably guessed that something was afoot between their father and Mrs Allen. Perhaps the discovery of the letter was an accident, perhaps not. If it was a deliberate act of snooping, it backfired nastily. We may wonder, but not wonder too long, given the authorship of that feeling phrase, who it was that found the incident so 'cruelly distressing'.

Perhaps in order to give the children time to accustom themselves to the situation, Charles Burney and his new wife continued to live mostly apart. By July 1768 it was no longer possible to hide the fact that Elizabeth was pregnant, but she still retained her spacious dower-house in Lynn and spent most of her time there. Fortunately, the Burney girls loved their new stepsister Maria Allen, and took their cue from her generous and optimistic view of the prospects of the new arrangements. Their devotion to their father was such, too, that they would not openly have said anything to hurt him. Fanny's wording is interesting when she describes how the sisters 'were all earnest to contribute their small mites to the happiness of one of the most beloved of parents, by receiving, with the most respectful alacrity, the lady on whom he had cast his future hopes of regaining domestic comfort'.[67] One gets the impression that even if Elizabeth Allen had been an ogress, the children would have made an effort for their father's sake. It does not mean that the shock of the news or their embarrassment was any the less.

For Fanny, writing in the 1820s as an old woman alone in her house in Mayfair, the recollection of this period provokes two strong associations: one the memory of her dead mother, abandoned, as it were, by the abrupt and unwanted change in the family's life, and the other of her own lost last chance at being given an education. The Paris plans for herself and Charlotte, kept on hold for years, were given up entirely when the new household shook down. Seven-year-old Charlotte went away to school in Norfolk, young Charles went to Charterhouse, but at sixteen Fanny was too old for schooling. Her third-person account in her biography of her father fails to contain the resentful disappointment she felt:

The second [daughter], Frances, was the only one of Mr Burney's family who never was placed in any seminary, and never was put under any governess or instructor whatsoever. Merely and literally self-educated, her sole emulation for improvement, and sole spur for exertion, were her unbounded veneration for the character, and unbounded affection for the person, of her father; who, nevertheless, had not, at the time, a moment to spare for giving her any personal lessons; or even for directing her pursuits.[68]

Much has been made of the violent antipathy that grew up between the second Mrs Burney and her stepdaughters, but the relationship started out well enough. Fanny's efforts to like her new stepmother, whom she immediately and without irony called 'Mama' or 'my mother', may not have been wholehearted (as is evidenced by the completeness with which she gave them up), but they were sincere. The new Mrs Burney recognised Fanny's sensitivity and singled her out as a possible ally, though typically, she seemed to be giving with one hand and taking away with the other when she remarked in company in the very early days of the new household, 'Here's a Girl will *never* be happy! *Never* while she Lives! for she possesses perhaps as feeling a Heart as ever Girl had!'[69] The new Mrs Burney's manner was emphatic, her opinions set and her voice loud. She was robustly unaware of getting on anyone's nerves, and, seen in a good light, this passed for artlessness. Certainly, Charles Burney loved and admired her uncritically – referring to her as 'my beloved' and 'the dear soul' in his memoirs[70] – and the girls greatly appreciated how much happier she made him. Proof of her fondness and partiality for Fanny is shown by her pathetic appeal to the sixteen-year-old to look after her baby if she should die (as she feared she might) in childbirth. The 'feeling' teenager could not but have been moved, both by the appeal and also by the role allocated to her as substitute wife to her father:

> Allow me my dear Fanny to take this moment (if there proves occasion) to recommend a helpless Infant to your Pity and Protection [...] & you will, I *do* trust you will, for your *same* dear Father's sake, cherish & support *His* innocent child – 'tho but *half* allied to you – My Weak Heart speaks in Tears to you my Love,[71]

The baby, a boy named Richard, was born safely in November 1768 and was much-loved by his half-sisters.

As late as 1773, Fanny was writing in her journal with genuine concern for her 'poor mother', whom she was nursing through a bilious fever: 'this is the third Night that I have sit [sic] up with her – but I hope to Heaven that she is now in a way to recover. She has been most exceeding kind to us ever since her return to Town – which makes me the more sensibly feel her illness'.[72]

This must make us treat with caution the suggestion first made by

Charlotte Barrett in the introduction to Madame D'Arblay's post-humously published *Diary and Letters*, and adjusted into fact by sub-sequent writers (including Thomas Macaulay, Virginia Woolf, Austin Dobson and Emily Hahn), that Fanny's stepmother disapproved so strongly of her 'scribbling propensity' that on her fifteenth birthday Fanny burned all her manuscripts and resolved to give up writing. The bonfire, which took place in the yard of the Poland Street house (with Susan, in tears, the only witness), seems to have been real enough, but the motives for it are cloudy. Fanny Burney first wrote about the incident in the dedication to *The Wanderer*, published in 1814, a piece of writing that seeks to justify the appearance of her latest novel by dramatising her vocation as in itself a kind of inextinguishable flame. Her motive for destroying the 'enormous' pile of early works was, she says, shame: 'ideas that fastened degradation to this class of composition' convinced her that novel-writing was a 'propensity' to be struggled against, an 'inclination' to be conquered only by drastic action: 'I committed to the flames whatever, up to that moment, I had committed to paper'.[73] She tells the story again nearly twenty years later in the long third-person narrative in her *Memoirs of Doctor Burney* that deals with her own writing history: 'she considered it her duty to combat this writing passion as illaudible, because fruitless. [. . .] she made over to a bonfire [. . .] her whole stock of prose goods and chattels; with the sincere intention to extinguish for ever in their ashes her scribbling propensity'.[74] Neither of these accounts, the only ones left by Fanny herself, indicates the influence of a third party; the first of them is specifically concerned with making a much larger statement – as we shall see later – about the value of the novel as a form. Mrs Barrett introduced the wicked stepmother into the story in her introduction to the 1842 *Diary*, describing how Mrs Burney's 'vigilant eye [. . .] was not long in discovering Fanny's love of seclusion, her scraps of writing, and other tokens of her favourite employment, which excited no small alarm in her'. Alarm and, it is implied, resentment.

Hindsight and wishful thinking, as we have seen, are likely to have coloured anything Madame D'Arblay told her niece about this period of her youth. The second Mrs Burney was unlikely to have had any influence at all over Fanny at the time of the bonfire (variously placed 'on my fifteenth birth-day', i.e. 13 June 1767,[75] 'from the time she attained her fifteenth year'[76] and 'in the young authoress's fifteenth year',[77] i.e. some time between June 1766 and June 1767). At these times, Fanny was barely aware of Elizabeth Allen except as an old family friend. Mrs Allen was still Charles Burney's secret *amour*; hardly in a position to 'inveigh very frequently and seriously against the evil of a scribbling turn in young ladies – the loss of time, the waste of thought, in idle, crude inventions'.[78] These sentiments, if ever uttered by Mrs Burney to Fanny, seem to belong to a later and more intimate period.

From the many self-conscious references in the diaries she began to write several months *after* the bonfire, it is clear that Fanny was going through a phase of experiment, the results of which often dissatisfied her (and tempted her to commit the journal itself 'to the Flames'[79]). Destroying her juvenilia could thus have had more to do with a resolve to write *differently*, rather than not write at all. Having read the contents of her bureau through to Susan, perhaps Fanny realised that she had written herself into something of a dead end with 'Elegies, Odes' et cetera. 'Caroline Evelyn' was a gloomy novel, and she was not feeling gloomy any longer. The fact that she wrote a sequel to 'Caroline Evelyn' which used the same characters but transfigured the story into a comedy is surely of significance. As an attempt to 'annihilate' the passion to write,[80] the purging bonfire, with its overtones of amateur witchcraft and spell-casting, was spectacularly unsuccessful, and was not repeated.

The journal Fanny started in March 1768 was the ideal testing ground for a variety of rhetorical styles, from the sublime (usually curtailed with self-deflating irony) to the commonplace. The first entry, in which she sets up her alter-ego, the 'romantick Girl' Miss Nobody, is pure performance, executed with brio by the 'backward' fifteen-year old:

> To Nobody, then, will I write my Journal! since To Nobody can I be wholly unreserved – to Nobody can I reveal every thought, every wish of my Heart, with the most unlimited confidence, the most unremitting sincerity to the end of my Life! For what chance, what accident can end my connections with Nobody? No secret *can* I conceal from No—body, & to No—body can I be *ever* unreserved.[81]

'I must imagion myself to be talking – talking to the most intimate of friends', Fanny had decided. The second entry attempts this ingeniously, with a send-up of 'girl-talk': 'O my dear – such a charming Day! – & then last night – well, you shall have it all in order – – as well as I can recollect'.[82] The diary allowed her to be skittish, serious, even dull: 'Nobody' was a tolerant audience, 'the most complaisant friend in the world – ever ready to comply with my wishes – never hesitating to oblige, never averse to any concluding, yet never wearried [sic] with my beginning – charming Creature'.[83]

The first years of the diary (patchily kept up) are the only part of Fanny Burney's huge output as a journal-writer that can be thought of as secret or confidential. Interestingly, they show that the sensitive, 'feeling' teenager actually possessed quite a cold eye. Here she is describing the family's cook's wedding:

The Bride. A maiden of about fifty, short, thick, clumsy, vulgar; her complection the finest saffron, & her Features suited to it[84]

and here a performance of Rowe's *Tamerlane* by the schoolboys of the Soho Academy:

the young Gentleman who perform'd Selima, stopt short, & forgot himself – it was in a Love scene – between her -- him I mean & Axalla – who was very tender – She – he – soon recover'd tho - Andrew whisper'd us, that when it was over – '*He'd lick her!* –' St[r]atocles amused himself with no other action at all, but beating, with one Hand, his Breast, & with the other, held his Hat.[85]

She didn't develop this mode of comic writing, but it clearly worked as a release valve for a highly intelligent teenager who was never allowed to utter a harsh word in public. 'Participation or relief'[86] were the two reasons she gave for keeping her early diary. 'I have known the Time', she wrote in 1771, 'when I could enjoy Nothing, without relating it'.

The creation of an imaginary confidante allowed Fanny to write the journal as if it were a series of letters; she went on to write letters to Samuel Crisp, in the avid correspondence that she started with him in 1773, as if she were writing a journal. To her sister Susan, she was to write journal-letters, blurring the distinctions further. The discovery of how fluid form could be was emancipating: Fanny Burney wrote a novel in letters that people said sounded like a play, and a play that ended up being partly reshaped into a novel. There were also tragic dramas that aspired to the condition of epic poetry and that weird hybrid, *Memoirs of Doctor Burney*, a biographical autobiography, using novel-writing techniques. It seems paradoxical that a writer who in her maturity was so anxious about the moral and intellectual acceptability of her works' content should grant herself this licence with form (and with style and usage too). Perhaps both stemmed from her perception of what was appropriate to her sex; 'lively freedoms' in her works were unthinkable, just as too much elegance might have seemed pretentious.

Fanny Burney's inventiveness with language is an aspect of her achievement that has been largely overlooked. Her work is so full of significant coinages, conversions, new compounds and new formulations that one commentator has felt moved to say that 'she seems worthy to stand alongside Pope, Dr Johnson and Sir Walter Scott as one of Bradley's "Makers of English" '.[87] Left to educate herself, Fanny had been inventing and adapting words from an early age, and grew up happy to adjust language to suit the requirements of the moment, as a sardonic journal entry from 1775 shows: 'Making Words, now & then, in familiar Writing, is unavoidable, & saves the trouble of *thinking*, which, as Mr Adison observes, we Females are not much addicted to'.[88] Family usage encouraged the habit of coinage: the Burneys employed quantities of catchphrases, nonsense terms and nicknames, for fun (a very new word) and the sheer pleasure of invention but also as a form of private language, a family code that was impenetrable to outsiders. The critic R.B. Johnson has deplored Susan Burney's 'barbarisms' and her father's 'passion for hybrid phrasing, and the pseudo-wit of made-up words': the whole family, he complained, 'was too impatient of solid culture to acquire sound literary taste'.[89] It may well be the case that this generation of Burneys was 'impatient of solid culture', though it is hard to see how the characteristic Burney letter style could have gained more than it would have lost from classical polish. Fanny's success as a novelist owes a lot to the quirky, 'unsound' family register which she reproduced in her journals and letters and took, in modified but distinctive and expressive forms, into her published works.

Fanny Burney's coinage of words, particularly evident in her early diaries, was mostly humorous and deliberately inelegant: 'snugship', 'shockation', 'scribbleration' – these words draw attention to themselves, and were meant to. More widespread, but less obvious to later readers – because her usages have been so well assimilated – are the examples in her work of parts of speech she has transposed or converted: 'to fight shy' is one such, 'to shilly-shally' (contracted from 'to stand shilly-shally'), 'beautify' (used intransitively), 'to make something of', and, going from verb to noun, 'take-in' and 'break-up'. She might have invented these forms, and was certainly the first person to record them. The 'common language of men' was of perennial interest to Fanny, and the realism of her novels derives in great part from her use of contemporary slang and colloquialisms (such as 'I'd do it as soon as say Jack Robinson,' which first appeared in *Evelina*[90]). Each of the novels relies heavily on the power of speech to reveal character and class, and contains long stretches of dialogue which are essentially satirical inventories of contemporary usage and abusage. In her 'elevated' style (usually reserved for the heroines' crises, when common language is abandoned altogether) she is conspicuously at her least inventive.

To quantify her impact on English and American usage would be extremely difficult, but some idea of it can be gleaned from the list of 'Additions to O.E.D. from the Writings of Fanny Burney'[91] compiled by J.N. Waddell, included as an appendix to this book. It shows how frequently Fanny formed verbs with -ise or -ize endings (diarise, scribblerise, journalise) and negative adjectives and adverbs, twenty-eight of which are listed in the *New English Dictionary* as first appearing in her work, including 'unobtrusively', 'unremittingly' and 'unamusing'. Waddell has also demonstrated the extent of her inventiveness,[92] from the possible first use of compounds such as 'school-girl' and 'dinner-party', to her borrowings from French later in life (after her marriage), which include 'maisonnette' and 'bon-bon', and her anticipations of Americanisms in words such as 'alphabetize' and 'tranquiliser'. The link between her personal register and forms that were emerging at the same time in eighteenth-century American English is particularly interesting. Many Americanisms deliberately subvert the mother tongue (or, some critics might say, distort it with ugly, overlong, philologically impure neologisms). It is a suggestive coincidence that Fanny Burney was writing her first novel during the early part of the American War of Independence, and that the infant nation was developing its characteristic language traits in the years when her novels, with their heavy reliance on slang, vogue and new words, had achieved cult status.

Fanny Burney's freedom with language reflects her self-image as an 'outsider' in literature and her defiance of conventional limitations in a manner that could be seen as rebellious, even revolutionary; but, as with her natural and powerful feminism, her sense of propriety, personal prejudices and deep conservatism all militated against her acknowledging this. The more she did acknowledge it, the more inhibited her writing became. Any connection with anti-conventionality, however abstract, was problematic for her, as we shall see in numerous instances. She deplored disrespect to authority, and was such an arch-Tory in her youth that even her father (not a man noted for his liberal politics) teased her with the nickname 'Fanny Bull'. But howevermuch her conservatism affected her behaviour socially, it never inhibited Fanny Burney from inventing words and phrases – 'John Bullism' itself is one of them.[93] As Wadell has remarked, her innovations 'reveal a relaxed enjoyment of language for its own sake, and an unashamed pleasure in its flexibility', and set her apart as a 'transcriber of the ordinary, as well as a pioneer in the unusual'. Whatever other anxieties Fanny Burney developed as a writer, language remained an area where she felt perfectly free.

Female Caution

In 1768, the year when Fanny began to write her diary, Hetty Burney and Maria Allen, aged nineteen and seventeen respectively, were making their entrances into the world. Fanny observed their progress with profound interest and a degree of ironic detachment. Both the older girls had plenty of admirers and indulged to the full the drama of playing them off against each other. Subsequent to every evening out there would be a trail of young men calling at Poland Street, some dull, some rakish, some unsure which girl to court, some, like Hetty's admirer Mr Seton, happy to talk to Fanny in her sister's absence, and to discover, as the chosen few did, how well the sixteen-year-old could keep up a conversation:

> [Mr Seton]: I vow, if I had gone into almost any other House, & talk'd at this rate to a young lady, she would have been sound a sleep by this Time; Or at least, she would have amused me with gaping & yawning, all the time, & certainly, she would not have understood a word I had utter'd.
> F. 'And so, this is your opinion of our sex? – '
> Mr S. 'Ay; – & of *mine* too.'[1]

'I scarse wish for any thing so truly, really & greatly, as to be in love', Fanny confessed to patient 'Nobody', but she didn't relish being the object of someone else's adoration. A 'mutual tendresse' would be too much to ask for – 'I carry not my wish so far'.[2]

Fanny was just reaching the age at which she was allowed to accompany the older girls to assemblies and dances, some of which went on all night. They would set off in the family coach and straggle home in hired sedan chairs at seven or eight in the morning. There were seldom any chaperones (sometimes because the girls had deceived their father into thinking there was no necessity for one, and he was too negligent to check). Fanny made her first serious conquest – a youth called Tomkin whom she didn't want – at the most sophisticated and risqué of the entertainments on offer to young women at the time, a masquerade. Masquerade balls were notorious as places of assignation, and excited widespread disapproval. Henry Fielding's brother, the famous magistrate Sir John Fielding, had been trying for years to close down the establishment run by Mrs Corneley, an ex-lover of Casanova. Contemporary engravings of her parties in Soho Square show some bizarre characters, including a man leading a live bear and a person dressed as (or rather, in) a coffin, with his feet protruding from the bottom and eyeholes cut in the lid. There is also a masquerader in the character of Adam, naked except for a shrubbery loincloth, which recalls the scandalous costume of Miss Chudleigh at the Venetian Ambassador's masquerade, who went as 'Iphigenia', wearing nothing but a piece of gauze.[3]

Fanny Burney had nothing quite so challenging to deal with at Mr Lalauze's masquerade in Leicester Square: there was a nun, a witch (who turned out to be a man), a Punch, an Indian Queen, several Dominoes and the predictable flock of shepherdesses. The Burney girls had spent the whole day dressing, Hetty in a Savoyard costume, complete with hurdy-gurdy, and Fanny (much less adventurously) in 'meer fancy Dress', a highly-decorated pink Persian gown with a rather badly home-made mask. Despite its flimsiness, the mask gave Fanny 'a courage I never before had in the presence of strangers'[4] and, as with Mr Seton, she 'did not spare' the company. According to the procedure at masquerades, everyone was obliged to support their character, passing from one person to another asking, 'Do you know me? Who are you?'[5] until partners had been chosen and the dramatic (or not) moment of unmasking arrived. Fanny's partner was a 'Dutchman' (Mr Tomkin) who had spent the evening grunting at her and using sign language. 'Nothing could be more droll than the first Dance we had after unmasking', she told Nobody later:

> to see the pleasure which appeared in some Countenances, & the disappointment pictured in others made the most singular contrast imaginable, & to see the Old turned Young, & the Young Old, – in short every Face appeared diferent [sic] from what we expected.[6]

The confusion of expectations and the burlesque aspects of the masquerade appealed strongly to Fanny's imagination, and her use of masquerade in her second novel, *Cecilia*, shows how well she appreciated its symbolic potential. In the novel, the heroine is tormented by her frustrated admirer Monckton, who is indulging his fantasies by dressing as a demon with a red 'wand'. She is forcibly detained by this supposed guardian, who never speaks, but uses his devilish character to intimidate the whole company. Cecilia describes this anarchic evening as one 'from which she had received much pleasure', and which 'excited at once her curiosity and amazement'.[7] The abdication of identity in the masquerade is seen as both exciting and dangerous.

Fanny Burney had a much less sheltered upbringing than most middle-class girls of her time, and the constant stream of musicians, writers, singers, actors and travellers that passed through the Burney household provided endless matter for amazement and speculation. It was a peculiarly worldly atmosphere for an unworldly, innocent-minded girl to observe, and she found it attractive without always being able to identify quite why. As a novelist, she developed a taste for drama and high colouring which some critics have seen as almost an obsession with the violence potential in genteel life.[8] The heroines of Burney novels are beyond reproach morally, but are constantly exposed to bizarre and outlandish events that the author is not afraid to depict as stimulating. This indicates a relish for experience which the novel form allowed Fanny Burney to emphasise and exaggerate – the freedom that the mask at Mr Lalauze's had given her not to hide her true colours, but to reveal them.

The habit of writing, whether it was her journal or creative 'vagaries', and the secretive solitude it required became such pleasures to Fanny that she resented other calls on her time. The social duties of adult life that obliged women to be forever receiving and returning visits and performing 'constrained Civilities to Persons quite indifferent to us'[9] left her cold. 'Mama' was very keen on these civilities (she no doubt saw them as essential in a household full of girls in the marriage market), and one of Fanny's outbursts in her journal hints at the tensions that were arising from the new regime:

those who shall pretend to defy this irksome confinement of our happiness, must stand accused of incivility, – breach of manners – love of originality, – & God knows what not – nevertheless, they who will nobly dare to be above submitting to Chains their reason disapproves, they shall I always honour – if that will be of any service to them![10]

The cryptic references to 'Chains' and 'defiance' indicate the dramatic terms in which the teenaged Burney girls saw their struggle against 'Mama' and her set ideas about a woman's destiny. At this point in her life, Fanny had no thought of her writings being published or even read by anyone other than 'Nobody', or Susan at the very most, but writing already defined her sense of autonomy, in terms both of what she wrote and the liberty she required to write it.

Fanny's invention of the deliberately trivialising term 'scribbleration' for her writing was a sort of disclaimer, disassociating herself from authorship, which was the preserve of the venerated 'class of authors'. Her father was about to join that class himself, in the same year (1769) that he finally took his doctorate in music at Oxford. When a friend called Steele suggested that Burney wasn't making enough of his new academic title, and urged him to change his door-plate, the new doctor replied, self-consciously slipping into dialect, 'I wants dayecity, I'm ashayum'd!'[11] Want of 'dayecity' – or the affectation of such – ran even stronger in his daughter. When her father was in Oxford for the performance of his examination piece, Fanny sent him some comic verses that she had composed to mark the occasion. He was so amused that he read them aloud to casual acquaintances in Oxford, and teased her when he got home by reciting them in front of the family. Fanny tried to snatch the verses from him, but he carried on, and all she felt she could do was run out of the room. Her delight that he was not angry at her 'pert verses'[12] made her creep back again, though, to hear his praises surreptitiously. It was a premonition of all her later fears and ambivalence about the reception of her work and her father's approval of it in particular.

Charles Burney's doctorate (which was, of course, soon brazened – Steele' s pun – on the Poland Street door) conferred an authority which was helpful to his self-esteem and to the new turn he wanted his career to take. In October his first book, a short, businesslike *Essay towards a history of the principal comets that have appeared since 1742*, was published.

The subject was timely and topical; astronomy was fashionable, and 1769 was the year in which Halley had predicted the return of his comet 'in confirmation of the theory of the illustrious Sir Isaac Newton'. But though Burney's little book shows his commercial instincts at work (it sold well enough to be reprinted the following year), it had a personal significance as well, being a form of homage to the dead Esther. Years before, she had made a translation of the French scientist Maupertuis's 'Letter upon Comets', purely from 'love of improvement', according to Fanny[13] (rather like Fanny's own youthful translation of Fontanelle). Esther's interest in astronomy had fuelled her husband's – she might well have been looking forward to the reappearance of the great comet herself. Charles Burney revised the translation and wrote his own essay as a companion piece, a gesture which was not lost on their daughter. In the *Memoirs* she describes the work as a *joint* project by her parents, and prefaces her remarks with the apparently irrelevant information that the second Mrs Burney was staying in Norfolk at the time of its production – as if the book constituted some kind of secret assignation between Burney and his dead wife. At the distance of more than fifty years, Fanny wrote portentously about her father's first step into print, and was in no doubt who should take the credit: her mother's pure 'love of improvement' had 'unlocked [. . .] the gates through which Doctor Burney first passed to that literary career which, ere long, greeted his more courageous entrance into a publicity that conducted him to celebrity'.[14]

The *Essay* was only a short work but it kept Dr Burney up late at night, and its completion was followed by an acute bout of rheumatic fever. The pattern of overwork, hurry and collapse during the composition of his books may have impressed the Doctor's daughter with the idea that writing was something urgent, difficult and heroic. Burney had by this time formulated the plan for his *General History of Music*, the first scholarly attempt in English to cover the development of the subject from ancient times to his own day. To choose a project so massive and challenging suggests that Burney had tired of dabbling and wanted a surefire ticket to fame (and fortune, of course), to be the author of a work which would virtually put itself beyond criticism on account of its novelty, authority and sheer size, and which, like the *Dictionary* of his admired Johnson, would contribute substantially to knowledge, in an age when all the best minds of Europe seemed engaged on writing works of reference.

Burney felt that his book would only make the proper impact if it derived from original research in the great music libraries of Europe, also that 'the present state of modern music' was the most important part of his subject. Armed with letters of recommendation from his influential friends to British officials in France and Italy, he set off on a six-month Continental tour in June 1770. It was an arduous but extremely productive journey, and though Burney was in a state of collapse on his return, he had met many famous and learned people, including Padre G.B. Martini in Bologna, the foremost musicologist of the time, the castrato Farinelli in Venice, the seventy-five-year-old Voltaire at Ferney (by an engineered accident), and in Paris Denis Diderot and the great Rousseau himself. The 'Man Mountain' was sitting in a dark corner, wearing a woollen nightcap, greatcoat and slippers, an informal reception which perhaps encouraged Burney to show him his plan for the *History*, which to the budding author's delight, and after a little initial resistance on Rousseau's part, went down encouragingly well.

Burney kept a detailed journal of his tour, and soon after his return to London began to think of publishing it as a money-spinner and as an advertisement for the forthcoming *History*. With the help of the girls, he had a manuscript ready within four months which was published in May 1771 as *The Present State of Music in France and Italy*. The market for 'tour' books was saturated at the time, but Burney's had the novelty of its focus on music and performers, as well as gripping passages about the difficulties of travel, such as this description of crossing the Apennines:

> At every moment, I could only hear them cry out 'Alla Montagna!' which meant to say that the road was so broken and dangerous that it was necessary I should alight, give the Mule to the Pedino, and cling to the rock or precipice. I got three or four terrible blows on the face and head by boughs of trees I could not see. In mounting my Mule, which was vicious, I was kicked by the two hind legs on my left knee and right thigh, which knocked me down, and I thought at first, and the Muleteers thought my thigh was broken, and began to pull at it and add to the pain most violently.[15]

The reviews of the book would probably have been good anyway, but Burney, in his acute anxiety to succeed, fixed the two most influential ones, in the *Monthly Review* and the *Critical Review*.[16] He described himself as a 'diffident and timid author',[17] but he had a ruthless streak, especially when it came to nobbling the opposition (as he did shamelessly when a rival *History of Music*, by Sir John Hawkins, appeared before his own). His later anxieties about his daughter's literary career centred on the possible critical reception of her books; he felt it better for her not to publish at all than to risk adverse reviews.

With their father's absence abroad in 1770, followed by the rush to write his book, and another long trip to Europe in 1772 to gather material for a sequel, the Burney children were left even more than usual in the undiluted company of their stepmother. While the Doctor was in Italy, Mrs Burney found and purchased a new home for the amalgamated Burney-Allen household. It was a large, luxurious house on the south side of Queen Square, an area familiar to the children from their long association with Mrs Sheeles's school (Burney's appointment there lasted from 1760 to about 1775). Fanny liked the open view of the villages of Hampstead and Highgate to the north, and rooms that were 'well fitted up, Convenient, large, & handsome', but regretted leaving Poland Street, which represented the old days of her parents' marriage.

One of the reasons for the move was to get away from the family's former neighbour Mrs Pringle, at whose house the Burney girls had met Alexander Seton, the baronet's son who had been so impressed with Fanny's conversational powers. His flirtation with Hetty had been so on-and-off for the past two years that she felt forced to give up seeing him altogether for her own peace of mind, and Mr Crisp's advice (backed up by 'Mama') was that the Burneys should end contact with Mrs Pringle too. Fanny was pained to cut her old friend, but did it all the same, and was ready with some lies when the puzzled matron asked what the matter was. In all 'difficult' dealings of this kind, the Burneys displayed unattractive qualities: panic, fudging and petty cruelty, such as in the case of their former friend Miss Lalauze, whom they treated with a species of horror after she was reputed to have 'fallen'. Their own struggle to sustain their upward mobility seems to have prevented them from behaving more magnanimously to such people 'however sincerely they may be objects of Pity'.[18]

Hetty recovered from her disappointment over Seton (and avoided having to join the new step-household) by marrying her cousin and fellow musician Charles Rousseau Burney in the autumn of 1770. Dr Burney was abroad at the time and unable to give his consent. He would not have approved the match; he was very fond of his nephew, a gentle, talented man, but knew as well as anyone how hard it was to make a decent living out of music. The marriage was happy, but never prosperous materially. Before long, Hetty was expecting the first of her eight children (the last of which was born as late as 1792). Her career as a harpsichordist was of course over. Fanny, as the eldest unmarried daughter, now acquired the title 'Miss Burney'.

At about the same time, Maria Allen was jilted by a young man called Martin Rishton. To cheer her up after this disappointment, Fanny wrote her a poem called 'Female Caution', which contains these stanzas:

> Ah why in faithless man repose
> The peace & safety of your mind?
> Why should ye seek a World of Woes,
> To Prudence and to Wisdom blind?
>
> Few of mankind confess your worth,
> Fewer reward it with their own:
> To Doubt and Terror Love gives birth;
> To Fear and Anguish makes ye known.
>
> [. . .] O, Wiser, learn to guard the heart,
> Nor let it's softness be its bane!
> Teach it to act a nobler part;
> What Love shall lose, let Friendship gain.
>
> Hail, Friendship, hail! To Thee my soul
> Shall undivided homage own;
> No Time thy influence shall controll;
> And Love and I – shall ne'er be known.[19]

This accomplished poem, which, strangely, has never found its way into any anthology of eighteenth-century verse, displays an advanced state of sexual cynicism in its eighteen-year-old author; men, she claims, do not have it in their nature to be constant, and are interested only in the process of conquest. Friendship (with women) is the only way to guarantee happiness; only among women can 'sensibility' and 'softness' survive undamaged. The fop and the cad were worrying social phenomena, coarse, worldly and unmarriageable. Fanny targeted such men in her novels and created heroes who presented a new 'feminine' ideal of masculinity, heroes who were (sometimes absurdly) super-sensitive, rational and gentle. Fanny admired, even idealised, older men such as Crisp, Garrick and the agriculturalist Arthur Young (who was married to Elizabeth Allen Burney's sister Martha), appreciated male gallantry and wit, and yearned romantically for an ideal male companion – but she didn't expect to find one. Her high standards were to cause her some trouble in an age when early marriage was the expected, and only really acceptable, fate of womankind.

Extrovert Maria Allen was the moving force behind several amateur theatrical productions in the Burney household and at Chesington in which Fanny was persuaded to take part, though few actors could ever have performed so consistently badly. Fanny was loath to perform in any way, being subject to terrible stage-fright that almost certainly originated in her stigmatisation as a 'dunce' in early childhood. Though at least one of the plays she took part in (Colley Cibber's *The Careless Husband*) was meant to be an exercise in overcoming stage-fright for the benefit of Dr Burney's former singing pupil Jenny Barsanti, who was giving up her career as a singer to become an actress (she went on to be the first Lydia Languish in Sheridan's *The Rivals*), nothing could distract Fanny from her own performance and its possible shortcomings. Howevermuch she wanted to join in with the gaiety and diversion of a family play-party, the moment when she had to appear, or speak, was one of disabling terror, as on this occasion at her uncle's house in Worcester, where her cousins were putting on a production of Arthur Murphy's *The Way to Keep Him*:

> Next came *my* scene; I was discovered Drinking Tea; – to tell you how *infinitely*, how *beyond measure* I was terrified at my situation, I really cannot [. . .] The few Words I had to speak before Muslin came to me, I know not whether I spoke or not, – niether [sic] does any body else: – so you need not enquire of others, for the matter is, to this moment, unknown.[20]

Fanny had a '*marking Face*'[21] and was a violent blusher. 'Nobody, I believe, has so *very* little command of Countenance as myself!' she complained to Susan on one of the many occasions when her 'vile Colouring' gave her acute embarrassment. The causes of her embarrassment varied enormously. It was *knowingness*, not innocence, that made her self-conscious in front of people such as Richard Twiss, a traveller who on his first visit to the Burney household in 1774 indulged in very 'free' conversation with Dr Burney about the prostitutes in Naples. Asked by Twiss whether she knew what he meant by a *ragazza*, Fanny records, 'I stammered out something like niether [sic] yes or no, because the Question rather frightened me, lest he should conclude that in understanding *that*, I knew much *more*.'[22] The inference of course is that she *did* know 'much more'. She certainly knew enough about John Cleland's erotic *Dictionary of Love* to be embarrassed by Twiss's reference to it on the same occasion. 'Questa signora ai troppo modesta', he said to Charles Burney of the blushing young woman he had been goading all evening, demonstrating the truth of James Fordyce's observation in his *Sermons* that many men find 'shyness' in women attractive sexually as well as morally. Fordyce implies that 'the precious colouring of virtue' on a girl's cheeks is the equivalent of showing a red rag to a bull: 'Men are so made,' he sighs complacently.[23] But Fanny was much more likely to have agreed with Jonathan Swift's acid judgement of female 'colouring': 'They blush because they understand.'[24]

Nevertheless she was highly resistant to sexual flattery, and too self-conscious to be vain. In her copious diary, she hardly ever mentions dress, although much of the needlework that the Burney girls, like all women of their class, were expected to do daily consisted in making and mending their own clothes. She disliked needlework and was not particularly good at it; if her clothes were ever eye-catching, it may not have been for the right reasons. Her best gown in 1777 was simply referred to as her 'grey-Green', presumably a silk or 'tabby', chosen to match the colour of her eyes.

Fanny Burney was quick to satirise the absurdities of fashion and personal vanity in her works: in *Evelina* the London modes provide plenty of humour, especially the mid-1770s fashion among women for high hair. In the novel, Miss Mirvan makes herself a cap, only to find that it won't fit over her new coiffure, and Evelina herself, the country girl agog at the novelty of going 'a-shopping, as Mrs Mirvan calls it'[25] (it was a very recently coined word), gives an insider's account of being pomaded, powdered and pinned:

> I have just had my hair dressed. You can't think how oddly my head feels; full of powder and black pins, and a great cushion on the top of it. I believe you would hardly know me, for my face looks quite different to what it did before my hair was dressed. When I shall be able to make use of a comb for myself I cannot tell for my hair is so much entangled, frizzled they call it, that I fear it will be very difficult.[26]

In Fanny's play *The Witlings*, the first scene is set in a milliner's shop, among the ribbons and gee-gaws that recur in her works as symbols of luxury and waste. The shop girls are slaves to appearances: Miss Jenny has no appetite because 'she Laces so tight, that she can't Eat half her natural victuals,' as one of the older women observes. 'Ay, ay', replies another, 'that's the way with all the Young Ladies; they pinch for their fine shapes'.[27] The unnaturalness of fashion struck Burney forcibly (as well it might in the age of hoops, stays, corsetry, high hair and silk shoes), but she also despised its triviality and the hold it had over so many women's lives, confirming them in the eyes of unsympathetic men as inferior beings. In her play *The Woman-Hater*, misogynistic Sir Roderick describes womankind as 'A poor sickly, mawkish set of Beings! What are they good for? What can they do? Ne'er a thing upon Earth they had not better let alone. [. . .] what ought they to know? except to sew a gown, and make a Pudding?'[28]

Each of Burney's novels contains some insight into the extent to which women are unfairly judged by their appearance. She was never very pleased with hers. Like all the Burneys she was very short – Samuel Johnson described her affectionately as 'Lilliputian'[29] – and slightly built, with very thick brown hair, lively, intelligent eyes and her father's large nose. She had an inward-sloping upper lip inherited from her mother (Hetty and Susan had the same), small hands and narrow shoulders. The portrait painted by her cousin Edward Francesco Burney in 1782 shows a gentle, intelligent and attractive face. She thought he had flattered her horribly, but how many portrait painters do not idealise their sitters, especially when, like Edward, the artist is also an admirer? His second portrait of her, painted only two years later (it now hangs in the National Portrait Gallery), has her face partly shadowed by an enormous hat. Her look is more thoughtful, slightly uncomfortable, but the benignly intelligent expression is the same.

Fanny Burney's short sight caused her trouble all her life and undoubtedly affected her behaviour. She became mildly paranoid about being scrutinised by other people because she couldn't see their expressions clearly and only felt really comfortable with things which fell within the circle of her vision, such as books, writing and intimate friends. Short sight affected her writing too; the novels are remarkable for the avoidance of physical description and heavy reliance on dialogue to delineate character. Fanny owned an eye-glass, but was often inhibited from using it; at Lady Spencer's in 1791 she 'did not choose to Glass' the company '& without, could not distinguish them'.[30] At court in the 1780s, the use of the eye-glass was, presumably, limited by protocol and many embarrassing incidents ensued when Fanny did not identify the King or Queen in time to respond correctly. She doesn't seem to have owned a glass in 1773 when she went to a performance at Drury Lane by the singer Elizabeth Linley one month before that siren's marriage to Richard Brinsley Sheridan; she could only make out Miss Linley's figure [...] & the form of her Face'.[31] By 1780, however, she could be pointed out at the threatre as 'the lady that used the glass'.[32] Understandably, she hated to have attention drawn to her disability, and scorned one of Mrs Thrale's acquaintance for suggesting that she could not see as far as the fire two yards away by answering his question 'How far can you see?' with a comical put-down; 'O – I don't know – as *far* as other people, but not *distinctly*'.[33]

Fanny's constitution was basically strong, but easily affected by nervous ailments and stress. '[H]er Frame is certainly delicate & feeble', Susan noted in her journal. 'She is quickly sensible of fatigue & cannot long resist it & still more quickly touched by any anxiety or distress of mind'.[34] Fanny endured remarkable pain, both physical and mental, in the course of her long life, and survived the appalling mutilation of the mastectomy she underwent for cancer in 1811 with astonishing tenacity and powers of recuperation, yet she appears to have been something of a hypochondriac in her youth, impressed with a belief in her own fragility and half-expecting to die young, like her mother. When Mrs Thrale once exclaimed against the idea of Fanny marrying a man old enough to be her father, Fanny replied, 'I dare say he will Live full as long as I shall, however much older he may be'.[35] The character of being frail, insubstantial, almost No-body, was oddly compelling, and she recorded with evident satisfaction the playwright Dr John Delap's remark in 1779 that she was 'the charmingest Girl in the World for a Girl who was so near being *nothing*, & they all agreed nobody ever had so little a shape before, & that a Gust of Wind would blow you quite away'.[36] The 'Girl' was, at this date, twenty-seven years old, unmarried, unhappy at being exposed to the public as a writer and not eating well.

Fanny's attitude to food and eating immediately suggests some sort of disorder. References to food in her journals and works are infrequent, and never enthusiastic or appreciative. She knew, as we have seen from *The Witlings*, about young women starving themselves to get into small-sized clothes; she also knew about bingeing. In *The Woman-Hater*, Miss Wilmot's unabashed relish for food is seen as a mark of her lack of feminine delicacy, and she characterises her old life of restraint and decorum as 'sitting with my hands before me; and making courtsies; and never eating half as much as I like, – except in the Pantry!'[37] Whether the Burney girls, singly or in gangs, raided the pantry in Poland Street or Queen Square is a matter for speculation, but in public Fanny was a very small eater. 'I seldom Eat much supper', she said to Twiss when he remarked on her pickiness.[38] The diaries show her at various times satisfied with one potato,[39] overpowered by the thought of a rasher[40] and alert to the grotesque aspects of ingestion, as a letter to Susan in March 1777 reveals:

Our method is as follows; We have certain substances, of various sorts, consisting *chiefly* of Beasts, Birds, & vegetables, which, being first Roasted, Boiled or Baked [...] are put upon Dishes, either of Pewter, or Earthern ware, or China; – & then, being cut into small Divisions, every plate receives a part: after this, with the aid of a knife & fork, the Divisions are made still smaller; they are then (care being taken not to maim the mouth by the above offensive weapons) put between the Lips, where, by the aid of the Teeth, the Divisions are made yet more delicate, till, diminishing almost insensibly they form a general *mash*, or *wad* & are then swallowed.[41]

This exercise in comic detachment is in part a send-up of the congenial dullness of life at Chesington Hall, intended to make Susan laugh, but it is revealing in other ways. While reducing the act of eating to its constituent parts, chewing over the very idea of eating, Fanny never touches on the sensual aspects – the smell, sight or taste of food. Food is simply matter to be made into smaller and smaller divisions 'almost insensibly', then swallowed in a 'mash' or 'wad'. She writes about eating as if it were a merely mechanical process, pointless and therefore slightly disgusting.

Fanny's small appetite (and her appetite for being small) was a form of self-neglect which had several other symptoms. Samuel Crisp complained about her unbecoming stoop and habit of sitting with her face short-sightedly close to the page when she was reading or writing. She was also criticised for mumbling, pitching her voice too low and being silent in company. Clearly, people felt she wasn't making enough of an effort, wasn't 'doing herself justice'; and they were right.

Fanny Burney was in no hurry to get married – in fact the idea filled her with dread. '[H]ow short a time does it take to put an eternal end to a Woman's liberty!' she had exclaimed, watching a wedding party emerge from the church in Lynn.[42] Her father was her idol, and she had no intention of quitting him. 'Every Virtue under the sun – is His!' she wrote unequivocally.[43]

Many men in the Burneys' wide and constantly shifting circle of acquaintance were attracted to Fanny, and she made several conquests despite her reputation for prudery and refusal to play the coquette, an activity she found degrading to both sexes. Like the heroines of her novels, she was confident that virtue was at the very least its own reward. Her 'quickness of parts' and sense of humour were only revealed to those men she felt worthy to appreciate them, such as Alexander Seton; others were shown the 'prude' front. This was as much a matter of propriety and fairness as anything else. 'I would not for the World be thought to trifle with any man', she once wrote to Crisp, and her lifelong behaviour bore out the sincerity of the remark.

The first proposal of marriage Fanny received, in the summer of 1775, provoked a crisis. The hopeful suitor, a Mr Thomas Barlow, was a decent, honest twenty-four-year-old, good-looking and reasonably well-off, who became earnestly enamoured of Fanny after one cup of tea in the company of some friends of Grandmother Burney. Fanny's aunts, sister and grandmother, in sudden, ominous collusion, strongly approved of the match, but Fanny was unmoved. She thought her polite rejection of Barlow marked the end of the story, but the opposition was marshalling its forces. Hetty had written to Crisp about the affair, and he wrote Fanny a long letter, blatantly working on what he imagined might be her worst fears. Did she, he asked, want to be

left in shallows, fast aground, & struggling in Vain for the remainder of your life to get on – doom'd to pass it in Obscurity & regret – look around You Fany [sic] – look at yr Aunts – *Fanny Burney* wont always be what she is now! [...] Suppose You to lose yr Father – take in all Chances. Consider the situation of an unprotected, unprovided Woman.[44]

Fanny replied to this harangue with courage. Pointing out how unwise Crisp was 'so earnestly to espouse the Cause of a person you never saw', she told him that she had resolved never to marry except 'with my whole Heart', be the consequences what they may. She was not so afraid of becoming an old maid that she could accept 'marriage from prudence & Convenience', and gently deflected Crisp's fears for her future provision by saying, 'Don't be uneasy about my welfare, my dear Daddy, I dare say I shall do very well'.[45] Did she think that her writing, still secret to all but Susan, might one day earn her money? Or was this an expression of confidence in her father, in whose career she had such a close interest? '[S]o long as I live to be of some comfort (as I flatter myself I am) to my Father', she grandly told Crisp, 'I can have no motive to wish to sign myself other than his & your [...] Frances Burney'.

Fanny's confidence collapsed, though, when her father suddenly added his voice to those urging her to reconsider Barlow's proposal. The suggestion that Charles Burney could live without her was a body-blow:

I was terrified to Death – I felt the utter impossibility of resisting not merely my Father's *persuasion* but even his *Advice*. [...] I wept like an Infant – Eat nothing – seemed as if already married – & passed the whole Day in more misery than, merely on my own account, I ever did before in my life[.][46]

73

The crisis resolved itself the next day in a tearful scene between father and daughter, during which Fanny declared that she wanted nothing but to live with him. ' "My life!" ' the Doctor exclaimed, kissing her kindly, ' "I wish not to part with my Girls! – they are my greatest Comfort!" ' Fanny left the room 'as light, happy & thankful as if Escaped from Destruction'.[47]

To Mrs Burney, the matter must have presented itself rather differently. The girls were not *her* greatest comfort, and seemed perversely determined not to marry well. Esther had made an impoverished love-match; in 1772 both Maria Allen and her seventeen-year-old brother Stephen shocked and offended their mother by runaway marriages – Maria with Martin Rishton, her former jilt, and Stephen with a girl called Susanna Sharpin. Now Fanny was declaring she would probably never marry, but wanted only to live with her father. With Fanny hunkering down after the Barlow episode as a possibly permanent fixture at home, relations between her and 'Mama' began to stiffen.

Progress with the *History of Music* was much slower than Dr Burney had anticipated, and although he was working at it obsessively and making as much use as possible of his daughters as secretaries and his new friend the cleric and scholar Thomas Twining as an adviser, it began to look as if he had taken on too much. He had other disappointments and difficulties at the same time, including the failure of his plans to found a school of music with the violinist Giardini and, a few weeks later, the publication of a raucous parody of his two books of travels (*The Present State of Music in Germany, the Netherlands and the United Provinces* had been published the prevoius year), satirising the credulity and affectation of earnest fact-gatherers such as the Doctor in a succession of absurd and often quite amusing 'musical' encounters around England. Burney was deeply alarmed and offended by the pamphlet, and is believed to have tried to suppress it by buying up the entire stock,[48] a drastic measure which (if he took it) did not prevent the work going through four editions in the next two years. In the *Memoirs* Fanny made as light of the incident as she could, though she betrays her strong feelings in metaphors of 'vipers' and 'venom'. According to her, the pamphlet 'was never reprinted; and obtained but the laugh of a moment',[49] but there was a great deal in the squib to touch her own feelings as nearly as it had the Doctor's.

If he, with his Oxford doctorate, could attract a lurid parody of his books about music, what treatment might not an uneducated female would-be novelist expect?

In the autumn of 1774 the Burneys were forced to leave Queen Square because of 'difficulties respecting its title'.[50] The house they moved to was right in the centre of town, on the corner of Long's Court and St Martin's Street, which runs south out of Leicester Square. Although the air was not so balmy as in Queen Square, with its 'beautiful prospect', and though St Martin's Street was, in Fanny's blunt words, 'dirty, ill built, and vulgarly peopled',*[51] there were many things to recommend the new address. It was convenient for the opera house and the theatres, the aunts in Covent Garden, Hetty and her young family in Charles Street and many of Dr Burney's fashionable friends (Sir Joshua Reynolds lived just round the corner in Leicester Square). It also had the distinction of having been Sir Isaac Newton's house, which alone would have recommended it to the astrophile Burneys. Newton lived there from 1711 to his death in 1727, and built a small wooden observatory right at the top of the property, glazed on three sides and commanding a good view of the city as well as the sky. '[W]e shew it to all our Visitors, as our principal Lyon', Fanny wrote in her journal ten days after moving in.

The Burneys were so proud of the connection with the great scientist that they thought of calling their new home 'Newton House' or 'The Observatory' as a boast. Charles Burney was particularly fond of dropping Sir Isaac's name into conversation, and displayed a certain ingenuity at creating occasions to do so. Once when a visitor broke his sword on the stairs Burney protested that they 'were not of my constructing – they were Sir Isaac Newton's';[53] and on Mrs Thrale's first visit to the house he said he was unable to 'divine' the answer to a query about a concert, 'not having had Time to consult the stars, though in the House of Sir Isaac Newton'.[54] As a sort of homage to their illustrious precursor, Burney spent a considerable sum having the observatory renovated. He did not, however, choose the chilly rooftop perch for his study (a small room adjoining the library on the first floor performed that function much more comfortably), and it was soon colonised by the children, Fanny

---

* Fanny's impression differs radically from John Strype's description of St Martin's Street in 1720 as 'a handsome, open Place, with very good Buildings for the Generality, and well inhabited'.[52]

adopting it as her 'favorite sitting place, where I can retire to read or write any of my private fancies or vagaries' – a substitute for her closet or 'bureau' of former days.

Of all the Burneys' homes, number 1 St Martin's Street is the most famous.* Dr Burney and his wife lived there for thirteen years, by the end of which the children, with the exception of their younger child, Sarah Harriet (born in 1772), had all left home. The house had a basement and three storeys each consisting of a front and back room, with a projecting wing to the rear on each floor. On the ground floor at the front was the panelled parlour where the family took their meals,† and behind it was another parlour (the kitchen, presumably, was in the basement). Above it, up the fine oak staircase, was the drawing room, with three tall windows looking onto St Martin's Street. This room was the most splendid in the house, and had an 'amazingly ornamented' painted ceiling, probably depicting nudes, since it seems to have been something of an embarrassment to the Doctor: 'I hope you don't think that I did it?' he said to one curious visitor, 'for I swear I did not!'[56] Sir Isaac's name was not invoked on this occasion. There had been three other owners since the scientist, one of them French.

The drawing room was separated from the library by folding doors which, when opened, provided a large and elegant space for the many parties and concerts which the Burneys soon began to hold at St Martin's Street. Dr Burney's library was extensive and highly specialised: when Samuel Johnson visited for the first time and abandoned the company to inspect the books, he would have found few volumes on any subject other than music (although he still preferred looking into books on music to attending the Burneys' informal concert which was the alternative entertainment). The library, also known as the music room, had a window looking down onto the small, overshadowed garden at the back and contained the Doctor's two harpsichords. Beyond it, in the part of the building which projected out at the back, was Burney's narrow workroom, grandly named 'Sir Isaak Newton's Study' (on hearsay), but commonly

---

* It was later renumbered 35. The house was condemned in 1913 and the site is now occupied by the Westminster Reference Library.
† This room in the Burneys' house has been reconstructed at Babson College, Wellesley, Massachusetts, using the original panelling and mantelpiece.[55]

known as 'the Spidery' or 'Chaos' and habitually so untidy with Burney's sprawl of papers that no guests were invited to look in.

On the top floor at the front was the main bedroom, used by Dr and Mrs Burney, with a powdering closet adjoining. The girls' bedroom was beyond it at the back, above the library. The three attic rooms, from which one gained entrance to the observatory, were probably servants' bedrooms and the nursery, with a poky stairway leading from the top floor. James was scarcely ever at home, but still had a room on the ground floor kept for him that opened onto the little garden; Charles junior probably slept there when he was home in the holidays from Charterhouse. Beyond 'Jem's room', opening onto Long's Court, was a small workshop, which Dr Burney rented to a silversmith. It is likely that the workshop created some noise and smell around the back of the house, a reminder of trade going on only just out of sight and earshot of the elegant drawing room. The back of the workshop and its yard would have been visible though from the girls' bedroom window and the east-facing side of the observatory.

The household in the autumn of 1774 consisted of the Doctor and his wife, both approaching fifty, Fanny (who, aged twenty-two, might not have been expected to be at home for much longer), Susan, aged nineteen, thirteen-year-old Charlotte, the lively six-year-old Richard and toddler Sally, then as always a rather neglected little girl. Small children were never going to be a novelty in the Burney household. When the family moved into St Martin's Street, Esther was only a few weeks away from giving birth to her third child, Charles Crisp Burney, having had Hannah Maria in 1772 and Richard in 1773, the first three of Dr Burney's eventual total of thirty-six grandchildren.

The move to St Martin's Street took place while Charles Burney was recuperating from another bout of rheumatic fever. He was confined to bed for weeks, but carried on work on the *History* by dictating to Fanny and Susan. The family did not hold a large party at the new house until March 1775 on account of this indisposition, but the publication of *The Present State of Music in Germany [. . .]* in 1773 had significantly increased Burney's standing as a writer as well as a historian of music, and there was no stopping the flow of illustrious visitors passing through London who wanted an introduction to him. Fanny's letters to Crisp in 1774 and

1775 contain many highly entertaining set-pieces describing some of these callers. The first was the most exotic, a young native of the Society Islands called Omai who had come to England on board the *Adventure* with James Burney. James, who had finished his training as an able seaman in 1771, had joined Captain Cook's second voyage to the Antarctic Circle the following year, returning to England in July 1774. He had mastered some Tahitian on the voyage home and was able to act as interpreter to 'lyon of lyons' Omai, who was fêted all round London, received by the King and invited to the houses of aristocrats keen to observe and display a living emblem of the nation's South Sea discoveries. Omai arrived at the Burneys' house in the company of Joseph Banks and Daniel Solander, the botanists who had accompanied Cook on his first circumnavigation of the globe. HIs manners impressed Fanny extremely favourably; even though he had very little English, the Polynesian 'paid his Compliments with great politeness [. . .] which he has found a method of doing without *words*'.57 Fanny sat next to him at dinner and noticed how unostentatiously alert Omai was to the feelings of others, glossing over the servant's mistakes and assuring Mrs Burney that the (tough) beef was actually 'very dood'. He 'committed not the slightest blunder at Table', and didn't fuss over his new suit of Manchester velvet with lace ruffles, although it was totally unlike his native costume (or the fantasy burnous in which he was painted by Reynolds during his visit). 'Indeed', wrote Fanny to Crisp, 'he appears to be a perfectly rational & intelligent man, with an understanding far superiour to the common race of us cultivated gentry: he could not else have borne so well the way of Life into which he is thrown'. With his spotless manners and spotless ruffles, Omai could not have been a more perfect example of Noble Savagery, showing up the gracelessness of the expensively educated 'Boobys' around him in a way that the future satirist found highly gratifying. 'I think this shews', she concluded grandly, 'how much more *Nature* can do without *art* than *art* with all her refinement, unassisted by *Nature*.'58

Their next notable visitor was one of the most famous singers of the day, the Italian soprano Lucrezia Agujari, known rather blatantly as 'La Bastardina'. Mozart had met her in 1768 and marvelled at her astonishingly high range: she had, in his presence, reached three octaves above middle C – a barely credible achievement. She was *virtuosa di camera* to the court of the Duke of Parma, whose master of music, Giuseppe Colla, 'a Tall, thin, spirited Italian, full of fire, & not wanting in Grimace',[59] was her constant companion. Susan Burney had got the impression – not unreasonably – that the couple were married, and that La Bastardina retained her maiden name for professional purposes. This led Hetty to cause the singer some consternation by enquiring if she had any children: 'Moi!' she exclaimed disingenuously, 'je ne suis pas mariée, moi!'[60]

The Burneys were of course all craving to hear Agujari sing, but Signor Colla explained that a slight sore throat prevented it. 'The singer is really a slave to her voice', Fanny noted in her journal; 'she fears the least Breath of air – she is equally apprehensive of Any heat – she seems to have a perpetual anxiety lest she should take Cold; & I do believe she neither Eats, Drinks, sleeps or Talks, without considering in what manner she may perform those vulgar duties of Life so as to be the most beneficial to her Voice.' Agujari was contracted at huge cost to sing at the Pantheon on Oxford Road (a new venue for concerts and assemblies that was proving immensely popular and in which Charles Burney had shares), and though she promised to return and sing for the Burneys at some later date, the possibility seemed remote. Months passed and they heard nothing of her, only jokes based on the story that she had been mauled by a pig when young and had had her side repaired with a silver plate. Lord Sandwich, First Lord of the Admiralty at the time, showed Charles Burney a satirical song he had written on the subject and wanted to have set to music. It was a dialogue between Agujari and the pig, 'beginning *Caro Mio Porco* – the Pig answers by a Grunt; – & it Ends by his exclaiming *ah che bel mangiare!*'[61] It is interesting to note that although the parody of her father's book had struck Fanny as scandalous, she was quite happy to join in and pass on jokes about Agujari's 'silver side'. It presented 'too fair a subject for Ridicule to have been suffered to pass untouched'.

It wasn't until June that Agujari did sing for the Burneys, and then all jokes about her person and criticism of her affectations were forgotten. 'We wished for you! I cannot tell you how *much* we wished for you!' Fanny wrote ecstatically to Crisp:

> I could compare her to nothing *I* ever *heard* but only to what I have heard
> of – Your Carestino – Farinelli – Senesino – alone are worthy to be ranked
> with the Bastardini. Such a powerful voice! – so astonishing a Compass –

reaching from C in the middle of the Harpsichord, to 2 notes *above* the Harpsichord! Every note so clear, so full – so charming! Then her *shake* – so *plump* – so true, so open! it is [as] strong & distinct as Mr Burney's upon the Harpsichord.[62]

Agujari certainly did not stint her hosts. She stayed for five hours, singing 'almost all the Time', arias, plain chant, recitative: 'whether she most astonished, or most delighted us, I cannot say – but she is really a sublime singer'. There was no more talk of their exotic visitor being 'conceitedly incurious' about her rivals: 'her Talents are so very superior that she cannot chuse but hold all other performers cheap'.[63] The generous free recital, the sublime voice, the plump shake had all done their work. Fanny and her sisters became Agujari's besotted devotees.

In his Surrey retreat, Crisp hung on these bulletins, especially the accounts of musical evenings. On one memorable occasion in 1773 recorded by Fanny, the party consisted of the violinist Celestini, the singer Millico and the composer Antonio Sacchini, 'the first men of their Profession in the World'.[64] Fanny could describe in detail evenings out, say at the opera, where they had gone to hear Agujari's rival Gabrielli, and reproduce the long discussions about the performances afterwards, with what seems to be remarkable accuracy. The guests at one of the Doctor's musical evenings that summer and autumn included Viscount Barrington, then Secretary at War, the Dutch Ambassador and Lord Sandwich, First Lord of the Admiralty, whom Charles Burney was no doubt trying to cultivate on James's behalf. This was exciting company for the Burney girls, and the fact that Fanny relished these evenings shows that her shyness was less potent than her curiosity. Some of their guests were outlandish, such as Prince Orloff, the lover of Catherine the Great, who arrived at St Martin's Street late on the appointed evening and squatted on a bench next to Susan, almost squashing her. His appearances in London had been the subject of much gossip, and here he was, dwarfing his hosts and dripping with diamonds, a portrait of the Empress indiscreetly flashing on his breast. Not that it was easy to see it – when the Burney girls were shown it the glare of the surrounding jewels was almost blinding; 'one of them, I am sure, was as big as a *Nutmeg* at *least*' Fanny wrote.[65]

Fanny's early diaries describe a life of seemingly uninterrupted gaiety in the company of her loving sisters, adored father and some of the greatest artists of the day. The '*abominably* handsome' Garrick continued to be a frequent visitor, loved by the whole family; on one occasion he picked Charlotte out of her bed and ran with her as far as the corner of the street. When he threatened to abduct the other girls 'we all longed to say, *Pray do!*'[66] But as the editors of Fanny's diaries have pointed out, the consistently cheerful portrait of life in St Martin's Street is deceptive, since most of the material relating to Fanny's stepmother was destroyed. From other sources, such as a letter to Fanny from Maria Rishton in September 1776, a different picture emerges:

> I knew you could never live all together or be a happy society but still bad as things used to be when I was amongst you they were meer children falling out to what they seem to be now ... You know the force of her expression. And indeed I believe she writes from the heart when she says she is the most miserable woman that breathes.[67]

When Mrs Burney was nervous and dictatorial, the girls responded with outward deference and private ill-will. She was perceived by them as grossly insensitive; perversely, this led them to treat her with gross insensitivity, almost as if they were testing her, trying to prove their worst apprehensions. A cabal formed against 'the Lady', and to his shame 'Daddy' Crisp joined it gleefully, going so far as to be 'excessively impudent' to her face and satirical behind her back, '*taking her off! –* putting his hands behind him, & kicking his heels about!'[68]

The portrait of Mrs Ireton in Fanny Burney's last novel, *The Wanderer*, seems to draw on many of the second Mrs Burney's supposed attributes (as well as those of Fanny's later *bête noire* at Court, Mrs Schwellenberg, whom she called Mama's double). The heroine of *The Wanderer*, Juliet, whom Mrs Ireton oppresses from sheer bloody-mindedness and sadism, is forced to act as 'humble companion', a symbolic representation of Fanny's subordination to her stepmother. An explanation for Elizabeth Burney's 'love of tyranny' is suggested in the story by Mrs Ireton's brother-in-law, who knew the old harpy in youth as 'eminently fair, gay, and charming!'[69] Perhaps the inextinguishable spleen of the Burney 'Family Scourge' was, like Mrs Ireton's, a kind of shock reaction to the withdrawal of sexual attention:

> without stores to amuse, or powers to instruct, though with a full persuasion that she is endowed with wit, because she cuts, wounds, and slashes from unbridled, though pent-up resentment, at her loss of adorers; and from a certain perverseness, rather than quickness of parts, that gifts her with the sublime art of ingeniously tormenting.[70]

Mrs Burney had plenty of fuel for sexual jealousy, not just at home among her stepdaughters (whom William Bewley had once described as Charles Burney's 'seraglio') but among the Doctor's pupils too. No doubt his male friends teased Charles Burney about his access to an endless supply of nubile young women, and perhaps not without cause: he appears in James Barry's 1783 allegorical painting *The Triumph of the Thames* surrounded by naked Nereids, and in C.L. Smith's caricature 'A Sunday Concert' in an obscenely suggestive pose in front of John Wilkes's daughter Mary. Burney was clearly susceptible to female charms: he became openly infatuated with the lovely Sophy Streatfield after her lover Henry Thrale was dead, to the extent that Mrs Thrale felt he was making a fool of himself.[71] Even Fanny noticed and joked about her father's ability to make 'conquests', though she saw it mostly as proof of his charm. But a wife would be likely to view such persistent 'charm' rather differently. Elizabeth Burney may have had much more to put up with in her marriage than we know.

❦ 4 ❦

An Accidental Author

*From the origin of her first literary attempt, [she] might almost be
called an accidental author.*

Fanny Burney, *Memoirs of Doctor Burney*[1]

Fanny's diary was not addressed to 'Nobody' for long. Craving news
from town and the company of his dear Burney girls, Samuel Crisp had
developed an apparently insatiable appetite for their letters, and singled
out Fanny's as the best. His attention was extremely gratifying to the
'little dunce' and encouraged her to invest time and effort in the correspondence. Her diary gradually modulated into a series of journal-letters
to the hermit of Chesington which Crisp felt free to circulate to his sister
and her friends.

While it stimulated Fanny to have a discerning and appreciative audience (in a way that addressing passive 'Nobody' could never do), there
was of course a danger that these semi-public letters might become
self-conscious. Fortunately, Crisp was not only a forthright man but
astute, and foresaw the kind of inhibitions to which Fanny might be
prey. 'I profess there is not a single word or expression, or thought in
your whole letter,' he wrote in the winter of 1773, when their correspondence was just taking root, 'that I do not relish':

– not that in our Correspondence, I shall set up for a Critic, or schoolmaster, or Observer of Composition – Damn it all! – – I hate it if once
You set about framing studied letters, that are to be correct, nicely grammatical & run in smooth Periods, I shall mind them as no others than
newspapers of intelligence; I make this preface because You have needlessly
enjoin'd me to deal sincerely, & to tell You of your faults; & so let this

declaration serve once for all, that there is no fault in an Epistolary Correspondence, like stiffness, & study – Dash away, whatever comes uppermost
– the sudden sallies of imagination, clap'd down on paper, just as they
arise, are worth Folios, & have all the warmth & merit of that sort of
Nonsense, that is Eloquent in Love – never think of being correct, when
You write to me.[2]

Crisp granted Fanny a licence to be natural, and the benefits were
enormous. He encouraged her to entertain him, not with anything fanci-
ful or affected, but with the events of her everyday life, written in her
everyday language, really as if she were talking to him. It was in their
degree of deviation from 'nicely grammatical' writing that he would judge
the vitality of her letters. Uneducated Fanny had appealed to the family
monitor to correct her faults, and he had replied that she wasn't to give
her style a moment's notice.

'Dash away, whatever comes uppermost': Fanny's letters to Crisp
became studiedly informal, making use of character sketches and long
passages of dialogue as a substitute for straightforward chronicling. The
success of the formula must have influenced her decision to cast the
latest of her 'writings' in epistolary form, and the sheer familiarity of
writing to Crisp suggested the story's central correspondence between a
young lady in the city (Evelina) and an old mentor in the sticks. Writing
a novel as a series of letters suited the author's circumstances, too. In a
household where there was little privacy, the excuse of 'writing a letter'
would have helped keep her compositions secret.

The epistolary novel was the most popular form of the day, and the
trademark of Fanny's literary hero, Richardson, though in *Evelina* she
uses it more cleverly than he. Having, like Richardson, presented herself
as the editor of the letters (thereby setting up the mild pretence of them
being real), she 'edits out' parts of the correspondence, plants references
in the text to 'missing' letters, has letters cross in the post, get diverted,
forged, delayed (notably in the case of the one from the heroine's dead
mother, pivotal to the resolution of the plot). The model of Fanny's real
correspondence with Crisp was most valuable, though, in discouraging
her from attempting too 'literary' a style. Evelina's breathless note to her
guardian on her arrival in London, for instance, has an irresistible realism:

This moment arrived. Just going to Drury-Lane Theatre. The celebrated Mr. Garrick performs Ranger. I am quite in extacy. So is Miss Mirvan. How fortunate, that he should happen to play! We would not let Mrs. Mirvan rest till she had consented to go; her chief objection was to our dress, for we have had no time to *Londonize* ourselves; but we teazed her into compliance, and so we are to sit in some obscure place, that she may not be seen.[3]

Evelina bears none of the marks of having been worked on for up to ten years, though in the *Memoirs* the author asserts that much of the story had been 'pent up' in her head since the time of the composition of 'Caroline Evelyn', the manuscript novel destroyed in Poland Street in 1766 or 1767.[4] A document in Charlotte Barrett's hand[5] (but presumably written under the supervision of her aunt) adds that the earlier story had featured several characters who reappear in the 'daughter' novel: Lady Howard, Mr Villars, Miss Mirvan, Sir John Belmont and Madame Duval. These characters were so real to Fanny that she couldn't help revolving their circumstances and personalities long after the manuscript containing their history had ceased to exist. 'My bureau was cleared,' she wrote, many years later, 'but my head was not emptied.'[6]

It is likely that *Evelina* was one of the 'writings' Fanny Burney mentions in her diaries of 1770, 1771 and 1772. The two following years were burdened with copying as Dr Burney hurried to finish the first volume of his *History*, and it was probably only after the publication of that book in 1775 that Fanny had much time for her own work. In the early stages, there was little motivation to write the story down, except perhaps a desire to circulate a readable manuscript among her siblings and the Chesington Hall set. 'Writing, indeed,' as Madame d'Arblay confessed later, 'was far more difficult to her than composing.'[7] Writing down also meant pinning down, and an end to the pleasurable composing process.

Nevertheless, in the summer of 1776, when Dr and Mrs Burney had gone to Bristol and Fanny was left to her own devices with only the toddler Sally and the servants for company, she settled down with a hitherto unknown single-mindedness and wrote most of what is now *Evelina*'s second volume. By the end of the year she was beginning to negotiate with publishers.

The step from indulging in private 'vagaries' to producing two volumes of a full-length novel and soliciting its publication is so momentous that we may well wonder what prompted Fanny Burney to take it, or even think of it. The reason given in the *Memoirs* does not sound like the whole truth:

> When the little narrative, however slowly, from the impediments that always annoy what requires secrecy, began to assume a 'questionable shape;' a wish – as vague, at first, as it was fantastic – crossed the brain of the writer, to 'see her work in print.'[8]

This makes it sound as if Burney was simply indulging 'a taste for quaint sports'[9] in a frivolous and ladylike fashion. She certainly could not have thought of openly adopting a *career* as a novelist in 1776 – for a middle-class woman it was simply not respectable – but anonymous publication was a possibility. Her knowledge of the printing trade made the business of soliciting publication less intimidating than it might otherwise have been, but when Joyce Hemlow says that 'the practice (almost the habit) of book-making that she had known for the last five years in her father's study must have been sufficient by the momentum of its progress to carry her on to the press',[10] she makes the publication of *Evelina* sound rather too much like a demonstration of Newton's second law. Fanny's sudden decision to finish and publish her novel seems to have been triggered by something more urgent and personal.

It is possible that something happened in the Burney family in 1776 that made it desirable or even necessary for Fanny to make some money quickly by hurrying into print. We are unlikely to find out what this might have been; Fanny burned her whole diary and most of her correspondence for that year and the next, noting in her papers that the material was 'upon Family matters or anecdotes' – as if that was sufficient to justify it being 'destroyed [. . .] in totality'.[11] But two years later, when she was accused by Mrs Thrale of having courted the attention she seemed to despise by soliciting publication, she said, 'My *printing* it, indeed [. . .] tells terribly against me, to all who are unacquainted with the circumstances that belonged to it.'[12] This reveals that there were 'circumstances' that forced Fanny to act against her inclination and publish.

Neither of the two family scandals that took place in the autumn of

1777 can completely account for the move. The first was the elopement of Mrs Burney's third child, Bessy Allen, who had been sent to Paris in 1775 for the improvement of her manners. Charlotte Burney, who was the same age as Bessy, was not sent with her as a companion; presumably they did not get on well. Mrs Burney was proud of her daughter and had intended, in Samuel Johnson's opinion, 'to enjoy the triumph of her superiority' over the Burney girls.[13] In August 1777 she had gone to Paris to bring Bessy home when the girl, sensing an end to her freedom, eloped with an adventurer called Samuel Meeke, a man reputed to be 'Bankrupt in fame as well as Fortune'.[14] The couple were married two months later in exactly the same place, Ypres, where Maria had married Martin Rishton. Mrs Burney had to return home on her own, shocked, anxious, ashamed and chagrined to the quick.*

The family had hardly recovered from this first shock when another disgrace hit the Burney household. Charles Burney junior had gone up to Caius College, Cambridge, in January 1777. Though he was fond of pranks, and lighthearted to the point of being feckless, Charles had a zeal for scholarship and an intellectual ability that outshone that of anyone else in the family. At Cambridge he was admitted to the University Library as a special privilege (it was not normally used by undergraduates at this date), but when a surprising number of classical texts began to go missing soon after his arrival, suspicion fell on him. The Under-Librarian decided to search his rooms secretly, an operation which had to be attempted during dinner since, as the College Bedmaker said, that was the only time Burney could be relied on not to be studying.[16] 'In a dark Corner' they found about thirty-five of the missing volumes, mostly sixteenth- and seventeenth-century editions of the standard classical authors, which had had the university arms removed from them and the Burney bookplate substituted. Other volumes, as it turned out, had been sold on, and when young Burney fled Cambridge after the discovery of his crime, a further box of stolen books was sent back to the library from London. In his few months at the university, he must have been stealing books almost all the time.

* Mrs Burney did not go straight to St Martin's Street, but to a friend's house, via Mrs Thrale's. Her reluctance to meet her stepdaughters casts an interesting light on relations between them. Johnson's interpretation suggests that Fanny and her sisters' hostility to 'Mama' was obvious: 'The consolations of [Burney's] girls must indeed be painful. She had intended to enjoy the triumph of her daughter's superiority. They were prepared to wish them both ill, and their wishes are gratified.'[15]

The shock at home was seismic, and none felt it more violently than the Doctor, who refused to see his son. Fanny's diary from this painful period has not survived, nor has Charles Burney's correspondence on the subject with his friend Thomas Twining, though Twining's replies indicate how much comforting and bringing to reason the bitterly disappointed father required.[17] At one point Charles seems to have considered disowning his son altogether, and he certainly thought of making him change his surname. Fortunately, when the first shock subsided, he dropped these drastic ideas. The problem of what to do with the reprobate remained, however. Charles junior was sent into exile to the village of Shinfield in Berkshire, presumably to a private tutor, from where he communicated forlornly with his sisters in St Martin's Street.

But young Charles's was not a brooding nature, and he recovered far quicker from this shameful episode than did the rest of his family. By the following spring he had been found a place at King's College, Old Aberdeen – a far cry from Caius, and in a Presbyterian country (which his father thought might be a further hindrance to his taking Holy Orders, as they still hoped he would some day). He was writing verses, such as 'Farewell to Shinfield', which indicate that his spirits were pretty well recovered:

> Let me shake off the rustic – & once more
> The gayer joys of college life explore.[18]

The 'gayer joys' in question may well have been what got him into trouble in his short Cambridge career, where any kind of high living would have very rapidly used up young Charles's small allowance. Ralph S. Walker, in his article on the thefts,[19] points out that when Charles junior's own son, Charles Parr Burney, was going up to Oxford, he warned him feelingly of 'three stumbling blocks: Gaming, Drinking and the Fair Sex', the greatest being gaming: 'Its fascinations are matchless and when they once influence the mind, their power is uncontrollable'.[20] This is surely the voice of experience, and perhaps young Charles did steal and sell the books in order to avoid owning up to debt at home.

Fanny puts a different slant on the matter in a letter written many years later to Charles Parr Burney (who had only just found out about the episode), in which she states 'the origin of that fatal deed to have been a MAD RAGE for possessing a library, and that the subsequent sale only occurred from the fear of discovery'.[21] Charles's bibliomania, which far surpassed his father's, resulted in him possessing at the time of his death in 1817 one of the most splendid private libraries of the age, which, along with his magpie hoards of old newspaper cuttings (ninety-four volumes) and an extensive archive of material relating to the history of the stage, formed a core collection of the new British Library. Fanny's suggestion that her brother suffered a pathological 'rage for possessing a library' seems psychologically convincing. In the days of his prosperity, he acquired books conventionally; when he was a student from the lower bourgeoisie, let loose in the treasure-house of a university library, he just acquired them anyway.

If Fanny was trying to make enough money from *Evelina* to bail out her brother, she failed, even though the twenty guineas she received from the publisher for the copyright seemed 'a sum enormous' to her at the time. She said later that she had given the proceeds of her first novel to her brother Charles, but his disgrace at university post-dates her rush to finish *Evelina*. Perhaps even at Charterhouse, where he stayed until the late age of nineteen, Charles had run into the kind of debt that seems to have burdened him as a student. It is even possible that he might have been desperate (from whatever cause) to the point of attempting suicide. There is a cryptic reference in Fanny's diary to a conversation with the writer Giuseppe Baretti in 1788, when Baretti used the image of 'running a dagger into your own breast'. This made Fanny shudder, 'because the dagger was a word of unfortunate recollection'.[22]* Is it possible, as Mrs Thrale heard on the grapevine the same year,[24] that Charles Burney junior was the model for the suicidal Macartney in *Evelina*, whom the heroine (later revealed to be his half-sister) discovers preparing to use a pistol on himself? The heroines of *Cecilia*, *Camilla* and *The Wanderer* undergo traumatic encounters with potential suicides too, and in each case the desperado is brandishing a weapon. There may have been something more painful behind her 'decision to print' than Fanny Burney was prepared to let anyone know.

*   *   *

---

* Fanny mentions daggers again in an emotional letter to her brother of 4 October 1814, a reply to his refusal to assume guardianship of Fanny's son Alex, who was facing rustication from college. At this significant juncture, she may have been trying to remind him of an old debt: 'O Charles – you have written me a dagger!'[23]

By the winter of 1776, Fanny had completed the first two volumes of her novel and had copied out at least one volume in the feigned, upright hand she developed to prevent recognition of the author of the manuscript. This was not as neurotic as it might seem. Fanny's handwriting was well known in the London printing shops from her extensive copying of her father's works, and as she would have no control over the production of her novel – should a publisher take it up – there was a real risk that her cover would be blown, or worse, that her father might be disgraced by association with the book.

The task of transcribing her text into the unnatural handwriting was irksome, and by Christmas 1776 she was losing patience with it. In conspiracy with Susan, Charlotte and Charles she had already approached the bookseller James Dodsley, but he had refused to consider an anonymous work. The next bookseller she fixed on was Thomas Lowndes, whose premises were in Fleet Street. Fanny felt she couldn't approach him directly, so using the Orange Coffee House in the Haymarket as a decoy address, she sent Charles as go-between, weirdly dressed up by his sisters to look as adult as possible and melodramatically concealed behind the pseudonym 'Mr King'. Fanny herself became the work's anonymous and genderless 'editor', writing to Lowndes, 'I have in my possession a M:S. novel, which has never yet been seen but by myself.'[25] She hoped to have the first two volumes 'printed immediately', with two more appearing later if they were successful. This might have been desirable to the young author, fed up with the slog of transcribing her half-completed manuscript and keen for cash; but Lowndes, unsurprisingly, wanted the thing complete. He returned volume one via 'Mr King', hoping to see the rest by the summer of 1777, but Fanny did not complete the book until November, staying up 'the greatest part of many Nights, in order to get it ready',[26] and it was not published until January of the following year. For one who claims to have had a 'vague' desire 'to see her works in print', it was an arduous process, requiring hard work, determination, patience and concentration.

The manuscript that finally found its way to Lowndes's shop late in 1777 was prefaced with three layers of anxious authorial disclaimer: first there was an ode dedicating the work to the 'author of my being' (Dr Burney) and explaining that anonymity was the only course open to one who 'cannot raise, but would not sink' the fame of a matchless parent; then there was a petition for clemency 'to the Authors of the Monthly and Critical Reviews', entreating them to remember that 'you were all young writers once'. Lastly there was a preface from 'the editor' of the book, admitting that though novels (with a few notable exceptions) were held in low regard, 'surely all attempts to contribute to the number of those which may be read, if not with advantage, at least without injury, might rather be encouraged than contemned'. Apparently forgetting the role of 'editor', she declared an intention not to copy the style of 'the great writers' (Johnson, Rousseau, Richardson, Fielding, Smollett and Marivaux) or to deal with 'the same ground which they have tracked'. She is of 'the vulgar herd', and they 'great'. Another reason why Fanny Burney's novel was unlikely to fit into the existing 'great' tradition was that she was female, but since the title page did not even feature the conventional anonymous credit 'By a Lady', that fact was hidden.

The novel tells the story of a seventeen-year-old girl, beautiful – of course – virtuous and naive, whose sheltered upbringing in Dorset under the protection of an elderly cleric, Mr Villars, is brought to an abrupt end by her entrance into London society in the company of aristocratic acquaintance. Villars is an anxious guardian: Evelina's grandfather, his former pupil, met an early death after a disastrous marriage to a 'lowbred and illiberal' serving-woman, having bequeathed the care of his baby daughter, Caroline Evelyn, to the old tutor. When the girl grew up, her reprobate mother, remarried and called Madame Duval, reclaimed her, but their subsequent life together in Paris was miserable. Caroline escaped into a hasty marriage to a profligate Englishman, Sir John Belmont, who abandoned his pregnant wife, destroying their marriage certificate and denying any connection with her. She died giving birth to a daughter, Evelina Anville, a surname invented by Mr Villars to cover the baby's unacknowledged parentage.

The eventual restoration of Evelina to her rightful name and identity, and the parallel story of her troubled courtship by courtly Lord Orville, provide the double framework within which Fanny Burney creates a vivid satire of eighteenth-century manners, told, for the first time, from a feminine viewpoint. The love story of Evelina is entertainingly perverse: as in *Pride and Prejudice* (which owes a great deal – possibly including its title* – to Burney's work), the couple start out by meeting at an assembly and getting on very badly. Endless accidents and misconceptions make Orville's poor opinion of Evelina, 'a poor weak girl!',[28] fall even further, and only through the passage of time, painfully good behaviour and the couple's persistent sexual attraction to each other are they eventually united.

Burney packed her 'little narrative' with matter, rather in the way that Dickens was to do a century later. There are sentimental scenes, 'sublime' scenes (notably the tear-jerking reconciliation between Evelina and her repentant father, Sir John Belmont), high drama, low comedy and a large cast of characters catering for all tastes. A great deal of the book's novelty and charm, however, comes from the sympathetic way in which Burney depicts the heroine's youth and inexperience. The scene at Evelina's first assembly is both funny and painful, for she is concentrating too hard on the formalities to behave any way other than idiotically. Her letters home to Dorset chart this frustrating 'entrance into the world' with an endearing candour that also performs an important ironic function: the reader sees (almost) all Evelina's troubles coming long before she does, from the manoeuvrings of her intemperate grandmother Madame Duval, to the dangerously plausible Sir Clement Willoughby's persistent attempts at seduction.

Evelina is at the mercy of appearances in every way, judged to be as vulgar as the company she is forced to keep, that of her meddling and exploitative grandmother and her self-seeking cousins, the Branghtons. Burney's portrayals of mean-spirited, selfish and socially ambitious characters immediately show where her genius lies. Years of studying the manners of the aspirant middle class (most notably, of course, her own father) had given her ample material to work on; her traditionally limited female upbringing added a claustrophobic intensity and weight of disgust to her observations. The Branghtons come in for particularly stinging satire. They are silversmiths (like the Burneys' own tenant in Long's Court), with premises on Snow Hill, near Smithfield. Their alertness to class signals is extreme – even the disposition of their accommodation

---

* The last chapter of *Cecilia* contains the words: 'if to PRIDE and PREJUDICE you owe your miseries, so wonderfully is good and evil balanced, that to PRIDE and PREJUDICE you will also owe their termination.'[27]

reflects it like a three-dimensional model. The Branghtons themselves live on the second floor, with a poor Scotch poet, Macartney, lodging in the garret and 'classy' Mr Smith in the former reception rooms on the first floor. The stratification is relative, of course. Only to a Branghton could Mr Smith be a model of gentility, and the poet, needless to say, turns out to be a man of sensibility and noble blood. Fanny Burney revels in exposing the small-mindedness of her vulgar characters, and Smith is the best of them all. 'Such a fine *varnish* of low politeness!' said Dr Johnson of his favourite, ' – such a *struggle* to appear a Gentleman!'[29] Smith is constantly on his guard, yet every word and action betrays him. He doesn't, for instance, like to lend his rooms to the grubby Branghton girls (who guilelessly admit how seldom they put on clean clothes). 'The truth is,' he explains, expecting to impress Evelina,

> Miss Biddy and Polly take no care of any thing, else, I'm sure, they should always be welcome to my room; for I'm never so happy as in obliging the ladies, – that's my character, Ma'am; – but, really, the last time they had it, everything was made so greasy and so nasty, that upon my word, to a man who wishes to have things a little genteel, it was quite cruel. Now, as to you, Ma'am, it's quite another thing; for I should not mind if every thing I had was spoilt, for the sake of having the pleasure to oblige you; and, I assure you, Ma'am, it makes me quite happy, that I have a room good enough to receive you.[30]

The Branghtons' ineradicable vulgarity provides much of the humour of the book. Forced to take a party to the opera, Mr Branghton is totally unprepared for the expense of the tickets and makes a scene at the booth, thinking he can haggle over the prices as he might with a fellow tradesman. His purchase of the cheapest possible seats, still in his view extortionately expensive, pleases no one in the party, for they have neither the satisfaction of hearing or seeing the performance properly, nor of being seen by the 'quality' in the pit. When the opera begins, their disappointment is intensified: 'Why there's nothing but singing!' Mr Branghton exclaims, and is disgusted by the realisation that it is all in a foreign language too. 'Pray what's the reason they can't as well sing in English?' he asks; 'but I suppose the fine folks would not like it, if they could understand it.'[31]

93

'The fine folks' come off rather worse than the vulgarians, although Burney's depiction of them is necessarily less convincingly observed. Lord Merton and his friends are all (except for super-virtuous Orville) as stupid as the Holborn crowd, and more culpable. Their affectations and excessive language are evidence of moral malaise; while they should be leading society (Lovel is a Member of Parliament and all the others landowners), their time is wasted in gaming, dangerous sports and dalliance. Evelina's blue-stocking chaperone, Mrs Selwyn, is the scourge of this set, endlessly showing up their ignorance and folly. When she suggests that they have a competition to see who can quote longest from Horace, none of the fops can join in, despite their expensive 'classical' educations: 'what with riding, – and – and – and so forth', says one of them, 'really, one has not much time, even at the university, for mere reading.'[32] But while Mrs Selwyn's 'masculine' learning and wit is the vehicle for many of the novel's home truths, the author makes clear that she finds it ultimately sterile. Mrs Selwyn is too busy 'reserving herself for the gentlemen' to function as the sympathetic mother-figure the orphaned heroine needs.

There is no doubt that Evelina's worth is only recognised at all by Lord Orville because she is also beautiful, but in this profoundly feminist novel Burney gives an original view of the conventional heroine – the view from the pedestal. Evelina's instant physical impact on other people – of which she is imperfectly aware – is shown as something of a liability (inflaming lustful men and making enemies of jealous women). It is her guarantee of attention, but at the same time an impediment to being truly *seen*. *Evelina* exposes – in a way undreamed of by earlier novelists – the double standards applied towards women, in whom everything but beauty and goodness are 'either impertinent or unnatural'.[33] The wit, Mrs Selwyn, is seen as unnaturally intellectual ('oddish'), and Evelina's grotesque grandmother, Madame Duval, as impertinently immodest; both commit the cardinal sin of being old. 'I don't know what the devil a woman lives for after thirty,' says dissolute Lord Merton, in one of the novel's bleakest remarks; 'she is only in other folks' way.'[34] The lovely young heroine's hold on her admirers will soon, it is implied, be turned to just such withering scorn, for women past their bloom are not just negligible but irritating – 'in other folks' way' – and a resented financial liability on some man or other.

The scene in *Evelina* in which the gambling-mad fops organise a race between two very old women is a graphic example of the point. Like the episode in which a dressed-up monkey attacks Lovel, it has been criticised for being excessive and unlikely, but this is not the case: gambling was the mania of the period and the occasions for it bizarre. There was one contemporary case of a gambler hiring a desperado to prove that people could live under water (the desperado drowned, so the gambler tried again with another), and another in which some members of Brooks's Club laid bets on whether or not a passer-by who had collapsed in the street was dead (no attempts were allowed to help him, which might have affected the outcome).[35] By these lights, the race between the two destitute old women in *Evelina* does not seem fantastical; Evelina's urge to step forward and help one who falls over is thwarted as 'foul play', for no one cares if the contestants die in the 'sport'. Who could be more disposable than a person who is not just poor, infirm and female, but also old?

Misogyny and sadism are linked throughout the novel, from the behaviour of the 'beaux' towards women in Marylebone's sinister 'dark walks' to the extraordinary ill-treatment of Madame Duval by Captain Mirvan and Sir Clement Willoughby. The two men, posing as highwaymen, waylay the coach in which Evelina and her grandmother are travelling merely to have an excuse to assault and humiliate the older woman, who is left bound in a ditch in such a state of dishevelment 'that she hardly looked human'.[36] Such scenes, intended as comic by the author, inevitably strike modern readers as both grotesque and revealing. Captain Mirvan seems in many ways a character from the earlier eighteenth-century school of rough and ready picaresque comedy, though Burney defended her portrait of him on the grounds that it was drawn from life (the ignorance of her brother James and his fellow sailors about 'modern customs' on shore[37] was presumably a running joke at home). This only renders the overall meaning of the book more ambiguous. If Burney really considered Mirvan – the main perpetrator of aggressive behaviour in the novel – to be an accurate expression of the social attitudes fostered in a male environment (the navy), his 'comic' status affords no excuse. Contemporary critics are surely right to view both the knockabout comedy and the romantic plot of *Evelina* as something of 'a consoling cover story', consciously or unconsciously hiding a far less acceptable tale of male violence and coercion.[38]

Much else in *Evelina* was 'drawn from life', often directly so. The novel contains a sort of guided tour of current fashionable amusements in London and the spa towns (here represented by Bristol, the only spa Burney had then visited), with scenes set in the Haymarket Opera House, Ranelagh, Marylebone Gardens, Drury Lane, Vauxhall, Cox's Museum and the Hampstead assembly rooms.* This didn't simply offer 'a fund inexhaustible for Conversation, observations, and probable Incidents',[40] but made the novel topical and glamorous in a way which Burney was correct to claim 'has not before been executed'.[41] Her expectation of remaining anonymous led her to draw freely on detail from her own experience. Her favourite performers, Garrick and the castrato Millico, appear in the novel in performances she had witnessed, and she includes a scene in a personally significant location, the Pantheon, the new winter assembly rooms in Oxford Road where Dr Burney was on the payroll and in which he had shares. Grandmother Sleepe's maiden name, Du Bois, is given to the put-upon male companion of Evelina's grandmother, Madame Duval, and the maiden name of her negligent godmother Frances Greville is given to the poet Macartney (who, as we have seen, may have been based on her brother Charles). In fact, so much in *Evelina* was recklessly transposed from Burney's own life that it is hardly surprising she later began to fear detection.

Before *Evelina*, the comic novel had been raucous and the novel of sentiment cloying; both types of book had tended towards obscenity, either through the sort of explicit sexuality displayed in Fielding, Smollett and Sterne, or Richardson's more insidious brand of prurience, which D.H. Lawrence memorably described as 'calico purity and underclothing excitements'.[42] There are no 'underclothing excitements' in Fanny Burney's novels, which is one reason why the burgeoning novel-reading class took to them so warmly. The novel, she proved, could be decent *and* amusing; indeed, Burney's moral satire derives a great deal of its power from the author's feelings of propriety, and the constraints this imposes on her. Her field of action is narrow, but within it she investigates carefully and critically.

---

* When Burney first tried to interest Lowndes in her novel, she pointed out that the first volume included 'a round of the most fashionable Spring Diversions of London', and that the second volume would cover 'Summer Diversions'.[39] Since at this stage she was planning a four-volume novel, it seems reasonable to assume that she was intending to cover the whole social year season by season.

The sophistications of *Evelina* were timely. In the 1770s some people thought that the novel had already outlived its usefulness, but Burney made it into a vehicle for refined entertainment. Just as Jane Austen was to outshine her literary heroine Burney, Burney herself had surpassed her hero Richardson with a work that can be seen as something of a rebuke to the male novelists who for decades had gorged on the theme of 'a young lady's entrance into the world' without ever realistically representing a young lady's sensibilities.

In the middle of January 1778, Fanny received a parcel containing proofs of the three volumes of her novel for correction from Lowndes, this time via Gregg's Coffee House in York Street, Covent Garden, which was now being run by her two aunts Ann and Rebecca Burney.[43] The new venue was necessitated by young Charles's dramatic fall from grace and removal to Shinfield, which also meant that a new go-between had to be found. Fanny chose obliging cousin Edward, who assumed the name 'Mr Grafton' for secrecy. The aunts, who might otherwise have become suspicious of the traffic with Lowndes going on at their address, also had to be let in on the affair. Their delight and pride in what Fanny was now referring to, with unconvincing insouciance, as her 'frolic' was gratifying to the anxious author, but the gradual widening of the circle of confidants was beginning to take the secret out of her control.

The actual publication of the book, on 29 January 1778, was a rather abstract affair. Fanny had the unbound and incomplete set of sheets from Lowndes, but didn't receive any finished copies for another six months. If the story she tells in the *Memoirs* is to be believed, she only found out that the book was ready for sale when her stepmother read aloud an advertisement of it in the newspaper at breakfast:

> This day was published,
> EVELINA,
> or, a Young Lady's Entrance into the World.
> Printed for T. Lowndes, Fleet-street.*

---

* This anecdote appears nowhere but in *Memoirs of Doctor Burney*.[44] In the *Early Journals and Letters* she simply says: 'A thousand little incidents happened about this Time [March 1778], but I am not in a humour to recollect them: however, they were none of them productive of a discovery either to my Father or Mother.'[45]

Charles Burney was not present at this breakfast, or he might have noticed, as Mrs Burney, buried in the paper, evidently did not, 'the conscious colouring of the scribbler, and the irresistible smiles of the two sisters, Susanna and Charlotte'.[46]

About six weeks passed without any news of the book's progress reaching St Martin's Street, and though the author would have us believe that this was just as she wished, it is clear that curiosity and impatience soon began to get the better of both her and her sisters. As soon as the Doctor and Mrs Burney left on a visit to Streatham Park on 13 March, the young women invited cousin Edward round to tea, and together they devised a plan to go to Bell's Circulating Library in the Strand to 'ask some questions about Evelina'.[47] When they got to the shop, which was one from which Charles Burney ordered new books, Fanny's nerve failed and all she could bring herself to 'ask questions' about were some magazines, only to find that there was an advertisement for *Evelina* on the back of one of them. This hard evidence of her book having made its own 'entrance into the world' was peculiarly disturbing to the young author, who made this interesting observation in her journal:

> I have an exceeding odd *sensation*, when I consider that it is in the power of *any* & *every* body to read what I so carefully hoarded even from my best Friends, till this last month or two, – & that a Work which was so lately Lodged, in all privacy, in my Bureau, may now be seen by every Butcher & Baker, Cobler & Tinker, throughout the 3 kingdoms, for the small tribute of 3 pence.[48]

The exposure she felt on this occasion was at least threefold: the social exposure of being read by tradesmen, artisans – even tinkers; a kind of sexual exposure suggested by these people (all men) being able to enjoy for a mere three pence what had hitherto been locked up in a young lady's bedroom; and, thirdly, the exposure of her inner self through the work. The last is the most significant, and this diary entry is a rare early articulation of the kind of questions about the psychology of creativity which preoccupied theorists and practitioners for much of the twentieth century. The idea of an artist 'carefully hoarding' what he wants to express in his work, then promiscuously giving it away, is just that so clearly analysed by Marcel Proust in his essays on Sainte-Beuve, where he says of authorship, 'it is the secretion of one's innermost life, written in solitude and for oneself alone, that one gives to the public. What one bestows on private life – in conversation, that is, however refined it may be [. . .] is the product of a quite superficial self, not of the innermost self which one can only recover by putting aside the world and the self that frequents the world'.[49] It is interesting to see Fanny Burney feeling this on the quick as she overheard Edward talking to the bookseller at Bell's. But as we shall see, her critical and analytical powers (manifesting themselves most often as an acute self-consciousness) were to a great extent to be her undoing. Usually the evidence of a writer's inhibitions is interesting – as, say, in the case of Coleridge – for the very reason that the inhibitions are, one way or another, eventually overcome. This was not so in Fanny Burney's case. She understood the conflict between inner and outer life too well for comfort, but was only able to resolve it partially, and her writing suffered in consequence.

While Edward Burney was at Bell's Library he may well have bought the copy of *Evelina* which he took off the next day to Brompton, where his brother Richard was convalescing from a fever, attended by the Worcester family nurse, Miss Humphries. Fanny, whose partiality for her cousin Richard is clear from several remarks earlier in the journal, was tempted to excuse herself from joining the party at Brompton when she discovered from Charlotte that the book, hotly recommended by both Edward and the Covent Garden aunts, was now in his hands. 'This intelligence gave me the utmost uneasiness,' she wrote in the journal. 'I foresaw a thousand dangers of Discovery, – I dreaded the indiscreet warmth of all my Confidents; & I would almost as soon have told the *Morning Post* Editor, as Miss Humphries.'[50]

But the visit went ahead, and had aspects of sentimental comedy which would have transferred very nicely onto the stage of Drury Lane, where Sheridan's *The Rivals* and *The School for Scandal* had been such recent successes. Even on the way up the stairs of the lodgings, Fanny could overhear Miss Humphries reading the book aloud, presumably to the invalid Richard. She had got as far as Mr Villars's consolatory letter to Evelina after her father has refused to acknowledge her (which is at the beginning of volume two, so they had read pretty far in one day): 'Let me entreat you, therefore, my dearest child, to support yourself with that courage which your innocency ought to inspire . . .'[51] 'How pretty that is!' Miss Humphries was commenting as the author entered the room.[52] 'I longed for the Diversion of *hearing* their observations', Fanny wrote in her journal, relating how she begged Miss Humphries to go on with the reading. It was highly gratifying to witness an audience enjoying her work so much. If this was publication, what had she to fear?

> I must own I suffered great difficulty in refraining from Laughing upon several occasions, – & several Times, when they praised what they read, I was upon the point of saying '*You are very good!*' & so forth, & I could scarce keep myself from making Acknowledgements, & Bowing my Head involuntarily.
> However, I got *off perfectly* safely.[53]

But, predictably, no sooner had Fanny appeared to 'get off safely' than a new anxiety presented itself to her overworking imagination: that Richard and Miss Humphries, who both seemed 'to have [*Evelina*] by Heart',[54] might talk about the book so much when visiting St Martin's Street that Mrs Burney would want to read it. Sooner or later, rumours about the book's authorship, or the truth itself, would reach her father. Delaying this moment was of prime concern. Fanny had already confessed to her father in the spring of 1777 that she was writing a book (although the Doctor, preoccupied at the time by a dispute with Fulke Greville over the money that had been paid to Arne back in 1748, seemed to have forgotten his daughter's confidence). The longer she was able to keep him in ignorance that it had been published, the more chance she had of influencing his judgement, and perhaps forestalling any serious criticism through its favourable reception by 'the world'.

And indeed, the judgement of the reviewers was far more favourable than Fanny had dared hope. The *London Review* was brief, but laudatory: 'There is much more merit, as well respecting stile, character and Incident, than is usually to be met with among our modern novels.'[55] The influential *Monthly Review* was more fulsome: 'we do not hesitate to pronounce [*Evelina*] one of the most sprightly, entertaining & agreeable productions of this kind which has of late fallen under our Notice. A great variety of natural Incidents, some, of the Comic stamp, render the narrative extremely interesting. The characters, which are agreeably diversified, are conceived & drawn with propriety, & supported with spirit. The Whole is written with great ease & Command of Language.'[56] The *Critical Review*, *Westminster Review* and *Gentleman's Magazine* also gave the book laudatory notices, and Fanny was right to think she had 'come off with flying Colours'[57] from the periodicals.

It is hard to appreciate just how low a profile most authors kept in the eighteenth century. Few authors were more famous or notorious than their works; in Fanny Burney's case, when even her gender was unknown to the publisher himself, never mind her name, age or station, the disparity between her fame and *Evelina*'s was even more extreme. While society women such as Mrs Cholmondeley were discovering the book and excitedly recommending it to their friends, while *Evelina* was the subject of gossip and speculation across London, it had almost ceased to exist for the author, who didn't even possess a copy, and had very little idea of the impact her work was having outside the small group of family confidants.

Fanny's ignorance of the book's progress was exacerbated by a bout of serious illness in the spring of 1778 which put her completely out of action for the better part of two months. She describes it as 'an Inflammation of the Lungs', which Dr Burney feared might turn tubercular, and which left her so enfeebled that she was hardly capable of moving. When the initial alarm was over, a long convalescence at Chesington was prescribed. Fanny went there in the first week of May, accompanied by Susan and Edward, who had to prop her up between them in the post chaise, and regularly apply salts to her nose. Samuel Crisp, who was himself infirm, gouty and a chronic pessimist, had probably resigned himself to never seeing his 'dear Fannikin' again after the dire reports from St Martin's Street; certainly, he was just as overcome by their reunion as she, and having kissed her hand, had to hurry away speechless.

Fanny's recovery was slow, but in June she began to feel well enough to continue her journal. One of the first conversations she chose to record was an example of Mrs Hamilton's niece Kitty Cooke in full spate against Mrs Burney, whom Kitty obviously felt should have brought Fanny to Chesington herself, rather than leaving the chaperonage to Edward and Susan: 'but you know, [three words effaced] what a thing it would be for a fine lady to bring a sick person!' Edward was clearly shocked by Miss Cooke's speech, as was Fanny, though she says she was too weak and tired to raise an objection. It seems unlikely that she would have objected in any case – Susan was uncomfortable, but only laughed nervously, and if Fanny had not secretly relished hearing criticism of her stepmother by someone they all considered 'utterly incapable of art', she need not have recorded quite so much of it. '"To be sure she [Mrs Burney] did well to stay away,"' Kitty rattled on, '"for she knows we none of us love her; she could only think of coming to mortify us; for one must be civil to her, for the Doctor's sake. – but she's such a queer fish, – to be sure, for a sensible woman, as she is, she has a great many oddities; & as to Mr Crisp, he says he's quite sick of her, d– her, he says, I wish she was Dead! for, you know, for such a good soul as the Doctor to have such a Wife, – to be sure there's something very disagreeable in her, – Laughing so loud, & hooting, & clapping her Hands, – I can't love her, a nasty old Cat, – yet she's certainly a very sensible Woman."' [58] No wonder Edward 'couldn't keep his Countenance' [59] at this outburst, so strongly dramatised by the diarist. If Miss Cooke's claim that 'none of us loves' the 'nasty old Cat' is shocking, even more so is her blurting out of Crisp's malicious private opinion of Mrs Burney, his view of her unworthiness as wife to the Doctor, and his wish that she were dead. And the more Fanny Burney tried to mitigate the effect in her diary by saying that Kitty was an 'unguarded Creature [. . .] without the slightest notion of the impropriety of which she was guilty', the more likely one is to believe that what Kitty says is also *true*.

Mrs Burney did not come off much better at Streatham, where her husband was enjoying a blossoming friendship with Mrs Thrale and her circle. In the classification tables of her acquaintances' qualities that Mrs Thrale was amusing herself with that summer, Elizabeth Burney scored an average '10' (out of twenty) for 'Worth of Heart', but a miserable 'o' under the heading 'Person, Mien & Manner'. [60] Perhaps the very insensitivity that Miss Cooke found 'disagreeable' provided Mrs Burney with some protection against the dislike of almost all her husband's family and friends – certainly she was given the cold shoulder as often as possible, which the Doctor could scarcely have failed to notice.

A letter from Mrs Burney to Fanny written around this time (and presumably kept as an exemplum, since Fanny wrote 'in the style of a certain Lady –' at the top of it) gives some idea of the odd manner that so riled Crisp and failed to impress Mrs Thrale. The whole letter is written in a jerky, inconsequential style, with many impenetrable coinages and cryptic references. At some points, Mrs Burney's sentences seem to run parallel to their meaning; she gives the bizarre impression of having made up both the vocabulary and the syntax as she went along. One example is a passage which presumably refers to Mrs Burney's youngest child, Sarah, who was then six years old: 'That nibbetting yepping thing snitch* stands gloring over my papers, & says she wonders what I am writing; but I tell her wondring is n't good for her – & to stop her yep have sent her for a wafer'. Or this, about the maid Betty, 'that Stothering Creter', whom Hetty Burney had recently dismissed: 'she'l never be good for anything while her eyes are open – the creter is to me aversion upon aversions – she was so rude the last time I drank tea with her mistress when I only wanted her to bring me up a glass of water – that tho' I went to the top of the Kitchen stairs & cried "is this body here"? half a hundred times she never made me any answer!'[61] Perhaps Betty was taking her cue from what she had overheard Hetty and her sisters say in private about 'the Lady's' embarrassing behaviour. Hetty herself clearly didn't feel inclined to reprimand her servant on this occasion.

The longueurs of convalescence at Chesington made Fanny restless. She had promised that Hetty would be allowed to read *Evelina* to Crisp – without disclosing her secret, of course – but began to want to witness his response to the book herself. Pretending that Hetty had introduced *Evelina* at Brompton, she tried to get Crisp interested in it, and eventually he agreed to have it read aloud. 'I found it a much more awkward thing than I had expected,' Fanny wrote in her journal; 'my voice quite faltered when I began it, which, however, I passed off for the effect of remaining weakness of Lungs; &, in short, from an *invincible* embarrassment, which I could not for a page together repress, the Book, by my reading, lost all manner of spirit.'[62] To avoid having to finish the book, she told him that the third volume was missing: 'To be sure, the concealment of this affair has cost me no few Inventions', Fanny reflected later. 'I have no alternative, but avowing myself for an authoress, which I cannot bear to think of.'

Fanny may not have understood at the time of writing *Evelina*, but soon learned, that guessing the authorship of an anonymous work was a common pastime among the London reading class: in her play *The*

* The printed version has 'wretch', but my reading of the manuscript is different.

Witlings, written in the year following the publication of *Evelina*, but never produced, Burney's Lady Smatter, a rather crudely caricatured blue-stocking, causes mischief by frivolously indulging in this game: 'I am never at rest', she says, 'till I have discovered the authors of every thing that comes out; and, indeed, I commonly hit upon them in a moment.'[63] By not including the words 'By a Lady' on the title page, Fanny Burney had presumably wanted her novel to be read without any gender prejudice; but it must also have been clear to her that any sensitive reader would guess the author's sex from the work. Apart from the obvious woman-centredness of the plot and viewpoint of *Evelina* and the physicality of much of the description, there is the whole force of the novelty of her portrayal of female sensibility. All Fanny could hope to conceal in the long term was her personal connection.

People in the Burneys' circle were starting to read the book, and Fanny listened avidly to reports of their opinions. Lady Hales and Miss Coussmaker were besotted with *Evelina*, apparently, and could hardly talk of anything else. But when Lady Hales declared that the author must be 'a man of great abilities', Miss Coussmaker replied firmly that 'the Writer was a *Woman*, for [. . .] there was such a remarkable delicacy in the conversations & descriptions, notwithstanding the grossness & vulgarity of some of the Characters, [. . .] that she could not but suspect the Writer was a Female, but, she added, notwithstanding the preface declared the Writer never would be known, she hoped, if the Book circulated as she expected it would, *he* or *she*, would be tempted to discovery'. Fanny Burney's private response was exultant: 'Ha! Ha! Ha! – that's my answer. They little think how well they are already acquainted with the Writer they so much honour.'[64] The trick seemed to be working.

Fanny was still very anxious about her father's possible disapproval, either of the work in particular or of the secrecy with which she had published it. There is no doubting the veneration she felt for her father – 'the author of my being', to use her suggestive phrase from the dedicatory verses to *Evelina* – but it had a neurotic edge which was absent from all the Doctor's feelings towards *her*. If she had conceived an illegitimate child she couldn't have tried harder to cover it up, and yet at the same time there is a perverse sense in which she was longing to 'come clean' with him about her authorship, and justify her efforts by openly winning his approval.

There was already speculation in Mrs Thrale's circle that the Doctor himself might be the author of *Evelina*, and Susan Burney must have realised that if the book came into his hands, he would immediately recognise the autobiographical incidents and allusions which Fanny had used. In what was a very well-judged and considerate piece of meddling – only revealed in a fragmentary memoir written by Dr Burney between 1792 and 1806 – Susan decided that the time had come to tell their father the secret while her sister was out of the way in Chesington.

The Doctor's benign reaction to the revelation (and his refusal to say how he was told) suggests that Susan and Charlotte presented the news as another family conspiracy, this time to alleviate Fanny's massive anxieties. In the wake of her illness, which they had all sincerely considered life-threatening, both the sisters and Dr Burney must have feared a relapse. The odd thing is that Fanny did not guess what had happened. When she received Charlotte's letter – 'the most interesting that could be written to me' – with the news that their father was reading *Evelina*, she paraphrased its contents thus:

> How this has come to pass, I am yet in the dark: but, it seems, the very moment, almost, that my mother & Susan & Sally left the House [to go to Chesington], he desired Charlotte to bring him the Monthly Review; [. . .] He read it with great earnestness, – then put it down; & presently after, snatched it up, & read it again. Doubtless his paternal Heart felt some agitation for his Girl, in reading a review of her Publication! – *how* he got at the *name*, I cannot imagine![65]

According to his own account, Charles Burney took up the first volume 'with fear & trembling',[66] but soon saw that the work was nothing to shame the family name further – quite the contrary. Susan passed on all his reactions to her sister, sitting agog over these letters in Chesington: he had begun reading it with Lady Hales and Miss Coussmaker; he admired Villars's pathetic style; he thought the preface 'vastly strong', and opined – clearly regretting his daughter's unworldliness on this count – that Lowndes had had a 'devilish good bargain' for his twenty guineas.

The further the Doctor went in the book, the more lavish his praise. By 16 June, Susan was reporting that he thought it 'the best Novel I know excepting Fielding's [*Amelia*], – &, in some respects, it is better than his!'

How much of a reader of novels Burney was is hard to ascertain: *Amelia* was the only novel he saw fit to keep in his library, and for all his genuine paternal pride over *Evelina*, he had no qualms about selling his set on to Lady Hales as soon as he had finished reading it.

Fanny heard with mixed gratification and amusement how *Evelina* was 'travelling in the Great World': it seemed that half of Lady Hales's acquaintance were blubbering over it at once. When she wrote to Lowndes at the end of June, asking to be allowed to make corrections to any further edition, his reply that he expected the first impression (of five hundred) to sell out by Christmas alerted her to the scale of its success: 'The Great World send here to Buy Evelina', the publisher replied excitedly to 'Mr Grafton'; 'A polite Lady said Do, Mr Lowndes, give me Evelina, Im [sic] treated as unfashionable for not having read it.'[67]

Meanwhile, the author herself sensed that although she had cleared the hurdle of her father's discovery remarkably easily, infinite further challenges opened up ahead:

> Indeed, in the midst of the greatest satisfaction that I feel, an inward *something* which I cannot account for, prepares me to expect a reverse! for the more the Book is drawn into notice, the more exposed it becomes to criticism & annotations.
>
> [. . .] Lord! what will all this come to? – Where will it End?[68]

❦ 5 ❦

Entrance into the World

In the summer of 1778, Hester Lynch Thrale was thirty-eight years old and expecting her twelfth child. She had already had to endure the deaths of seven children, and this last baby, Henrietta Sophia, was also destined to die very young. Mrs Thrale had been married for fifteen years to the brewer and Member of Parliament for Southwark, Henry Thrale. Though the marriage was outwardly successful, it was not happy: 'it would have been difficult to find a bride and groom who were more temperamentally unsuited to each other', James Clifford has written of the alliance between Thrale, the taciturn businessman, and his cultured, high-spirited Welsh heiress. Thrale displayed towards his wife few of the qualities that endeared him to his friends, one of whom, the playwright Arthur Murphy, praised his 'goodness of heart' and 'amiable temper'.[1] Mrs Thrale saw another side of him, coldness and neglect, and had to tolerate his many infidelities and bouts of venereal disease. In the early years of the marriage, which had been arranged by the couple's families with no regard to the personal preferences of either party, there was little opportunity for Hester to cultivate her interest in literature, or exercise her skills as a poet and wit. Dr Johnson was to say to her later that she had lived at this period 'like My Husband's kept Mistress, – shut from the World, its pleasures, or its Cares'.[2]

After the Thrales' introduction to Dr Johnson in 1765, via their mutual acquaintance Murphy, an easy friendship was established. Johnson was soon a regular visitor at the brewer's house in Southwark and comfortable estate at Streatham Park, Surrey. The Thrales were a godsend to 'the Great Cham', whose bluntness and acerbity did not go down well in polite society any more than did his lumbering form and unrefined, erratic manners. Howevermuch he was revered for his literary achievements, Johnson often cut a lonely and vulnerable figure. The wealthy and broad-minded Thrales, though, accommodated his oddities with ease, and a particular friendship soon grew up between the Doctor and Mrs Thrale. Something of an outsider herself, Hester Thrale provided Johnson not only with the free run of her household and ideal conditions in which he could work, but also with a degree of protection against his chronic melancholy. Shrewd and good-humoured, she was not intimidated by the great man's ex-cathedra manner, and no doubt played on his sensibility 'to the influence of female charms', as Boswell rather grudgingly put it,[3] once saying that she felt her power over Johnson's spirits and his readiness to confide 'such Secrets as [he has] entrusted to me'[4] derived from her sex. Johnson needed equally a confidante and a protectress; Mrs Thrale required an outlet for her strong affections, good sense and intellect.

The coterie of 'Streathamites' that grew up around Johnson's almost permanent residence at the Thrales' home included Garrick, Murphy, Joshua Reynolds, William Seward and James Boswell. Charles Burney had been mixing in this exalted society for about a year and a half by the time *Evelina* was published, but his veneration for Johnson went back much further. He had written some rather obsequious fan mail to the great lexicographer when the *Dictionary of the English Language* was about to appear in the early 1750s, and visited him at the Temple in 1760, where the star-struck music-teacher surreptitiously removed some bristles from Johnson's hearthbrush as a souvenir to take back to Norfolk, ostensibly on behalf of his friend William Bewley.* The connection was kept alive by Burney with some difficulty: Johnson's scorn for music was well known – 'it excites in my mind no ideas, and hinders me from contemplating my own'. Though Johnson received Burney's books with grace and, after the publication of the second one, increasing interest, music was not a subject ever likely to elicit his full attention.

Charles Burney's introduction to Henry Thrale in 1776, and his subsequent engagement to teach music to the Thrales' eldest child, Hester (always known as Queeney), created a marvellous opportunity for him to meet Johnson regularly at Streatham Park on far less unequal terms

---

* Bewley was later referred to by the Streathamites as the 'Broom man' on account of this story, which was one of Boswell's favourites, perhaps because it showed someone in an even more advanced stage of Johnson-mania than himself.

than before. The Thrales, who were generous hosts, were enjoying their most affluent period; they had already added an impressive new library wing to the house, and in 1777 they had a small lake with an island built in the grounds and reconstructed a two-mile gravel walk around the property. The household's prospects seemed fair in every way (although the unpredictability of Thrale's profits from his brewery in fact made their finances quite volatile), and Burney was intensely gratified by the chance to share something of their luxurious and easy lifestyle.

Burney had been appointed as a music-master, but was soon asked to Streatham as a guest. Mrs Thrale had taken to him with characteristically wholehearted enthusiasm. 'Such was the fertility of his Mind, and the extent of his Knowledge; such the Goodness of his Heart and Suavity of his Manners', she wrote in her journal *Thraliana*, 'that we began in good earnest to sollicit his Company, and gain his Friendship.'[5] Burney was just as eager to cement the connection, and within weeks of his first invitation to Streatham he had invited Johnson and Mrs Thrale to St Martin's Street for the visit which, as we have seen, so impressed his daughter. Mrs Thrale went to the considerable expense of buying a new harpsichord for Burney's use at Streatham, and was delighted with his capacity to fit in with the unpredictable Dr Johnson, whom he flattered with his attentiveness and sincere admiration. In Mrs Thrale's private classification system (in which Mrs Burney had come off so poorly), Johnson's 19 out of 20 for 'Scholarship' far outshone the historian of music's 8; but Burney was awarded 19 for 'Good humor', where Johnson scored 0. '[F]ew People possess such Talents for general Conversation', she wrote of her new friend in the autumn of 1777.[6] Her journals show occasional annoyance at Burney's over-anxiety to please, but also bear witness to the depth of her affection for him: 'My Heart [. . .] runs forward a Mile to meet my dear Doctor Burney', she wrote. 'If ever the – Suaviter in Modo, fortiter in Re – resided in mortal Man, tis surely in Doctor Burney'.[7]

By the summer of 1778 the friendship had already survived one tricky episode. After the fiasco of Bessy Allen's elopement the previous October, Mrs Burney had come straight from France to the Thrales, who were on holiday in Brighton, expecting to find her husband there. But Dr Burney had already gone home to London, and when the distraught Mrs Burney arrived it was impossible for her to conceal the cause of her anguish from Mrs Thrale, despite the risk of public humiliation. Mrs Thrale could not resist passing on the scandalous news in a letter to Johnson the next day, but however much she played sarcastically on Mrs Burney's former pride in her 'fine daughter', the woman's genuine unhappiness – 'greater & more real Distress have I seldom seen'[8] – not only prevented Mrs Thrale from really exploiting the information, but rather drew out her sympathy. Dr Burney's own letter to Mrs Thrale on the subject a few weeks later displays a scorn for the hypocritical condolences he and his wife had received from some of their acquaintances that suggests Mrs Thrale had treated him and his wife much better:

[Mrs Burney] is now in Town, but invisible; 'tis humiliating to tell melancholy Stories abt one's Self, & more so to hear People pretend to pity one, when we know they have no more Feeling than *Punch*. I hate to think of the Trick that has been played her, & still more to talk about it.[9]

The even more melancholy story of young Charles's disgrace at Cambridge remained a closely guarded secret from Mrs Thrale, although she noticed that the whole Burney family 'colour and fret at the mention of him'.[10] Mrs Thrale's heart might be running out to meet 'dear Doctor Burney' all the time, but the music-master remained cautious underneath his charm, always aware, as were his children, of the precariousness of his favoured position.

Fanny, more alert than anyone to her father's social standing, was never more anxious about it than at this point in her life, when she had the power to affect his reputation dramatically one way or the other. 'I, as *myself*, am nobody', she wrote once he knew about her authorship, 'but as *your* spawn, I could easily make myself *known* & have power to disgrace'.[11] When father and daughter met at Chesington for the first time after 'the *Fact*'[12] was acknowledged between them, her tearful relief at his approbation had been so violent he thought she was going to collapse. She threw herself into his arms and 'cried *à chaudes larmes* till she sobbed', Burney recollected in his unpublished fragmentary memoir. 'The poor humble author I believe never was happier in her life'.[13] It is hard to square this scene of near-prostration with *happiness*. It seems more like nervous exhaustion, bordering on hysterics. Fanny herself, recounting the same incident in her journal of 23 June 1778, admits that there was more than mere relief to her response: 'the length of my illness, joined to severe mental suffering from a Family calamity which had occurred at that period, had really made me too weak for a joy mixt with such excess of amazement'. The editors of the *Early Journals* footnote this entry with the speculation that the 'Family calamity' might have been 'some aftershock of Bessy Meeke's elopement', though nine months had passed since then – time enough for a half-sister to recover from a clandestine marriage, one would think. Charles junior's disgrace and possible suicide attempt seem more likely causes of 'severe mental suffering', but the only clue is that it concerned 'Family'.

Charles Burney was longing to get some credit at Streatham from the family's only benign secret, the authorship of *Evelina*, and as the only one of the cognoscenti who had not been bound with solemn oaths '*by all they hold most sacred* [. . .] never to reveal it, without my consent',[14] he was the weakest link in the chain (though we know that the oath had also been broken by Susan). Even with Fanny's reluctant permission to use his judgement over the matter, Burney realised that it would be extremely risky to introduce the subject of *Evelina* at the Thrales' himself, but also that among that novel-devouring crew he probably wouldn't have to wait long before someone else mentioned it.

The exact sequence of events here becomes difficult to unpick from the neatened version handed down to posterity in the *Memoirs* by Madame d'Arblay, whose 'entrance into the world' in the summer of 1778 became, retrospectively, the cornerstone of her fame – 'more like a romance' as she was to say, 'than anything in the book that was the cause'.[15] Fifty pages of her biography of her father are devoted to the publication of her own novel *Evelina* (compared with three pages on the Doctor's *General History of Music*); they form in effect a book-within-a-book, with a disingenuous preamble about the 'devoir due to the singleness of truth' and a separate dedication to Sir Walter Scott and Samuel Rogers, whose visit to her in 1826, as we shall see, alerted the elderly Madame d'Arblay to some of the variant stories going around by that date. The fact that it was clearly important to her to 'correct' the version that Scott and Rogers had heard (recorded by Scott in his diary[16]) didn't prevent her from changing it again for publication in the *Memoirs* on the grounds that she had spoken to Scott and Rogers 'incoherently, from the embarrassment of the subject, and its long absence from her thoughts'.[17] This admission that she was not, aged seventy-four, a reliable witness to her own life story does not sit easily among the surrounding protestations that she is about to set the record straight once and for all.

The version that Madame d'Arblay wanted to authorise placed heavy emphasis on the involvement of Samuel Johnson, the affability and sentimental pride of her father, her own youth, modesty and reticence, the apparently miraculous qualities of her book to elicit praise in high places and the relative unimportance of Hester Thrale except in confirming the opinions of others. In it she tells how her father came home to St Martin's Street one evening during her long stay at Chesington with the news that while they were at tea in Streatham, Dr Johnson, 'see-sawing on his chair', had suddenly come out with the remark that Mrs Cholmondeley 'was talking to me last night of a new novel, which she says has a very uncommon share of merit; Evelina. She says she has not been so entertained this great while as in reading it; and that she shall go all over London to discover the author'.[18] In this version, Mrs Thrale replied that she too had heard the book recommended, and, at Johnson's further insistence on Mrs Cholmondeley's good opinion, made it clear she would get herself a copy. Charles Burney, scarcely able to contain his pleasure, added archly that he had heard of the book and 'read a little of it – which, indeed – seemed to be above the commonplace works of this kind'.[19] As he said later to Susan (who immediately wrote an account of their conversation to Fanny), this mentioning of his daughter's book was 'just what I wished but could not expect!' and, far from being something to hide from his grand friends, owning authorship 'would be a credit to [Fanny] – and to me! – and to you! – and to all her family!'[20]

Since the original letter from Susan (existing in fragmentary form in the Berg Collection) includes the detail of Dr Burney saying to Mrs Thrale that the book 'will do [. . .] for your time of confinement', this incident must have taken place before the birth of Henrietta Thrale on 21 June. The editors of the *Early Journals and Letters* place the following letter from Fanny to Susan (dated 5 July) as a response to it:

meeting Mr Crisp ere I had composed myself, I *tipt him such a touch of the Heroicks*, as he has not seen since the Time when I was so much celebrated for *Dancing Nancy Dawson* [...] He would fain have discovered the *reason* of my skittishness[.][21]

The reference is to the hornpipe tune made popular in *The Beggar's Opera* in 1759 by the dancer Nancy Dawson, and which is better known now as the nursery song 'Here we go round the mulberry bush'. It is the tune to which Fanny used to dance her wild jigs 'on the Grass plot' at Chesington in her youth, as Crisp fondly recalled,[22] although there is nothing to suggest that she actually *danced* on this occasion, let alone around a tree. According to the two sources, Susan's letter and Fanny's account in the *Memoirs*, no one at Streatham had actually read *Evelina* yet (apart from Dr Burney), and though the young author might well have felt elated by her work having come to Johnson's notice, it doesn't explain the reference further on in the same letter to Mrs Thrale's '*eloge* [...] that not only delights at *first*, but that proves more & more flattering every Time it is considered'. No *éloge* (praise) of any sort is recorded in the *Memoirs*, where Mrs Thrale, barely aware of the existence of *Evelina*, is cast in the unlikely role of slowcoach, or in the existing copy of Susan's letter. The only *éloge* likely to have provoked Fanny's excited response is included in a letter from Susan wrongly dated 7 instead of 4 July by Annie Raine Ellis in her 1898 edition of the *Early Diary* which records a conversation between Mrs Thrale and Charles Burney when Dr Johnson was not present. Mrs Thrale is recommending a new novel, *Evelina*, to her friend and his wife which Queeney read to her during her last confinement (i.e. around the end of June): she liked it 'VASTLY – is EXTREMELY pleas'd with it [...] 'tis very clever I assure you [...] there's a vast deal of humour & entertainment in it', adding, more thoughtfully, 'there's a great deal of human *Life* in this Book, & of the Manners of the present time. It's writ by somebody that knows *the top & the bottom* – the *highest & lowest* of Mankind.' The demonstrative pronoun could indicate that Mrs Thrale had fetched her copy to pass round; certainly she pressed Mrs Burney to take the book home to St Martin's Street, neither woman realising, as Fanny observed in her journal, that the original manuscript of the novel had been there some time.

Although the *Memoirs* version of the story makes it look as if Johnson was the prime mover in publicising *Evelina*, Mrs Thrale was the first of her circle actually to read the book, and Johnson only did so after she had virtually forced him to by putting a copy in his coach in late July. The incident of Johnson 'see-sawing' on his chair could have taken place quite some time before 21 June, as Charles Burney admitted to knowing Fanny's authorship by 4 June, but he could have been told earlier. This would leave several weeks between the book being mentioned casually by Johnson and Mrs Thrale's '*éloge*' to Dr and Mrs Burney, rather than both these things having happened at once, as their juxtaposition in Fanny's letter can be read to imply,[23] or Mrs Thrale's *éloge* not having happened at all, as in the *Memoirs*.*

The wonderful news that Johnson had read and liked the book only reached Fanny on 3 August (along with the infuriating information that Anna Williams, the blind poet who lived with Dr Johnson at Bolt Court, also knew her 'poor mauled to pieces secret'). He was full of praise for *Evelina*, saying to Mrs Thrale that there were 'passages in it that might do honour to Richardson'. The letter 'almost Crazed' the author 'with agreeable surprise':

> it gave me such a flight of spirits, that I Danced a Jigg to Mr Crisp, without any preparation, *music*, or explanation, to his no small amazement & diversion. I left him, however, to make his own comments, upon my friskiness, without affording him the least assistance.[24]

This little account of her second 'touch of the Heroicks' within the month is the basis for the best-known anecdote about Fanny Burney, the story (told for the first time in the *Memoirs*) that she danced for joy around a mulberry tree when she heard Johnson's praise of her first book. It is a charming picture; the impromptu ecstatic dance seems to illustrate perfectly Burney's sense of elation at her achievement, and her release from the anxieties and inhibitions that constrained so much of her behaviour. There are a number of things about the story, though, that indicate it isn't strictly true. The mulberry tree only appears in the *Memoirs*; one assumes there was such a tree at Chesington and that it was much more important to Fanny than to Crisp, who never mentions

---

* There remain the references to Dr Johnson and Mrs Cholmondeley in Fanny's delighted reply from Chesington, which seem to have no basis in the preceding letter from Susan; but as this letter has a defaced first page and seven lines deleted at the end, it isn't impossible that there was some reference hidden there to their earlier remarks about the book.

one. Six months after the *Evelina* revelations, in a letter about the difficulties Fanny might face in trying to avoid grossness in her writing
(specifically in the comedy she was then planning), he wrote: 'Do You
remember about a Dozen Years ago, how You Used to dance Nancy
Dawson on the Grass plot[?]'.[25] If she had repeated this performance
only six months before on receipt of the news about Johnson, why did
Crisp not mention that occasion rather than harking back a dozen
years?

Dancing 'Here we go round the mulberry bush' was clearly something
Fanny did 'in her days of adolescence'[26] in fits of strong animal spirits,
and Johnson's approbation revived just such a surge of wild energy. 'She
was very young at this time', Walter Scott recorded in his journal in
1826, having just been told the story on his first visit to Madame d'Arblay.
In 1778 Fanny wasn't 'very young', she was twenty-six, but there is a
poetic truth in her story. The composition of *Evelina* could be said to
have begun when Fanny Burney *was* very young indeed, with the composition of the destroyed 'mother' novel, 'Caroline Evelyn', and to be the
result of youthful spirits urgently requiring expression. If the mulberry
tree story shows signs of having been tampered with to make it neater and
more expressive of this gratifying moment in her life, one is disinclined to
criticise its author too roundly. Perhaps it is more important to remark
on this occasion what a talent she had for story-telling, rather than
lamenting too much her shortcomings as a historian.

Although Fanny Burney wrote it out of the *Memoirs*, Mrs Thrale's opinion
of *Evelina* was of enormous moment to the new author. It was the most
important notice she felt it possible for her book to attract from the
literary world (not really believing Johnson would ever read it), and her
response, in the same letter to Susan, was a queer mixture of elation and
anxiety:

> I am now at the *summit* of a high Hill, – my prospects, on one side, are
> bright, glowing, & invitingly beautiful; – but when I turn round, I perceive,
> on the other side, sundry Caverns, Gulphs, pits & precipices, that to *look
> at*, make my Head giddy, & my Heart sick! – I see about me, indeed,
> many Hills of far greater height & sublimity; – but I have not the strength
> to attempt climbing them; – if *I* move, it must be in *descending*![27]

'Caverns, Gulphs, pits & precipices', 'sublimity' – Burney is employing the language of the picturesque twenty years before the Romantics, and might be suspected of a romantic self-indulgence here too, if she did not go on to a fairly shrewd anticipation of the possible consequences of such startling early success:

> [W]ould a future attempt be treated with the same mercy? – No, my dear Susy, quite the contrary, – there would not, indeed, be the same *plea* to save it, – it would no longer be a *Young Lady's first appearance* in public; – those who have met with less indulgence, would all *peck* at any new Book, – & even those who most encouraged the 1st offspring, might prove Enemies to the 2d, by receiving it with Expectations which it could not answer[.]

The reception of this putative second attempt was what concerned her, not its composition. Fanny took for granted that she would keep on writing, and there is evidence that she was already engaged on another work at this point, as she mentions 'Letters, Italian' and 'some of my own vagaries'[28] as the occupations which made Crisp refer to her ironically that summer as 'the scribe' and 'the authoress'. Writing was already a way of life for her, however unpleasant the thought of public exposure might be and however many objections her anxious mind might present:

> I have already, I fear, reached the *pinnacle* of my Abilities, & therefore to *stand still* will be my best policy: – but there is nothing under Heaven so difficult to do! – Creatures who are formed for motion, *must* move, how-ever great their inducements to forbear.[29]

Charles Burney had intended to flatter and please his daughter when he passed on, through Susan, his opinion that Mrs Thrale and Mrs Cholmondeley 'were *d–d severe*, & *d–d knowing*, & *afraid* of praising *à tort & à travers* as their opinions are liable to be quoted, which makes them extremely shy of speaking favourably'.[30] Fanny was more likely to interpret these remarks as threatening, an indication of how high the stakes were being raised. She anticipated the shock Mrs Thrale might feel at the discrepancy between mousy Miss Burney's behaviour and the riotously satirical nature of her novel. Having a thieving brother or an eloping stepsister was nothing compared to being identified as the only begetter of Madame Duval or Captain Mirvan. '[I]f you do tell Mrs Thrale', she wrote to her father on 8 July in a letter clearly meant as gentle warning to him, 'won't she think it very strange where I can have *kept Company*, to draw such a family as the Branghtons, Mr Brown & some others? [. . .] I am afraid she will conclude I must have an *innate vulgarity of ideas* to assist me with such coarse colouring for the objects of my Imagination'.

It seems likely that Fanny herself, as much as anyone, was troubled by this discrepancy. The 'old lady' had kept her public behaviour under strict control her whole life, while letting her powers of observation and imagination develop as they would. It was unnerving – subversive – to be a prude and a satirist at one and the same time. Her imagination could easily produce ideas that were innately vulgar, shocking and grotesque – indeed, as she acknowledged in the same letter, her writing would have been anodyne otherwise: 'Not that I suppose the *Book* would be better received by [Mrs Thrale], for having Characters *very pretty & all alike*: [. . .] I should build my defence upon Swift's maxim, *that a Nice man is a man of Nasty ideas*.'

Only two days before this Fanny had been deliberately teasing Daddy Crisp at Chesington, saying that her father had divulged to her profoundly secret news about the authorship of *Evelina*. Crisp demanded to be told immediately, at which Fanny insisted upon his guessing.

> 'I can't guess, said he – may be it's *You*.'
> Oddso! thought I, what do you mean by that? – 'Pho, nonsense! cried
> I, what should make you think of me?'
> 'Why You look guilty.' answered he.[31]

This 'horrible Home stroke' was laughed off by Fanny, with some difficulty. Crisp could read her face like a book – 'deuce take my looks! [. . .] I shall owe them a grudge for this!' – and would have found her out instantly, she imagined, had he witnessed her reading her recent letters from home. But she determined to spin out the game with him a little longer – at least until he had finished reading the book – and clearly enjoyed the 'ridiculous' scenes in which she was 'almost perpetu-ally engaged' with him.

Elsewhere the machinery of publicity that Charles Burney had set in motion rolled on. He wanted to tell Lady Hales, and Mrs Cholmondeley, and of course all the Streathamites. Susan reported hearing Mrs Burney's bursts of laughter through the door as the book was read aloud to her in bed by her husband. The kind and praising letter that arrived soon after from Fanny's erratic stepmother made up for the preceding anxiety: 'Good God! – to receive such a panygeric [sic] from the quarter from which I *most* dreaded satire!' Fanny wrote in her journal when this new hurdle had been cleared.[32]

When Mrs Thrale was told about the book's authorship she must have felt slightly foolish at first, for her *Thraliana* entry is reserved by comparison with the former *éloge*:

> I was shewed a little Novel t'other Day which I thought pretty enough & set Burney to read it, little dreaming it was written by his second Daughter Fanny, who certainly must be a Girl of good Parts & some knowledge of the World too, or She could not be the Author of Evelina – flimzy as it is, compar'd with the Books I've just mentioned [Richardson, Rousseau, Charlotte Lennox, Smollett and Fielding].[33]

She warmed to the book again, though, when Johnson's approval was certain. She had left the first volume in his coach for him to read on the way back to London, and he borrowed the second by return, saying later that 'Harry Fielding never did anything equal' to it.[34] This was Mrs Thrale's cue to promote the book further, and her newly-discovered connection with the author through 'her' Dr Burney seemed to proffer a stake in its success. She read the funny bits aloud to 'whoever came near her',[35] and was happy to pass on the quaint news about the book's authorship.

It was only a matter of weeks before Mrs Thrale invited the new lioness to dine at Streatham Park on one of the Thursdays when her father would be there to teach Queeney. To the 'accidental author', this was 'the most *Consequential* Day I have spent since my Birth'.[36] She spent an unpleasant journey in the coach from Chesington along the dry and dusty summer roads to Streatham, 'really in the Fidgets' about her reception. It was a fair guess that Dr Johnson would be there, living as he did '*almost wholly*'[37] with the Thrales. She was so nervous that she hardly noticed what handsome Streatham Park looked like on this first visit, apart from the fact that it was white.

Mrs Thrale, who emerged from the paddock, dressed informally in a muslin jacket, said nothing of *Evelina*, for which Fanny was extremely grateful. Even when the subject was broached later, while she and Fanny were alone in the library together, Mrs Thrale only reported Johnson's conversation the night before, and no one, surely, could take exception to that? 'Mr Johnson repeated whole scenes by Heart!' Mrs Thrale told her almost silent young guest, who was studying the bookshelves to hide her embarrassment. 'O you can't imagine how much he is pleased with the Book.'[38] There was little Fanny could say in reply to this, even if she had been able to raise her voice above a whisper.

It was a relief when Mr Thrale came in from his ride and Fanny was left with the magnificent library to herself for a few minutes. She had 'just fixed upon a new Translation of Cicero's Laelius' when the library door opened and the Thrales' other guest, William Seward, walked in. 'I instantly put away my Book', Fanny recorded in her journal, 'because I dreaded being thought studious and affected'. It would have been provoking to be taken for a blue-stocking, like Elizabeth Montagu and her associates.

William Seward was part of the inner circle at Streatham, handsome, rich and slightly eccentric. He was only five years older than Fanny, and unmarried, but if there had been any idea of matchmaking in Mrs Thrale's mind that day, nothing was to come of it. Beside the fact that he had prevented Fanny from enjoying a quiet hour or so poking about the Thrales' library, Seward made the mistake of launching straight into conversation about *Evelina*, the book with which Miss Burney had 'favoured the World' (and which just happened to have been left lying about on the library table). Compared with Mrs Thrale's sidelong approach and delicate address, this seemed grossly ill-mannered, but for once Fanny's response was more irritated than ashamed. Seward must have been puzzled when she sat firmly turned away from him in disgust, answering him curtly, if at all.

What made this day at Streatham 'the most Consequential' for Fanny was dinner, which began fashionably late in the afternoon. When the small party went in, she was disappointed that Dr Johnson had still not appeared. Mrs Thrale put Fanny and her father on either side of her, with a place left empty on Fanny's other side, saying graciously that she was sure it would give Johnson great pleasure to sit there. Fanny had been given the seat of honour.

When Johnson finally arrived, her anxieties were forgotten in the rush of 'delight & reverence' she felt towards him. She was determined to listen as avidly as possible – as avidly as she had heard his disciple Mr Boswell did to every word that fell from the great man's lips. She could then report back faithfully to her sisters and Daddy Crisp, who all, like her, venerated Johnson as 'the acknowledged Head of Literature in this kingdom'.[39] She had seen him twice before, and was prepared for 'the cruel infirmities to which he is subject; for he has almost perpetual convulsive motions, either of his Hands, lips, Feet, knees, & sometimes of all together'. When Johnson took his place beside her, the short-sighted Fanny was not put off, although it was the first time she had got such a close view of 'a Face the most ugly, a Person the most awkward, & manners the most singular, that ever were or ever can be seen'. She did not put this in her diary in order to denigrate Johnson, but to wonder at it. That this unlikely vessel should house such a great mind seemed highly interesting to her, in a world full of people far too ready to judge everything by appearances.

Johnson and Mrs Thrale dominated the conversation, each spurring the other on in a way that Fanny's subsequent diary entries show to be typical – Mrs Thrale often starting up a subject, Johnson pronouncing upon it and Mrs Thrale capping his aphorisms with some light or witty rejoinder. They were both very fond of quoting, and they were both very fond of each other. The ease and relaxation of the relationship gave the Streatham table-talk its peculiar sparkle, and if other guests seldom got a word in edgeways, it may be because they were far too busy being entertained. 'How we laughed!', 'We all laughed', Fanny writes continually.

Johnson made his first acknowledgement of Fanny's authorship when refusing one of Mrs Thrale's mutton pies (which he never ate anyway) with the gently absurd remark, '"I am too proud *now* to Eat of it; – sitting by Miss Burney makes me very proud to Day!"'[40] Mrs Thrale was quick to tease him over this by warning Fanny to '"take great care of your Heart if Dr. Johnson attacks it!"' '"What's that you say, Madam?"' he replied. '"Are you making mischief between the young lady & me already?"' It seemed like a conspiracy to delight their guest, especially since they were just as quick to drop the subject and take up another instead. Now Dr Johnson was half-recalling an epitaph, now Mrs Thrale quoting a French poem, and Johnson retaliating in Latin. Sitting between these two indefatigable wits, Fanny must have had to turn her head to and fro continually, like a spectator at a particularly fast game of tennis.

For all one's doubts about Fanny's veracity, especially in the *Memoirs*, the conversation she records in her journal of Johnson and Thrale does at least have the virtue of being sharply and consistently characterised; even if what she writes is not word-for-word what they said, either because of failure of memory or deliberate doctoring, at least it is very convincingly reconstructed. The speeches attributed to Johnson in her journal are the least tinkered with of any material appearing subsequently in the *Memoirs*. That is not to say that she doesn't make mystifyingly trivial adjustments to his words in the later publication, but it does suggest that she feels some sense of obligation to keep her original record of his speech fairly intact.

The 'Consequential' dinner gave rise to some delightful table-talk. Of Garrick, Johnson said that he '*looks* much older than he is: for his Face has had double the Business of any other man's, – it is never at rest, – when he speaks one minute, he has quite a different Countenance to what he assumes the next.' 'O yes,' Mrs Thrale replied, 'we must certainly make some allowance for such *wear* & *Tear* of a man's Face.' Sir John Hawkins, who was to be Johnson's first biographer (much to Boswell's irritation), was next under discussion. As the author of a rival *History of Music*, Hawkins was a sore subject with Charles Burney, who no doubt laughed as loud as anyone at Johnson's illustration of Hawkins's meanness. On the first night of his admission to the same club as Johnson,[*] Hawkins, quite against the spirit of the institution, begged off paying his share of the supper, as he had not eaten any of it. 'And *was* he excused?' someone asked. 'O yes', replied Johnson, 'for no man is angry at another for being inferior to himself! we all scorned him, – & admitted his plea. For my part, I was such a fool as to pay my share for

---

[*] It could have been the Ivy Lane Club or 'The Club'; they were members of both.

the *Wine* though I never tasted any. But Sir John was a most *unclubable* man!'⁴¹ Johnson's coinage particularly pleased Fanny: 'How delighted was I to hear this *master of Languages* so unaffectedly & sociably & good naturedly *make* Words, for the promotion of sport & humour!' The same journal entry contains one of Fanny's own notable coinages, 'agreeability'; the OED cites her diary as the first use of the word since Chaucer. 'Surely *I* may make words, when at a loss', she observed with evident satisfaction, 'if *Dr. Johnson* does.'⁴²

The two surviving accounts of this first Streatham evening have some interesting dissimilarities, with plenty of extra commentary of all kinds inserted in the *Memoirs* account to substantiate Fanny's early impressions of the great man.* In this version, Dr Burney manages to interject a couple of aphoristic speeches which his daughter omitted to notice the first time around in the journal; but the most glaring difference is in the number and quality of Johnson's supposed references to *Evelina*. In the journal, he makes only one. Relating how he witnessed a lady at an inn quarrelling with a waiter over a measure of ale, Johnson comments, 'Now *Madame Duval* could not have done a grosser thing!' Everyone laughed at this, and, miraculously, Fanny experienced none of her usual symptoms of embarrassment: '*I* did not *glow* at all! nor *munch fast*, – nor look on my plate, – nor lose any part of my usual composure!'⁴³ She was grateful to Johnson for his delicacy at keeping her work in mind without explicitly mentioning her authorship; indeed she was so impressed by the gentle flattery of everyone at the table that she was even prepared to think she might have judged Seward too harshly.

In the *Memoirs*, Johnson mentions the book far more frequently and knowingly. The guests seem conspiratorial with their 'sympathetic sim-per's and 'resistless' laughter, which is far from the delicacy Burney remarked in her journal, and she laughs with them, but inwardly feels 'embarrassment', 'shame' and 'unwillingness to demonstrate my con-sciousness'.⁴⁴ One of Johnson's reported remarks about the book has been relocated from a dinner conversation which the journal records two weeks later, another appears nowhere but in the *Memoirs*. Madame

---

* The account in the *Memoirs* is passed off as a quoted letter to Crisp, though none such survives. One suspects that Madame d'Arblay chose to redraft the journal as a 'letter' in order to retain the more dramatic first-person narrative and present tense.

d'Arblay clearly thought it would make a better story to amalgamate these incidents; in the process she inadvertently exposes the sham form of the whole *Memoirs* version, trying to pass it off as another of her inexhaustible supply of 'letters to Crisp'.

When the sexes were segregated at the end of the meal, Mrs Thrale took the opportunity to press Fanny to come for a much longer visit, and as William Seward handed her into the chaise later, he too expressed a desire to see her at Streatham again. 'I was loaded with civilities from them all', Fanny wrote in her journal. She may not have spoken much or attempted to impress herself on the company, but she had shown herself to be as appreciative and good-humoured as her father; Mrs Thrale and her friends could take Fanny Burney's other qualities quite literally *as read*.

Charles Burney was in high spirits on the journey back to London, and could talk of nothing but his daughter's success: 'he told me that, after passing through such a House as that, I could have nothing to fear. Meaning for my Book.' On her delighted return to St Martin' s Street after months away, and her reunion with all three sisters, Fanny heard even more good news: Sir Joshua Reynolds had sat up all night to finish *Evelina*. He and his sister – along with half of London, it seemed – were very keen to know who the author was.

This news about Reynolds prompted Fanny to go to Lowndes's book-shop herself at the first opportunity (with her stepmother as accomplice) to see what sort of gossip it was possible for a curious reader to pick up. The results were encouraging: despite Mrs Burney's formidable powers of persistence, Mr Lowndes could tell them nothing about the author of *Evelina*. '"I have no honour in keeping the secret"', Fanny records him saying,

> 'for I have never been trusted. All I know of the matter is, that it is a Gentleman of the other End of the Town.'
>
> And *that*, thought I, is *more* than even the *Author* knows![45]

Fanny spent most of her time in the shop pretending to read, much as she had done on her visit to Bell's with Edward and her sisters, but she was fascinated to see her publisher at last, if not exactly meet him (which she never did). He had an 'air of consequence & authority', and was now busy telling Mrs Burney how he had for a time suspected *Evelina* to be the work of Horace Walpole (who published *The Castle of Otranto* anonymously), and had tried to find out the author himself many times, without success: '"to tell You the truth, Madam,"' he said 'with a most important Face', '"I have been informed that it is a piece of *secret History*: &, in that case, it will never be known!" This was too much for me', Fanny recalled in her journal. 'I grinned irresistably; & was obliged to look out at the shop Door till we came away.'[46] She seemed to have pulled off an impossible trick, 'entering the world' to the sound of trumpets, while remaining snugly incognito. No wonder she grinned.

Daddy Crisp, who had eventually heard the astonishing news about the novel from Charles Burney, felt, like many others, that since the reception of *Evelina* had been so favourable, Fanny ought to be taking possession of her fame. '[Y]our perturbation ought to be in a great Measure at an end', he wrote when he heard of her success at Streatham. 'When You went into the Sea at Tinmouth, did not You shiver & shrink at first, & almost lose your breath when the Water came up to your Chest? – I suppose You afterwards learn'd to plunge in boldly overhead & Ears at once, & then Your pain was over – You must do the like now; & as the Public have thought proper to put You on a Cork Jacket, your Fears of drowning would be unpardonable.'[47] What he says would seem very reasonable – if Fanny had merely been *shy*. What it does not take into account is why she really valued her anonymity, which was because it gave her the freedom to write as she wanted to, without inhibitions.

No one seemed prepared to believe that Fanny's reticence was anything more than affectation. On her first long visit to Streatham, which took place in late August, Mrs Thrale followed her up to her room one night after an uncomfortable scene when one of the dinner guests, a Mr Lort, had started up a conversation about *Evelina*. Fanny begged Mrs Thrale not to reveal to him or anyone further her secret – thinking she still had a secret worth the name. Mrs Thrale laughed at this naivety:

'Poor Miss Burney! – so you thought just to have played & sported with your sisters & Cousins, & had it all your own way! – but now you are *in for* it! — but if you *will* be an Author & a Wit, – you must take the Consequence!'[48]

Fanny protested her sincere desire to remain anonymous. But if this wasn't affectation, Mrs Thrale said astutely, it had to be 'something *worse*':

'an over-delicacy that may make you unhappy all your Life! – Indeed you must *check* it, – you must get the better of it: – for *why* should you *write* a Book, *Print* a Book, & have every Body *Read* & *like* your Book, – & then sneak in a Corner & disown it!'[49]

Mrs Thrale had made another 'horrible home stroke', and they both knew it. Fanny spent a miserable night '*worked* by the certainty of being *blown* so much more than I had apprehended, & by seeing that, in spite of all my efforts at *snugship*, I was in so foul, I won't say *fair*, a way of becoming a *downright* & *known* scribler'.[50] However kind and supportive Mrs Thrale was – 'had I been the *Child* of this delightful woman; she could not have taken more pains [to] reconcile me to my situation'[51] – Fanny was beyond reconciliation. *Snugship* was what she needed and wanted. Whatever social advantages were to accrue from her entrance into the world, nothing could compensate for the powerful inhibitions any publicity was going to impose on her creative life.

⚜ 6 ⚜

Downright Scribler

Mrs Thrale set about cultivating Fanny Burney as her protégée with remarkable rapidity. Fanny's first long stay at Streatham began at the end of August 1778 and lasted a fortnight, with a break of just over a week at St Martin's Street before she returned to the Thrales. All winter she came and went between Streatham and London – Chesington was ignored completely. At Streatham Park, which Mrs Thrale soon began to refer to as her new friend's 'home', they spent as much time as possible in each other's company, walked the grounds, visited neighbours, gathered exotic fruits from the glasshouses and vegetables from the kitchen garden, dressed and undressed together, 'confabing'[1] all the time. Fanny, with her good sense and appreciative laughter, her modesty and her unthreatening appearance, was the perfect foil to the lively older woman. Being exactly between the ages of Mrs Thrale and her daughter Queeney, who had turned fourteen that September, Fanny performed the useful function of buffer zone: surrogate daughter to the one, and sister to the other. Queeney's chilly manner with everyone (including her music-teacher) was a source of sadness and irritation to her demonstrative mother. Perhaps Mrs Thrale thought that Fanny's company would melt her a little. Certainly she thought she was gaining an ally in the household.

A decisive factor in Fanny's instant adoption as a member of the Streatham coterie was the way she got on with Samuel Johnson. There was a romantic susceptibility in Johnson which Boswell found difficult to recognise, but which emerged quickly in sympathetic female company. His gallantry was reserved for those women he perceived as good-hearted and unaffected. Where he found these qualities he could be extraordinarily tender and affectionate (just as his rebukes to 'silly' women were notoriously harsh); the whore Bet Flint (much to Fanny Burney's surprise) had impressed Johnson as much as any woman for her 'stock of

Honesty' and '*high notions of Honour*'.² Johnson had suffered several unrequited passions in his early life and a troubled marriage to Elizabeth Porter, his senior by twenty years, who had died in 1752. The wistfulness in his later friendships with women (especially young women) suggests long practice in the suppression of his sexual feelings and a resigned awareness of how repellent his strange manner and twitching, scrofula-scarred face might be to those of tender sensibilities. By the time Fanny Burney met him in 1778, Johnson seems to have given up making love to women, but sometimes made pets of them instead.

When Fanny paid her first long visit to Streatham, Johnson seemed to have decided in advance that he was going to like her. He and Mrs Thrale treated her with flattering lack of ceremony, assuming their wonted familiarity with each other, quite as if she had been part of the household for years. Neither of them raised the subject of *Evelina* at all on the first day, or forced conversation out of their guest on any topic. It is interesting that Johnson's initial remarks to Fanny were about food; her thinness and frail appetite must have struck him. At tea he '*made*' her eat a piece of cake by holding it out 'with an odd, or absent complaissance' [sic]³ until she took it, and at supper insisted that she have a couple of eggs and a rasher, although she protested her lack of hunger (the Streatham dinners were so lavish this is easily believable). The next morning, Johnson was all apology, saying he had passed a poor night, 'restless & uneasy, & thinking all the Time of Miss Burney! – Perhaps I have offended her, thought I, perhaps she is angry; – I have seen her but once, & I talked to her of a *Rasher*! – Were You angry?'⁴ His humour cloaked a genuine unease, for Johnson hated to give offence where none was due. '[Y]ou must not mind me, Madam', he said by way of explanation. 'I say strange things, but I mean no harm.'

Johnson's manner towards Fanny was almost immediately demonstrative, sometimes abruptly so. The same morning, he snatched her hand and kissed it, calling her a *Tartar*, then put his hand on her arm as he spoke to her. After only a couple of days' acquaintance, he was asking 'Evelina' to cuddle up to him on the library sofa: 'he took me almost in his arms, - that is, *one* of his arms, for *one* would go 3 times round me, – &, half laughing, half serious, he charged me *to be a good Girl!*'⁵ His embracing of Fanny, his insistence on feeding her up, his mode of address – calling her 'my little Burney' and 'my dear love' – may strike the

modern reader as patronising, even slightly distasteful. But where Johnson's behaviour was most demonstrative, it was least open to doubt. One
can't imagine him behaving in a similar fashion towards Hester Thrale,
with whom his relations were much more complex and adult, and to
whom he had confessed disturbing masochistic fantasies of which he was
painfully ashamed.[6] For Johnson to pat or stroke Mrs Thrale in public
would have been out of the question, virtually obscene.

Johnson's famous description to Boswell of an ideal pastime as 'driving
briskly in a post-chaise with a pretty woman' is a comically displaced
sexual fantasy of an intense but self-mocking kind. He and the 'pretty
woman' never arrive at their destination (to travel hopefully, after all, is
better than to arrive); and yet, being Johnson's, the fantasy requires more
of the woman than mere 'prettiness': 'she should be one who could
understand me, and would add something to the conversation'.[7] He found
these qualities immediately in Dr Burney's daughter, so well self-taught in
'the art of pleasing', so ready to laugh till she was 'sore'[8] at his stories,
and also, once the ice had broken between them, full of stories of her
own, told with relish and an unmistakable talent for mimicry.

So much of Johnson's conversation with (or around) Fanny is recorded
in the journals that while she is busy setting down an accurate picture of
him, much of what he says reflects on her, especially her moral character –
of which, naturally, she is scarcely conscious herself. Johnson was a severe
judge, and having heard some of his cutting remarks about the young
poet Hannah More's flattery and the flustered, silly sayings of a Miss
Brown, Fanny decided that the best way to avoid making a fool of herself
was to evade answering any of his questions about books or reading.
This was partly cowardice and partly modesty, as she genuinely felt
unworthy to voice her opinions in the presence of one whose erudition,
intellect and phenomenal memory had made him the most venerated
man of letters of his day in England. Puzzled by never seeing her with
a book in her hand, Johnson solemnly asked Fanny one day if she did
actually love reading, as he had been led to believe. 'I have taken Notice',
he said, 'that she never has been reading whenever I have come into the
Room.'

Sir, quoth I, courageously, I am always *afraid* of being caught Reading,
lest I should pass for being *studious*, or *affected*, & therefore, instead of

making a *Display* of Books, I always try to *hide* them, – as is the case at this very Time, for I have now your Life of Waller under my Gloves, behind me![9]

Johnson's later description of Fanny as 'a spy'[10] shows that he came to understand that her reserve was neither affectation nor ineptitude. When he teased her about the prospect of meeting Elizabeth Montagu, the 'Queen of the Blues' – '*Down* with her, Burney! – *down* with her! – spare her not! attack her, fight her, & *down* with her at once!'[11] – his battle metaphor was not entirely facetious. Nothing was less likely than Miss Burney giving the famously scholarly blue-stocking a rough time over the teacups, but as Johnson knew, Fanny had the critical acumen to identify Mrs Montagu's pretensions, and the humility and manners not to expose them socially. She would never be a 'wit' in the true sense (quite apart from the fact that, then as now, conspicuous wittiness was considered profoundly unfeminine), but could bring a wit's destructive energy to bear in her work. As Mrs Thrale remarked, 'Miss Burney looks so meek, & so quiet – nobody would suspect what a comical Girl she is: – but I believe she has a great deal of *malice* at Heart.' 'Oh she's a Toad! – cried the Doctor, Laughing, – a sly Young Rogue! with her Smiths & her Branghtons!' Once Johnson had begun on the theme of *Evelina*, apparently, there was no stopping him, much to the delight and astonishment of its author, who noted down every word (and possibly more) in her diary. 'O Mr Smith, Mr Smith is the Man! cried he, Laughing violently, Harry Fielding *never* drew so good a Character! – such a fine *varnish* of low politeness! – such a *struggle* to appear a Gentleman! – Madam, there is *no* Character better drawn *any* where – in *any* Book, or by *any* Author.'[12]

When Fanny heard Sir Joshua Reynolds's niece Mary Palmer say that both Mrs Cholmondeley and Sir Joshua 'should be frightened to Death to be in her Company, because she must be such a very nice observer, that there would be no escaping her with safety',[13] she commented to Susan, 'what strange ideas are taken from mere *Book-reading*!' This was disingenuous, for although the idea of being feared personally on account of her novel's satirical power had not occurred to Fanny (secure as she had been in the expectation of a permanent anonymity), she understood the nature and possible extent of that power perfectly well. She wanted everything her own way: she wanted to be studious without appearing so (as with the concealment under her gloves of Johnson's *Life of Waller*); she wanted to pass judgement on society without incurring its reciprocal scrutiny; and she wanted to be able to write exactly as she pleased without having to alter her cautious, prudish personality to fit the products of her imagination. When things slipped out of her control, her reaction bordered on hysteria. On 7 December 1778 (about six weeks after *Evelina* had gone into a second edition) a pamphlet appeared, the second part of a verse satire called *Warley*, addressed to Sir Joshua Reynolds and containing the lines (spoken as if by Reynolds):

> Will your metre a Council engage or Attorney
> Or gain approbation from dear little Burney?[14]

This flat-footed couplet could hardly have been tamer, but because a footnote identified 'dear little Burney' as 'The Authoress of Evelina', Fanny treated it as if the nameless fate she had been dreading all year had finally come upon her. She suspected, probably rightly, that Johnson himself had unconsciously had a hand in her exposure, fond as he was of passing on Reynolds's remark 'that if he was conscious to himself of any trick, or any affectation, there is Nobody he should so much fear as this little Burney!'[15] The bearer of the bad news was, appropriately, Elizabeth Burney, who, with her usual disregard for finer feelings, brought a copy of the pamphlet into the house and showed it to her stepdaughter 'with a loud & violent laugh'.[16] 'I can never express how extremely I was shocked', Fanny wrote to Susan, admitting in the same sentence that she had been too agitated to read the lines of the satire in question. She hardly needed to read them; she was inwardly convinced *Warley* was a 'vile poem'. She couldn't eat, drink or sleep, she claimed, for more than a week 'for vehemence of vexation'.[17] Her father tried to comfort her, as did Johnson, who called specially at St Martin's Street. Mrs Thrale's letter on the subject, which Fanny preserved and marked with the words 'A spirited, charming & rational Remonstrance on the unavailing disturbance of F.B. at being proclaimed an *Author*',[18] betrays considerable impatience with Fanny's over-nice sensibilities: 'I pity your Pain, but do not mean to soothe it [. . .] I have lost seven Children and been cheated out of two thousand a Year [by the remarriage of an uncle to whom she had been heir], & I cannot, indeed I cannot, sigh & sorrow over Pamphlets & Paragraphs.'

Though it looked as if Fanny was being missish about this incident, her agitation was genuine, and came from a deep source. There were now so many people in the know about her authorship (the latest batch included Lord Palmerston and all Mrs Cholmondeley's set, Dolly Young in King's Lynn, the Worcester Burneys and everyone at Howletts, Lady Hales's home) that Fanny had begun to refer to them as 'the *Evelina Committee*'.[19] Everywhere she went, she was treated to impersonations of Madame Duval and the Branghtons, jokes about monkeys, absurd gossip linking her with Samuel Johnson and earnest quizzings about her method: 'But *where*, Miss Burney, *where* can, or could You pick up such Characters? – *where* find such variety of incidents, yet all so natural?'[20] A journal entry of this period acknowledges that her response to celebrity was likely to be misinterpreted: 'I part with this my dear, long loved, long cherished *snugship* with more regret than any body will believe, except my dear sisters who *Live with* me, & know me too well & too closely to doubt me'. *Snugship* meant freedom of choice and freedom of movement. She hadn't needed to look at the *Warley* satire because what it represented was more important than what it actually said. Within a few short months she had had to acclimatise to every variety of impertinence, from being cross-examined at parties by people to whom she had had no formal introduction, to being publicly exposed in a lampoon and even credited (if that is the word) with the authorship of a salacious novel, *The Sylph* (generally thought to be the work of Georgiana, Duchess of Devonshire), which Lowndes was craftily advertising alongside *Evelina*. On the whole, though, she was coping with celebrity very well and was glad to hear, after a fashionable party at Mrs Cholmondeley's, that society's general verdict on her was positive. This was a relief, but not at all how she had intended things to work out.

Mrs Thrale had two schemes in mind for her new friend: to marry her off well and to persuade her to write for the stage. The first of these projects must have seemed more pressing, and in fact Mrs Thrale already had a candidate lined up, her husband's wealthy and profligate nephew Sir John Lade. Charles Burney's negligence over finding husbands for his daughters was rather glaring. By 1778, Hetty was the only one of the

Burney girls to be married, and that was a love-match to her impecunious cousin – hardly an ambitious move. But when Mrs Thrale reported her husband's approval for 'giving Miss Burney to Sir John Lade', Fanny's exclamation of horror could have been heard, she imagined, all the way back to St Martin's Street. Sir John Lade would have been purgatory; even William Seward, who had taken advantage of the candleless darkness after one Streatham dinner to take hold of Fanny, and who was becoming a regular caller at St Martin's Street, was not a very serious contender. Marriage was still far from Fanny's thoughts. It would have broken up the intimacy of the sisters at home (which Hetty's marriage to another Burney had only minimally disrupted), and seemed worse than unnecessary. In her next journal-letter to Susan, Fanny remarks on her own 'indifference to all things but good society', and says nothing would make her marry except for love, if that: 'O if [Mr Thrale] knew how *little* I require with regard to money, how *much* to even *bear* with a Companion!'[21]

Mrs Thrale's second plan was much more to Fanny's mind. 'Have you begun your Comedy?' she asked at every opportunity, promising 'to *ensure* [...] success' through her contacts and patronage. Johnson's opinion was sought too, but Fanny hardly needed such encouragement. The rapidity with which she got to work on her play *The Witlings* in the winter of 1778 suggests that she had been giving such a project serious thought for a long time. It was almost a year since she had finished *Evelina*, and during the long months of convalescence at Chesington she had had plenty of time to revolve ideas for a drama. When she met Arthur Murphy at Streatham in February 1779 (he was Mrs Thrale's favourite and a highly respected dramatist of the day) he offered to give her 'any advice or assistance in my power'[22] should she think of writing a comedy. She had already had the 'decisive' encouragement of Richard Brinsley Sheridan himself, who astonished her when he turned up unexpectedly at the Reynoldses' in January and said he would be 'very glad to be accessory'[23] to any comedy Fanny might write:

Sir Joshua. She has, certainly, something of a knack at Characters; – *where* she got it, I don't know, – & *how* she got it, I can't imagine, – but she certainly *has* it. And to throw it away is – – –

Mr. Sheridan. O she *won't* – she will write a Comedy, – she has promised me she will!

Fanny Burney at the age of thirty, painted at Chesington Hall
by her cousin Edward Francesco Burney in the summer of 1782
following the success of her second novel, *Cecilia*.

Dr Charles Burney, by Sir Joshua Reynolds (1781), the portrait commissioned by the Thrales and bought thirty years later by Charles Burney junior. Samuel Johnson objected to the sitter's showy doctoral robes: 'We want to see *Burney* & he never comes to me in that dress'.

Fanny's mother Esther Sleepe Burney. This is the miniature by Gervase Spencer which Charles Burney commissioned in 1749 and which was instrumental in securing Fulke Greville's approval of the match.

Mrs Elizabeth Allen of King's Lynn, by an unknown artist. In 1767 she became Charles Burney's second wife and Fanny's stepmother.

Left: The Burneys' house at the corner of St Martin's Street and Long's Close. At the date of the picture (1811) it was being used as a hotel. The building was demolished in 1913.

Right: A view looking north into the observatory at the top of the house, where the young Fanny Burney composed many of her 'vagaries', including *Evelina*. The drawing was made for a Newton souvenir print and dates from before the Burneys' residence.

Samuel Crisp, painted by Edward Francesco Burney in the year before his death, 1782.

'Abominably handsome' David Garrick, painted by Jan van der Gucht in 1769. All the Burney girls were in love with him at this date, along with most of the capital's playgoers.

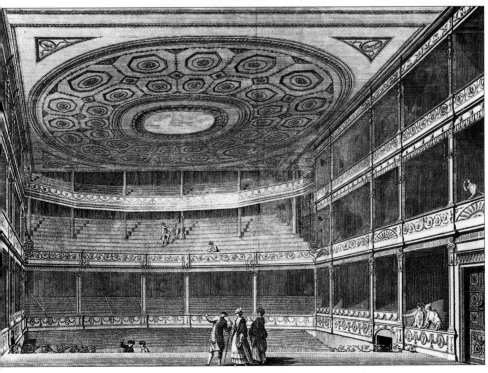

Drury Lane Theatre in 1775, much as Fanny Burney would have known it when she saw Garrick play Abel Drugger, Bayes and his great Shakespearian roles.

Left: Fanny's younger brother Charles, painted by Daniel Gardner, a friend and neighbour of Dr Burney. The painting probably predates Charles's disgrace at Cambridge in 1777, after which he was *persona non grata* for some time.

Below Left: Fanny's beloved sister Susan, in a miniature probably dating from the period of her engagement to Molesworth Phillips in 1781.

Bottom Left: A miniature of Fanny Burney painted by John Bogle in 1783, at the time of her infatuation with George Cambridge.

Hetty Burney at the harpsichord with her cousin Charles Rousseau Burney (later her husband) and uncle Richard Burney, the dancing-master.

Above: An engraving of a masquerade at Mrs Corneley's in Soho Square, where fancy dress and undress were indulged with enthusiasm. In Fanny Burney's opinion, 'nothing could be more droll'.

Below: Dr Burney in the corner of C.L. Smith's 'A Sunday Concert' (1782), exercising his charm on John Wilkes's daughter Mary. The castrato Gasparo Pacchierotti, idolised by the Burney girls, is the figure standing nearest the keyboard.

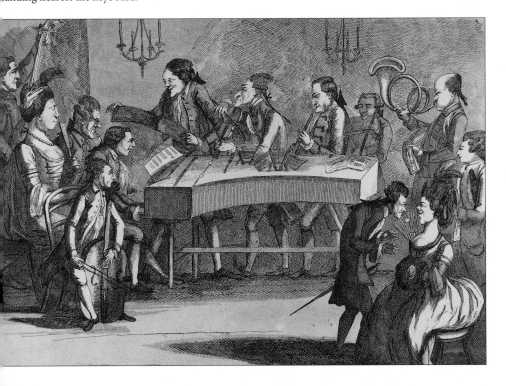

Joshua Reynolds's handsome portrait of Hester Thrale and her daughter Queeney, painted in 1781, shortly after Fanny Burney first met them.

Right: An unflatteringly realistic view of Samuel Johnson by Thomas Trotter (1782), given to Fanny Burney by the sitter. When Johnson saw the drawing he is said to have exclaimed, 'Well, thou art an ugly fellow, but still, I believe thou art like the original.'

The burning of Newgate Prison during the Gordon Riots of June 1780. The Burneys' house was only a mile and a half away.

F:B. O Good God! – if you both run on in this manner, I shall – –

I was going to say *get under the Chair*, but Mr. Sheridan, interrupting me with a Laugh, said 'Set about one? – very well, that's right!'[24]

Sheridan, Murphy, Reynolds, Johnson, Mrs Thrale, Samuel Crisp and her father were all of the same mind, and it was a powerful cabal. '[H]ow *amazing*, that this idea of a *Comedy* should strike so many!' Fanny wrote to Susan, not needing to mention to her beloved sister and confidante how long she might have been harbouring the idea herself. When Johnson teasingly suggested as far back as August 1778 that Fanny had already started to write a play – 'What a rout is here, indeed! – She is writing one up stairs all the Time' – she privately acknowledged that this was another home stroke: '"True, true Oh King!" thought I.'[25] Although she didn't admit to composing *The Witlings* until the beginning of 1779, she was probably writing in secrecy well before then. As Johnson remarked astutely, '"Who ever knew when she began Evelina?"'

There are other reasons to think that *The Witlings* was actually quite well-formed already by this point, in the author's mind if not on paper, and they are detectable in the play itself, particularly in the crudity of its satire surrounding the 'female wits' – 'a formidable Body', as Mrs Thrale noted in her diary, '& called by those who ridicule them, the *Blue Stocking Club*'.[26] Mrs Thrale herself was often a guest of the blue-stocking hostesses Mrs Vesey, Mrs Chapone and Mrs Montagu, the wealthy and cultured author of *Essay on Shakespeare* and *Dialogues* and the acknowledged 'Queen of the Blues'. Hester Thrale recognised any invitation from these ladies as an intended honour, but stayed on the periphery of their acquaintance, happy with her own very different kind of entertaining at Streatham. The Blues' rather priggish insistence on intellectually and morally 'improving' conversation made their meetings stilted and pretentious by comparison with those of 'The Club' and the Streathamites, or with Dr Burney's soirées at St Martin's Street. Even Fanny Burney, for all her interest in propriety and regulation, was not to enjoy the high-minded, teetotal evenings she spent *chez* Montagu with more than a rather abstract happiness.

But howevermuch Mrs Thrale and Dr Johnson joked about the pompous wording of their invitations to 'Blue' events, they recognised Mrs Montagu's status and respectability, and wanted to introduce Fanny to her at the first opportunity. Johnson joked with Fanny that he and she would have to '*study our parts* against Mrs Montagu comes'.[27] The visit, when it happened, was only a qualified success. Mrs Thrale's motivation in the business was partly selfish, for she was keen to promote her own protégée against Mrs Montagu's, Hannah More. She also wanted to defend her own puffing of *Evelina*, and told for the umpteenth time the story of how Edmund Burke, the great politician, had started reading the book at seven one morning, and stayed up all the next night to finish it. Next thing, Mrs Thrale, carried away by her own rhetoric, was blurting out that the author of this highly-honoured volume was none other than Miss Burney herself, causing Fanny to run out of the room.

One can imagine that this kerfuffle did not impress Mrs Montagu, and neither, when she got round to reading it, did *Evelina*: 'Mrs Montagu cannot bear Evelina – let that not be published', Mrs Thrale wrote to Johnson on 19 October; 'her Silver Smiths are Pewterers She says, & her Captains Boatswains'.[28] If this dismissive remark (with its emphasis on the book's *vulgarity*) had been relayed to Fanny at the time, she would never have had the courage to enter the same room as its esteemed author. She felt humble enough at the prospect, remarking in her journal that 'a woman of such celebrity in the Literary world, would be the *last* I should covet to converse with, though one of the *first* I should wish to listen to.'[29]

The portrait of 'female wits' in *The Witlings* is far from this respectful, even reverential tone. Lady Smatter and Mrs Sapient are shown as mean, hypocritical, shallow, unfeeling and stupid, the former 'a Woman whose utmost natural capacity will hardly enable her to understand the History of Tom Thumb', the latter characterised by speeches beginning 'for in *my* opinion', followed by a truism or banality. The Club itself is described by the play's hero, Beaufort, in a passage cancelled from the first scene, as

the most fantastic absurdity under Heaven. My good aunt has established a kind of Club at her House, professedly for the discussion of literary Subjects; and the Set who compose it are about as well qualified for the Purpose, as so many dirty Cabbin Boys would be to find out the Longitude. To a very little reading, they join less Understanding, and no Judgement, yet they decide upon Books and Authors with the most confirmed confidence in their abilities for the Task.[30]

This is not the kind of representation one would expect from a young writer who was on the edges of such a group herself. It is an unsympathetic, satirical, lively *outsider's* view (this was one of the strong objections to it later), and by the winter of 1778 Fanny Burney was an outsider no longer. Dr Burney had been a sporadic attendant at 'Blue' parties since 1773, when the second volume of *The Present State of Music* prompted Mrs Vesey to cultivate his acquaintance. The robustness of the satire in *The Witlings* probably derives more from Dr Burney's impressions of the Blues than from Fanny's own. The only surviving copy of the play is an 'exceptionally neat'[31] fair copy, presumably post-dating May 1779, which was when Fanny finished writing the earliest version, and the deletion of Beaufort's speech suggests that second thoughts about the satire had already set in.

There is no doubt that writing for the stage was one of Fanny Burney's longest-held ambitions, and that success as a playwright would have been far more gratifying to her, and probably more lucrative too, than success as a novelist. The composition of *The Witlings* was not, as it might seem from the perspective of an age that values the novel so highly, a step down from *Evelina*, but a progression towards solid literary fame. Many people had remarked on the dramatic qualities of *Evelina*, and it is odd to think that Fanny Burney may have considered her most famous work as an apprentice piece for a career as a dramatist.

The Witlings has not yet been produced, and was published for the first time in 1995, 216 years after its composition. Fanny wrote at least eight other plays, only one of which, *Edwy and Elgiva*, was performed in her lifetime, and that, as we shall see, was a one-night fiasco. She can hardly be said to have fulfilled her ambition to be a playwright. But her sheer persistence (trying to alter *The Witlings* for half a year in the hope of salvaging something from the project) and her sensitivity to failure in this field (she, not the theatre management, withdrew *Edwy and Elgiva* after its first performance) indicate how much she wanted to succeed.

The failure of *The Witlings* is a sorry story, since the play has many virtues. The plot turns on the loss of fortune, and subsequent collapse of marriage prospects, of an orphan heiress called Cecilia, whose fiancé, Beaumont, is under the guardianship of the head 'witling', his aunt, Lady Smatter. Other members of her 'Esprit Club' include Mrs Sapient, the peddler of truisms, Codger, a man so pedantic he has to retire to work out the order in which he is going to relate his sister's news, and a would-be poet called Dabler, whose works include 'On a young lady blinded by Lightning':

> Fair Cloris, now depriv'd of Sight,
> To Error ow'd her fate uneven;
> Her Eyes were so refulgent bright
> The blundering Lightning thought them Heaven.[32]

Lady Smatter wants her nephew to abandon Cecilia once she is (apparently) bankrupted, but he staunchly refuses; a series of accidents, however, leads Cecilia to think he has renounced her, and she sinks into despair and the lodging-house of vulgar Mrs Voluble, where she contemplates her future as companion to a gentlewoman. The plot concludes lamely with the arrival of a letter informing Cecilia 'that my affairs are in a less desperate situation than I had apprehended', and the lovers are reunited, partly because of the machinations of Beaumont's friend Censor (a role crying out for Garrick, though the great Roscius was ailing, and died before the play was finished).

The limp ending is just forgivable because the rest of the play is so stuffed with jokes and absurd comic scenes, such as one in which Mrs Sapient has to hide in a cupboard containing all the household clutter Mrs Voluble threw out of sight before her arrival. In the scene where the Esprit Club meets, the ladies stand up one at a time in exasperation with Codger, producing some dance-like comic business and showing Burney's well-developed sense of stagecraft. There are several inventive elements too, such as ending the first scene mid-sentence and having Codger often begin but never quite finish the story of his Aunt Deborah's poultry. Domestic messiness and housewifely hypocrisy had never been shown on stage before; nor had any dramatist opened a play in a milliner's shop, a particularly female environment and 'a ridiculous and unmanly situation'[33] for a gentleman like Censor to be forced to enter. As in *Evelina*, Fanny was being inventive and uncompromisingly woman-centred.

In this she was fulfilling the criteria set down in two letters of advice that Samuel Crisp wrote her in November and December 1778. Crisp, clearly pleased at Fanny's success among the Streatham lions but sensitive to his loss of influence over her, adjured her to grasp the moment and 'act vigorously (what I really believe is in your power) a distinguish'd part in the present [scene]'. Her friends would not always be around her, nor so influential: 'You will then be no longer the same Fanny of 1778, feasted, caress'd, admir'd [. . .] When You come to know the World half so well as I do', warned the Hermit of Chesington, '& what Yahoos Mankind are –, you will then be convinc'd, that a State of Independence is the only Basis, on which to rest your future Ease & Comfort.' This very sensible advice is perhaps surprising to hear from an elderly man to a young woman, whose traditional expectations of 'future Ease & Comfort' would have rested in marriage or an inheritance. He is basically telling her that since she has the talent to be a writer, she should make the most of it and reap all the advantages, material and personal. His words are echoed in the concluding speech of *The Witlings*, in which Beaumont eulogises 'self-dependence' as 'the first of Earthly Blessings':

> since those who rely on others for support and protection are not only liable to the common vicissitudes of Human Life, but exposed to the partial caprices and infirmities of Human Nature.[34]

Beaumont's words are all the more noteworthy for being somewhat at odds with the outcome of the play, in which, after all, the heroine fares very badly on her own and is only saved *ex machina* by a cheque for £5000 and marriage to the hero. But as an ending it is far more thoughtful, one might say daring, than the conventions required.

Crisp's second letter seemed to retract much of the encouragement he had offered earlier. He was alarmed that Fanny wanted to try a Comedy, for he couldn't see how it was properly achievable by a woman. 'I need not Observe to *You*', he wrote,

> that in most of Our successful comedies, there are frequent lively Freedoms (& waggeries that cannot be called licentious, neither) that give a strange animation, & Vigour to the same, & of which, if it were to be depriv'd, it would lose wonderfully of its Salt, & Spirit – I mean *such* Freedoms as Ladies of the strictest Character would make no scruple, openly, to laugh

at, but at the same time, especially if they were Prudes, (And You know You are one) perhaps would *Shy* at being known to be the Authors of.[35]

Crisp was voicing the common prejudice that 'Salt & Spirit' were 'natural & expected' in men's writing (and guaranteed to amuse even 'Ladies of the strictest Character'), whereas the only kind of writing suitable for a woman to put her name to was something 'very fine-Spun, all-delicate', like the bloodless sentimental comedies of French theatre. The latter were respectable, but deadly dull, as Crisp acknowledged by quoting from Pope: 'We cannot blame, indeed, – but we may Sleep!' To steer a path between the two would be virtually impossible, and Crisp's advice was that Fanny should think of writing another novel instead, a form in which he could see great potential:

In these little entertaining, elegant Histories, the writer has his full Scope; as large a Range as he pleases to hunt in – to pick, cull, select, whatever he likes: – he takes his own time; he may be as minute as he pleases, & the more minute the better; provided, that Taste, a deep & penetrating knowledge of human nature, & the World, accompany that minuteness. – When this is the Case, the very Soul, & all it's most secret recesses & workings, are develop'd, & laid as open to the View, as the blood Globules circulating in a frog's foot, when seen thro' a Microscope. – The exquisite touches such a Work is capable of (of which, Evelina is, without flattery, a glaring instance) are truly charming. – But of these great advantages, these resources, YOU are strangely curtailed, the Moment You begin a Comedy[.][36]

Fanny valued his advice, but didn't act on it (another reason to suppose she had already gone past the stage of deciding whether or not to write a play). Her reply comes close to a manifesto:

Every word you have urged concerning the *salt & spirit* of gay, unrestrained freedom in Comedies, carries conviction along with it, – a conviction which I feel in trembling! should I ever venture in that walk publicly, perhaps the want of it might prove fatal to me: I do, indeed, think it most likely that such would be the Event, & my poor piece, though it might escape Cat calls & riots, would be fairly *slept off the stage*. I cannot, however, attempt to *avoid* this danger, though I *see* it, for I would a thousand Times rather forfeit my character as a *Writer*, than risk ridicule or censure as a *Female*. I have never set my Heart on Fame, & therefore would not if I *could* purchase it at the expence of all my own ideas of propriety. You who *know* me for a *Prude* will not be surprised, & I hope not offended at this avowal, – for I should deceive you were I not to make it. If I *should* try, I must e'en take my chance, & all my own expectations may be pretty easily answered![37]

At first glance this looks like an admission that Fanny is prepared to surrender her artistic integrity to her sense of propriety in a sacrificial act of daughterly deference; whereas she is actually making a distinction between the traditional kind of comedy that Crisp was thinking of and the kind she intended to write herself, which was, indeed, also the only kind that she felt *able* to write naturally. Her distinction between 'Writer' and 'Female' in herself is interesting. His assumption that 'unrestrained' in dramatic writing equals 'unfeminine' equals 'successful' is challenged by her hope that what is natural to herself could also be successful. If her play were to be 'slept off the stage', so be it; her inner confidence must have been strong enough to override this consideration.

The Witlings was completed by the beginning of May 1779. Fanny showed it first to her father and next to Mrs Thrale, who could not have failed to recognise a rough caricature of herself in Mrs Sapient, and whose private comments on the play in the *Thraliana* are subdued:

> one has no Guess what will do on a Stage, at least I have none; Murphy must read an Act tomorrow, I wonder what he'll say to't. I like it very well for my own part, though none of the scribbling Ladies have a right to admire its general Tendency.[38]

Murphy apparently liked the parts of the play that he saw (although he didn't ask after the rest of it until December). Charles Burney, according to Mrs Thrale, liked the play 'vastly',[39] but his comments about it must have led Fanny to believe it would benefit from improvement, for she began revising the text immediately. On 2 August, Dr Burney read the play in front of a party at Chesington that consisted of Crisp, Mrs Gast, Susan, Charlotte, Mrs Hamilton and Kitty Cooke, a real gathering of the old 'homely home'. Fanny was not present (she had to stay in London to nurse Hetty), but awaited their verdict eagerly. The note her father sent the same evening ought to have alerted her to a poor reception: he told her that they weren't yet ready to comment. Kind Susan, seeing the storm ahead, wrote as soon as she could, describing the reading. The fourth act (that is, the Esprit Club scene) was, she said 'upon the whole that wch seemed least to exhilarate or interest the Audience'.

The letter that the 'Daddies' sent together several days later has not survived, but from her reply it is clear that it advised Fanny in the strongest possible terms to abandon *The Witlings*. This was an appalling shock; she 'expected many Objections to be raised, a thousand errors to be pointed out, & a million of alterations to be proposed; – but – the *suppression of the piece* were words I did *not* expect'.[40] The disapproval of Crisp, who was as much a figure of authority to Charles Burney as to the Burney children, had clearly swayed the Doctor's own opinion from liking *The Witlings* 'vastly' to collaborating in the 'Hissing, groaning, catcalling Epistle'[41] he and Crisp sent to persuade Fanny of the play's faults. Their main objection was to the depiction of the Blues, although they also said that *The Witlings* too closely resembled Molière's *Les Femmes savantes* (a play Fanny was quick to point out she had never read, and couldn't even spell correctly[42]), that people expected better of the author of *Evelina*, even that the political situation was so fraught that the play-going public might not be in the mood or in sufficient funds to indulge a new playwright that year.

But the satire of the Blues was the sticking point, and Crisp was justified in objecting to its crudity. He felt Fanny had at her disposal 'an inexhaustible Fund of Matter' from which to compose 'a most spirited, witty, Moral, Useful Comedy without descending to the invidious, & cruel Practice of pointing out Individual Characters, & holding them up to public Ridicule'.[43] Nobody had admitted until then that, whatever the author's intentions, the 'female wits' in Fanny's play would be identified instantly as Mrs Montagu (who, like Lady Smatter, was wealthy and had a nephew for heir) and Mrs Thrale. 'As it is,' Charles Burney wrote to his daughter at the end of August, 'not only the Whole Piece, but the plot had best be kept secret, from every body.'[44]

Fanny's response indicates that she hadn't really wanted or expected

Crisp and her father to criticise her work minutely, but simply to give her an impression of 'the general effect of the Whole'.[45] Now that they had picked it to pieces, however, she had no option but to abandon the project – or at least, that was what duty dictated. The terms in which she submitted to the Daddies' judgement betray a determination to prove them wrong, one way or another: 'the best way I can take of shewing that I have a true & just sense of the *spirit* of your condemnation, is not to sink, sulky & dejected, under it, but to exert myself to the utmost of my power in endeavours to produce something less reprehensible.'[46]

Back at Streatham, Mrs Thrale was impressed and no doubt relieved by the sacrificial gesture, noting in the *Thraliana* (with her characteristic quirk of writing as if she had not mentioned it before): 'Fanny Burney [. . .] resolves to give up a Play likely to succeed; for fear it may bear hard upon some Respectable Characters'.[47] But Fanny had clearly invested so much in the play that it was impossible to let it drop entirely. Her letters to Crisp and to her father were full of quotations from and references to her rejected characters, and within weeks she was 'new modelling' the play,[48] presumably to exclude the Esprit Club and elaborate the love story. She wrote to Crisp, trying to pre-empt his disapproval, that a new version of *The Witlings* was her only chance of bringing anything out that year, and that with 'hard fagging' she might just manage it. His response was almost explosive:

> my dear Fanny, for God's sake, don't talk of *hard Fagging*! It was not *hard Fagging* that produced such a Work as Evelina! – – – it was the Ebullition of true Sterling Genius! you wrote it, because you could not help it! – it came, & so You put it down on Paper! [. . .] Tis not sitting down to a Desk with Pen, Ink & Paper, that will command Inspiration.[49]

For all the robust tone and good intention of Crisp's argument, Fanny must have recognised the flaws in it immediately. It was all very well for him to hold up *Evelina* as an example of 'true Sterling Genius', but she was never going to be able to replicate the conditions under which that book had been composed. Crisp himself had encouraged her not to sigh after the old anonymity but exploit her celebrity; left to her own devices, she would have gone ahead with her play and not been reduced to 'hard fagging' at all. On one hand, he adjured her to be professional – but what could be more professional than 'sitting down to a Desk with Pen, Ink & Paper', as Dr Johnson did so doggedly almost every day of his adult life? And as for having written *Evelina* in some kind of mystic haze – 'you wrote it, because you could not help it!' – only Fanny could ever be the judge of *that*.

In the past, Crisp had urged Fanny to trust her own judgement, and make sure her work was *'all your own – all of a Piece'*,[50] but now he wasn't just expecting her to act on other people's (i.e. his) criticism, but to accept their (also his) ideas for her next work. Why didn't she write a play about Mrs Thrale's neighbours, the Pitches family? he asked. The descriptions of them in her letters had left him 'quite animated'.[51] He could imagine a 'Moral, Useful Comedy' being made out of such material, and even rather heavy-handedly fed her a title: 'their whole Conduct might be term'd, the Right Road to go wrong'.[52] Wisely, Fanny did absolutely nothing with this suggestion. Instead she worked on at *The Witlings* while she tried to come to terms with its rejection, then gradually gave it up.

Fanny had been so sure of success that she had made no secret of writing her play, and by the new season in the autumn of 1779, people began to expect to see it advertised. On her visit with the Thrales to Brighton in the summer, she had talked about the work to the Reverend Dr John Delap, whom she now called her 'Brother Dramatist', and was surprised to find herself already treated like a rival by another playwright, the prolific and highly successful Richard Cumberland.* When Fanny returned to Brighton in October, Delap asked how her play was going, and she had to say she 'had determined not to risk it'.[53] Guessing that he would deduce from this that Sheridan had seen it and disapproved, Fanny reflected gloomily that everyone would jump to the same conclusion. Delap's own play, *The Royal Suppliants*, had been worked over and over for the past five years and only reached the stage in the spring of 1781, favoured with an epilogue by Murphy and a prologue by Hester Thrale. This must have rubbed salt in the wound rather for Fanny, who had been promised even better – a prologue by Johnson! – and who, on

---

* Cumberland's jealousy towards any rival, real or imagined, earned him the scorn of, among others, Sheridan, who caricatured him as Sir Fretful Plagiary in *The Critic*, first performed on 30 October 1779.

account of her superior knowledge of the theatre and stagecraft, was frequently asked to advise Delap on his work.

The general expectation that Miss Burney was preparing a play persisted some time, and led to at least one wrong attribution of an anonymous play to her – *The East Indian*,* which ran for ten nights at the Haymarket in the 1781–2 season.[54] But the potential for public embarrassment was something that the Daddies don't seem to have thought of when they passed the death sentence on *The Witlings*. To Fanny, who bore her disappointment over the affair very secretly, it must have been clear that her father and Crisp might not always be the best brokers of her literary reputation in future; especially not Crisp, whose own attempt at drama, after all, had been such a flop.

In the short term, Fanny found a way to use some of the rejected material, though in a very different form. If you subtract from *The Witlings* the blue-stocking plot, what is left is the story of an heiress called Cecilia who loses and then regains her fortune and marries a man who has been true to her through all vicissitudes: in short, the plot of Fanny Burney's second novel, *Cecilia*. The triumph of this novel was still to come, however. For the moment there was only the bitterness of seeing an excellent piece of work miscarry, and her living, breathing characters being locked back into the bureau, perhaps only destined for another bonfire: 'good Night Mr. Dabler! – good Night Lady Smatter, – Mrs. Sapient, Mrs. Voluble, – Mrs. Wheedle – Censor – Cecilia – Beaufort, – & you, *you great Oaf* Bobby! good Night! good Night! –'.[55]

The relationship between Fanny and Mrs Thrale did not develop into a true intimacy, though each of them habitually pretended that it had. Fanny had been in awe of Mrs Thrale for years, and seems to have found the older woman's sudden adoption of her alarming and intemperate. There is nothing so likely to kill admiration in someone who is chronically self-deprecating as to be 'taken up' by the object of their idolatry. To this perverse brand of disappointment was added Fanny's uncomfortable awareness of her inferior education and class. The literary talents of the two women were so divergent that neither feared comparison on that

---

* The title, and possibly the content, of this play could not have pleased 'Sir Fretful Plagiary' Cumberland much; his own most famous work was *The West Indian*.

score, but literary taste was another thing, and made Fanny anxious. Her manners too, she knew, would be constantly monitored by Mrs Thrale for evidence both of her 'low race' origins and of any attempts to cover them up. Her nervousness on all these counts often caused Fanny to behave in a way that *did* seem studied and affected, very like Queeney, in fact, who in Fanny's eyes was a misunderstood girl towards whom she began to feel increasingly friendly.

The two writers confided more candidly in their diaries than in each other. Mrs Thrale, whose remarks in *Thraliana* almost always sound harsher than reports of her public speech and opinions, made a dismissive judgement of Fanny in February 1779:

> [Dr Burney's] Daughter is a graceful looking Girl, but 'tis the Grace of an Actress not a Woman of Fashion – how should it? her Conversation would be more pleasing if She thought less of herself; but her early Reputation embarrasses her Talk, & clouds her Mind with scruples about Elegancies which either come uncalled for or will not come at all.[56]

This sounds like a chilly first impression, but it was written after the two women had spent the better part of the previous five months in each other's company, laughing and joking and going about everywhere together. The tone is horribly at variance with that of Fanny's whole-heartedly admiring journal entries after the first Streatham visit:

> I *fear* to say all I think at present of Mrs. Thrale, – lest some *flaws* should appear by & by, that may make me think differently: – & yet, why should I not indulge the *now*, as well as the *then*, since it will be with so *much* more pleasure? – In short, my dear Susy, I do think her *delightful*: she has *Talents* to create admiration, – *Good humour* to excite Love, *Understanding* to give Entertainment, – & a *Heart* which, like my dear Father's, seems already fitted for another World![57]

It is odd that Fanny felt such reckless admiration for Mrs Thrale, yet in her company gave the impression of being tiresomely self-obsessed. Fanny's love for Mrs Thrale modulated over the years into appreciation, but she remained convinced of her erstwhile patroness's essentially good nature. Fanny's analysis of her character in *Memoirs of Doctor Burney* (written almost fifty years later) helps explain her diffidence towards Mrs Thrale if, as seems likely, she had formed these impressions quite early on:

> [Mrs Thrale] had a sweetness of manner, and an activity of service for those she loved, that could ill be appreciated by others; for though copiously flattering in her ordinary address to strangers, because always desirous of universal suffrage, she spoke of individuals in general with sarcasm; and of the world at large with sovereign contempt.
>
> Flighty, however, not malignant, was her sarcasm; [. . .] her epigram once pronounced, she thought neither of that nor of its object any more[.]⁵⁸

Fanny intended the *Memoirs* to be a final account, with all that implies of both Last Judgement and score-settling. In them, she applies to her early friendships the analytical and critical powers which she rarely displayed at the time. In conversation she never attempted to outshine the great figures around her, whereas Mrs Thrale was a true Wit and extravagantly devoted to making brilliant talk. Both women's public behaviour was deceptive, and deceived the other. The *Thraliana* are powered by a cynicism that few of Mrs Thrale's acquaintance would have recognised from the 'sweet', 'flattering' hostess of Streatham Park, but one should not deduce from this that she was a hypocrite. Her journal (more of a commonplace book, really, with flights into controlled confession) is an extraordinary testimony to her struggle to extract as much pleasure as possible from a difficult life. Henry Thrale was two-faced in a malign way, unaccountably cruel and negligent towards Hester, but solid and admirable to outsiders. Mrs Thrale's loveless marriage, almost yearly pregnancies, the mortal dangers these put her in and the tragic deaths of so many of her children made her impatient of people like Fanny who over-dramatised small problems, and by the summer of 1779 the strains in their friendship were beginning to show. 'Fanny Burney has been a long time from me, I was glad to see her again', Mrs Thrale wrote when recovering from the stillbirth of a son in August,

> yet She makes me miserable too in many Respects – so restlessly & apparently anxious lest I should give myself Airs of Patronage, or load her with

the Shackles of Dependance – I live with her always in a Degree of Pain that precludes Friendship – dare not ask her to buy me a Ribbon, dare not desire her to touch the Bell, lest She should think herself injured.[59]

Mrs Thrale was so charming and adept socially that Fanny never seemed to detect this strain of disapproval, which amounts at times to scorn. When on their return from Brighton in November Mr Thrale was taken ill (with another of the apoplectic fits he had been suffering for a year or two), Mrs Thrale felt Fanny's response of going into mild hysterics at an inn in Reigate was less than helpful. When the party got back to Streatham Park, Fanny took to her bed for a week with 'something that She called a Fever', as Mrs Thrale put it.[60] 'Mrs Thrale Nursed me most tenderly, letting me take nothing but from herself', Fanny recorded gratefully in a letter to Susan, though the exclusive treatment had not actually been intended to flatter. The *Thraliana* reveal the uncomfortable fact that by acting as 'Doctor & Nurse, & Maid' Mrs Thrale was actually trying to placate the servants – all flat out with the crisis over her husband's stroke – lest they should resent the little hypochondriac upstairs. '[A]nd now –' Hester noted sarcastically, 'with the true Gratitude of a Wit, She tells me, that the *World thinks the better of me* for my Civilities to her. It does! does it?'

To the outside world, nevertheless, Fanny was presented more and more as Mrs Thrale's pet and protégée, and when she accompanied the Thrale family on their long visit to Tunbridge and Brighton in October 1779, Mrs Thrale took every opportunity to show off the new authoress and repeat the stories, now smooth with telling, of her 'discovery'. *Evelina*, which had now been out for eighteen months and was into a third edition, had a massive following among the socialites gathered in Brighton, and Fanny couldn't hide her pleasure at it: 'I am prodigiously in Fashion', she wrote home to Susan, who must have felt increasingly left out of her sister's success. One young lady was '*Dying* with impatience to see *me*, because she *idolizes* Evelina [...] – she *looks* at me as if it was an *heaven* to see me, *Addresses* me as if it was an *Honour* to speak to me, & *listens* to me as if it was an *improvement* to hear me! [...] In short, she has just such a youthful & mad enthusiasm about me as you & I, at her Age, should have had about Richardson'.[61] It is interesting that Fanny felt companionship with the girl, as a fellow reader, rather than with

Richardson, as a fellow novelist. The young fan, incidentally, was Augusta Byron, future aunt of the poet. Another girl Fanny met on this trip was Elizabeth Pilfold, who thirteen years later gave birth to Percy Bysshe Shelley.

The most interesting news about *Evelina* was how well it was selling. As soon as they arrived in Brighton, Mrs Thrale had called at Thomas's bookshop on the Steyne to register the names of her party – the accepted method of 'checking in' to the social life of the town, as the Brighton Master of Ceremonies consulted these lists in order to draw up invitations to the assemblies and balls. Mr Thomas's rival bookseller, Bowen, told Mrs Thrale that 'trade' gossip considered *Evelina* 'a Book thrown away [...]! – all the Trade cry shame on Lowneds [sic], – not, Ma'am, that I *expected* he could have known its worth, because that's out of the question, – but when it's *profits* told him what it was, it's quite scandalous that he should have done nothing! – quite ungentlemanlike indeed!'[62] If Lowndes had sold all his copies of the three editions of *Evelina* already published (which, judging by the scarcity of the book in the shops, is not unlikely), and if he had kept the price at the nine shillings per set he was charging for the first edition, he would already have netted £810 from the manuscript for which he had given 'Mr Grafton' twenty pounds. Perhaps bookseller Bowen was hoping that Miss Burney might allow him to print her next novel. Fanny was remarkably stoical about the lost income from her book, probably because she was so relieved at the magnificent reception it had met with. Direct sale of the copyright had been the only option when she wished to remain anonymous, but she knew that if she ever used this method again, she would drive a much harder bargain.

On this trip to Brighton Fanny went sea-bathing 'almost Daily'.[63] It was an increasingly popular pastime for young women, at once bracing and voluptuous. The bathers were taken to the water in 'machines' pulled along by professional female attendants and either soused with water or lowered into the sea to splash about. Fanny had first submitted to sea-bathing in Teignmouth in 1773 'to *harden* me',[64] and it seems to have worked; on this trip to Brighton with Mrs Thrale she relished the bathing, and in 1782 at the same resort said that the operation 'now gives me nothing but animation and vigour'.[65]

There are signs that she was becoming 'hardened off' in other ways too. She was constantly pointed out by passers-by on the Steyne and ogled at routs and balls, especially by Cumberland's daughters, whom Queeney gamely volunteered to stare back at. Fanny chose not to dance on any of these occasions, not wishing to be 'Watched & *commented upon*',[66] but though she protested about this first exposure to real celebrity, there are touches of complacency about her new-found fame.

The holiday mood in Brighton was subdued by the persistent fears of an imminent invasion by the French and Spanish, whose combined fleets had been in the Channel since August. The American war had dragged on with no sign of a victory, and with France and Spain at war with Britain and the League of Armed Neutrality about to range Russia, Sweden and Denmark against Britain too, times were beginning to feel dangerous as well as difficult. The Thrales had had two poor years with the brewery business, and a tax bill in 1778 of £2000 (although this hadn't prevented them going on their extended tour or planning an even more ambitious one for the next year). Dr Burney found his own work harder to come by, and like Crisp, arch prophet of doom, thought that the country was gradually sliding into ruin.

One of Mrs Thrale's Streatham neighbours, a gentleman named Rose Fuller, whose quirky manner of speech always amused Fanny,* had lamented the worsening political situation thus: 'Why very bad! very bad, indeed! quite what we call poor old England! – I was told, in Town, – Fact! – Fact, I assure you! – that these Dons intend us an Invasion this month! – they & the Monsieurs intend us the respectable salute this very month, – the powder system, in that sort of way! – Give me leave to tell you, Miss Burney, this is what we call a disagreeable visit, in that sort of way!'[67] It was more to Fanny's taste to lampoon Rose Fuller than to worry about what he was saying. She was beginning to enjoy her position in the Thrale entourage and the insights it gave her into a different social set, whose absurdities were endlessly entertaining. Here is her account of a General Blakeney, reading the newspaper:

Now he would cry 'Strange! strange! that!' presently – 'What stuff! I don't believe a Word of it!' – a little after 'O Mr. Bate! I wish your Ears were

* It found its way into several of her works – see especially the character of Litchburn in 'Love and Fashion'.

Cropt!' – then, 'Ha! Ha! Ha! – *Funnibus! Funnibus*, indeed!' And at last, in a great rage he exclaimed 'What a fellow is this! to presume to arraign the conduct of persons of Quality!' [...]

Soon after, he began to rage about some Baronet whose title began *Sir Carnaby* – 'Jesus! he cried, what names people do think of! – here's another, now, – Sir Oenesiphorus Paul! – why now what a Name is that! – poor human Beings here inventing such a Name as that: – I can't imagine where they met with it! – it is not in the Bible.'[68]

Of course there is no telling how much or how little the conversations in her journals were tinkered with or sent up in the writing (remembering Fanny's skill as a mimic), but whichever way, they are impressive as works of art even if not as feats of memory. Much of this 'eavesdropping' writing was for Susan's benefit, and sought to reproduce scenes Fanny wished she and her sister could have experienced together. To Dr Johnson, however, whom she (wrongly) felt required more formal correspondence, Fanny wrote a pitifully false-sounding note about how she had nothing to report worth his attention. She had already earned his displeasure by writing a postscript to one of Queeney's letters, 'a silly short note, in such a silly white hand, that I was glad it was no longer', as Johnson complained to Mrs Thrale.[69] There was quite a rift opening up between her gay, intimate private writing and the very unnatural style she was beginning to adopt for 'serious' audiences.

❦ 7 ❦

Cecilia

All through the autumn of 1779 Fanny was worrying about the letter she had sent to Sheridan earlier in the year promising him a play for the winter season. By Christmas she could not put the matter off any longer and persuaded her father to call on the playwright and pass on the message that 'what I had written had entirely dissatisfied me, and that I desired to decline for the present all attempts of that sort'.[1] When Dr Burney did this, however, Sheridan's response was to insist on seeing what had already been done; it suited him far better, he argued, to work with an author on an unfinished manuscript than to battle over revisions to a supposedly complete text. Dr Burney's resolve vaporised immediately and he came home telling Fanny he had changed his mind and thought she should take up the playwright's tempting offer at once.

This reversal, just when Fanny had managed to quash all her former ambitions, could scarcely have been more disturbing. Sheridan had asked Charles Burney's permission to call on Fanny to discuss the play, and in anticipation of his visit she began hurriedly revising *The Witlings* one more time. She felt 'violently fidgeted' about it, and wrote to Crisp in something of a panic, probably hoping he would command her to stop. But the magic of Sheridan's name worked powerfully on Crisp, too, and though he admitted that his young friend's brutal cuts to the play had left little to work on, he suggested she might be able to scrounge some decent new plot-lines out of Colley Cibber's memoirs. Thus Fanny's two mentors showed again the limitations of their usefulness, or even common sense. Her disappointment in them was evident; she even went as far as making an overt criticism of her father's part in the matter, saying he was 'ever easy to be worked upon'.[2] Fortunately, Sheridan never made his call, and the mutilated play to which Fanny had taken a disgust was left to rest in peace.

With the long death of *The Witlings*, Fanny's career as a 'scribler' seemed in danger of coming to an end. Though her father was keen for her to consolidate the success of *Evelina* with another book as soon as possible, Fanny had never had so little time to herself. All her leisure was taken up compiling long accounts of celebrity social life in letters to Samuel Crisp and her sister. She had never before been so busy doing nothing, having to think about clothes, hair and caps, visiting and jaunts.

In April 1780 she accompanied the Thrales on another long trip, this time to Bath. They travelled in style, in a coach and four with a post chaise behind for Mrs Thrale's two maids, and two menservants on horseback, and took a house at the end of South Parade, overlooking the River Avon. Everything about the arrangements was luxurious, and Henry Thrale, his pocketbook permanently open, insisted that Fanny order anything she wanted from the Bath milliners and dressmakers, as freely as Queeney and Hester did. Fanny was flattered, but exhibited her usual scruples, only accepting Mr Thrale's largesse when he 'absolutely insisted' on it.[3] Perversely, the idea that Fanny was freeloading struck Mrs Thrale most forcibly whenever their gifts were refused, but a letter from Fanny to Queeney on the subject, written almost twenty years later, hints at the difficulty of being on the receiving end of the Thrale beneficence:

> my pride was dearer to me than her [Mrs Thrale's] gifts, which were forced upon me whether I would or not, & which hurt me inexpressibly, frequently with a raillery that showed she discredited the sincerity of my resistance. But I valued our friendship too much for any serious dispute – & all other she overpowered.[4]

The two months in Bath were mostly spent visiting; Mrs Montagu and another famous 'Blue', Mrs Elizabeth Carter, were in town, as well as a host of fashionable ladies, retired bishops and elderly beaux taking the waters. It was the kind of company that Mrs Thrale had correctly judged would have bored Dr Johnson, but not Fanny. As in Brighton, Fanny stayed with the card-playing matrons much of the time, and refused to dance at the dances. She joked that she was becoming 'old-cattish',[5] and it was true: at almost twenty-eight she was taking up position on the outskirts of middle age. The next generation of young society girls (who admired Miss Burney's book to distraction) had some surprising new preoccupations. One, a 'Miss W—', was an atheist, whose views (by Hume out of Bolingbroke) profoundly shocked the pious novelist; another was Augusta Byron, Fanny's romantic young fan from Brighton. She observed these two young women of the coming age with attention, keeping their traits, manners, even dialogue in mind for almost thirty years, when they reappear recognisably in the characters of Eleanor Jodrell and Aurora Granville in her last novel *The Wanderer*, published in 1814.

'Miss Burney was much admired at Bath', Mrs Thrale wrote in her journal a few weeks later; 'the puppy Men said She had such a drooping Air, & such a timid Intelligence; or a timid Air I think it was, and a drooping Intelligence.'[6] Mrs Thrale's flashes of malice towards her young friend were understandable; she was having a strenuous year travelling to and from health resorts with her ailing and moody husband, entertaining his friends at Streatham and campaigning on his behalf in Southwark for the coming parliamentary election 'like a Tigress seizing upon every thing that she found in her way', as Johnson wrote to Queeney.[7] Her efforts went unrewarded by any tenderness from 'Master', who openly said his only comfort was his beautiful young mistress, Sophy Streatfield. Relations with Queeney were as bad as ever – 'Miss despises me', her mother wrote dramatically – and Fanny Burney, who had been drafted in to leaven the spirits of this company, was not proving quite grateful or useful enough. Though Fanny half-convinced herself that she was now almost one of the family (she had begun to refer to Mr Thrale as her 'dear Master' in imitation of Hester), she seems not to have appreciated how ill and unhappy the Thrales were. Mrs Thrale noted with a strange kind of satisfaction how 'disgusted' one of her friends was 'at Miss Burney's Carriage to me' in Bath. 'I love her dearly for all that', she conceded in *Thraliana*, '& I fancy She has a real regard for me, if She did not think it beneath the Dignity of a Wit, or of what She values more – the Dignity of *Doctor Burney's Daughter* to indulge it. Such Dignity!!'[8]

The rather uncomfortable holiday came to an abrupt end in the second week of June when reports reached Bath of serious disturbances in London. Stage-coaches arriving from the capital had 'No Popery' chalked on them, and shocking reports followed that riots had been going on for almost a week, aimed primarily at Roman Catholic targets and ostensibly in protest at the Catholic Relief Act, a relatively mild piece of legislation that had been passed the previous year. Next day in Bath the same 'No Popery' message was appearing around the city, and within hours bets were being laid on whether the new Roman Catholic chapel would be attacked, which it was overnight.

The Thrale party had already decided to leave, but speeded up their preparations when Mr Thrale was identified in a local paper (wrongly, of course) as a Catholic. Clearly there was some connection in the public mind between the brewing trade and Catholicism which Thrale's political rivals sought to exploit. A distiller in Holborn (a known Catholic) had been one of the prime targets of the riots in town; when his property was burned, it exploded and sent rivers of liquor into the streets, which some of the mob drank themselves to death on. Free drink was not the main motive for the violence, though, since brewers' homes were as vulnerable as their premises (one non-Catholic brewer had his house in Turnstile Alley fired because the mob said he brewed 'popish beer'). The Thrales' brewery in Southwark, worth an astonishing £150,000,[9] was already under threat, they heard in Bath; the rumour about Thrale being a papist seemed to doom it to destruction. The family decided to make their way across country towards Brighton, whence, if necessary, Mr Thrale could embark for the Continent.

Though Fanny had to flee Bath with the Thrales, her thoughts were of course with her own family, from whom she had no news until she reached Brighton. The letters from Susan which awaited her there contained astonishing accounts of the riots, the most violent civil disturbance of the century in London. More damage was done in one week of mob rule than in Paris during the whole of the French Revolution; hundreds of properties were destroyed and 290 citizens died. The initial protest, led by the fanatical Lord George Gordon, took place on 2 June, but the Burneys in St Martin's Street only got wind of the trouble on the evening of the fifth when Charlotte came back from the Reynolds's in a fright, saying that a mob was out breaking the windows of suspected Catholics. Soon after, they heard an affray nearby; it was Sir George Saville's house on the north side of Leicester Square being attacked (Saville had introduced the Catholic Relief Bill into the House of Commons). The family watched in fear from the observatory at the top of their house as the huge bonfire of Sir George's household effects lit up the whole square.

The next evening the rioting came even closer. The coach in which

Susan was returning from Lady Hales's was surrounded by a mob in
Leicester Square that was blocking the narrow entrance to St Martin's
Street. She was taken the long way round and got home to find Mrs
Burney and Charlotte both almost hysterical; only half an hour before
'many hundred people' had charged past the house on their way to the
house of Justice Hyde at the bottom of the road. Susan counted six fires
made of Hyde's belongings, reaching as far as the junction with Orange
Street – only a stone's throw away:

> When Hyde's house was emptied of all its furniture, the mob tore away
> the windows and window-frames and began to pull up the floors and the
> pannels of the rooms [. . . At last] the Ringleaders gave the word and away
> they all ran past our windows to the bottom of Leicester Fields with lighted
> fire-brands in their hands like so many Furies, [where] they made one
> great bonfire. [They continued their work of destruction] till between two
> and three in the morning.[10]

Susan, Hetty and her husband Charles Rousseau Burney were watching
from the drawing-room windows. The crowd dispersed, but a gaggle of
men and women remained in St Martin's Street shouting 'No Popery!'
Next thing, the crowd was pointing towards the little group in the window
and shouting 'They are all three papists!':

> 'For God's sake', cried poor Hetty, 'Mr Burney, call out No Popery or
> anything!' Mr Burney accordingly got his hat and huzza'd from the
> window. It went against me to hear him, though it seemed no joke in the
> present situation of things to be marked out by such wretches as papists.
> 'God bless your Honour', they then cried, and went away very well sat-
> isfied.[11]

This sort of intimidation was widespread. All over London, people
were wearing the Protestant blue ribbon as a passport through the crowds.
Horace Walpole, who had come up from Strawberry Hill to observe the
riots, said he was 'decking myself with blue ribbons like a May-day
garland'[12] before going out onto the streets. City merchants lit up their
houses at night as a supposed gesture of sympathy with the rioters, and the
words 'No Popery' were on everyone's lips, however unenthusiastically.

Money was being extorted from householders on a grand scale, and after the storming of Newgate Prison, then the King's Bench and the Fleet, the streets were full of criminals ready to take advantage of the complete breakdown of law and order.

Mrs Burney, terror-stricken, wanted the whole family to decamp at once to Chesington, but the others worried that the house on St Martin's Street would be lost if they left it. The threat of fire from nearby properties was their greatest anxiety (the premises at the back of the house were rented at this date to a Roman Catholic china-dealer), and after the complete destruction of Lord Mansfield's house in Bloomsbury Square, with its priceless library and manuscript collection, Charles Burney naturally began to fear for his papers and books (Fanny presumably feared for hers too). When they tried to move their valuables to Hetty's, however, they found that the rioting had spread to Covent Garden, and the two old aunts in York Street were cowering in the coffee house, having had an ominous symbol chalked on their door by accident. The Burneys' Italian friends had taken down their door-plates for fear of being victimised, and such was the mindless momentum of the riot that the French Protestant chapel next door to the Burneys' house was also under threat for a time, from the simple association of France with Catholicism. Every evening Susan went up to the observatory, saw fires on all sides and heard 'huzzas, shouts and firing, and shrieks from some of these terrible scenes of fury and riot'.[13] Charlotte had made a parcel of all her most important possessions, ready to evacuate the house at a moment's notice, but Susan put the job off – it was too depressing.

By 9 June, when troops arrived in the city, order began to be restored. George Gordon was arrested and sent to the Tower,* fresh earth was laid on the road to Blackfriars Bridge and the bloodstains were obliterated from the walls of the Bank of England with a quick coat of whitewash.

The Thrale party reached Brighton and heard all this news on 18 June, by which time London was quiet again. Fanny was desperate to rejoin her family and left for the capital as soon as possible with Mrs Thrale, who went up to survey the damage to the brewery and to reward a servant who had quick-wittedly diverted the mob. She expected Fanny

---

* Astonishingly he was not executed for his incitement of the mob, but lived long enough to become a convert to Judaism.

to return with her to Brighton and was disappointed when her offer was declined. The violence of the riots and the danger her family had suffered in her absence made Fanny begin to think that she had let Mrs Thrale 'overpower' her life too long. She had missed Susan terribly, and the lively social life of home (which was, frankly, much more interesting than Brighton or Bath); she also missed reading and writing in peace and being of practical help to her father. Living as Mrs Thrale's handmaid had been unproductive and ultimately unrewarding. With eyes newly opened to what she valued most, Fanny's instinct was to re-establish herself at home.

On 10 January 1780 a letter from Captain Charles Clerke of the *Resolution* reached London. It had been written the previous June in Kamchatka and travelled overland to St Petersburg, thence to Berlin. By the time it reached its destination, Clerke himself was dead, a fact that was rather overshadowed by the news his letter carried. It told how Captain Cook and four of his Marines had been killed 'on the 14th of February last at the island of O'Why'he [Hawaii], one of a group of new discovered Islands in the 22nd Degree of North Latitude, in an affray with a numerous and tumultuous Body of the Natives'.[14]

It was only when James Burney returned home, nine months after this news had been received and twenty months after the event, that his family heard the details of Cook's death. The *Resolution* and *Discovery* had made a long stay at Hawaii from November 1778 to early February 1779, revictualling prior to another trip north in search of a north-west passage through the Arctic Circle. During this stay, Cook had been involved in 'strange ceremonies' on the sacred platform known as the Morai, which are thought to have identified Cook with a native deity. The British party did not take the local religion very seriously, however, and heedlessly desecrated the Morai when removing for firewood both its wooden paling (which Cook had bargained for) and some of its idols (by mistake). Nevertheless, they set sail peacefully at the end of their furlough. A couple of days out, the *Resolution* sprang her mast and the two boats had to return to Kealakekua Bay on 11 February, where they met with an inexplicably hostile reception. Neither James Burney nor his colleagues understood the malign significance to the Hawaiians of any unscheduled return of the 'god'.

The *Discovery*'s cutter went missing overnight, and suspecting the natives of theft (they were as shameless a set of pilferers as the British were 'bargainers'), Cook decided to blockade the bay and go on shore to demand its return with a sergeant, nine Marines and his Lieutenant of Marines, Molesworth Phillips. The atmosphere on board the British ships was tense. The sight of armed native warriors assembling on the clifftops and the sound of conch shells being blown were unambiguously warlike, and at the instigation of a trigger-happy young officer, William Bligh (later captain of the *Bounty*), the sailors began sporadically firing at native canoes, which led to a chief being killed. Other native leaders, finding that Cook was not on board either British ship to receive their complaints about this, set off to find him, and half an hour later Burney and his companions heard firing on shore. The *Resolution* fired in response, and looking through a telescope from the deck of the *Discovery*, Charles Clerke could see the fracas that broke out on the shore as Cook and his party attempted to bring the King, Terreeoboo, back with them as a hostage. In the confusion and bloodshed, several of the Marines decided it would be better to flee to the launches than to risk trying to defend themselves with muskets (which took at least twenty seconds to reload). Phillips stood his ground longer than any of his men, though stabbed in the shoulder with a spear and pelted with stones. He was a strong swimmer, and helped his colleague Jackson into the pinnace before making for a more distant cutter himself.

Lieutenant John Williamson had long since left in the launch, saying later that he had interpreted Cook's hand signal from the rocks as an order to retreat. Burney and the others on the *Discovery* saw, aghast, that Cook was left unprotected and reeling from the attack of the crowd, in which four Marines were killed. Cook received a blow from a club and fell into the water, where he struggled (like most sailors, he could not swim) and was struck again. He was probably already dead when the natives pulled him out of the water, but they finished him off extravagantly, in what turned quickly into a ritual mob killing.

The reprisals that followed this shocking event were swift and bloody, but the main concern of Clerke, who took over command of the expedition, was to mend the *Resolution*'s mast and get away as soon as possible, having recovered what they could of their colleagues' remains. Lieutenants Burney and King were sent on this dangerous and gruesome mission, but found nothing on shore. The next day a parcel containing some of Cook's remains was delivered to the *Resolution*, provoking disgust and further retaliation. Another parcel, containing Cook's hands, scalp, skull and some bones was delivered later, and on 23 February, having given what burial honours they could to their murdered captain, the deeply dispirited British party set sail from Kealakekua Bay.

Of the officers involved in Cook's fatal mission, Phillips came off by far the best, and assumed the role of hero. Somehow he became known as the man who had shot Cook's main assailant, though by the time Cook was attacked, slipping on the rocks at the edge of the water, Phillips would have already been in the water, his musket abandoned and sword drawn. Phillips consolidated his reputation as the dead leader's champion by challenging Williamson – who was universally regarded as the villain of the piece for failing to stand his ground – to a duel. This ended unsatisfactorily, and they gave the matter up (through the intervention of a fellow-officer, whom G.E. Manwaring suggests was Burney[15]), though another fight broke out between the two men when they were provisioning at the Cape on the way home.*

When the two ships finally came up the Thames in October 1780, they were besieged by sightseers and well-wishers. Henry Thrale went to visit James on board the *Discovery*, and invited him to Streatham next time Fanny was going there. Dr Johnson also intended to visit James and see the celebrated ship.[17] James was soon home in St Martin's Street, telling his astonishing stories over and over. A kind of 'South Sea fever' gripped London; John Webber's pictures from the voyage were on display, as were curiosities from the South Seas, New Zealand and China. Mrs Thrale had an extremely expensive and elaborate court dress made, based on a native Hawaiian garment that James had brought back – the grebe-skin and gold trimmings alone cost £65 (compared with a manservant's annual wage of about seven guineas[18]). Fanny went to see Webber's pictures,

---

* Phillips and Burney must have viewed with amazement and anger the relative ease with which Williamson found subsequent promotion in the Navy. While Burney's petitions for work in the 1790s fell on deaf ears, Williamson was honoured with the command of the *Agincourt* in the action later known as the battle of Camperdown in October 1797. In strange repetition of his abandonment of the shore party at Kealakekua Bay, Williamson removed the *Agincourt* from the action, leaving the *Ardent*, on which many died, unsupported. At his court martial in December that year, charges of 'cowardice and disaffection' were not proved, but negligence was 'proved in part' and Williamson was rendered incapable of ever serving again.[16]

and was even more impressed by her brother's colleague Lieutenant King, 'one of the most natural, gay, honest and pleasant characters I ever met with';[19] but the 'lyon of lyons' was Molesworth Phillips, proudly bearing the scar on his shoulder where the native spear had struck. He had become a close friend of James on the voyage, and was introduced to the Burney family at the earliest opportunity. It was a fateful step. The twenty-five-year-old Irishman, whom Samuel Crisp, with his eye for male beauty, approvingly declared 'fine made, tall, stout, active, manly-looking',[20] made a bee-line for Susan. Within two months she and Phillips were engaged to be married.

'Bone idle, slack and amiable' is how one writer has described Phillips,[21] but at the time of his marriage to Susan Burney in January 1782 no one had any doubts about him (it would have seemed almost unpatriotic). Mr Crisp was impressed by Phillips's odd talent for making models 'with a degree of neatness and accuracy that cannot be surpassed',[22] and later in life the ex-Marine was often to be seen at the British Museum, 'lounging and offering advice', in the words of his former shipmate Rickman's daughter Mrs Lefroy: 'He had a turning machine and made small vases after the antique, using perhaps a dozen different kinds of wood, relics of his distant voyages'.[23] Phillips's attraction to Susan was undoubtedly fuelled – and possibly even suggested – by his deep feelings for her brother James, a friendship which lasted for life and which transcended family ties, even surviving the seemingly unforgivable events preceding Susan's death. When James died in 1821, Phillips, ostracised by the rest of the Burneys because of his treatment of Susan, commissioned a bust of his old friend and shipmate that he kept with him always, and his last request was to be buried in the same grave as Burney.*

Faced with evidence of such devotion in friendship, it is difficult not to suspect that there was perhaps some sexual attraction between Burney and Phillips, albeit the eighteenth-century taboo on acknowledging or discussing sexual relations allowed a latitude to *feeling* that we find difficult to appreciate and are prone to misinterpret. As with the later problem of whether James Burney and his half-sister Sarah Harriet committed

---

* James Burney was buried at St Margaret's, Westminster, in 1821 and Molesworth Phillips in 1832, but there is no record of the gravestone positions or memorial inscriptions of either. The churchyard was grassed over in 1881.

incest, we can only substitute caution for certainty. Sibling and pseudo-sibling love was strong in an age when parent–child relationships were always at risk of being cut short by early death; it was often intense and exclusive, especially between members of the same sex, who were thrown so much in each other's company. The bosom-friendship of Fanny and Susan is a case in point: there was '*but one soul* – but *one mind between you*; – you are *two* in *one*',[24] and they shared everything, 'the same House, Room – Bed – confidence & life'.[25] We tend to view such relationships, and the heightened language used to describe them, as either quaint or suspicious – (*vide*, to take one example of many, the recent controversy over Jane Austen's relationship with her sister Cassandra[26]) – transposing them into the mores of our own day with significant distortion. And of course the distorting effect works both ways. Most covert sexual relationships in the eighteenth century would have been too carefully disguised for us ever to recognise them as such, though the prevalence and popularity of, for instance, the incest theme in novels of the period (including Fanny Burney's[27]) is just one indicator of how the collective unconscious of the day was working.

The strength and durability of the bond between James Burney and Molesworth Phillips is of more relevance to us than its precise nature. Life at sea, which for men like James Burney began very early in life, ended early too, leaving decades of retirement on half-pay in domestic situations that could only strike the former mariners as insipid and unreal. It is hardly surprising, given the traumatic and peculiar nature of their shared experiences in the South Seas, that Burney and Phillips stuck together self-protectively afterwards. They had seen first hand, and been threatened with, violent death; they had endured extremes of weather and the privations of long sea voyages (where fricassee of rat was a delicacy only the officers were allowed); they had been among the first Europeans to set eyes on the other-worldly ice-scapes of both the Arctic and the Antarctic, had met and consorted with exotic and utterly foreign people, and had doubtless seen, perhaps joined in, countless scenes of coarseness and brutality as well as of heroism and comradeship. From the 1780s onward, James Burney showed signs of disturbance, restlessness with his home life and an inability to further his career; Phillips metamorphosed into a gambler, drinker and philanderer.

Dr Burney displayed caution about his favourite daughter's engagement in 1780, despite Phillips's hero status. Phillips was confident of a large income when his uncle died, but he didn't have it yet, and Dr Burney, always realistic on matters of household economy, withheld his consent to the marriage all through 1781, not convinced that there would be '*de quoi manger* very plentifully', as Fanny put it to Mrs Thrale. 'For my own part, I think they could do very well. [. . .] there is not any part of our family that cannot live upon very little as cheerfully as most folks upon very much'.[28] It was not perhaps the height of tact to say this to a woman who had just spent a small fortune on a ridiculous dress and even more on the set of Reynolds portraits that now adorned the walls of the library at Streatham Park, but Fanny took pride in the family self-sufficiency and Susan's choice, like Hetty's, of love over materialism.

The news of Susan's engagement made Mrs Thrale think that she would 'slip pretty readily into the Susannuccia's place' in Fanny's affections,[29] but no one was ever going to do that. Fanny genuinely liked Phillips (as they all did at that date), and was confident that Susan would be happy with this man who was to succeed her as 'closest friend and companion'.[30] But privately, the prospect of losing her sister was traumatic. Fanny naturally feared for Susan's future well-being. A woman of such a small frame and frail health would run a high risk of dying as a result of childbirth, or from a consumption, as their mother had done. Was not Hetty, a much more robustly healthy person, already looking 'like the Edge of a wornout knife', according to Crisp,[31] after ten years of marriage and six children? How could Susan survive the inevitable pregnancies and confinements?

Fanny had selfish reasons, too, of course, for dreading the forthcoming separation. Charlotte, who was almost ten years her junior, was an eccentric, delightful girl, but not yet a suitable substitute for Susan: 'our likings and dislikings, are often dissimilar', Fanny wrote sadly to Susan; 'with *you* all seemed the same as myself'.[32] Sarah Harriet was still only a child, and not delightful at all: her early nickname 'Queerness' seemed likely to stick. In the shrinking Burney household there would be no one with whom Fanny could conspire against Mrs Burney's malign presence, no one to complain to or take comfort from.

Elizabeth Burney was 'grown more sour than ever' according to Crisp,[33] and a great deal of treason was being talked about her at Chesington. 'Nothing is said that she does not fly in a Passion at and Contradict!'

complained Charlotte, the object of her stepmother's 'extremest hatred'; '*Whatever is, is Wrong!* that's her Maxim. I think she ought to be indicted for *Living*: for she is a Nuisance to Society'.[34] Susan had no intention of living at St Martin's Street ever again. As wife of a Captain of Marines, she faced an itinerant life, expected 'to pack up her bundles, and trudge along with him, except he should be commanded abroad'.[35] During Phillips's foreign postings she had arranged to live at Chesington.

Perhaps as an escape from the gloomy prospect ahead, Fanny threw herself into work on another novel. The composition of the first draft of *Cecilia* lasted almost exactly the duration of Susan's engagement, and was executed with manic bursts of overwork and collapse. For weeks at a time during the winter of 1780–1, Fanny shut herself up to write, overseen with oppressive attention by the two 'Daddies'. Charles Burney was an especially hard taskmaster. He imagined that his daughter could work the same way he did himself – night and day – without the advantage of amanuenses to take dictation at midnight or relieve the drudgery and discomfort of quill writing. Crisp on the other hand, having little experience of writing professionally, failed to perceive any difficulties at all. As far as he was concerned, it was tantamount to a paid holiday

> to sit by a warm Fire, and in 3 or 4 months (for the real time she has stuck to it closely, putting it all together, will not amount to more, tho' there have been long Intervals, between) gain £250 by scribbling the Inventions of her own Brain – only putting down in black and white whatever comes into her own head, without labour drawing from her own Fountain.[36]

By the end of February, however, Fanny was half-dead from 'the eternal fagging of my mind & Brains'. '[M]y hand scarce rests an Hour in the whole Day', she wrote to Susan from Chesington,[37] yet she was still only at the end of the first volume. When Mrs Thrale made an impulse visit and saw how ill and exhausted her friend had become, she scolded Dr Burney for putting too much pressure on his daughter, and made him let her come home for a rest. The plan filled Fanny with dread, as she explained to Susan:

I am *afraid* of seeing my father. Think of a whole volume not yet *settled*, not yet begun! [. . .] I cannot sleep half the night for planning what to write next Day, & then next day am half dead for want of rest![38]

Work was suspended for much of the spring, and there was another illness in September, brought on, as even Crisp understood, by overwork. After the frivolity and socialising of the previous two years, 1781 was proving arduous and unhappy for Fanny. Hetty's latest baby, Henry, died in August, and the fortunes of James and Charles were thwarted. James was appointed Captain of the *Latona*, but got no prize on his first commission; reprobate young Charles, despite his degree from Aberdeen, was refused ordination by the Bishop of London. In April Henry Thrale suddenly dropped dead in the house he had rented for the season in Grosvenor Square, on a day when half of fashionable London was invited there for a party. His widow was required to sell up the brewery business almost immediately; a complex and dispiriting task. She retired exhausted to Streatham, with Johnson, Fanny and others of the old circle in attendance, but it must have been clear to all of them that the great days of entertaining there were over. Apart from generating the huge wealth that had allowed the Thrales' magnificent hospitality, 'Master' had been the perfect foil to his wife, sincerely admired by their friends, and missed.

By the second winter, Fanny's novel did not seem near completion, and Crisp was threatening to keep her at Chesington until it was done. She joked with Susan that she might have to elope from Chesington Hall – as Susan was perhaps beginning to think she would have to do from St Martin's Street. Dr Burney was still dithering about consenting to her marriage, but Phillips, promoted to Captain that autumn, had waited long enough. The long engagement ended in a rapidly-arranged wedding, sending Fanny into a panic that she wouldn't be home in time for it. Still her main fear was of displeasing her father. She dreaded his 'cold looks' if she went back without the book done. 'I will scrawl Night & Day, if I *can*', she wrote to Susan,[39] and after another burst of unremitting labour, managed to finish enough of the novel to get permission to be home for Christmas. She had been made to feel incompetent, though working at remarkable speed: at about 300,000 words in five volumes, *Cecilia* was almost twice the length of *Evelina*, and was completed in only a year and a half.

The hurry in which Fanny wrote *Cecilia* meant that she had to abandon some of her more ambitious plans for the novel. From a letter of Crisp of 27 April 1780, it is clear that she had been thinking of writing about an 'unbeautiful clever heroine, beset all round for the sake of her great fortune'. It is not possible to determine whether this radically different idea was one of the desperate late revisions to *The Witlings* or an early sketch of the new novel; as we have seen, the two projects melted into one another, and though the heroine of the novel was originally called Albina, her name was later changed to that of the play's heroine, Cecilia. In the surviving early drafts, Albina is rather sharper-tongued than Cecilia, but nothing indicates whether or not she was conceived as 'unbeautiful'. By the final draft, Fanny had defaulted to convention, and Cecilia emerges on the page radiantly lovely outside and in. The fate of an 'unbeautiful clever' woman had to wait until the next novel to be attempted, and even then the character in question was a secondary one.

The orphaned Cecilia's intelligence, virtue and maturity (far greater, at twenty, than any of her supposed guardians) puts her in a class above the naive heroine of Burney's first novel and emphasises the deliberate break she strove to make between the two books. If the Daddies thought they would get another *Evelina* by sitting Fanny down in front of the fire for a couple of months, they were wrong: *Cecilia* is a novel about complex moral problems and perverse practical ones, lacking both *Evelina*'s light-heartedness and tendency towards farce. *Cecilia* was more concerned with *humours* than humour, and when Johnson praised 'the grand merit' of the book being 'in the *general Power of the whole*',* he acknowledged its quite different ambitions and achievements from her first attempt at the form.[40]

Cecilia is about birth and wealth, symbolised in the heroine's inheritance, which depends on her retaining the family name (Beverley) after marriage. Unfortunately, the man she falls in love with is the last in line of an etiolated aristocratic family who retire behind a pulled-up drawbridge every night and would rather see their son dead than lose their

---

* Johnson's remark could be seen as a rather slovenly generalisation; he had only read one volume of *Cecilia* at the time and, as with *Evelina*, there is no proof he ever finished reading the novel. Macaulay's conviction, expressed in his famous review of Madame D'Arblay's *Diary and Letters* and repeated by many later commentators, that Johnson helped revise the manuscript, even wrote parts of it, is wholly untenable.

own ancient name. Out of this rather unpromising framework for a thwarted romance Burney creates a series of situations that show the limitations of virtue in a world actively ranged against it. Cecilia consistently behaves not just 'correctly' but well, yet is subject to numerous vicissitudes (mostly arising from the combined attractions of her person and her fortune) on her way to securing the affections of the hero, Delvile. He is a much more complicated and attractive character than *Evelina*'s flawless Orville, and towards the end of the novel his conflicting thoughts are represented almost as thoroughly as those of the heroine – a highly unusual development. Also very unusually, the plot is not 'resolved' but horribly complicated by the lovers' union. Delvile has to choose between two evils: losing his parents' approbation or losing Cecilia. His suggested compromise of making a secret marriage renders both bride and groom profoundly uneasy, and when the wedding is dramatically stopped midway, it is almost a relief that their better judgement has prevailed, however frustrating to the romantic plot. Their second (successful) attempt at getting married is not a scene of triumph but of disabling anxiety. Cecilia listens 'mechanically' to the words of the service and looks round the church 'with a sort of steady dismay in her countenance'.[41] This was certainly not what the average reader of romantic fiction would have expected; weddings in that genre are proof that the plot has reached its happy ending.

Burney defended the realism of the love story in the following terms: 'the hero and heroine are neither plunged in the depths of misery, nor exalted to UN*human* happiness. Is not such a middle state more natural, more according to real life, and less resembling every other book of fiction?'[42] Her concern to create probable plot and character was somewhat at variance with the necessity of filling such a long book with sufficient drama. *Cecilia*, like both of Burney's subsequent novels, would have appealed far more to later audiences if it had been shorter; its five volumes were a gesture towards a waning convention, the monumental novels of Richardson in particular. *Evelina* had only three volumes, and it was that book's relative concision which the next generation of novelists sought to emulate.*

---

* George Austen, sending his daughter Jane's first novel to the publisher Cadell, specifically described it as 'about the length of Miss Burney's Evelina'.[43]

The advantage of length was that it allowed a mass of characters and a multiplicity of action that Mrs Thrale likened to 'a Camera Obscura in the Window of a London parlour'.[44] Few eighteenth-century novels have such historical interest as *Cecilia*, with its absorbing attention to the detail of London social life, contemporary fashions, attitudes and talk. Sex and money are the main targets of the satire; with the exception of the hero, the men in *Cecilia* are seen in a poor light as useless guardians, selfish sons and brothers, sexual predators, fortune-hunters, wastrels, hysterics and cheats. Their misogyny is presented more subtly than in *Evelina*, but Mr Monckton's cynical marriage to an ageing rich widow is arguably an act of far greater aggression than Captain Mirvan throwing Madame Duval into the ditch. Madame Duval was a straightforward grotesque, but Lady Monckton is shown to have once been just as the heroine now is, and her sour dislike of Cecilia, incomprehensible to the younger woman, is a premonition of what's to come at the hands of a man such as Monckton. 'An old woman', the baronet Sir Robert Floyer opines, in terms redolent of the fops in *Evelina*, 'is a person who has no sense of decency; if once she takes to living, the devil himself can't get rid of her.'[45]

Money and the movement of money between different levels of society is viewed with profound cynicism: the £20 owed to indigent Mrs Hill by the supposedly rich but spendthrift Harrels comes to symbolise the inequity in fact and in law between the various classes. The sum is too small to register in the minds of the Harrels; they depend on credit for everything and live at the expense of people like the Hills, too poor to be able to be bankrupt (a theme Burney returned to on a grand scale in *The Wanderer*). The Harrels are essentially money-addicts, constantly extorting cash from their ward and spending it in absurdly extravagant ways, such as the masquerade,* a triumph of surface over substance. Harrel's repeated threats to commit suicide tire even the susceptible heroine after a time, but his dramatic death at Vauxhall Gardens comes as all the more of a shock because of it. Mr Briggs (supposedly a portrait of the sculptor Joseph Nollekens, a friend of the Burneys whose parsimony was legendary), another of Cecilia's guardians, shows the same pathological attitude to money, but with very different symptoms: he is

---

* See Chapter 3.

so mean that he loves even his own dirt as a kind of crop (it indicates how much he has saved on soap), and is commodity-minded about everything, from the chances of getting Cecilia a husband – 'Not very easy, neither; hard times! men scarce! wars and tumults! stocks low! women chargeable!'[46] – to the very language he uses, pared down to its miserliest forms.

Cecilia's awareness of class, money and birth is acute, as it was for the author: she understands exactly her position relative to genteel but poor Henrietta Belfield and proud Mrs Delvile (a strong character based fairly obviously on Hester Thrale). When Cecilia finally takes possession of her estate, which has been eroded and threatened by her guardians during her minority, Burney has a chance to suggest how virtuous people with access to money (specifically, women) might affect society at large for the good. Cecilia coming into her inheritance is a protracted feminist fantasy of self-determination; all a woman needs, Burney seems to be saying, is several thousand a year and an estate of one's own.

Cecilia, which is set in the year of its composition, 1780, and contains many up-to-the-minute fashion and artistic references (including a homage to the singer Pacchierotti, a friend of the Burneys), draws on aspects of *haut-bourgeois* life observed by Fanny since her rise to fame. The kinds of conversation she had been recording in her Brighton and Bath journals appear in sharper focus here, coming from the mouths of a wide cast of society women, wits and misanthropes, such as the worldly Monckton, garrulous Miss Larolles (a favourite of Jane Austen) and spirited, sardonic Lady Honoria Pemberton. However, the middle-class characters proved again to be Burney's forte: Mrs Belfield is a wonderful study in misplaced ambition, Simkins in Uriah Heep-like cringing and Hobson the acme of a successful tradesman's complacent vulgarity:

'I take every morning a large bowl of water, and souse my whole head in it; and then when I've rubbed it dry, on goes my wig, and I am quite fresh and agreeable: and then I take a walk in Tottenham Court Road as far as the Tabernacle, or thereabouts, and snuff in a little fresh country air, and then I come back, with a good wholesome appetite, and in a fine breathing heat, asking the young lady's pardon; and I enjoy my pot of fresh tea, and my round of hot toast and butter, with as good a relish as if I was a Prince.'[47]

Burney's dealings with booksellers produced some gentle satire on the trade; she was obviously thinking of Lowndes and his twenty guineas when a bookseller in *Cecilia* says, 'we pay very handsomely for things of any merit, especially if they deal smartly in a few touches of the times',[48] and of her own career when she observes that authors 'must feel our way, with some little smart *jeu d'esprit* before we undertake a great work'.[49]

The range of characters, themes and incidents in *Cecilia* makes one suspect that Dickens as well as Thackeray (who admitted his debt to Burney) learned something from this remarkable novel, unjustly considered in our own day the inferior of its predecessor. Apart from having a thoroughly absorbing story, *Cecilia* contains touches of psychological realism that were truly *novel*. In the following passage, the lovers have just been parted after Delvile's duel with Monckton:

> Grief and horror for what was past, apprehension and suspense for what was to come, so disordered her whole frame, so confused even her intellects, that when not all the assistance of fancy could persuade her she still heard the footsteps of Delvile, she went to the chair upon which he had been seated, and taking possession of it, sat with her arms crossed, silent, quiet and erect, almost vacant of all thought, yet with a secret idea she was doing something right.[50]

This brilliant description of the kind of torpor brought on by shock, with Cecilia straining to hear the lost footsteps and instinctively taking shelter in the chair where Delvile last sat, shows Burney's imagination and worldly knowledge in perfect unison. That the set-piece scenes of violence and dramatic action in *Cecilia* (such as Harrel's suicide, Mrs Delvile bloodily bursting with emotion and Cecilia running mad through the streets of London) develop from realistic beginnings such as this explains why *Cecilia* is such a powerful book, never being overset by its own melodrama (of which there is plenty towards the end) and only once, in the tableau of weeping children around the heroine's sickbed, seriously lapsing into sentimentality.

The excessive speed at which Fanny composed this monumental work increased her fears for its reception, and as with *Evelina*, she sought to deflect criticism in an introduction, cast as a fable of Genius and Vanity.

Possibly because it went much further than a conventional 'curtseying preface', Fanny eventually decided not to publish the piece; significantly, it shows her awareness of what a modern psychologist would call the problem of self-appointment. She identifies herself with the ranks of authors who have Inclination (to the point of excess) rather than Ability, which is an 'unconscious' gift to few, who 'possess [it] without effort, & [...] without trouble'.[51] To authors like herself, writing is far from trouble-free – it is a kind of drug which both agitates and dissatisfies the addict/writer: 'his accustomed occupations become irksome, his former pleasures, insipid; the smallest praise has powers to enchant, the slightest criticism to distract him'. This was admitting too much for comfort. Begun as a pre-emptive strike against the *Critical*, the *Monthly* and the *Gentleman's Reviews*, Fanny's introduction to *Cecilia* had somehow turned into a statement of her own vulnerability: 'all [the youthful author's] ideas of Happiness & of Misery are centred in Fame & Disgrace, & in the *Author*, the *Man* is lost'.

Fame and disgrace haunted Fanny as much as ever, though she had, fortunately, developed some tolerance of publicity since the publication of *Evelina*. She could now hear out strangers' praise with polite resignation, be 'attacked and catechised' by the curious without running out of the room, and sounded almost pleased to be 'poked [...] in with all the *belles esprits*' in some verses about contemporary women writers that appeared anonymously in the *Morning Herald*. Perhaps she knew, or suspected, that the author was in fact her own father.* He was almost bursting with pride and had bragged to half of London about his daughter's forthcoming book (Mrs Thrale dealt with the other half): 'he is fond of [*Cecilia*] to enthusiasm, and does not forsee the danger of raising such general expectation', Fanny wrote anxiously to Susan.[53] Though she was not named on the title-page, Fanny's authorship of *Cecilia* was known to everyone well before publication. But Charles Burney was enjoying the advantages of Fanny's success too much to be discreet about it. He had been invited to Court (where he hoped to be appointed soon as

---

* This was proved by the discovery of the manuscript, with corrections and additions, among his posthumous papers. Fanny noted at the time of their publication that her father 'carries them constantly in his pocket, and reads them to every body!',[52] but imagined that his pride derived from seeing 'Little Burney's quick discerning' lauded in print.

Master of the King's Band) and, as Crisp reported, was 'now at the Top of the *Ton*. He is continually invited to all the great Tables, and parties, to meet the Wits and Grandees, without the least reference to Music.'[54]

Dr Burney had sold the copyright of the novel to the bookseller Thomas Payne while Fanny, as bridesmaid, was accompanying Susan and her husband on their honeymoon at Chesington in January 1782. The Burneys and Paynes were already on friendly terms. James was paying court to Payne's younger daughter, Sally, and married her three years later. Perhaps this introduced too great an element of goodwill into the sale of *Cecilia*. Payne paid £250 for the copyright, a sum Crisp marvelled at, but which was once again underselling Fanny's work considerably. Dr Burney and his daughter were naively surprised to discover later that Payne's first edition of *Cecilia* was of two thousand copies, four times that of *Evelina*, and that his profits from that edition alone would have been in the region of £500 (as calculated by Dr Johnson).

Fanny rushed to copy and revise her manuscript during the first half of the year, and Payne printed up each volume hot from her hands. 'I would it were in my power to defer the whole publication to another spring', Fanny wrote to Crisp, frustrated at the lack of time she had to polish the work, 'but I am sure my father would run crazy if I made such a proposal'.[55] The book was published in June 1782 and sold out almost immediately. *Cecilia* seemed to please everyone, the reviewers, the *ton and* the intellectuals – Edward Gibbon purportedly read it in one sitting and Burke, the foremost orator of the day, thought so highly of it that he wrote the novelist a fan letter, offering his 'best thanks for the very great instruction and entertainment I have received from the new present you have bestowed on the public'.[56] The morality of the book also won the approval of Mrs Delany, a highly respectable elderly author-ess who was close to the Royal Family, and probably through her recom-mendation *Cecilia* came to the notice of the Queen, who, after having it vetted by a bishop, allowed her daughters to read it – the first novel ever to penetrate that far into the Royal Household.

Crisp was impressed not just by the very favourable critical reception of *Cecilia*, but by its material success, noting with approval that the publishers Payne and Cadell were intending to present the author with a 'handsome pair of Gloves' over and above the 'bare price stipulated' of £250.[57] Two months after the publication of the novel, Crisp arranged his own treat for Fanny. He commissioned a portrait of her by her talented cousin Edward, who arrived at Chesington Hall in August with a carriage-load of materials and produced the charming, 'horribly flattering' portrait in Van Dyke dress which now hangs in the gallery at Parham Park, Sussex. Crisp also sat to Edward Burney that summer, his portrait finding its way into Fanny's possession in 1792 on the death of Kitty Cooke. Perhaps he commissioned it because he suspected he hadn't much longer to live. He had been a martyr to gout and rheumatism for years (he and his sister Mrs Gast were even thinking of trying out the new-fangled electrification treatment for the latter), but in the early months of 1783 he went into decline. When he died in April the whole Burney family was plunged into grief for the loss of their kind, cultured and benevolent friend. 'That *all but* matchless man' continued to haunt Fanny's works in various guises, but the old retreat of Chesington Hall was never the same again.

❄ 8 ❧

Change and Decay

Since the death of her husband, Mrs Thrale's future had been the subject of speculation in London society. She was still only forty, witty, famous and presumed very rich (though her finances in fact took a sharp downward turn in 1782 because of the resolution of an old family lawsuit). Although nothing was less likely, many outsiders were convinced that she and Dr Johnson would marry; Boswell was mischievously suggesting it as soon as Henry Thrale's funeral was over,* and her name had been linked with Johnson's in the newspapers, as well as with William Seward, the brewer Samuel Whitbread and Queeney's admirer Jeremiah Crutchley. 'Deluged with proposals' as she was,[2] Mrs Thrale declared firmly that she had no intention of marrying again except for love; and love was something she claimed never to have experienced.[3] To the members of her coterie, however, the prospects of Mrs Thrale remarrying or Mrs Thrale staying single were equally alarming. Either way the charmed circle at Streatham Park was doomed to break up.

All through 1782 it was clear that Johnson's dependence on Mrs Thrale was beginning to grate on her nerves. Age and infirmity were turning the venerable Doctor into something of a liability, and the difficulties of looking after him, overseeing Thrale's estate, dealing with the executors (of whom Johnson was one) and her continuing lawsuit made Hester restless and unhappy. In the autumn she took the dramatic decision to go and live in Italy for three years with her daughters, to give up the London house they had been renting and to let Streatham Park to Lord Shelburne.

The news stunned her friends. Fanny Burney, like most of them, had

---

* And composed some scurrilous verses to support his speculation.[1]

come to look on Streatham as 'my other home, and the place where I have long thought my residence dependent only upon my own pleasure', as she told Susan. 'If I was to begin with talking of my loss, my strangeness, [. . .] I should never have done.'⁴ And if Fanny, who had known the family such a short time, felt this strongly, how much more devastating a loss it was for Samuel Johnson, who had been protected by the Thrales for more than fifteen years.

Johnson's bitterness at his abrupt abandonment increased his irascibility and caused some painful scenes when Mrs Thrale, Fanny Burney and he were visiting Brighton together that autumn. He humiliated one old acquaintance in company and snapped at another; '[he] has really frightened all the people, till they almost ran from him', Fanny reported in November,⁵ noting that 'Mrs Thrale fares worse than any body.' Johnson was pointedly excluded from almost all the party's evening invitations and got so tired of being left on his own at the lodgings that he even attended a ball one evening, saying pathetically, 'it cannot be worse than being alone'⁶ (a sentiment with which Fanny heartily disagreed). He was still benevolent towards his 'little Burney' and planted noisy kisses on her cheeks, but it is not to her credit that in return she was beginning to feel embarrassed to be seen in the sick old man's company, and disloyally tried to avoid sitting next to him on one occasion because of 'the staring attention he attracts both for himself and all with whom he talks'.⁷

Mrs Thrale's restlessness and her choice of Italy as destination were due to her increasing regard for the singer Gabriel Piozzi, who had become a regular visitor to Streatham in 1780 when he was appointed Queeney's singing-master. Since their unpropitious introduction at the Burneys' house two years before, Mrs Thrale had radically changed her view of the elegant Italian, whose company had helped cheer and divert her through the difficult last months of Henry Thrale's life. For his part, Piozzi was grateful to Mrs Thrale for her respectful (if rather ignorant) appreciation of his talents, having been treated as little better than a mountebank by aristocratic patrons in the past. Piozzi's protracted absence in 1781 during the early months of Mrs Thrale's widowhood only served to confirm her admiration of him. She had developed a strange fantasy, based on his supposed resemblance to her father, that Piozzi was her secret half-brother. It was a way to displace and perhaps diffuse the strong feelings Piozzi's company aroused in her, 'emotions one would not be without', as she put it rather forensically, 'though inconvenient enough sometimes'.[8] Just how 'inconvenient' remained to be seen. Mrs Thrale soon came to perceive Piozzi as the man who could transform her life, her ideal companion. She foresaw with clarity all the objections that would be raised at the suggestion of a match with someone so far below her in class, 'parts' and wealth, and listed the drawbacks carefully in *Thraliana*, but concluded:

> I live a quiet Life, but not a pleasant one: My Children govern without loving me, my Servants devour & despise me, my Friends caress and censure me, my Money wastes in Expences I do not enjoy, and my Time in Trifles I do not approve. [E]very one is made Insolent, & no one Comfortable.[9]

Essentially, she had already fixed on marrying Piozzi.

Fanny Burney was the first to guess that Mrs Thrale had fallen in love, and was keen to appear sympathetic when the news was broken to her in Brighton. Queeney, however, made no attempt to conceal her disgust. Almost eighteen and in the marriage market herself, it is not surprising that she found her mother's behaviour inappropriate. '[M]ade an Eldest son of'[10] in her father's will, with a fortune of about £50,000 (far more than her mother's), she had taken on the role of guardian of the family honour. No doubt she felt that her mother would have been more suitably employed brokering marriages for her heiress daughters than indulging herself in a profoundly embarrassing liaison with the music-master. Fanny, too, was horrified at the prospect of scandal ahead. When Mrs Thrale, 'in a Transport of Passion' showed her the outpourings about Piozzi in her journal, Fanny's response – when she had finished crying herself 'half blind' over them – was harsh behind its cajolery, as Mrs Thrale recorded:

> [Miss Burney] said there was no resisting such pathetic Eloquence, & that if she was the Daughter instead of the Friend, She should even be tempted to attend me to the Altar. [B]ut that while she possessed her Reason, nothing should seduce her to approve what Reason itself would condemn: that Children, Religion, Situation, Country & Character – besides the

diminution of Fortune by the certain loss of 800£ a Year were too much to Sacrifice to any *One* Man.[11]

Perhaps Fanny thought this little lecture (with its prudent parenthesis about income) would sway her friend, but as the months passed, Mrs Thrale's ardour for Piozzi only increased, as did Queeney's antipathy. Once rumours began to go round, the Thrale family friends and trustees marshalled their forces against the proposed Italian journey (on which Piozzi was to be guide), backing Queeney vigorously. The atmosphere in the household became extremely tense, Queeney coldly asserting that her mother was deluded, Mrs Thrale responding with impassioned pleadings, tears and fainting fits.

Fanny, who was intimate with both parties and had heard all the gossip and slander going about, counselled Mrs Thrale to marry Piozzi immediately rather than damage her reputation – a very Burneyan solution – but the affair dragged on unresolved all year, Mrs Thrale torn between powerful self-interest and her sense of duty to her 'unfeeling' daughters. A terrible crisis seemed to have settled the matter by *force majeure* when in the spring of 1783 Mrs Thrale's youngest child, four-year-old Harriet, died of measles and Cecilia, two years older, was stricken with whooping-cough. Piozzi, anxious to avoid the emotional fall-out, refused to see the distraught mother and left the country soon after, much to Mrs Thrale's friends' relief. But Hester sank into a stasis of unhappiness so alarming that Fanny feared a complete breakdown. Mrs Thrale had retreated to Bath, where she expected and craved Fanny's company, but Dr Burney, anxious as ever to disassociate himself from anything 'improper', refused to let his daughter go to her.

Fanny could not condone her friend's passion for Piozzi, but defended her good nature. 'Though her failings are unaccountable and most unhappy', she wrote to Susan,[12] 'her virtues and good qualities [...] would counterbalance a thousand more'. Privately, Fanny was shocked by the letters she was receiving almost daily from Bath: 'Dear, lost, infatuated Soul! [...] how *can* she suffer herself, noble-minded as she is, to be thus duped by ungovernable passions!'[13] Indeed the spectacle of a mature woman giving vent to passionate feelings – even publicising them – sent a general shudder round polite society: 'there must be really some degree of *Insanity* in that case', Mrs Chapone wrote to William Weller Pepys, echoing Mrs Montagu's verdict of 'lunacy', 'for such mighty overbearing Passions are not natural in a "Matron's bones" '.[14]

In November Mrs Thrale collapsed after nursing her twelve-year-old daughter Sophia through a dangerous illness, and Queeney began to fear for her sanity as well as for her life. In the epic ego-struggle she had been playing out with Queeney, Mrs Thrale's threat-cum-battle-cry, 'Death or Piozzi!', seemed about to come true. Before the end of the year, the family had agreed a compromise: Mrs Thrale could marry Piozzi as long as the four surviving children, now wards of court, did not have to live with her.

What Piozzi thought about the matter is difficult to ascertain. Mrs Thrale was convinced of his regard for her, but to the outside world he seemed a cold and oddly undemonstrative lover (rather like Henry Thrale, in fact). Having heard at the end of 1783 that the marriage could go ahead, he waited months before setting out from Italy, and only arrived in England to claim his bride the following June. 'The excuse of Roads, &c, makes me sad, – little as is my haste for his arrival', Fanny wrote to Queeney in February 1784, 'yet it seems to me such *coolness*; – did not my Father travel home through Italy in December?'[15] The delay was profoundly humiliating to Mrs Thrale, and probably did more to disgust her friends than any of the former objections to Piozzi's nationality, religion or profession.

Though her behaviour was later vilified by Mrs Thrale, Fanny showed what seems sincere concern for her friend all through this emotionally charged and well-publicised affair. She was a consistent adviser and trustworthy confidante, refusing to tell even Susan about the details of the case until July 1784. She made no secret of her misgivings (which were, after all, no more than the obvious objections which Mrs Thrale herself had enumerated) yet withheld judgement on Piozzi, whom she admitted she hardly knew, leaving Mrs Thrale the benefit of the doubt about the reluctant bridegroom's actual intentions. Right up to Mrs Thrale's marriage to Piozzi at the end of July 1784, Fanny was her 'sweet' friend and mainstay, writing in the warmest terms to Susan about their 'incurable affection'.[16] A shocking reversal was in store, as Fanny described in a letter to Queeney written fourteen years later:

[Mrs Thrale] bore all my opposition – which was regularly the strongest the utmost efforts of my stretched faculties could give – with a gentleness, nay a *deference* the most touching to me – till the marriage was over – And then – to my never ending astonishment, in return to the constrained & painful letter I forced myself to write of my good wishes – she sent me a cold, frigid, reproachful answer, in entirely a new style to any I had ever received from her, to upbraid me that my *congratulations were not hearty!* As if I could write *congratulations* at all! *or meant* to write! How gross must have been such hypocrisy![17]

Dr Johnson had ranted against the remarriage, Dr Burney had cringed at it, but though they and some of Mrs Thrale's other male friends did far less to accommodate the match than did Fanny, Fanny's inability to write a sufficiently artificial note that could be read with complacency by both Mr and Mrs Piozzi was judged so ungenerous that it cost her the whole friendship. After one more exchange of letters, she was dropped, abruptly and completely. 'I am convinced from the moment of the nuptials she shewed him [Piozzi] all my Letters, & probably attributed to me every obstacle that he had found in his way', Fanny wrote to Queeney in 1798, trying to account for it.[18]

The very fact that Fanny was entering into explanations like this so long after the event rather scotches the idea that she and Queeney had been in cahoots at the time. Her friendship with Queeney lasted a lifetime and in many ways suited Fanny better than the friendship with Hester, though it lacked the alluring ardour and aggravation of the latter. It was based on mutual esteem and shared remembrance of the old days at Streatham, but there was a cause for real sympathy too. Mrs Thrale's alliance with Piozzi (rich middle-aged widow marries badly-off middle-aged professional musician) was almost a replica of the match between Mrs Elizabeth Allen and Charles Burney. Dr Burney could not have failed to make the connection himself, though his condemnation of the Piozzi marriage seems particularly hypocritical in this context.

Fanny too was aware of the parallels, and they stretched her sympathies all ways. Given her professed view of Mrs Allen having made the running with the widower Charles Burney, Piozzi must have seemed in many ways like her father; Mrs Thrale, her admired friend, was, on the other hand, taking up the disgraceful role of impassioned matron. Ultimately, Fanny could not condemn or condone either of them. The only person for whom she could feel unreservedly sorry was Queeney, who like Fanny herself had been forced to contemplate not simply the existence but the power of a parent's sexuality. She had had to witness the apparent betrayal of a beloved dead parent by the living one, and accept changes which she thoroughly disapproved. Fanny and her sisters seem to have suffered their stepmother as a kind of purgatory which proved how much they loved their father, but theirs was a muddled kind of moralism compared with Queeney's unequivocal denunciation of her mother. Fanny more than forgave her father's faults, she glorified them – as we shall see in the history of her biography of him – but the fact that she never criticised Queeney's treatment of Mrs Thrale is interesting. In Queeney's abusive resistance to the changes foisted on her by her mother's remarriage, Fanny might possibly have found something to admire.

In the way of such things, it took some months for Fanny to realise that she was not going to hear from Mrs Piozzi again. The loss of her friend came at a particularly difficult time (as her reference to her 'stretched faculties' hints), when Fanny was still mourning for Crisp, anxious about Susan and sadly witnessing the decline of Dr Johnson. The great Lex-ophanes never completely recovered from a stroke in 1783, and on his return to London from Lichfield in the summer of 1784 sank steadily. Fanny had visited him at his home in Bolt Court several times the previous autumn, but Johnson still felt neglected. Her prim excuse (in her diary) for staying away was that the house was usually too full of male visitors for her to call on Johnson in comfort now that old Anna Williams was dead and could not act as chaperone. It is just as likely that she shrank from the prospect of hearing Johnson's views of the Piozzi scandal. William Seward (whom Fanny might also have been trying to avoid) was always attempting to sound her on this subject, and other old acquaintances of Mrs Thrale, such as Lady Frances Burgoyne, seemed to think that Fanny, as proxy to the errant widow, deserved 'painful conferences'[19] of recrimination. In the last ever interview she had alone with Samuel Johnson, Fanny tentatively introduced the subject of Mrs Thrale, presumably hoping that her two old friends could make peace before Johnson died. She got a dusty answer.

I had seen Miss T. the day before.

'So,' said he, 'did I.'

I then said, 'Do you ever, sir, hear from her mother?'

'No,' cried he, 'nor write to her. I drive her quite from my mind. If I meet with one of her letters, I burn it instantly. I have burnt all I can find. I never speak of her, and I desire never to hear of her more. I drive her, as I said, wholly from my mind.'[20]

This was on 28 November 1784. Fanny made several more attempts to see Johnson, but he was by then too ill to see her. Bolt Court was full of people trying to pay their last respects or catch the great man's dying words. On one occasion, Fanny waited alone in a cold parlour rather than have to talk to anyone else, and hovered on the stairs for reports from the sick-room from Johnson's manservant Frank Barber.

Johnson's obvious fear of death troubled Fanny profoundly: 'Good and excellent as he is, how can he so fear death?' she wrote, revealing – along with great unworldliness – her own powerful if narrow-minded piety; 'Alas, my Susy, how awful is that idea!'[21] Three days before Johnson died on 13 December, she was relieved to hear reports of his apparent change of mind 'from its dark horror'. 'Good, and pious, and excellent Christian – who shall feel [hope] if not he?'[22] Despite this professed confidence in the afterlife, Fanny rather proudly noted that on the day of the funeral 'I could not keep my eyes dry all day'. As with many of her contemporaries in that sentimental era, Fanny's capacity for 'feeling' overrode strictly pious behaviour, a tendency that was to be heartily condemned by the coming generation of evangelically-minded Burneys.

Ten days after Johnson's funeral, Fanny went to a party at Mrs Chapone's, the first she had attended in months, but she felt very subdued. 'How melancholy will all these circumstances render these once so pleasant meetings', she wrote in her diary, referring to the deaths and losses of the past year. Something else was weighing on her spirits, though, which was all the worse for having, in its beginnings, held out the promise of better days to come. All the time during which Mrs Thrale had been agonising over Piozzi, Fanny herself had been suffering the long-drawn-out agonies of an unrequited love that left her depressed, embittered and, probably for the first time in her life, feeling bleak about the future. The man she had fallen in love with was a twenty-eight-year-old

cleric called George Owen Cambridge, whom she had met among the
Blue-stockings. In the early 1780s the Blue-stocking 'Club' – deliberately
not a men's-style, exclusive club at all – was at the height of its modish-
ness, and Fanny was a regular at 'Blue' parties held by Elizabeth Vesey,
eccentric wife of the MP Agmondesham Vesey. Mrs Vesey's set included
Mrs Garrick, Burke, Reynolds and Horace Walpole, the most flamboyant
literary figure of the day, whom Fanny described as 'gay, though caustic;
polite, though sneering; and entertainingly epigrammatical'.[23] Mrs Vesey
fancied herself less stuffy than her rivals Mrs Montagu and Mrs Boscawen.
At her soirées, the chairs were placed in odd groupings round the room
to break the convention of sitting in a circle, as Hannah More described
in her comic poem 'The Bas Bleu', dedicated to the hostess:

> See VESEY's plastic genius make
> A Circle every figure take,
> Nay, shapes and forms, which wou'd defy
> All Science of Geometry.[24]

As a result, 'Away dull Ceremony flew': a dozen different conversations
could be going on simultaneously, generating a sense of vivacity and
plenty of noise. Horace Walpole called Mrs Vesey's overcrowded parties
'Babels' or 'Chaos',[25] and Fanny records evenings of 'almost riotous gaiety'
at Mrs Vesey's house. It was not in the least like Streatham: the hostess
was more an object of amusement than a wit in her own right, artlessly
trying on Lady Spencer's strange new hearing aids – ear-shapes in silver
– which dropped out whenever she moved, or lamenting the death of a
new friend in absurd terms: '"It's a very disagreeable thing, I think,"
said she, "when one has just made acquaintance with anybody, and likes
them, to have them die."' As Fanny recorded, 'This speech set me grin-
ning so irresistibly, that I was forced to begin filliping off the crumbs of
the macaroon cake from my muff, for an excuse for looking down.'[26]

That 'Blue' parties had lost something of their original intensity and
pretentiousness shows how much more relaxed women writers had
become about their status during the preceding decade. Hannah More's
'The Bas Bleu', which was circulating in manuscript at the end of 1783,
emphasises the pleasure that female 'kindred souls' were beginning to
find in 'alliance'; a slightly surprising tribute to sisterhood from the

woman who was later one of Mary Wollstonecraft's loudest and most persistent critics. The poem mentions many of the 'Blues' by name, and ends with a description of a Blue party's vital ingredient, 'Attention', which William Weller Pepys thought was a portrait of Fanny Burney:

> Mute Angel, yes: thy looks dispense
> The silence of intelligence;
> Thy graceful form I well discern,
> In act to listen and to learn:
> 'Tis Thou for talents shalt obtain
> That pardon Wit would hope in vain.[27]

'The compliment is preposterous, because the description is the most flattering', Fanny wrote in her journal,[28] though it is easy to see how Pepys made his guess – Fanny had always been a good watcher and listener, absorbed by the minutiae of her own and other people's behaviour. Observation had been the basis of her art as well as the source of her neuroses – she *was* all 'Attention'. This habit of observing was to cause her great pain in the affair with George Cambridge. She would have been much happier both during and after the whole business if she had been less consciously alert.

The first thing that Fanny did not fail to notice about Cambridge was that he and his father, the wit Richard Owen Cambridge, always seemed to be present at Mrs Vesey's when she herself was invited, and she soon began to believe they were seeking her out on purpose. Richard Owen Cambridge, well-known in his day as the author of a satirical poem, 'The Scribleriad', and editor of a magazine called *The World*, was rich, cultivated and owned a large house by the river at Twickenham; his son George, later Rector of Elme and Archdeacon of Middlesex, was three years younger than Fanny, handsome, intelligent and modest. What attracted Fanny to him were his extremely good manners and his apparent sensitivity, though in the light of what happened – or rather, didn't happen – later, perhaps she was misreading even these early signs. Young Cambridge forbore to talk about her novels, so Fanny imagined he understood her better than anyone else:

He neither looks at me with any curiosity, nor speaks to me with any air of expectation; two most insufferable honours, which I am continually receiving. [. . .] If I met with more folks who would talk to me upon such rational terms, – [. . .] with how infinitely more ease and pleasure should I make one in those conversations![29]

Nothing could have been more likely to win Fanny's admiration than delicacy about her authorship. George Cambridge was present one evening in January 1783 at the house of Tory hostess Anna Ord when the writer Soame Jenyns set about Fanny with 'an eulogy unrivalled' of *Cecilia* that 'would have drawn blushes into the cheeks of Agujari or Garrick'.[30] Mr Cambridge senior protested that she should not feel embarrassed by such attention from a man of judgement and sense like Jenyns, but this was no comfort to Fanny. His son, however, came over to her as the party was breaking up and said how sorry he had been on her behalf. The next morning he called at St Martin's Street and engaged her in charming, but general, conversation – all of which she noted down word for word in her journal. It was perfect conduct-book behaviour.

In the circles Fanny and George frequented, any possible romance was sure to be anticipated, encouraged (or deplored), commented upon and generally overseen by their friends. George Cambridge's admiration for Miss Burney, and hers for him, were obvious to most observers very early on. He seemed to follow her everywhere; they laughed at the same things, finished each other's sentences, had 'the same expression, & same smile!'[31] It was no surprise to their friends (though a dreadful shock to Fanny) when their names were linked in a newspaper gossip item in the spring of 1783.[32] Casting round to guess which of the 'Blues' could have betrayed them to the papers so disloyally, Fanny suspected William Weller Pepys again, the man to whom she had attributed some satirical verses about learned ladies in the *Morning Herald* the previous year which mentioned her.[33] But the critic Margaret Anne Doody has suggested the paragraph could, like the poem, quite easily have been the work of Charles Burney, perhaps hoping to spur young Mr Cambridge into action.* Who-

---

* Another small circumstance supports this only too credible theory. In the spring and summer of the same year, Fanny had her portrait painted in miniature by John Bogle, whose wife was a friend of Mrs Burney. The miniature was a form particularly associated with love-tokens because it was designed to be worn or carried about the person; such portraits were very commonly commissioned at the beginning of or during engagements. Apart from patronising a friend's husband and celebrating the famous authoress of *Cecilia*, Dr and Mrs Burney might have intended the portrait as a gift for Fanny's intended.

ever published the gossip about Fanny and George, it had no effect on the young cleric's behaviour, which was as pleasant, partial and as provokingly non-committal as before.

In the meantime, George's father had become such an ardent admirer of Fanny that many of her friends began to suspect *he* was in love with her. When the Cambridges invited Fanny and her parents to Twickenham Meadows for a day in the summer of 1783, the whole family must have thought of it as the start of pre-nuptial socialising; but what Mr Cambridge had in mind was a *tête-à-tête* with the authoress of *Cecilia*, whom he monopolised shamelessly the whole time. All his conversation came round to her book. All the felicity of his life, he said, consisted in female society. What a pity she could not stay a month, he said, rather than just a day. Her sister, Mrs Phillips . . . now there was another very attractive woman.

The slowness with which the 'romance' between Fanny and George Cambridge progressed puzzled everyone, Fanny most of all. Even her published diaries, carefully pruned of embarrassing revelations, show how soon in the friendship she began to note down signs of 'Mr G.C.'s preference for her. Her unpublished journals go much further, revealing how 'tremblingly alive' she was to his every word and gesture, and what elaborate feats of interpretation she could perform in order to corroborate her inner conviction that he was as much in love with her as she was with him. Susan, the recipient of dozens of tormented letters on the subject of 'G.C.', surely found it as painful as we do to read page after page of feverish wishful-thinking such as this: 'I am *greatly* mistaken if he was pleased at seeing me [. . .] decamping. [. . .] If you had seen with how irresolute an air he followed me in my retreat with his Eye, & turned entirely round to look after me, you *must* have concluded he was provoked at my departing in such a manner';[34] or this: 'His smile, indeed, had as much of pain as of pleasure in its expression; – what it meant, I can not tell, but it was a look of so much unaccountable consciousness as I cannot easily, if ever, forget.'[35]

Over the months of their acquaintance – spreading alarmingly into years – Fanny became convinced that it *could* only be a matter of time until George Cambridge declared himself. Pathetically and humiliatingly, she hung on in the belief that only delicacy and sensitivity (which she imagined he had in great store) were holding him back. No proposal ever took place, though Fanny thought he 'seemed irrepressibly attached to me, – and has been deemed honourably serious by all our mutual acquaintance'.[36] *Seemed, deemed* – her disbelief is palpable, added to which was the shame of 'all our mutual acquaintance' thinking likewise. Fanny became more puzzled when she tried to analyse his behaviour, which she considered 'long past all mere impeachment of *trifling*', but George Cambridge's manners must have been smooth and plausible enough to conceal anything:

> He loves me? I said internally, else he would not return in less than a week. No, he means nothing. Yet so interested his air & look, so gay, animated, & undisguised the pleasure he received in our conversation [. . .] How *astonishingly* does he deceive me, if he went not from the House impressed with the most flattering sensations towards me . . . Yet firmly I believe I *am* deceived.[37]

Of course the last thing Fanny could do to bring matters to a head was *act*: the courtship process required real or affected passivity from women until some sort of declaration had come from the man. And yet in the situation she found herself relative to George Cambridge, he was the effeminately passive party, she the ardent, watchful lover. It is interesting that in her next novel, *Camilla*, which is in effect a lengthy dramatisation of the difficulties of interpreting love-signals, it is the hero Edgar, not the heroine, who experiences the kind of bewilderment that Fanny herself experienced over George Cambridge.

In January 1784, George's sister Kitty was mortally ill, and Mr Cambridge broke the news to Fanny with a warning for her to 'bear up against this misfortune as *he* did'.[38] Fanny had but one fault, Mr Cambridge declared, 'and that is too much feeling. You must repress that, therefore, as much as you can'. Though this was primarily advice about how to brace herself for the death of his daughter, it is possible to see in Mr Cambridge's words a veiled caution about 'too much feeling' with respect to his son, too. But Fanny was by this time in the grip of an obsession which no amount of advice or rationalising could ameliorate. She had tried snubbing George – he looked hurt; she tried avoiding him – he turned up uninvited; she tried to banish all thought of him from her mind – and found her mind filling up again with anxious fourth and fifth thoughts. Truly, hope deferred maketh the heart sick. While Mrs Thrale waited for her tardy lover to join her in Bath, Fanny Burney was in just as fervid and unhappy a state of mind, though instead of coolness, poor Fanny had to suffer 'torturing uncertainties' from George Cambridge's unremitting but ultimately meaningless attentions. Though she congratulated herself that her behaviour towards him had been exemplary, the passions he had secretly aroused in her were hardly less strong than the passion she had so loudly criticised in Mrs Thrale.

At several times during those three years she felt intensely bitter about the insensitivity of the 'sensitive' young cleric, yet guilty that her own assumptions had possibly been too forward, too 'knowing' and indecorous, inviting cynical interpretation, like Swift's of the apparently coy female blush. She vacillated between thinking that the whole affair had been a dreadful delusion on her part and that Cambridge had in fact practised 'endless deceit & treachery' on her.[39] In the spring of 1784, her nosy and prudish friend Anna Ord had heard definite rumours that the couple were about to marry, which provoked this outburst from Fanny to her sister, full of angry emphases:

> some thing must have been very wrong in somebody's management, & I will not think it my own! – Neither, indeed, could it be my own; – were the rumour the effect of my behaviour, it could only be called a flirtation, – a coqueting, – &c., – a Marriage is never settled but in consequence of conclusions from the Man's behaviour.[40]

Cambridge's 'behaviour' seems to have been made up of gestures rather than words. If – as is highly unlikely – he and Fanny ever discussed their feelings for each other, no record remains of it. The wordlessness of the affair was its most torturing aspect for Fanny, endlessly keeping the interpretation of 'G.C.' open to question. There was a neurotic element to this that seeped into her work in a particularly damaging way. Her later novels are clogged with details of physical gestures, as if 'conduct' in its most literal, physical forms was of more interest to her than action, and could provide a satisfactory substitute for plot and character. Camilla can be read as a dictionary of body-language, much of it casual or meaningless, The Wanderer as the ultimate novel of inaction, a book in which the heroine's ideas of propriety induce a wordless, sighing, glancing, blushing stasis.

Despite several attempts to forget all about George Cambridge, Fanny kept meeting him in company, and the wounds of the affair did not heal for years. In the meantime, her siblings were moving on, and with the prospect of marriage and Twickenham Meadows receding, Fanny was in danger of being stranded for ever at St Martin's Street with only her father, stepmother and unsympathetic half-sister Sarah for company. Charles Burney junior had married in 1783. Having failed to get accepted for ordination, he had become a schoolmaster in Chiswick, where he fell in love with the headmaster's daughter, Sarah Rose (known in the family as 'Rosette'). On his father-in-law's death three years later, Charles took over the school, moved it from Chiswick to Hammersmith, and at last began to build up his career as a schoolmaster and classical scholar.

James's career, on the other hand, had been going downhill since his voyages with Cook and his uninspiring stint as Captain of the *Latona*. In 1782 he had been appointed Captain of the *Bristol*, head of a convoy of East India Company supply ships bound for India via the Cape of Good Hope. This was his last commission; James was brought home in June 1785, ostensibly on grounds of ill-health (a 'chronic liver obstruction', according to the log[41]) and was retired on half-pay the same year, aged thirty-five. Dr Burney was still angry about this more than twenty years later, blaming James's liberal politics (and possibly loud mouth) for his inability to rise in the navy: '*Painism* & politics had been his ruin', the Doctor wrote warningly to Charles junior in 1808, 'instead of being an admiral to wch his standing entitled him [. . .] he was upbraided for his political principles – & laid on the shelf for the rest of his life.'[42]

Certainly, James's humanitarianism cannot have endeared him to the authorities during the naval mutinies of the mid-1790s, when he sent a defence of the seamen's position (unsolicited, of course) to the First Lord of the Admiralty. Justice demanded a more equitable distribution of prize money between officers and men, he wrote, more liberty on shore and a closer check on punishments, the misapplication of which 'is too well known to require proof. I served in a ship where every one of the maintopmen were stripped and flogged at the gangway for no other cause than that another ship in company got her topgallant yards up first, and not for any wilful negligence on the part of our men'.[43] This kind of outspokenness must have infuriated cautious Dr Burney, but, as Joyce Hemlow points out in her edition of Fanny Burney's *Journals and Letters*, he probably never knew that James had given the Admiralty far more solid grounds to dismiss him, since he had been guilty of disobeying orders.[44] How is not entirely clear, but the *Bristol*'s movements around the Indian coast seem more erratic than were strictly necessary to avoid the French forces under Suffren which were patrolling the waters around Ceylon. Unlike the soldierly Molesworth Phillips, James Burney was not anxious to get advancement through military glory (he played a very minor part in the action off Cuddalore in June 1783), but kept his eye on the main chance. Fanny artlessly mentions in her 1771 diary the fact that James had taken private '*merchandise*' with him on his first trip to India.[45] Perhaps he was indulging again in a spot of private trading in the 1780s, and perhaps there was more of the would-be wheeler-dealer in 'Admiral Jem' than has survived in the family records.

Whatever his actual insubordination,* James's naval career was over by 1785, and he seems to have known it – the huge travel expenses he claimed for his home journey from Weymouth to London have the look of an act of spite against the Admiralty. As soon as he got back, he retreated to Chesington, which even without Crisp was where he felt most at home. His wedding with Sally Payne took place at Chesington Church in September. Bride and groom were both described in the register as being 'of this parish'; Sally had in fact moved out to Chesington Hall the month before, which is perhaps why neither Dr Burney nor Fanny attended the wedding. James and Sally's first baby, Catherine (known as Kitty) was christened in the same church ten months later; her date of birth is unknown. The couple settled at Chesington Hall for several years, much to the pleasure of the ageing Mrs Hamilton and Kitty Cooke, after whom, presumably, the baby was named.

The week before James returned to England in 1785, another ship

---

* Possibly the fact that he unilaterally changed the rendezvous agreed between the Admiralty and the East India Company.[46] James's protestations of surprise that the Admiralty had been dissatisfied with his management of the convoy ring very false, and his 'clarification' of the events of 1782, in a series of petitioning letters in 1806 and 1807, is anything but clear. Still hopeful of winning back the trust of the Admiralty, he didn't understand how dead the issue was for them. On the back of one of his letters wanting to know why his enquiries are unanswered, one Admiralty official has written: 'This person's Name is not on the List of Officers', with his secretary's response underneath, 'A Superannuated Captain at 12d/a'.[47]

from India had landed, carrying the Governor-General, Warren Hastings, fetched home to stand trial for fraud in what was to become the most famous and long-running legal battle of the period. With Hastings was his personal surgeon and confidant, forty-one-year-old Dr Clement Francis, who nursed an interesting secret ambition. He had read a novel called *Evelina* while he was in India, and admired it so much he had resolved to marry its authoress. He had probably met James Burney at some time in the previous three years; it is hard to see how he could otherwise have gained an introduction to the household in St Martin's Street as quickly as he did. It was not the authoress of the family, however, with whom he forged a rapport, but her younger sister Charlotte. Clement Francis was sixteen or seventeen years her senior, but this didn't seem to put Charlotte off, and his income must have been enough to satisfy Dr Burney because, unlike in Hetty's and Susan's cases, no objections were made to the match. The couple married in February 1786 and settled in Norfolk. Recalling the wedding day, Susan wrote to Charlotte of Fanny's unenviable fate, returning to 'that solitary Newton House!'[48] Without cheerful Charlotte, it would be solitary indeed.

With the new marriages came children: Charles's wife gave birth to their only child, Charles Parr Burney, in 1785, and Charlotte's first baby, a girl with her own name (who grew up to be the first editor of her aunt's diaries), was born, like her cousin Kitty, in 1786. Hetty had five surviving children by this date and Susan two, a daughter called Frances and a son called Norbury.

Susan's little boy was so named because his mother had gone into labour unexpectedly while visiting Norbury Park, the home of her friends and neighbours in Mickleham, the Locke family. William Locke, a direct descendant of the philosopher John Locke, and his beautiful German wife Frederica, were to play an important part in the Burney sisters' lives. Almost as soon as they met in 1784, Mrs Locke, who was two years older than Fanny, five older than Susan, developed an intense sentimental friendship with both sisters which Charles Burney, for one, found rather cloying. Highly-strung to the point of being almost unstable, Mrs Locke caused her husband some anxiety, but Fanny and Susan, both women of feeling, could hardly get enough of 'Fredy's 'soft & insinuating manners',[49] and the three women spent much of the summer of 1784 very happily together in and around Norbury.

The Lockes' house at Norbury Park was brand new and had been decorated in the height of *avant-garde* elegance. Its situation on top of a hill above the Dorking gap gave long views down the Mole Valley in one direction and as far as London the other. It had been built by Thomas Sandby in the mid-1770s, but was only really finished in 1783 with the completion of its famous Painted Room, a drawing room whose walls were decorated with full-scale landscapes in *trompe l'oeuil* fashion to blend with the real landscape (fashionably 'improved') visible through the bay windows. The illusion was meant to be of sitting entirely in the open air. The corners of the room were painted to resemble the trellising of a summer-house or belvedere, the doors concealed in the design and even the carpet chosen in green, to imitate grass. It was an elegant, elaborate fantasy room which provided an ironic twist to great-grandfather Locke's empiricism, his belief that knowledge comes initially only through the senses and that no art is superior to nature. Though Pevsner says of the Painted Room '[i]t would be difficult to find a better example anywhere of the late C18 Englishman's delight in nature',[50] it surely showed a yet stronger delight in artifice and nature tamed.

Fanny thought Norbury Park 'paradise' and the Lockes the ideal family, with their beautiful house, grounds, children, and their intelligent and sensitive conversation. Dr Burney had long admired John Locke as England's foremost metaphysician, an equal to Newton in his personal pantheon, so he had no objection to the friendship, despite some sarcastic references in a letter to Thomas Twining to 'Paradise Regained'.[51] William Locke represented the acceptable face of liberalism, enlightened and mannerly, whose views began to work on Fanny whether she realised it or not at the time. 'The serenity of a life like this smoothes the whole internal surface of the mind', she wrote while staying at Norbury in the autumn of 1784. 'My own, I assure you, begins to feel quite glossy.'[52]

The Lockes' kind hospitality was particularly welcome to Fanny because of an imminent separation from Susan which in fact lasted less than a year, but which at its start threatened to be permanent. Fanny's emotional dependence on her sister was greater than ever during and after the Cambridge affair, as is evident in a plangent letter of 3 October 1783:

I seem dissatisfied with myself, and as if I had not made the most of being with you. Yet I am sure I cannot tell how I could have made more. Were

I but certain of meeting you again in any decent time – but I have a thousand fears that something will interfere and prevent that happiness; and there is nothing like being with you, my Susy – to me, nothing in the world.[53]

Susan's frail health broke down in 1784, and on the doctors' recommendation of a warmer climate the Phillipses decided to move to Boulogne. Fanny had some difficulty understanding the necessity for her going so far: even if Susan got better, there was no guarantee of her return, and if she worsened, it would be difficult for any of the family to reach her quickly. The slowness of the post was a torment, and Fanny became preoccupied by Susan's absence in ways more usually felt for a lover. 'My heart was very full [. . . your] image seemed before me upon the spot where we had so lately been together',[54] she wrote on the first day of the separation, as if she had prematurely seen her sister's ghost.

An important new friendship Fanny made in these years was with Mary Delany, widow of Swift's friend Dr Patrick Delany. Mrs Delany had been born in 1700, married twice, and had gained a reputation in her second widowhood as one of the 'Old Wits' – an indication that to be 'Blue' was not entirely new. She was also an amateur artist, specialising in découpage, embroidery and shell-work, the decorative fad of the period. With her accomplishments, intelligence and refinement Mrs Delany was, according to Edmund Burke, 'a pattern of a *perfect* fine lady, a *real* fine lady, of other days',[55] and she reminded Fanny forcibly of her grandmother, Frances Sleepe. In the person of this benign and cultured woman, Fanny at last re-established a truly maternal figure in her life. When Mrs Delany's bosom friend the Duchess of Portland died in the summer of 1785 and the old lady sank under the weight of her grief, it was Fanny's 'feeling' solicitude that helped her through the bereavement and set the seal on their own friendship. They spent long afternoons together, talking about the past or looking through Mrs Delany's boxes of old letters from Swift and the poet Edward Young. Soon, Fanny was spending so much time at Mrs Delany's house in St James's Place that a bedroom was set up for her there.

Like Fanny, Mrs Delany had been 'bashful to an extreme' in her youth, 'even blameably so', to quote her husband's judgement in 1757.[56] Despite being a superior harpsichordist and dancer, nothing would induce her to display her talents in public. 'She could not bear the attention of others to her', Dr Delany continued, but 'blushed and fluttered herself into a confusion.'[57] Mrs Delany was the personification of eighteenth-century female propriety, described by Burke as 'the highest bred woman in the world, and the woman of fashion of all ages',[58] but there was nothing vapid or anodyne in her character. She had 'bottom' as well as refinement, and her autobiography is full of surprises, from her frank description of her first husband's vices to outbursts such as this against modern men in general:

> Would it were so, that I went ravaging and slaying all odious men, as that would go near to clear the world of that sort of animal [. . .] moneyed men are most of them covetous, disagreeable wretches; fine men, with titles and estates, are coxcombs; those of real merit are seldom to be found.[59]

This from the 'highest bred woman in the world', ultra-conservative friend of the Royal Family, model of propriety, gives us, like Fanny Burney's own vituperativeness on the same subject, pause for thought. It serves to remind us that the bounds of propriety in the eighteenth century were 'wider than historians have been apt to admit', as Amanda Vickery amply demonstrates in her study of the subject.[60] It also indicates that a system which upheld 'separate spheres' for the sexes left many women feeling frustrated by the behaviour of the opposite 'sphere' and powerless to influence it. Novel-writing provided a rare opportunity for women to contribute to the debate in a really active way, albeit the examples of feminine excellence their books posit strike us now as passive and somewhat insipid. 'Prim' is the word we now link with 'proper', but for eighteenth-century women, propriety was a hotly contentious issue. A novelist like Fanny Burney was in the front line of an ongoing battle to defend and extend 'polite' values, a consideration which should cast a slightly different light on her gentility, politeness and even prudery.

Mrs Delany's illness in 1785 following the Duchess of Portland's death had been drawn to the attention of the Queen, whose regard for the old lady was such that she offered her a pension of £300 a year and a grace-and-favour house in St Alban's Street, Windsor, opposite the main gate of the castle. The King himself oversaw the decoration and fitting up of the house, even to laying in a supply of pickles – an amusingly frugal choice, perhaps intended for use on royal visits, since their Majesties were well-known as being plain eaters. As soon as Mrs Delany was settled in Windsor with her teenaged great-niece Mary Ann Port, the Queen became a regular visitor. Fanny was excited to be moving at the edges of such exalted society; through Mrs Delany she had met the late Duchess of Portland, Horace Walpole, Lady Weymouth (the Queen's lady-in-waiting) and a host of other titled people. Now she shared a friend with the Queen.

Fanny was impressed by the marks of royal condescension and the Queen's generosity towards Mrs Delany, however oddly conceived it was at times. When the weaver-bird that was Mrs Delany's only memento of the Duchess died, the Queen sent one of her own birds as a substitute, thinking that Mrs Delany might never notice the difference. Fanny, who had been the person who discovered the bird dead in its cage, had to state outright to the Queen's messenger that there was no point trying to deceive the old lady, however poor her sight, and that the Queen's bird might be accepted as a replacement, but not palmed off as a substitute. The fact that the Queen didn't think anyone could tell the difference between one caged bird and another was, in view of what was about to befall Fanny, somewhat ironic.

During the frequent royal visits to her house in Windsor, Mrs Delany puffed her young friend's talents assiduously, knowing how well *Cecilia* had gone down with the princesses, and she spoke highly of Miss Burney's delicacy and taste, clearly signalling to the Queen that she might grant her an audience. The royal interview seemed about to happen by default when the Queen called unexpectedly on a day when Fanny was also visiting, but the prospect of being introduced was simply too much for the ardent royalist 'Fanny Bull', who fled to her room, 'quite breathless between the race I ran with Miss Port and the joy of escaping'.[61] Two days later, when Miss Port, Mr Dewes (a nephew of Mrs Delany), and his young daughter were all assembled very casually in the drawing room of the house, a 'large man, in deep mourning' walked in without ceremony and shut the door behind him. Fanny was the first to see him, Miss Port the first to recognise him as the King.

The whole party, apart from Mrs Delany and the King himself, became extremely self-conscious, trying so hard to be inconspicuous that they didn't dare move from the positions in which he had surprised them. Fanny's first impression was that they were behaving like people playing a children's 'statue' game, her next, interestingly, that they were as artificially disposed as actors:

> It seemed to me we were acting a play. There is something so little like common and real life, in everybody's standing, while talking, in a room full of chairs, and standing, too, so aloof from each other, that I almost thought myself upon a stage, assisting in the representation of a tragedy, – in which the King played his own part, of the king; Mrs Delany that of a venerable confidante; Mr Dewes, his respectful attendant; Miss P[ort], a suppliant virgin, waiting encouragement to bring forward some petition; Miss Dewes, a young orphan, intended to move the royal compassion; and myself, – a very solemn, sober, and decent mute.[62]

The burlesque tone of this was typical of Fanny's first reports back to her family about meetings with the King and Queen, which became more frequent as the months went by. The informality of their visits to Mrs Delany allowed Fanny an intimate view of the monarch and his wife. The King's simplicity, forthright manner and earnestness implied 'a character the most open and sincere':

> He speaks his opinions without reserve, and seems to trust them intuitively to his hearers, from a belief they will make no ill use of them. His countenance is full of inquiry, to gain information without asking it, probably from believing that to be the nearest road to truth.[63]

Fanny's description of this artlessness, and the King's attentive expression, inviting the spontaneous revelation of 'truths', make him sound childlike in conversation with her. His characteristically quick and disjointed speech reminded her so forcibly of how it was represented in contemporary lampoons that she had trouble keeping a straight face during their first conversation, which was on the subject of *Evelina*:

> [C]oming up close to me, he said,
>   'But what? – what? – how was it?'

'Sir?' – cried I, not well understanding him.

'How came you – how happened it – what? – what?'

'I – I only wrote, sir, for my own amusement, – only in some odd, idle hours.'

'But your publishing – your printing – how was that?'

'That was only, sir, – only because –'

[...] The *What!* was then repeated, with so earnest a look, that, forced to say something, I stammeringly answered –

'I thought – sir – it would look very well in print!'

I do really flatter myself this is the silliest speech I ever made![64]

Fanny's new familiarity with the nation's first family was more a matter of amazement even than pride. Her guide to Court etiquette, written to Hetty in December 1785, was designed to reassure her own family that her head had not been turned:

Directions for coughing, sneezing, or moving, before the King and Queen.

In the first place, you must not cough. If you find a cough tickling in your throat, you must arrest it from making any sound; if you find yourself choking with the forbearance, you must choke – but not cough.

In the second place, you must not sneeze. If you have a vehement cold, you must take no notice of it; if your nose-membranes feel a great irritation, you must hold your breath; if a sneeze still insists upon making its way, you must oppose it, by keeping your teeth grinding together; if the violence of the repulse breaks some blood-vessel, you must break the blood-vessel – but not sneeze.

In the third place, you must not, upon any account, stir either hand or foot. If, by chance, a black pin runs into your head, you must not take it out. [...] If [...] the agony is very great, you may, privately, bite the inside of your cheek, or of your lips, for a little relief; taking care, meanwhile, to do it so cautiously as to make no apparent dent outwardly. And, with that precaution, if you even gnaw a piece out, it will not be minded, only be sure either to swallow it, or commit it to a corner of the inside of your mouth till they are gone – for you must not spit.[65]

In short, all normal life, all natural behaviour is suspended in the royal presence. Critics have made much of the aggression of this letter; in its highly indulgent grotesquerie they see signs of Fanny's inner anger at a life of self-repression. Julia Epstein thinks it displays 'Burney's deep resentment of her powerlessness' in the face of her father's social ambitions for her at Court,[66] though it pre-dates the first signs of those ambitions by half a year. It is important to note that the letter was written before Fanny had any personal knowledge of Court life at all; her information about protocol at this date came solely from Mary Delany. Fanny could indulge this violent satire because she did not in any way feel personally implicated in it.

In the same letter, she had mentioned jokily to Hetty how pleasant it would be to gain 'preferment' if that meant getting 'a handsome pension for nothing at all'.[67] No doubt, the spectacle of Mrs Delany being showered with gifts, money and a house full of pickles had given Fanny a rosy image of royal patronage, but it was an uncharacteristic act on the part of the royal couple, so noteworthy as to be mentioned in the King's obituary.[68] On the whole, the King and Queen liked to get value for money, whether from things, like the hard-wearing, no-nonsense uniform which was *de rigueur* for the men at Windsor, or from people, like Mrs Delany (a cynic might, after all, question the generosity of granting a lifetime annuity to an eighty-five-year-old). Fanny's 'blossom of an idea' of sudden wealth, being released from dependence on her father and stepmother and allowed all the time in the world in which to write or please herself, was an engaging fantasy, but unlikely to be satisfied by 'Mr and Mrs King' – who, it might be remembered, are seated in Gillray's satirical cartoon 'Temperance enjoying a Frugal Meal' below an empty picture-frame bearing the title 'The Triumph of Benevolence'. Far from offering a way out of 'attendance and dependence', Fanny's association with the Royal Family condemned her to even more of both.

Susan and Fredy Locke had seen what was coming, though Fanny dismissed their speculations as absurd. When in May 1786 Charles Burney was called to Windsor by Lemuel Smelt, a former deputy-governor to the royal princes, and told to bring Fanny with him, the Doctor and his daughter both imagined that it was he and not she who was in line for 'preferment'. Aged sixty, Burney was showing no signs of ambition-fatigue. Through the intervention of Burke in the dying days of the Fox–North coalition, he had been appointed organist of Chelsea College, a post offering a very small salary but with the possibility of providing free accommodation in the future within the college – a valuable perk.

The post Burney coveted most, though, was to be Master of the King's Band. He had been passed over before (unfairly, in his view, of course) but when the latest holder of the office, John Stanley, died in 1785, Burney was convinced that the job was his for the asking. He had presented the King with an elaborately bound copy of his account of the 1784 Commemoration of Handel (the monarch's favourite composer) as a reminder of his musical *and* literary worth, and began to make enquiries about the succession as soon as Stanley was dead. Mr Smelt advised him to appear on the Terrace at Windsor – the long walk on which the Royal Family promenaded in public – as a 'hint' to the King, but when the royal party appeared they passed by the Doctor without speaking to him. It was Fanny who was honoured with a conversation, even though she had been trying to hide behind her hat. She was embarrassed by her consciousness of her 'real errand', to promote her father's career: 'The very idea of a design, however far from illaudable, is always distressing and uncomfortable',[69] she wrote, indicating once again how often she acted against her own judgement and instincts to please 'il Padre'. When the King and Queen had spoken to her and moved on, the Doctor hung around for some time, chagrined by the evident failure of his expectations. Fanny hoped that the marks of favour shown to herself might be some-thing 'to build upon', but was distressed by how 'conscious and depressed' her father was. 'There is nothing that I know so very dejecting as solici-tation', she wrote in her journal. 'I am sure I could never, I believe, go through a task of that sort.'[70] Charles Burney had been soliciting all his life, and it *was* degrading. Only his adoring daughter could have seen his constant efforts towards advancement in the light of heroic endurance. Elsewhere, the Doctor was known as 'The Hare with Many Friends', an unflattering reference to John Gay's poem in which the Hare's popularity is of no practical use at all in a crisis ('Her care was never to offend;/ And every creature was her friend'[71]).

A few weeks later the bombshell dropped when Mr Smelt requested a private interview with Fanny on behalf of 'a great personage' – the Queen – 'who had conceived so favourable an opinion of me as to be

desirous of undoubted information, whether or not there was a prob-
ability she might permanently attach me to herself and her family'.[72] In
other words, Fanny was being offered a place at Court, with apartments
in the castle, a salary of £200 a year and a footman. Fanny's face must
have fallen so much at this speech that Smelt immediately made it clear
that it was (just) possible to refuse. He himself was extremely surprised
at her reaction: 'I saw in his own face the utmost astonishment and
disappointment', Fanny wrote to Charlotte Cambridge, desperately asking
advice on how to proceed (and at the same time obliquely communicating
her predicament to George Cambridge). No wonder Mr Smelt was astonished. As people kept reminding Fanny over the coming weeks and
months, places at Court were coveted by 'thousands' of candidates, and
rarely if ever offered to someone of her low rank in life and negligible
birth. Smelt would have expected her to be overcome with pleasure,
self-satisfaction and gratitude rather than dread and repugnance.

Fanny was fully sensible of the honour being done her (or rather her
father, as the appointment was clearly a form of compensation to *him*),
but she saw with lightning clarity that life as a courtier would mean the
end of 'all possibility of happiness'. The word 'permanent' made it sound
like a life sentence; attendance on the Queen was to be 'incessant', and
confinement to the Court 'continual'. For someone like Fanny, 'to whom
friendship is the balm, the comfort, the very support of existence!'[73] it
would be hell on earth, a world away from her 'blossom of an idea' of
getting an obligation-free pension. Smelt's suggestion that he could send
back a respectful excuse to Her Majesty and keep the whole matter
secret, even from her father, would have been jumped at by anyone less
duty-bound and less strictly honourable than Fanny. But the mention of
her father, and Smelt's insinuation that she could further his interests
by accepting the invitation (i.e. she could damage them by refusing),
removed any real power of choice. By the next morning, she was already
speaking in the passive tense of when the affair would 'be decided', and
by the evening, when she received a summons from the Queen at Windsor, the future began to close in on her. 'I now see the end', she wrote
to Miss Cambridge in despairing tones; 'I see it next to inevitable.'[74]

Fanny's appointment as Second Keeper of the Robes was settled with
brutal speed. Within a month of the invitation, she was in residence at
Windsor, at just the time she had been expecting to go to Norbury to

spend the summer with the Lockes and Susan. In her new position, she would be able to invite close friends and family to the castle, but not go out herself, and her panic as the last days of freedom ticked by is evident in a letter to her father: 'I shall want to decamp the very instant I have it in my power', she told him, waiting for the castle business to be settled.[75] Part of the preliminaries involved a visit to her future apartments in the Queen's Lodge and a pep-talk from the retiring robe-keeper, Mrs Haggerdorn, who had come to England in 1761 with Queen Charlotte's entourage from Strelitz. German was still the main language spoken around the Queen; Fanny's superior, Juliana Schwellenberg, only spoke English on sufferance, and then badly.

Mrs Delany was delighted at the 'honourable and delightful employment' offered to her young protégée, 'for such it must be near such a Queen'.[76] Fanny kept very quiet during the general rejoicing: 'Every body so violently congratulates me, that it seems as if *all* was gain', she wrote to Charlotte in June. 'However, I am glad they are all so pleased. My dear father is in raptures; that is my first comfort. Write to wish him joy, my Charlotte, without a hint to him, or any one but Susan, of my confessions of my internal reluctance and fears.'[77] Thus the sisters conspired to bolster their father's feelings one more time. For all her protestations about how kind and dear a father Charles Burney was, Fanny was convinced of two things: that he would neither understand her position nor treat her sympathetically if she acted against him: 'To have declined such a proposal would [. . .] have been thought madness & folly, nor, indeed, should I have been *permitted* to decline it, without exciting a displeasure that must have made me quite unhappy.'[78]

Charles Burney took some of the credit for his daughter's preferment, by which he was profoundly flattered and gratified. The Doctor venerated the monarchy and saw nothing but pleasure ahead in Fanny serving them; he also saw plenty of opportunities for her to solicit favours for himself and his sons. Burney's biographer Roger Lonsdale is right to say that there was no conscious cruelty involved in his eagerness to deprive Fanny of her liberty and peace of mind, but to conclude that 'his excitement rendered him temporarily insensitive to all other considerations'[79] is possibly too forgiving. What was this 'excitement' in truth other than unseemly fervour for recognition and self-promotion? And what was temporary about its manifestations?

In his essay on Madame d'Arblay's life and work, Thomas Macaulay was in no doubt that Dr Burney's 'transported [. . .] delight' on this occasion was a damning indictment of him as a parent, and that he suffered delusions of 'infantine vanities and chimerical hopes':

[Charles Burney] seems to have thought that going to Court was like going to heaven; that to see princes and princesses was a kind of beatific vision; that the exquisite felicity enjoyed by royal persons was not confined to themselves, but was communicated by some mysterious efflux or reflection to all who were suffered to stand at their toilettes, or to bear their trains.[80]

Macaulay declared that the Court section of Madame d'Arblay's diaries enraged him on her behalf. This is probably exactly the response, consciously or not, which Fanny Burney wanted to provoke in a reader of her diaries, whether that reader was herself, Susan, or some unknown person in the future. Her 'loyal' attention to the detail of Court life was, like everything else in that voluminous work, a form of self-justification. Having read the published *Diary and Letters* in the 1840s, Macaulay was withering about the King's boorish literary judgements and the Queen's amazing meanness at sending out a servant to buy books cheaply off second-hand stalls, marvelling 'in how magnificent a manner the greatest lady in the land encouraged literature'.[81] To draw the foremost novelist of the day into this company was, he felt, perverse; the £200 she received a year was no compensation for the loss of income through writing, and Fanny was clearly not the kind of 'woman of fashion' who might have made a *useful* wardrobe attendant: '[T]hough Miss Burney was the only woman of her time who could have described the death of Harrel, thousands might have been found more expert in tying ribbands and filling snuff-boxes', he concluded rationally.[82]

Macaulay's indignation at Fanny Burney's fate was sadly not felt by any contemporary champion. There is plenty of evidence that she still hoped George Cambridge might save her, but his failure to step in with a last-minute proposal of marriage, his failure, in fact, to react at all to the news of her imminent 'banishment', struck her as '*coldness of Heart, innately* unconquerable, & a *selfishness of disposition* which to nothing can give way'.[83] It is perhaps not surprising that at a period when she was suffering so much from her own slavery to duty, she imagined that

Cambridge ought to show a similar selflessness. Her strong language indicates that she knew finally that the 'romance' was over. This knowledge must have added sharpness to a situation that was already extremely painful. When she wrote to Susan that she would now have to give up 'all my most favourite schemes, and every dear expectation my fancy had ever indulged of happiness adapted to its taste',[84] we get a glimpse of how much Fanny Burney had been living on her hopes.

It is significant that the metaphor that her fate suggested was that of a marriage. The preparations were ironically similar, as she wrote to Charlotte from St Martin's Street:

> I am now *fitting out* just as you were, and all the maids and workers suppose I am going to be married, and snigger any time they bring in any of my new attire. I do not care to publish the affair, till it is made known by authority; so I leave them to their conjectures, and I fancy their greatest wonder is, *who* and *where* is the *sposo*; for they must think it odd he should never appear![85]

On the fateful day of leaving home, she went first to Mrs Ord's house where the inferior Burney carriage was swapped for a suitably grander one (with their own coach following as a baggage-van). They set off for Windsor, Mrs Ord and Dr Burney both in very good spirits, Fanny ominously quiet and subdued. As they walked from Mrs Delany's house to the Queen's Lodge fifty yards away, the new courtier was on the verge of prostration:

> I could disguise my trepidation no longer – indeed I never had disguised, I had only forborne proclaiming it. But my dear father now, sweet soul! felt it all, as I held by his arm, without power to say one word, but that if he did not hurry along I should drop by the way. I heard in his kind voice that he was now really alarmed; he would have slackened his pace, or have made me stop to breathe; but I could not; my breath seemed gone, and I could only hasten with all my might, lest my strength should go too.[86]

Charles Burney was worried enough to stay until Fanny had seen the Queen and been shown her apartment by Mrs Schwellenberg. Fanny took pains to assure him that everything had gone well, and let him conclude that her former indisposition had been nerves about the day's formalities. This satisfied her father, who shook off his apprehensions in a trice. '[H]is hopes and gay expectations were all within call', Fanny wrote with devastating perspicuity in her account to Susan, 'and they ran back at the first beckoning.'[87] Dr Burney went back happy and proud to dine with Mrs Delany and Mrs Ord, while Fanny faced her life at Court in a spirit of grim determination:

I am *married*, my dearest Susan – I look upon it in that light – I was averse to forming the union, and I endeavoured to escape it; but my friends interfered – they prevailed – and the knot is tied. What then now remains but to make the best wife in my power? I am bound to it in duty, and I will strain every nerve to succeed.[88]

Retrograde Motion

In her new capacity as Second Keeper of the Robes, Fanny Burney was required to wait on the Queen at least three times a day and assist in dressing her. The day began at six when Fanny rose and prepared for the Queen's first, less formal, dressing; it ended at about midnight when the consort went to bed. The junior robe-keeper's tasks were boringly simple: she had to hold items of dress ready for the Queen, place ribbons, hair ornaments and jewels, put on or take off the Queen's powdering gown so that the hairdresser could come and create a suitably high and mighty 'head'. During this operation, which could take an hour or more, the Queen generally read the newspapers.

The Queen had initially resisted the fashion for powdered hair when she arrived in England in the 1760s, but gradually it had become a staple of Court dress. In England Court dress took pride in being behind the times; only here could you see still the huge side-hoops and heavily-embroidered sacques that Mrs Montagu said made women resemble state beds on castors.[1] While Marie-Antoinette was leading the French Court into a shocking state of *déshabille*, Charlotte of Mecklenburg-Strelitz preferred formality in all things.

The Queen was no beauty and had no interest in personal display. By the time Fanny Burney knew her, 'the bloom of her ugliness', as Horace Walpole wickedly put it, was only just going off. She had some unattractive habits – two of the young ladies-in-waiting at this time used to lampoon the way she wiped her dirty nose across her hand after taking snuff;[2] she was inelegant, even coarse, but at the same time the Queen was a stickler about matters of form and procedure. An awareness of this made the new robe-keeper nervous and clumsy: 'I have even [. . .] and not seldom, handed her her fan before her gown and her gloves before her cap!' Fanny confessed at a later date.[3] Such things were 'of moment' to the Queen.

The first few times that Fanny was summoned to the dressing room, she was given nothing to do at all: Mrs Schwellenberg and Mrs Thielky, the Queen's wardrobe woman, who between them were also responsible for the ordering and maintenance of the Queen's dresses, were perfectly able to manage alone, and whenever by some accident only one of them was in attendance, the Queen simply helped put her own clothes on. Fanny might well have imagined that she would have plenty of time left over to herself at Court, but not only did her undemanding occupation take up, because it broke up, the whole day, but she found in the first months at Windsor that she was very often late or unready when the bell rang, she had so little to do but prepare to wait. When alone, Fanny was so torpid from depression that she wasted 'moment after moment as sadly as unprofitably'.[4] Wasting time was ingrained in Court culture. When a Major Price congratulated her on the success of her first month, Fanny replied, ' "I only do nothing; that's all!" ' to which he answered, ' "But that [. . .] is the difficulty; to do nothing is the hardest thing possible." '[5]

Fanny had a drawing room and bedroom on the ground floor of the Queen's Lodge, the barracks-like building inside the Windsor Castle complex which had been built the previous decade on the site of Queen Anne's former lodge. It had been designed with George III's large family in mind: all the princesses, from the twenty-year-old Princess Royal down to three-year-old Amelia were kept strictly within the Court and unable, through the Royal Marriage Act, to make anything other than dynastic marriages approved by their father. The inevitable result was that although Queen Charlotte produced thirteen healthy children, not one legitimate grandchild survived the King, and after his sons George and William had succeeded, the throne passed across to William's niece, the Duke of Kent's daughter Victoria. King George III was uxorious and a devoted family man, but his large household was not a very happy one: the older princesses apparently 'hated and feared' their mother,[6] and came to resent their restricted lives (only one of them ever married legitimately, though there were clandestine relationships later). The princes, glaringly absent from Court, pursued lives of dissipation as far as they could. The Prince of Wales was the black sheep of the family, with his factitious cultivation of Whig politics and his support from the 'fast' Devonshire House set. Needless to say, Fanny's sympathies were all with his parents.

Fanny's rooms looked out onto the castle's Round Tower and had a window opening into the park. She had a maid and an incompetent servant called John at her disposal, some books (though she had never owned many, on account of her father's library being so good) and at least two hours in the day to herself. She soon learned, though, that there was no such thing as privacy or leisure at Court. Other courtiers came constantly to the door for tiresome *tête à têtes*; some, like Margaret Planta, a Swiss woman who was English Reader to the princesses, were pleasant enough, others less so. Fanny Burney was not what they had expected, and they let her know it. When a Mrs Fielding, of the Bedchamber, came to wish Fanny 'joy' on the second day,

> I saw in her face a strong mark of still remaining astonishment at my appointment. Indeed all the people in office here are so evidently amazed, that one so unthought of amongst them should so unexpectedly fill a place to which they had all privately appropriated some acquaintance, that I see them with difficulty forbear exclaiming 'How odd it is to see you here!'[7]

There were social obligations among the courtiers for which Fanny was unprepared and which she resisted, naively expecting to be able to establish her own patterns of behaviour by the simple expedient of ignoring broad hints, or even direct summonses when they were not directly to do with her job. She was not prepared to admit how much bad feeling this might have caused, nor how it showed up the difference in 'breeding' between herself and most of her colleagues. The equerries with whom she was expected to take tea every evening were recruited almost exclusively from younger sons of the aristocracy and had gentlemanly manners, but nothing much in common with a middle-class musician's daughter. Fanny neither spoke nor ate much in front of them (insinuating she was there on sufferance), and her withdrawn manner was put down to dullness or prudery. The ladies-in-waiting were all aristocratic and kept their distance, and it soon became clear that Fanny was unlikely to find any kindred spirits among her fellow courtiers. At the end of her first half-year she was told with evident congratulation by the princesses' French Reader, Monsieur de Guiffardière, that she had now seen just about everything there was to see of life at Court, and that 'the same round will still be the same, year after year, without intermission or alteration'.[8] This was meant to be reassuring.

The most unfriendly and obstructive of her new colleagues was the one with whom Fanny had to spend most time, Juliana Schwellenberg, the senior female among the German courtiers. 'Schwelly', as one of the equerries disrespectfully called her, had spent her whole adult life in the service of the Queen and had established a very effective power-base at Court. She did not take kindly to 'Miss Bernar', whose lack of interest and pleasure in Court society was a clear criticism of the system. Their antipathy was strong and immediate. After the first month, Fanny was meeting Mrs Schwellenberg's frequent outbursts of bad temper with obdurate silence, and was maliciously lampooning her absurdly rep-etitious speeches in the long journals she was sending once a month to Susan and Fredy Locke: '"Upon my vord!" – "I tell you once!" – "Colonel what-you call, – I am quite warm!" – "Upon my vord! – I tell you the same!" – "You might not tell me such thing!" – "What for you say all that?"'[9] There was, however, little humour to be extracted from the situation. Mrs Schwellenberg, probably sensing that Fanny craved privacy above all else, seemed bent on imposing her company as much as possible. Every evening was spent *à deux* with this ignorant and unpleasant woman, and they were obliged to take most of their meals together. Fanny soon realised that Mrs Schwellenberg expected her 'not to be her colleague, but her dependent deputy! not to be her visitor at my own option, but her companion, her humble companion, at her own command!'[10]

Even Mrs Delany was struck by Mrs Schwellenberg's pointed rudeness towards Fanny, and having endured one evening of it, told Fanny she 'would positively come no more, unless I would exert and assert myself into a little more consequence'.[11] But Fanny knew how futile it was to confront such 'wretched tempers'. The comparison with 'The Lady' was strikingly obvious. 'O Heaven! – how depressing', she wrote despairingly to her sister, 'how cruel to be fastened thus again on an Associate so Exigeante, so tyrannical, & so ill disposed!'[12]

There were occasional releases from the new life; Mrs Delany's house in St Alban's Street was a welcome refuge from the stifling atmosphere of the Lodge, but since, like Charles Burney, Mrs Delany derived little but pleasure from Fanny's appointment, a brave face was required to greet her. Fanny was granted leave by the Queen to visit Chesington one weekend (where memories of Crisp plunged her into melancholy), and received several visits from her father, on one of which they called on the Astronomer Royal William Herschel at his house in Slough, and had the extraordinary experience of being allowed to walk through his partially-constructed forty-foot telescope, the largest at that date ever devised: 'it held me quite upright, and without the least inconvenience; so would it have done had I been dressed in feathers and a bell hoop – such is its circumference',[13] Fanny wrote (interestingly using dress as a form of yardstick). Such diversions were rare however, and tended to disturb Fanny. 'I tried to feel happy', she wrote on parting with Fredy Locke after a visit, 'but I hardly knew how to describe – nor wish to do it – how far I am from all the sweet peace that belongs to happiness, when I see that sweet friend who brings me almost piercingly near what she has not power to make me reach.'[14]

By the turn of the year, Fanny was using a metaphor which, unknown to her, was current among the princesses at Windsor, too, and resolving

to relinquish, without repining, frequent intercourse with those I love; – to settle myself in my monastery, without one idea of ever quitting it; – to study for the approbation of my lady abbess, and make it a principal source of content, as well as spring of action; – and to associate more cheerily with my surrounding nuns and monks.[15]

If she willed herself to do so, she could – surely? – get used to this horrible new life. It might just be a matter of practice, like the ability to walk backwards out of the King's presence, which she watched Lady Charlotte Bertie perform with consummate elegance:

For me, I was also, unluckily, at the upper end of the room [. . .] However, as soon as I perceived what was going forward, – backward, rather, – I glided near the wainscot, (Lady Charlotte, I should mention, made her retreat along the very middle of the room,) and having paced a few steps backwards, stopped short to recover, and, while I seemed examining some other portrait, disentangled my train from the heels of my shoes, and then proceeded a few steps only more; and then, observing the King turn another way, I slipped a yard or two at a time forwards; and hastily looked back, and then was able to go again according to rule, and in this manner, by slow and varying means, I at length made my escape. [. . .]

Since that time, however, I have come on prodigiously, by constant practice, in the power and skill of walking backwards, without tripping up my own heels, feeling my head giddy, or treading my train out of the plaits [. . .] and I have no doubt but that, in the course of a few months, I shall arrive at all possible perfection in the true court retrograde motion.[16]

Fanny's unhappiness at Court was exacerbated by her anxiety about protocol. The many small mistakes she made in her first six months of service loomed as large in her anxious mind as capital offences, and she became abnormally alert and unforgiving about other people's lapses, too. On a royal visit to Oxford in August 1786, she took profound offence at not being formally received by any of the hosts at Nuneham Courtney (who were all, of course, engaged receiving the King and Queen), and cut Lady Harcourt when she finally met her. Wandering disconsolately round the Harcourts' house with Miss Planta, she became mildly hysterical and refused to speak to anyone to whom she had not been introduced by a suitable host. Mrs Thrale's former scorn of 'such dignity!' comes to mind, but now it had taken on a manic edge. The lack of welcome at Nuneham simply rubbed in the fact that Fanny was no longer a guest in such houses, but a servant. Like the bell that called her at Windsor and her first wages, it was a symptom of a 'strange degradation'.[17]

She experienced an even worse panic on the Queen's birthday in January 1787, when a ball was held at St James's Palace. Fanny left the assembly at the appointed time, in order to attend the Queen, but got lost in the palace's labyrinthine courtyards and corridors almost immediately. Blind, lost, unprotected, uninformed and late (again) for the Queen of England, whose jewels she was meant to take charge of, Fanny gave herself over to a sort of hysterical despair. She couldn't find her own chair-men so had to hire a hackney-chair, manned (in her opinion) by two drunkards. When she asked to be taken to St James's Palace (where she already was) the cabbies decided that the lady meant South Audley Street, and set off. Fanny thought she was being abducted and began to scream. She was rescued and helped to the right part of the palace (eventually) by a young clergyman who had been trying to assist her earlier, but whom she had repulsed because he was a stranger. This bizarre incident, written up at great length in the diary, is disturbing to read because so much of Fanny's distress (not to say all of it) seems to have been self-inflicted. She panicked and ran into risk immediately (her account strongly emphasises the likelihood of assault, rape or murder) rather than accept the assistance of a clergyman to whom she had not been properly introduced.

Any reader of *Cecilia* will be struck at once by the parallels between this scene and that in the novel when the heroine runs away from an 'inebriated' coach driver and, lost in London streets at night, has her pockets picked, is locked into an attic by strangers and descends rapidly into madness. The episode in the novel is effective because the reader knows of Delvile's mortal danger and the heroine's incommunicable anxiety on his behalf; the contrast between her secret knowledge and the infuriating unconcern of ordinary observers (or their exploitation of her) is credible and highly dramatic. In Fanny Burney's real-life 'mad scene', however, the only contrast is between her idea of her own sense of extreme vulnerability and the actual dangers faced. The story is all effect and no cause – or at least the cause is irrational. The incident underlines the fragility of Fanny's state of mind just a few months into her long incarceration at Court; it also suggests some of the damage that was being done to her imaginative processes. Both her later novels, but especially *The Wanderer*, show a deteriorating grasp on how to make a crisis plausible in fiction.

Had Fanny not admired the Queen so much she might have found some release for her overwrought feelings in a spirit of rebellion, but the only outlet she allowed herself was in her communications with Susan and Mrs Locke, both of whom were unsympathetic to the Queen. To everyone else she presented a subdued but uncomplaining front. Inwardly, Fanny felt herself dwindling away, both physically and mentally, and at the turn of the New Year in 1787 made the desperate resolution to 'wean myself from myself – to lessen all my affections – to curb all my wishes – to deaden all my sensations'.[18]

She was losing her ability to deal with even simple matters, such as what to do about a letter from the distinguished French novelist, Madame de Genlis. Fanny had been immensely impressed by de Genlis when they met in 1785, but dark rumours about her morals now seemed to make her a dangerous associate. When Fanny tried to ask the Queen's advice (i.e. permission) on whether to answer the letter or not, she was so nervous that her voice failed and she had to retreat behind her mistress's chair, 'that she might not see a distress she might wonder at'. Fanny knew this was strange, even psychotic, behaviour, and that her mind was 'enfeebled [. . .] by a long succession of struggling agitations'.[19] Her Majesty, predictably, told her to have nothing to do with Madame de Genlis.

The challenge to convey to Susan and Fredy her mental sufferings at Court produced some of Fanny Burney's most acute writing – her description of Fredy Locke bringing her 'almost piercingly near what she has not power to make me reach' was one example, another was her novel expression to describe Mrs Schwellenberg's effect on her ego, 'little i am fairly as one annihilated'.[20] Fanny could evoke the symptoms of her 'forcible emotions' powerfully, but didn't want to analyse their cause, and in contrast all her language about the Royal Family is vacuous and sentimental. The word that recurs with nauseating frequency is 'sweetness', but there are quantities of 'charming' and 'gracious' too. It was as if – just as with her father – Fanny's critical faculties were being deliberately suspended in this special instance, and the vacuum filled with hyperbole.

Fanny was one of the few people who genuinely admired Queen Charlotte (another, surprisingly, was Susan's husband Molesworth Phillips[21]): she considered her a model of propriety and was impressed by her lack of airs and graces. This partly explains her readiness to solicit and defer to the Queen's advice on personal relationships (which was severely cautious), manners (cold) and taste in literature (stodgy). Asking the Queen's advice, even on trivial matters, was a fail-safe way to avoid the blame and opprobrium Fanny had begun to fear from the exercise of free will.

Of the various things that gradually impelled Fanny Burney to adopt 'the worst [prose style] that has ever been known among men'[22] for grand or formal performances, the Queen's influence cannot be discounted. During the long years at Court, Fanny's anxieties were focused on pleasing this highly conventional, non-intellectual German woman who didn't like novels. To begin with, the anxiety was about practicalities, movement, manners and procedure, then about morals and later about the moral value of writing. After Fanny had left Court service in 1791, with a pension dependent on the Queen's pleasure, the anxiety persisted. She knew that everything she wrote from then on would have to pass muster with her patroness, whose taste was for 'improving' literature. The first novel that Fanny wrote after leaving the Queen's service was dedicated to the consort, and the nervous convolution of the dedication demonstrates what she had come to feel was required on such occasions, a development of the 'white hand' that Dr Johnson had once found so objectionable:

> MADAM,
>
> That goodness inspires a confidence, which, by divesting respect of terror, excites attachment to Greatness, the presentation of this little Work* to Your Majesty must truly, however humbly, evince; and though a public manifestation of duty and regard from an obscure Individual may betray a proud ambition, it is, I trust, but a venial – I am sure it is a natural one.[23]

The Court did not offer any models of good English. The King himself was bilingual, but few courtiers were. German was the language used intimately and as a blocking device for private conversations (as Fanny experienced often in the Queen's dressing room). There were also factional registers that performed the same function in English: the Prince of Wales's friends had their own form of code to conceal their Whiggishness (not that they were heard much at Court), and no doubt a lot of what the equerries were saying to each other derived from public-school jargon and other exclusive cant. In these conditions, Court rhetoric, traditionally florid and enervated, served as the only common currency. It expressed perfectly the artificiality of Court life: its rhetorical affectations mirrored the repetitiousness, rodomontade and retrogression of courtly behaviour itself. As Fanny recognised in a line of a ballad she wrote at this time for the Lockes' son William – 'Void was the scene, blank, vacant, drear!' – there was a direct connection between her state of mind and the rhetorical style she happened to use. She disliked the line she had written, but implies that she actually *couldn't* change it. It was 'a tautology so expressive of the tautology of my life and feelings'.[24]

Fanny was constantly hearing another sort of bad English, too: the Queen's. Her Court diary respectfully ignores the Queen's foreign accent – a courtesy not extended to 'Schwelly' or any other German-speakers

---

* It is a thousand pages long.

around the Court, whom Fanny satirised freely. Earlier diary entries about her first meetings with the Royal Family at Mrs Delany's in 1785 showed her alert to all the Queen's peculiarities of speech, accent, idiom and cadence. 'Her language is rather peculiar than foreign', Fanny noted then;[25] 'She speaks English almost perfectly well, with great choice and copiousness of language', but 'her emphasis has [a] sort of change-ability'.[26] Few examples remain of Queen Charlotte's speech in this objective phase of Fanny's diary, but they betray an essential lack of elegance; for instance:

'For me, I never have half time enough for things. But what makes me most angry still, is to see people go up to a window and say, "What a bad day! – dear, what shall we do such a day as this?" '[27]

or

'I am always quarrelling with time! It is so short to do something, and so long to do nothing.'[28]

The Court entries smooth over these oddities, endowing Queen Charlotte with perfect grammar and syntax. Here is the Queen's opinion, as reported by Fanny in her more reverential period, of the recently published *Letters to and from the late Samuel Johnson, LL.D*:

[O]nce I said to the Bishop of Carlisle that I thought most of these letters had better have been spared the printing; and once to Mr Langton, at the Drawing-Room, I said, 'Your friend Dr. Johnson, sir, has had many friends busy to publish his books, his memoirs, and his meditations, and his thoughts; but I think he wanted one friend more.' 'What for? ma'am', cried he; 'A friend to suppress them', I answered.[29]

This is an unlikely speech from the woman who another time asked Fanny to check her private diary 'to tell her if it was English'.[30] The Dedication of *Camilla*, and so much of Fanny's subsequent public writing, addresses someone who could appreciate the meaning and moral of a book in English, but on whom purity of diction and delicacy of expression were almost entirely lost.

*   *   *

Fanny had taken up her position at Court in the hope that her real function would be to read to the Queen and discuss literature. Her first request to read, however, was marred by her usual stage-fright at any sort of performance: 'my voice was less obedient than my will, and it became so husky, and so unmanageable, that nothing more unpleasant could be heard'.[31] A month later, in a ill-conceived attempt to bring her father's work to the Queen's notice, she requested from home a copy of *The Present State of Music in Germany*, probably thinking that the passages about Handel, the King's obsession, would go down well. Charles Burney, who had vehemently defended his book in 1773 against those who accused him of anti-German prejudice, thought rather differently about it now it was suggested as reading-matter for the Queen. But the opportunity was too good to miss, and he sent Fanny a copy straight away, with all the 'sensitive' passages about German lack of genius marked in pencil, so she could avoid them when reading aloud.

This plan backfired unpleasantly when the Queen asked to borrow the book for the Princess Royal. 'It is all over with us for ever!' Fanny wrote dramatically, fearing her father's imminent disgrace. She made up an elaborate lie to explain the markings, saying they were proposed revisions which he had sent for her to inspect. Nothing awful came of the incident because evidently none of the Royal Family bothered to read the book – not even the Princess Royal, who thought the marked sections indicated Fanny's favourite passages! – but Fanny's profound unease about soliciting patronage seemed fully justified. Later in her Court career she appealed to the Queen on behalf of both her brothers, and though the petitions were heard with 'some concern & compassion'[32] they were not successful, and laid open to scrutiny James's and Charles's past sins and present failures. The net effect, felt most acutely by Fanny, was not to raise the Burneys up but to expose their shortcomings.

Though Fanny longed to be rescued from her situation at Court, Charles Burney clearly thought of the arrangement as permanent. In 1787 the organist's apartments at Chelsea College became vacant and Dr Burney decided to move his wife and remaining unestablished child, fifteen-year-old Sarah Harriet, out of St Martin's Street at last (although he kept the lease on until 1789.[33]) Sarah was a gawky and unhappy girl who had been brought up, according to Maria Rishton, in 'a perpetual state of Warfare' with her mother.[34] Her brother Richard, reputedly the most handsome and charming of Charles Burney's children, had not stayed long at Winchester School, despite his early patronage by Dr Johnson and Mrs Thrale. Between 1781 and 1783 he and Sarah had been sent to Switzerland to learn some French; little else is known of his adolescent years until the summer of 1787, by which time he had removed to India. Mystery and whiffs of scandal surround the circumstances of this, but as nothing has been left in the Burney archive to elucidate 'beautiful Dick's virtual disappearance from the family, it is impossible to define the nature of 'all his transgressions', cryptically referred to in Susan's journal of 1789.[35]* In July 1787, Charles Burney received 'a letter fm India – which he told us [the Phillipses] he dreaded to unseal'.[39] Dr Burney and his wife were clearly anxious about their son, and almost certainly disappointed in their expectations of him. Dick's marriage to one Jane Ross on her fifteenth birthday in November 1787 (he was an elderly nineteen) cannot have gone down well at home; he was the fourth of Mrs Burney's five children to make a clandestine teenage match.† Dr Burney later revealed that his youngest son was 'one of those who have married natives'.[40] This does not necessarily mean that Jane Ross had any Indian blood; she was a Christian,[41] and likely to have been connected with the Indian Civil Service, which Dick Burney joined when he first reached Calcutta. One of their numerous children was described by Fanny in 1820 as having a 'Complection a little Indian',[42] which could indicate anything from being half-caste to having a suntan. Initially at least, the union was considered by Susan a 'very faulty step, & very probable to be not only his own ruin but that of his poor Companion',[43] but though he died at the early age of forty, Dick's exemplary career as headmaster of the Orphan School at Kidderpore, earnest Christianity (he

* Joyce Hemlow extrapolates from Susan's remark that Dick was 'involved in misdemeanours and difficulties'.[36] Her further suggestion that the dissolute younger brother Lionel Tyrold in *Camilla* is based on Dick Burney is taken up by the editors of the *Early Journal and Letters*, who state as if fact that Dick 'was exiled to India, probably because of libidinous conduct which may have led to resultant victimization by blackmailing and debts'.[37] As the editor of Sarah's letters, Lorna J. Clark, points out, there is no evidence to support this surmise, or the identification of Dick with Lionel Tyrold.[38]
† Presumably Dick witheld the information from home for some time: Susan Burney's reaction to the news in her journal is dated June 1789.

converted to Methodism) and apparently happy marriage seem to have proved her fears wrong.*

Mrs Schwellenberg, who suffered from asthma, stayed in town for several months in 1787, and during her absence Fanny became much better acquainted with the equerries and left lively sketches of their conversation in her diary. These vignettes are the first signs that she was becoming relaxed enough to observe her surroundings in the way that had previously been second nature. A holiday atmosphere broke out whenever 'Schwelly' was absent; there were even fits of laughter and flashes of wit around the tea-table from time to time – nothing to that of Mrs Thrale, Garrick, Johnson or Walpole, of course, but welcome in the chilly 'monastery'. The equerries worked on three-month shifts, so the company was always changing, and in January 1788 one of them, Colonel Stephen Digby, came back into duty after nursing his wife in her fatal illness the previous summer. By a strange coincidence his wife, Lady Lucy Fox-Strangways, had been the very child at Mrs Sheeles's boarding school in Queen's Square who had taken Fanny under her wing in the months following Esther Sleepe Burney's death in 1762. These poignant recollections helped draw Fanny closer to Colonel Digby, who despite his gouty foot, ruined teeth and taste for melancholic literature appealed strongly to her. His sensibilities seemed much finer than other men's, and his sorrows made him interestingly vulnerable. Soon the damaged widower was visiting her as often as he could.

Fanny made a rare public appearance at the first day of the notorious eight-year trial of the former Governor-General of India, Warren Hastings, which began on 13 February 1788 on a specially constructed 'set' in Westminster Hall. Hundreds of peers, politicians and society people flocked to hear the great orators of the day, Burke and Sheridan, fling accusations of fraud and extortion at Hastings from a charge sheet of phenomenal length. As a spectacle the trial was unrivalled; the galleries were crowded with the nation's great and good, including many old

---

* Dick Burney's monument in the Mission Burial Ground, Park Street, Calcutta, says he 'eminently exhibited the characteristics of an enlightened tutor and a spiritual guide'. Whatever his 'transgressions', they seem to have been overcome very early on. By 1790, his mother was gushingly thanking his friends Mr and Mrs Charles Grant for having 'recovered my son',[44] and correspondence between Dick and his parents is mentioned at intervals on the family grapevine.

friends of the Burneys such as Sir Joshua Reynolds and Jeremiah Crutch-ley from Streatham. The Queen was incognito in the Duchess of New-castle's box (it is interesting how few people could recognise members of the Royal Family before the age of photography) and saw Fanny conversing at great length with William Windham, Opposition MP and a member of the prosecution. Fanny's disturbance at talking to this amiable and intelligent man, whom she had met in society before her incarceration at Windsor, was nothing to her distress at seeing Edmund Burke also among the prosecution 'managers', loosing his unrivalled oratorical powers against Hastings. His campaign which led to Hastings's impeachment the previous year had disgusted Fanny, who had met the former Governor-General at her brother-in-law Clement Francis's house in Aylsham and was his ardent supporter. Fanny's naivety is evident again here, both in her conviction that Hastings was innocent because 'he looked with a species of indignant contempt towards his accusers, that could not, I think, have been worn had his defence been doubtful'[45] and in her puzzlement at Burke's apparent perversion of his genius. 'Mr Burke has no greater admirer!' she said to Windham, thinking no doubt of her extreme gratification at his former admiration of *her*, 'that is what disturbs me most in this business!' Windham's reply was another 'home' stroke: 'I am then really sorry for you! – to be pulled two ways is of all things the most painful.'[46]

When Mrs Delany died that spring, in her eighty-eighth year, Fanny's only pleasure in life at Court died too; years of obscurity and unhappiness stretched ahead. And life at Court took a darkly dramatic turn later that year when the King fell seriously ill. A long visit to Cheltenham in the summer, to take the waters, had done nothing to cure his sporadic 'bilious attacks', nor his hyperactive 'flow of spirits', as Fanny described it.[47] After a particularly bad 'bilious attack' in October, the King called in his chief physician, Sir George Baker, who attributed the illness to the fact that the King had worn damp stockings and eaten four large pears. Despite this comfortably trivial diagnosis, the symptoms did not subside and the royal party's routine return to Windsor from Kew after their weekly audience at St James's was delayed by several days. When Fanny met the King at the end of the week, she was alarmed at the change in him:

I had a sort of conference with his Majesty, or rather, I was the object to whom he spoke, with a manner so uncommon, that a high fever alone could account for it; a rapidity, a hoarseness of voice, a volubility, an earnestness – a vehemence, rather – it startled me inexpressibly[.][48]

The King himself knew that something was amiss; he was mildly delirious, couldn't walk properly, sleep or speak, and said to one of the ladies-in-waiting, Lady Effingham, with a frankness and familiarity that was also one of his symptoms, 'My dear Effy [. . .] you see me, all at once, an old man.'[49] Fanny feared that he was on the verge of 'a great fever', others that his whole constitution was breaking down, though none of this was discussed openly. 'Nobody speaks of his illness, nor what they think of it', Fanny wrote in her diary.[50] The word 'mad' was not mentioned at all.

Sir George Baker kept taking the King's pulse and occasionally examined his urine, but in truth had no idea what the matter was. 'Unformed gout', was one theory, and the wet stockings remained another. It wasn't until the 1960s that the likely cause, porphyria (a genetically passed-on condition), was investigated by Ida Macalpine and Robert Hunter in their book *George III and the Mad-Business*. In the crisis of 1788–9, the Court doctors simply sat tight, treated the symptoms as best they could and hoped the King's illness would pass before a definite diagnosis became necessary.

An article in the *Morning Herald* on 5 November however revealed to an anxious nation the fact that the King had been delirious during his 'indisposition'. This was a dangerous leak, reckoned 'treasonable' by the Queen, who was terrified by recent developments and their implications for the future. The same day, the Prince of Wales appeared at Windsor ready to assess the situation for himself, but his presence agitated the King to such an extent that at dinner he broke 'into positive delirium',[51] attacked the Prince and sent the Queen into violent hysterics. After this, the doctors persuaded the King to be separated from his wife at night (clearly she was frightened of him by this time), but he kept bursting in unexpectedly, sometimes raving, abusive and foaming at the mouth. A more drastic removal followed, with the Queen and princesses sealed away in a distant set of rooms. 'I am nervous', the King said meekly after this dramatic episode; 'I am not ill, but I am nervous: if you would know what the matter is with me, I am nervous'.[52]

The new arrangements at Windsor, overseen by the Prince of Wales, changed the whole tenor of Court life. The equerries were on call most of the time outside the King's room, but the Queen's women had less to do and Fanny found herself often alone. The usual routine ceased, and with it the usual flow of news and gossip; no one went out of the castle, everyone seemed isolated in their quarters, waiting to see how the situation would develop. '[A] stillness the most uncommon reigned over the whole house', Fanny wrote to her sister. 'Nobody stirred; not a voice was heard; not a step, not a motion. I could do nothing but watch, without knowing for what: there seemed a strangeness in the house most extraordinary.'[53]

In the first week of the King's illness, Fanny had begun writing again 'in mere desperation for employment'.[54] It was a tragic drama, eventually titled *Edwy and Elgiva*, based on the story of the short-lived Anglo-Saxon King Edwy as told by Hume in his *History of England*. She did not, however, stick at the play with enthusiasm; at this stage it was more of a vent for her overwrought feelings than an intentional work of art. She saw Colonel Digby rather more often than before, because he took advantage of the disruption to the usual routine to invite himself to tea or dinner without notice, slipping away if Mrs Schwellenberg appeared. Fanny seemed to have forgotten all her earlier scruples about being unchaperoned in a room with a man, but she deluded herself if she thought no one noticed or minded. Their friendship even made its way into the King's unstoppable flow of speech: '[Mr Digby] is as bad as any of them,' he had said on 20 November, 'for he's so fond of the company of learned ladies, that he gets to the tea-table with Miss Burney, and there he stays and spends his whole time.'[55]

All the equerries had been called into service during the crisis at Windsor, but the royal household was soon to be drastically reduced. Windsor was felt by the politicians and doctors alike (some of whom were now receiving death threats from the public) to be too exposed a residence; Kew, with its large private gardens and seclusion, would be a better hideaway for a noisy, delirious monarch. The Court moved at the end of November, packing up hastily, 'as if preparing [...] for banishment'[56] and cramming into the smaller palace very uncomfortably. Nothing was ready, everywhere was cold, and the usual disposal of apartments had been changed by the Prince of Wales (who rode over in advance and chalked names on the doors) to accommodate a suite of sick-rooms on the ground floor for the King and an empty set of rooms above him (ostensibly to ease the King's rest, but much more likely to ease everyone else's). Fanny's new room was at the end of a servants' passageway, up a winding staircase with a makeshift coal-hole at its foot. The great advantage was its distance from Mrs Schwellenberg, who was being exceptionally difficult. Colonel Digby liked its isolation, too, and took the liberty of using the room as a study-cum-bolthole, sitting reading Mark Akenside's poetry to Fanny while she got on with her endless needlework, like an old married couple.

The sentimental bond she found with Digby helped Fanny through the terrible winter at Kew. One of her jobs was to take the Queen a report from the doctors first thing every morning; this often entailed a long wait in a cold, wet passageway (Mrs Schwellenberg having refused to let her sit in the parlour) and then having to break bad or indifferent news to her mistress. The King's relapses during November and December made everyone fear that his illness would be too prolonged to enable him to keep the throne. The Prime Minister, Pitt, and the Chancellor, Thurlow, had been shocked by the King's deterioration when they attended the Privy Council that signed permission for the Court's removal to Kew. To prevent the Opposition gaining power through their patron, the Prince of Wales, the Government had to stall for time and keep reports about the King's health as non-commitally optimistic as possible. Pitt was now prepared to concede the need for a Regency, as long as he could restrict it, keeping his party in government. Everything hung on the bulletins from the sick-room, where the desperate struggles of the Regency crisis were seen in microcosm, with the only 'Opposition' doctor, Robert Warren, gloomily prognosticating no hope of a recovery and Francis Willis, the Queen's favourite, saying quite the opposite.

Dr Willis, a well-known 'mad-doctor' from Lincoln, had been called in as a last resort in December and was soon imposing a draconian regime on 'the loved Royal sufferer',[57] as Fanny referred to the King. Emetics and febrifuges, blisters and bark were applied liberally, and increasingly the King was 'put under coercion'[58] in a strait-waistcoat or on the sinister 'Restraining Chair' which had been built for him. The Willises – father and two sons – took over the care of the monarch exclusively; none of the pages or equerries was allowed access without permission, and their own asylum attendants were brought in to help 'coerce' the violent, sleepless and abusively ranting King. No wonder Fanny experienced the 'severest personal terror' of her life[59] when she accidentally came across the King and his warders in the grounds of Kew Palace one morning in early February. To see him was not only forbidden, it was dangerous, and she set off at speed, looking for somewhere to lose herself among the garden's 'little labyrinths'. To her horror, though, the King had spotted her and she could hear him in pursuit, calling out her name 'loudly and hoarsely'. But Fanny was too terrified to stop, even when she heard Willis's voice begging her to:

> 'I cannot! I cannot!' I answered, still flying on, when he called out 'You must, ma'am; it hurts the King to run.'
>
> Then, indeed, I stopped – in a state of fear really amounting to agony. I turned round, I saw the two Doctors had got the King between them, and the three attendants of Dr Willis's were hovering about. They all slackened their pace, as they saw me stand still; but such was the excess of my alarm, that I was wholly insensible to the effects of a race which, at any other time, would have required an hour's recruit.[60]

Fanny felt later that forcing herself to walk towards the King that day was 'the greatest effort of personal courage I have ever made'. To her relief, he looked benign instead of angry, 'though [with] something still of wildness in his eyes'; he spread out his arms to embrace her (she imagined she was about to be attacked) and kissed her cheek, a most extraordinary gesture. The doctors 'simply smiled and looked pleased',[61] and the King entered into a rambling conversation with Fanny, during which he sang bits of Handel in a croaking voice and became tearful remembering Mrs Delany. 'I have lived so long out of the world, I know nothing!' he said, plying Fanny with questions about his friends and staff until the doctors and attendants gently persuaded him to come away. She was moved by the evidence of improvement, and having first reported 'almost all' of this strange encounter to the Queen (omitting the kisses, presumably), spread it quickly around the Court, much to the delight of the Willises. Though the Regency Bill was in print the following week, it was put off, and before the month was out His Majesty was slowly getting back to normal. By 10 March, only five weeks after Fanny's chase with 'Mad King George' around Kew gardens, the first medallions had been struck, celebrating his full recovery. For the time being, the Regency debate was over.

A royal progress around the West Country was organised for the summer of 1789, part convalescence and part triumphal parade, which Fanny was elected to join. Colonel Digby was also of the party, which set off towards Weymouth via the New Forest in late June. All along the route, people came out to watch the procession and vehicles were parked by the roadside, 'chariots, chaises, landaus, carts, waggons, whiskies, gigs, phaëtons – mixed and intermixed, filled within and surrounded without by faces all glee and delight'.

> At Winchester the town was *one head*. I saw Dr Warton, but could not stop the carriage. The King was everywhere received with acclamation. His popularity is greater than ever. Compassion for his late sufferings seems to have endeared him now to all conditions of men.[62]

Buglers dressed quaintly in forest-green greeted the royal party as it entered the New Forest, and 'God Save the King!' was heard everywhere. At Weymouth, which had given itself over to a protracted holiday, the words appeared on patriotic caps and bandeaus, 'all the bargemen wore it in cockades; and even the bathing-women had it in large coarse girdles round their waists. It is printed on most of the bathing-machines, and in various scrolls and devices it adorns every shop and almost every house in the two towns'.[63] There was no getting away from the loyal prayer: even when the King bathed in the sea, there was a group of musicians hidden in an adjacent bathing machine to strike up the anthem as soon as his convalescent royal flesh hit the water.

It wasn't until they had been in Weymouth for several weeks that Fanny, and most of the King's party, had any idea of what was taking place in France during this momentous month. Miss Planta's brother-in-law joined them on 26 July with news of 'confusion, commotion and impending revolution';[64] slowly they began to read and hear of the fall of the Bastille and the arrest of King Louis XVI. 'Truly terrible and tremendous are revolutions such as these', Fanny wrote to her father later that year:

There is nothing in old history that I shall any longer think fabulous; the destruction of the most ancient empires on record has nothing more wonderful, nor of more sounding improbability, than the demolition of this great nation, which rises up all against itself for its own ruin – perhaps annihilation. Even the Amazons were but the *poissardes* of the day; I no longer doubt their existence or their prowess; and name but some leader amongst the destroyers of the Bastile, and what is said of Hercules or Theseus we need no longer discredit. I only suppose those two heroes were the many-headed mob of ancient days.[65]

By contrast the crowds that surged round the royal party as it progressed from Weymouth to Exeter were strikingly loyal, affectionate and indulgent (the theatre audience at Weymouth sat patiently waiting for the King and Queen until eleven o'clock one evening before a performance by Mrs Siddons could begin); their 'honest and rapturous effusions' caused Fanny to cry 'twenty times in the day'.[66] George III hadn't been so popular in years.

Colonel Digby, whose family seat, Sherborne Castle, was included in the royal tour, was present much of the time, though less attentive to Fanny than before. '[H]is dauntless incaution had now given way to fearful circumspection',[67] she noted, though she found it impossible to credit Court rumours that the Colonel intended to marry one of the maids of honour, the young, lovely and rich Charlotte Gunning. Fanny felt that her intimate friendship with Digby was too sincere ever to be broken, whoever the object of his romantic affections might be. She was realistic enough to see that Digby's 'high family' and his first wife's 'still higher connections' made her an unlikely candidate for second wife, but couldn't anticipate being dropped entirely: '[I am] firmly impressed with a belief that I shall find in him a true, an honourable, and even an affectionate friend, for life',[68] she had written in August 1788.

As with George Cambridge, she was wrong. Digby proposed to Miss Gunning during the West Country tour and they were married in January 1790. Digby, in the time-honoured way of the male in such circumstances, avoided Fanny like the plague thereafter, though he expected her to socialise with his wife. It was a bitter disappointment and another public humiliation for the Second Keeper of the Robes, now in her thirty-ninth year, who tried to put a brave face on the matter, but was writing privately to Susan in terms redolent of her anger at George Cambridge: 'He has committed a breach of all moral ties, with every semblance of every virtue!' [...] 'never has any Mask more completely done its office of Duping!'[69]

Life at Court after this second jilting became insupportable to Fanny, and she began to discuss with Susan the means by which she could resign her post on grounds of ill-health, plans she referred to as her 'Visions'. She bravely broached the subject with her father when they met at the annual Handel Commemoration in May 1790, letting him know for the first time how miserable she had been in the Queen's service. His remorseful response bound her to him more than ever before: ' "I have long," ' he cried, ' "been uneasy, though I have not spoken; ... but ... if you wish to resign – my house, my purse, my arms, shall be open to receive you back!" '[70]

Having thus acquired, in her quaint but revealing phrase, 'permission to rebel', Fanny began to think that the end of her ordeal was in sight and dutifully exerted herself to make some last attempts at soliciting favours for her family through the Queen. James, who thought he could have command of a frigate simply for the asking, perhaps impressed Lord Chatham more with his hubris than his suitability; by the end of 1790 the war was over, and James never worked again. Charles's case was more sensitive, but no more successful; he failed to win the head-mastership of Charterhouse and was refused the mandate degree he needed to take Holy Orders. His father's response to this humiliation makes a significant connection between writing and freedom from patronage: 'You, my dear lad, have still one revenge in store, wch is to produce some literary work, wch with diligence & good conduct shall make your enemies ashamed'.[71] The only fail-safe way to advance in life and wreak 'revenge' on those who kept you down was to create something entirely on your own.

Fanny prepared a statement about her wish to leave Court for the Queen, but lacked the nerve to hand it in. It seemed that the only people *not* to have noticed her condition were the Queen and Mrs Schwellenberg; elsewhere 'there seemed about my little person a universal commotion'.[72] The Warren Hastings trial, which she attended at least seven times that year, brought her into contact with a number of her friends, who were appalled at how haggard she was looking, and the effects of her 'seclusion from the world' had even attracted the attention of the press, who 'dealt round comments and lamentations profusely'.[73] Fanny was fading dramatically, displaying psychosomatically-enhanced symptoms of a cough, breathlessness, fever and weight-loss that were redolent of both consumption and a wasting disease, such as anorexia nervosa. Like Mrs Thrale with her desperate formula, 'Death or Piozzi!', Fanny had set up a dangerous bargain with herself: 'resignation of place or of life was the only remaining alternative'.[74]

Mrs Thrale herself (now Mrs Piozzi) was back in England and enjoying the success of her new career as an author (she had published four books between 1785 and 1789, including her *Anecdotes of the late Samuel Johnson LL.D*, which led the field in Johnsoniana). She heard the rumours about Fanny's sufferings, but was unconvinced by them: '*my* Notion always was that her Majesty confided in, & loved the little cunning Creature as I did: while *She*, to cover her real Consequence at Court, pretended disgust & weariness among her friends.'[75] Mrs Piozzi was clearly much more embittered towards her than Fanny could have guessed: when they met by accident, at Norbury Park in the late 1780s and at St George's Chapel, Windsor in 1790, the older woman was polite but distant. (The latter was the occasion when the Queen made Fanny cringe by asking, 'Who was that *painted foreigner*?') Mrs Piozzi could be as powerful an enemy as she had once been a friend, and her view of Fanny's attachment to the Queen was distinctly uncharitable: 'no one possesses more powers of pleasing than She does, no one *can* be more self-interested, & of course more willing to employ those Powers for her own, and her Family's Benefit'.[76]

It took Fanny seven months to propose her resignation to the Queen, but the Queen was unconvinced of any necessity and simply let the matter rest. Fanny relapsed despairingly, taking hartshorn, opium and Dr Willis's (unspecified) 'violent' medicines to relieve her debilitating symptoms: 'so weak and faint I was become, that I was compelled to put my head out into the air, at all hours and in all weathers, from time to time, to recover the power of breathing, which seemed not seldom almost withdrawn.'[77]

It was during this dreadful year that Fanny returned to the composition of her tragedy *Edwy and Elgiva*, finding dismal solace in the plight of her murdered heroine. She did not harbour any ambitions for this 'almost spontaneous' work[78] – in fact she wasn't sure it was a 'work' at all – but she finished a first draft in August and went straight on to start another play in the same vein. By June 1791 she had three tragedies half-written and a fourth begun: 'I could go on with nothing; I could only suggest and invent', she wrote in her journal, indicating how restless and obsessive this spurt of composition actually was:

> The power of composition has to me indeed proved a solace, a blessing! When incapable of all else, that, unsolicited, unthought of, has presented itself to my solitary leisure, and beguiled me of myself.[79]

Fanny Burney's 'Court plays', which were not published until 1995, have little claim to literary or dramatic merit but have attracted critical attention on account of their vivid symbolism and the clues they offer to their author's subconscious feelings. There is no evidence that at the time of writing Fanny intended them to be staged or printed; in their early drafts they could perhaps be better described as effusions than dramas, disparate fragments of blank verse that the author had organised into a familiar form. Like Crisp's *Virginia*, these are plays that favour speech over action. The climax of *Edwy and Elgiva*, for example, is reported rather than seen on stage: ''Twas horrible! – the cries of Elgiva,/ Torn from her home and husband, rent the Heavens', Sigebert says of the heroine's abduction. 'Who could have viewed unpitying her despair?'[80] Certainly not the audience, from whom it is hidden. In the same play, there are no fewer than twenty-three scenes in the fifth act, all taking place in the same unspecified 'forest'. Indeed, in the composition of these plays, Fanny seems to have forgotten everything she ever knew about dramatic structure and the writing of blank verse – consistently bad in each – and to have given herself over to her 'fits' of composition as she might to a drug. She made the analogy of possession clear in a diary entry for May 1791 that speaks of the works themselves as having the power of composition, as if she experienced them as incubi rather than as inspirations: '[they] seize me capriciously; but I never reprove them; I give the play into their own direction, & am sufficiently thankful, in this wearing waste of existence, for being so seized at all'.[81]

The tragic dramas are all set in the distant past and share very similar themes: civil strife, the constraint of women, filial duty and sacrificial marriage. *Edwy and Elgiva* and *The Siege of Pevensey* made use of historical subjects adapted from Hume's *History of England*, the former tapping into the late-eighteenth-century nationalist vogue for the Anglo-Saxon period. *Hubert de Vere* ('a pastoral tragedy') and the fragmentary *Elberta* were Gothic romances which the author may have wished to dignify by setting in the thirteenth and eleventh centuries respectively. Each play features a heroine who quickly falls victim to the political and sexual power-struggles of the men around her, and each contains a malign authoritarian as *agent provocateur* and a weak or prevaricating 'protector' figure whose shortcomings expose the heroine to danger and, in all but the case of Adela in *The Siege of Pevensey*, death. The repeated themes of constraint, monasticism and forced marriage are fairly obviously metaphors for Court life and the impositions it laid on Fanny's personal and creative liberty. Her passively suffering heroines face the same choice between death or submission that she had come to see as the stark reality of her own situation.

Margaret Anne Doody, in her exhaustive psychological interpretation of the tragedies,[82] has found in them evidence of violent resentments towards George Cambridge, Stephen Digby and, most of all, Charles Burney, the 'protector' who had failed to protect or rescue, whose alterego de Mowbray in *Hubert de Vere* is his own daughter's murderer. The question of 'protection' is an interesting one, since the dutifully self-sacrificial daughters in these plays all end up, in a reversal of natural law, protecting their fathers' feelings, honour or lives (again, this is reminiscent of Crisp's *Virginia*, the manuscript of which Fanny had inherited). In *The Siege of Pevensey*, Adela's father is so sensitive to the violence a forced marriage between her and de Warenne would entail that she volunteers to enter a convent to save him from the temptation to commit suicide. Far from asking 'permission to rebel', the women in these tragedies accept their fate – which is to be badly protected, or not protected at all, by someone less capable or less responsible than themselves.

The language of the plays encourages psychoanalytical interpretations; at times it resembles confessional, or even 'automatic' writing. Here is Dunstan in *Edwy and Elgiva* in the scene following the plot's (invisible) climax:

I feel petrified! – My King! – rash Youth,
Why would he thus provoke – What are these men?
They shrink – they know – or fear me – Hah! a Corpse
Perhaps 'tis Elgiva – yes 'tis ev'n so!
Her lifeless frame – that deed is surely done.[83]

And here Elgiva, in the draft of a sub-Shakespearean lament over her forced divorce from Edwy:

The Song of Joy let Treach'ry Sing
Vice is now to Mirth inclin'd,
Bring me Myrtle, Lawrels bring,
Bind their Brows, their Tresses bind.
Hark I hear of Death the knell; –
Hist! of Ghosts I hear the Yell
Murmuring in the Swelling Wind.[84]

The state of distraction which the author may be trying to convey in these characters' speeches is out of her control; *she* is too distracted herself to write it. Doody thinks that the plays reveal 'a truly suicidal streak' in their author, immured in a Court that had come to resemble an asylum for the insane, and speculates that Burney may have really feared going mad herself. There is certainly an air of desperation about these pieces, an artistic letting-go, as if Fanny was daring herself to see what would happen. Her distressed and dying heroines are abandoned in a variety of graveyards, dense forests or wildernesses, physically or mentally wounded, waiting for 'the doom of death' with 'swelling bosoms' panting for 'some finer, lighter, purer region'.[85] They are also, more completely, 'abandoned' in their inflated language and nightmare visions. Fanny seems to have anticipated the worst excesses of the coming vogues for 'Gothic' and Romanticism.

Her misgivings about her tragedies were obvious from the start. 'Believe me, my dear friends,' she wrote to Susan and Mrs Locke only months after leaving Court, 'in the present composed & happy state of my mind, I could never have suggested these Tales of Woe; – but having only to connect, combine, contract, & finish, I will not leave them undone.'[86] It was perhaps an unfortunate instinct. Though her tragedies were never going to be viable commercially (unlike her comedies), Fanny seems to have valued them because they were written *in extremis*. In her later novels she adopted much the same style for the episodes of high drama, and it worked no better there, but it is clear that 'spontaneous' writing, uncontrolled and empty though it was, struck her as somehow truthful to strong feeling.

The Court plays may have performed a valuable function by letting Fanny dwell on the fantasy of suicidal sacrificial death without actually having to go through with it. Even in her worst period of physical debilitation, she displayed a strong instinct for self-preservation and surprising will-power. When the Queen offered her a holiday instead of retirement, she refused, incurring temporary displeasure of the sort she wouldn't have dared weather before. Elsewhere, opinion was moving strongly in sympathy with the ailing Second Keeper. The subject had become prime gossip among the London intelligentsia, and was flamboyantly indulged by James Boswell when he turned up at Windsor one Sunday in October 1790 to beg for a look at Fanny's correspondence from Dr Johnson for his forthcoming biography (which she refused). William Windham, who was marshalling members of The Club to petition Dr Burney on the subject, said that Fanny's release from Court had become 'the common cause of every one interested in the concerns of genius & literature',[87] a recognition of how highly regarded Miss Burney's achievements really were in the outside world.

Of course, the agitations of Oppositionists like Windham were dangerously open to misinterpretation, but fortunately there was not time for the matter to become overtly political; Fanny's resignation was gradually accepted by the Queen, and after many delays and setbacks she was released from duty on 7 July 1791, almost five years to the day since she had entered the castle with such fear and trembling. 'My Heart was a little sad, in spite of its full contentment', Fanny wrote to Susan when she arrived at Chelsea College, but she soon began to revive.

Her father had set up a desk for her in his study (now called the Grubbery), which he was prepared, for the first time ever, to share. With his great task of the *History of Music* completed (the third and fourth volumes came out together in 1789), some of the urgency had gone out of the Doctor's work habits and he was happy to have a companion with whom to read, work and compare progress. There was no talk of Fanny becoming his amanuensis again – Sarah had inherited that function for a time, and the Doctor had paid help too when he needed it. But the apartment at Chelsea College was not very large, and a certain claustrophobia must have struck them all at the start of the new arrangement. Fanny and her half-sister Sarah – aged thirty-nine and nineteen respectively – had nothing in common except a desire for solitude in which to read and write; now they had to share a bedroom. What Mrs Burney thought of the unexpected readmission of her stepdaughter into her household is not recorded.

✤ 10 ✤

Taking Sides

When Fanny Burney left Court in the summer of 1791 with a pension of £100 a year, she was a mature and independent woman emerging, as it were for the first time, into a changed and changing society. In this year of the first publication of *The Rights of Man*, between the fall of the Bastille and the onset of the Terror, there was much more widespread tolerance of radical ideas among the English intelligentsia than Fanny could have imagined from within the walls of Windsor Castle. Some of the Burneys' acquaintances had become out-and-out republicans, among them the poet William Mason, Mary Gwynn* and the scholar Catherine Macaulay. James Burney had shocked his father with his 'Painism', Charles Burney junior had become a close friend of William Windham and the Whig Lord Spencer, and now Susan seemed to be following their lead, and that of William and Fredy Locke, with an ardour for democracy that posed a great challenge to her conservative sister. Fanny had jokingly referred to 'you Republicans of Norbury & Mickleham!'[1] in a letter to Susan written while she was touring the West Country with Mrs Ord in August 1791, but Susan did not take the remark lightly, and it provoked a series of exchanges which show the sisters for the first time in profound disagreement. 'France is doubtless at present in a state of confusion & anarchy wch is grievous', Susan wrote, in uncharacteristically sombre vein:

> – *à tel pris* I cd not have wished for any revolution – but since it has been effected, I wish its support & success from a persuasion that whatever disturbance or distress it May have occasioned a few living Individuals . . .

* Footnote: Goldsmith's 'Jessamy Bride', formerly Miss Horneck and wife to one of the equerries at Court.

Millions yet unborn, & Millions who still exist will be lastingly benefited – that abuses very intolerable & very shocking to humanity will no longer be tolerated – that the great Mass of the French nation (wch does not consist in Dukes & Counts) will be relieved from oppressions cruel towards the sufferers & disgraceful to the great Aristocrates by whom they have been inflicted.[2]

These surprisingly teleological sentiments were triggered by Fanny's account of a group of French aristocrat refugees she and Mrs Ord had met at an inn in Winchester. The plight of the 'Poor Wanderers' horrified Fanny: 'is THIS LIBERTY! – where one side alone predominates thus fiercely? [. . .] alas – in France, it seems to *me* but a change of despotism'.[3] 'What Tyranny', Susan answered, 'does there appear in the new Code of Laws? – What Tyranny has the National Assembly sanctioned?' though she had to concede misgivings over the new assembly, 'wch seems to me to consist of a very VERY inferiour set of Men, who by their republican & insolent spirit will I fear endanger the new Constitution more than all the efforts of the aristocratic body'.[4] It was disturbing for Fanny to hear these set and earnest opinions from the 'sister of her soul'. As a believer in absolutes, she could not account for 'wrong' ideas taking root in 'bosoms so pure as my Susan's & Mr & Mrs Lock's': 'My Mind revolts at differing essentially from the THREE MINDS I *most revere*'.[5]

The Revolution in France was 'the only topic which those who had either hearts or heads could, at that time, discuss',[6] its increasing militancy observed and debated in obsessive detail by the English intellectual class. Fanny records long conversations on the subject with Windham and with Edmund Burke, the publication of whose *Reflections on the Revolution in France* the previous year had led to a renewal of their acquaintance. 'Kings are necessary,' he told her, in his pragmatic new spirit of reaction, '& if we would preserve peace & prosperity, we must preserve THEM.'[7] The likelihood of the Bourbons adapting to constitutional monarchy was not great, however: when Louis XVI was forced to swear his continuing allegiance to the Constitution or don a red 'liberty' cap to please the crowd, it was as a gesture of humiliation, not a foretaste of reform.

When she was visiting Arthur Young and his wife in Suffolk in the autumn of 1792 Fanny met a distinguished refugee from France, the Duc de Liancourt, who impressed her with the story of his dramatic escape from France in an open boat. There had been a price on the Duc's head since his attempt to rouse his regiment in support of Louis XVI following the massacre of royal guards and attendants in the Tuileries on 10 August 1792. At almost exactly the same time, another group of Constitutionalist refugees intimately bound up with the events of 10 August were arriving in Susan Phillips's neighbourhood in Surrey: the Princesse d'Hénin and her lover the Comte de Lally-Tolendal took a house in Richmond, the Princesse de Broglie was staying in West Humble and a group including Madame de Châtre, Matthieu de Montmorency and the charismatic ex-Minister of War Louis de Narbonne (purportedly a natural son of Louis XV) had rented Juniper Hall, a large house in a damp valley at the foot of Box Hill, about three quarters of a mile out of Mickleham village.

Juniper Hall was a former coaching inn that had been extended and redesigned in the 1770s. It now had two new wings, a landscaped garden and an elegant drawing room in the Adam style designed by the amateur artist Lady Templetown, a friend of Fredy Locke. It was part of the Juniper Hill estate, owned in 1792 by a lottery-owner called Jenkinson, but the Hall was never used as a family home, despite the expensive improvements. In his far superior property about a mile and a half away, Norbury Park, William Locke heard the local gossip that the Hall had been leased to 'French *papishes*' who were thought unlikely to pay their way.[8] As an anti-xenophobic gesture, Locke immediately offered to stand surety for the rent of Juniper Hall, and made a point of befriending the new colony of exiles. He also made a prudent appearance at a rally in Epsom that December of the gentlemen, yeomen and farmers of Surrey 'for the purpose of expressing their Loyalty to the King, and their attachment to every Branch of the present happy Constitution in Church and State'.[9] In days of suspended diplomatic relations with France and increasing official anxiety about Jacobinism and sedition, Locke didn't want his friendliness towards the odd collection of destitute aristocrats in Mickleham to be taken amiss.

Among the refugees at Juniper Hall was Narbonne's devoted friend Alexandre d'Arblay, a thirty-eight-year-old career soldier from Joigny in Burgundy who had served as Adjutant-General under Lafayette in the Army of the North campaign against Austria that year and who had made his way via Holland and Harwich to London after the capture of

Lafayette at Longwy. Susan Phillips, delighted to meet a lieutenant of her hero, described d'Arblay to her sister thus:

> a true *militaire, franc et loyal* – open as the day – warmly affectionate to his friends – intelligent, ready, and amusing in conversation, with a great share of *gaieté de coeur*.[10]

D'Arblay's long career in the army had begun at the age of fourteen, but though hard-working and dedicated, he lacked the sort of drive that worldly success requires, and his ascent through the ranks had been slow.[11] He was a cultivated man, a music-lover who liked to compose a little poetry, and seems to have been happier obeying orders than giving them. D'Arblay was honourable, courageous and intensely loyal but had an unlucky streak which a critical observer might interpret as a certain lack of competence. He was in charge of the guards at the Tuileries, for instance, the night in June 1790 when Louis XVI and his family made their ultimately unsuccessful escape to Varennes. If there was a plot among the officers to allow the King to escape, d'Arblay seems to have been kept in ignorance of it. It is impossible not to suspect that he was being set up as a stooge on this occasion. If the King had not been recaptured, d'Arblay's life would almost certainly have been forfeit.

D'Arblay's open manner, sensitivity and charm, however, endeared him to many people. He often visited the Phillipses' cottage on the main street in Mickleham, and Susan sent long accounts of their conversations to her sister. D'Arblay seems to have given up the idea of being able to return home to France and saw, with prescience, the unlikelihood of a lasting peace within thirty or even forty years: 'I see no hope of peace in my unhappy country during my lifetime', he told Mrs Phillips sadly, 'The People are so *vitiated* by the breakdown of law – by disorders of every kind – by the constant sight of blood'.[12] Fanny, writing back to Susan, carefully interpreted the stranger's words as fuel for her anti-liberal feelings, saying they should be read to 'all English Imitators of French Reformers [. . .] New *Systems*, I fear, in States, are always dangerous, if not wicked; Grievance by grievance, wrong by wrong, must only be assailed, & breathing time allowed to old prejudices, & old habits, between all that is done.'[13] To Mrs Locke's similarly enthusiastic letters about the Juniper Hall set, Fanny replied, 'Your French Colonies are truly attractive – I am sure they must be so to have caught *me*, so substantially, fundamentally, the foe of all their proceedings while in power'. Again, this apparent concession to emotion was prelude to a form of reproach: '[W]hat of misery can equal the misery of such a Revolution! – I am daily more & more in charity with all fixed Governments.'[14]

Fanny went to stay at Norbury Park in mid to late January 1793 and it was there that she finally met the French exiles, whose cultivation and good manners impressed her very favourably. The timing of their meeting was fortuitous, for it meant that she had a chance to form an opinion of both d'Arblay and Narbonne before the awful news reached London on the morning of 24 January of the execution of Louis XVI three days earlier. The whole Juniper Hall community was in shock, complicated, on the part of the émigrés, by guilt, fear and the need to demonstrate their disapproval and distress. Fanny wrote to her father that her new acquaintances had been 'almost annihilated – they are for-ever repining that they are French, &, though two of the most accomplished & elegant Men I ever saw, they break our Hearts with the humiliation they feel for their guiltless *BIRTH* in that guilty Country – "Is it possible" cries M. de Narbonne, "that you, Mr Lock, retain one jot of goodwill towards those who have the shame and misery of having been born French?" '[15] Narbonne looked jaundiced with shock, and d'Arblay, 'from a very fine figure & good face, was changed as if by Magic in one night' to 'meagre' and 'miserable'. Howevermuch the friendly Lockes and Phillipses might sympathise with their plight, none of the émigré party knew how the wider English community would treat them now, and in truth no objective person could have failed to connect the Constitutionalists with the regicides, albeit indirectly. With the expectation of war getting stronger every day, they holed up at Juniper Hall, waiting on events.

At this critical juncture in the progress of the Revolution, Fanny ceased to cavil at her friends' liberalism. Possibly with a sense of relief at being again unanimous with Susan, she transferred her full support and sympathy to the 'guiltless' émigrés. She wrote to her father that, with the exception of George III's illness, she had 'never been so overcome with grief & dismay for any but personal & family calamities',[16] and requested her mourning clothes to be sent from Chelsea immediately, so that she could appear among the Juniperians without shame. She must have realised that in her father's opinion no amount of mourning could obscure the treasonable nature of these dangerous French liberals, and that he would deeply disapprove any further fraternisation with them. Yet Fanny was suddenly quite ardent in their defence. In the light of the rapidly developing intimacy between herself and the Chevalier d'Arblay over the next month, it seems that she had probably fallen in love with him at first sight, and was already, in this first letter to her father mentioning d'Arblay, adopting the methods of special pleading that characterise her correspondence with him over the next few months as she tried (fruitlessly) to change Dr Burney's mind about the 'French sufferers' at Mickleham.

The community at Juniper Hall was enlivened by the arrival towards the end of January of Anne-Louise-Germaine de Staël, twenty-six-year-old daughter of Jacques Necker, the French King's former Minister of Finance. Madame de Staël had recently given birth to a son at her parents' home in Switzerland, but the months in Paris preceding that confinement had been fraught with personal danger. As the author of an admired study of Rousseau (published in 1788) and wife of the Swedish Ambassador to Paris, Madame de Staël had enjoyed a prominent role in Parisian intellectual life; her salon was a meeting-place for Constitutionalists and she used her influence to aid the safe passage of many refugees out of France during the turbulent autumn of 1792. When she tried to leave Paris herself, however, she had to run the gauntlet of the mob and was taken before Robespierre, accused of betraying the Revolution. Only her diplomatic status (and considerable personal bravery in standing up to Robespierre) got her safely away.

She brought with her to Juniper Hall not only these dramatic histories but further news about 'the saint like end of the martyred Louis', as Fanny styled it; how the King's last words were drowned out by drums on the orders of Santerre and how the eight-year-old Dauphin pleaded in vain to be allowed to beg mercy for his father before the Convention. These affecting tales, told by the charismatic young authoress, inspired a warm response from Fanny: 'She is one of the first women I have ever met with for abilities & extraordinary intellects', she wrote to her father,[17] this despite the Duc de Liancourt's warnings that Madame de Staël was 'one of the most offensively presumptuous women in the world, though of distinguished talents'.[18]

It is not surprising that Fanny's letters of this period are full of superlatives: the company at Juniper Hall, which also briefly included the former Bishop of Autun, Charles Maurice de Talleyrand Périgord, was the most brilliant and animated that she had known in her long experience of distinguished and famous people. Even unobtrusive Monsieur d'Arblay was described as 'one of the most delightful Characters I have ever met, for openness, probity, intellectual knowledge, & unhackneyed manners'. If Fanny was already enamoured of the gentle chevalier, with his large dark eyes, dark eyebrows and greying hair, receding at the front but flowing down over his collar behind in the new informal style, it seems very likely that he had fallen for her as quickly. By the end of their second week of acquaintance, he had suggested – *insisted* – that he become her tutor in French, which she accepted gladly. She forbore to mention that she already read and wrote the language very well.* Clearly she hadn't been speaking much French in front of the foreign grandees, constrained by her unconquerable shyness, or 'folly of fear', as she described it to Mrs Locke.[20] Monsieur d'Arblay teased her gently about this: 'Since as your friends are quite ignorant of your knoledges in the french language, the are been surely surprised of your unexpected improvement.'[21] There was no question, however, of not going ahead with the lessons. Fanny was amply motivated, writing to her new 'Master of the Language', 'I have never had a real desire to write, speak or hear French until now'.[22] The lessons became two-way, and therefore, of course, more frequent, with each party composing short 'themes' or essays in the language of the other, and sending them for correction and improvement. '[O]ur lessonings are mutual', Fanny wrote to Mrs Locke, '& more entertaining than can easily be conceived.'[23]

The *thèmes* that Fanny and Monsieur d'Arblay exchanged between February and April 1793 were never formal or particularly educational, but from the start a substitute for correspondence, often more intimate and immediate than their later actual correspondence. The two 'students' had agreed to write on whatever they liked (or could express), which in Monsieur d'Arblay's case was often a simple commentary on what was

---

* Joyce Hemlow suggests that Fanny had taught herself French as early as 1764,[19] and it is clear – to take only one example – from her exchanges with the refugees in Winchester, as detailed in the diary of August 1791, that she understood French with great ease.

going on around him in the drawing room at Juniper Hall. One of his *thèmes*, a note to Fanny (with her subsequent corrections added in square brackets) has a charming immediacy, and a strong French accent:

'Why do'nt you get down? [come down] every body in the drawing room calls after you [asks for you]. Some thought you were gone to Darking. Some others, you had got a Sittkness; at last [others that you had got a sickness at least]. – Mr Narbonne was affraid to finding you [was afraid of finding you] low-spirited, and all the society schew [shewed] an uneasiness wich I have desired to put an end [uneasiness to which I desired to put an end].'[24]

Fanny's replies were lively, confident, even playful. D'Arblay was soon calling her his 'Master in gown', but his English seems, if anything, to have got worse under her tutelage, and when he had anything important to convey he always did it in French, establishing early on the language they would speak most often together in their strange bilingual marriage. The significance of this 'simple, yet curious' first phase of their courtship was such to Fanny that the *thèmes* were especially carefully preserved among her papers, 'to obviate their [the next generation] being Dupes of false accounts'.[25]

Fanny's immediately strong feelings for Monsieur d'Arblay undoubtedly coloured her view of the whole Juniper community. Madame de Staël, who was delighted to find the famous authoress of *Cecilia* among her new English neighbours, reminded Fanny particularly of Hester Thrale, whom she resembled 'exactly [. . .] in the ardour & warmth of her temper & partialities [. . .] but she has infinitely more depth, & seems an even *profound* politician & metaphysician'.[26] Narbonne, Fanny wrote to her father, 'bears the highest character for goodness, parts, sweetness of manners & ready wit', and as for Narbonne's devoted Monsieur d'Arblay, he was surely 'one of the most singularly interesting Characters that can ever have been formed. He has a sincerity, a frankness, an ingenuous openness of nature that I had been injust enough to think could not belong to a French Man.' To Mrs Locke, she admitted that something like Juniper-fever had taken hold of her: 'I am always exposing myself to the wrath of John Bull when this coterie come in competition. It is inconceivable what a convert M. de Talleyrand has made of me; I think him now one of the first members, & one of the most charming, of this exquisite set. Susanna is as completely a prosilyte. His powers of entertainment are astonishing both in information & in raillery. We know nothing of how the rest of the World goes on.'[27]

Unfortunately, the rest of the world went on with a rather less admiring view of the émigrés at Mickleham, and back in Chelsea, Charles Burney read his daughter's eulogies with growing alarm. France had declared war on Britain and Holland at the end of January 1793, and the new Aliens Bill required the registration (and surveillance) of all these suspect Frenchmen. Worse still, though Dr Burney did not doubt Madame de Staël's intellectual status or 'captivating powers', he had heard rumours about her moral character from the Burkes and Mrs Ord, who, with her close connection to the Court, was someone to take particularly seriously. He did not, in his immediate reply to Fanny, dwell on the gossip, which was that Madame de Staël had a 'partiality' for Narbonne, but warned her that Necker's former administration and those associated with it were currently 'held in greater horror by aristocrats than even the members of the present Convention'.[28] He advised both his daughters to have as little to do with Madame de Staël as possible and to make any excuse to avoid staying at Juniper Hall.

Fanny responded with a spirited, not to say gushing, defence of the Constitutionalists. In her opinion they had been horribly misrepresented by Jacobins ('that fiend-like set') and the corrupt *noblesse* alike. Anti-Constitutionalist propaganda made little impact on Fanny any more – she had heard it all discussed at Juniper Hall – but the scandalous possibility that Madame de Staël and Narbonne could be lovers had never crossed her mind. Her reasons for thinking it 'a gross calumny' show her prejudice and unworldliness at full stretch:

she [Madame de Staël] loves [Monsieur de Narbonne] even tenderly, but so openly, so simply, so unaffectedly, & with such utter freedom from all coquetry, that if they were two Men, or two women, their affection could not, I think, be more obviously undesigning. She is very plain; – he is very handsome; – her intellectual endowments must be with him her sole attraction.[29]

Fanny's assumption that there are certain 'rules' about sexual attraction (not to mention her apparent ignorance of the existence of homosexuality, and what was and wasn't 'undesigning' between people) seems extraordinarily naive in a woman brought up among demi-mondaines and bohemians, and must colour our view of all her stated opinions about other people's sex lives. This is particularly relevant to the scandal over the elopement, four years later, of James Burney and his half-sister Sarah. On that occasion, Fanny's first instinct that something awful must be going on was quashed by her disinclination to think 'something awful' *possible*. As an adolescent it was not so surprising that Fanny took people at face value (one remembers how little trouble the Italian soprano Lucrezia Agujari had convincing the Burney girls of her purity); as an adult she never really understood that denying the obvious about one's sex life was the polite way of admitting to it.

Though she was a prude herself, Fanny naturally enough found other prudes rather dull; thus her horror of immorality was forever coming into conflict with her attraction to charming, affable, sexy people. Sometimes it took years for the penny to drop even halfway. The relationship between the Princesse d'Hénin and Lally-Tolendal (living together quite openly in Richmond in 1792) was still puzzling Fanny in 1815, when she began to suspect that they might have a 'secret marriage'. Even when the case was notorious, such as that of Lady Elizabeth Foster, bosom friend of the Duchess of Devonshire and mistress of the Duke of Devonshire, charm was able to win over Fanny's deep initial distaste, and she ended their first meeting in August 1791 'in fervent wishes that calumny, not truth, may have condemned her, & in something like a fascinated feel in her favour'.[30] It was one of Fanny's strengths that she was aware of this susceptibility and the confusedly 'mixt sensations of pain & pleasure' it caused: the stories she had heard about Lady Elizabeth and the Devonshires 'made me shudder at their power of pleasing', but 'the excellence of the behaviour & manner I witnessed, contradicted them all & rendered these objects of defamation patterns of virtue!'[31]

Others were not quite so easily swayed. Charles Burney had received a letter from his old friend James Hutton[32] expressing his extreme disquiet at learning of Fanny's association with Madame de Staël, whom he heard had come to England 'to intrigue here, and [...] to follow Mr de Narbonne'.[33] Fanny should avoid any connection with such 'an Adulterous

Demoniac', who could only be intending to exploit her celebrity in a way 'most horrible Prejudicial to Fanny'. Hutton's letter, sent on by their father, caused Fanny and Susan great disturbance. While apparently holding to her opinion that Madame de Staël was being 'cruelly calumniated, & truly worthy of every protection & support',[34] Fanny made no delay in arranging to return to London and sent her excuses to Juniper Hall, begging off the latest of Madame de Staël's fervent invitations with the excuse of a sore throat. Mrs Locke, who was back in London with her family for the season, had also sent news about scandal being attached to Madame de Staël's name. The sisters wrote to her in distress, not knowing what to believe of their charming and brilliant French friends. Fanny's remark seems particularly melancholy, weighted, as it undoubtedly was, by anxieties about the grounds of her relationship with d'Arblay: '& we had been liking & loving these exquisite people more & more every day without suspicion or controul!'

Reports of Fanny's 'indisposition' and imminent departure from Mickleham brought Monsieur d'Arblay to the Phillipses' cottage in person, eager to see her once more and ascertain whether he could continue to send her *thèmes*. These tokens of his concern and the affecting farewell note he sent her the same day – 'my feelings are too strong – farewell my dear Master!'[35] – must have made the parting from Mickleham even more wrenching. Fanny went back to joyless Chelsea, to her disgruntled father, ailing stepmother and the shared room with Sarah, wondering if anything would come of this extraordinary ignition of feeling, or if the Surrey idyll was already over.

Fanny continued to plead the cause of Madame de Staël at home, and thought (unlikely though it was) that she was slowly converting her father and stepmother to her own point of view. At the same time, she moved quickly to limit any damage done to her reputation, getting an audience with the Queen within days and arranging to dine with Mrs Ord and spend an evening with Lady Hesketh. Feeling against Madame de Staël was strong in London, and Fanny had to endure the congratulations of people like Hutton who felt she had done well 'to forsake those Devilisms'.[36] She used the *thèmes* to sound out d'Arblay on the subject: 'Opinion here', she wrote, dramatising her own trouble coming to terms with the dilemma, 'says she is neither an emigrée nor banished – – M.

de N[arbonne] has seduced her away from her Husband and Children!
– – in vain I point out the difference in customs; the reply is always "She
is a Woman, she is a Mother!" '[37] This was an implicit challenge to
d'Arblay to declare his attitudes to marriage and adultery, whether or
not he was going to reveal to Fanny his revered friend Narbonne's secrets,
which he undoubtedly knew. His answer was delicate and diplomatic,
carefully shifting the ground of the argument to avoid what he knew
would alienate Fanny, open discussion of Madame de Staël's sexual
morals. He reminded her instead of Madame de Staël's outstanding personal qualities: 'Nothing can match her charitableness, humanity and
generosity and the need that she feels to exercise them.'[38] Madame de
Staël's marriage had not been happy, like many other marriages of convenience among the French aristocracy, but, he pointed out, it would
not only be wrong but barbaric to blame her for that. Not everyone
could aspire to the domestic happiness presented by the Lockes, although
d'Arblay made it clear that *he* aspired to it. As for the question of the
nature of the relations between Madame de Staël and Narbonne, he
answered, doubly negative, that though he couldn't swear that it had
never been 'the most intimate possible', he could assure Fanny that at
present it was nothing but 'the most respectable friendship'. Presumably
d'Arblay knew or suspected that two of Madame de Staël's children were
fathered by Narbonne, but of course he was never going to tell this to
Fanny. It is also unlikely that he thought the affair was over (Madame
de Staël's letters of the period prove that it wasn't). Perhaps he hoped
that the phrase 'the most respectable friendship' could be stretched to
describe their public behaviour, which was certainly decorous. D'Arblay
was a man of fine conscience, and would not have relished telling this
half-truth to the woman he wanted to marry, but neither would he have
wanted to betray Narbonne's trust or break up the friendship between
Fanny and Madame de Staël, whose society, he vowed on his honour,
he could recommend 'to my wife, or my sister'.[39]

The problem over how to treat Madame de Staël acquired a new
urgency when the whole Juniper Hall party arrived in town in the second
week of March 1793. Madame de Staël called, naturally enough, at Chelsea
College to see Fanny, who was at her recently widowed sister Charlotte's
house in Sloane Street, probably trying to dodge the meeting. Convention
dictated (to conventional people, at any rate) that a visitor wait in her

carriage until her compliments, or simply her name, had been acknowledged by the person she had come to visit. Madame de Staël overrode
this formality and gained entrance to the College, where a stunned Mrs
Burney (reputedly even more of an anti-liberal than her husband) had
to make conversation with her for a quarter of an hour, the minimum
that politeness demanded. Unfortunately, while Madame de Staël was
still in the Burneys' apartment, Mrs Ord called (but was not introduced).
Going on to Sloane Street subsequently, Mrs Ord was horrified to find
Madame de Staël's carriage there ahead of her again, proof that Fanny
was still on good terms with the scandalous Frenchwoman. She refused
to go into the house, but sent her name in via the servant and waited
outside, rather preposterously, for the duration of the 'adulterous
demoniac's visit. Fanny was galled to think the whole story would quickly
reach the Queen's ears (undoing the benefit of her recent audience), but
couldn't help warming to Madame de Staël again as soon as they were
together: 'this poor ardent woman – who was so charming, so open, so
delightful herself, that, while with me, I forgot all the mischiefs that
might follow, & that threatened with a broad aspect'.

The chief mischief that might follow from Fanny falling out of favour
with the Queen would have been the loss of her pension, her sole depend-
able income now that she was only making about £20 a year from the
invested profits of *Cecilia*. This small independence, approximately
reckoned (by Mr Locke) as what a curate could just about live on, had
suddenly taken on a new importance to Fanny, and it is not surprising
that she became extremely anxious to protect it. D'Arblay had no money
at all. All his property ('something immense, but I never remember the
number of hundred thousand livres', as Susan had reported[40]) had been
seized by the Convention in 1792 and he had been living off his friends
ever since, presumably with some small pocket-money from Narbonne,
who dramatically swore he would share his last pound with his faithful
companion. Narbonne had been offering his (and d'Arblay's) services to
all the people of influence they met, the latest being 'the Royal highness
the duck of glocester', as d'Arblay informed Fanny in one of his *thèmes*.
'We have not the foolish opinion – to be very interesting defensors of
this happy country, but we want to pay our debt for the kind reception
we receive'.[41] They also, naturally enough, wanted some kind of financial
security.

Without such security, d'Arblay was honour-bound not to press his suit with Fanny any further, and he did not make any attempt to call on her while he was in London with Madame de Staël's party. His feelings seeped through in the *thèmes* he kept writing, however: 'Pray you, my dear *Master in all*,' he wrote on 23 March, 'to be convinced that your exercises give me very much pleasure, and never any trouble. Let us be blessed with our friendship and never vexed by it.' Relations between Fanny and d'Arblay looked in danger of stalling just at the point when d'Arblay might have been expected to declare himself. What she did next – which was to offer to lend him £100 without interest – brought events to a head rather rapidly. No doubt she intended the gesture to seem casual and truly *without interest*; it also implied that she had lots of money to spare (and could therefore support both of them in the future). D'Arblay, of course, could not accept her offer, nor the £10 banknote and coins sent with it, but if his pride was hurt (and it is hard to see how it could not have been) he did not allow any sense of that to taint his reply. Instead he wrote her an account of his latest effort at finding gainful employment, a proposal to set up a 'Corps d'artillerie à Cheval' to help defend the English coast, which he hoped the government would accept. Mr Locke had tried to indicate to d'Arblay the extreme unlikeliness of this happening, and that the best he could hope for would be an appointment as Agent for one of the French corps recruiting in England at the time. Locke understood far better than his artless friend that the position of the Juniper émigrés not only precluded any government-sponsored job, but presented an extremely risky prospect to any prospective employer or patron, with, at the very least, the possibility of the situation in France changing at any moment and the émigré aristocrats all decamping without ceremony to reclaim their property. The prospects for d'Arblay were truly unpromising. Unless by some miracle he found a job in England, his only means of survival would be to follow Narbonne around.

D'Arblay himself was the last person, figuratively and literally, to see his situation in these stark terms, and his letter to Fanny of 31 March about his prospects is unaffectedly optimistic. He thought that if the cavalry plan could be proposed to Pitt, and if Fanny exerted her influence at Court, his worries would be over. What, he asked, in hesitant phrases, did Fanny think of this proposal, on which his hopes of gaining independence in England rested? It was, as Fanny was in no doubt, d'Arblay's roundabout way of proposing marriage.

'O my dearest *dear* Susan!' Fanny wrote in delighted turmoil to her sister, 'what would I not give to have you with me at this moment! You to whom alone I could open my Heart – labouring at this instant with feelings that almost burst it.' She had sent only a short friendly note to d'Arblay, playing for time. What she needed was to talk the whole situation over with her sister. The money problem was not, surprisingly, on her mind at all:

> I will be quite – quite open – & tell you that Everything upon Earth I could covet for the peculiar happiness of my peculiar mind seems here united – were there not one scruple in the way which intimidates me from listening to the voice of my Heart – Can you not guess what it is? – I wish him a *younger Partner*. I do not wish myself richer – grander – more powerful, or higher born, – one of his first attractions with me is his superiority to all these considerations – no, I wish myself only to be *younger*: I should then, I believe, with difficulty start a single objection, thinking of him as I think – His nobleness of character – his sweetness of disposition – his Honour, Truth, integrity – with so much of softness, delicacy, & tender humanity – except my beloved Father & Mr Lock, I have never seen such a man in this world, though I have drawn such in my Imagination.[42]

Susan thought the age question of no real moment. She had gathered that d'Arblay was thirty-nine (actually he was still thirty-eight until May 1793), and anyway, 'his appearance makes him judged much older'.[43] Susan was delighted at the prospect of this romantic match, but foresaw that their father might oppose it: 'But – but – but – You do not wish yourself richer you say! – Ah my Fanny! – but that wd be essentially requisite in such a union – your single £100. per ann – his – Alas! his *NOTHING* – How wd it be possible for you to live?'[44] Fanny's reply was ardent and immediate: the high romance of the sacrifice necessary was very appealing to her: 'Were he secure of only Bread & Water, I am very sure I should gaily partake them with him. How the World would blame me at first, I well know; but his worth, in time, would make its own way, & be my vindication. This, however, is all Utopian now – & I must not let him divine it.'[45]

Throughout the early weeks of April, d'Arblay and Fanny kept missing each other at the Lockes' and at Charlotte's house in Sloane Street, but Fanny thought it just as well, as she anticipated the difficulties of behaving normally in company. Nothing between her and d'Arblay was properly agreed at this point, and she felt that 'repressing all personal discussions'[46] would allow him to back out without shame if he changed his mind. D'Arblay had no such scruples and was desperate to talk to Fanny, turning up uninvited at Chelsea College on a series of pretexts, which caused some raising of eyebrows among the family (especially Sarah, who was immediately intrigued by the French visitor). During one of these *tête à têtes*, in which Fanny had been trying unsuccessfully to stop him saying anything at all, d'Arblay asked as a special favour for her *tablettes*, the erasable notebook made of bound ivory sheets in which she jotted down drafts of letters and memoranda. He must have noticed these at Juniper Hall, for she had thought of it already, and bought him a brand-new set. But d'Arblay didn't want the new one, he wanted the one she had used, which he received with delight. Like his gift to her soon afterwards of an old pen, it showed a certain sensuality. It also reflected his perception of Fanny as a *writer*, specifically as the author of *Cecilia*, which several of the Juniperians had read. He had heard her referred to as 'Cecilia' (probably by Madame de Staël) and wanted her to inscribe it on his tablets. 'So that isn't your real name?' he said 'drolly' when she declined,[47] reminding us that though he presumably knew Miss Burney's Christian name, he had never yet had the opportunity to use it.

D'Arblay was keen to meet Dr Burney, and Fanny could not refuse, though she knew it would be extremely painful to see her father snub him. She got the Doctor's grudging permission to be introduced that evening, after a dinner at the Lockes' to which both she and d'Arblay were invited. A situation as nicely problematic as any in Fanny's novels arose when d'Arblay asked to ride back to Chelsea in the carriage with Fanny alone. She agreed, very hesitantly, but alert to the impropriety of travelling alone with a man in a carriage, tried to get away without him. D'Arblay caught up with her, however, before she reached the carriage steps:

I had already taken hold of Oliver's arm – &, the instant I was in, he began putting up the steps! [—]

'Ah ha!,' cried M. D'Arblay, – &, leaping over them, got into the Coach, seating himself opposite to me.

I believe Oliver's surprise was equal to my queerness! [—]

'Where is he to go, Ma'am?' cried he.

'To Chelsea,' I answered. – And the door was shut – & off we drove.[48]

Monsieur d'Arblay was in a very emotional mood, and alarmed Fanny by saying how impossible he would find it not to speak his mind to her father. She had only just persuaded him of the folly of doing any such thing when he was off on the subject of the joys of a retired life in the country with *une personne*, to which Fanny was 'obliged to make him no answer at all, but say something quite foreign'.

'Mais! mais! he cried, a little impatiently, laissez moi parler! – laissez – permettez – –'

'Non! non! non! non!' I kept crying – but, for all that – he dropt on one knee – which I was fain to pretend not to observe – & held up his hands folded, & went on –

I begged him to say no more then quite fervently.[49]

Poor d'Arblay took this as evidence that Fanny had had a change of heart, and 'flung' himself back in the carriage's furthest corner. However, he was not one to brood, and was soon 'bending from his little *Boudoir*', as Fanny comically described it in her journal, and laughing at an idea he had had to evade her strictures. She had forbidden him to speak to her intimately in French:

'– ainsi – I *will speak English*! &, in this language – I may pray you – you can't refuse me I pray you – that you be –'

'O oui! oui! oui!' cried I, laughing too, parlons d'autre chose! –'

'Non! non! cried he, – be – be – My *dear* Friend! – My *dear -EST!* –'

Their mutual laughter, the acknowledgement that they were playing a game and the surreal detail of the lovers having reversed languages, give this scene in the carriage peculiar charm. Fanny had been waiting all her life for someone as open, earnest and romantic as this, but had never imagined such a gentle hero. Where another more worldly or ill-intentioned man might have taken advantage (almost on principle) of the absence of any chaperone, d'Arblay's conduct was wildly innocent, ardent without being in the least threatening. The middle-aged sweethearts emerged from the carriage at Chelsea College causing just as much surprise to the Burneys' servant as they had done to the Lockes', but now this was a detail which Fanny could enjoy observing, rather than tremble at. She knew her behaviour was above reproach, and she had decided to marry d'Arblay.

While her father could hardly prevent her from marrying, the withholding of his approval inevitably overshadowed the prospect for her. In the section of the *Memoirs* dealing with this period, Fanny lets slip that religion, politics and 'the dread of pecuniary embarrassment' were not her father's only objections: he also nursed 'a latent hope and belief in a far more advantageous connexion'.[50] Whether he had any particular suitor in mind is not clear, but it is possible he harboured hopes of William Windham, whose admiration for Fanny was obvious and who had been corresponding with Dr Burney for some years.

When d'Arblay invited himself to tea at Chelsea College, Charles Burney did not hide his grudgingness: '[He] prepared himself, drily, & *sans commentaire*: my Mother was taciturn, but oddly smiling [. . .] Sarah was flightily delighted'.[51] No doubt Sarah, who was to introduce into her first novel, *Clarentine*, a character named the Chevalier de Valcour, clearly based on d'Arblay, was enjoying the occasion in her own way. D'Arblay was on top form, 'light, gay & palpably in inward Spirits', as Fanny reported to Susan, and either unaware of his hosts' antagonism or too happy to be received into the bosom of Fanny's family to care. But Charles Burney, who had been such a good-hearted and good-natured guest himself at so many dinner tables, had the grace to recognise d'Arblay's efforts (and genuine pleasure). He melted a little as the evening went on and fetched out various treasures from his library to share with the enthusiastic foreigner. It is impossible not to feel sorry for Burney, faced with the loss of his most devoted daughter to a Roman Catholic liberal Frenchman, or for Fanny, given this glimpse of their compatibility: 'Ah, my dearest Susanna! – with a Mind thus formed to meet mine – would my dearest Father listen ONLY TO HIMSELF, how blest would be my lot!'[52]

During the courtship, the atmosphere at Chelsea College was strained. Mrs Burney was at her most 'capricious' and seemed to Fanny to be trying to catch her out by ostentatiously leaving the room almost every time Monsieur d'Arblay called. Only by forcing Sarah to stay put could Fanny thwart 'the confounding & detecting effect' she assumed was 'meant to be produced & pointed out by la Dama'. The implication that 'la Dama' was an old hand at intrigue and assignations herself would not have been lost on Susan, the recipient of this report, nor would the unpleasant observation that Sarah Burney's interest in Monsieur d'Arblay's visits seemed to be one of 'watchful *malice*'.[53] Charles Burney himself was infected with this spirit of ill-will, and drew up a list of the factions in France (including the Constitutionalists) for d'Arblay to define, with the enquiry if there were any more. The sarcasm of this did not reach d'Arblay, but was absorbed by Fanny, the go-between, who also had to invent thanks from her father to her lover for his earnest efforts.

Susan remained Fanny's mainstay at this extraordinary time, reading both sides of the lovers' correspondence (copied for her by Fanny) and entering fully into the spirit of conspiracy. It was an odd situation in which Susan was not just letter-bearer, letter-reader and general go-between but substitute fiancée too, having her hand kissed and listening to the outpourings of the frustrated Chevalier. 'Is it possible my dearest Susan can talk of *postage* to me at such a time?' Fanny wrote with true lover's impatience, 'when you have only time for one Line, send it me off, as you prize my peace.'[54]

D'Arblay's duty to Narbonne meant that his fate was tied up with that of a very active, ambitious and influential man who might at any moment draw them both back into war or intrigue. The defection of General Dumourier to the Austrians at the beginning of April had quashed Narbonne's latest plan to join a proposed counter-revolutionary movement, but there were to be dozens of similar alarms. Exile in Surrey had made the émigrés look like people of leisure; Fanny was having to consider for the first time what it might be like to be married to a soldier, and one of the wrong nationality. D'Arblay's remarks about how much cheaper life was in France raised the question also of where they might end up living.

D'Arblay was not, for all his charm, a practical or resourceful man.

His enthusiasm for a succession of money-spinning schemes flared up and died down unpredictably. Probably his wildest dream, and one of the longest-cherished in the spring of 1793, was that the widowed French Queen Marie Antionette might – with a change of government! – be once again in a position to grant pensions to worthy candidates, amongst whom he counted himself, naturally. He came to speak of this money as if it were only a matter of time before it would be in his hands. Fanny did not seem to be worried about d'Arblay's lack of realism, possibly because she was already inwardly confident of being able to support them both by her writing. What did give her cause for concern were the outbursts of emotionalism she witnessed in d'Arblay. On one occasion he became quite maudlin about the Locke girls' measles, and warned Fanny that he was sometimes 'moody [. . .] throwing myself here, there and everywhere restlessly'.[55] She became too agitated to remember later exactly what else he had said, writing, 'I am frightened at the susceptibility that binds me – perhaps more than any other thing – to enter into all his feelings!'[56] It is interesting not only that her phenomenal memory shut down at this point, but that she saw the danger of her own sensibilities being altered by sympathy with his.

With the departure of Madame de Staël at the end of May (called back to her husband and their property at Coppet, near Lausanne), the Juniper Hall party was breaking up. Having found no prominent position in England, Narbonne intended to leave as soon as was practical, but understanding that something was afoot, he made no demands on d'Arblay to accompany him. D'Arblay himself seemed to have all but given up job-hunting by the summer. His conversation was mostly about cottages and he seemed eager to embrace a life of retirement. Loyal lieutenancy had always been his strong suit; he had done it for Lafayette and Narbonne. Now he imagined a cosy domestic version of the same thing, perhaps undertaking a little light secretarial work for his famous wife (he had extraordinarily neat handwriting) or making a French translation of her next book – the one whose proceeds they would live on. What could be more romantic than love in a cottage with a writer of romances, or more satisfyingly philosophical in an age of revolution than simply sitting tight and cultivating one's garden, à la Candide?

A rapid and successful return to authorship was clearly the only way ahead for Fanny, but she needed some peace in which to test out ideas for a new book. Mickleham was out of the question while Madame de Staël was still there, issuing invitations to the last. The best place to ensure privacy was the old 'homely home', Chesington, and Fanny went there at the end of May with some notes for a novel. The house was sadly run-down, but 'my good little dumpty fat square short round Mrs Hamilton' was just as kindly welcoming as ever, as of course was 'her young niece, Miss Kitty, who is only 63'.[57] James Burney was there too, trying to recover from the long illness and subsequent death in April of his eldest child, seven-year-old Catherine. To Fanny he looked ten years older and 'grievously altered' by the blow. There is no mention of his wife Sally or four-year-old son Martin, but James often went about on his own. Fanny remarked that he was so often at Chelsea College he 'almost lives' there,[58] and since 1787 he had been making surprise visits to the Phillipses at Mickleham, apparently looking round the area for a house to rent. Much of his erratic behaviour and some of his remarks on those occasions indicated that all was not well with his marriage, even in those early days. Susan hoped that 'all that might have made [James and his wife] mutually wretched' had been overcome and that 'every year will endear them to each other',[59] but there were worse disruptions to come.

The new book that Fanny felt pressured to write was doomed to be something of a compromise. She said later* that *Camilla* was based on jottings made during her time at Windsor – hardly her happiest or most productive period. The sense that she was using this book to ingratiate herself with the Royal Family is evident in the fulsome dedication to the Queen, an honour that Fanny solicited (unlike Jane Austen, who kicked against having to dedicate *Emma* to the Prince Regent twenty years later). The book thus had several burdens to bear before a page had been written.

Work was interrupted in May by a visit from d'Arblay, for which preparations began days in advance:

Mrs Hamilton ordered half a Ham to be boiled ready; – & Miss Kitty trimmed up her best Cap, – & tried it on, on Saturday, to get it in shape

---

* She was answering a query by the King, quoted in a letter to Charles Burney of 5–6 July 1796, after the book was published.

to her face. She made Chocolate also, – which we drank up on Monday & Tuesday, because it was spoiling: – 'I have never seen none of the French Quality,' she says, 'and I have a *purdigious Curosity* [sic]; though as to Dukes and Dukes Sons, and these high top Captains, I know they'll think me a mere country Bumpkin. *Howsever*, they can't call me worse than *Fat Kit Square*, and that's the worst name I ever got from any of our english polite Bears.'[60]

Despite the cap and the chocolate, Monsieur d'Arblay's arrival still took them by surprise:

the French *top Captain* entered while poor Miss Kitty was in *dishbill!* [*déshabille*] & Mrs Hamilton finishing washing up her China from Breakfast! A Maid who was out at the Pump, first saw the arrival, ran in to give Miss Kitty time to escape – for she was in her round dress *nightcap*, & without her roll and curls – However, he followed too quick – & Mrs Hamilton was seen in her linen gown & mob, though she had put on a silk one in expectation, for every noon these 4 or 5 days past – & Miss Kitty was in such confusion she hurried out of the Room. She soon, however, returned with the roll and curls, & the Forehead & Throat *fashionably* lost, in a silk Gown.[61]

With roll and curls firmly in place, Kitty Cooke and Mrs Hamilton never left the room during the whole visit, much to d'Arblay's chagrin. They were immensely impressed by the French 'top Captain' and his history of war, revolution and escape. Quizzing Fanny later about him, Mrs Hamilton was moved to tears. It was only now that she'd actually set eyes on one of the émigré gentry, she said, that she could really begin to believe there had been a Revolution after all! To which Miss Kitty agreed: '"I purtest I did not know before but it was all a Sham!"'[62]

Fanny harboured few illusions over d'Arblay's chances of employment. She also realised that matters in France could take a whole generation to be sorted out, and that his property there should be discounted from their plans. But this hard-headed realism balked before the power of her desire to go ahead and marry the indigent Frenchman come what may. As a middle-aged spinster daughter Fanny was still prey to her family's plans for her, the latest of which was that she should go and live as companion to Charlotte, who had been left with the care of three very young children at the death of her husband, Clement Francis, in 1792. Marriage would mean a final release from such threats of dependence, escape from Chelsea College and, at last, a share in Susan's apparently charmed life at Mickleham. 'You all *MUST* know', she wrote to Susan and the Lockes with emotion, 'that to *ME* a crust of Bread, with a little Roof for shelter, & a FIRE for warmth, *NEAR* YOU, would bring me to peace, to happiness – to all that my Heart holds dear, or ever, in any situation, could prize.'[63]

Once Madame de Staël had left Juniper Hall the place all but shut down, and Narbonne and d'Arblay took to dining every day at the Phillipses' cottage, much to Captain Phillips's annoyance. He had his own view of the relationship between his wife and the foreign gentlemen, and it was not charitable. The property he had inherited at Belcotton in County Louth, which was vulnerable to the maraudings of nationalist rebels, took him off to Ireland frequently, but every time he came back it must have seemed as if his wife had perversely strengthened the already unwelcome intimacy with the Juniperians. D'Arblay especially, with his almost constant visits, his petting of the children and relish for lachrymose *tête-à-têtes* with Susan, was obviously not to be trusted.

Discussion of the income problem exercised all Fanny's and d'Arblay's friends at Mickleham, but only Susan saw that the solution lay with Fanny: '*print, print, print!*' she urged. 'Here is a ressource – a certainty of removing present difficulties'. 'Yes, I would', Fanny replied, '– if my own Mistress – & either for myself, or by – even by subscription'.[64] By 'for myself' she meant at her own expense, which would be out of the question if she married d'Arblay. To publish by subscription meant opening a list and soliciting funds in advance, as her father had done for his *History of Music*. Though Fanny did not relish such a method of publication, any chance to make cash quickly was not to be sneered at any longer. Narbonne had thoroughly alarmed d'Arblay by exclaiming that the life the couple envisaged together would kill Fanny. If she was so delicate that she could not defy public opinion over Madame de Staël, he noted – with a touch of resentment – what hope of her surviving the social and material deprivations of life 'comme – des Paysans!'?[65] And how would they support their children? It was the first time anyone had broached *that* problem. Fanny and d'Arblay had idealised the struggle with poverty as a lovers' trial, but at forty-one, Fanny was still young enough to have quite a sizeable family. Had not La Dama surprised them all by giving birth to Dick at the age of forty-three and Sarah at forty-seven?

Fanny tried to heal the rift with her father by showing him the few pages of her new novel, whose heroine at this date laboured under the name 'Betulia'. He was pleased, with the writing and with the gesture, but nothing was going to alter significantly his dim view of Monsieur d'Arblay. He withheld his consent when d'Arblay formally applied for it, citing the 'precarious tenure' of his daughter's income, his own professed inability to help them financially, 'the distracted state of your own country, and the almost hopeless state of your party & friends'. To Locke he replied at greater length and in sad agitation: 'All the self-denying virtues of Epictetus will not keep off indigence in a state of society, without the assistance of patrimony, profession, or possessions of [sic] on one side or the other.' No one was better qualified than Dr Burney to know what a struggle it could be to maintain 'a *family establishment*' from scratch, but perhaps he had been too good an example of the triumphantly self-made man to impress his daughter with anything other than her own ability to succeed likewise.

The way in which Fanny was writing to d'Arblay indicates that parental approval was not, by this stage, uppermost in her thoughts:

You desire to know if I have weighed well how I could support an entirely retired life, &c –

Here comes a great *YES!* I have considered it thoroughly – but it was not at Ches[ington] – No; I considered it upon receiving your first Letter [31 March]; & my thoughts have never since varied.

Situation, I well know, is wholly powerless to render me either happy or miserable. My peace of mind, my chearfulness of spirits, my every chance of felicity, rest totally & solely upon enjoying the society, the confidence, & the kindness of those I esteem & love. These, I am convinced, will at all times be successful; – every thing else has at all times failed.[66]

It is not surprising that d'Arblay found this letter 'charmante', showing as it does Fanny's ardour, good humour and commitment. On 21 June she left London for Epsom, where she was going to meet the Lockes at

Bracebridge's Inn and be taken on to Norbury Park. It was presented to Dr and Mrs Burney as yet another visit, but this time Fanny had no intention of coming home.

A begging letter from Susan, the family's darling, made Dr Burney submit to the inevitable and send a grudging consent (presumably an upsetting document – it was not kept), and at seven a.m. on 28 July 1793 Fanny and her 'bien meilleur Ami' were married at St Michael's Church, Mickleham. It was a small party: Susan and Captain Phillips, the Lockes, Narbonne and James Burney, who stood in for his father and gave away the bride. Two days later the couple went through a Roman Catholic ceremony at the Sardinian Chapel in Lincoln's Inn Fields, a precaution against any future property disputes in France, then went back to Mickleham to start their married life in modest rented rooms in a farmhouse on Blagden Hill.

⚜ 11 ⚜

The Cabbage-Eaters

The reaction to Fanny's marriage was almost universally one of surprise. Mrs Burney alone said she had seen it coming; other members of the family who had been kept out of the secret, such as Maria Rishton, isolated in Norfolk by her misanthropic husband, were amazed and amused at the prospect of 'our vestal sister' taking such a plunge in middle age.[1] Some friends of the family, such as Mrs Ord and James Hutton, were appalled, but Fanny no longer worried about their disapproval. 'I fear my good old friend Mr Hutton imagines me *a mere poor miserable Dupe, taken in by an artful French avanturier,*' she wrote with spirit to her stepmother. 'If he thinks so, it is *he,* – Heaven be praised! – is the Dupe! – which I bear with great philosophy, if one of us must be Dupe'.[2]

The d'Arblays' wedding present from William and Fredy Locke was the lease of a five-acre plot of land on the Norbury Park estate, on which the newlyweds intended to build themselves a house. D'Arblay drew up some elaborate plans in his exceedingly neat hand, but the project didn't begin for years due to lack of cash. 'How the matter will terminate I know not', Fanny wrote to her father in the summer of 1793 as she listened to the builder pouring cold water on d'Arblay's amateur architecture; 'at present the contest is lively, & M. d'Arblay's want of language, & the man's want of ideas, render it, to me, extremely diverting'.[3] Everything was 'extremely diverting' to the enraptured bride, even not having a home of her own. The couple were conspicuously and besottedly in love.

After four months at Phenice Farm on Blagden Hill, the d'Arblays found much more private lodgings in a cottage on the main street in Great Bookham called 'Fair Field' (which they renamed 'The Hermitage'). They lived in this cramped but cosy house for the next four years, with their few prized possessions, such as the copy of Van Dyke's *Sacharissa* in oils by Mrs Delany and Edward Burney's portrait of Samuel Crisp, some cheap cane furniture and spare household goods lent by the Lockes and Phillipses. 'Can Life, [Monsieur d'Arblay] often says, be more innocent than ours? or happiness more inoffensive?'

> – he works in his Garden, or studies English or Mathematicks, while I write, – when I work at my needle he reads to me, & we enjoy the beautiful Country around us, in long & romantic strolls, during which he carries under his arm a portable walking Chair, lent us by Mr Lock, that I may rest as I proceed.[4]

Even in the early days, there were threats to this life of quiet retirement, for d'Arblay's honour and inclination made him want to respond to developments such as the gathering of monarchists in Toulon in 1793, routed in December by the forces of the Convention under the command of the young Napoleon Bonaparte. Some of d'Arblay's friends had decided to risk the return to France to retrieve property or rejoin family; he himself had hardly any family left except a surviving younger brother, François, and a beloved uncle in Joigny.* The desire to make contact with his remaining kin must have been strong, as was the desire not to lose touch with his friends and the Constitutionalist cause for which they had risked so much. Fanny did not interfere in these matters of conscience and duty, but dreaded a rekindling of her husband's 'military ardour'.[6] Everything they heard about life under the Terror in France and everything they read in the papers (received second-hand from the Lockes and the parson) was alarming, and lent weight to Fanny's belief that a return to France would mean certain death for d'Arblay. French visitors passing through Bookham had dramatic and pathetic tales to relate. The Chevalier de Beaumetz, an associate of Talleyrand, told the d'Arblays of his flight from murderous agents of the Convention and his narrow escape by hiding himself under a pile of rubbish in an attic. Fanny retold his story in gripping 'thriller' style in a letter to her father,[7] revelling in its intrinsic drama: 'as the Gang approached, higher & higher, nearer &

---

* His parents and elder brother were all dead long before the Revolution, and his only sister had died in 1792 or 1793, a fact he probably didn't yet know.[5]

nearer, he heard a woman exclaiming "O, you'll find him – I'm sure he's in the House."'

Fanny made a surprising return to print in the first winter of her married life, her first publication for eleven years, with a pamphlet called *Brief Reflections Relative to the Emigrant French Clergy*. This cause had been taken up by a committee of charitable ladies (with Dr Burney acting as secretary) and had already been the subject of pamphlets by Burke and Hannah More and a poem, 'The Emigrants', by Charlotte Smith. Fanny's appeal to 'the Ladies of Great Britain' to send money to support the refugee priests was a mixture of conventional morality and sensationalism. She described (on what authority we may wonder) the 1792 massacre of priests in the Église des Carmes thus:

> the murderers dart after them: the pious suppliants kneel – but they rise no more! they pray – and their prayers ascend to heaven, unheard on earth! Groans resound through the vaulted roof – Mangled carcases strew the consecrated ground – derided, while wounded; insulted, while slaughtered – they are cleft in twain – their savage destroyers joy in their cries – Blood, agony, and death close the fatal scene![8]

Charles Burney, significantly, loved this rhetoric: 'I never liked anything of your precious writing more', he wrote to the author in congratulation. His praise was enough to encourage Fanny to develop the style for other grand subjects – sometimes more appropriately than others.

Brief Reflections is interesting for its clear statement, in the 'Apology', of Fanny's views on the role of women. If she had read Mary Wollstonecraft's extraordinary feminist polemic of the previous year, *Vindication of the Rights of Women*, she does not mention the fact in her extant letters or journals. It is highly likely that she avoided the book, or read only enough to condemn it, as she had done other 'dangerous' literature in the past, such as Goethe's *Sorrows of Young Werther*. Wollstonecraft's acute analysis of female conditioning and subjugation was indeed so radical that it was relatively easy, at this date, to dismiss it as Jacobin ranting; but even women writers, like Fanny Burney, who did not want to dignify Wollstonecraft's work by engaging with it directly, can be seen to be reacting to it, reaffirming their own ideas or formulating them perhaps for the first time. Fanny's position, as set out in the 'Apology', seems at first sight to be a restatement of received wisdom about 'the distinct ties of [women's] prescriptive duties' to the home and their unsuitability for 'forming public characters' (rather rich coming from 'the author of *Evelina* and *Cecilia*', as she identified herself on the title page), but she was assertive about the superior role that women had to play within their restricted field. They should not be 'mere passive spectatresses' of life, but active in the refinement and practice of morality,

> since the retirement, which divests them of practical skill for public pur-
> poses, guards them, at the same time, from the heart-hardening effects of
> general worldly commerce. It gives them leisure to reflect and to refine,
> not merely upon the virtues, but the pleasures of benevolence; not only
> and abstractedly upon that sense of good and evil which is implanted in
> all, but feelingly, nay awefully, upon the woes they see, yet are spared![9]

This was as unlike Wollstonecraft as it was unlike Wollstonecraft's opponent Hannah More (who famously said of the idea of 'Rights', 'there is perhaps no animal so much indebted to subordination for its good behaviour as woman'[10]). Fanny's was an egalitarian view of sorts, if pre-scriptive: women were the conscience of society, men its functionaries. She was basically claiming *all* the moral high ground for her sex in return for any 'heart-hardening' participation in 'worldly commerce', which would contaminate women, on whom private virtue and social progress depended. Fanny Burney was making over 'conduct-book'-style ideas from the old century for use by a new generation to whom James Fordyce and his kind looked impossibly old-fashioned. It was reactionary but assertive, and actually had a greater immediate impact on the coming age than did Wollstonecraft, whose time was yet to come. In Burney's post-1790s novels, her tragedies and her one political tract, all of which promote the idea of moral responsibility as a more powerful weapon for women than political rights, we can see the emergence of the 'Victorian' ideal of womanhood that in fact took hold well in advance of Victoria's reign, and which found its most famous expression in the idea of 'the Angel in the House'.

Married life at Bookham was blissfully happy and amusing. Monsieur d'Arblay made strenuous efforts to *cultiver son jardin*, hoping that enthusiasm would make up for ignorance. Unfortunately, he couldn't tell weeds from vegetables, and dug up a whole asparagus bed; he also planted strawberries thinking they would crop the first year: 'our Garden, therefore, is not yet quite the most profitable thing in the World', Fanny wrote to her father, 'but M.[onsieur] assures me it *is* to be the staff of our Table & existence'.[11] D'Arblay's passion for redesigning and transplanting threatened at one point to wipe out all signs of life in The Hermitage's little plot and orchard, neither of which ever seemed to impress visitors quite as much as he felt they deserved. Fanny was appreciative, though, and patient with his mistakes. She enjoyed watching him trying to cut the hedges with martial swipes from his sabre and giving wheelbarrow rides to Susan's two-year-old son William. Her own attempts at cooking had been disasters, and they soon got a maid to do it. Some 'asparagrass, most fortunately overlooked by my Weeder' was sent to Chelsea as humorous acknowledgement of their incompetence, but one crop did survive to grace the d'Arblays' own table: cabbages, of which they had a glut in the spring of 1794 because they didn't identify them early enough. They ate cabbage for a week with more voluptuous pleasure than is easily imaginable, exulting in self-sufficient pride and joy: 'O, you have no idea how sweet they tasted! we agreed they had a freshness & a goût we had never met with before.'[12]

During the summer of 1794, Fanny suffered 'bilious attacks' and fatigue which neither she nor her doctor recognised as symptoms related to early pregnancy. The medical man 'gave no opinion' even when he examined his patient in the middle of June, when Fanny could have been as much as thirteen weeks pregnant; for her part, she was either ignorant of the symptoms (which is unlikely, given her closeness to her sisters) or used to such irregular periods that missing three of them did not surprise her. This dysmenorrhea (a condition associated with anorexics and of course, more generally, with the menopause) might help explain some of her mysterious chronic ailments, fevers and prostrations during the preceding years.

Monsieur d'Arblay was delighted at the news when it was finally confirmed, though, like Fanny, fearful for her well-being. Dr Burney was delighted too; he had more than made up the breach that had caused them all such unhappiness around the time of the d'Arblays' marriage and had quite warmed to his son-in-law subsequently, no doubt influenced by the charming descriptions of their married life in Fanny's letters home.

Dr Burney had begun to lend d'Arblay books from the 'Chelsea circulating library',[13] and now looked forward with glee to the prospect of romping with the 'Bookham Brattikin'. The full return of affection from her beloved father made this period truly happy for Fanny, and was further confirmation, if she needed it, that her own judgement about what was best for herself had been superior to his.

Naturally enough, as the birth approached Fanny became extremely anxious about her chances of survival, and began a farewell letter to her husband which is a touching memorial of their mutual love, praising 'the chaste, the innocent, the exemplary tenour of your conduct, & the integrity, the disinterestedness, the unaffected nobleness of your principles & sentiments. – Heaven bless you, my d'Arblay! here & hereafter!'[14] Such parting words were not, however, necessary; the baby, a son, was born without complications on 18 December 1794, and three weeks later his mother described herself as 'wonderfully well'.[15] Even in this first letter about him, Fanny remarked on 'a thousand little promises of original intelligence' in the little bundle at her side. He was christened Alexander Charles Louis Piochard d'Arblay, but was soon known to his parents as 'the Idol of the World'.[16]

It is hardly surprising that during the autumn and winter when the baby was born, Fanny had barely time or inclination to attend to an important episode in her professional life, the first and only production of one of her plays. It is ironic that though *The Witlings* had been shelved and none of her later comedies ever reached the stage, one of the strange, half-finished tragedies that she composed at Court was chosen for production. The Court dramas had been circulating among the family and had struck young Charles Burney as saleable (unlike *Brief Reflections*, all of the profits of which had gone to the priests' charity). He had contacted the actor John Philip Kemble on his sister's behalf, knowing how strapped for cash the d'Arblays were, and met with immediate success; Kemble liked *Hubert de Vere*, but Fanny preferred *Edwy and Elgiva*, and it was this play which was rushed into production in January 1795 with a cast that included Kemble himself and his sister Mrs Sarah Siddons in the leading roles. Rehearsals were late and patchy and at no point was the author, who had given up her only copy, required or allowed to alter the play. It went on, for its first and only performance on 21 March 1795, in an essentially unactable form.

Fanny came up to town to see the play having been ill for weeks with a painful abscess on the breast which had forced her to wean the baby. Drury Lane Theatre had been magnificently redesigned, and the pantomime playing with *Edwy and Elgiva*, *Alexander the Great* (featuring a cast of hundreds and two live elephants), had been composed specially to show off the dimensions of the new stage. No such care had been taken over the main piece, however. At the back of Sheridan's box, 'wrapt up in a Bonnet & immense Pelice',[17] Fanny settled down with Susan, d'Arblay and her brother Charles to witness a farcical representation of her already flawed work.

Despite the efforts of Kemble, Siddons and Robert Bensley, who played Dunstan, the rest of the cast seemed hardly to know their lines at all, and the prompter's voice was 'heard unremittingly all over the House', as the reviewer for the *Morning Advertiser* noticed.[18] The actor playing Aldhelm seemed to be making up his speeches as he went along, and the whole cast 'made blunders I blush to have pass for mine', as Fanny wrote of the distressing evening to her old friend Mary Ann Port (now Mrs Waddington). Mrs Siddons lost no time in describing the performance to Mrs Piozzi: 'In truth it needed no discernment to see how it would go, and I was grievd that a woman of so much merit must be so much mortified. The Audience were quite angelic and only laughed where it was *impossible* to avoid it.'[19] Bursts of laughter went up when Edwy cried out 'Bring in the Bishop!', which the audience chose to interpret as punch rather than a prelate; they hooted when the King asked what brought Sigibert rushing onto the stage and he answered, 'Nothing'; and they fell about at the tragic conclusion when a countryman suggested putting the dying heroine behind a hedge. This proved 'a very accommodating retreat', as the reviewer of the *Morning Herald* related:

> for, in a few minutes after, the wounded lady is brought from behind it on an elegant couch, and, after dying in the presence of her husband, is carried off and placed once more 'on the other side of the hedge'. The laughter which this scene occasioned [. . .] was inconceivable.[20]

This sort of reception would have half-killed Fanny in former years, but it is interesting to see how much more resilient to criticism she had become. Her response was more irritated than ashamed: 'a more wretched

Fanny's brother James Burney. An engraving of the bust by Joseph Nollekens (modelled from a death-mask) which Molesworth Phillips commissioned immediately after James's death.

John Webber's reconstruction of *The Death of Captain Cook*, showing Lieutenant Molesworth Phillips on the ground in the centre, firing at Cook's assailant.

Queen Charlotte, by William Beechey, 1796 – the only
official portrait that gives any idea of what Walpole
meant by 'the bloom of her ugliness'.

The Royal Terrace at Windsor Castle in 1783, with the Royal Family
promenading on it. In the background is the newly-built Queen's Lodge,
where Fanny Burney lived for most of the years 1786 to 1791.
Engraving by James Fittler after George Robertson.

James Gillray's caricature of George III and Queen Charlotte, 'Temperance enjoying a Frugal Meal' (1792), a satire on the royal couple's parsimony.

The trial of Warren Hastings in Westminster Hall, engraving by R. Pollard after E. Dayes. On the opening day of the trial, 13 February 1788, Fanny Burney was seated in the Great Chamberlain's box at the upper end of the hall, facing the same way as the picture does. The defendant, and the 'managers' of the trial – including Burke, Sheridan and William Windham – were in the boxes in front of her.

Mary Delany, by John Opie,
'a pattern of a perfect fine lady'
who was the friend of Swift in her youth
and of George III in her old age.

Frederica Locke, by Dowman. Fanny and
Susan adored her, but her intense manner was
not to everyone's taste: Dr Burney thought
there was 'a *viscosity* in their friendship'.

Norbury Park soon after its completion in the 1770s.
The Painted Room looks out from the opposite side of the house.

Alexandre Piochard d'Arblay,
a pencil drawing thought to be by
William Locke Junior, c.1792-3.

The charismatic
Germaine de Staël,
by Gérard.

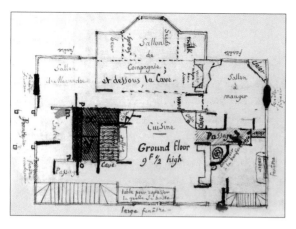

Monsieur d'Arblay's sketch plan of the interior of Camilla Cottage, showing his keenness for cupboards and the position of the stove 'à la Rumford'.

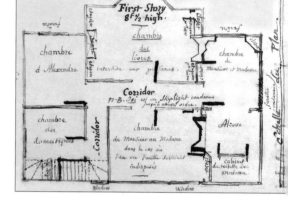

The only surviving image of Fanny's son Alexander d'Arblay (c.1815), as shadowy and unrevealing as he was in real life.

Carl and Horace Vernet's mildly misleading portrait of the retired Lieutenant-General d'Arblay taking his rest from battle, 1817.

...r Burney in old age, when ill-health and bereavement had soured his temper considerably, by John Nixon.

Left: Charlotte Broome in the early nineteenth century. She was the last of the siblings to predecease Fanny.

Fanny's favourite niece and executrix Charlotte Barrett in old age, a photograph probably dating from the 1860s.

Portrait of Frances Burney by an unknown artist. The strange frill at the neck of the dress may have been necessary to hide the scars from her mastectomy in 1811.

performance [. . .] could not be exhibited in a Barn,' she told Mary Waddington, echoing the reviewers' amazement at the sloppiness of the production. She took immediate action to withdraw the piece '*for alterations*'.

The reviews of *Edwy and Elgiva*, which Fanny read with close attention, also denounced the style of the play as 'nauseous bombast', revealing 'nothing of Poetry, and [. . .] often inelegantly familiar, or ridiculously absurd'.[21] Oddly enough, neither this criticism nor the humiliating night at Drury Lane deterred Fanny from hoping that not just *Edwy and Elgiva* but *Hubert de Vere* and the fragmentary *Elberta* might at least be published, if not produced.[22] Like Crisp with *Virginia*, she continued to think them viable works of art.

The summer before the *Edwy and Elgiva* fiasco, at just about the time when Fanny would have discovered she was pregnant, she had begun to write her new book in earnest, spurred on by the absolute necessity of making money. It was not to be a 'novel', a denomination which she felt 'gives so simply the notion of a mere love story, that I recoil a little from it', and which, significantly, 'was long in the way of Cecilia, as I was told, at the Queen's House'.[23] It was to be '*sketches of Characters & morals, put in action*, not a Romance', and was to contain several 'sermons' pointing up the moral in no uncertain terms. Fanny Burney knew her market, and had noted the current popularity of tract-writing – especially the kind so successfully earning a small fortune for Hannah More. But if Fanny thought she could prevent *Camilla* from turning into a romance simply by inserting a few sermons, she was wrong. Despite her stated intentions, the love-tangles of the central group of young people dominate the book. She was struggling against her instinct to entertain, and the results were predictable: 'It's a delightful thing to think of perfection,' as one of the characters in the novel itself remarks, 'but it's vastly more amusing to talk of errors and absurdities.'[24]

The speed at which the book was written certainly prevented the author from organising her material more coherently, but perhaps the most interesting touches in *Camilla* might have been lost too had the author, determined on a 'work' of moral value, had time to correct it. Fanny finished the book – which is about 350,000 words long – in a period of less than two years that also included the birth of her child and her subsequent illness. She was aware that it sprawled too much and said she was 'almost ashamed to look at its size',[25] but had really enjoyed its composition (unlike the struggle with *Cecilia*), reporting to d'Arblay, 'it is so delicious to stride on, when *en verf!*'[26] This stream of ideas carried along with it matter that had been on her mind for many years, from travel notes dating as far back as her jaunts with the Thrales, to observations on female education, the distresses of unrequited love, the new Young Man, the evils of gambling among women (thinking of the Duchess of Devonshire and her set) and the state of marriage.

Camilla Tyrold is the second daughter of a Hampshire rectory, beautiful, charming, warm-hearted and selfless, whose only faults reside in her youthfulness and inexperience. The favourite of her amiable buffoon uncle, Sir Hugh Tyrold, Camilla is replaced as heiress to his estate by her younger sister Eugenia, towards whom Sir Hugh feels profound remorse, having not only caused her to fall off a seesaw and deform her back and legs (a scene lampooned in *Northanger Abbey*), but also having exposed her to the smallpox, by which her looks are ruined. Camilla, whose sisterly feelings are as strong as any Burney's, is not in the least concerned for her own loss of fortune, unlike her beautiful cousin Indiana, Sir Hugh's ward, who is also disinherited to compensate Eugenia. Money and beauty, and the sudden loss of both, are the powerful forces that work on the group of young people at the heart of the book: the Tyrold sisters, Lavinia, Camilla and Eugenia, their feckless brother Lionel, their handsome, heartless cousins Indiana and Clermont Lynmere, and the old family friend Edgar Mandelbert.

Edgar, described by Joyce Hemlow as 'the greatest prig in English literature',[27] makes a very unsatisfactory hero. Aged only twenty when most of the novel's action takes place, his behaviour is of such stuffy rectitude that even the author begins to lose patience with him, allowing the most lively woman character, Mrs Arlbery, to call him 'a pile of accumulated punctilios' and 'that frozen composition of premature wisdom'.[28] Edgar is heir to a Norbury-esque estate called Beech Park; he loves Camilla (at a respectful distance) and elects very early on to marry her. However his cynical and misogynistic mentor, Dr Marchmont, persuades the young man to submit Camilla to a 'probationary interval' during which, he is convinced, any young woman will prove herself unworthy of his charge. Edgar's quick submission to this advice is the frail thread on which the subsequent plot depends. Like much in *Camilla*, it is unlikely, and certainly earned the scorn of whoever wrote in Jane Austen's copy of the novel, 'Since this work went to the Press a circumstance of some Importance to the happiness of Camilla has taken place, namely that Dr Marchmont has at last died.'

Most of the action of the novel depicts Camilla's adventures in society 'on probation' and how open to interpretation her actions are to Edgar's anxious eyes. Just over halfway through the book, the couple reach an 'understanding' and become engaged, only to break it off very soon afterwards when Edgar suspects that his fiancée is soliciting the attentions of the fop Sir Sedley Clarendel. The painful restitution of mutual esteem would be moving if Edgar were allowed some normal twenty-year-old characteristics. As it is, he behaves more like a plain-clothes policeman than a lover, following Camilla from resort to resort, ready to have his worst fears about her character proved right.

Though there are plenty of parent and pseudo-parent figures in this book, Burney's obsession with unguided or badly-guided youth remains as strong as in *Evelina* and *Cecilia*. Here the Tyrold parents, like Burney's own, are seen as perfect – yet oddly disabled. Their marriage is described thus in the opening pages (in language typical of Fanny's newly-reformed style):

> distinctness of disposition stifled not reciprocity of affection – that magnetic concentration of all marriage felicity; – Mr Tyrold revered while he softened the rigid virtues of his wife, who adored while she fortified the melting humanity of her husband.[29]

But even this exemplary couple (whose 'distinctness of disposition' is of exactly the kind Burney recommended in *Brief Reflections*) expose their family to danger for no good reason, and are so intimidatingly virtuous that their children feel incapable of turning to them for help when it is needed. Mrs Tyrold is an especially interesting authority-figure, 'unaffectedly beloved' yet 'deeply feared by all her children',[30] in the same way that Dr Burney was. Her moral superiority to every other character is of so harsh a nature, the precepts by which she lives so chillingly severe, that she seems inhuman and unsympathetic, almost as if she were, like Burney's own mother, dead. It is a parallel emphasised by the fact that Mrs Tyrold is absent for a large part of the story, 'taken from them' to nurse her brother abroad, and that Camilla's first contact with her on her return is as a disembodied voice in an inn and later as a ghostly 'vision' hovering by her daughter's sick-bed. Natural mothers are conspicuously absent from all Fanny Burney's works, and here, on the only occasion she attempts to depict one, impossibly other-worldly.

Mrs Tyrold's submission to her husband's will, and through him to the irresponsible whims of Sir Hugh, seems perverse and irrational, but her moral perfection includes the virtue of knowing her place:

> she never resisted a remonstrance of her husband; and as her sense of duty impelled her also never to murmur, she retired to her own room, to conceal with how ill a will she complied.
>
> Had this lady been united to a man whom she despised, she would yet have obeyed him, and as scrupulously, though not as happily, as she obeyed her honoured partner. She considered the vow taken at the altar to her husband, as a voluntary vestal would have held one taken to her Maker; and no dissent in opinion exculpated, in her mind, the least deviation from his will.[31]

If this obeisance were not a major cause of the Tyrold family's misfortunes, one might be able to admire its rigour; as it is, Mrs Tyrold's submission weakens the moral force of the work beyond repair in the eyes of modern readers at least (and of some contemporaries – Horace Walpole hated this novel), for what use is superior judgement if it is wilfully not exercised?

Though Camilla is nominally heroine of the story, the most truly heroic character is her deformed sister, Eugenia. Here at last we see Burney tackling the idea she had first broached to Crisp in the early 1780s of a 'clever *unbeautiful* heroine, beset all around for her great fortune', though she still didn't quite dare place this excellent subject centre-stage. Through Eugenia's 'extraordinary personal defects'[32]* and their violent contrast with her cousin Indiana's perfect beauty, Burney explores the demoralising effects on women generally of society's obsession with good

---

* Fanny uses exactly the same words in the *Memoirs* to describe the Burneys' beloved old friend Dolly Young's appearance.

looks and their irrational, irresistible 'magnetic effect'. Both girls are 'stunning', for different reasons; the scene in which Clermont Lynmere comes home from abroad to meet his intended bride, not knowing of her deformities but only of her accomplishments, is brilliantly handled. He is *stunned* into an unbelieving silence, which silences Eugenia's loving family, too, who realise for the first time the power of outward appearances. Inwardly, Indiana is shallow and selfish while Eugenia is not just refined and pure-minded but highly educated too; part of her special treatment has been a 'masculine' education at the hands of Dr Orkbourne, the absent-minded and obsessive scholar employed by her uncle (purportedly a joke portrait of Dr Burney). She has all the 'feeling' feminine qualities and yet is a trained philosopher, the perfect mate for a truly sensitive and worthy man. It is another of the book's moral anomalies that Edgar, who is set up as a masculine ideal of virtue, recognises Eugenia's superior worth but chooses to marry bubbly, pretty Camilla instead. Melmond, the emotional young romantic who is at first bewitched by Indiana but finds true happiness with Eugenia, therefore rather confuses the ending by beating the hero at his own game.

The most imaginative part of the story is the depiction of Eugenia's pained recognition that, contrary to the moral thrust of the book, which lauds patience and fortitude, she would do *anything* to change her looks. No amount of philosophy can compensate the fifteen-year-old girl for the disgust and abuse she excites everywhere she goes. The depression she falls into because of this doesn't last long because she is 'brought to her senses' by her father lecturing her on the subject (the chapter is called, uninvitingly, 'Strictures on Deformity'), but though Mr Tyrold ostensibly wins the argument, the reader's sympathy remains entirely with the girl.

When Fanny referred to her manuscript as '4 *Udolphoish* volumes',[33] she didn't simply mean to compare its size with that of Ann Radcliffe's Gothic bestseller, published in 1794, which she had admired greatly. Fanny's previous novels had revealed a taste for violence and grotesquerie, but *Camilla* was the first to contain deliberate elements of horror. As Margaret Anne Doody points out, the Gothic climax of the novel shares the intensity of Burney's tragic dramas and also something of their emotional excesses; Camilla is isolated from her family by her shame at

running into debt and, in a sequence of nightmarish episodes that emphasise her ostracism (including an eerie return to her uncle's empty, abandoned mansion), she finally collapses at a significantly named 'half-way
house'. Here she teeters on the brink of death, unrecognised and
unclaimed until an accident alerts Edgar to her identity. Fanny had
already toyed with a sort of false Gothic earlier in the novel (notably in
the moonlight scene where Mrs Berlinton appears like a ghost, and
Camilla's visit to the absurd Gothic garden created by Mr Dubster for
his roadside villa), but in the final chapters she decided to pull out all
the stops. Camilla not only witnesses a hushed procession bringing a
murdered man into the inn (he turns out to be her wicked brother-in-law,
Bellamy), but in this house of the dead enters a state of morbid delirium,
in which, having prayed for death, she has a vision of impending
judgement:

> another voice assailed her, so near, so loud, so terrible . . . she shrieked at
> its horrible sound. 'Prematurely', it cried, 'thou art come, uncalled, unbid-
> den; thy task unfulfilled, thy peace unearned. Follow, follow me! the
> Records of Eternity are opened. Come! write with thy own hand thy claims,
> thy merits to mercy!

Camilla is required to write down her 'deserts' and her 'claims', after
which her eternal doom will be rapidly revealed.

> A force unseen, yet irresistible, impelled her forward. She saw the immense
> volumes of Eternity, and her own hand involuntarily grasped a pen of
> iron, and with a velocity uncontroulable wrote these words: 'Without
> resignation, I have prayed for death: from impatience of displeasure, I
> have desired annihilation: to dry my own eyes, I have left . . . pitiless, selfish,
> unnatural! . . . a father the most indulgent, a Mother almost idolizing, to
> weep out their's!'[34]

Wherever she looks, these words are before her eyes, but when she
comes to write down her claims to mercy, the pen makes no impression

– in other words, there are no mitigations to her 'crimes'.* She is urged on by the voices to turn over the page and read her doom, but wakes up from this nightmare, 'labouring under the adamantine pressure of the inflexibly cold grasp of death', just in time *not* to read the inevitable judgement – eternal damnation. The fantastic elements of the vision should not blind us to the fact that Fanny was trying to convey what to her was a plain and incontrovertible truth (in a form she knew would be more powerful than another 'sermon'): that despair is a mortal sin which will wipe out any claims to divine mercy. In this climax to her 'Picture of Youth', as the novel is subtitled, she was earnestly attempting to warn the younger generation, so bombarded with impious and revolutionary ideologies, that the consequences of their actions were of the utmost seriousness.

In order to raise as much money as possible from *Camilla*, Fanny agreed to publish it by subscription, which necessitated publicity and a businesslike attitude towards the book's commercial value. Her friends Mrs Boscawen, Mrs Locke and Mrs Crewe managed the list for her (and gathered three hundred names before publication, including those of Hannah More, David Hume, Burke, Hastings, Mrs Piozzi and a whole regiment of dukes and duchesses); the Burney men busied themselves with the business side, negotiating with printers and publishers. Fanny needed these agents, but showed more true *nous* than all of them put together; her remark to her brother, that she considered her '*Brain* work as much fair & individual property, as any other possession in either art or nature'[36] shows an appreciation of the value of 'intellectual property' long before copyright law had even been thought of. Almost twenty years after the appearance of *Evelina* and fourteen years after *Cecilia*, the family were all too aware of the huge profits that were still being made for other people by those books, and were determined to maximise the benefits for the d'Arblays this time. As her brother Charles said to Fanny, 'What *Evelina* [. . .] does now for the Son of Lowndes, & what *Cecilia* does for the Son of payne, let your third work do for the Son of its Authour.'[37]

---

* The passage has been wishfully interpreted as an allegory of the heroine's 'inability throughout the novel to speak or write clearly', and of female creative problems in general by the critic Julia Epstein,[35] the title of whose study of Fanny Burney, The Iron Pen, derives from it. A pen of iron, it might be necessary to point out here, was an engraver's tool.

Fanny heard via Mrs Schwellenberg (who had become very friendly since Fanny's retirement from Court) that the Queen had enjoyed the book, but in the outside world responses were mixed. Dr Burney had indulged his usual practice of trying to fix at least one good review, writing anxiously to his son Charles, 'The work [. . .] must do credit, not only to Fanny, but to us all'.[38] As it turned out, the worst review was the one he had tried to influence in the *Monthly*, co-written by his close friend Ralph Griffiths, which freely criticised the book's length, structure, faulty grammar, Gallicisms and crank vocabulary (such as 'stroamed', 'flagitious' and 'fogramity'). 'M' (Mary Wollstonecraft) in the *Analytical Review* thought the book contained 'parts superior to any thing [the author] has yet produced',[39] but that overall it was not a success; elsewhere critics praised the usefulness of such a work to young people but withheld any very loud or strenuous praise. 'This novel is not such as we expected,' the *Critical* said reservedly. Privately, Dr Burney had heard much harsher judgements, to his fury. The printer Robinson had told him 'there was but one opinion about [*Camilla*] – Mme d'Arblay was determined to fill 5 Volumes – & had done it in such a manner as wd do her no credit'.[40]

Though Fanny admitted she was 'a good deal chagrined' by the reception of her book (and took the criticisms to heart, continuing to revise *Camilla* well into the 1830s), she comforted herself with the knowledge that 'Camilla will live and die by more general means'.[41] She had raised about a thousand pounds through subscription and sold the copyright to Payne, Cadell and Davies for another thousand soon after publication (the book went on to sell four thousand copies by November). The thousand pounds for the copyright was a record sum at the time (though it must be pointed out that the author did not receive all the money at once), and the profits from *Camilla* kept the d'Arblays afloat for some years. To her father, who was much more piqued by the reviews than she, Fanny sent on Charles junior's consolatory couplet,

> Now heed no more what Critics thought 'em
> Since this you know – All people bought 'em.[42]

Among the list of subscribers were Fanny Burney's fellow-novelists Ann Radcliffe and Maria Edgeworth and a 'Miss J. Austen' of Steventon in Hampshire. Austen was only twenty when *Camilla* was published, and four months later she began writing her own first adult work, a novel called 'First Impressions' (later *Pride and Prejudice*), the manuscript of which was circulating among the Austen family by August 1797. In her famous defence of the novel in *Northanger Abbey* (which, as we shall see later, was almost certainly addressed specifically to Madame d'Arblay), Austen singled out *Camilla*, along with *Cecilia* and Maria Edgeworth's *Belinda*, as examples of works in which 'the most thorough knowledge of human nature, the happiest delineation of its varieties, the liveliest effusions of wit and humour are conveyed to the world in the best chosen language'.[43] Austen was a devoted fan of Burney, and seems to have particularly admired *Camilla* (along with *Sir Charles Grandison*, it is the novel most frequently mentioned in her letters), reusing several situations and jokes from it in her own much more famous work. Any close reader of *Camilla* who is familiar with *Pride and Prejudice* will get a feeling of *déjà lu* from the similarity of Sir Sedley Clarendel's haughty behaviour at the provincial ball to that of Darcy at Meryton; Camilla's detention at Mrs Arlbery's house because of the rain to that of Elizabeth Bennet and her sister at Netherfield; and the musical ineptitude of Indiana, who 'with the utmost difficulty, played some very easy lessons' on the piano-forte,[44] to that of Mary Bennet, who so famously 'delighted us long enough'. The fate of Mr Bennet is foreshadowed in Mrs Arlbery's warning to Macdersey that the man who chooses a pretty, silly wife to gratify his own sense of superiority will end up 'looking like a fool himself, when youth and beauty take flight, and when his ugly old wife exposes her ignorance or folly at every word'.[45] Even the famous first sentence of Austen's book finds an echo in Burney's: '[It is] received wisdom among match-makers, that a young lady without fortune has a less and less chance of getting off upon every public appearance',[46] and the main narrative of both books – couple get engaged but then break off and struggle back together – is of course identical.

There are connections from *Camilla* to other Austen novels too: to *Emma*, which like *Camilla* features a charming, imperfect heroine and a disapproving monitor/lover, and to *Persuasion*, in which the famous Lyme Cobb accident recalls Indiana Lynmere coquettishly insisting on jumping into the yacht without assistance. The very title of *Pride and Prejudice* is thought to derive from Burney's repeated use of the phrase in the closing pages of *Cecilia*.[47] These evidences of influence are easily traced through

Austen's reading, but there are other, more enigmatic echoes in Austen of Burney which are more difficult to account for, notably the strange similarity of Fanny Price's experience in the famous 'Lovers' Vows' episode in *Mansfield Park* with the account in Burney's early diary of her own terrifying amateur debut in *The Way to Keep Him* in Worcester back in the 1770s. There is, more particularly, what looks like a pastiche of Madame d'Arblay's frequent use of the terms 'caro sposo' and 'cara sposa' in Mrs Elton's affected talk in *Emma*. In a fascinating article tracing the 'in-group language' common to the Burney and Austen families, 'Sposi in Surrey',[48] the critic Pat Rogers elucidates the connection between the two writers through the d'Arblays' friends and neighbours at Bookham, the Reverend and Mrs Samuel Cooke. Mrs Cooke was a first cousin of Mrs Austen, Jane's mother, and the reverend gentleman was Jane's godfather. Jane Austen knew Bookham and its environs well (*Emma* is set in this part of Surrey), and kept in touch with the Cookes all her life. Rogers's conclusion that she might have got to hear 'more about the Burney household than we have recognized'[49] through her friendly relations with the Cookes' daughter Mary, a teenager in the 1790s, is certainly suggestive. Fanny d'Arblay was a frequent visitor to the Cookes' rectory (The Hermitage is just across the road from Bookham Church), and while she was particularly fond of Mrs Cooke, she found Mary 'stiff and cold'. It is not beyond the bounds of possibility that Mary was passing on her impressions of their famous literary neighbour to her Hampshire relations, all of whom, it might be remembered were 'great Novel-readers & not ashamed of being so',[50] and that her reports might have concentrated on the more embarrassing or ridiculous titbits that she heard drop from the novelist's mouth.

The happy community of Lockes, Phillipses and d'Arblays in Mickleham and Bookham was short-lived. Though Susan loyally kept from her family her husband's worst 'eccentricities' of temper, debt and fidelity, it was clear as early as 1794 that there were serious problems in the marriage. Ever since inheriting the Belcotton farm, Major Phillips had harboured plans to move back to Ireland, and got near to doing it several times. Susan was, of course, averse to the scheme, and though Fanny hoped the matter would blow over, she had seen enough of the Major at close quarters by this time to begin to be wary of him. His behaviour was dangerously unpredictable, she wrote to her father, '*hovering*, though in forms so frequently contradictory that it is impossible to fully fix any stable judgement, either upon the real intent, or the internal causes. Sometimes the aspect is that of a terrible break up, at others the wilfulness of a restless mind that loves to spread confusion, cause wonder, & displace tranquility.'[51]

In the autumn of 1794 Phillips removed his elder son, nine-year-old Norbury, from Charles Burney junior's school in Greenwich and later in the year took him to Dublin and placed him with a private tutor. It was the first stage in a staggered removal of the whole family. In June 1795, amid tearful scenes, Susan and her other two children, Frances and William, left their cottage in Mickleham for good and moved to London, where they lodged with James and Charles in turn. The makeshift arrangements suggest that they were expecting to have to leave for Ireland any minute; the fact that the arrangements lasted over a year suggests that Susan was doing everything possible to postpone that evil hour.

In October 1795, Phillips took the rash step of resigning his commission as a Major of Marines, ostensibly because of 'insuperable avocations in Ireland', though Fanny was convinced that was a pretence.[52] His friend James Burney tried to talk him out of it (having lived for twelve years on half-pay himself he knew the difficulties), but Phillips had made up his mind, and what's more, seemed unconcerned about the consequences. He spent much of the winter and spring of 1795–6 in County Louth, supposedly preparing Belcotton for his family's reception, and came back to collect them in August, having promised Susan that he would bring Norbury with him. Had he done so, it seems very likely that Susan would have tried to effect a separation from her husband at this point, but Phillips knew that the boy was his only real bargaining counter, and so left him behind in Ireland.

Susan's distress was extreme when she realised the choice facing her: to stay in England against her husband's wishes and possibly never see her son again, or to remove to unknown, distant Belcotton with the 'half-mad & unfeeling M[ajor]', as Dr Burney was now calling his son-in-law,[53] who, incidentally, had extracted a massive £2000 loan from the Doctor the previous year and showed no signs of paying it back.

Fanny and Charlotte met their sister in secret at Charlotte's lodgings in Downing Street on 11 September, after which Susan wrote:

the terrible struggle is over – I think I shall be capable of submitting as you would have me – not from *mere* despondence – but from something better – that despondence may not at times seize me I do presume to hope ... but I intend to subdue it when I can, & to make such efforts as I am able to support myself.[54]

It seems, amazingly, that Fanny and Charlotte had advised their sister to obey her husband's wishes, even though she was clearly frightened of him and wanted a separation. Nothing could override a wife's and mother's duty in Fanny's eyes, even the happiness of her beloved Susan. She gave similarly 'rigidly Virtuous advice' to Maria Rishton the following year, saying that 'the only *Indispensible* Cause of Marriage Seperation' was death.[55] However *'Justifiable'* the complaint, a wife 'forfeited, by her marriage vow, the right of positively quitting [her husband], if she could not obtain his consent'. These harsh pronouncements, worthy of Mrs Tyrold, were all very well coming from one who had married so happily and knew nothing of domestic tyranny or abuse. One might have thought that her own experience of duty-bound incarceration at Court would have made Fanny more sympathetic to her sisters' distresses, except that she had (sensibly) not felt obliged to test her own principles quite so far in her own case. The sermonising of *Brief Reflections* and *Camilla* (which, ironically, she was only able to indulge because of her own separation from a tyrannical 'spouse', the Queen) seems to have made Fanny think of herself as a moral oracle who could not be heard condoning anything other than the most rigidly correct behaviour. The only comfort she could offer Susan were images of the sentimental reunion awaiting in Ireland with her adored son Norbury, and the prospect of a speedy return.

None of Susan's family was prepared to stand up to Phillips, especially not Dr Burney, who though enraged at the treatment of his favourite daughter, let the 'half-mad' Irishman bear her away to a country on the verge of a violent rebellion. 'I had no hope of working upon his wrong-headed & tyrannical spirit by anything I cd say or do,' he said limply, '& there was great reason to fear the making bad worse, by putting him out of humour, since we *must*, circumstanced as we are, submit.'[56] Susan and the children left London with Phillips on 14 October 1796, having said goodbye to the Lockes and Fanny at Norbury Park a week earlier. Fanny had run up to the gallery alone to watch from the window until the chaise was out of sight.

Susan had not yet reached Dublin before the Burneys had to face another family crisis at home. Elizabeth Allen Burney, who had been ailing for some time, suffered a lung haemorrhage in the summer of 1796 and by September was bedridden and dosing heavily on laudanum. She died, aged seventy-one, on 20 October, and was buried in the grounds of Chelsea College six days later. Charles Burney was devastated by his loss and entered a state of stupefaction very similar to that he had suffered in 1762 after the death of Esther: 'I sit whole hours with my hands before me, without the least inclination or power to have recourse either to such business, or amusemts as I used to fly to with the greatest eagerness', he wrote to his friend Christian Latrobe, and to Thomas Twining, 'who can calculate my loss?'[57]

Fanny, who went up to Chelsea as soon as she heard the news and spent a fortnight with her grieving father, was anxious about his weak, miserable condition and protracted mourning. Her long jealousy of Elizabeth Burney, kept sharp by loyalty to her own mother's memory, had always prevented her from acknowledging her father's true admiration and love of his second wife; now it prevented her from sympathising with the Doctor's profound bereavement. In her view, his misery was due to the superior 'tenderness of his pitying nature', not 'penetrated affections'. Deep sorrow, she stated categorically, was 'impossible' in the case.[58] Indeed, she was insensitive enough to suggest that 'La Dama' had been such a malign influence on the household at Chelsea College that her death was more a matter for rejoicing than tears; Sarah, she thought, was showing marked signs of improvement already, and her father's better nature, suppressed since the days of his first marriage, would soon reassert itself. The prospect was elating, and she wrote to d'Arblay, who had been left holding the baby in Bookham, that he would soon 'know that Father' for the first time:

> He evidently wishes to call all his Children about him, to receive & bestow the affections long pent or restrained, rather than manifested & indulged. His Heart has never been shut, but his ARMS now are opened again[.][59]

Fanny harped on these views at length to various members of the family, and developed other theories, including the shamefully self-aggrandising notion that her own departure from Chelsea in 1793 had left Charles Burney unprotected from his wife's temper, and that 'from that period, our so long-enduring Father became more clear sighted to her frailties, &, indulgently as he continued to bear them, ceased to persuade himself that he had nothing to bear.'[60] There is a note of sour triumph in this that is particularly distasteful. It is unlikely that Fanny ever read such testimonies as Dr Burney sent to Twining and his other friends during these months, describing Elizabeth as 'bosom friend & rational companion of 30 years, who had virtues, cultivation, & intellectual powers, sufficient to make home not only desirable, but also preferable to places where amusement is sought & promised'[61] (if she *had* read them in her father's posthumous papers, they probably wouldn't still exist). That she and her father held radically different views of Elizabeth Burney was something Fanny would rather deny than confront. She simply could not believe that he had ever been in love with this woman, just as he couldn't see (or chose to ignore) the very strong antipathy his second wife aroused in his first wife's children. Fanny's readiness to shape the past to obliterate these uncomfortable differences and re-imagine her father's feelings for him is ample warning of how she was to behave as his biographer.

Fanny suggested various projects to distract her father from his grief, one of which was to collect and revise his poems. This kept 'the monster' of depression at bay for a while, though Dr Burney later destroyed the ambitious long poem he began at this time, a versified history of astronomy. Fanny also attempted to cheer him with letters about her happy family life at Bookham, where everything to do with the 'Bambino' seemed newsworthy: his teeth, his toddling, his 'gibberish lingo'.[62] She was the archetypally doting mother, and described the antics of Alex with minute attention. She wrote at length and with pride of the three-year-old boy's presentation at Court in the spring of 1798, unwittingly revealing how unused the child was to discipline (the Queen, on that occasion, seemed far from amused with 'My little Rebel' and his restlessness.) However, Fanny could also laugh at her own maternal fondness and send up 'the wonderful wonders with which [the baby] makes *even his own parents* astonished by his wit & vivacity'.[63]

The d'Arblays were finding The Hermitage unsuitable as a permanent home and decided to go back to their plan to build a house on the land offered by the Lockes. It was not the most auspicious time to do so; with the war going so badly for Britain in 1797, goods and services were extremely expensive and there were serious fears of invasion as troops massed on the northern French coast. The establishment of the Directory had turned the tide of the Revolution, and Bonaparte's spectacular military success in Italy, along with his conquest of Belgium and Holland, made France the most powerful country in the world. It must have been strange for d'Arblay to witness this from the position of an exile. It was clear that his cause – constitutional monarchy – was becoming obsolete, and that he was in danger of having nowhere to return in his changed country. In August 1796 he received news of his younger brother's death in action in Spain two years before, fighting for the Republic of which he had been an ardent opponent. D'Arblay ruminated on the irony of this, and the hard choices which those left behind in France during the Revolution had had to face. Uncle Bazille in Joigny was now his last surviving relation in his native land, and little Alex in Bookham the last of the d'Arblay line.

D'Arblay threw himself with ardour into overseeing the construction of their new house in West Humble, which was only about a mile and a half's walk from Norbury Park. 'My Chevalier almost lives in his Field', Fanny reported to her father. '[H]e dreams now of Cabbage Walks – potatoe Beds – Bean perfumes & peas' blossoms.'[64] D'Arblay took responsibility for the grounds (the builders don't seem to have encouraged him to help *them*), digging a ha-ha to keep the cow off the cabbages and a well that had to be taken to a depth of a hundred feet before they struck water.

'Camilla Cottage', the name Dr Burney gave the new house, had a kitchen and three small, high-ceilinged reception rooms on the ground floor, a cellar beneath and four bedrooms and a 'chambre des livres' on the first floor (though they still didn't own many books). D'Arblay had included in his plans a bedroom to be used 'dans la cas où l'un ou l'autre seraiant indisposés',[65] which as at The Hermitage allowed Fanny a room of her own if required: 'such a dear refuge – so uncommon & so consolatory'.[66] He also gave the little house (which was tall and thin, like himself) 'Rumford-style' improved-efficiency fireplaces, a skylight in the roof and plenty of 'large fenêtres', though they had barely moved in before Pitt's window-tax forced them to block up four. Nevertheless, the d'Arblays were extremely proud of their first home, paid for entirely from Fanny's 'Brain work'.

On moving day in October 1797, d'Arblay went ahead on foot and had a fire burning in the grate to welcome his wife and child, who arrived by chaise. Alex was delighted to play in the empty rooms, still damp from being freshly plastered, and his parents were equally happy with their first meal of bread, cut with a garden knife, and eggs boiled in the only saucepan. They ate this sitting on the only piece of furniture in the house, a bench left by the carpenters. 'We dined, therefore, exquisitely', Fanny wrote in triumph, '& drank to our new possession from a Glass of clear water out of our new Well.'[67]

Camilla Cottage might have been 'lilliputian', in Fanny's description,[68] but it had not been cheap to build. D'Arblay estimated the cost at £1,300 – for which sum they could have bought a much larger property freehold. D'Arblay had overspent, thinking that he was likely to get some money from France soon, either from the change in government (subsequently overturned by *coup d'état* in September 1798) or his brother's estate (which ended up being confiscated by the state). Fanny was always anxious about her husband's poor money-sense and tendency to be led astray by 'bargains & temptations'.[69] Despite the *Camilla* savings, she was dreading the builders' final accounts, and in January 1798 had begun on another 'scribbling business' to meet their rising debts. She had decided to try writing for the stage again (much quicker than another five-volume novel), and the result was a comedy called *Love and Fashion*.

The plot of *Love and Fashion* centres around the choice facing the heroine, Hilaria Dalton, of marriage to wealthy old Lord Ardville or young, not-so-wealthy Valentine, the son of Ardville's elder brother, Lord Exbury (who has been forced to retrench to pay the debts of his other son, Mordaunt). The outcome is obvious from the start, so it is hardly a *dramatic* play, but Burney enjoyed returning to the *Camilla* themes of materialism and marriage in what is essentially a comic sermon about the importance of conjugal compatibility. The temptations of mercenary marriage for young girls are strong: 'to be made mistress in a moment of mansions, carriages, domestics – To have Time, Power and Pleasure cast at once at their disposal', but as Valentine points out baldly, such ties are 'radically dishonest'.[70] Hilaria, who begins as a frivolous, greedy girl whose idea of poverty is a 'pitiful' eleven thousand a year, has a comic solution to the choice between Love and Fashion (i.e. Money): 'If the regard of Lord Ardville be sincere – why can he not settle half his wealth upon me at once, without making me a prisoner for life in return?' She loses this flippancy through forced exposure to country life and Valentine's virtues, which make her 'attend to Nature' for the first time, and is rewarded by getting not just the young, good husband, but a fortune too, since Ardville repents his sins and makes Valentine his heir.

Love and Fashion is a much less inventive and amusing comedy than its predecessor, *The Witlings*. The secondary characters, which include a trio of domestics who open the play, each have traits which are established quickly and stuck to doggedly – a crude form of comic writing. There is a send-up of Gothic in the 'ghost' scene and the appearances of the 'Strange Man', who turns out to be a bailiff, but this sort of joke is too subtle for the rest of the play, which includes John-Bullish speeches from Lord Exbury directed straight at the gallery: 'Is This a Land where spirit and Virtue shall want Protection?' with the heartfelt coda, which could be called The Burney Principle, 'What is there of Fortune or distinction unattainable in Britain by Talents, probity, and Courage?'[71] Overall, *Love and Fashion* would have needed quite a bit of rewriting before being staged, as Thomas Harris, manager of Covent Garden, suggested in his generally enthusiastic correspondence with Burney about the play in 1798 and 1799. The weakest scene, which may well be among the ones Harris wanted to revise, is a sentimental episode between two rustics, a Hay-Maker and a Wood-Cutter, who are looking forward to married life together in virtuous poverty. 'How will I rub, and clean, and brighten my platters, and my pans, and my nice red bricks, to make them all shine, and look sightly, to welcome thee!' the young girl says to her manly but lust-free boyfriend. Hannah More herself couldn't have written with more patronising sentimentality of the rural poor.

While Fanny Burney was composing this hymn to companionate marriage, more marital disruptions were taking place within her family. Charlotte displeased their father profoundly by marrying again without his approval. Her first husband, Clement Francis, had left her independent and well-provided-for – so much so that Ralph Broome, her new suitor, seemed suspiciously like a fortune-hunter to Dr Burney and James.

They were still trying to find out about his finances when Charlotte went ahead with a secret marriage in March 1798. Broome, an ex-Captain in the Bengal Army, was a left-wing political pamphleteer, author of a successful satire on the Hastings Trial known as *Simpkin's Letters* (properly *Letters of Simpkin the Second, Poetic Recorder, of all the Proceedings upon the Trial of Warren Hastings*, 1789). He had been married before and was the father of an illegitimate daughter by an Indian woman, a fact which both Hetty Burney and Maria Rishton thought 'disgusting'. Fanny was torn between doubts about her younger sister's judgement, which she thought at best rather romantic, and a pragmatic hope that all would turn out well now that the unbreakable knot had been tied.

Elsewhere in the family there were worse disruptions to come. In the spring of 1798 Maria Rishton finally got her husband's agreement to an amicable separation, under the terms of which she received enough money to set up her own house eventually at Bury St Edmunds. The example of this (relatively) easy solution to an unhappy marriage (the Rishtons had no children to complicate the matter), and Charles Burney's readiness to give Maria temporary refuge in his apartments at the College, must have helped precipitate James Burney's decision in the autumn of 1798 to leave his wife and family for good. He had been spending more and more time away from home in the preceding years, often going about with his half-sister, Sarah Harriet, now twenty-six. While Elizabeth Burney had been alive, James had not been welcome at the College. Mrs Burney harboured dark suspicions of the special friendship that was emerging between the superannuated tar and her wilful, independent-minded daughter, ideas that lodged in Dr Burney's mind, but which he could not credit at the time. After 'La Dama's death, James appeared at his father's home frequently and seemed happily re-established as 'the best good fellow & kindest Brother imaginable', to use Fanny's phrase.[72] But it is clear that as the months went by, the Doctor began to wonder if his late wife had not perhaps been right to suspect that something highly inappropriate was going on.

James's suggestion, in September 1798, that he might leave his own home and come and board with his father, met with an immediate and disgusted response from the Doctor, who flatly refused to agree, not so much because of James's intended abandonment of his wife and children (the younger of whom was not yet two), but because the move would indicate 'an improper Attachment' to Sarah Harriet.[73] James's response to this was to go home and pack. The following day, 2 September, he and Sarah Harriet ran away together.

Controversy surrounds the nature of this elopement, which sent shockwaves through the Burney family – all of whom, interestingly, initially assumed that the couple were committing incest, and all of whom eventually came round to thinking they hadn't. The secretive quality of James and Sarah's departure, Sarah's 'happy & flighty' state on the day and her sinisterly satisfied smiles when quizzed by her half-sisters in the following months all helped convince the family of the worst. Biographers and editors of the Burneys have followed suit ever since with the assumption of incest, except for the editor of Sarah Harriet's letters, Lorna J. Clark, who has put the case for a less sensational alternative: that Sarah and James, who were both independent-minded and rebellious people, simply found they had common cause in wanting to run away (James from his family responsibilities, which had oppressed him for years, Sarah from her dead-end life at Chelsea), and chose to do so together. Clark's argument includes the facts that James and Sarah both denied any love-involvement; the family began to dismiss their own worst fears as soon as they had contact again with the runaways; the suspicion of incest had originated with 'La Dama'; and – the strongest point in Clark's view – James's wife Sally welcomed her husband back in 1804 and got on very well with Sarah Harriet afterwards.

There is much to be said for all this, though it might deprive the Burney family history of another animating sex-scandal. The Burneys were worldly people and reliable detectors of sexual guilt. One feels that the rehabilitation of Sarah and James at the end of their five-year experiment in cohabitation could only have taken place because the odd couple were understood to be just that: odd, but not wicked. Sarah Harriet had many reasons for wanting to leave home. She had seen little of her father's legendary charm and much of his curmudgeonliness, especially in the years since 1790 when old age, the war, family disappointments, the conclusion of his life's work and the death of his wife had changed the Doctor almost beyond recognition. He did not find his youngest child very congenial, and let her know it, treating her on occasion with 'bitter raillery or Harshness'.[74] It is little wonder that this spirited, eccentric woman, who thought of herself as ugly, 'queer' and unlikely to marry, responded with a form of passive rebellion, taking care not to be any good at things that might tie her to Chelsea as dogsbody spinster daughter. She couldn't copy, sew or keep house, and would much rather read to herself than aloud to anyone else. In 1796, very soon after the appearance of *Camilla*, Sarah Harriet's first novel, *Clarentine*, was published. It was reasonably successful (though not taken very seriously within the family), and served to show Sarah Harriet that she didn't necessarily have to stay under her father's protection for life. She went on to write four more novels over the next three decades, eking out a life of genteel poverty and proud independence on the proceeds.

From her letters, one can deduce that Sarah Harriet did not have the necessary guile or patience to keep up a false front on the subject of her relations with James. Her intolerance and free criticism of other people's sexual misdemeanours also suggests she wasn't sensitive to it. She was easily dissatisfied, tactless, restless and could be difficult company. None of her later jobs as a governess and lady's companion lasted very long, and she made a poor co-boarder in her one experiment of that kind. The five-year residence with James, in a series of fairly disreputable lodgings and with little money, probably came to an end because she had had enough of it; unlike when impassioned couples split up, Sarah and James seem to have had no hard feelings about the change, and remained very fond of each other. Her search in life, as she articulated later, was not so much for love, from which she seemed to think her looks debarred her, as for 'a gentle, rational, & friendly associate',[75] and her letters, especially the later ones, show her sighingly resigned to 'Old Maidism'.

But in the autumn and winter of 1798 this was cold comfort to the Burney family, especially to Dr Burney, who fumed at the ingratitude and defiance of the unfilial pair threatening to bring disgrace on them all. Any mention of James or Sarah changed his mood abruptly; he wished not to speak of them again. His daughters kept secret from him their efforts to keep in touch with the runaways (unrewarding though these were, since James himself felt aggrieved about his father's treatment of *him*), and the Burney sisters' correspondence in this period is full of concern for their father, who had been left, after Maria Rishton's departure from Chelsea College in 1799, with no one to look after him.

The necessity of finding 'some female society & care'[76] for old Dr

Burney suggested a hopeful scheme to Fanny. If Major Phillips could be persuaded to release Susan, she would make the perfect companion for her father at Chelsea. Fanny probably intended this to be presented to Phillips as a temporary expedient; little else seemed likely to make him agree to a separation. Dr Burney, not surprisingly, was delighted with the idea. He had not previously been able to admit that Susan's marriage was beyond repair, but if her 'sweet temper, tender heart, sound judgement, exquisite taste, integrity & acquirements' might be put to good use sweetening his dotage, he was very keen to get her back. If he had acknowledged the misery of Susan's situation earlier, such an action might have been of some use, but by the spring of 1799 it was already too late.

Susan had been careful to play down the difficulty of her life at Belcotton, to avoid both alarming her family and risking her husband's anger. Belcotton was cold, damp and isolated, and Susan and her two children (Norbury was in Dublin with his tutor) were often left there alone while Phillips was out with his friends or pursuing his handsome second cousin and neighbour Jane Brabazon. Phillips was a tyrannical and belligerent man, a heavy drinker and gambler who had no qualms about getting into debt (his huge loan from Dr Burney was never repaid, and he frequently called on James Burney for handouts). Susan had reason to believe that he had interfered with her letters to Norbury in the past and might be monitoring her letters home now; her correspondence with her sisters therefore became circumspect and evasive, making use of conspiracy tactics from the past, such as the use of code names (one of hers was 'Mrs le Blanc'; Phillips was referred to as 'the Climate', or 'le Temps') and removable 'cuttings' at the edges of the writing paper.*

Still, Fanny had little idea of how poor her sister's health had become. Her hopes and '*violent* wishes'[77] were centred on getting Susan back to England, which she did not believe was really possible before order had been properly restored in Ireland after the uprising of 1798. The Major put off his wife's 'visit' to Chelsea from season to season, and cold-heartedly exploited the family's increasing desperation in order to extort money from them for supposed travelling expenses.

---

* Some of these melancholy documents, slips of paper typically about an inch and a half deep and filled with minute writing, are preserved in the Berg Collection.

In the autumn of 1799 Fanny heard with mixed delight and dread that Phillips had finally decided to let Susan go because of the state of her health. Though she was sure that Susan would revive as soon as she got back to England, the prospect of her starting a journey at the beginning of winter was so alarming that Fanny offered to go over to Ireland herself to nurse her rather than risk her setting out. D'Arblay went up to town to lodge £50 at Coutts's bank in Susan's name towards these expenses; the Lockes also sent money secretly.

However, Susan's journey went ahead in early December while she was still very weak; she only got as far as Dublin before she had to retire to bed again for weeks, waiting to regain enough strength to continue. She was by this time desperate to get home, probably because she knew she was dying. She left these fears unspecified in her letters, and Fanny could only interpret the references to 'something [. . .] which has happened' as possibly connected with 'a danger she has never yet apprehended from rebels'.[78]

The Phillipses, with their seventeen-year-old daughter Fanny and eight-year-old son William, set out from Ireland at last in terrible weather at the end of December, not sure whether the yacht they had borrowed would put in at Parkgate or Holyhead. Charles Burney junior, who had volunteered to go and meet his sister and bring her home in 'a proper travelling Chaise' instead of one of Phillips's cheapskate contraptions, reached Chester by the mail coach on Boxing Day with his fourteen-year-old son Charles Parr Burney and heard that his sister and her family had sailed on to Parkgate, though when he got there he heard that they had been blown back to Holyhead. Charles set off along the north Wales coast road in the snow, only to find that the boat had gone on to Parkgate after all, and he had to hurry back towards Chester again. When he finally found his sister, in lodgings in Parkgate on 2 January 1800, she was not surprisingly much the worse for the long, cold sea-voyage. Charles's first impression was that Susan, emaciated, coughing violently and suffering from dysentery, 'could not live two days'.[79]

Susan must have rallied enough by the following day for Charles to have justified his rather extraordinary decision to take Phillips and the children to Liverpool for the weekend, leaving his sister at Parkgate to gain some strength in peace. When they got back on the night of Sunday, 5 January, Susan's forty-fifth birthday, she seemed 'apparently better',[80] but she spent the night in great pain and was so ill the next morning that she didn't recognise or attempt to speak to her brother, and died a few hours later.

Meanwhile, preparations had been going ahead at Chelsea to receive the travellers, and at West Humble Fanny was waiting impatiently for news from her father and looking forward with anxious excitement to 'embracing my dearest Susan in your arms & under your roof', not knowing her sister was already dead. The letters from Parkgate arrived on the ninth; Charles had written to his father, Phillips to the Lockes, asking them to 'communicate this intelligence to Mrs D'Arblay'. The Chevalier heard the news first; he had called at Norbury Park that morning on his way to London, and had to turn back.

'Tis wonderful to me my dearest Fredy that the first shock did not join [our souls] immediately by the flight of mine,' Fanny wrote soon afterwards to Mrs Locke, 'but that over – that dreadful – harrowing – never to be forgotten moment of horrour that made me wish to be mad – over – the ties that after that first endearing period have shared with her my Heart come to my aid.'[81] The d'Arblays set off from Surrey immediately, hoping to reach Parkgate in time to see the body and attend the burial, but the roads were snowy and the mails from London to Chester all booked up until the twelfth. They were forced to retreat to Chelsea, where they heard later that the funeral had taken place while they were kicking their heels there on the tenth. Charles had been the only mourner.

So the new century began for Fanny in seemingly irreparable heartbreak. As an old woman, annotating letters she intended to pass on to her heirs, she marked the little note she had sent her father on 9 January 1800 in anticipation of meeting Susan again, 'These were the last written lines of the last period – unsuspected as such! – of my perfect Happiness on Earth.'[82]

❧ 12 ❧

Winds and Waves

Fanny was numbed by the shock of her sister's death. For the first few days she could not cry at all, only scream to give 'some vent to the weighty oppression upon my soul'.[1] The blow was 'deadly – irreparable – it strikes at the root of happiness'; '[I] still sometimes think it is not – & that she will come – & I paint her by my side – by my Father's', she wrote miserably to Fredy Locke from Chelsea.[2] Dr Burney had to hide in his room for more than twelve hours after the d'Arblays reached Chelsea, literally unable to face them. When he eventually appeared at the parlour door, he wore 'a look of unutterable anguish'. His eyes were shut and he was muttering, 'I dread to see *you*, Fanny! I dread to see *you*!'[3]

There was nothing sublime or transcendent about Susan's death to mitigate the tragic waste, and the idea of 'merciful release' was little comfort, as the family had all been convinced of her imminent recovery. Though piety dictated that it had been the will of God, Fanny couldn't accept the death 'chearfully, nor [...] regard it otherwise than as a Chastisement!'[4] Dr Burney was so overcome that he couldn't go into public for three months. His only consolation was that Phillips had agreed to let his son William go to Charles Burney's school in Greenwich, and Fanny Phillips was coming to live at Chelsea College. Fanny hoped to 'mentally adopt' her beautiful young niece; Dr Burney, who said 'he will never part with her',[5] was intent on some compensatory spoiling, the results of which caused a deal of trouble later.

Once back in West Humble, Fanny also shut herself indoors until d'Arblay took matters into his own hands and engineered a meeting with the Lockes in order to break the 'hard spell which seemed to obstruct returning consolation'.[6] The results were cathartic: 'overpowered' by the sight of William Locke, Fanny sank to her knees – 'I was compelled to let my sorrow – my gratitude – & my anguish take their own way.'[7] This must have been an intimidating sight. As Mrs Sheeles had noted all those years before at the death of her mother, Fanny grieved unlike anyone else.

Fanny felt *unhinged* by the force of her misery, to the extent that her faculties were impaired. 'I have lost my power of retaining & retailing', she wrote to Hetty in late March, '& my recollections & ideas all run – I know not how – incoherently against one another'.[8] More significantly for her lifelong habit of journalising and letter-writing, she had lost her closest confidante and earliest reader. The 'power of retaining & retailing' gradually came back to her, but the motivation to practise it had for the most part gone.

Meanwhile, the production of Fanny's comedy *Love and Fashion* was going ahead at Covent Garden. She had sent a copy of the play to her brother Charles in the spring of 1799, and heard in October that Thomas Harris wanted to put it on the following March. Harris expressed surprise that Madame d'Arblay hadn't tried her hand at comedy before (clearly he knew nothing of *The Witlings*), as she had 'a genius for it!',[9] and praised Hilaria as 'the first female character on the English stage: – quite drawn from nature'.[10] More to the point, he was offering £400 for the manuscript.

Fanny left the matter in Charles's hands, and did not expect to have anything more to do with the production. She told Harris that she wanted the play to remain anonymous, but while the d'Arblays were still in London after Susan's death, staying at Esther's house in Beaumont Street,* a notice appeared in the *Morning Chronicle* stating that 'Madame d'Arblay, *ci-devant* Miss Burney, has a Comedy forthcoming at Covent-Garden'.[11] The leak was galling, not least because Fanny didn't want the failure of *Edwy and Elgiva* to spoil her chances of a fresh start as a playwright. Worse than that, the article sent Dr Burney into a panic. He demanded not only that Fanny withdraw the play, but also that the newspaper print a 'contradicting paragraph'.[12] The Doctor's extreme response is only partly explicable by a desire not to expose the family

---

* Charles Rousseau Burney and his family, struggling as hard as ever to make ends meet, had moved there from Titchfield Street in 1798.

name to any sort of publicity during their mourning for Susan. Was this the first he'd heard of Fanny's comedy? If so, she must have deliberately hidden it from him.

This seems very likely in the light of the letter Fanny wrote to her father following his outburst against any play being produced. She had moved swiftly to retrieve the manuscript from Harris, but clearly intended only to postpone rather than cancel the play's appearance on the stage (Harris himself expected to use it the following season). Fanny knew the reasons underlying her father's 'most afflicting displeasure', and had anticipated such a response. Since in her letter – the most assertive she ever wrote to her father – she doesn't once mention Susan's death it is clear that, in her opinion at least, family delicacy was not the point at issue. The issue was Dr Burney's chronic lack of confidence in her abilities and judgement, and she had had enough of it:

> Your goodness, your kindness, your regard for my fame, I know have caused both your trepidation, which doomed me to *certain* failure; & your displeasure that I ran, what you thought, a wanton risk. But it is not wanton, my dearest Father. My imagination is not at my own controll, or I would always have continued in the walk you approuved. The combinations for another long work did not occur to me. Incidents & effects for a Dramma did. I thought the field more than open – inviting to me. The chance held out golden dreams. The risk could be only our own for – permit me to say, appear when it will, you will find nothing in the principles, the moral or the language that will make you blush for me. A *failure*, upon these points only, can bring *DISGRACE* – upon mere control or want of dramatic powers, it can only cause *disappointment*.[13]

She pointed out, in a way guaranteed to flatter and cajole, that she had followed her father's example by wanting to be an author in the first place, and then by 'ranging' from one kind of writing to another. It was not *her* career only, but 'our career' – both the credit and the blame could be shared. 'Come on then, poor Fan', she wrote to him, articulating his ideal response, 'The World has acknowledged you my offspring – & I will *disencourage* you no more. Leap the pales of your paddock – let us pursue our career.'[14]

In truth, Fanny could no longer *afford* to be 'disencouraged' from writing and needed to leap into whatever 'paddock' promised some decent grazing. The loss of income from *Love and Fashion* was serious for the d'Arblays, and had important repercussions. With the overthrow of the Directory in November 1799 and Napoleon's establishment as First Consul soon after, change was afoot once more in France. Though d'Arblay had resolved years before not to return home while France was still at war with England, nor to serve against his wife's country, he was more impatient than ever to make a proper contribution to supporting his family. When he heard, late in 1800, that he had been removed from the proscribed list of émigrés in April and that there was a chance to salvage about £1000 from his French property, he was delighted and set out immediately for Holland to make out a procuration (Holland was the nearest country at peace with France from which he could do so). Unknown to d'Arblay, he was already too late to claim his property, but he returned to Camilla Cottage full of high hopes.

When hostilities ceased between England and France in October of the following year, Monsieur d'Arblay was overjoyed. By a strange twist of fate the French plenipotentiary who came to London to begin negotiations for the peace was an old army comrade of d'Arblay, Jacques-Alexandre-Bernard Lauriston, who was now a General and in high favour with Napoleon. Lauriston promised to put in a word with the First Consul over the matter of d'Arblay's pension and status, and the erstwhile Chevalier (now referred to officially as 'Citoyen d'Arblay') began planning a return to France with his wife and child immediately. All through October he went up and down to London, arranging passports and tickets, while Fanny, 'much hurried, & much perplexed',[15] tried to adjust to the idea of spending the winter in France. She understood that d'Arblay had to make the journey 'as a thing of course', but found it hard to share his excitement: 'on my side, many are the drawbacks – but I ought not, & must not listen to them'.[16] When Alex, now six years old, became ill with 'worm-fever' the same month, Fanny had a rock-solid reason to stay at home. Though she hated to be parted from her husband, there was no question of moving Alex during his illness, and d'Arblay made the journey to Paris alone in early November.

The return to France after almost ten years was exciting, surprising and stimulating to d'Arblay. In Joigny he was received with rejoicing as a long-lost son; there was 'beaucoup de gaieté et surtout de bruit' in his uncle's household. The youngest generation of cousins were about the same age as Alex, and d'Arblay longed to bring his son 'home' and settle in the beautiful valley of the Yonne. In Paris he met many of his old friends, all of whom had spent a far more active and profitable decade than he: Lafayette, imprisoned for years in Omlutz, was now being sought after by First Consul Bonaparte, and another former army friend, Louis-Alexandre Berthier, later Prince de Wagram, had made a spectacular rise to Minister of War. Berthier, like Lauriston, was a General, while d'Arblay was a shelved Maréchal du Camp, scrabbling after old pension rights. Even to an unambitious man like the Citoyen, these examples of success among his peers were a spur to action.

Restoration of the Bourbons, it seemed, was a lost cause, and most of the old Constitutionalists had transferred allegiance to Bonaparte. Madame de Staël and Narbonne were both thriving under the new regime; less successful, but surviving, were Lally-Tolendal, Montmorency and the former Princesse d'Hénin, last seen driving round Mickleham in a clapped-out cabriolet, now living in a small but elegant hôtel on the rue Miroménil.

As Fanny read her husband's excited letters from Paris, she realised that his visit was likely to make him discontented with their life of quiet retirement in England. She wrote him long replies full of advice, pointing out that there was no need to 'change our system', since the peace would make it easy to travel to and from France. She also insinuated that it would be difficult for her to earn money abroad from her writing (which was all too true), and that their immediate future depended on the success of the plans she had for the new comedy she had been writing during d'Arblay's absence (she was also revising *Camilla* in the hope of a new edition and trying to revive Harris's interest in *Love and Fashion*). Always more of a realist than her husband, she saw little chance of him regaining his 'many lost rights': 'What business, in which Money has any part, is ever executed as speedily as hoped?' she wrote to her father; 'I am the less philosophic in this delay [to d'Arblay's return], as I have myself, no expectations of ultimate success.'[17]

Her letters to her husband had a resigned tone, however. Fanny intuited that change was in the air, and sincerely wanted d'Arblay to do whatever he thought best: 'the more I reflect, the more I feel *I* can know no *happiness* but *yours*! – *misery* I may taste in many shapes; but *Happiness* & *you* are linked, for *me*, inseparably.'[18] His patience and selflessness through his long exile deserved reward, whatever her personal fears and misgivings about a 'renewed public sort of life':

> Do as you JUDGE best, & FEEL happiest, & I shall be best content. Yes, my dearest best loved Friend, your long forbearance – your waiting my wishes for the PEACE, call for my liveliest gratitude, & shall ever meet it, by an entire concurrence with your own decision for our future life.[19]

The comedy Fanny had been writing in the winter of 1801 was *A Busy Day*, but *The Woman-Hater* also belongs to this period. Far from being 'years of quiet' during which 'Mme d'Arblay [was] happily occupied with her maternal responsibilities and, when time permitted, with her literary career', as the editor of the *Journals and Letters* describes the period 1793–1801,[20] it was a time of almost non-stop literary composition: *Brief Reflections*, revisions to *Edwy and Elgiva* and the other Court dramas, *Camilla*, three comedies and the tentative beginnings of a new novel. *The Woman-Hater*, written between 1796 and 1802, incorporates some themes from *The Witlings*, updated to take in the contemporary debate on the role of women in society and embellished with elements of sentimental drama. Two characters from *The Witlings* reappear, Bob Sapling and Lady Smatter, misquoting and showing off her little learning as before, but in *The Woman-Hater* she is an isolated figure of fun. The focus of this satire is Sir Roderick, the sour old misogynist who, like Dr Marchmont in *Camilla*, is smarting from being jilted in the distant past (in Sir Roderick's case, by Lady Smatter*. Sir Roderick will not suffer women on his property at all, but his desire to avoid them has become such an obsession that he talks of little else. He has a wildly exaggerated idea of female helplessness (and conversely of male power) – 'if they fall into a ditch, they are drowned, – and if you don't put the meat into their mouths, they are starved!'[21] – and sees women as useless whether they are educated or not:

> Either you [women] know nothing, and a poor fellow, when noosed, might as well have the charge of a baby, or you know something, and he must

---

* Burney specifies in the play that it is seventeen years since this incident, interestingly the same interval as that between the composition of *The Witlings* and the first draft of *The Woman-Hater*.

pay for it with the peace of his life: for if you once take to a Book, or a Pen – his House may go to rack and ruin; his children may have the rickets; his dinners won't be half dressed, and his servants may dance rigadoons.[22]

Sir Roderick's attitudes are infectious. Old Waverley, his obsequious friend, lives in such fear of any dealings with women that when by accident he meets the virtuous Sophia Wilmot and her mother Eleanora, wronged wife of Lady Smatter's brother, he interprets their actions as soliciting for sex. He subsequently tries to 'rescue' Sophia from vice, which occasions some slightly risqué scenes and *double entendres* about prostitution and 'paupau women' (something of a departure for the prude playwright, who presumably intended this play, too, to be staged anonymously).

Young Waverley, Sir Roderick's heir, is so desperate to break free from the woman-hating zone in which he has grown up that he plans to marry the only gentlewoman he has ever met, Lady Smatter, even though he doesn't love her and is certain to be disinherited because of the match. Fortunately, he meets Sophia before he can carry out his elopement. She and her mother have come in search of Sophia's father, Wilmot, who is about to depart for the West Indies. Wilmot is another jealous misogynist whose misinterpretation of his wife's 'feeling' behaviour many years ago made him cast her off. But unknown to him, Eleanora took their daughter with her and substituted the nurse's child, a raucous, sensual, unintelligent girl who has been brought up as 'Miss Wilmot'. The untangling of this family romance, the reuniting of a chastened Wilmot with his noble wife and lovely daughter, and the capitulation of Sir Roderick to the charms of Lady Smatter (comically effected with very little difficulty in the closing minutes), make an undemanding, entertaining play that shows the author perfectly at ease 'doing what I have all my life been urged to, & all my life intended, writing a Comedy'.[23]

A Busy Day, which Fanny was writing during her separation from d'Arblay in 1801, has the distinction of being the only one of Fanny Burney's comedies to have been staged – albeit 192 years after composition. When the Show of Strength company put it on in a pub theatre in Bristol in 1993 (with a revival in London the year after), a reviewer in *The Stage* described the play as 'at least as scathing as anything from

Goldsmith – and considerably funnier'.[24] The only surviving manuscript is in d'Arblay's hand, so presumably Fanny did not finish the play until she was reunited with him in France. That she intended to present it to Harris is clear from the draft cast-list she drew up, all members of the Covent Garden company. But circumstances intervened again to thwart her career as a dramatist: *A Busy Day* must have been among the 'unprinted works' that she was forced to leave behind in Paris until their final removal in 1815, since the only manuscript she is known to have taken out of France in the period 1802–15 was that of her novel *The Wanderer*. By then, the play was dated and Harris was dead.

The action of this splendid comedy takes place in London on the day when both the hero, Cleveland, and heroine, Eliza Watts, are returning from the East Indies. Unknown to either of their families, they have already met, fallen in love and become engaged. Eliza, the daughter of a self-made City trader, comes from an uneducated low-class background (her father was originally an errand boy and her mother a housemaid), but she has been adopted and brought up in India by a wealthy and cultivated elderly gentleman, Mr Alderson (a distant bachelor-monitor, rather like Crisp), whose recent death is the cause of her return to England. Cleveland, an aristocrat, has been sent out to India to make his own fortune, though by rights he should inherit one from his selfish uncle Marmaduke, who has mortgaged the family estates due to bad management. The reason for Cleveland's recall (which he only hears on arrival) is for him to be married off by the uncle (his guardian) to a skittish heiress, Miss Percival.

Since Sir Marmaduke and his wife Lady Wilhelmina Tylney are monumental snobs and the Watts family are vulgar 'Cits', it soon becomes clear that there is going to be a violent clash between the families. Anticipation of this moment keeps the hero and heroine in suspense until Act 5, when Miss Percival, piqued by Cleveland's rejection of her, manoeuvres the disparate parties into the same room. 'Bless me! what people are these?' Lady Wilhelmina exclaims:

Sir Marmaduke. I can't imagine: unless those – (*pointing to Mr Watts and Mr Tibbs*) are two new men out of livery.
Lady Wilhelmina. Impossible she can have chosen two such grotesque figures. Besides, what do they stand there for? And look at those strange

Women! how extraordinary! I can't turn my head round, but that odd body made me a courtsie![25]

The Wattses retaliate by talking loudly of their showy new coach:

Miss Watts (aloud). I wonder if our Coach stops at the Door.
Mrs Watts. I hope never a Cart, nor nothing, will drive against it, for the paint's but just new put on, and it cost sich a deal!
Miss Watts (whispering). La, Ma', you're always talking so saving! Can't you speak about our servants? I dare say *(aloud)* Robert's forgot to tell Thomas to order Richard to stop.
Mrs Watts. Yes, I dares to say Robert's forgot to tell Thomas to order Richard to stop.[26]

The Wattses are lovingly satirised: Mr Watts in his scruffy scratch wig clings to recollections of how much more controllable his wife and daughter were when they were poor; his wife, on the other hand, is obsessed with maintaining the visible signs of wealth. Peggy, their daughter, has seen just enough of the grand world to intuit how vulgar her family appears, but unlike her sister she doesn't have the taste or refinement to rise above it. Her adoption of pretentiously romantic names for herself and Eliza, 'Margerella' and 'Eliziana', is comically thwarted by her parents' inability to remember them correctly; her embarrassment over this and her family's many other shortcomings recalls the Miss Branghtons' similar concern with impressing 'the quality' in *Evelina*, a work that has many echoes in the play.

'The Quality', as represented by the Tylneys, frivolous Miss Percival, Cleveland's dissipated younger brother Frank and his goofy boon-companion, Lord John Dervis, are a hopeless, enervated set; the constant references in their conversation to debts, tenures and mortgages emphasise that they are members of a class living on borrowed time as well as borrowed money. Money, and only money, matters in this cynical world; Cleveland's and Eliza's virtues would count for nothing if Eliza did not happen to be heiress to Mr Alderson's £80,000 and therefore, ultimately, acceptable to the Tylneys.

Only money can control the anarchic effects of class fluidity that the play depicts in a rather surprisingly radical way. The compact between the serving class and those who pay them is precariously maintained: when Mr Watts (who looks like a gentleman, but isn't) fails to tip the porter in Act 1, the porter immediately drops his deferential manner. Only the intervention of good-natured Joel Tibbs, who has neither got 'so high up in the World' as his 'Cit' cousin nor come from 'so low down',[27] prevents the disgruntled porter from becoming violent. The waiters at the gaming-house in Act 1 are insolent and unhelpful (their stage directions include 'exit sneering', 'exit yawning' and 'exit loiteringly'), and the gentleman's valet in Act 3 is so elegant that he is mistaken by the Wattses for his master; both have taken on the affectations of their employees. But none of their behaviour is seen as culpable insubordination because their 'betters' are so lax.

The servants of the late Mr Alderson are correspondingly loyal and devoted, particularly the Indian Mungo, a fascinating character who does not appear at all (probably because of the restrictions of the all-white Georgian stage). At the waiters' incredulity that they should have to help him or even talk to him – 'What, the Black?' – Eliza resolves to 'treble' her care of him in future 'for the little kindness you seem likely to meet with here'. Her (white) female servant Deborah, who has been in India many years, makes the depressing reply:

> Why that's very good of you, my dear young lady, to be so kind to him, being my late master's wish: but, for all that, these gentlemen mean no harm, I dare say; for after all, a Black's but a Black; and let him hurt himself never so much, it won't shew. It in't like hurting us whites, with our fine skins, all over alabaster.[28]

Deborah's dismissal of Mungo's sensitivity hides another interpretation: perhaps his hurts 'won't shew' because he is already black with them, like an all-over bruise. The treatment of natives in the colonies and at home would have been a sensitive point to press with a contemporary audience just waking up to the horrors of the slave trade and the responsibilities of a would-be empire. Burney was brave to dwell on it at some length in *A Busy Day* and to return to it in *The Wanderer*.

A Busy Day looks like a typical eighteenth-century comedy in the tradition of Murphy or Sheridan, but its concern with social conscience as well as social consciousness marks it out as a much more modern play. Aristocratic Cleveland's move downwards into the trading class has not just filled his purse but broadened his mind. He knows the value of money *and* understands the means of production and has picked up a set of unimpeachably humanitarian principles on the way. Nurture must perfect nature; Cleveland is both cultured and practical, Eliza refined, unaffected and sensitive, unlike her newly-wealthy family, who have the trappings of 'class' with none of its *agrémens*. Both hero and heroine are moving into an idealised 'middle' class from opposite directions. Burney's premise, as expressed by Cleveland almost exactly halfway through the play, is a restatement of the Burney Principle that 'Elegance, as well as talents and Virtue, may be grafted upon every stock, and can flourish from every soil!'[29] There is no swapped-cradle dénouement (as in *The Woman-Hater*) that will expose Eliza's superior birth and save us from having to include the Wattses in the imagined aftermath of the play: she *is* a Watts and Cleveland is (almost) a Tylney – a disturbing and very effective resolution to this clever satire on social mobility.

Back in Paris, d'Arblay was hoping that his influential friends would help him get a job in London as commissioner of French commercial relations in England, but first he needed to sort out his pension and *retraite*. When he wrote to the First Consul, however, he was told that he would have to serve on at least one campaign for the Republic before he could expect to be paid for *ci-devant* services, and Bonaparte suggested he join an expeditionary force setting out for the colony of Santo Domingo (Haiti) to put down the rebellion of the Negro slave leader Touissant-L'Ouverture. D'Arblay agreed, glad to have the chance of promotion to Brigade Commander and an honourable exit from the army. He came home to England in January 1802 to fit himself up for the campaign, spending a small fortune – 220 guineas – on his new uniform and equipment and securing the correct passports and papers for an absence of over a year. Fanny of course was terrified at the prospect of her husband risking his life in the 'pestilential' climate of the Caribbean, not to mention the fact that she had little sympathy with the French cause, and thought the rebellious slaves had very likely been 'ill-used'.[30] She felt strongly enough about the issue to include a footnote in the *Memoirs* exculpating her husband from any insensitivity to it: 'The Culpability, or the Rights of the insurgents [in Santo Domingo], could make no part of the business of the soldier; whose services, when once he is enlisted, as unequivocally demand personal subordination as personal bravery'.[31]

The same argument about 'personal subordination' did not, however occur to the d'Arblays in relation to action against the British, from which they naively imagined Monsieur d'Arblay might be excused. Before setting out for France again, d'Arblay took the precaution of writing to the First Consul to make it clear that though he was happy to accept the Santo Domingo commission, he would never fight against England. Bonaparte was not impressed. When d'Arblay arrived in Paris, with his hundreds of guineas'-worth of equipment in tow, he found that his commission had been cancelled.

This was not only a blow to his pride and his expectations (he thought of it as 'cette disgrace'), but forced a huge disruption on his wife and child. D'Arblay's latest passport, issued in connection with his military service, prevented his return to England for another year. If the family was not to be separated all that time, there was nothing for it but for Fanny and Alex to join him in Paris.

Fanny faced the prospect of leaving her precious home in West Humble and moving abroad for up to eighteen months with stoical resignation, fortified by relief that d'Arblay was not going to Santo Domingo after all. She set about arranging for Camilla Cottage to be let and, on William Locke's advice, spent quite a bit of money sprucing it up to attract the right sort of tenant (it must indeed have seemed quite Spartan to the Lord of Norbury Park). The Lockes asked Fanny to take with her back to Paris a protégée of theirs, six-year-old Adrienne de Chavagnac, who was going to be reunited with her émigré parents. Little did Fanny realise that she herself was about to become a sort of refugee, detained in France not for one year, but ten. It was as well that she didn't know this when she bade the Lockes, her father and siblings goodbye on 14 April 1802, and caught the Paris diligence with Alex and little Adrienne from the White Bear Hotel on Piccadilly.

Though she was unassisted, unaccompanied, uncomfortable about the language and had two excited children to look after, Fanny's first ever journey abroad passed off pretty well. Sea-sickness made the Channel crossing a misery, but as soon as they arrived at Calais, Fanny was absorbed by the novelty of the scene. She and the children wandered out into the streets of the town and felt perfectly safe – much to her surprise: Fanny admitted that she had 'conceived an horrific idea of the populace of this Country, imagining them all transformed into bloody monsters'.[32] On their two-day journey to Paris, she was further impressed by the kindness and good manners of the villagers she met at every *relais*, piously rejoicing at Bonaparte's recent restoration of freedom of worship in the Concordat. By the time Madame d'Arblay fell into her husband's arms at the coach stop on rue Nôtre Dame des Victoires she was already feeling less apprehensive about what life would be like in this alien land.

D'Arblay had found an apartment in the Hôtel Marengo, near the Champs Élysées, then a relatively retired spot 'entirely out of the violent bustle & close air of Paris', as Fanny described it to her father. Narbonne lived nearby, and visited frequently, though Fanny was less ready to encourage a renewal of friendship with Madame de Staël, or with the novelist Madame de Genlis, who was also re-established – very success-fully – in the French capital. The d'Arblays' near-neighbour Madame d'Hénin came to visit the Hôtel Marengo on Fanny's first day there, bringing tea and a teapot. Fanny was to see a great deal of this friend in the coming months, who tirelessly showed her the sights of Paris and found her a reliable *femme de chambre*.

The new French fashions for light drapery, translucent muslins and minimal underwear were not quite as shocking as reports in England had led Fanny to expect, but all the same it was obvious that Madame d'Arblay, now aged fifty, was never going to wear them. Madame d'Hénin and the maid looked at Fanny's wardrobe in horror, as Fanny reported back amusedly to Miss Planta in Windsor:

> *This* won't do! – *That* you can never wear! *This* you can never be seen in! *That* would make you stared at as a curiosity! *THREE* petticoats! No one wears more than one! STAYS? every body has left off even corsets! – Shift sleeves? not a soul now wears even a chemise! &c &c. – In short I found all that I possessed seemed so hideously old fashioned, or so comically rustic, that as soon as it was decreed I must make my appearance in the *grande monde* hopeless of success in exhibiting myself in the *costume francais*, I gave over the attempt, & ventured to come forth as a Gothic *anglaise*, who had never heard of, or never heeded, the reigning metamor-phoses.[33]

Fanny had no desire to enter Parisian society and hoped to ride out her visit to France in modest obscurity. The new meritocracy created by Napoleon was an intimidating group, flaunting money and titles for the first time in years. There was no way in which the d'Arblays could compete with those who had flourished under the Directory and who now, like General Hulin (who had served as a Captain *under* d'Arblay before the Revolution), appeared at parades and reviews decked out in astonishingly showy uniforms, while d'Arblay was in a scruffy old coat and 'complete undress'.[34] Although France was still nominally a republic, Napoleon's elevation to Consul for life in 1802 – a stepping-stone on his way to becoming Emperor two years later – was ushering in a new epoch of national confidence and pride. Bonaparte's face was on everything, from medallions to barley-sugar sticks, and his fame was awe-inspiring, as Fanny soon had the chance to witness and experience herself. Only a fortnight after her arrival in Paris, d'Arblay secured tickets for a review of troops in the Tuileries at which the First Consul was going to preside. The crowd was extremely large, and short-sighted Madame d'Arblay would have seen nothing at all if she hadn't been identified as a foreigner and given one of the best places (an example of French good manners which impressed her deeply):

> At length, the two human hedges were finally formed, the door of the Audience Chamber was thrown wide open with a commanding crash, a vivacious officer-Centinel – or I know not what, nimbly descended the three steps into our Apartment, & [. . .] called out, in a loud & authoritative voice, 'Le Premier Consul!' [. . .] I had a view so near, though so brief, of his face, as to be very much struck by it: it is of a deeply impressive cast, pale even to sallowness, while not only in the Eye, but in every feature, Care, Thought, Melancholy, & Meditation are strongly marked, with so much of character, nay, Genius, & so penetrating a seriousness – or rather sadness, as powerfully to sink into an observer's mind[.][35]

The review in the Tuileries took place when the Peace of Amiens between England and France was scarcely two months old, and when Fanny could dwell on Bonaparte's abstract virtues without worrying too much about his martial ambitions. She began to feel very differently about the First Consul as the prospect of war built up again the following year.

The small circle of 'female worthies' with whom Fanny associated were mostly middle-aged *ci-devant* aristocrats like Madame d'Hénin and Madame (formerly Vicomtesse) de Laval, who had little money with which to enjoy the sophisticated cultural life of Paris but who maintained a genteel, intelligent and mutually supportive society of their own. Madame de Tessé, sixty-five-year-old former lady-in-waiting to Marie-Antoinette, was of this company, a lady whom d'Arblay described as 'one of the first Women of the best French society';[36] her niece, Adrienne de Noailles, was the resourceful and heroic wife of d'Arblay's former commander Lafayette (to whose rural retreat, La Grange, the d'Arblays were invited in June 1802). The elderly abbess Catherine de Fay de Latour-Maubourg was also of this circle with her niece Madame de Maisonneuve, who became one of Fanny's closest friends in France. Fanny was fortunate to have a member of her family living in Paris at this time too: Hetty's daughter Maria had moved there recently with her husband Antoine Bourdois (affectionately known to little Alex as 'Bood'), a well-off native of Joigny and old friend of the d'Arblay family. The match between him and dowerless Maria Burney had been engineered by Fanny and her husband several years before and had proved a great success. It was a relief to have this charming and familiar young couple living within easy reach on the rue de Choiseul.

As Fanny had predicted, d'Arblay was seriously considering a permanent 'change of system', and, perhaps encouraged by the ease with which Fanny had made friends, soon came up with a plan to spend six months of every year at Camilla Cottage, four months in Paris and two in Joigny. He didn't realise (because she hid it as well as possible) how increasingly important retirement was to his wife. When they spent a fortnight with the Bazille clan in Joigny in late June, Fanny found the visit almost intolerable. She loved the Bazilles and appreciated the fuss they made of their nephew and his family, but the small-town life that d'Arblay thrived on destroyed her sense of well-being as much as had Court life, as she wrote in comic exasperation to Hetty:

> M. D'arblay is related, though very distantly, to a quarter of the town, & the other 3 quarters are his friends or acquaintance: & all of them came first to see me; next to know how I did after the journey; next were all to be waited upon in return; next came to thank me for my visit; next to

know how the air of Joigny agreed with me; next to make a little farther acquaintance; & finally to make a visit of congé.[37]

'Interruption, & visiting' were still Fanny's idea of hell.

Just as they couldn't decide where to live, the d'Arblays also had a continuing struggle over which language was going to predominate in their household, since neither of them was truly bilingual. D'Arblay's letters to his wife are in French, hers mostly in English, but English was the language they spoke at home – at least, it was when they were in France. Fanny could understand and read French very well by now, but was frustrated at her lack of fluency in speech. 'You have hardly an idea what a check it is to my *declamatory powers* that if I think of speaking, I cannot utter a word!' she wrote to Fredy Locke. 'All my eloquence hangs on being surprised into an harangue, before I consider in what language I am delivering it'.[38] She found the effort of speaking French tiring and boring: 'my voice is as wearied of pronouncing as my brain is wearied in searching words to pronounce'.[39] The resulting tongue-tie was like a return to her silent, blushing youth.

It wasn't only her 'declamatory powers' that were checked in this period; Fanny also felt that for some reason or other her 'epistolary spirit' had 'flown'.[40] 'I never wrote so few letters in my life', she said[41] – nor, she might have added, got so few replies. Her father, now approaching his eightieth year, was no longer a good correspondent, and despite resolutions with Hetty, Charlotte and Fredy Locke to keep a letter always on the stocks, ready for any opportunity to get it transported across the Channel, there was something deadening about the delays involved.

Within a couple of months of Fanny's arrival in Paris the d'Arblays moved from the Hôtel Marengo to the airy suburb of Monceau because of Alex's persistent illnesses in the city; in October 1802 they moved again, to 54 rue Basse, a house built into a hill overlooking the Seine at Passy.* They bought this 'queer, irregular, odd house'[42] in order to have some property in France to substantiate d'Arblay's citizenship, since his

---

* Rue Basse, now called rue Raynouard, has housed many famous people, including Benjamin Franklin, Jean-Jacques Rousseau and, in the nineteenth century, Honoré de Balzac. The Maison Balzac, with its rustic garden and views over the river, stands in the plot adjacent to the d'Arblays' former home.

hopes of reclaiming his land in Joigny had failed.* 'It is just the place for such odd folks,' Fanny wrote to Mrs Locke, 'for we *descend* to enter it.'[43] The cottage was mostly unfurnished when they moved in, and they had to send the builders away due to lack of cash, but Fanny liked the privacy of owning her own home, which became another 'hermitage'. Presumably uncle Bazille helped out with the purchase; it is hard to see how else the penniless d'Arblays could have afforded it, cut off from Fanny's small Court pension and the even smaller amount of rent they were owed at Camilla Cottage, which had only attracted a three-month let. D'Arblay's own hopes of a pension were eventually realised in April 1803, through the offices of Lauriston again, but amounted to a mere £62 10s a year, half what he was expecting.

Fanny had been planning to return to England in October 1803, but events overtook her. War between France and England was imminent. On 12 May, the day the British Ambassador Lord Whitworth left Paris, the dramatist Bertie Greatheed called on the d'Arblays in Passy for the first time and found Monsieur in 'the greatest agitation'. Madame kept to her room, clearly in no state to entertain. 'This approaching war seems quite to overset them,' Greatheed wrote in his journal, 'so linked are they to both countries that to separate from either is ruin and to hold both impossible.'[44] His observation was perspicacious: the d'Arblays' loyalties were painfully confused. 'War [...] seems inevitable,' Fanny wrote the same day to Fredy Locke, '& my grief – I, who feel myself now of Two Countries – is far greater than I can wish to express.'[45]

With the declaration of war on 16 May 1803, there was no longer any question of choice in the matter of where the d'Arblays' were going to live. Now it was Fanny's turn to be an alien in an enemy country. Bonaparte decreed on 22 May that all Englishmen and women in France between the ages of eighteen and sixty were to be considered prisoners of war. Severe travel restrictions and coastal blockades cut off any chance of Fanny keeping in touch with her family in England except by getting letters smuggled through on the very rare occasions when they could place them with trustworthy travellers. In 1804 she wrote only one letter to England – to her elderly father – and in 1807 she mentioned two that

---

* It had been purchased from the state during his exile and could only be bought back at a massively inflated price.

were 'antiques that had waited 3 or 4 years some opportunity'. There was little chance of knowing, under these circumstances, if letters got to their destination or not, or whether they passed through the censor's office on the way. Dr Burney was completely dissuaded from writing to Fanny because of his fear of her vulnerability, and advised the rest of the family not to risk writing to Paris either. He imagined that Fanny, with her Court and social connections in England, could easily be suspected of spying.

The d'Arblays therefore lived in a strange news blackout that lasted nine years. Letters that did trickle through from family and friends in England kept off politics and the war; consequently the d'Arblays didn't even hear of the British victory at Trafalgar until 1812 – seven years after the battle. Similarly, Fanny had no idea until long after the event that her half-brother Richard had died out in Calcutta, aged only forty; that Sarah and James had finished their experiment in cohabitation in 1803 (James went back to his family and Sarah went off to be a governess in Cheshire); that Ralph Broome had died in 1805, leaving Charlotte widowed for the second time; that in 1807 her favourite niece, Charlotte Francis, had married a man called Barrett thirty years her senior and her most beautiful niece, Fanny Phillips, had found a husband rich enough to pay her debts and satisfy her extravagant tastes. Queeney Thrale had married too, at the age of forty-three. Her husband was Baron (later Viscount) Keith, Admiral of the White, the distinguished Commander-in-Chief of the Channel Fleet in the later stages of the Napoleonic war. Queeney's mother, Mrs Piozzi, had begun a correspondence and friendship with Marianne Francis, Charlotte's second daughter, a pious, self-possessed young woman who never married but devoted herself to private study and philanthropy. Perhaps it is just as well that Fanny did not know how she had been replaced in Mrs Piozzi's affections by her niece, nor of how often gossip about 'Madame Dab' was passed along to Streatham Park via this channel.

There was little for the d'Arblays to do after the outbreak of war but keep their heads down, but with no chance of money coming from England and no recourse to their most reliable source of income, Fanny's pen, the family was in a worse financial position than ever. In March 1805 d'Arblay began work on a salary of about £150 a year as a humble *rédacteur* in the Ministry of the Interior, a post he kept right through to the Restoration. After the first few months of pen-pushing he was so restless that he was briefly tempted by Narbonne's suggestion to join Napoleon's Polish campaign, but his principles and his chivalrous respect for his wife's feelings prevented him from doing so. Fanny's implacable objection to militarism and her reluctance to let d'Arblay risk his life in battle clashed once again with the family tradition, instincts and training of her frustrated soldier husband.

The health and education of Alex was a constant preoccupation of both his parents, who fussed continually over their hyperactive, precocious *sauvage*. Fanny was a firm believer in preventive medicine (they had submitted Alex to the risky new smallpox vaccination in 1798), and had always been keen on dosing her child up. The treatments she mentions giving him in these years in Paris include her old favourites, James's powders and bark, as well as saline draughts, asses' milk, red port infused with garlic, rhubarb and senna (together), sulphur, cream of tartar with honey, and raw turnip juice. No wonder the child felt sick most of the time and looked as thin as a 'live skeleton'.[46] And while his mother hung over his bedside, administering turnip juice on a spoon, his father was anxiously monitoring the boy's studies and trying to rectify bad habits such as his obsessive interest in mathematical problems, which kept the child awake at night. Alex's absent-mindedness, asociability and general lack of connection with the outside world were already marked at the age of ten.

The d'Arblays devoted a great deal of energy to their son's education, but the time came when he began to out-learn them. Fanny had been planning to send him to his uncle Charles's school in Greenwich on their return to England, but their detention in France necessitated finding him a place locally. Being possessive, anxious parents, unwilling 'to relinquish entirely Our home system',[47] they persuaded Monsieur Sencier, the head of the pension on the rue Basse, to take Alex for mornings only. After only ten months of this dual regime, the boy won four first prizes at the end-of-year examination, for Mythology, Version, Thème and Bonne Conduite, much to his parents' delight and pride. Neither Fanny nor d'Arblay seemed to anticipate any problems that might arise from Alex always being odd-man-out at school – the only *externe*, a skinny *anglais*, a winner of prizes for *Bonne Conduite*. The degree of control his parents exerted over him was extraordinary. At the age when d'Arblay himself had joined the army, Alex was being treated to evenings of family reading, his father carefully censoring 'all such passages as might tarnish the lovely purity of his innocence by any dangerous impressions'.[48]

When the d'Arblays had to move back into the centre of Paris in the winter of 1806 to alleviate the unpleasantness of commuting (d'Arblay had been walking to and from his office in the sixième arrondissement along the muddy lanes to save money), Alex of course had to move schools. Monsieur Hix's big school of almost two hundred boys was primarily for boarders, but again the d'Arblays made an exception of their son and insisted on sending him as a day pupil, this time on grounds of his health. Alex performed even better here than at Passy, but at a cost. Not surprisingly, the boys in his class developed a strong dislike of the little swot, and his superflux of merit points was deeply resented. The disaffected pupils were soon petitioning that d'Arblay be moved up to the next class, as Fanny related with misplaced pride in a long account to her father:

> one of them called out aloud 'Au quatrieme, D'Arblay!' M. Hue angrily demanded who spoke? upon which 12 hands were held up, & 12 voices 'Au Quatrieme, d'Arblay! This was so near a mutiny, that M. Hue was going to inflict some severe punishments, when all in a body lifted up their hands, & joined in the Chorus 'Au quatrieme, d'Arblay! il est trop fort pour nous!'[49]

The teacher backed down at such a show of force, and referred the matter to the headmaster, but when the class was told yet again that they only had to work hard to get the same success as 'petit d'Arblay', they took matters into their own hands and threatened to beat him up in the playground if he didn't either volunteer for a transfer or stop swotting. Alex took the latter course and quickly turned himself into 'the idlest & most wanton Boy of the Class!'[50] to appease his persecutors. His parents only found this out just in time to force him back 'to his good old way' before the exams. At the school prizegiving Alex carried off six first prizes and was so laden with books and laurel crowns that he made the audience of 1200 people give 'a burst of approbation such as was given to no one else' – so his mother said. She and d'Arblay were swollen with pride at their child's success: d'Arblay was 'forced to cover his face with his handkerchief from a joy amounting almost to shame', as Fanny put it, and she – who had previously feared her child 'might disgrace himself' – couldn't see for tears. It was indeed a very poor look-out for Alexander, as Madame d'Arblay herself realised later, singling out 'those 6 fatal prizes' as having 'turned his understanding into presumption, & his application into caprice'.[51]

During her forced sojourn in France, Fanny worked sporadically on her fourth novel, *The Wanderer*. In the dedication to the book she reveals that it had been 'planned and begun [...] before the end of the last century!',[52] put aside, taken to France in 1802 and composed in patches over the next decade. With no chance of publication in the foreseeable future, there was no necessity to finish the book, and perhaps no desire to finish it either. The long, flexible story seems to have acted as a form of entertainment for Fanny as well as an occupation, a substitute for all the letters, conversations and gossip she was missing with her English intimates. Unfortunately *The Wanderer* suffered from its leisurely, aimless, episodic composition; without the pressure of a deadline that had knocked all her preceding novels into shape, Fanny's new story merely sprawled.

Fanny had all but stopped writing a diary or journal, replacing it with memoranda, jottings and lists of visits, correspondence and reading. In the past she had composed her journal from notes made on the day (this had become a habit during the Court years); now she made very few notes and never bothered to elaborate them. 'Could I write more frequently, or with more security that I write not to the Winds & the Waves, I would characterise the whole set to you, & try to make us yet shake hands in the same party', she wrote to her father in 1810 of her friends the 'female worthies'.[53] But there didn't seem any point in even beginning such a task.

The silence was broken occasionally, most notably when Fanny had to undergo an appalling operation, without anaesthetic, in 1811. Since the abscess which developed in 1794, she had suffered recurrent 'breast attacks' – painful inflammation of the right breast – in 1804 and 1806 (and possibly at other times which she forbore to mention). A regimen of fasting and asses' milk helped her get through these bouts of illness, but the problem did not go away and by 1810 she had a painful lump in her right breast which by the following year was the size of a fist. After much agonised consultation and protracted attempts at a medicinal cure, it was decided to consult a surgeon, whose alarming diagnosis was that 'a small operation' might be necessary. Fanny's delicacy was as much affronted at the thought of the indignities and exposure ahead as of the pain, and there was a further delay while she hoped to cure herself by diet and quiet living. Unfortunately, nothing but bad news reached her during this period, of the deaths of William Locke and Princess Amelia and of King George's final collapse into illness (leading to the establishment of the Regency in 1810). Her state of mind had always had a direct effect on her health, and at the next consultation, which was with Napoleon's celebrated army-surgeon Dominique-Jean Larrey, the need for an operation was pronounced vital: the growth was cancerous.

In the medical culture of the day, exposure of a female patient's body to examination was not insisted on, and it is highly likely, given Fanny's temperament and her stated 'dread & repugnance' of medical intervention 'from a thousand reasons *besides* the pain',[54] that Larrey had not actually seen the affected breast until he was just about to cut it off. The consultation and decision-making that went on between the doctors over Madame d'Arblay's prone body on the day of the operation certainly suggest it was the first opportunity any of them had had to examine the tumour, and even then, they didn't *touch* it. It has been suggested in recent years that the fact that the patient, then aged fifty-nine, survived for twenty-nine years after her mastectomy indicates that the lump was benign and that total amputation may not have been necessary.[55] The mastectomy was itself of course a life-threatening operation, from the dangers of haemorrhaging and infection (not to mention the trauma of excruciating pain in this pre-anaesthetic age). Without Larrey's expertise at suturing and his pioneering surgical techniques, perfected on dozens of battlefields in the Napoleonic era, Fanny would very likely not have survived this cure for a possibly benign tumour.

The events of the day itself – 30 September 1811 – were recorded by the patient in extraordinary detail in an account written between six and nine months later.[56] It was addressed to her sister Hetty, but was intended to be circulated among her immediate family in England, and because she had both her husband and son fair-copy it for her – a task which d'Arblay found traumatic – it could be rightly thought of as primarily addressed to *them*. Step-by-step she re-enacts the 'never-ending' wait for the doctors to arrive, the preparation of the bed, bandages, sponges and two old mattresses to soak up the blood, the arrival of the cabriolets 'one – two – three – four – succeeded rapidly to each other in stopping at the door', then the sudden entrance of the seven doctors, all dressed in black, the weeping nurses, the doctor's imperious commands to his assistants 'en militaire' and the horrible moment of having to undress in front of them.

> [E]verything convinced me [. . .] that this experiment alone could save me[.] I mounted, therefore, unbidden, the Bed stead – & M. Dubois placed upon me the mattress, & spread a cambric handkerchief upon my face. It was transparent, however, & I saw, through it, that the Bed stead was instantly surrounded by the 7 men & my nurse. I refused to be held; but when, Bright through the cambric, I saw the glitter of polished Steel – I closed my Eyes. I would not trust to convulsive fear the sight of the terrible incision.

The style is an odd mixture of reportage and melodrama, relating all the facts with forensic accuracy but underpinning them with a symbolic language of intrigue, mystery, sacrifice and assault. The elements of colouring – the sinister '7 men in black' arriving like assailants and surrounding the bed as soon as the victim's face is covered, the threat of restraint, the glinting steel – might be considered unnecessary in a piece of writing which, the author claimed, was only written in order to correct any false reports her sister Hetty might encounter (from whom she might hear 'false reports' on this subject is hard to imagine). In her instructions about how the account of the mastectomy could/should be circulated, Fanny was very concerned not to have her father, Fredy Locke or Miss Cambridge read or know anything of the matter. (This was easily effected, and none of them ever found out what she had endured.) Her real motive in telling all but her most vulnerable friends about this dreadful event was clearly something different – a desire to shock. She goes on:

> a terror that surpasses all description, & the most torturing pain. Yet – when the dreadful steel was plunged into the breast – cutting through

veins – arteries – flesh – nerves – I needed no injunctions not to restrain my cries. I began a scream that lasted unintermittingly during the whole time of the incision – & I almost marvel that it rings not in my Ears still! so excruciating was the agony. When the wound was made, & the instrument was withdrawn, the pain seemed undiminished, for the air that suddenly rushed into those delicate parts felt like a mass of minute but sharp & forked poinards, that were tearing the edges of the wound – but when again I felt the instrument – describing a curve – cutting against the grain, if I may so say, while the flesh resisted in a manner so forcible as to oppose & tire the hand of the operator, who was forced to change from the right to the left – then, indeed, I thought I must have expired. I attempted no more to open my Eyes, – they felt as if hermettically shut, & so firmly closed, that the Eyelids seemed indented into the Cheeks.

This blood-curdling description is surely one of the most extraordinary pieces of 'reminiscence' ever committed to paper. Like the operation, the account goes on for a long time, and Fanny spares nothing: 'the Knife rackling against the breast bone – scraping it!', the mutilated breast so excruciatingly sensitive that she could *feel* the doctor's hand poised over it 'though I saw nothing, & though he touched nothing'. 'I have two total chasms in my memory of this transaction, that impede my tying together what passed',[57] Fanny notes with slight regret of her lapses into unconsciousness. She wants to share it all, recall everything with a tenacity of attention which reaches to the very edges of consciousness: 'When all was done, & they lifted me up that I might be put to bed, my strength was so totally annihilated [. . .] my hands & arms [. . .] hung as if I had been lifeless.'

The question why Fanny Burney decided to write the operation up in retrospect and in such detail is answered in great part – but not completely – by her obsessive need to control other people's interpretation of her life. Most diarists or self-biographers would have drawn the line, though, at such a subject. First, there are the artistic difficulties: how do you convey pain convincingly? How can you transcend what is so personal? Of what use is it? Bodily functions and bodily ailments have never made good subjects for art. Fanny made no attempt to record anything about the birth of Alexander, which up to this date was the most traumatic physical event of her life; childbirth has no moral, which is why writer-mothers have avoided it as an unrewarding subject. There *is* a moral, of a kind, in Fanny's mastectomy narrative. It symbolises all the other occasions in her life when she had 'submitted to the knife' and bowed to fate or to the will of others. It demonstrates the persistence of her individual consciousness and independent thought even when duty and prudence dictate submissive or passive behaviour. The value of Fanny's narrative as a rare patient's-eye view of radical surgery has been acknowledged by medical practitioners and historians of medicine,[58] but its greatest value is as a testimony to the inviolability of the ego.

The Wanderer

Fanny had made an attempt to leave France for a brief holiday in England in 1810 (probably spurred by her worries about her worsening breast disease), but was prevented from going because of 'a universal Embargo' on traffic in the Channel.[1] The mastectomy in 1811 and its uncertain aftermath clearly added urgency to her desire to go home, and her next attempt to do so took place in the summer of 1812, as soon as she was sufficiently recovered from the initial trauma of the surgery. Alex was going with her. He was approaching the age of conscription and his mother was keen to get him as far away as possible from Napoleon, who was then preparing to invade Russia. Fanny intended to deposit Alex at university in England, see her family for a few months and return to sit out the rest of the war with her husband in Paris.

The journey had to be undertaken by stealth, using passports for North American destinations on a ship whose captain was prepared to make an unscheduled (and illegal) call at Dover. When they reached Dunkirk, expecting to set sail almost immediately on the American boat *Mary Ann*, Madame d'Arblay and her son were kept waiting six weeks while the captain tried to get as many more clandestine passengers for England as he could. Fanny wrote to d'Arblay asking him to send on her manuscript of *The Wanderer* to relieve her 'vapid and uninteresting leisure'.[2] The novel 'filled a small portmanteau' already, and d'Arblay packed it up with as much care 'as if every page had been a Bank note', which was of course exactly what the d'Arblays hoped them to become.

Fanny and Alex left France on 14 August and because of calms in the Channel took two days to reach the English coast. Unknown to the crew and passengers of the *Mary Ann*, the United States had declared war on Britain in June; the boat was duly seized by the British ship *Castilian* and brought in to Deal, not Dover as had been secretly planned. In an odd repetition of the confusion surrounding Susan's return from Ireland, Charles Burney junior was waiting in the wrong port – Dover – and stayed on there three days. Fanny, meanwhile, had delayed writing to her father to tell him of her return until she was back on English soil, for fear of the letter miscarrying. Now she calculated that he would need a few days to prepare for them at Chelsea. She had some old friends in Deal who were happy to entertain her: Lady Lucy Foley, a frequent visitor to the Lockes at Norbury Park, and her husband Admiral Sir Thomas Foley, who was commander of the port. Fanny delighted in the sound of English 'ringing in my ears' all through her first dinner at the Foleys' house. It was there that she saw a plate decorated with a likeness of Lord Nelson's head and the word 'Trafalgar' written underneath and had to ask her hosts what 'Trafalgar' meant.[3] Nothing could better illustrate the effects of the news blackout in France.

After a few days, and still ignorant of each other's whereabouts, Charles junior set off from Dover and the d'Arblays set off from Deal. They met up by accident on a common outside Canterbury when Charles put his head into the carriage and called his sister by name, and travelled on together to Chelsea, 'Oh! with what reciprocation of Joy!'

When Fanny reached the Chelsea College on 20 August she was in such a state that she couldn't recognise the servants or even remember which direction to go: 'To Chelsea – George comes down – Beckey on stairs – In to Padre – on Sofa – Chairs & Tables removed'.[4] The long-awaited moment of 'ecstatic delight' at seeing her father, who had moved the furniture to shorten the last few moments of their separation, was much more of a shock than Fanny had anticipated. She hadn't known of the paralytic stroke suffered by the Doctor in 1806 which had affected one of his hands and depressed his spirits. He was shockingly altered, thin and feeble-voiced, his head 'completely bent, and hung helplessly upon his breast [...] his whole appearance manifesting a species of self-desertion', as she recalled later.[5] In marked contrast to the old days, Dr Burney now preferred solitude to company, never went out if he could help it and took all his meals alone in his room. Fanny struggled to conceal her dismay at her father's deterioration, not realising that she was actually seeing him at his best. Her nephew Clement Francis, now a student at Cambridge, thought the Doctor was looking twenty years younger because of his daughter's return from France.[6]

The day after arriving at Chelsea, Fanny was reunited with James, Charles, Fanny Phillips (now Mrs Charles Raper) and twice-widowed Charlotte, who was 'almost overpowered with tender feelings' at seeing her sister once more.[7] The homecoming was marked with long, confidential talks and family parties everywhere but Chelsea College (since the Doctor had lost his appetite for them). James, apparently content to be home with his wife and daughter, had in Fanny's absence begun to write an acclaimed five-volume *General History of Voyages to the South Seas* (the most famous volume of which was the fourth, *History of the Buccaneers of America*), as well as works on civil defence, navigation and whist – a pastime he indulged extravagantly with his friend Charles Lamb and his circle.* Charles Burney junior, appointed chaplain to George III in 1810, had retired from teaching to one of his livings at Deptford and was hoping for promotion to a bishopric. All Fanny's siblings had aged a great deal during the decade of her exile: Hetty was now sixty-three and Sarah Harriet was a confirmed spinster of forty, the author of three novels, returned from a series of jobs as a governess to live with her father again at Chelsea.

The nieces and nephews were all adult by this time (except Charlotte's sickly youngest son, Ralph Broome), and observed their famous aunt and her son with curiosity. Marianne Francis, Charlotte's intellectual daughter, had already passed on to Mrs Piozzi her sister's opinion that 'my aunt d'Arblay is grown *fat*, & has a foreign accent; i.e., talks like a Frenchwoman speaking *remarkable good English*.'[8] The authoress Mary Berry also thought that Madame d'Arblay had put on weight, but used the old-fashioned term '*embonpoint*', which she considered 'very advantageous to her face'.[9] Alex, now a tall and silent seventeen-year-old, struck Marianne as 'a very expressive, dark-eyed, intelligent creature – a perfect bookworm', and seemed to his cousin Clement 'a prodigy in mathematics' who 'would shine in an English university'.[10]

A portrait by an unknown artist in a mid-Victorian frame, upon which the name 'Frances Burney' and her birth and death dates appear, dates

---

* Sally Burney, his wife, was affectionately caricatured by Lamb in his essay 'Mrs Battle's Opinions on Whist' in *Elia*. The essay is a celebration of how to take one's pleasures seriously.

from approximately this period. If authentic, it is the latest image we have of the author. There is much to encourage the identification: facially the subject looks very like Fanny as she appears in Edward Burney's portraits of 1782 and 1784, and her hair has exactly the same texture, bulk and style. The peculiarities of the subject's clothes are also suggestive. The hat that covers her lightly powdered or naturally greying hair is of a romantically extravagant 'cavalier' design which was never exactly fashionable. The first thing Fanny noted when she landed in England in 1812 was that she was the *only* woman at the Foleys' assembly in Deal wearing a hat of any description. She didn't just cling on to the old habit of wearing hats all the time when away from home, but specifically favoured *big* hats that would hide her face as much as possible: 'I beg only a *brim*, or enlargement, or some thing to shade the Phiz', she had written to Hetty in 1799, refusing the gift of a new small bonnet. 'As soon as you, who live in the *midst of things*, can exclaim, "I would not wear it for the World!" it will just suit me.'[11] One is reminded of Fanny's comic description of herself in 1802 as a 'Gothic anglaise', a term which seems particularly applicable to the dress in the portrait, which is in the pre-Revolutionary corseted style but with a scarf tied under the bust as a half-hearted gesture to neo-classical *chic*. The oddest element in this concoction is the deep pleated frill which has been attached to the neck of the dress. This, too, was never fashionable and actually looks rather absurd, but such an expedient would have been necessary on all Madame d'Arblay's dresses after 1811. Her old bodices, with their low necklines filled in with translucent fichus, would all have shown her mastectomy scar.

The 'wretched health' that Marianne Francis noticed was the weakness, pain and sensitivity to cold and damp which Fanny suffered as a result of her mastectomy, her survival of which the family rightly regarded with awe. Though she was in fact to outlive almost all of them, Fanny was 'in a most *dangerous* state'[12] in the autumn of 1812, and was cosseted and indulged by everyone. 'The avidity of my dear Family in our present union is as yet beyond any controlling', she wrote to d'Arblay at the end of September. 'I am never an hour out of the arms of one or another of the affectionate tribe'.[13]

Many people wanted to see the returned exile: old friends like Lady Crewe, Sheridan, the ageing Joseph Banks and the writer Anna Barbauld, and others who wished to be introduced for the first time, including the novelist Maria Edgeworth and the poet Samuel Rogers. Thomas Jefferson Hogg met Fanny in 1813 and wanted to introduce her to his friend Shelley. It is hard to imagine that she would have liked the notorious young atheist poet, or he the ageing 'bundle of conventionalities', as Hogg described her later. Hogg noted disappointedly that Madame d'Arblay talked 'wholly about herself'.[14]

Fanny was so exhausted by the round of parties that she was soon obliged to keep to her room for one day in two to 'recruit', though, typically, she rallied quickly in congenial company. Some invitations were virtually impossible to refuse, such as one from the infamous Princess Caroline of Wales, whose separation from her husband, now Prince Regent, and estrangement from the rest of Fanny's beloved Royal Family made hers an uncomfortable acquaintance. (The fact that Dr Burney was also included in this particular invitation and wanted to go, contrary to custom, was probably the only reason Fanny accepted.) One of the other guests, Thomas Campbell, left an interesting account of the occasion, noting the glaring differences between the Princess's gaucherie and the novelist's composure:

> [Madame d'Arblay's] manners are highly polished, and delicately courteous – just like Evelina grown old – not bashful, but sensitively anxious to please those about her. I sat next to her, alternately pleased and tormented with the Princess's naïveté, and Madame D'Arblay's refinement. [Y]ou would love her for her communicativeness, and fine tact in conversation.[15]

What Campbell describes is not just *correctness* in manners but a true delicacy, developed to a fine art through years of painful self-awareness. His appreciation of her 'fine tact' and refinement would have gratified Madame d'Arblay profoundly.

The ghosts of two old friendships came back to haunt Fanny on this trip to London. Hester Piozzi, widowed for the second time in 1809, had been persuaded by Marianne Francis that Madame d'Arblay wanted a reconciliation, or at least an exchange of civilities, but having called once when Fanny was out, she didn't try again. Madame de Staël was in town too, but Fanny made no attempt to see her. Her novel *Corinne* (1807) had made de Staël famous internationally, and her works of criticism had placed her in the mainstream of European romanticism. Fanny had followed her career with great interest and admiration, but felt that it would be hypocritical to renew their old acquaintance, even though de Staël was now 'received by all mankind', as Fanny wrote to Mary Ann Waddington, adding sardonically '– but that, indeed, she always was – all womankind, I should say'.[16]

While staying with her brother Charles at Sandgate, Kent, Fanny was introduced to the philanthropist and social reformer William Wilberforce (a friend of Marianne Francis through her great-uncle Arthur Young), and had '4 Hours of the best conversation I have, nearly, ever enjoyed':

> He was anxious for a full & true account of Paris, & particularly of Religion & Infidelity, & of Buonaparté & the Wars & of all & every Thing that had occurred during my Ten years seclusion in France: & I had so much to communicate, & his drawing out, & comments, & Episodes, were all so judicious, so spirited, so full of information, yet so benignly unassuming, that my shyness all flew away, & I felt to be his confidential Friend, opening to him upon every occurrence, & every sentiment, with the frankness that is usually won by years of intercourse.[17]

Wilberforce's long campaign against the slave trade had resulted in the Abolition Act of 1807, and he was a prominent member of the increasingly influential 'Clapham Sect' of Evangelical Christians, to which Marianne Francis also belonged. In the violent age through which they were living, a pious and active humanitarian like Wilberforce inspired Fanny's deepest respect. Her ten years of obscurity in exile had prevented her from making friends among such people, or playing any part herself in the philanthropic movements of the day which so obviously interested her. She had been 'forcibly struck' on her return to England that 'sacred themes, far from being either neglected, or derided' (as she felt they were in France) 'are become almost common topics of common discourse'.[18] As she walked along the Sandgate ramparts discussing religion and politics with Wilberforce, under the shadow of the Martello towers which Pitt had ordered to be built against the threat of a French invasion, the intellectual deprivations of her years in France must have come home strongly.

As it was, all Fanny had to show for her long exile was the incomplete manuscript of *The Wanderer*, which lay untouched in its portmanteau for some months after her arrival in England. Early in 1813 she suddenly set to work on it again with a vengeance. Uncertain of the length of her stay in England, which was dependent on the progress of the war with France and Alex's establishment at university, she hurried on with the book in the hope that she could get it through the press. In the spring of 1813, she began to discuss with her brother Charles the possibility of auctioning the rights to this 'work' (as with *Camilla*, she was unwilling to call it a *novel*), and eventually agreed a sale of the rights to the firm of Longman, Hurst, Rees, Orme and Brown in Paternoster Row. The deal looked good, but in fact gambled a large amount on *The Wanderer* going into several editions. Fanny was to receive £500 on delivery of the manuscript and two further payments of £500 in the eighteen months following publication. She would be paid for up to five subsequent editions, but only after each sold out, with a possible maximum income of £3000 if the book was successful.

Expectations of Madame d'Arblay's new work were high, as one reviewer later recalled: 'We can hardly remember an instance when the public expectation was excited in so high a degree, as by the promise of a new novel from the pen of their old favourite, Madame D'Arblay.'[19] As early as December 1811 Lord Byron had heard with amazement that a thousand guineas was being asked for the book; by September 1813 most of literary London knew that Longman had 'paid £3000' for the rights. Even provincial Miss Austen was joking about *The Wanderer* in relation to her own newly-published *Pride and Prejudice*: 'Poor Dr Isham is obliged to admire P.& P. – & to send me word that he is sure he shall not like Mde Darblay's new Novel half so well.'[20]* Madame d'Arblay's long residence in France led people to expect an autobiographical *Zeitroman*, perhaps a satire of manners under Napoleonic rule, an *Evelina* or *Cecilia* for the Revolutionary period. The book's title set up certain obvi-

---

* It is worth noting that Austen was passing on this news to her sister Cassandra from Cassandra Cooke, the Austens' and d'Arblays' mutual friend in Great Bookham, who while on holiday in Brighton had been discussing both novelists with Dr Edmund Isham (then Warden of All Souls). Austen goes on to remark: 'Mrs C[ooke]. invented it all of course.' Assuming 'it' to refer to *The Wanderer*, not to Dr Isham's opinion of *Pride and Prejudice*, this sounds like a sly jibe against Madame d'Arblay, suggesting that there was already a joke current between the Cookes and the Austens connected with Mrs Cooke's ideas being plagiarised. Mrs Cooke was by this time an author herself. Her novel *Battleridge* was published in 1799.

ous expectations about its plot which were only just satisfied by the heroine's meanderings around southern England. Moreover, the title plugged into the overpowering current of romanticism surging through the art and literature of the 1810s. So many writers and artists had used the trope of the solitary 'wanderer' in these years (Goethe, Friedrich Schlegel and Wordsworth among them) that it was already in danger of becoming a cliché.

By the later stages of composition Fanny was obsessively adding 'MORE & MORE last touches to my work, about which I begin to grow very anxious'.[21] No one knew better than she what a hotchpotch it was, two-thirds of it composed at intervals over the previous fifteen years and the last 60,000 words poured out in a rush since her return to England. But money was a serious consideration again, with the costs of Alex's education facing the impoverished d'Arblays. Alex had been sent to cram towards a Cambridge scholarship in Mathematics at Charles Burney junior's school in Greenwich, now run by Charles junior's son, Charles Parr Burney. An English university education still seemed the safest way to avoid conscription for their son in France, but without a scholarship the d'Arblays doubted they could afford it. After a great deal of shameless manoeuvring and string-pulling by his mother (including an appeal to the Queen), Alex was elected to a Tancred Scholarship at Cambridge, worth £120 a year, and went up to Caius College in October 1813.

Alex's superior abilities had been so assiduously puffed by his mother before their arrival in England that it is not surprising that he failed to live up to the Burney family's expectations, nor to the standards later demanded of him at Cambridge. His poor performance at school in Greenwich was put down to the difference between the French and English mathematical systems, but while this clearly contributed to his difficulties, it was by no means the whole story. Charles Parr Burney was unimpressed by his cousin's French schooling and lamented that the youth was not 'more careful, – more regular, – more systematick, – more TIDY'. When Alex got to Caius, these shortcomings were shown up immediately. Typically, he followed a period of concentrated work and achievement (in this case, matriculating at Cambridge) with a complete falling-off of interest and effort. Unlike his cousin Clement Francis, who was two years ahead of him at Caius, Alex was not a committed scholar and by the end of his first term was in such trouble with his tutor that he was in serious danger of being sent down. His late arrival at his mother's lodgings on Lower Sloane Street that Christmas alerted her to trouble: he had been kept back to fulfil various college 'impositions' for absence and lateness. Fanny resorted to constant monitoring of her errant son's work and hired a private tutor (at considerable expense) to keep him at his studies all through the vacation.

Alex's difficulties at Cambridge puzzled and distressed his mother, who had always been confident that he would excel. Every academic success of his sent her into raptures about 'the Honour!' involved, which she bruited abroad without a grain of modesty or restraint. His failures, which she covered up assiduously, inevitably struck her as personal humiliations. She tried to excuse them on grounds of Alex's disrupted education, 'absence of mind' and (increasingly) frail health, but his really dangerous frailty was, at this age, somewhat harder to identify.

Alex's difficulties at the university, old Charles Burney's failing health and the imminent publication of *The Wanderer* had kept Fanny in England for more than a year. There were also some troublesome business affairs to sort out. Fanny's pension from the Queen, which had been paid to Dr Burney's banker in her absence, had got entangled in her father's accounts and was, essentially, untouchable. A worse loss financially was Camilla Cottage, which the d'Arblays had been worrying over for years. Dr Burney advised them not to sell it, but to retain the cottage for the rent, however small, and to provide Alex with 'a little freehold in his Native Country'[22] which might be of value in the future. This presupposed that the d'Arblays had a freehold to hang on to or dispose of, but in October 1813 William Locke junior informed them through his solicitor that he was selling Norbury Park (which he had inherited on his father's death three years before), and that the land upon which Camilla Cottage was built was included in the sale. Locke was offering to buy the cottage for its appraised value, £640.

The d'Arblays were shocked by the news that the freehold did not in fact belong to them, having misunderstood the nature of their friends' wedding gift back in 1793. They had spent more than £1000 building the cottage, much more repairing and maintaining it, and had banked on selling the property at a profit. Young Locke's offer struck them as an insult rather than what it really was, an unnecessarily generous gesture towards two unbusinesslike old family friends.

The resulting quarrel between the d'Arblays and the Lockes casts an interesting light on Fanny's character. Monsieur d'Arblay, angered by the apparent injustice of the forced sale, fired off a series of letters which caused deep offence at Norbury Park. Not surprisingly, Fredy Locke defended her son's position: in law, he was not obliged to buy the cottage from his tenants, nor was any purchaser obliged to compensate the d'Arblays for their overspending on the house and failure to notice that they had never been granted the freehold. Fredy Locke's letters to Fanny at this time were conciliatory and sympathetic, but her defence of William struck Fanny as a form of betrayal. She wrote back in the role of 'The Wife who firmly believes that no human being that breathes has a higher sense of honour than her husband',

> & that even the 3 Ang[e]l friends whom she forever deplores. Mr – Locke – Mrs. Delany – & her Sister –
> No, nor all the angels that now surround them – had not, & have not intentions more pure.[23]

This absurd rhetoric, with its crude appeal to Fredy's feelings towards her dead husband and friends, provoked a restrained criticism from Mrs Locke, who had anticipated an '*apology*, if I may use the word, for an unusual manner, which I cou'd not but feel most painfully'.[24] But an apology was exactly what no one could ever extract from Fanny d'Arblay. She had kept a copy of her own letter marked 'an answer to a most unlooked for Letter of Reproach from my dearest Intimate Friend in her misconceived resentmt of Monsieur d'Arblay's high & forcible reclamation to Wm. Locke Junr'. Resentment towards Monsieur d'Arblay could only ever, in Fanny's eyes, be 'misconceived', and reproaches undeserved. Her sense of her own rectitude, veracity and moral superiority – and those of her nearest and dearest – was unassailable.

Meanwhile, Monsieur d'Arblay continued to write plangent letters from his office at the Ministry of the Interior in Paris. The armistice of June 1813 between France and the Allied forces of England, Russia and Prussia lasted only two months, and the renewal of hostilities in August made travel between England and France as difficult and the mail as slow as ever. It took weeks for d'Arblay's letters to arrive bearing such news as Narbonne's death on active service at Torgau in Austria and Victor

Latour-Maubourg's near-fatal injuries during the battle of Wachau. Keeping up with the details of the war became an obsession for Fanny, but in her desire to be thorough, she never quite caught up with the very latest information. Her father had kept piles of newspapers and periodicals for her to go through, which she was determined to read in order, as Sarah Harriet observed with amusement to Charlotte Barrett:

> [Madame d'Arblay] reads Newspapers from morning till night: but Newspapers of three or four weeks back, & will not let you say a word to her of recent events. 'O, don't tell me – I shall come to it – I am reading up to it!' And by the time she *has* read up to it, some newer intelligence will probably have arrived, which will make what we are now rejoicing at appear stale, & put it all out of our heads. [. . .] Who can be much interested to hear her talking so big of a partial skirmish, who knows that a momentous general engagement has so recently taken place? – These are oddities that are – that are – rather – odd![25]

'At a time like this,' Fanny wrote to Mrs Locke, 'all public news, good or bad, of a Warlike nature, fills me with almost equal alarm.'[26] In February 1814, with the Allies sweeping towards Paris, the fall of Napoleon seemed imminent. D'Arblay, like many other terrified residents of Paris, was steeling himself for a long siege, but on 30 March the Allies entered the capital and three days later *The Times* pronounced that 'Everything announces the winding up of the great Drama.' On 11 April the amazing news reached London that Bonaparte had abdicated.

The triumphant fireworks that went off in London that night were clearly visible in Dr Burney's apartment on the top floor of Chelsea College, and provided a strange counterpoint to the scene inside. On the previous day, Fanny had hurried to the college on hearing the news that her father had taken a turn for the worse, and was distressed to find the old man in a sort of trance and incapable of recognising or responding to her. His last coherent action was to make his way to the window, which overlooked the hospital's burying ground where his second wife lay, and after a long contemplation of the scene to open his arms wide and say, 'All this will soon pass away as a dream!'[27] While Fanny was taking in the solemnity of this moment, the servants used the opportunity of the Doctor's arms being suddenly extended to remove his wrapping gown and get him ready for bed. Charles Burney died two days later in his sleep, less than a fortnight before his eighty-eighth birthday.

Fanny refused to the very end to believe that her father was dying, and even when he was dead insisted on being left alone with the corpse in the hope that someone had made a mistake: 'I forced them to let me stay by him, & his reverend form became stiff before I could persuade myself to believe he was gone hence for-ever.'[28] The idea of Madame d'Arblay *forcing* the doctors, servants and other members of the family to indulge this slightly grotesque final audience could either be interpreted as profoundly pathetic (in the manner of King Lear) or inappropriately egocentric. It was a scene she was to enact almost exactly at her husband's deathbed and which, many years later, her son took pains to avoid being replayed over his own dying form.

The Doctor's will caused trouble among his children because he left large bequests of £1000 or more to Hetty, Fanny, Sarah Harriet and Susan's daughter Fanny (Phillips) Raper, but only £200 apiece to James, Charles and Charlotte. Hetty and Fanny, as residuary legatees, were heirs to his savings, running to some seven or eight thousand pounds. They also benefited from the sale of the Doctor's property, including his library, sold later in 1814 for a total of £2353, and had possession of his manu-scripts, letters and unpublished memoirs, which were expected to be a continuing source of income. No wonder that Charlotte (whom the Doctor had mistakenly imagined well-off by her two widowhoods) felt hurt and excluded from her father's good wishes, and that James, the disregarded eldest son, was infuriated and resentful. Certainly James's treatment seemed like punishment from beyond the grave for having failed to please his father either in his politics or his private life. Fanny and Hetty attempted to placate their brother with offers of money from the old 'Irish mortgage', the loan to Molesworth Phillips which was being recovered at last by litigation (perhaps not the most tactful offer, since Phillips was still James's friend), but he refused to be mollified. The will 'seems to have cast a kind of general though undefinable cloud over the Family Harmony', Fanny wrote sadly to Charlotte in June.[29]

The Doctor had lived just long enough to see the publication of *The Wanderer* at the end of March 1814, but probably never read its fulsome dedication to him, an unusually frank statement on the author's part of her own history as a novelist and her persistent anxieties about the form which she had done so much to develop. Her defence of the novel as 'a picture of supposed, but natural and probable human existence' which 'holds [...] in its hands our best affections [...] exercises our imaginations [...] points out the path of honour; and gives to juvenile credulity knowledge of the world, without ruin, or repentance' is rather overset by the succeeding denunciation:

> in nothing is the force of denomination more striking than in the term of Novel; a species of writing which, though never mentioned, even by its supporter, but with a look that fears contempt, is not more rigidly excommunicated, from its appellation, in theory, than sought and fostered, from its attractions, in practice.
>
> So early was I impressed myself with ideas that fastened degradation to this class of composition, that at the age of adolescence, I struggled against the propensity which, even in childhood, even from the moment I could hold a pen, had impelled me into its toils[.][30]

By 1814 few people shared her association of the novel with 'degradation', and Burney herself admits in the same piece of writing that she only came to hold novels in low esteem because there were so few of them in her father's library – from which she deduced that the whole class must be 'condemned'.

Her irrationally low opinion of the novel found a rational challenger in her younger admirer, Jane Austen, whose idea of the form's potential had, ironically, been shaped by works such as Miss Burney's own. The famous authorial defence of the novel in Chapter Five of *Northanger Abbey* (not published until after Austen's death in 1817) states the case clearly, and seems to be a direct retort to Fanny Burney's anxious remarks in *The Wanderer*:

> I will not adopt that ungenerous and impolitic custom so common with novel writers, of degrading by their contemptuous censure the very performances to the number of which they are themselves adding – joining with their greatest enemies in bestowing the harshest epithets on such works, and scarcely ever permitting them to be read by their own heroine, who, if she accidentally take up a novel, is sure to turn over its insipid pages with disgust. [...] Let us leave it to the Reviewers to abuse such

effusions of fancy at their leisure, and over every new novel to talk in threadbare strains of the trash with which the press now groans. Let us not desert one another; we are an injured body. Although our productions have afforded more extensive and unaffected pleasure than those of any other literary corporation in the world, no species of composition has been so much descried.[31]

Unlike Austen, Fanny Burney never achieved a sense of belonging to a mutually supportive professional 'body' or gave herself up to the dangerous luxury of providing readers with 'extensive and unaffected pleasure'. Burney obviously knew how to write a bestseller, but seems to have wanted to renounce that knowledge for the purpose of achieving greater literary seriousness, implying in the Dedication to *The Wanderer* that she aspired to the same 'grandeur, yet singleness of [. . .] plan' in her 'work' that characterises epic poetry, 'that sovereign species of the works of fiction'.[32] Her reasons for doing so seem inextricably linked with her chronic neuroses about performance and professionalism, issues dealt with at length in *The Wanderer*; but they were bad reasons, and Austen was right to object to them.

The Wanderer or Female Difficulties tells the story of a young refugee from France during 'the dire reign of the terrific Robespierre' who joins a group of English men and women as their open boat prepares to leave the French coast by stealth one night in 1793. The girl's appearance is unpromising: she is dressed raggedly and partially covered in bandages and patches. As the light rises, her companions are able to see that her skin is 'dusky' like that of a Creole, but she refuses to satisfy anyone's curiosity about her origins, purpose or even her name, maintaining a silence that some on the boat find infuriating and suspicious and others, like the young anti-heroine of the book, Elinor Joddrel, and her companion Albert Harleigh, consider fascinating and suggestive.

Through Elinor's patronage and protection, the stranger is assimilated into the social circle represented in microcosm on the boat. Travelling with Elinor and her aunt Mrs Howel via Dover and London to Lewes in Sussex, the 'Incognita' gradually loses her black and shabby appearance (a disguise adopted to effect her escape), emerging as an exceptionally beautiful white woman. Though she maintains her refusal to explain her business in England, she seems to be a gentlewoman of high class and excels in various genteel accomplishments, such as needlework, singing and playing the harp. For a time she is tolerated by her hostess as a curiosity, but eventually Mrs Howel and her friends begin to suspect that 'Ellis' – the name they have given her, based on the initials 'L.S.' which appear on a letter – is an adventuress, and she is ejected from their society with threats.

In contrast to the vulgar jealousy and mean spirit of these middle-class women (who are primarily concerned to get rid of Ellis 'without letting the servants know the indiscretion we have been drawn into, by treating her like one of ourselves'[33]), the Wanderer finds immediate sympathy with the aristocrats she meets in Brighton, Lady Aurora Granville, Lord Melbury and Albert Harleigh. Harleigh has admired the 'Fair Unknown' ever since he saw her playing Lady Townley in an amateur production of Vanbrugh's *The Provok'd Husband*. Not only did she look beautiful in the role, with her 'fine form [. . .] and animated complexion', but was transformed in voice and manner, giving Harleigh a tantalising glimpse of the discrimination, sensibility and intelligence concealed beneath the persona of silent, mysterious 'Ellis'.

Harleigh's increasing admiration for Ellis soon provokes Elinor Joddrel into an intense sexual jealousy. Up to this point, Elinor has not thought of Harleigh as a lover (she was formerly engaged to his younger brother Dennis), but her passion, once acknowledged, becomes violent and headstrong. Elinor, the frank and outspoken enthusiast of 'this glorious epoch' of revolutionary freedom, has no qualms about declaring her feelings to Harleigh, but sadistically does so using Ellis as go-between. She thereby inhibits a similar declaration of love between Harleigh and Ellis, and makes Ellis the vehicle of Harleigh's pained refusal. Elinor's response to his rejection is to attempt suicide with a poniard soon after, 'a smile triumphant though ghastly' playing about her lips.

When Elinor runs away and Ellis is forced to support herself alone, the novel enters a long phase of describing the difficulties and dangers faced by an unprotected woman looking for respectable employment. Unlike Cecilia in *The Witlings*, for whom even the threat of having to work is traumatic, Ellis is totally exposed to the conditions of the market, the humiliation of having to solicit work, the expense of conducting it, the physical and mental exertions of the work itself and the difficulty of getting paid correctly or on time. As Ellis's first job is as a teacher of the harp, Burney is able to include many observations on the life of a music-teacher obviously derived from her father's experience (as well as from that of a young woman whose talents and enterprise she had admired in Bath in 1780, 'a taylor's daughter, who professes musick, and teaches so as to give six lessons a day to ladies, at five and threepence a lesson'[34]). The note of genuine grievance in *The Wanderer* on the hard lot of performers and artists rings true not just for Charles Burney and his family of dancing-masters, actors and painters but for that other kind of performing animal, the writer: 'The better he performs, the harder he has worked', kind-hearted Giles Arbe says in defence of the artist; 'he does not execute what is easiest, and what he likes best, but what is hardest, and has most chance to force your applause. He sings, perhaps, when he may be ready to cry; he plays upon those harps and fiddles, when he is half dying with hunger; and he skips those gavots, and fandangos, when he would rather go to bed!'[35]

Ellis's need to work is only temporary; when her circumstances are revealed (some 300,000 words into the book) and she is restored to the protection of her guardian, the experiences she has undergone as a music-teacher, seamstress, milliner and lady's companion will be put behind her. But Burney dwells on them at great length for fairly obvious reasons: though the heroine of *The Wanderer* and her immediate circle are all wealthy or aristocratic, Burney's real subject (and audience) was that section of English society which Ellis passes through as a 'wanderer', the new and vulnerable bourgeoisie, particularly its female members, caught between the old regime of dependence and idleness and the increasing necessity to be self-dependent. Times had changed, and Burney was aware of how inadequate traditional female 'accomplishments' were in the new world order, as her heroine states with vigour:

> How few, [...] how circumscribed, are the attainments of women! and how much fewer and more circumscribed still, are those which may, in their consequences, be useful as well as ornamental, to the higher, or educated class! those through which, in the reverses of fortune, a FEMALE may reap benefit without abasement! those which, while preserving her from pecuniary distress, will not aggravate the hardships or sorrows of her changed condition, either by immediate humiliation, or by what, eventually, her connexions may consider as disgrace![36]

The economic status of women and the vexed question of their rights are dealt with exhaustively in *The Wanderer*, making this Burney's most political novel by far. Though the book is set in 1793, the date of her *Brief Reflections*, Burney had adjusted her views during the revolutionary period and brought different ideas to bear in her novel – or rather, different ways of opposing the radical feminist view. In *Brief Reflections*, she had argued the necessity of protecting women from 'the heart-hardening effects of general worldly commerce' in order to preserve their moral superiority, but by the time she wrote *The Wanderer* it had become clear that women could no longer count on such protection. When Admiral Powel says to Ellis that 'the devil himself never yet put it into a man's head, nor into the world's neither, to abandon, or leave, as you call it, desolate, a woman who has kept tight to her own duty', he is speaking as a representative of the old school and of idealised past manners. His words are undercut not just by his own behaviour but that of the other supposed male 'protector' figures in the novel, particularly Ellis's guardian, the Bishop, for whose safety Ellis is expected to make any sacrifice, like the heroines in Burney's tragic dramas.

The decline of the 'protection' offered to women had left the idea of separate spheres in tatters, as *The Wanderer* amply illustrates. The alternative was for women to become self-sufficient, though the trials of Burney's heroine show how nearly impossible, in practice, that was. The Wanderer is 'a being [...] cast upon herself, a female Robinson Crusoe, [...] unaided and unprotected, though in the midst of the world, [...] reduced either to sink, through inanition, to nonentity, or to be rescued from famine and death by such resources as she could find, independently, in herself'.[37] Ellis's passivity and sufferance of ill-treatment (which at many points actually *provokes* 'difficulties' rather than solves them) is very much at variance with the power of this authorial statement at the end of the book. Her reward for her many trials is to be married quietly to Harleigh (a man who has been shown to be her moral inferior, as is everyone else in the story) and to be allowed to forget all about self-dependence for ever. Her conventional exit from the world of 'female difficulties' is therefore at odds with the implied message that a system which imposes such mental, economic and social restraints on women is a system ripe for change.

Latter-day readers latch on to this message with relief, though it is unlikely that Burney consciously wanted to be the bearer of it. The self-dependence she advocated was at risk of being confused with the impious self-worship she believed to be at the heart of the new feminism. The arguments of the libertarians are thoroughly represented in *The Wanderer* by the novel's strongest female character, Elinor Joddrel, whose rash behaviour, melodramatic egotism and wrong-headed pursuit of Harleigh mark her out as attractive but dangerous. Burney is very much in two minds about Elinor: on the one hand, she is that object of horror for the author, 'an agreeable infidel', whose real-life model, the 'Miss W[—]' Burney met in Bath back in 1780, had seemed 'a shocking sight, [. . .] with her romantic, flighty and unguarded turn of mind, what could happen to her that could give surprise?'[38] On the other hand, Elinor displays the same spirit of longing after social justice that Susan Phillips and the Lockes had exhibited in the early stages of the French Revolution. Elinor reappears at regular intervals in the novel in scenes of high melodrama, dressed as a 'foreign man' at Ellis's subscription concert (where she again tries to stab herself), embracing her own prepared tomb in a graveyard at night (where she tries to shoot herself), yet her disruptive presence does not sufficiently detract from the plain sense of what she says about the rights of woman: 'which all your sex, with all its arbitrary assumption of superiority, can never disprove, for they are the Rights of human nature; to which the two sexes equally and undeniably belong'.[39]

For the book to be unequivocally moral, Burney had to condemn this lively character and the 'fatal new systems' she represents. As in *Camilla*, where *despite* the author Eugenia emerges as the true heroine (in the eyes of modern readers, at least), there is a sense of Burney again being somewhat out of control of her material. Elinor argues the rationalist case articulately, but makes no converts to infidelity, while Harleigh's earnest but intellectually spineless pleadings about the immutability of Truth and his argument for immortality from the persistence of consciousness in sleep effects Elinor's capitulation almost at once. Like Eugenia's apparent submission to her father's rhetoric about 'deformity' in *Camilla*, this rings very false indeed.

Elinor's loquaciousness and self-indulgent theatricality set her apart from the other characters in the book as an oddity or aberration. She is a full-blown romantic while they derive from the old comedy of manners so dear to Fanny Burney's heart. Sir Lyell Sycamore, a wicked baronet, is of the same class and style of seducer as Sir Clement Willoughby in *Evelina*; Mr Tedman, the businessman, is a vulgarian like Briggs in *Cecilia* or Mr Watts in *A Busy Day*; Harleigh is another vapid male paragon like Edgar Mandlebert in *Camilla*. As before, Burney builds up a huge cast of secondary characters whom the heroine observes in picaresque style, but in *The Wanderer* there is an important difference. Perhaps Evelina was the only one of Burney's heroines to display any believable flaws which are remedied in the course of the narrative. 'The Wanderer' displays none whatsoever. First known as 'The Incognita', then 'Ellis', and finally revealed to be 'Juliet Granville', unacknowledged daughter of an English Lord (and half-sister to Lady Aurora and Lord Melbury), the heroine changes name, status, form, colour and class with such frequency that her real identity, when discovered, seems of little importance. Her 'wandering' through society becomes just that, a vague and aimless exercise. There is little humour in *The Wanderer*, and little true satire. What replaces the satire is a form of bald social criticism (of the conditions of the rural poor, of the treatment of working girls, of racial and sexual prejudice) which makes the book valuable as a socio-historical text today but which did not satisfy those readers and reviewers in 1814 who had been awaiting another comedy from the pen of Madame d'Arblay.

The Wanderer was a serious critical failure. The first edition sold out before publication (on the expectation that had been aroused), but the subsequent reprint fell flat, and three years later the publishers, much to their chagrin, were left to pulp the copies they had overprinted in 1814. The novel was brought back into print in 1992 as a feminist rediscovery (and is popular with students), but prior to that new lease of life was almost universally derided as a really bad novel. Even Macaulay, keen to anatomise the poor style of *Memoirs of Doctor Burney*, passed over *The Wanderer* with a kind of weary disbelief, like an exhausted angel of death: it was 'a book which no judicious friend to her memory will attempt to draw from the oblivion into which it has justly fallen', he wrote in his essay-length review of the posthumous *Diary and Letters*.[40]

Contemporary reviewers bemoaned the book's 'most unnecessary length', 'trifling and tedious' dialogues and insufficiently '*modern*' ideas.[41] The style of *The Wanderer* was particularly criticised: 'If we had not been assured in the title-page, that this work had been produced by the same pen as Cecilia,' wrote John Wilson Croker in the *Quarterly Review*, 'we should have pronounced Madame d'Arblay to be a feeble imitator of the style of Miss Burney';[42] and William Hazlitt wrote even more forthrightly in the *Edinburgh Review* that 'There is little other power in Miss Burney's novels than that of immediate observation; her characters, whether of refinement or vulgarity, are equally superficial and confined.' There were many private expressions of disappointment, too; Sir Walter Scott regretted that 'Madame D'Arblay has certainly made a miss',[43] while Byron rather more forcefully dismissed the book as 'feminine trash'.[44] Fanny's friends hardly knew what to say about the novel. 'You read the "Wanderer", I doubt not, with as much surprise and disappointment as I did,' William Weller Pepys wrote to Hannah More three months after publication; 'but as we both have so much regard for the author, we must be faithful, and not quote each other's opinion on that book.'[45]

The unhappy truth was that the plot of *The Wanderer* was improbable and badly structured, and the style and language quite astonishingly awful. Nothing in the novel is directly or simply put. Instead of the wind blowing through the trees, zephyrs agitate the verdant foliage of venerable branches. 'The feathered race' does not sing but issues warbling sounds celestial 'from the abode of angels, or to that abode chanting invitation'.[46] It is a book in which cheeks are mantled with 'the varying dies of quick transition of sentiment', and where joy irradiates the hero's countenance to such an extent that he feels obliged to bend his eyes to the ground:

> But their checked vivacity checked not the feelings which illumined them, nor the alarm which they excited, when Ellis, urged by affright to snatch a second look, saw the brilliancy with which they had at first sought her own, terminate in a sensibility more touching[.][47]

Joyce Hemlow has described this style as 'a double swelling, present in neither romantic nor eighteenth-century writers, and peculiar to Madame d'Arblay alone',[48] a hybrid between the generalised diction of the eighteenth century and the loosening of control associated with 'romantic' writing. Professor Hemlow has also noted the influence of French on Burney's English (her constant use of the phrasal genitive, such as 'the presage of Harleigh', 'the house of Mrs Maple', for instance), a phenomenon less charitably described by George Saintsbury in 1913 as 'a lingo which suggests the translation of an ill-written French original by a person who does not know English'.[49] Alex d'Arblay's private opinion was that his mother had 'no doubt originally conceived' *The Wanderer* in French;[50] but while this may account for some of the novel's stiltedness, it doesn't excuse the insistent sentimentality of the writing, nor its peculiarly unpleasant fusion of hyperbole with euphemism. There had been elements of this in *Camilla*, in *Brief Reflections* and in the Court dramas. Much worse was to come in *Memoirs of Doctor Burney*.

Monsieur d'Arblay had rushed over to England to be with his wife when he heard the news of her father's death in April 1814. The peace was signed on 30 May and Napoleon, apparently vanquished for ever, was exiled to Elba. With the imminent restoration of the Bourbon monarchy, it was time for Fanny and her husband to make important decisions about the future. They both harboured fantasies of d'Arblay landing an important diplomatic post in England, but there was in reality never any chance of that for the humble civil servant. Fanny clearly did not want to go back to live in France, but d'Arblay at last saw a chance for promotion and perhaps restoration for himself to his old status under the new regime. Though he had sworn allegiance to the Republic in 1800 in order to get a passport, and had accepted the post offered him on the Santo Domingo expedition by Napoleon in 1802, d'Arblay now proudly claimed that he had been 'constant dans mes refus'[51] throughout the period. All he *had* actually refused was to serve against his wife's country, whichever system was in power, but now he wanted some political credit for his years in the doldrums.

That chance seemed to come in June 1814 when d'Arblay (who had returned to France alone the previous month) was offered a place in the Garde du Corps of the new King, Louis XVIII, brother of the murdered Louis XVI. D'Arblay was thrilled and honoured, though it is hard to see why: he was ranked only as a Sub-Lieutenant and the pay was derisory, scarcely enough to cover the expenses of his elaborately embroidered new uniform, plumed helmet, weapons and the two warhorses required. The Garde du Corps, made up of middle-aged émigrés and *ci-devants* like d'Arblay, was in fact a bit of a joke amongst professional soldiers and was never taken seriously as a fighting unit. D'Arblay's satisfaction with his new position indicates that he was significantly out of touch with matters both military and political. His old acquaintance Talleyrand, at this date the most powerful man in France, was certainly not impressed by d'Arblay's preferment. The two men met frequently at the house of Madame Laval, where d'Arblay kept petitioning the Foreign Minister on the subject of his hoped-for 'consulship'. It is a mark of d'Arblay's naivety that he thought he was making progress with this scheme when Talleyrand told him that his name had been 'put on a list'.[52]

As for being a Constitutionalist, as he claimed in the 1790s, it seems that Chevalier d'Arblay was emerging at the other end of the revolutionary period as an out-and-out monarchist and reactionary. Of course, many of his former associates had moved with the times – notably Narbonne, who had died serving as Napoleon's aide-de-camp, and Talleyrand, whose astonishing series of pragmatic volte-faces almost beggared belief. Mathieu de Montmorency-Laval was the only one of d'Arblay's old associates to have ended up further to the right than he – Montmorency had 'got religion' and helped to found a Masonic-style order of 'Chevaliers de la Foi' in the service of Church and King. Madame de Staël was, if anything, more liberal than before, and her new salon, which included Lafayette and her current lover, Benjamin Constant, was actively critical of the restored monarch.

D'Arblay's commitment to a career in the army was constantly compromised by his tender solicitude for the feelings of his pacifist wife. She contemplated his return to military service with horror. D'Arblay had turned sixty in the summer of 1814 and was not particularly fit or healthy. He hadn't ridden a warhorse for twenty-two years. Fanny understood how 'highly gratifying' the new position in the royal service was to her husband, but privately hoped for a speedy return to 'civil domestic life'.[53] Unfortunately, d'Arblay was so happy with his appointment to the 'Maison du Roi' that he began to drop hints that Alex should join him in the same service. The boy had, after all, miserably failed his end-of-year exams at Cambridge, and perhaps it was time to call a halt to his expensive English education. As a Lieutenant in the Garde du Corps, Alex could earn about 12,000 francs a year and possibly gain preferment in the royal household or the diplomatic service. Such a move would give him 'inexprimable bonheur', d'Arblay wrote to his wife; in fact, he had to admit, he had already put Alex's name down for it.

Alex himself resisted this offer firmly, and Fanny thought it so impractical that she was almost dismissive. The question remained of what was to be done about their son, though, and d'Arblay's impatience to act exercised Fanny all through the summer of 1814. She had reached some conclusions about Alex's character which must have been painful to admit: 'he thought – & still thinks – he could, & can, do *what* he pleases *when* he pleases. This perverse secret vanity casts him upon indolence & whim, & he never begins any thing, little or Great, in time, or with sufficient diligence to make it even possible to obtain Success.'[54] To her sympathetic brother Charles, who had become one of the most highly respected Greek scholars of his day, Fanny confided that she thought her son had 'something *morbid* in his constitution that *paralyzes his charac-ter*'.[55] She wondered whether or not to remove Alex with her to France, begging the excuse of his name being on the Duc de Luxembourg's list of supernumerary officers, or else move herself to Cambridge to oversee Alex's studies personally. Both Alex and his father were unequivocally against this. D'Arblay came over to England again in October 1814 in order to take Fanny home with him to Paris, and Alex was left to his own strange devices and desires.

When Monsieur and Madame d'Arblay returned to France in November 1814 they expected to enjoy their first ever period of peace and comfort there together, with a Bourbon King once more on the throne and a new regime opening out the prospect of honour and promotion for the ageing Chevalier. But everything seemed to go wrong from the first. On the way from the boat to the hotel in Calais, d'Arblay was the victim of a hit-and-run accident when a cart knocked him down and landed him a severe blow on the chest. His recovery was slow and the effects of the injury long-lasting. Back in Paris, the couple soon faced the threat of separation again when d'Arblay was ordered to a four-month residence at the garrison in Senlis, thirty miles north of Paris. While he was at home arranging for Fanny to join him there (she was *not* looking forward to life in the officers' mess), news reached Paris of Napoleon's daring escape from Elba on 26 February. It was received in the city with a curious apathy, which Fanny was puzzled to share. Even when it was known that Napoleon had re-entered France with his small army of followers, Parisians went about their business as usual and the d'Arblays carried on taking their daily drives in the Bois de Boulogne in the elegant calèche Monsieur had bought the previous year. Fanny tried to account for this 'species of stupor' in terms of over-exposure to such alarms during the previous twelve years:

> the idea of Napoleon was blended with all our Thoughts, our projects, our Actions. The greatness of his Power, the intrepidity of his Ambition, the vastness of his conceptions, & the restlessness of his spirit, kept suspense always breathless, & Conjecture always at work. [. . .] how could I for a moment suppose he would re-visit France without a consciousness of success, founded upon some secret conviction that it was infallible [? . . .] Unmoved, therefore, I reposed in the general apparent repose, which, if it were as real in those with whom I mixt as in myself, I now deem for All a species of Infatuation.[56]

However, as Napoleon moved quickly northwards meeting little if any resistance, royalist troops began to gear themselves for action. D'Arblay warned his wife to be prepared to leave the city without him at short notice and made her promise to use the protection of their old friend Madame d'Hénin (who had resumed her pre-Revolutionary title of Princesse) in such an eventuality. Fanny agreed with extreme reluctance. Privately, she was determined to hang on as near her husband as possible until the last minute.

D'Arblay himself was in his barracks at the Tuileries with the Garde du Corps during most of these anxious days in March 1815, expecting any minute to set out to fight Bonaparte. He came back to the rue Miroménil on the nineteenth exhausted and depressed by the collapse of confidence in the loyalist camp, and spent the afternoon in 'military business' which Fanny took care to avoid overhearing. The couple seem to have had a compact not to offend each other's sensibilities on the extremely delicate matter of Fanny's pacifism: 'I was always silent upon this subject', she wrote later, detailing the events of this day. '[I was] well aware that while his Honour was dearer to him than his life, my own sense of Duty was dearer to me also than mine.'[57] Dutiful 'acquiescent stillness' was, however, only really achievable when Fanny kept herself in willed ignorance. When d'Arblay received his orders to march later that day and had to part from his wife, very unsure whether they would ever see each other again, she could not resist watching his departure from the window:

There, indeed, behold him I did – but Oh with what anguish! just mounting his War Horse – [...] loaded with pistols, & equip'd completely for immediate service on the field of Battle – [...] I had not the most distant idea he was thus armed & encircled with Instruments of Death – Bayonets – Lances – Pistols – Guns – Sabres – Daggers – oh! gracious God! what horrour assailed me at the sight! I had only so much sense & self-controul left as to crawl softly & silently away[.]⁵⁸

Fanny had hitherto dwelt on the dangers which her husband would face as a soldier; here, on the eve of the troubled 'Hundred Days' of Napoleon's return, she contemplated, as if for the first time, his active participation in the process of war that so appalled her. D'Arblay seemed such a *gentle* man in peacetime, with his poetry-writing habits and fondness for painting and gardening, that Fanny found it very difficult to accept his professional manner (of which she had seen so little) as anything other than an aberration. The contrast had struck another observer, the English dramatist Bertie Greatheed, when he met d'Arblay at a men-only dinner in Paris in 1803. Greatheed described d'Arblay as 'a pleasant and a handsome man, very intelligent and bears a most excellent character [...] kind hearted, even tender, I believe, till on the command of another man he thinks it his duty to banish every feeling of humanity from his soul, and become more terrible than the tigre of Sumatra'.⁵⁹ After-dinner conversation probably revealed more of this side of d'Arblay's character to Greatheed in an hour than Fanny ever saw in their whole married life. She would have been horrified by Greatheed's description of her beloved *ami* as 'a thorough soldier with all his open rough virtues, and honourable murders on his head'.⁶⁰ Honour was the virtue by which she excused all her husband's military activity, but it was safely abstract; the idea of him ever having actually killed or even harmed another human being would have been too much for her to bear. When she did have intimations of her husband's part in the brutal 'exterminating contest' of war, as on the occasion of their parting in Paris, he appeared to her almost monstrous, 'so cold, so hard, so changed'.⁶¹ Her desolation after he left had as much to do with this sudden revelation as with the separation itself:

The street was empty. The gay constant Gala of a Parisian Sunday was changed into fearful solitude. No sound was heard, but that of here &

there some hurried footstep, on one hand hastening for a passport, to secure safety by flight; on the other rushing abruptly from, or to some secret concealment, to devize means of accelerating & hailing the entrance of the Conqueror. Well in tune with this air of impending crisis was my miserable mind, which from Grief little short of torture sunk, at its view, into a state of morbid quiet, that seemed the produce of feelings totally exhausted.[62]

It is little wonder that the 'bewildered' Madame d'Arblay scarcely knew what to do when the Princesse d'Hénin called soon afterwards to tell her they would be leaving the capital that evening. With only one spare dress (she was still in mourning for her father) and a basket of clean underclothes, she set out to say goodbye to Madame de Maisonneuve, at whose house she received a hurried note from her husband: 'My dearest amie, all is lost! – I can say no more at present. For God's sake leave as soon as possible'.[63] At the Princesse's house, Lally-Tolendal was begging his mistress to hurry, but another difficulty had arisen: there were no horses for hire to pull the Princesse's heavily-laden Berlin, the government having requisitioned them all. The anxious party, including Fanny, the Princesse, a femme de chambre, valet and two postillions, was only able to leave Paris at about eleven at night when they secured the loan of four horses for the first stage out of town.

Unknown to his wife, d'Arblay had left the city in similar confusion. At the review of troops at the Tuileries that day, the Garde du Corps had been expecting, with all the other royalist brigades, to march south to join the Duc de Berry and stage a battle against Napoleon. In fact the King, galloping past their ranks in an open carriage, was on his way *north* to Lille. Napoleon was already at Auxerre (very near d'Arblay's native Joigny), and the Duc's army had disintegrated. Suddenly, the whole army was on the run, the Maison du Roi straggling after the King's party with the vague idea of regrouping in Lille.

At the same time, Fanny and the Princesse wound their way towards the Belgian border in a zigzag route through Roi, Amiens, Arras, Douai and Tournai, using the Princesse's passport and passing Fanny off as 'famille', or, on one tricky occasion, as another 'femme de chambre'. The roads were oddly empty in the early stages but after Douai the women passed some groups of soldiers whom they peered at with anxious enquiry. The troops hardly seemed to know which side they were on. 'Some times they called out a "Vive! – "', Fanny noted, 'but without finishing their wish; and we repeated – that is we bowed to the same hailing exclamation, without knowing, or daring to enquire its purport.'[64]

It wasn't until they reached Tournai that they heard Louis XVIII had fled northwards. There was no information about his entourage, but while Fanny was wandering about the town trying to find a way to post letters, she saw a liveried carriage which she found out belonged to the Prince de Condé. Hoping to get information about the Maison du Roi from the Prince or his companion the Comte de Vioménil, she accepted the help of a man to whom the Princesse had been talking. This 'benevolent strange Chevalier' was, unknown to Fanny at this point, none other than François-René de Châteaubriand, the famous writer and controversialist, on his way to join the King's government in exile. Together they found de Vioménil eating his supper at an inn, but, without taking his eyes off his plate, the Count would only divulge that the King had by now crossed to Ghent. Fanny returned disappointed to her lodgings with the obliging stranger.

Châteaubriand's 1801 romance *Atala* was one of the cult books of the age and had 'bewitched all the reading females into a sort of idolatry of its writer'. When Fanny was properly introduced to him later the same day, she enlarged rather tactlessly on the superior merits of his 1811 *Itinéraire de Paris à Jerusalem*, but it was probably all one to Châteaubriand, who maintained 'an air of gentlemanly serenity'[65] on the subject of which was the greatest of his great works.

The Princesse and her party reached Brussels on 24 March, still without news of d'Arblay. After five frantic days of enquiry, a letter finally arrived from d'Arblay to Madame de Maurville, the Princesse's cousin (at whose house they were staying), explaining that he was ill with fever at Ypres. The Maison du Roi had been disbanded unceremoniously when the King realised that it would be impossible to enter Belgium with household troops and that he could no longer afford to fund them anyway. Officers who felt willing to pay their own expenses were invited to follow the King, which d'Arblay, predictably, had chosen to do. Unfortunately, he had been forced to abandon all his expensive war-gear – including the horses – at Béthune when a false alarm of imminent action drew his compagnie in a different direction. Nevertheless he intended to press on to Ghent when well enough to do so.

Armed with this information, Fanny decided to stay put in Brussels and wait to see how and where she could be reunited with her husband. As she recovered from the ordeal of her flight from Paris, she began to regret more and more the loss of her possessions there, which, she felt sure, would be looted or destroyed by the Bonapartists. Foremost among her treasures were the mass of manuscripts she had brought over from England, including her father's memoirs, Susan's letters and journals, all the family papers with which she had been entrusted and her own diaries of the past forty-seven years – 'all of my own inedited mss! – of my whole life!'[66] For such an archivally-minded person, the prospect of having lost all these precious documents was extraordinarily upsetting, and she returned to the subject again and again in long letters to d'Arblay and to her family.

For the first weeks of her four months in Brussels Fanny was sharing a house with the Princesse d'Hénin and Lally-Tolendal. Brussels was filling up with Allied troops, but war had not yet been declared on Napoleon, who had entered Paris on 20 March and now held defensive positions in the north of France. The cautious, conspiratorial atmosphere of Brussels was as remarkable as the inertia that had struck Paris a few weeks before. No one really believed that Bonaparte was conquerable – he was certainly not predictable – and though the Allies were gathering force in Belgium, their overall strategy remained obscure.

Fanny's most heartfelt wishes were granted when d'Arblay arrived unannounced in Brussels in late April, having been granted a *congé* to visit his wife. He looked terribly ill, 'thinned & changed inconceivably',[67] but despite their terrible anxieties about each other and about their son (who had left Cambridge for the foreseeable future due to the outbreak of a putrid fever there) they snatched some pleasures together, including a concert attended by the Queen of the Netherlands at which the Duke of Wellington impressively stopped his officers singing an encore to 'Rule, Britannia!' The sight of so many foreign troops enjoying some eve-of-battle jingoism prior to invading his native land cannot have been comfortable to d'Arblay, howevermuch his wife thought that without the presence of Wellington 'all public Hope would be lost'.[68]

D'Arblay was also painfully aware how quickly the Bourbon cause was losing ground among his old friends. The liberal faction, anticipating the need to find a moderate alternative to both Louis XVIII and to Napoleon, was now backing 'M. d'O' – Louis-Philippe, Duc d'Orléans – who had already been discussing with the English Prince Regent how to bring about a successful second restoration in France. The Princesse d'Hénin was one of many Constitutionalists who were now rooting for Orléans; they included Lafayette, who had come out of his retirement at La Grange and had just been elected Deputy for Seine-et-Marne, with whom the Princesse was again in correspondence. While he was in Brussels visiting Fanny, d'Arblay must have had an argument with Lally-Tolendal and the Princesse about their new allegiances, because before leaving he felt it desirable to move his wife out of the shared house and to a small apartment on the Marché au Bois. In the following weeks it became clear to Fanny that her old friends were avoiding her. '[Y]our last *vivacité* has made a sore impression', she wrote to d'Arblay a month after his departure. 'The tide can no longer, I fear, be stopt! the round Letter [Orléans] makes way perceptibly!'[69] But for the Chevalier, who had rather burnt his boats by accepting a position in the Bourbon royal household, it was a tide he felt honour-bound to resist.

In this strangely isolated state, Fanny stayed on in Brussels while d'Arblay returned to Ghent, whence he was almost immediately transferred to duty at Trèves (Triers) to mediate between the anti-French Prussian army and the French population in the lower Rhine. He and his handful of fellow-officers were also meant to be finding requisitions and volunteers (i.e. deserters) for the ailing royalist army, but once in faraway Trèves they seem to have been rather forgotten by their superiors as events on the other side of the Netherlands came to a crisis. All through June and July 1815, Sub-Lieutenant d'Arblay was completely dependent on his wife's letters from Brussels for news of the campaign of which he was meant to be part.

Much of what Fanny heard in the weeks prior to Waterloo was, of course, wildly inaccurate or speculative. Refugees and deserters strayed through Brussels, each with a different tale to tell, but as Fanny wrote later, 'nothing was known – every thing was imagined'.[70] A 'British under-officer' assured her that the Allies were aiming at 'the *surrender*, by the Inhabitants, *of Buonaparte* or the *Destruction of all France*'.[71] Another strangely apocalyptic rumour was that Wellington had sixteen million artillery rockets at his disposal that would leave France 'a burning heap of ashes!'[72] Brussels continued to fill up with British troops, clearly in readiness for some 'inexpressibly dreadful' confrontation, but at the same time there was a strange lull in Bonaparte's activities. 'How awful is this pause!' Fanny wrote to her husband. 'How, & in what manner will it terminate? I shudder – but try vainly to run from the subject'.[73]

The answer to her question came soon enough. Fanny was woken in the night on 15 June by confused noises in the street and the sound of a bugle. On her way back from the post office the next day she stood in a doorway to let a body of troops pass by only to find that it was not one troop but the whole company of the Brunswickers, dressed in full uniform and clearly going off to battle. That day and the next the sound of cannon began (from Quatre Bras) and the whole town became anxiously alert. The differences of opinion between Fanny and her friends were instantly forgotten in the common crisis, and she spent 17 June going between one and the other of them, the Princesse d'Hénin, Madame de Maurville, Madame La Tour du Pin and the Boyds (an English couple with five daughters Fanny had befriended during her stay), 'joining in & changing plans 20 times in an Hour'.[74] 'All the people of Brussels lived in the streets', she wrote memorably in her 'Waterloo Journal':

> Doors seemed of no use, for they were never shut. The Individuals, when they re-entered their houses, only resided at the Windows: so that the whole population of the City seemed constantly in Public view. Not only Business as well as Society was annihilated, but even every species of occupation. All of which we seemed capable was to Enquire or to relate, to speak, or to hear.[75]

Early in the morning of the eighteenth, Mrs Boyd and her daughter Ann appeared at Fanny's door in a panic, saying that the news was bad and that they were leaving immediately for Antwerp by barge. Fanny hurriedly packed her few things and went on foot to the Boyds' house (there were no carriages to be had at all), from where they set out for the wharf. On the way they heard 'a growling noise like distant thunder',[76] and in a few minutes were overtaken by a long procession of carts and baggage wagons, full of men and machinery. The barge was ready, but the wharf was so crowded that Mr Boyd left his womenfolk in an inn while he tried to find the boat's master. He came back with the news that Wellington had ordered the evacuation of Brussels, and all water-transport had been requisitioned for wounded officers. Fanny and her friends had no choice but to return to their apartments in the town, walking against a tide of wounded soldiers, the sound of cannon louder in their ears than ever, the shock-waves from the guns only nine miles away powerful enough to break windows in some of the houses.[77]

News of the battle changed dramatically twice during the day: first it was said that Wellington and Blucher had been victorious, then that Napoleon was working at Wellington's right wing and was expected to take Brussels in the morning. At one point, Fanny saw a captured General tied to his warhorse whom the crowds were proclaiming as Bonaparte (it was the Comte de Lobau). Soon after, there was a howl 'violent, loud, affrighting & issuing from many voices':

> I ran to the Window, & saw the *Marchée aux Bois* suddenly filling with a rushing populace, pouring in from all its avenues, & hurrying on, rapidly, & yet in a scrambling manner, as if unconscious in what direction: while Women with Children in their arms, or clinging to their cloathes, ran screaming out of doors: & cries, though not a word was ejaculated, filled the air: and, from every house, I saw Windows closing, & shutters fastening: – – all this, though long in writing, was presented to my Eyes in a single moment and was followed in another by a burst into my Apartment, to announce that *the French were come!*[78]

Fanny rushed off to rejoin the Boyds, but the streets were too full of people and she ended up at Madame de Maurville's house on the rue de la Montagne. Together they received a very encouraging first-hand account of the battle from an English Commissary who had just arrived from the scene, but even he had to admit that the outcome was not absolutely sure and that the battlefield was in 'excessive disorder'.[79] The French that had been mistaken for invading hordes approaching the town earlier in the day were in fact hundreds of prisoners who were being herded into Brussels. But rumour was more powerful than fact, and had a louder voice: 'The crowds in the streets, the turbulence, the inquietude, the bustle, the noise, the cries, the almost yells – though proceeding, I now believe, only from wanton Boys, mingling with disorderly females, or frightened mothers, kept up perpetual expectation of annoyance'.[80]

During the evening of the eighteenth Fanny went back to the Boyds', intending to try to set off again with them by barge very early the next morning (Mr Boyd, a wealthy merchant, must have bribed someone handsomely to secure this boat). She could not sleep, so sat up writing an account of her terrifying day to her husband:

> We none of us go to Bed, but they are all gone to lie down, in their cloaths; & I have tried to do the same, but excessive inquietude prevents my sleeping. I must now make up this confused scrawl, with repeated petition for a Line to Made *de Burney, poste restante*, Anvers. Heaven bless & preserve you, O mon ami![81]

Before she had finished this letter, an English officer brought further evidence that the enemy had been routed and that Brussels was saved. This persuaded Fanny to stay put in Brussels, where she had at least the comfort of being able to send and receive letters from Trèves. The Boyds tried to argue with her, but it was no good: 'They wondered at my temerity, & probably blamed it; but there was no time for discussion, & we separated.'[82]

Temerity is indeed a word not often associated with Madame d'Arblay, but she displayed it here, along with a shrewd awareness of what the real personal dangers were. 'If B[onaparte] does not obtain Brussels by a Coup de Main', she wrote the next day to George III's daughter Princess Elizabeth (with whom she had begun a correspondence on her return to France in 1814), 'he can only obtain it by the loss of Paris – since, if he stays longer away, the allies will enter in his absence, – & the Victory of a Town will cost him a Kingdom.'[83] All her other acquaintances had left Brussels by this time except Madame de Maurville (who thought Fanny had gone to Antwerp), and she was forced to spend a day in 'a sort of hopeless seclusion' on her own in her apartment, waiting for confirmation of the victory. This only came on the twentieth, two days after the battle of Waterloo itself, when Fanny's confidence was rewarded with copious news of 'the matchless Triumph of the matchless Wellington'.[84]

Once the threat of invasion was over and Wellington and Blucher had gone on towards Paris, civilians began filtering back into Brussels. The scale of the victory became clearer, and so did the scale of the devastation: thousands of bodies were lying in the midsummer sun on the battlefield where a new army, of local peasants, was employed digging graves for the 'Piles of Dead – heaps, Masses, hills of Dead!'[85] The wounded were still coming in four days after the battle on every conceivable kind of vehicle and being billeted all round Brussels in churches, workhouses and private homes. The town had become, in Fanny's phrase, a 'Walking Hospital':[86] 'For more than a week from this time, I never approached my Window but to witness sights of wretchedness', she wrote in her journal. 'Maimed, wounded, bleeding, mutilated, tortured victims of this exterminating contest, passed by every minute: – the fainting, the sick, the dying & the Dead, on Brancards, in Carts, in Waggons, succeeded one another without intermission.'[87] The sick or maimed prisoners were left till last and arrived in Brussels in a state which distressed Fanny, who was spending 'half the day' in the makeshift hospitals, winding lint for bandages: 'the blood that dried upon their skins & their Garments, joined to the dreadful sores occasioned by this corrosive neglect, produced an effect so pestiferous, that, at every new entry, Eau de Cologne, or vinegar, were resorted to by every Inhabitant, even amongst the shop-keepers, even amongst the commonest persons, for averting the menaced contagion'.[88] The authorities' assurances that everything possible was being done for these 'poor wretches' did not particularly convince her.

Fanny's letters to her husband, still at his distant post in Trèves, become noticeably more excited at the approach of the peace on 26 June and the prospect of the speedy re-enthronement of Louis XVIII. It must have been humbling for d'Arblay to hear the news this way, especially at a time when all faithful royalists might have been expecting some reward. Despite persistent requests to the Minister of War, de Feltre, to be reunited with the Maison du Roi, d'Arblay never got an answer to any of his letters, and was chagrined to hear that the King's entourage had re-entered Paris in triumph without him. He seemed to have been altogether forgotten.

Even had d'Arblay been younger and more dynamic, his prospects under the Bourbon re-restoration would have been poor. His son Alex, who had spent the whole of 1815 drifting from one friend's house to another because of the fever at Cambridge, gave a youthfully sarcastic but astute summary of the situation in a letter to his mother:

The King is in the hands of the Jacobins – of his Brother's murderers –
of Buoney's friends – of a set of ruffians – Fouché at the head – the crafty
Talleyrand &c is it likely that such men should call such loyal subjects as
my Father round the throne? And what honour to him *if he was asked* to
mix with such people? such company? [. . .] What can we expect from a
superannuated Monarch, an *Esclave couronné* ruling a demoralised nation
with revolutionary Ministers?[89]

Fanny did not record her response to this disrespectful view of the
monarch for whom her husband was prepared to give 'the last drop of
his blood'.[90] She and her son were never quite on the same wavelength.
She disliked his habit of quoting poetry at her in his letters, 'apropos to
nothing, copied from printed Books!'[91] This seemed actually insulting at
a time when Fanny craved hard news from England or sympathy for her
own plight, the seriousness of which Alex did not appear to recognise.
His rhapsodic manner seemed a symptom of his general moral malaise,
as Fanny told him in no uncertain terms:

Your expressions [upon a return to Camilla Cottage in 1815] lose much
of their effect by being over strained, *recherchée*, & *designing* to be pathetic.
We never touch others, my dear Alex, where we *study* to shew we are
touched ourselves. I beg you, when you write to me, to let your pen paint
your thoughts as they rise, not as you seek for, or labour to embellish
them. I remember you once wrote me a letter so very fine from Cambridge,
that if it had not made me laugh, it would most certainly have made me
sick.[92]

There was a long silence from Alex after this letter. His reply, on 24
May (now missing, possibly destroyed because of its contents), must have
expressed a certain pique at his mother's criticism, because in her next
letter she refers to 'that touch of *l'amour propre* that makes you so
sensitive to my attack upon a few laboured flowers of rhetoric'.[93] Her
cheery dismissal of his 'sensitivity' indicates some of the ways in which
Madame d'Arblay might have been alienating her son for years. From
the time of his going to Cambridge onwards, her anxieties about his
'apathy' and 'inertia' had cast a shadow over everything, even his successes. Just as his apparent laziness and 'secret vanity' annoyed her, it is

clear from his letters of this period that there were things about his parents (such as their political naivety) that exasperated Alex in return. But it seems safe to say that he probably kept his mother in ignorance of anything too close to his heart, fearing the intrusiveness of her interest and attention.

The generation gap exacerbated these difficulties. Alex's parents were actually old enough to be his grandparents, and he was obviously more influenced by the taste and manners of his own age than theirs. He idolised the work of his romantic contemporaries Byron and Lamartine, and was the first person (of many) to recommend to his mother a novel called *Waverley*. The immediate success of Scott's novel must have made a painful contrast with the reception accorded *The Wanderer* in the same year. Alex may have felt ashamed by the bad reviews his mother's book had attracted; he was staying with his uncle James all through the spring and summer of 1815 when Hazlitt's stinging attack on Madame d'Arblay was published in the *Edinburgh Review*, provoking James to break off his friendship with the reviewer. Alex's response was very different. On 1 May he sat down, 'for want of any better occupation', to write a long private critique of 'the last work of The Author of Evelina', pointing out some of the 'spots in her Sun':

> The Author seems to have found it necessary to concentrate [the English language] with painful conciseness, and to shorten off with elaborate quaintness that which literally translated from the French sentence, as she no doubt originally conceived, would not have had in English the same elegance.[94]

Amusing as it is to see the phrase 'painful conciseness' applied to *The Wanderer*, a novel of some 400,000 words, one understands what Alex means when he translates one of the book's phrases into French and it suddenly becomes elegant. 'The Author of Evelina', to use Alex's impersonal term, had described one of her characters as having 'the strong recommendation of being wholly natural; a recommendation as rare in itself as success is in its deviations'.[95] 'Its deviations' particularly irritated Alex, but he showed that in translation the phrase could be turned into a neat French apothegm: 'Il est aussi rare d'être naturel que de reussir sans l'être.' There is no evidence that Alex ever showed his mother his

critique of *The Wanderer* – which is notably more concerned with minutiae like the above than with the book's larger meaning. It was probably
much more satisfying not to show her. Given their quarrel over 'strained'
and 'natural' style, his choice of example seems a particularly subtle form
of revenge.

By early July in Brussels, Madame d'Arblay was tentatively looking forward to a reunion with her husband and a return to Paris, though, as
she wrote to Mary Ann Waddington, 'the changes which this country
has now for so long a time gone through, have been so astonishing, so
sudden, so unexpected, That they take at least away all presumption, if
not all confidence in public transactions. This is no siecle for those who
love their home, or who have a home to love', she continued. ' 'Tis a
siecle for the Adventurous, to whom Ambition always opens resources;
or for the New, who guess not at the Catastrophes that hang on the rear,
while the phantom Expectation allures them to the front.'[96]

Unknown to Fanny, a catastrophe that would put back all their plans
had befallen her husband the day before she wrote her wistful letter to
Mrs Waddington. A new horse had dealt d'Arblay a violent kick to the
right leg as he approached it in the stables (where the horse was eating
oats), and the injury had become infected. D'Arblay had developed a
fever, and by the time Fanny heard about all this ten days later he was
very ill and desperate for her to join him. She packed her few things and
set off immediately in a diligence to Liège, the first stage towards Trèves.

Later, Fanny was to wonder at the rash speed with which she set
off from Brussels alone on the two-hundred-mile journey across the
Netherlands and the Prussian Rhineland via Liège, Cologne, Bonn, and
then south to Coblenz and Trèves. 'I can scarcely myself now conceive
how I found the courage to combat the obstacles I continually encountered', she wrote nearly ten years later when she was composing her
lengthy 'Journey to Trèves';[97] 'But I was so absorbed by an anxiety that
had nothing to do with myself, or my situation, that both were nearly
driven from my thoughts & my calculations'.[98] With no protection, no
contacts in any of the towns on the way, very little money and very little
knowledge of German, it is certainly remarkable that Fanny – a woman,
it must be remembered, who was once rendered hysterical by a sedan-
chair ride from one end of St James's Palace to the other – undertook

this long and hazardous journey. She had problems with the authorities all the way: every stop seemed to harbour some power-crazed minor bureaucrat ready to find fault with her papers and threatening to send her back in the direction from which she had come. She dealt with these people with surprising *sang froid*, dropping the name of d'Arblay's commander, General Kleist, as often and in as authoritative a manner as possible. In Cologne she passed herself off as a Frenchwoman to avoid the delays and alarms of red tape. In Coblenz she had to trail round the town at night in the rain trying to get the necessary visas. In Bonn she almost missed the coach when she got lost in the city's winding streets and only found her way back to her hotel when she recognised a gaudily-painted statuette in a corner niche. It was a damned close-run thing:

> I saw that the Coach was just departing! The Horses harnessed, every passenger entered, & the Drivers with their whips in hand extended! – Oh my God! what an escape! & what thankful Joy & Gratitude I experienced![99]

The remarkable views from the coach window of the famous river Rhine as she travelled from Bonn to Coblenz made Fanny believe she was entering 'regions of enchantment':

> we passed through such stupendous mountains on each side, that the Rhine & its Banks, which constituted our Road, made the whole of the valley; while stately Rocks, of striking forms, & hanging woods, of exquisite beauty, invited, on one side, our gaze & admiration; & prospects eternally diversifying varied our delighted attention on the other.[100]

But this was no Grand Tour. The picturesque splendour of the 'falling Turrets & scattered fragments, moss grown, & widely spread around' on the summit of almost every hill were not 'the indispensible effect of all conquering, irresistible Time' but war ruins, as Fanny understood all too well. They gave 'as much interest & as great a charm to the scene, as they caused, on the other hand, sorrow, resentment: & even horror to the reflections'.[101]

After Coblenz, all pleasure went out of the journey. Fanny had almost entirely run out of money and was only able to secure a place on the coach by deferring payment until Trèves. After the 'exquisite felicity' of her reunion with d'Arblay on the evening of 24 July, she was able to see for herself the damage done by his accident. He was still in great pain, had round-the-clock nursing and had to keep his leg raised all the time. In the morning, he was lifted from his bed onto a sofa and wheeled to the window, where he remained all day, 'the poor tortured Leg always lifted up, & immoveable, & the whole person in a state of cruel constraint from apprehension of any motion that might cause a fresh shock'.[102] To pass the time until her husband was well enough to leave Trèves, Fanny took day trips alone around the city and down the Moselle. D'Arblay was meanwhile trying to secure a recall from duty, but as before, he had great difficulty getting any response from his superiors in Paris, who had lost all interest in the few men scattered on the Prussian frontier. Eventually he received confirmation of his recall and the papers necessary to get himself and his wife back to Paris. He also received, simultaneously, confirmation of his promotion to Lieutenant-General and his *retraite*: d'Arblay was being officially retired.

Thus d'Arblay's unspectacular military career came to an end. He and Fanny left Trèves in mid-September and began an arduous journey back to France in their own calèche, with all d'Arblay's luggage hanging off the back to allow maximum leg-room under the leather apron. Perhaps there was some prestige to be had from returning home from the war dramatically wounded – however those wounds had actually been received. But there was little honour or glory in d'Arblay's return. The insolence of the Allied border-guards, and of a Prussian sub-officer at Thionville in particular, enraged the Lieutenant-General and embarrassed his wife. The humiliation of having to re-enter his native land by the permission of foreigners and to see, as Fanny put it, 'the vision of Henry V revived, & Paris in the Hands of the English!',[103] must have hurt him far more even than his mangled leg.

The d'Arblays were relieved to find their possessions in the rue Miroménil intact and the town full of their former friends and neighbours. They did not intend to stay in Paris long, however. With the Lieutenant-General's retirement and the continuing instability in France, they had decided to move back to England, to some spa town perhaps, where they could attend to d'Arblay's health. They didn't tell their friends their long-term plans, but passed off their impending departure as a temporary expedient; the many visits they received in Paris that month therefore took on the nature of secret last farewells. The Latour-Maubourgs, Madame de Maisonneuve, the Princesse de Poix and Madame La Tour du Pin were all friends who 'had wrought themselves, by innumerable kindnesses' into Fanny's affections, and she was extremely sorry to leave them. 'The vivacity & obligingness of the Really high bred French' had led her to prefer French society in many ways to English, even during the extremely volatile period she had lived through in that country. In polite society, politics could always be overridden by manners (or trampled underfoot by manners, depending on your point of view); it was therefore easy to associate again with the Princesse d'Hénin and Madame de Maurville, 'who had not yet forgiven my escape from them at Brussells [i.e. her moving out of the shared house] – – but came to me with unfailing kindness'.[104] Lafayette, too, was among the callers to d'Arblay's sick-bed who despite political differences retained a real affection for his former comrade-in-arms; and Monsieur Larrey, another political opponent, but revered by Fanny for his surgical expertise (and created a Baron by Napoleon for his remarkable services on the field), was on hand to tend the injured leg. Even Talleyrand was not completely beyond the pale. Fanny, who hadn't seen him since his visit to the Juniper colony in 1793, recognised the great man when she attended Madame de Laval's drawing room, and stopped by his chair on her way out. 'Monsieur de Talleyrand has forgotten me, but no one forgets him,'[105] she said, and left immediately. '[I] saw a movement of surprize by no means unpleasant break over the habitual placidity, of the nearly imperturbable composure of his general – & certainly *made up* countenance,' she remarked uncharitably.[106] But she was glad to have spoken to him, for old times' sake: 'O what Days were those of conversational perfection! of Wit, ingenuity, gaiety, repartee, information, badinage, & eloquence!'

The d'Arblays left Paris for Calais in the calèche and arrived in Dover on 17 October 1815, both terribly ill and shaken by a rough crossing. They went straight to Deptford to visit Charles, then on to meet Alex at Sablonière's Hotel in Leicester Square. Fanny never set foot on French soil again.

❧ 14 ☙

Keeping Life Alive

On their return to England in 1815, the d'Arblays settled in a pleasant ter-
raced house at 23 Great Stanhope Street, Bath. The fashionable spa town
suited Fanny and her 'poor *Boiteux*'[1] very well, being cheaper than London
and more genteel. In Louis XVIII's lavish dispersal of honours during the
Hundred Days d'Arblay had been made a Count, but he chose not to use
his title in England (except at the bank and the War Office). He and Fanny
simply couldn't live up to the social expectations of being 'titled' – nor did
they want to.

Soon after arriving in Bath Fanny discovered that there were several
of her old acquaintances from her travels with Mrs Thrale and Mrs Ord
still living in the city 'in perfect preservation',[2] and in the autumn of 1815
Mrs Piozzi herself was living in Gay Street, a few hundred yards from
the d'Arblays' lodgings just north of the Circus. Fanny felt compelled to
call on her, but the reception she met with was frosty. Mrs Piozzi was
wearing mourning, as she had done permanently in the six years since
Piozzi's death, and other people's attitudes to her late husband remained
the benchmark by which she judged them overall. When Mrs Piozzi sold
off the contents of Streatham Park in 1816, she kept only two of the
magnificent set of portraits by Reynolds, those of Henry Thrale and
Arthur Murphy, the latter 'the only friend who had been equally attached
to both my husbands'.[3] All the others, including the portraits of Dr
Burney, Garrick (both bought by the acquisitive Charles Burney junior),
Dr Johnson and the double portrait of herself and Queeney were ultimately disposable.*

---

* Charles Burney junior reported the progress of the Streatham Park sale in a series of letters to
Fanny (in the Comyn collection). His observations must have given her pain, for included in the
sale were the copies of *Evelina* and *Cecilia* which the author had presented to Mrs Thrale. The first
leaf of the latter (on which Fanny would have written an inscription) had been torn out; in the
former, 'From the Scribler' was annotated by Mrs Thrale, 'N.B. *Scribler with one B*, Madame Dab!'

Fanny, on the other hand, still carried with her 'whithersoever I go'[4] a locket which Mrs Thrale had given her years before, containing a lock of Hester's hair wound together with a lock of Susan's. Two years later, Fanny and Mrs Piozzi had another meeting which was more successful – in Fanny's view, at least. To the end of her life, Fanny believed that some sort of restitution had been made, but the older woman revealed in her commonplace book that she remained cynically unmoved:

My perfect Forgiveness of l'aimable Traitresse, was not the act of Duty, but the impulsion of Pleasure rationally sought for, where it was at all Time sure of being found – In her Conversation. I will however not assist her Reception in the World a *Second* Time –[5]

Life in Bath was never comfortable for d'Arblay, whose wound continued to pain him and who had many reservations about settling in England. He saw little reason for staying if their son did not make a success of his university career; Madame d'Arblay therefore made it clear to Alex that it was for her sake as much as his own that he should 'procure Honour & Independence'[6] – she certainly did not want to live in France again, although she conceded (in theory) to a yearly visit.

Alex did not respond well to being nagged, as his mother well knew: 'he pines, he sickens, or rebels, under mental or intellectual restraint', she wrote to Lady Keith.[7] Though she monitored his work relentlessly and made him socialise in Bath during the vacations, Alex responded with 'sighing & moaning',[8] and returned to his obsessive life of recreational mathematics, chess and solitude as soon as he was back in Cambridge. He distressed his mother by rarely answering her letters until she was in a complete panic (this did not necessarily take long), but perhaps reasoned that there was not much to answer to communications such as this:

Have you Cocoa?
Have you got *Shoes*?
Do you take a *Rhubarb* pill from time to time?
an *analeptic* if you have any headache?
a *black* one if Nature is coy?[9]

Alex had difficulty applying himself to learning – it was not something he had ever had to do. His memory was as astonishing as his mother's (at about this time he recited to Charlotte Barrett the whole of Pope's 'Lines to an Unfortunate Lady' to illustrate a point about his translation of it into French, which he also recited), but he lacked any particle of her drive towards self-improvement.

Alex was forced to transfer from Caius to Christ's College in the Michaelmas term of 1816, and at the same period had to resign the Tancred scholarship because neither he nor his parents had understood it was for students taking a medical degree. Fanny knew that without the entrée to a Cambridge fellowship granted by a high degree Alex's chances in life were not going to be good, and that there was not enough money to maintain him otherwise. D'Arblay had the same worries about his son, but thought of a different solution. Despite his poor health, d'Arblay made a three-month visit to France in the summer of 1816 to visit his family (Fanny stayed behind to watch over Alex), during which he rapidly evolved a scheme for Alex to marry the beautiful daughter of one of his wealthy old friends from Joigny. The attraction of this idea to the ageing and ailing General is easy to see – it would have re-established the d'Arblay blood-line in its native country, solved the problem of money-earning for Alex and possibly, by removing that worry and making him take on responsibilities he had hitherto shirked, woken the dreamy youth out of his indolence. But Fanny objected strongly to any marriage of convenience, a shockingly old-fashioned, even barbaric practice in her view (as d'Arblay should have known from her works). Apart from thinking that Alex was far too young and immature to be married, she insisted on him 'seeing, selecting, chusing, wholly for him-self'[10] when the time came, just as his parents had been able to do. She urged d'Arblay to keep even the suggestion of such a match secret from their son, and he reluctantly gave in. He returned to England in November with little to show for his troublesome journey apart from a small amount of back-pay and an attack of jaundice.

Continuing problems with his pension – which was reduced because he was living abroad and which he was required to collect in person – necessitated d'Arblay's return to France in the summer of 1817. It was on this, his last journey home, that he arranged for the completion of his portrait painted in oils by the brothers Carl and Horace

Vernet.* Posterity was on his mind: 'People will always remind Alex who his mother is, but not who his father was!' he said rather sadly. 'I have had this portrait made and dedicate it to him so that he doesn't forget me.'[12]

In the Vernets' picture, the Lieutenant-General appears in full dress uniform and medals, seated as if on the edge of a battlefield, with a warhorse behind him looking nobly animated, and a battle scene featuring a dragoon and guns in the background. Even making allowances for convention, this representation could only seem absurd, not to say fraudulently self-aggrandising, to anyone who knew the history of d'Arblay's war. The horse, certainly, recalled the source of his injury, but not its banal circumstances. The obvious implication of the picture is that d'Arblay had been at Waterloo or one of the other major battles of the Hundred Days, instead of being posted about as far away from the action as possible, doing little more than keeping his equipment polished and having dinner with General Kleist.

D'Arblay left among his papers a neat sketch-plan of the battlefield of Waterloo which oddly substantiates the impression that he was present at the battle. 'These sketches of the field were taken on the spot from the Summit of a perpendicular bank immediately above the high road from Brussells to Genappe in the front of the British position', he wrote by way of explanation on 'Plate B'. *Who* was 'on the spot', and *when*, is not stated. If on one of his trips to France in 1816 or 1817 d'Arblay made the tourist pilgrimage to Waterloo that was so popular in those years, he never mentioned it in his surviving letters or wrote home from any location on that route. The only other way that he could claim his picture was made 'on the spot' would be if it was a copy of one so made. Charles Parr Burney had been among the first deliberate tourists, arriving in Brussels in July 1815 while his aunt was still there. It is possible that d'Arblay derived his information from someone like Charles Parr who had seen the field and perhaps made sketches of his own, or from an 'official' representation, such as appeared in illustrated magazines and

---

* It is not clear when this portrait was begun, but it was probably during d'Arblay's 1816 trip. His comment in late June 1817 that 'poor Vernet has not yet finished my portrait' betrays a certain impatience, and Fanny's response, 'let me not pass another Winter without it,' shows it was begun at least a year before.[11]

public exhibitions, 'dioramas' and 'panoramas'.[13] The two-part structure of his sketch, which is meant to represent a 360-degree all-round view, and the description of the parts as 'plates' rather support the latter suggestion.

When d'Arblay went back to France in the summer of 1817 on what was intended to be his annual visit, Fanny decided once again to stay home to monitor Alex, who was approaching his finals, yet, 'unwatched, un-urged, does *NOTHING!*'[14] They joined a group of his Cambridge associates on a 'reading party' that summer in Ilfracombe, North Devon, where Fanny gradually learned from Alex's young tutor, Edward Jacob, the extent of her son's laziness at the university. Alex was no longer in a position to achieve high honours, Mr Jacob admitted. His habits were obsessive and his lifestyle alarmingly unhealthy, almost neurasthenic, as Fanny reported anxiously to her husband:

[He would] never partake of any meal; but go on with whatever he is about till he feels gnawn with hunger [. . .] never go to Bed, till his burnt out candles leave him suddenly in the dark! & then, his clothes hardly taken off, & no night cap on his head, he rolls himself between the Bedcloaths, falls into a quick sleep of fatigue; but quickly awakens from it, cold, shivering, or feverish.[15]

Even allowing some latitude for maternal hyperbole, Alex's behaviour was clearly abnormal and unhealthy. 'Morbid' was again the word that suggested itself to the anxious parent: 'There is something, I firmly believe, in his obstinate feelings more *morbid* than *wilful* bad habits'.[16] It cannot be ignored that Alex's symptoms have similarities to those of a drug or alcohol addiction, specifically opium addiction, so commonplace at the time (when opium was the main ingredient in patent remedies for anything from teething pain to cholera). Most households had opium in some form among their medicines, and its widespread use as an analgesic makes it highly likely that Monsieur d'Arblay was taking some form of opiate for his bad leg and his recent chronic bowel pain, just as Fanny had been dosed up with laudanum at various times in her life, notably at Court and during and after her mastectomy. She had been encouraging Alex to take his analeptic pills and 'a *black* one if Nature is coy' – the colour is associated with many opium preparations such as the Black

Drop (a favourite tipple of Lord Byron) and the Black Draught. Alex's listlessness, which was to become more marked as the years went by, bears a resemblance to certain side-effects of opiates – 'A dull, mopish and heavy Disposition [. . .] Anxieties and Depressions of Spirits'.[17] That he was melancholic and depressive is certain, but the exact causes – and how he coped with them – remain obscure.

It is perhaps not surprising that during their holiday in Ilfracombe, Fanny ended up putting her own life in danger through sheer inattention. She had gone with her dog Diane to a part of the shore known as the Wildersmouth, a steep-sided bay at Capstone Point to which there was access only at low tide. She was so absorbed in picking up pebbles for d'Arblay's mineral collection, thinking of him far away in France and of their problematic child, that she failed to notice when the exit to the cove was cut off by the incoming tide. According to her own lengthy account, written up six years later as her 'Ilfracombe Journal', Fanny took refuge from the sea on a small, steep island with a grassy top, which she assumed would lie above the high-water mark. As the sea boomed into the bay, however, she found it more difficult than she had anticipated to reach the safety of the grass, even going on all fours. The steep and slaty rock cut her hands and feet and bruised her knees, she said, and her long dress must have been a handicap, too. She reached a point very near the top, where her head was on a level with the grass, but could go no further and had to haul the dog up by the collar (ingeniously using the handle of her parasol). They were forced to stay put, balanced precariously on a ledge, unable to move. Using her eyeglass, Fanny tried to see whether the tide had turned, but to her horror realised it was still rising, and that there was no vessel anywhere in sight: 'All was vacant and Vast! – I was wholly alone, wholly isolated.'[18]

The dramatic colouring in Madame d'Arblay's account heavily emphasises the picturesque and romantic potential of the scene and turns it into a mortal struggle with the forces of Nature – she might have been Manfred on the Jüngfrau rather than an old lady on a rock:

The next Waves reached to the Upper end of my Chamber, which was now ALL SEA, save the small Rock upon which I was mounted! [. . .] The Wind roared around me, Pushing on the Waves with a frothy velocity that, to a bye-stander, – not to an inmate amidst them! – would have been beautiful [...] A Wave, at length, more stupendous in height, in breadth, in foam, & in roaring noise than any which had preceded it, dashed against my Rock as if enraged at an interception of its progress, & rushed on to the extremity of this savage chamber, with a foaming impetuosity from which I felt myself splashed. This Moment I believed to be my last of Mortality!'[19]

The tide was on the turn, however, and Fanny was saved by hanging on to the rock for ten hours[20] until she heard voices from the clifftop, Alex's among them.

That was her story. Another very different (and much shorter) version of the incident exists, in a letter solicited by the collector F. Leverton Harris from the son of John Le Fevre, a student friend of Alex's who was one of their party. According to Le Fevre, Alex had come to him in some distress when he began to worry about his mother's absence. Le Fevre suggested that Madame d'Arblay might have got caught by the tide in some bay or other (exactly what had happened), and the two young men set out along the cliffs to search. Eventually they spotted the old lady on the sand in a bay below, returned to Ilfracombe and rescued her by boat. Le Fevre's son Baron Eversley dispenses with the rest in a few sentences: 'My father said that the lady's account of her adventure was greatly exaggerated. She was in no real danger. The sea had not come up to her. She was not clinging to the rocks – She was seated on the sand – The incident of the little dog Fidèle was an invention so far as my Father recollected.'[21]

Le Fevre's downbeat account of the day, though it has obvious slips such as calling the dog Fidèle rather than Diane (he was thinking perhaps of Fidel, the dog in *Cecilia*), sounds the alarm about Madame d'Arblay's veracity again. On investigation, the presence of the dog seems highly unlikely. According to Madame d'Arblay's note-form diary Diane whelped (one puppy only) on or just before 24 September,[22] the same day that she records her 'Adventure terrific on A Rock at Ilfracomb!' The bitch's unplanned pregnancy had been the source of a rather cruel joke between the d'Arblays against their old friend Madame de Staël, who had a child by a 'secret husband' in 1812. Fanny had noted going to 'Capston with Diane' twice before this date – on 16 and 17 September – but it is highly improbable that the dog would have been out on a long excursion so soon after having a puppy. If, as Le Fevre said, the dog's involvement was 'an invention', it is a pretty shameless one, full of guilefully particular detail such as the use of the parasol handle as a hoist. And if Madame d'Arblay was 'inventing' the presence of Diane, it is all too likely, as Le Fevre claimed, that the rest was 'greatly exaggerated'.

Madame d'Arblay's account seems to bear as much upon the time when it was composed (1823) as the time it describes. In the mid-1820s the dog Diane was a constant companion and solace to her widowed owner, more reliable and attentive than Alex, as Madame d'Arblay overtly stated ('I have always a delighted Companion in Diane, though I have not always my Minister'[23]). She wrote up her Ilfracombe adventure as a *devoir* to her late husband, who, as we shall see, asked Fanny during his final illness to make a record of such events for their friends and for posterity. The Ilfracombe Journal can be seen therefore as a piece of retrospective prophecy, the Germanic-sounding 'Wildersmouth' representing the jaws of death and the inrushing flood-waters Madame d'Arblay's uncontrollable fears about separation from her husband and son. The imminent 'death' she foresees for herself in this nightmarish fantasy is *survival*, her intense and wholly justifiable terror of being alone, cut off from the familiar world, looking out on nothing but the blank sea of extinction. In a letter to her sister Hetty in 1825, Fanny declined to return to Ilfracombe not because it reminded her of being caught by the tide in Capstone Bay (an incident she never mentions in her many retrospective references to Ilfracombe in her letters of the 1820s) but because the landscape was too strongly associated with the solitary walks on which she read letters from her absent husband 'such as scarcely any one ever received, & as no one breathing ever more tenderly more devoutly valued'.[24] Well might she look back on those letters with a pang once the absence had become permanent and reunion after death was all she had to look forward to. D'Arblay had written to her from Calais at the beginning of their separation in the summer of 1817:

> The sea lies between us, my darling Fanny, but I trust that soon we will be reunited, and anyway nothing can ever come between our hearts – I swear it on mine.[25]

✳   ✳   ✳

1817 saw the beginning of the wave of family deaths which blighted the last twenty years of Fanny Burney's life. In April of that year she witnessed the death of fifteen-year-old Ralph Broome, Charlotte's only child by her second husband, when Charlotte and her family came to Bath in their latest attempt to find a cure for her consumptive son. Charlotte bore the death with apparent fortitude: 'she scarcely permits herself to deem it a misfortune,' Fanny wrote with admiration, 'so deeply religious is her sense of his own eternal advantage from the change'.[26] Such piety was certainly a useful specific against bereavement; Fanny seems not to have had it in as great a degree as her sister, who in turn was regarded by her Evangelically-minded daughters, Charlotte Barrett and Marianne Francis, as falling short of the Christian ideal. Many of their older relations, worldly uncle Charles, for example (though a cleric), were judged by both the nieces to be hopelessly materialistic and sensual.

These differences were highlighted in the winter of 1816 when Fanny was composing the epitaph for her father's memorial tablet in Westminster Abbey. Her fulsome tribute to the Doctor's personal and professional virtues met with a mixed response among the family, many of whom (Marianne Francis most strongly) felt it inappropriate to stress his worldly achievements on a sacred memorial. Fanny defended the wording of her tribute vigorously, but had never met with so much opposition before. It was a surprise to her that no one else in the family seemed to share her view of their father as 'Unrivalled Chief and Scientific HISTORIAN of his Tuneful Art', whose 'High Principles' and 'Conscience without Reproach' had 'Prepared, through the whole tenor of his Earthly Life, with the mediation of our Blessed Saviour, his Soul for Heaven'.[27] The relegation of the deity to a parenthesis did not strike her as inappropriate, nor the superlative adjectives describing her father's principles and achievements, which clearly irritated her brother James and embarrassed Charles junior. He cavilled at references to Dr Burney's powers of conversation and 'self-acquired accomplishments', a misleading term, in Charles's opinion, given the Doctor's years at Chester Free School and his apprenticeship under Arne. The phrase did not finally appear on the memorial stone when it was laid in the North Choir of the Abbey in the summer of 1817, but Fanny made it clear that she would return to the subject in the biography of her father she intended to write. In her view, Dr Burney's 'indefatigable *self-directed* industry' was not simply admirable in itself, but the key to his character.

Hard-drinking, kind-hearted Charles had been complaining for some time of pains in the head, and died of a stroke at the age of sixty just after Christmas 1817. He left behind a treasure-house of books and manuscripts, which was assessed by a committee of experts (including Thomas Payne's son, also a bookseller called Thomas) on behalf of the British Museum and subsequently bought for the nation. Charles's library included the earliest printed editions of every Greek classic 'and several of the scarcest among the Latins', and almost four hundred manuscripts, including two Greek gospels (tenth and twelfth century), fifteenth-century copies of Callimachus and of Ptolemy's Geography, and, the star item, a late-thirteenth-century copy of the *Iliad*, formerly belonging to the antiquarian Townley. The whole collection was valued at £14,500 – truly 'a sum enormous' – and was bought by negotiation with the heir, Charles Parr Burney, for the bargain price of £13,500. It was at this date that Charles Parr found out about his father's youthful theft of books at Cambridge and decided not to write the memoir he had been planning, for fear of dragging the story into public notice. The question remains, though, how his father, on a clerical schoolmaster's income and within forty years, had managed to acquire 'probably the most complete [classical library] ever assembled by any man'.[28]

D'Arblay had returned from France in October 1817 'altered – thin – weak – depressed – full of pain'.[29] In Paris he had consulted Baron Larrey, who said there was no need for an operation, but he was being prescribed treatments conventional for a stricture of the rectum, which suggests that he may have been suffering from cancer.[30] Whatever the cause, the symptoms were extremely painful, and by the winter of 1817 d'Arblay must have suspected that he was mortally ill.

The Lieutenant-General cut a nobly pathetic figure that December when he was presented to the elderly Queen Charlotte at the Pump Room in Bath on her first ever Royal Progress without the failing, blind King from whom she had been separated for several years. D'Arblay was having so much trouble merely standing that some ladies offered him their seats, but of course he felt unable to accept and endured the torture of the morning as well as he could, speechless with pain. He was clearly trying his best for Fanny's sake; she had been looking forward to this mark of favour with an ardour reminiscent of her father's for all things royal. One would think that she had never known the inside of a palace or cavilled at the fatuity of Court life. The details of the morning were lovingly recalled in her journal, written retrospectively after d'Arblay's death. Old, ugly, unexciting Queen Charlotte is described in terms fit for a deity:

> she rose to make her round, & with a Grace indescribable, &, to those who never witnessed it, inconceivable; for it was such as to carry off Age, Infirmity, sickness, diminuitive & disproportioned stature, & Ugliness! – & to give to her, in defiance of such disadvantages, a power of charming & delighting that rarely had been equalled.[31]

It was d'Arblay's first presentation to the Queen – a long-awaited public acknowledgement – and it was also his last public appearance. Fanny was bursting with pride, so much so that in her account she dwells on the Queen's inconceivable graciousness at greater length than on poor d'Arblay's heroic endurance of it. She records with delight that the Queen had so much small-talk with d'Arblay that only 'a word sufficed for those who remained'; she also notes that d'Arblay's exertions were such that he had to retreat and collapse on a bench as soon as the Queen had finished with him, and that the rest of the day was spent 'in bodily misery'. There is something monstrous in this valuation of royal attention unless you happen to believe fervently, as Fanny did, in the Divine Right of Kings. When, subsequent to this Bath meeting, the Queen sent her a gift of some rather dull books and a pair of candlesticks, Fanny wrote in thanks: 'the honoured signature of my beloved Royal Mistress – my venerated Queen, I have pressed to my lips & my Heart, & shall prize as my first possession to the end of my life'.[32] (However, neither the books nor the autograph appears on the list of treasures in her will.)

Fanny was not able to accept the seriousness of d'Arblay's condition, and even chose to think that he might be exaggerating, though this was far from the truth. The private diary he kept between February and April 1818[33] reveals the extent of his physical sufferings, his anxieties for his wife and son and his intuition that he was dying. D'Arblay's love for Fanny and understanding of her character shows itself more clearly than ever in his concern to prepare her for the inevitable, just as her refusal to acknowledge what he was trying to tell her in the latter half of 1817 is testimony to her equally strong feelings for him. She was so sure she could not possibly outlive her 'meilleur ami's death that there was really no point in anticipating it.

The result of her denial was, however, to impede his recovery. In January 1818 d'Arblay demanded a consultation with a surgeon, but by then he was far gone in his disease. 'My Invalid was right!' Fanny wrote in distress to Mrs Locke; 'measures were required that had far more happily been employed sooner! – alas alas.'[34] Still she maintained a false optimism in front of her sister Hetty (who was living at this date near Bath with her daughters Maria and Sophia) and in front of the invalid himself, whom she continually tried to rally. It was only when d'Arblay had received the last rites from the local Roman Catholic priest and began to tell Fanny his dying wishes that she 'dared no longer oppose to him my hopes of his recovery'. She heard his counsel 'with deluges of long restrained tears', at last 'awakened to a sense of his danger'.[35]

D'Arblay was of course deeply concerned about his wife's likely reaction to his fast-approaching death. He adjured her to seek support from her sisters and friends, to solidify her friendships with the Queen and princesses, to keep as much as she could in the world and not to clam up as she had done so damagingly after Susan's death in 1800: '*Parle de moi!*' he urged her, as Fanny recalled in her long 'Narrative of the Illness & Death of General d'Arblay', 'Parle – et souvant. Surtout à Alexandre; qu'il ne m'oublie pas!'[36] He also instructed her to write up some of the critical episodes of their later life together, guessing that the process would have some therapeutic benefit for her.

Alex, who had graduated from Christ's as tenth Wrangler in January 1818 and had been elected a Fellow of the college in March, was called back from Cambridge at the end of April to see his father once more. The Lieutenant-General was still in possession of his faculties and able to give his son a blessing, but Fanny was by this time in a state bordering on distraction and so desperate to see symptoms of recovery that she was even prepared to wake her husband up with sal volatile when he fell into unconsciousness. The doctor, unsurprisingly, took a dim view of such behaviour. On 3 May d'Arblay leant forward, took Fanny's hand between both of his and said, 'I don't know if these are my last words, but this will be my last thought – Our Reunion!'[37] He did speak again, even attempting a pleasantry about the way Alex plumped up his pillow, but these were his last words to his wife, chosen with great care and sincere feeling. Thoughtful and selfless to the last, d'Arblay provided Fanny with the only possible comfort with which to face her coming bereavement.

D'Arblay died in his sleep later that day while his wife and son were in the room, watching, though neither of them realised when the actual moment of death came. Ironically, Fanny had mistaken his calm for 'a favourable crisis' that might turn the course of her husband's illness. Hours passed, during which she noticed 'a universal stillness in the whole frame such as seemed to stagnate – if I so can be understood – all around'.[38] She called for their servant Payne, convinced that 'this sleep was important' (as indeed it was), and was astonished when the woman slipped off during the next hour of waiting, telling Alex she 'would go and take her tea!' Fanny did not dare look for her husband's pulse or touch his lips, but felt that his hands were turning cold, so covered them with new flannel. Payne – and presumably Alex, too, since he did not stop the servant leaving – saw what Fanny simply could not bear to see, that d'Arblay was already dead.

Confirmation of the death was made by the doctor, Mr Tudor, soon after. 'How I bore this is still marvellous to me!' Fanny wrote later, in an extraordinary reconstruction of the effects of the shock; 'I had always believed such a sentence would at once have killed me':

> I had certainly a partial derangement – for I cannot to this moment recollect any thing that now succeeded with Truth or Consistency; my Memory paints things that were necessarily real, joined to others that could not possibly have happened, yet amalgamates the whole so together, as to render it impossible for me to separate Truth from indefinable, unaccountable Fiction. Even to this instant, I always see the Room itself changed into an Octagon, with a medley of silent & strange figures grouped against the Wall just opposite to me. Mr Tudor, methought, was come to drag me by force away; & in this persuasion, which was false I remember supplicating him, with fervent humility, to grant me but one hour, telling him I had solemnly engaged myself to pass it by his side.[39]

This hallucinatory experience, more peculiar in its details than any of the 'visions' she had written in her fiction, marked Fanny Burney's passage into a long declining widowhood. Her marriage to d'Arblay had lasted twenty-five years, and despite all the vicissitudes of their separations, illnesses and privations during that period, they had remained utterly devoted to and dependent on each other. Back in 1793 Fanny had praised her lover's 'nobleness of character – his sweetness of disposition – his Honour, truth, integrity with so much of softness, delicacy, & tender humanity'.[40] Remarkably, she spoke of him in almost exactly the same terms a quarter of a century later, with an apparently unquenchable freshness of appreciation and love. Even the wording of the memorial tablet which she paid to have erected in Walcot Church expressed a persistent sense of incredulity at her good fortune:

> But who shall delineate his noble Character?
> The Spirit of his Valour, or the Softness of his Heart?
> [. . .] The PURITY of his INTEGRITY: the TRANSPARENCY of his
> HONOUR;
> or the indescribable charm of his Social Virtues!

Madame d'Arblay only remained in Bath a few months following the death of her husband. She gave Alex the choice of where they should live, and he decided on London, a good choice, since Fanny had never lived in the capital with d'Arblay; her loss, 'though *Internally* forever the same' would not be 'so acutely goaded on by All that is *external* also' there.[41] She was too distraught to be able to tolerate any avoidable distress, and shunned Bath after she left it in September 1818. As much as ten years later she could still be overset by the unexpected sight of one of their old friends, and could never mention her husband's name in letters without breaking down into exclamation marks and silence.

The house she found in the capital was at 11 Bolton Street, a quiet, narrow road off Piccadilly to the north, handy for the greenery and fresh air of Green Park and within easy reach of her brother's household in James Street, Westminster. The first weeks there were 'the most forlorn that can be conceived even by the darkest Imagination!', as she described them to her sister:

> a seclusion complete from all but sorrow – save, my dear Hetty, Prayer
> & Future Hope. Without those, I think I had surely sunk. And with them,

this solitary affliction was so nearly heart-breaking, that I seemed to myself living in a Hearse! – – Yet I did all I could – & walked out daily with Diane – & made short visits to James street very frequently – but the long – dreary afternoons & Evenings were always alone.[42]

Fanny remained very 'nervous and low', as her niece Charlotte observed,[43] for the whole of the first year of her widowhood and hid herself from public as much as possible. For the first time in her life, writing had become 'a great toil to me – it is ungenial – *recollective* – laborious – recollective!'[44] She could not bear to listen to music, nor did she want to be in the company of small children. The organ at church 'dissolved' her. 'Oh my dear Charlotte!' she wrote to her sister in the spring of 1819, 'What havock in all my existence has that dread dread blow occasioned!'[45]

Fanny's life came to revolve around the small group of family and friends within easy reach; she did travel to see her sisters Hetty and Charlotte, but these outings were rare, long-planned and postponed if the slightest illness or difficulty presented itself. James and his wife Sally were only a short walk away, and she had frequent visits from Susan's daughter, Fanny Raper, who lived in Chelsea (and was by now the author of a novel, *Laura Valcheret*, and a pamphlet, *Pastoral Duties*, published in 1814 and 1818 respectively). Her cousin Edward Francesco Burney, now almost sixty, niece Fanny Burney (Hetty's daughter), Mrs Locke, Amelia Angerstein (*née* Locke) and the Cambridges were also faithful visitors. George Owen Cambridge was now Archdeacon of Middlesex and one of the Ecclesiastical Commissioners, a useful patron for Alex, who had taken Holy Orders in the year of his father's death. The Cambridges' semi-adoption of the fatherless youth probably had something to do with the fact that they had no children of their own, but may also have reflected residual feelings of guilt on the part of George Cambridge for the pain he had caused Fanny back in the 1780s. Remarkably, she had become one of their most admiring friends.

Fanny was more grateful than ever for the support of her affectionate family and friends: 'I am very glad of your correspondences', she wrote to Hetty. 'They keep Life alive.'[46] One of the few solid comforts of these years when Fanny was living in discreet retirement in Mayfair was that her friendships with the princesses blossomed. Since the death of their mother in 1818 the princesses were enjoying a modest amount of freedom for the first time. Their father was still alive, but incapacitated and kept in confinement at Windsor; their brother, the Prince Regent (after 1820 King), had proved a much more generous and liberal head of the family. The princesses were all middle-aged by now: the eldest, Charlotte, was married to the King of Württemburg; her sister Elizabeth (with whom Fanny was in correspondence) to the Prince of Hesse-Homburg; and Mary to the Duke of Gloucester. None of these was a love-match, unlike the secret relationships, possibly secret marriages, which are thought to have been going on between Princess Augusta and an Irish officer, Brent Spencer, and Princess Sophia and one of the King's equerries. Princess Sophia was even rumoured to have borne an illegitimate child to her beau in 1800, an item of gossip that didn't become widespread until 1829. It is unlikely that Fanny knew or heard much about any of these scandalous suggestions in the early 1820s, or credited them if she did. She accepted the princesses' friendship gratefully and was treated with flattering familiarity by them in return. 'I received not only consent, but command to come forth in that Form where it had never before made its entrée', she wrote amusedly to her sister and niece,

> & Mobbled, & Muffled, & Hooded, & Bas Chapeaued, I presented myself at Kensington Palace – to the no small wonder, no doubt, – & probably Horror, of the Heralds preceding my ushering into Presence, – who, having received orders to take care I caught no cold, came forward as the royal vehicle drove up to the Gates, Two pages with a large umbrella in front, & two footmen to each touch an elbow in the rear, – & two underlings spreading a long carpet from the Coach steps onward to the Hall, – – & all, no doubt, inwardly, sniggering when they saw it was for such a Figure of Fun![47]

Fanny's main occupation in the years following d'Arblay's death was to fulfil her promise to make a comprehensive record of certain episodes for posterity. The retrospective 'journals' she composed as a result – covering her experiences in Dunkirk and Brussels and the journey to Trèves in the years 1812–15, her presentations to Louis XVIII in London in 1814 and to his sister the Duchesse d'Angoulême in Paris the same year and her 'Ilfracombe Adventure' – run to several hundred pages. It must have struck her when she had completed this task that she was halfway to having finished an autobiography. In the same period, she was at last getting down to the job of sorting her father's voluminous manuscripts. She had originally imagined that it would be a relatively easy task to select from his correspondence a book's-worth of material and to write an accompanying memoir. However, when she first inspected the papers closely (on the ill-fated Ilfracombe holiday in 1817) she was severely disappointed by (as she said) the poor quality of the letters both to and from Charles Burney's many famous friends. She reported back to Hetty that there were 'Few [. . .] not fit to light Candles', and that it simply wouldn't be worth the effort of 'about 3 years hard reading' to provide 'about 3 quarter's of a hour's reading' for others.[48] She persuaded Hetty that they should abandon the project, though Hetty had been hoping to derive some income from the manuscripts, a matter of importance to her since the death of her husband, faithful Charles Rousseau Burney, in 1819.

Whether or not Madame d'Arblay genuinely felt disgusted at the literary shortcomings of Dr Burney's papers or not is impossible to say, but it seems likely that her strong revulsion at her father's letters and memoirs (of which there were some twelve 'cahiers') was complicated by the portrait which emerged from them, which was very much at variance with her own idealised view. She had hoped that the Doctor's memoirs would show him 'the Carressed, sought, honoured & admired Friend' of the greatest men of his age, 'as much loved & esteemed as if he had been the Universal Patron of them all'.[49] It is not surprising, therefore, that she was disappointed. The 165 fragments of original memoir that remain show Charles Burney at his most unassuming, relaxed and self-mocking about his early efforts to make a name for himself in the professional music world. Fanny judged his reminiscences of merely 'local interests of the day, now sunk from every memory, & containing Nothing that could either benefit or amuse a single Reader by remaining on record'. She stressed to Hetty how thoroughly she had scoured the material, twice, for anything 'that may be usefully, or ornamentally, Biographical', but that all the rest, which she considered 'utterly irrelevant, or any way mischievous',[50] she had destroyed.

'Mischievousness' seems to have been the real sticking point. Fanny was surprised that her father had not taken more care with the disposal of his papers, 'an omission that has often astonished me, considering the unexamined state of his private memorandums, & the various papers that could not have been spread, even in a general Family review, without causing pain, or Confusion'.[51] Clearly there were things in them that gave *her* cause for 'pain, or Confusion'.[52] It is unlikely that Charles Burney would have revealed specific secrets such as his cohabitation with Fanny's mother before their marriage, but there may have been clues to rouse his daughter's suspicions (she was very reticent about letting Hetty see the material for herself), and there would certainly have been matter relating to the Doctor's second wife which contradicted Fanny's ideas about her. When Fanny reported to her sister that she had 'dissected this multifarious Work' and 'removed all that appeared to me peccant parts',[53] it was no coincidence that she was employing the same adjective she had used to describe the life-threatening 'atoms' of her cancer. In their mutilated state, the Doctor's memoirs were left, for the time being, to rest in peace.

In the summer of 1821 James Burney was finally promoted to the rank of Rear-Admiral on the retired list. He had reached the top of the retired Captains list through seniority many years before this without promotion, but no one in the Burney family was in the mood to view the long delay as a humiliation. Her brother's new rank afforded Fanny more solid pleasure than anything had for years, far more than she ever derived from her own title of Comtesse (which she seems only to have used to spare the princesses' servants' feelings). She began to call herself 'the Admiral's sister', and to fill her letters to James and his wife with arch references to his new status.

The family's pleasure was short-lived, however. James dropped dead in November of the same year, aged seventy-one, and the three widowed sisters, Hetty, Fanny and Charlotte and their half-sister Sarah were left as the only remnant of the old Burney family. James's death brought back into view an unwelcome survivor of the old days, Molesworth Phillips. Phillips had married again in 1800, scandalously soon after Susan's death, but abandoned his second wife, Ann Maturin, and their children and had been openly keeping a mistress in London for some years. James had stayed loyal to him despite his sisters' disgust towards the 'unfeeling wretch'. Phillips was often to be seen at James Street, and was followed there on one occasion by bailiffs and arrested for the non-payment of his wife's house-rent (which kind James stumped up, unsurprisingly).[54] It was Phillips who assumed the role of chief mourner after James's death, helping to organise the funeral (which the sisters did not attend) and arranging – but not paying – for a bust to be made of the dead man.[55]

Alex did not get an appointment in the Church until he was almost thirty years old, despite the active support of friends such as George Cambridge. Because of the Peace, the Church was flooded with young clergymen all competing for a relatively small number of livings, and it was necessary to gain a name as a preacher in order to advance. Alex's preaching style was not to everyone's taste – certainly not his mother's, who confined her praise to his clear delivery (something that would have concerned her, since Alex was prone to 'stuttering and hesitation' in his ordinary speech[56]). She was alarmed to hear from her sister Hetty that Alex was thought by some observers to be deliberately affecting a style of theatrical declamation, perhaps in direct imitation of 'a particular actor'[57] (Alex was a great admirer of Edmund Kean and of Talma). Addicts of pulpit 'enthusiasm' were less difficult to please. When Charlotte Barrett went to hear Alex preach at Ely Cathedral in 1823, some of the ladies in the congregation were 'in raptures'. Whether this was actually because of the sermon, or the sermoniser's expensive French clothes, slim figure and meticulously curled hair is impossible to tell.

Alex's long wait for a curacy was as much a matter of indolence on his part as anything else, and suggests that he had misgivings about his chosen career. In 1821 he had travelled to Switzerland with his Cambridge mathematician friends Charles Babbage (later the inventor of an analytical machine now thought of as the forerunner of the computer) and John Herschel, son of the astronomer. The trip, which was meant to last only a few weeks, extended to nine months when Alex left his friends and went on an impromptu solitary walking tour around Lake Geneva and to Mont Blanc. The mountain impressed him forcibly – as it had most romantic and poetical young travellers of the time, Coleridge and Shelley among them – and he gave himself over to writing an 'Ode on Mont Blanc' (in English) and later a 'Dithyrambe' (in French) on the same subject.* Unlike his interest-

---

* William Hazlitt made a sardonic observation on the banality of the subject in 1825: 'The Crossing of the Alps has, I believe, given some of our fashionables a shivering-fit of morality; as the sight of Mont Blanc convinced our author [Tom Moore] of the Being of God – they are seized with an amiable horror and remorse for the vices of others.'[58]

ing translations of Lamartine into English and Byron into French, Alex's own poetry tended to swell uncontrollably:

> La Pensee! Elle seule atteste ta Puissance
> Roi du Monde et des Dieux!
> Plus que de ces Rochers l'Amphitheatre immense,
> Plus que le Firmament, et la magnificence
> De ses points radieuse.[59]

The quantity of Alex's poetry that has survived in the family archive and, more tellingly, the meticulous care with which he reworked, revised and rewrote it, suggests that he had serious ambitions in this field. In Paris, he had alarmed Madame de Maisonneuve by saying that he would like two more years of 'wandering' before even looking for a curacy. His mother was naturally 'not quite easy' at all the 'wandering' that had gone on already:'If you repeat on those summits 3 or 400 lines of DeLille, or 3 or 4 odes of Le Brun', she wrote to him, using an all-too-appropriate metaphor, 'your Enthusiasm may make you bound too high or leap too low for your Equilibrium'.[60]

Fanny was desperate for her son to come home, secure a job and find 'some distinguished Fair one'[61] to marry. Having protested for years that he was too young and immature to marry, she now saw marriage as one of the only possible remaining cures for Alex's 'oddity'.[62] Since the death of her husband, too, she had developed a strong desire to see the family secure in another generation, and fantasised about grandchildren reading her journals and set-piece memoirs in some 'Fire-side Rectory' in the future. The task of memorialising, which became her main work and *raison d'être*, depended of course on there being heirs to hand it down to. 'Look me out a fair Belle Fille who may gently be my Friend', she told Alex, with shameless selfishness, 'as well as delightingly yours, & fix permanently your Happiness, your Character, & your Fame'.[63]

Over the next ten years Alex fixed on at least three young women whom he said he wanted to marry, but nothing came of his ardent and fleeting passions. Two were granddaughters of Fredy Locke, Cecilia Locke and her cousin Caroline Angerstein, the other was a Miss Sarah White. It is not surprising that the Reverend d'Arblay, dandified, poetry-spouting curate-in-theory, was not considered an appropriate suitor by the Locke family or the wealthy Whites. Even his own family had their doubts about 'poor dear Alex' as a potential husband. When Marianne Francis detected that he was 'deeply smitten' with her niece Julia Barrett (Charlotte Barrett's daughter), she wrote to warn her sister about it. 'For all his cleverness', she didn't think that Alex was 'at all nice enough' for his beautiful cousin.[64]

In 1824 Alex was appointed to a curacy at last, of the new Camden Chapel, with a salary of only £150 per year and accommodation in the parish. The Cambridges were present with Madame d'Arblay on the day in August 1824 when Alex was to preach the inaugural sermon at the consecration of the chapel. The Bishop had completed the consecration, the morning service was over, but the congregation waited in vain for the appearance of the preacher. 'I felt myself tremble all over', Fanny reported to Charlotte:

> The Archdeacon [...] quite *shook*, himself, with apprehension, – he thought Alex had lost his Sermon – or had suddenly conceived a new end for it! – & Mrs Moore believed he was siezed [sic] with affright, & could not conquer it – Finally – the last verse finished – & no Alex! Mr Wesley* ran & re-ran over the Keys, with *fugish* perseverance – & I was all *but* fainting – when, at length, – the New Camdenite appeared. I was never more relieved.[65]

This was characteristic of Alex's behaviour in general – 'always just in time to be too late', as he said himself[66] – and of his performance as a minister in particular. Typically, he didn't begin writing his sermons until the last moment and would stay up all night to finish them. Once his servant had to wake him on a Sunday morning as the chapel bell tolled, and there were to be many unscheduled absences from his duties at Camden which did not endear the new curate to his flock. Alex's insouciance about his duties contrasted violently with his mother's embarrassingly thorough brand of worrying. She had visited St Paul's Cathedral *three times* in the weeks prior to Alex giving a sermon there in 1823, just to look at the pulpit from which her son would speak.

The fusspot side of Madame d'Arblay's nature seemed mostly reserved

---

* S.S. Wesley, the famous organist and composer.

for Alex. To her nieces and friends she often appeared remarkably lively and cheerful for a woman in her seventies. Julia Barrett described to her grandmother the 'pleasantest possible evenings' with Aunt d'Arblay. 'She tells such amusing stories as you well know – sometimes repeats poetry – takes off all the curious people she used to know &c that you can easily imagine how pleasant it is'.[67] Charlotte Barrett remarked how her aunt was 'in excellent health & spirits, takes long walks without fatigue, puns & jokes, & enters into all our little intrigues, & is as Mama says, one of the youngest in our party'.[68] Marianne Francis, a slightly less charitable observer than her sister or niece, left another valuable description of her aunt from this period, the only one to remark on Madame d'Arblay's acquired *Frenchness* and the fact that even when ill the old lady was an almost unstoppable talker:

> I called on Aunt d'Ary, & found her very kind & willg to see me, & pleased at my comg & waitg on her a little, but very feeble & full of cough, & *would* talk so much, & in her animated, handclaspg, energetic french way, that I was quite alarmed, & findg she expected her Dr every moment, left her, the moment there was a knock at the door, on purpose that she might cease to talk, the worst thg that she can do but impossible, I see, to prevent.[69]

The mid-1820s seem to have been relatively happy years for Fanny because of the frequent company of Charlotte, her daughters and grand-daughters. She had been called 'the Old Lady' when she was a child on account of her reserve, but as a *real* old lady Fanny became an accom-plished raconteur and seems to have developed a taste for being the centre of attention. 'All her merry stories set her, & us laughing for the hour together,' Julia Barrett wrote to her sister Henrietta,

> but sometimes in the midst of her *grave* ones, Grandmama [Charlotte] falls asleep, & when she wakes again, Aunt d'Arblay insists upon my telling all the story over again, up to the point where Grandmama fell asleep – Only fancy how appalling! to have to tell Aunt d'Arblay's stories before her face![70]

The comical picture of Charlotte nodding off during the *grave* tales and her sister obligingly running through them all again when she woke up also gives a hint of how forceful – even, Julia implies, *intimidating* – Fanny had become. Having to tell 'Aunt d'Arblay's stories before her face', and get them right, and match her skills as an entertainer was clearly no laughing matter.

Madame d'Arblay had lived long enough to enjoy a second wave of celebrity as the survivor of a bygone literary age. Among the visitors at Bolton Street who were introduced by her friend and neighbour Samuel Rogers (probably the most ardent literary networker of his day) were the poet George Crabbe and Sir Walter Scott, the latter an admirer of Fanny's 'uncommonly fine' first two novels (though he had rated *The Wanderer* 'a miss'). Rogers was surprised that Madame d'Arblay hadn't heard of Scott's lameness: 'when he limped towards a chair, she said, "Dear me, Sir Walter, I hope you have not met with an accident?" He answered, "An accident, madam, nearly as old as my birth."'[71] Scott was impressed with Madame d'Arblay's 'simple and apparently amiable manners with quick feelings' and her old-world *agrémens*, as he recorded in his diary:

[She is] an elderly lady with no remains of personal beauty but with a gentle manner and a pleasing expression of countenance. She told me she wished to see two persons – myself of course being one, the other Geo. Canning. This was really a compliment to be pleased with, a nice little handsome pat of butter made up by a neat-handed Phillis of a dairy maid instead of the grease fit only for cart-wheels which one is dosed with by the pound.[72]

The reference to the Foreign Secretary, Canning, was probably connected with Fanny's concern about the progress of the Greek War of Independence.* For all her talk about retirement, Fanny liked to keep abreast of events. Being sought out by the most famous novelist of the day was highly gratifying to the elderly authoress, who took the opportunity to recount to her guests the history of the publication of *Evelina*. The mulberry tree story (purportedly from 1778) makes its first appearance in Scott's record of the day: 'The delighted father [Charles Burney] obtained a commission from Mrs Thrale to purchase his daughter's work

---

* Lally-Tolendal had asked her to promote the cause of the refugee Constantine Sevastopulo – he visited Bolton Street three times in 1826.[73]

and retired the happiest of men', he wrote in his diary. 'Made. D'Arblay said she was wild with joy at this decisive evidence of her literary success and that she could only give vent to her rapture by dancing and skipping round a mulberry tree in the garden.'[74] If Madame d'Arblay had told this story before, it is odd that it hadn't seeped into print earlier, or got into circulation in the way that the less memorable (and untrue) story of Dr Burney 'having brought home [Fanny's] own first work and recommended it to her' had done already. When the mulberry tree incident appeared in the *Memoirs* six years later, it had changed in one significant way from the version told to Scott, and had become even more 'tellable'. The revised reason for Fanny's 'rapture' is given as the fact that 'Doctor Johnson himself had deigned to read the little book.'

It was in this year, 1826, and very probably on this visit by Walter Scott and Samuel Rogers, that Madame d'Arblay 'received an intimation'[75] that the publishers of Chalmers' *General Biographical Dictionary* were intending to include an article on Dr Burney in their next volume: 'they had only forborne to do [so earlier]', her informant told her, 'from respect to intelligence [. . .] that I [Madame d'Arblay] always intended bringing the work to light.' This startled Fanny into action. She began preparing her father's correspondence for the press immediately (they were mostly letters *to* him), and was ready to have the text copied before she found out that a legal precedent in an 1813 copyright case disallowed the publication of letters without their writer's permission. Most of the material she had intended for her book – letters from Johnson, Twining, Greville, Mrs Thrale and others to her father – was not hers to publish, unless she contacted the heirs, which she seemed to think was impossible.[76] She was therefore in a quandary, convinced on one side that 'rivals' were likely to bring out a biography of Charles Burney 'mangled in a manner disagreeable to all his Race',[77] and on the other side having little to go on for a book of her own apart from her own memories, since she had destroyed so many of her father's papers.

The fact that Madame d'Arblay felt pressured to write something – anything – about her father as quickly as possible goes a long way towards explaining why *Memoirs of Doctor Burney* is such an awful book. That she knew it was faulty is evident from the fact that she considered deferring publication till after her death. Alex and Charles Parr Burney both objected to a delay, on the grounds that none of the younger generation would be qualified to defend the 'many things' in the book 'that might be disputed'.[78] But as the date of publication approached, Fanny's misgivings increased. 'O I was so tired of my Pen!' she wrote of the effort it had cost her; 'Should my Readers be as fatigued of its product! – And nothing is more likely, for Ennui is as contagious as Yawning'.[79]

When the *Memoirs* were published in November 1832 it was to almost universal scorn. 'Surely such a quantity of unmixed nonsense never was written before', Baroness Bunsen wrote to her mother,[80] while Maria Edgeworth deplored the book's 'pedantry and affectation': 'Whenever [Madame d'Arblay] speaks of herself some false shame, some affectation of humility or timidity, or I know not what, [. . .] spoils her style'.[81] It was obvious to everyone that the author's portrait of Charles Burney was absurdly idealised, and the book did nothing but harm the reputation Fanny had been so keen to foster. The Doctor was presented as a heroic figure whose achievements were almost unrivalled: 'allowed throughout Europe to have risen to the head of his profession; and thence, setting his profession aside, to have been elevated to an intellectual rank in society, as a Man of Letters [. . .] with most of the eminent men of his day'.[82] Bleached of the very things that gave Burney his charm – his natural gaiety, vulgarity, energy and unstoppable drive – he came over as a faultless, bloodless prig. Fanny's apology in the closing pages of her work for the potential dullness of her father's perfection is an astonishing admission of her own delusions on this subject:

> to delineate the character [. . .], with its FAILINGS as well as its EXCEL-LENCIES, is the proper, and therefore the common task for the finishing pencil of the Biographer. Impartiality demands this contrast; and the mind will not accompany a narrative of real life of which Truth, frank and unequivocal, is not the dictator.
>
> And here, to give that contrast, Truth is not wanting, but, strange to say, vice and frailty! The Editor, however, trusts that she shall find pardon from all lovers of veracity, if she seek not to bestow piquancy upon her portrait through artificial light and shade.[83]

The note of surprise suggests that the only person Fanny was in danger of convincing was herself. She seems to have made a mental shift from thinking that there were things the public had no right to know about her

father to believing that those things actually *were not*. The deliberate suppression of many facts and the distortion of others in the *Memoirs* went far
beyond what filial piety could excuse. And as with Fanny's self-censorship
of her judgement of Queen Charlotte, what rushed into the vacuum was
hyperbole and a form of grandiloquent euphemism, a style which Macaulay
roundly denounced as 'the worst [. . .] that has ever been known among
men. No genius, no information, could save from proscription a book
so written'.[84] Fanny's description of the meeting of her parents (which,
it might be remembered, took place at a 'hop' in Hatton Garden) illustrates both the otiose style and the hagiographical approach:

> Who shall be surprised, that two such beings, where, on one side, there
> was so much beauty to attract, and on the other so much discernment to
> perceive the value of her votary, upon meeting each other at the susceptible
> age of ardent youth, should have emitted, spontaneously, and at first sight,
> from heart to heart, sparks so bright and pure that they might be called
> electric, save that their flame was exempt from any shock?[85]

The convolutions of the *Memoirs* seem symptomatic of Fanny's unease
with the project as a whole. As Macaulay said when he wrote on this
painful subject later, the book revealed 'not [. . .] a decay of power, but
[. . .] a total perversion of power'.[86] There is, indeed, something almost
deranged about a biographer who claims that her work represents '[not]
a thought' by her subject 'that I knew not to be authentic',[87] when she
has tampered with all the evidence. 'It can be stated with confidence that
hardly a single quotation from Burney's papers in her *Memoirs* escaped
her interference', Roger Lonsdale has said in his biography of Fanny's
father. And as he has demonstrated, the 'interference' often takes the
form of ludicrously exaggerating Fanny's own importance in her father's
life; Lonsdale gives the example of the King and Queen asking after the
Doctor's family in 1802, 'particularly of Made d'Arblay, & Miss Phillips',
which Fanny adjusted so that it read 'Their Majesties then both condescended to make some inquiries after my family, though by name only
after my daughter d'Arblay'.[88]

Such crimes were hidden, but the author's egotism and 'affectation of
humility' were obvious to any reader. Maria Edgeworth had noted
Madame d'Arblay's 'strange notion that it is more humble or prettier or

better taste to call herself the *Recluse of West Humble* or *your unworthy humble servant* or *the present memorialist* than simply to use the short pronoun *I*'.[89] To the charge of personal vanity, John Wilson Croker added that of 'literary vanity', accusing Madame d'Arblay of the deliberate suppression of dates to insinuate that she was much younger than twenty-six when *Evelina* was published. Croker had gone as far as applying for Fanny's baptismal certificate from the vicar of St Margaret's, King's Lynn. He found a willing accomplice there, for Stephen Allen was still the incumbent, and very much resented Fanny's portrait of his mother in the book. The issue of Fanny's birthdate became something of a red herring, however. It was easy to prove that Madame d'Arblay had never *deliberately* lied about her age in the *Memoirs*, and her supporters used this to dismiss Croker's criticisms as a whole. But much of what he had said was valid, especially on the subject of Fanny's suppression of original documents. Macaulay realised the justice of some of Croker's remarks and politely passed by the opportunity to defend Madame d'Arblay in print in 1833, even though he detested Croker and might have been expected to jump at the chance to score against him.* Macaulay reserved his opinions on Madame d'Arblay until after her death when, in his essay on the *Diary and Letters*, he felt free both to criticise her shortcomings and praise her real achievements.

What were the reasons for Fanny's deplorable performance in the *Memoirs*? Senility is out of the question; she could still write perfectly naturally in her private correspondence long after 1832. Bad taste and bad judgement are part of the answer, as is her residual terror of her father. But it also seems to me significant that the *Memoirs* represent the nether end, almost the logical conclusion, of Fanny's persistent neurosis about authorship. Though it was her last published work, it was in one important respect a long-deferred, long-dreaded *debut*. With the exception of the pamphlet *Brief Reflections*, the dedication to *Camilla* and the preface to *The Wanderer* (all notably stilted), Fanny had always been able to hide her own voice in fictional forms, whether poetry, novels

---

* Macaulay and Croker were both, at this date, Members of the House of Commons and involved in parliamentary controversy over the 1832 Reform Bill. They also had a number of long-running literary feuds, notably over Croker's edition of Boswell's *Life of Johnson*. 'I *detest* him more than cold veal,' Macaulay once said of his rival.[90]

or plays. The nearer these were to her natural modes of expression – such as the correspondence in *Evelina* – the more comfortable she felt, but the important thing was that they were *fiction*. When she had to speak unequivocally in her own voice, the same sorts of terrors and inhibitions afflicted her that had disabled her at every public performance throughout her life. It was like the moment when the curtain went up on those amateur dramatics long ago, and Fanny was 'discovered Drinking Tea' alone on stage. She knew she looked unnatural, she suffered, but couldn't do anything to save herself.

Hetty Burney did not live to see the *Memoirs* published, nor did Frederica Locke. 1832 was a terrible year for Fanny, which also saw the deaths of her nephew William Phillips and her forty-two-year-old niece Marianne Francis. Clement Francis junior had died three years before, and two of Hetty's daughters, Cecilia and Fanny, were also dead. Charlotte Barrett, now in her forties, was the only one of Charlotte Burney's four children left alive. With the next generation disappearing before their eyes, the two elderly sisters, Fanny and Charlotte, drew together for comfort.

One final and irreparable heartbreak lay in store for Fanny – the death of her son and heir. In the sad story of Alex d'Arblay's wasted and apparently unhappy life, it is hard not to conclude that he suffered from the very 'Wertherism' that his mother had identified in her novels as the greatest evil of the age. In the mid-1830s, when he had just turned forty, a crisis was brewing in Alex's affairs. His long absences from duty at Camden Chapel had so tested the patience of some of the parishioners that as early as 1832 they were getting up a petition to have the curate dismissed. But still Alex spent months away, often in hotels, a circumstance which the editors of the *Journals and Letters* think 'a symptom perhaps of nervous weariness or some deviation'.[91] At home at 1 Half Moon Street (where she had moved in 1829),* Madame d'Arblay had got into the habit of reading the 'epistolary litters' on her son's desk, ostensibly to prevent important business being overlooked by him. Perhaps

---

* An interesting reference to these premises survives in P. Cunningham's *Handbook of London* (1850): 'I remember Madame D'Arblay (Fanny Burney) living on the east side of the street, in the last house overlooking Piccadilly. Her sitting-room was the front room over the shop, then a linendraper's, now a turner's, shop.'[92]

she discovered more than she bargained for. She professed to believe that her son was indulging in solitary recreation during his unscheduled absences, but clearly feared that there was some more dangerous 'manie' being pursued: 'O be careful for *watch* is the word!' she wrote to him mysteriously when he was staying in Brighton in 1834; 'Let nothing *strange* occur'.[93]

A long poem which Alex composed in 1833, 'Urania, or The Spirit of Poetry', suggests that one of the things that was depressing the clergyman-poet was the failure of his literary ambitions. The poem ends with the lines:

> Grant but one flash of heavenly light,
> One hour of inspiration's might,
> Then plunge him in the shades of night,
> To be forever free.[94]

The willingness to bargain eternity against 'one hour of inspiration' and the equation of death with freedom are unexpectedly bleak ideas for a pious man to entertain. The poem shows that Alex was subject to strong passions, which are expressed almost exclusively in negative images: 'Shame veiled her conscience-clouded brow/For whom was spread the lure'; '. . . on the havoc she had made/I saw false beauty smile', and so on. At the beginning of 1835 Sarah Harriet Burney had heard gossip that a Mrs Clara Bolton, wife of a society doctor, had 'conceived a mad fancy' for Alex d'Arblay. 'She is reported to be very handsome, immoderately clever, an Astrologer, even [. . .] She is very entertaining, & has something of the look of a handsome Witch'.[95] 'The Sibyl', whose husband had a house very near the d'Arblays in St James's Square and another in Dover, had been the mistress of Benjamin Disraeli a few years before, and was now soliciting her former lover on Alex d'Arblay's behalf to get him promoted to a better job than his one at Camden. Even Alex's mother was drawn into a correspondence with Disraeli on the subject, though at this point she had no idea what role 'Mrs George Buckley Bolton' played in the lives of either man.

That Mrs Bolton had a powerful hold over Alex is indisputable. A copy of part of a letter to Alex 'of Mrs B' (whom I take to be Clara Bolton), received on 4 April 1835, shows a manipulative woman at work:

My friend M.A.S is very good & we often talk of you – I am convinced if you liked her & popped, you would be accepted [...] if I held out to you she was a genius, I should lie – nor is she enthusiastic – her nature is formed in a different mould [...] – there now – do you not intend giving us a look ere we leave – we may never meet again under such happy circumstances – the steamboat runs regularly to Dover & comes in one hour less than the coach – do come next week if possible – contrive & give the boobys the slip.[96]

Alex was peculiarly vulnerable to such a call from 'the Sibyl' at that time; a day or two earlier he had received from his mother the harshest letter she had ever written him, betraying exasperation and disgust with her incurably negligent son:

What is all this conduct, Alex? & What does it *mean*? if a *Joke* – does it not go too far [...]

If it be from *worn-out affection* – helas! – then, it is from mere, though perhaps unconscious Indifference –

What a Change! – And why did you say write the other day 'My Nature is so very affectionate –'

To *whom*, Alex?[97]

Alex was stirred by this to take the only sort of action that would guarantee to placate his mother. Astonishingly, within three weeks, he not only let Mrs Bolton introduce him to her pliable friend 'M.A.S.', but had proposed and was accepted.

Madame d'Arblay's reaction was all he could have hoped. 'Take my tenderest – & delighted Benediction, my dearest – dearest Alex!' she wrote ecstatically from London.[98] Though alarmed by 'the precipitancy with which you have hurried into so solemn an engagement', she was prepared to swallow all her misgivings at the prospect of at last seeing him settled. Oddly, though, Alex seemed in no hurry to show off his fiancée. Madame d'Arblay had to wait until July to meet her.

'M.A.S.' was a Miss Mary Ann Smith, of Croom's Hill, Greenwich, who may have been a teacher at a private school in Dover.[99] When Charlotte Barrett met her she described Mary Ann as 'very kind, gentle & pleasing – not really *pretty*, but nothing *unpretty*'.[100] Sensible, pious, modest and – as it turned out – endlessly patient, Mary Ann won her prospective mother-in-law's affection immediately: 'my beloved Charlotte I have seen the young lady – & she has put me in Heaven!' Fanny wrote excitedly to her sister.[101] Alex himself did not seem to feel the same degree of enthusiasm about his bride-elect, however, and it is impossible not to suspect that the whole matter of his engagement was one of convenience, to win a reprieve from disappointing his mother. By the end of the year her pleasure at the betrothal had worn away and she was more than ever distressed by Alex's continued unexplained absences and neglect of both herself and Miss Smith. An undated letter, thought by the editors of the Journals to be a reply to a frantic one from his mother on 15 December 1835, shows the depths of depression to which Alex was sinking. It seems to be addressed to his mother, but is more like a confessional effusion written under the influence of drink, drugs or desperation:

A deep deep gloom has laid hold of me & God knows if I shall ever shake it off –

The more I pine in solitude the worse it grows

Poor generous noble May! Her fresh heart her happiness ought not to be put at stake upon one whose spirit is broken whose soul is fled – [. . .]

O my dear dear Mammy how – – beautiful your patience your forbearance has been – How unworthy I feel of it – how it cuts me to the Soul

Why have I fled from you who alone can even attempt to console me –

O it is a madness – a delirium without a name –[102]

While Alex had absconded into his romantic nightmare of dejection and melancholy, Mary Ann and Madame d'Arblay became closer by the day. Mary Ann was long-suffering, but no fool, and wrote candidly to Fanny in January 1836 about her fears for Alex and 'the influence' (presumably that of Mrs Bolton) 'that has sunk into apathy so fine, so noble a mind – but he will recover dearest Madme D'Arblay & be again the comfort to you he has been & to me he will ever be *all* & *every* thing'.[103] Charlotte Barrett had heard rumours that led her to guess that Alex 'had some *Chère Amie* – many people suspect as much from his conduct', as she wrote to her mother. 'It would be far best to marry Miss Smith directly'.[104]

But Alex did not marry Miss Smith. In March 1836, he resigned at last from his post at Camden and the search began again for a suitable living or lectureship. Through the good offices of George Cambridge, he was appointed minister of Ely Chapel, a thirteenth-century church (originally, and latterly, known as St Etheldreda's) in a neglected backwater of Holborn. The chapel had been out of use for some years, and when it was reopened in the late autumn of 1836 it was still damp, cold and unwelcoming. The Reverend d'Arblay came down with a violent form of 'flu after the Christmas services which turned to a high fever. By the middle of January he was sinking, and when Archdeacon Cambridge called at Half Moon Street to see Alex, he was not invited in. Madame d'Arblay's message was that she felt her son's case was 'hopeless', and that 'by poor Alexander's express wish she did not go to his Bedside'.[105] Alex did not want a repetition of the scenes at his father's and grandfather's deathbeds.

It seems appropriate that the only surviving portrait of Alex d'Arblay as an adult is a shadowy silhouette. Mysteriously solitary to the end, he died alone in his room on 19 January 1837, with his poor rejected mother alone in another part of the same house.

'I cannot describe the chasm of my present existence – so lost in grief – so awake to Resignation – so inert to all that is proffered – so ever & ever retrograding to all that is desolate! – I am a non-entity!'[106] Fanny Burney was eighty-four when her son died, a cruelly advanced age at which to lose her only child. Among her friends and relations she appeared to be 'a pattern of Resignation to the Divine Will',[107] but from her diaries and notebooks of the time she seems to have been more numbed than resigned. 1837 was 'the most mournful – most *earthly* hopeless, of any and of all the years yet commenced of my long career!'[108] Alex's expensive library, his papers, his chattels and his debts were now all her responsibility, and she was at a loss to know what to do with 'this killing mass of constant recurrence to my calamity'.[109] The papers, adding to her vast archives of unsorted manuscripts that had belonged to her sister, her father and her husband, presented a huge problem to the bereaved old lady. She was unwilling to destroy so much material 'that may be amusing & even instructive [. . .] for future times' – and which was now her only posterity – but the task of examining it was by this time simply beyond her powers. Not only was she tormented by 'all that was recollective', but her eyesight, which had been deteriorating steadily throughout the 1830s, was now near 'total Eclipse'.[110]

Worst of all, she was plagued by bitter misgivings and self-reproaches about her son. Even a cursory examination of his poems and letters would have shown her (if she had not already understood it) the extent of his melancholia. A remark in one of Charlotte's condoling letters had arrested her and provoked some miserable self-examinations. Charlotte had said that Alex was 'no match for the World', and that it seemed 'a mercy for him to be taken to Heaven'.[111] 'You thought it a *mercy* he was taken while yet watched & cherished in This world of which he so little knew how to combat the ways & arts', Fanny replied in distress. 'I could read no more! – I had often, transiently admitted that idea – but recoiled from it with shuddering & anguish'.[112]

Mary Ann Smith, probably realising that her fiancé's heartbroken parent would not have long to live, offered to come and live with Madame d'Arblay. After some resistance (Fanny was worried that it was too self-sacrificial a gesture on Mary Ann's part) an arrangement was agreed, and in August 1837 (a month after the young Queen Victoria had acceded to the throne) Madame d'Arblay moved to a new address in Mount Street, which she and Miss Smith intended to share. When Mary Ann moved in the following year, the two women soon evolved a *modus vivendi* that ensured they both remained independent – 'that each may have time for our separate business or fancies' – yet had the comfort of each other's company if need be. This mitigated the pain of Fanny's evenings previously spent alone in 'lassitude & weariness' and long days spent trying 'to *persecute* myself into a new existence that might somewhat repair the havoc of calamity upon the worn-out old one'.[113]

Fanny was fated to endure one more bereavement. Her sister Charlotte, having travelled from Brighton to visit her in the summer of 1838, took ill and died in lodgings in Mount Street on 12 September at the age of seventy-six. At the beginning of 1839 Fanny wrote in her diary, 'One more melancholy year let me try – since for some hidden mercy it seems granted me – hidden – for all Life's happiness is flown with my Alexander.' Though feeble, depressed, almost blind and still sporadically subject to 'breast attacks' that required blistering and bleeding of the old wound, Madame d'Arblay soldiered on through her last year. Despite her fondness for Mary Ann Smith, she did not adopt her as heir – that role was taken by Charlotte Barrett, her tender, clever and sympathetic niece. In the new will Fanny drew up that year, Charlotte was entrusted with 'my [. . .] immense Mass of Manuscripts collected from my fifteenth year [. . .] with full and free permission according to her unbiassed taste and judgment to keep or destroy them'.[114] Generous annuities were bequeathed to Sarah Harriet and to James's eccentric son Martin, smaller bequests to a host of nephews, nieces and friends. Charles Parr Burney was left the residue of Dr Burney's papers and Charlotte's son, Richard Barrett, was made residuary legatee of the estate and of Madame d'Arblay's manuscripts.

In the summer of 1839 Madame d'Arblay's health relapsed and she took to her bed. In November Charlotte Barrett came from Brighton to nurse her and the family gathered round, expecting the old lady to die at any moment. Fanny rallied and held on, though her attention was wandering, and when her nieces tried to read to her she said to them, 'My dear, I cannot understand a word – not a syllable – but I thank God, my mind has not waited till this time.' 'Her kindness remained as ever,' Fanny Raper recalled, 'though it became more and more distasteful to her to receive us – she could not endure the exertion of speaking.'

By an odd coincidence, or – perhaps – a strange effort of will, Fanny Burney held on to life until 6 January 1840, the day upon which Susan had died exactly forty years before, and which she had kept as a solemn memorial day of prayer and meditation ever since. Her last recorded words to her nieces were, 'I know I am dying, but I am willing to die; I commit my soul to God, in reliance on the mercy & merit of my redeemer';[115] but these were not her only thoughts. Among the kind words for the nieces and pious hopes for herself, there were still instructions, directions and matters of business about where to find the keys to unlock her boxes of papers. Part of her mind was on posterity to the last.

POST MORTEM

Charlotte Barrett was nervous about the publication of her late aunt's *Diary and Letters* in 1842, and it seemed with good reason. Croker continued his campaign against the author with a stinging attack in the *Quarterly* on her 'extravagant egotism', and many other reviewers followed suit. Madame d'Arblay's vanity, according to the *Eclectic Review*, 'obtrudes itself in almost every page, and frequently leads to prolixity, and minuteness of detail, which is wearisome in the extreme'. Within the family, Sarah Payne, James Burney's daughter, was 'very sensitive' about the publication, and told her friend Henry Crabb Robinson that it was 'a great reproach to Mad d'Arblay that she should record nothing but the conversation that respected herself, be it praise or blame – and that nothing else even of Johnson's or Burke's conversation made any impression on her'.[1] Like the accusations of self-absorption (an odd criticism to level at a diarist), this was hardly fair. What really seems to have upset the readers and reviewers of 1842 was not so much that Madame d'Arblay's diaries were self-centred as that they were relatively artless and unpolished, that they revealed 'the conversations of eminent people' like Johnson and Burke to be sometimes conversations of 'ordinary mediocrity'.[2] No one wanted to know what Dr Johnson had said about rashers and mutton pies.

Of the 'tautology and vanity' of the diaries Sarah Harriet Burney had this to say to Robinson: 'In her life, [Madame d'Arblay] bottled it all up, & looked and generally spoke with the most refined modesty, & seemed ready to drop if ever her works were alluded to. But what was kept back, and scarcely suspected in society, wanting a safety valve, found its way to her private journal. Thence, had Mrs Barrett been judicious, she would have trundled it out, by half quires, and even whole quires at a time'.[3] Sarah Harriet implies that her half-sister was only able to appear 'unoffending and unenvious' in public because in private she was self-regarding. Though it is unpleasantly put, there is some truth in this:

labouring under the belief that authorship and gentility, performance and sincerity, were not compatible, Fanny Burney's public behaviour and private writing did not intersect very much at all.

Sarah Harriet, a novelist herself, knew all about 'safety valves' for a woman's private feelings, but clearly thought those feelings shouldn't be served up raw to the public. Fanny Burney, presumably, felt differently about her diaries: not simply that they provided 'participation or relief' at the time of writing, but that the ultimate revelation of her private thoughts was valuable and illuminating, that they complemented or completed the picture offered to posterity in her works. The story of the secret composition and publication of *Evelina* became central to her autobiography because the circumstances and difficulties of authorship were critically important to her, 'more like a romance', to quote her own revealing phrase, 'than anything in the book that was the cause'.[4] Her seventy-year diary therefore served as an elaborate apology for her public performances, 'proof' that her inhibitions were social rather than artistic.

For this very reason, Burney's diary fascinates modern readers as much as her novels do. They show that 'the Mother of English Fiction', as Virginia Woolf called her, was an anxious and vulnerable pioneer. As early as 1810 Anna Barbauld, in one of the first critical works of its kind, wrote that 'Scarcely any name, if any, stands higher in the list of novel-writers than that of Miss Burney',[5] but four years after this Burney herself was still talking of novels as 'degraded'. Had she lived to read Macaulay's claim, in 1843, that her work had 'vindicated the right of her sex to an equal share in a fair and noble province of letters', she would probably have taken exception both to the judgement and the wording, so unfortunately reminiscent of the title of Miss Wollstonecraft's book. What she expressed in the negative to Samuel Crisp in 1779 apropos *The Witlings* – 'I would a thousand times rather forfeit my character as a writer, than risk ridicule or censure as a Female' – held true throughout her life: she put a huge value on private life, friendships, family duties and her own behaviour *'as a Female'*, and to some extent deliberately neglected her potential as a writer. Even in her most famous and admired novels, *Evelina* and *Cecilia*, there are elements of wilful amateurism, a sprawling quality which she herself always put down to hurry but never attempted to rectify. Her revisions of *Camilla*, though they went on for decades, never seriously addressed the many structural and stylistic faults of that book. In a sense, she left it to Jane Austen to revise *Camilla*. Having played out in her own life the struggle to make female novel-writing respectable, her successors reaped the benefits.

I am uncomfortably aware of all the stories untold in this biography, the dense patterning of information, misinformation and anecdote in the Burney papers that because of the demands of biography to tell an (artificially) coherent and approximately chronological story has had to remain obscure. There is more than ever to know about Fanny Burney and her circle: reading the existing material is an occupation in itself, and scholars grow grey in its service. I believe that Burney's anxiety to record her life in sometimes minute detail was not simply a compulsive habit but a form of acknowledgement that experience has a complex texture and that the truth about it is elusive. Few writers leave themselves so exposed to posterity as she has done. There is a sort of courage in it, just as there is courage in her frank admission, after the death of her husband, that Truth and Fiction were sometimes 'indivisible' in her mind.

Burney must have doubted that anyone, even her niece, would have read through all her papers – the residue, it must be remembered, of a much larger original archive. I have come to view the quantity of infor-mation that she left behind as an ironic challenge to anyone presuming to have the last word on this complex, wordy woman. As Fanny Burney understood all too well, 'precise investigation of the interior movements by which I may be impelled' was of questionable value, for, as she wrote in the rejected preface to *Cecilia*:

> the intricasies of the human Heart are various as innumerable, & its feelings, upon all interesting occasions, are so minute & complex, as to baffle all the power of Language. What Addison has said of the Ways of Heaven, may with much more propriety & accuracy be applied to the Mind of Man, which, indeed, is
>
> Dark & Intricate,
> Filled with wild Mazes, & perplexed with *Error*.

APPENDIX A

Fanny Burney Undergoes a Memory Test

Fanny Burney's powers of memory, on which she prided herself and which formed the basis of her reputation for accuracy, can be demonstrated in part. Fanny was present at the first day of the trial of Warren Hastings in 1788 and heard the opening speech by the Lord Chancellor, Lord Thurlow, which she tried to recall later for her father and sisters because she felt that the newspapers had printed it 'far less accurately than I have retained it, though I am by no means exact or secure'.

Fanny Burney's account of Lord Thurlow's speech is as follows:

> Warren Hastings, you are now brought into this Court to answer to the charges brought against you by the Knights, Esquires, Burgesses, and Commons of Great Britain – charges now standing only as allegations, by them to be legally proved, or by you to be disproved. Bring forth your answers and defence with that seriousness, respect, and truth due to accusers so respectable. Time has been allowed you for preparation, proportioned to the intricacies in which the transactions are involved, and to the remote distances whence your documents may have been searched and required. You will still be allowed Bail, for the better forwarding your defence, and whatever you can require will still be yours, of time, witnesses, and all things else you may hold necessary. This is not granted you as any indulgence: it is entirely your due: it is the privilege which every British subject has a right to claim, and which is due to every one who is brought before this high Tribunal.[1]

Also present at the trial were at least three shorthand writers making a transcription of the speech for the official record. Taking theirs as the most literally accurate version available, and comparing Fanny's with it, one can see that she has reproduced Lord Thurlow's argument closely and repeated certain key words and phrases:

Warren Hastings

You are called upon, after every expedient allowance, for your defence. You have had bail: you have Counsel. Much time also has been granted you – becoming well the circumstances of your case.

For the matter in the Charges is most momentous, and the dates are remote since the occurences in those charges alleged against you are said to have been committed.

These advantages you must understand, while you feel. – You are to deem them not as an indulgence of this House – but the fair claim of right – a concession of nothing, but what you have in common with all around you – what every British subject may ask, and every British tribunal must allow.

Conduct your Defence, therefore, in a manner that may befit your station, and the magnitude of the charges against you. – Estimate rightly the high character of those you have to answer – the Commons of Great Britain! – who, at once, perhaps, attach likelihood to doubt – and enforce authority, certainly, on accusation.'[2]

The order of the material varies, and the style of Fanny's version is more grandiloquent than the transcription, but the only difference in substance is her reference to 'remote distances', where Lord Thurlow spoke of remote dates. The two accounts are almost exactly the same length. As Fanny was not, presumably, trying consciously to memorise the speech at the time of hearing it (she could not have seen the unsatisfactory newspaper account until the next day), her reconstruction of it seems to have been remarkably good.

APPENDIX B

Additions to O.E.D. from the writings of Fanny Burney

The following list was compiled by J.N. Waddell, to whom and to the publishers of *Notes and Queries*, where it first appeared in February 1980, I am indebted. References are to first editions of the novels.

absorbment, sb. [not in *O.E.D.*] 1795 *Journals*, III, 99 my illness & weakness & constant absorbment in the time of its preparation.

acquaintance, v. [not in *O.E.D.*] 1799 *Journals*, IV, 339 Mrs Milner, of Mickleham, who has a son, by a former husband, now Colonel FitzGerald, & aid de Camp to the Duke of York (& probably of the staff you met at Walmer Castle) has sent me, lately, a message to desire we should acquaintance.

alphabetize, v. [*O.E.D. Alphabetize*, v., 2., 1880–] 1796 *Journals*, III, 171 I have now 6 proofs to correct just arrived – & all my list to alphabetize.

anecdote, sb. [*O.E.D. Anecdote*, 2.b.: only example of *anecdote* as a collective noun, 1826] 1794 *Journals*, III, 50 Why what an exquisite Letter, my dearest Father! – how full of interesting anecdote, & enlivening detail!

applause, sb. [*O.E.D. Applause*, sb. 1.: last example of *applause* in the plural, 1725] 1791 *Journals* I, 30 That great old City is too narrow, too populous, too dirty, & too ill paved, to meet with my sublime applauses.

bavardage, sb. [*O.E.D. Bavardage*, 1835–] 1801 *Journals*, V, 73 'I suppose, Mama, if the ladies rule every body in France, even if there is a man of quality, that meets with a lady, that happens to be a beggar, he must let her govern him?' Shall I ask your pardon for all this bavardage?

betake, v. [*O.E.D. Betake*, v., 4. b., –1641] 1797 *Journals*, IV, 50 Muff betook to the Coal hole, & there seemed to repose with native ease.

bluism, sb. [*O.E.D. Bluism*, 1822–] 1795 *Journals*, III, 101 I am quite delighted at your progress in this bluism; it was always to your taste.

bob-jerom, sb. [*O.E.D. Bob*, sb.¹ 10, 1782 only] 1796 *Camilla*, II, 261 The effect of this full buckled bob-jerom, which stuck hollow from the young face and powdered locks of the Ensign, was irresistably ludicrous.

break down, v. [*O.E.D.* 1st Suppl., *Break*, v., 50, d., 1837–] 1778 *Evelina*, I, 101 we had not proceeded thirty yards, ere every voice was heard at once, – for the coach broke down!

break–up, sb. [*O.E.D. Break-up*, sb., 1795–] 1794 *Journals*, III, 79 Sometimes the aspect is that of a terrible break up, at others the wilfulness of a restless mind that loves to spread confusion, cause wonder, & displace tranquillity.

briefly, adv. [*O.E.D. Briefly*, adv. 2, –1611] 1801 *Journals*, IV, 488 we take in stores for nearly a year at a time, from the difficulty of procuring any thing briefly, & as wanted.

canter, v. [*O.E.D. Canter*, v.², 4., 1845–] 1796 *Camilla*, III, 135 Sir Sedley Clarendel drove his own phaeton; but instead of joining them, according to the condition which occasioned the treaty, cantered away his ponies from the very first stage.

chaoticism, sb. [not in *O.E.D.*] 1795 *Journals*,
III, 114 M. d'A. has arranged himself a
Study in our little Parlour, that would be
after your Heart's content, for literary
chaoticism.

coach-party, sb. [*O.E.D. 2nd Suppl., coach,
sb.* 6., 1957–] 1778 *Evelina*, II, 140 The
coach–party fixed upon consisted of
Madame Duval, M. Du Bois, Miss
Branghton, and myself.

coque-sash, sb. [not in *O.E.D.*] 1802 *Journals*, v,
366. The young ladies were all dressed
alike, very simply, & very elegantly in
white muslin, with white shoes,
coque-sashes, & their hair in ringlets.

cuisiniere, sb. [*O.E.D. Cuisinier*, 1859–] 1802
Journals, V, 251 the Maid whom M.
D'Arblay had engaged for me, as 'femme
de chambre, to coiffer, dress, work &c, &
as cuisiniere.

cultivate with, v. [*O.E.D. Cultivate, v.* 5. d., 1772
only] 1799 *Journals*, IV, 368 How I wish
you may cultivate with him! – what you
give of his debate with M. de Calonne
concerning the abominable Sieyes (for
abominable I hold him to be) is very
interesting.

dabble, sb. [*O.E.D. Dabble, sb.*, 1871–] 1800
Journals, IV, 402 should it happen I should
be able to fix a time for this Honour
which her very sweet Royal Highness does
the little dabble when you should be at
liberty to shake hands with me.

damper, sb. [*O.E.D. Damper*, 1, b., 1804–] 1782
Cecilia, V, 57 'a few oysters, fresh opened,
by way of a damper before dinner'.

destinationing, vbl. sb. [not in *O.E.D.*] 1814
Journals, VII, 350 I grieve not to put this in
the hands of my dear Brother, for his own
use, or at least, destinationing, & decision.

detail, v. [*O.E.D. Detail, v.*, 1., 1841–] 1799
Journals, IV, 283 I think you would not
disapprove were we to commune upon it
together; but I cannot detail longer, from
uncertainty what may strike you.

diarize, v. [*O.E.D. Diarize, v.*, 1827–] 1793
Journals, II, 100 I will now regularly
Diarize to my beloved Susan from the
moment of our parting.

diminisher, sb. [*O.E.D. Diminisher*, –1637] 1799
Journals, IV, 297 Resentment is a powerful
diminisher of sorrow, in diminishing the
feelings that first excited it.

diminuendoing, vbl. sb. [*O.E.D.* 1st Suppl.,
Diminuendo, v., 1901–] 1797 *Journals*, III,
343 How I should like to see your beautiful
Quarry – I think your monumental
diminuendoing very exactly exemplary.

dine out, v. [*O.E.D. 2nd Suppl., Dine, v.* 1. b.,
1816–] 1796 *Camilla*, I, 250 'Miss Camilla!
you won't think of dining out unknown to
Sir Hugh?'

disciplinarianism, sb. [*O.E.D. Disciplinarianism*,
1872–] 1832 *Memoirs*, III, 60 These were
circumstances to exile common form and
royal disciplinarianism from those great
personages.

distance, v. [*O.E.D. Distance, v.*, 4. c., 1786
only] 1796 *Camilla*, IV, 270 Miss Margland,
seeing nothing in him that marked fashion,
strove to distance him by a high
demeanour.

dizzying [*O.E.D. Dizzying, ppl. a.*, 1804–] 1796
Camilla, III, 90 'You waft me from
extreme to extreme, with a rapidity
absolutely dizzying.'

do spite [*O.E.D. Spite, sb.*, 1. a., –1658] 1778
Evelina, II, 71 'he's always been doing me
one spite or other, ever since I knew him'.

duberous, a. [*O.E.D. Duberous, a.*, 1818–] 1791
Journals, I, 20 My dearest Fredy, I think,
has full as strong a propensity to the
antique as myself; but I am a little
duberous as to my Susanne.

dutify, v. [not in *O.E.D.*] 1797 *Journals*, IV, 30 I
come frm her wth the most dutiful duty
that ever was dutified.

egotism, sb. [*O.E.D. Egotism*, 2., 1800–] 1796
Camilla, I, 183 the egotism which urged
him to make his own amusement his first
pursuit.

elbow, v. [*O.E.D. Elbow, v.*, 4. b., 1833–] 1796
Camilla, V, 17 Clermont, now, elbowing his
way into a group of gentlemen.

Englishism, sb. [*O.E.D. Englishism*, 1855–] 1802
Journals, V, 217 that Englishism of reserve
for which I am so noted in the Circles in
which I am known.

Englishize, v. [*O.E.D. 2nd Suppl., Englishize, v.*,
1858–] 1799 *Journals*, IV, 344 How happy
should we be if the whole party were to
come, & Englishize again the Major.

enrage, v. [*O.E.D. Enrage*, v., 2., –1782] 1795 *Journals*, III, 125 I entreat you, my dear Carlos, not to enrage, – I could not withstand the united voices that chorussed against your counsel.

far from it [*O.E.D. Far*, adv., 1. d., 1882–] 1796 *Camilla*, I, 157 'Yes; you hold it in antipathy, don't you?' 'No, indeed! far from it.'

fascinately, adv. [not in *O.E.D.*] 1832 *Memoirs*, II, 30 Then, how fascinately she condescended to indulge us with a rondeau!

follow up, v. [*O.E.D. Follow*, v., 21. b., 1794–] 1792 *Journals* I, 251 He meant to follow this up with some daring effort to serve the King – but he had soon intimation that his own doom was fixed.

formalize, v. [*O.E.D. Formalize*, v., 5. b., 1856–] 1791 *Journals*, I, 103 a little chat with them was all my entertainment; for though Mrs Boscawen & Dr Russel were also there, the circle was formalized by Lady Amherst.

French grey [*O.E.D. French*, A. 3., 1862–] 1798 *Journals*, IV, 232 The dear Princess was seated on a sofa, in a French Grey riding Dress, with pink lapels.

fudge, sb. [*O.E.D. Fudge*, B. 2., 1797–] 1796 *Camilla*, II, 89 'How did you like my sending the Major to you? was not that good fudge?'

gay-looking [*O.E.D. Gay*, A. 9., 1897–] 1778 *Evelina*, I, 46 Presently, after, a very gay-looking man, stepping hastily up to him.

gentilize, v. [*O.E.D. Gentilize*, v.,¹ 2, 1679 only] 1796 *Journals*, III, 214 the Horses being sufficiently gentleized by 18 miles at a stretch not to be alarmingly frisky.

gipsy-looking [*O.E.D. Gipsy*, sb., 4., 1824–] 1802 *Journals*, V, 231 old women selling fruit or other eatables; Gipsey-looking Creatures with Children tied to their backs.

gladify, v. [not in *O.E.D.*] 1798 *Journals*, IV, 146 O that he would come & mortify upon our bread & cheese, while he would gladify upon our pleasure in his sight!

glass, v. [*O.E.D.* 2nd Suppl., *Glass*, v., 4. c., 1935–] 1791 *Journals*, I, 43 their names were all mentioned by Mrs Pointz, but I did not choose to Glass them, & without, could not distinguish them.

grand-dad, sb. [*O.E.D. Grand-dad*, 1819–] 1782 *Cecilia*, V, 71 'Must, must!' cried Briggs, 'tell all his old grand-dads else.'

hob-nob, v. [*O.E.D. Hob-nob*, v., 1., 1828–] 1814 *Journals*, VII, 361–2 Rain, or Illness, shall alone, then, prevent my hob nobing in a dish of tea with my dear Brother.

inappeasable, a. [*O.E.D. Inappeasable*, a., 1840–] 1803 *Journals*, VI, 469 the consideration I meet with in this Country, from my evident & inappeasable distress upon this subject.

inarticulated [*O.E.D. Inarticulated*, ppl. a, 2., 1824–] 1796 *Camilla*, II, 348 The if almost dropt inarticulated: but he added – 'I shall make some further enquiries before I venture to say any more.'

inquire out, v. [*O.E.D. Inquire*, v., 6., –1790] 1814 *The Wanderer*, V, 233 'Rawlins, order Hilson to enquire out the magistrate of the village'.

intercourse, v. [*O.E.D. Intercourse*, v., 2., –1571] 1799 *Journals*, IV, 289 I hope to receive one, & to be again upon terms of affection & intercoursing, – though, alas, no more of faith or approbation.

irreflection, sb. [*O.E.D. Irreflection*, 1835–] 1832 *Memoirs*, II, 173 She was rather, therefore, from her scoff of all consequences, a child of witty irreflection.

John Bullism, sb. [*O.E.D. John Bullism*, 1796–] 1791 *Journals*, I, 8 After a little deliberation, we were now touched to shake off a part of the John Bullism that had encrusted us, & to ask them to our sitting Room, to drink Tea.

jump, v. [*O.E.D. Jump*, v., 8., 1815–] 1796 *Camilla*, I, 361 Edgar, somewhat agitated, occupied himself with jumping the little boy.

kinspeople, sb. [*O.E.D. Kinspeople*, 1866–] 1796 *Camilla*, IV, 150 'caring about the wide world, so, when we know nothing of it, instead of one's own uncles and nephews, and kinspeople!'

litter, sb. [plural use not in *O.E.D.*] 1801 *Journals*, IV, 504 two Tables – one to keep the Wall, & take upon itself the dignity of a little tidyness, the other to stand here – there – & every where, & hold litters.

lodging-hunting, vbl. sb. [O.E.D. Lodging, vbl. sb., 6., 1879–] 1796 Camilla, III, 153 a message from Mrs Arlbery, who always breakfasted in her own room, to announce that she was going out lodging-hunting.

lunch, sb. [O.E.D. lunch, sb.,² 2., 1829–] 1812 Journals, VII, 46 She has engaged me to her house on Tuesday, for a Lunch, with the Miss Berrys.

lunch-party, sb. [O.E.D. 2nd Suppl., Lunch, sb.,² 3., 1884–] 1812 Journals, VII, 52 I have also been at Lady Crewe's to a Lunch party made for my meeting the Miss Berrys.

lunch-dinner, sb. [O.E.D. Lunch, sb.,² 3., 1878–] 1797 Journals, IV, 36 This morning M. Bourdois has been here, to a lunch dinner, & M. d'A is walked off with him.

maisonnette, sb. [O.E.D. Maisonette, 1818–] 1793 Journals, III, 2 We have not yet begun our Maisonette in Norbury Park: M. d'Arblay is his own Architect.

make oneself up [O.E.D. 2nd Suppl., Make, v., 96. i. (b), 1808–] 1778 Evelina, I, 97 'I suppose you'd have me learn to cut capers? – and dress like a monkey? – and palaver in French gibberish? – hay, would you? – And powder, and daub, and make myself up, like some other folks?'

M.P., sb. [O.E.D. M.P., 1809–] 1801 Journals, V, 106 The Chancellor gave in his language the rebuke he loved not to give to a M.P. & so powerful an antagonist, as Mr Sheridan.

nothingist, sb. [O.E.D. Nothingist, 1890–] 1797 Journals, IV, 45 Your Collection of learned Wights at the Royal Society stopt my breath – though the 'Nothingists' gave it me back.

nothingly, a. [O.E.D. Nothingly, a., 1833–] 1802 Journals, V, 187–8 God knows how little I shall ever think of our losses, & how NOTHINGLY they are.

nudging, a. [sense not in O.E.D.] 1796 Camilla, I, 198 'She's not a bit like a lady of fortunes, with that nudging look.'

opera buffa, sb. [O.E.D. Opera, 3., 1880–] 1801 Journals, V, 267 Madᵉ d'henin made a party for us all to meet again the next day, & go to the Opera Buffa.

parade, v. [O.E.D. Parade, v., 3., 1809–] 1796 Camilla, IV, 230 She kept, therefore, her seat, looking steadily straight down the water, and denying herself one moment's glance at anything, or person, upon the beach: little imagining she ingrossed, herself, the attention of all who paraded it.

pas seul, sb. [O.E.D. Pas, 2., 1870] 1813 Journals, VII, 70 I know not exactly how many fandangos, or pas seul's, I may dance, but I cannot deny myself, upon such an occasion.

pinky-winky, a. [O.E.D. Pinky, a.¹, 1817–] 1814 The Wanderer, II, 293 'I should sooner take her for my wax-doll, when she's all so pinky-winky.'

plain sailing [O.E.D. Suppl., plain sailing, sb., 1823–] 1796 Camilla, I, 73 the rudiments, which would no sooner be run over, than the rest would become plain sailing.

play, v. [O.E.D. Play, v., 22. c., 1850–] 1796 Journals, III, 157 Bambino & I have played our Ball up to the Top of the Bed, & nobody can reach it.

post-chaise-and-four [O.E.D. Post-chaise, sb., 1840–] 1796 Camilla, III, 7 I then followed him to the little lane to the right of the park, where I perceived an empty post-chaise-and-four in waiting.

re-encourage, v. [O.E.D. Re-encourage, v., –1670] 1782 Cecilia, V, 172 'You must then be angry with yourself, next', said Cecilia, anxious to re-encourage her.

re-hear, v. [O.E.D. Re-hear, v., 2., 1815–] 1799 Journals, IV, 297 He has taken the amazing trouble & toil of copying the whole, from the pleasure the interview gave him! though he may always re-hear it DE VIVE VOIX!

self-acquitted [O.E.D. Self-, 2., 1847–] 1814 The Wanderer, III, 107 their honour was self-acquitted and self-applauded.

self-desertion, sb. [O.E.D. Self-, 1. a., 1823–] 1796 Camilla, V, 454 will no worthier wish occur to thee, than to leave it to its sorrows and distress, with the aggravating pangs of causing thy afflicting, however blamable self-desertion?

self-enclosed [O.E.D. Self-, 3. a., 1876–] 1814 The Wanderer, IV, 240 Juliet passed three days, self-inclosed.

shake hands, sb. [*O.E.D. Shake*, v., 22., 1811–]
1800 *Journals*, IV 436 William will be much
pleased by a private congratulatory shake
hands from you in his own Apartment.

showable, a. [*O.E.D. Showable*, a., 3., 1823–]
Journals, VII, 157 a Credential to shew, in
your own hand writing, with an excuse for
your sudden absence, that you did not see
or write yourself. It was most fortunate
that bit was shewable, for it gave propriety
to the Measure.

sight-seeker, sb. [*O.E.D. Sight*, sb.¹, 16, 1844–]
1814 *Journals*, VII, 438 But for Heaven's
sake send him no more sight–seekers, who
expect 'The Hero' to give dinners, & shew
Lyons!

skipping-rope, sb. [*O.E.D. Skipping-rope*, 1836–]
1802 *Journals*, V, 388 He interests himself
warmly about them, since he has seen the
Cuttings, especially of the skipping ropes.

social-cheerful, a. [*O.E.D. Social*, a., 11.; no
examples of compounds before 1890] 1800
Journals, IV, 404 I have found my sadness
so extreme – so depressing to all exertion –
so mischievous to all the purposes of
social-chearful life.

stram, v. [*O.E.D.* 1st Suppl., *Stram*, v., 1846–]
1792 *Journals*, I, 209 He bowed without
looking at her, & she strammed away, still,
however, keeping in sight.

tartine, sb. [*O.E.D. Tartine*, 1826–] 1804
Journals, VI, 477 I have given no more
medicine – plenty of tisanes &c, & tartines
of Honey & salad are all he has taken.

tea-paper, sb. [*O.E.D.* 1st Suppl., *Tea*, sb., 9. a.,
1884–] 1814 *Journals*, VII, 488 If you write
to me again upon a scrap that can hardly
arrive – I shall answer upon a bit of Tea
paper.

thank you, sb. [*O.E.D. Thank you*, b., 1887–]
1792 *Journals*, I, 174 He looked even
extremely gratified at these first voluntary
words, & Bowed expressively a thank you.

tinies, sb. [*O.E.D. Tiny*, a., B. 2., 1863–] 1797
Journals, III, 326 He always selected the
littlest for his first donation, & stopt &
hesitated before he could persuade himself
to give at all to any bigger Children, if they
came accompanied by tinies.

totter, v. [*O.E.D. Totter*, v, 5., –1693] 1814 *The
Wanderer*, V, 120 'a dimple of yours

demolishes all their work, and again totters
me down to your feet!'

tranquillizer, sb. [*O.E.D. Tranquillizer*, 1822–56]
1800 *Journals*, IV, 402 I find, however,
USEFUL employment the best tranquiliser.

unamusing, ppl. a. [*O.E.D. Unamusing*, ppl. a.,
1799–] 1794 *Journals*, III, 43 He found it
very unamusing to have a Walk without
any but, & be always obliged to turn short
back.

unappreciable, a. [*O.E.D. Unappreciable*, a.,
1822–] 1801 *Journals*, V, 21 my dear
Charlottina, whom I regard as an
unappreciable consolation & delight to
you.

unconvenience, sb. [*O.E.D. Unconvenience*,
–1635] 1796 *Camilla*, II, 305 'I've made no
other, on account of the unconvenience of
dressing.'

undefinably, adv. [*O.E.D. Undefinably*, adv.,
1886–] 1796 *Camilla*, V, 470 While wrapt
up in this reverie, poignantly agitating, yet
undefinably soothing.

underbred, sb. [*O.E.D. Underbred*, 2. b., 1880–]
1814 *The Wanderer*, IV, 105 even the
poisoned shafts of malice are less
disconcerting to delicacy than the
unqualified bluntness of the curious
underbred.

underminingly, adv. [*O.E.D. Underminingly*,
adv., –1601] 1832 *memoirs*, III, 176 The
accumulation of the whole had, slowly and
underminingly, brought him into the state
that has been described.

undisquisitionable, a. [not in *O.E.D.*] 1791
Journals, I, 22 I shall enter into no
disquisitions of what is nearly proved
undisquisitionable.

ungenial, a. [*O.E.D. Ungenial*, a., 1. b., 1815–]
1797 *Journals*, III, 354 what a blessing you
keep well! & then the Climate is not very
ungenial.

ungenially, adv. [*O.E.D. Ungenially*, adv.,
1858–] 1814 *Journals*, VII, 457 O drive, as
fast as you can, this William Locke, who
has broken so ungenially upon your
happiness, from your mind.

unGrecian, a. [*O.E.D. UnGrecian*, a., 1847–]
1799 *Journals*, IV, 359 William there may
see Noses to his mind – & if difficult
already, make himself 10 times more so

with every ungrecian one he sees.

unjulyish, a. [not in *O.E.D.*] 1799 *Journals*, IV, 312 I am very glad the Weather was so good. It was particularly kind of it, for I am sure it has been very unjulyish since.

unmarked, a. [*O.E.D. Unmarked*, ppl. a., 1. b., 1815–] 1791 *Journals*, I, 103 Our visit to Mrs Montagu turned out very unmarked; I met my good Mrs & Miss ord, & a little chat with them was all my entertainment.

unpleasure, sb. [*O.E.D. Unpleasure*, 1814–] 1792 *Journals*, I, 111 I told him, very truly, of the pleasure with which I had re-entered his Roof – but I write the unpleasures that followed!

unrobustify, v. [not in *O.E.D.*] 1795 *Journals*, III, 103 I have been able to see her but twice! – the roads are so indifferent, & we are both so unrobustified as yet.

unspoil, v. [see *O.E.D. Unspoil*, v.¹: sense not in *O.E.D.*] 1778 *Evelina*, II, 42 'And what good will that do now? – that won't unspoil all my cloaths.'

unsystematized [*O.E.D. Unsystematized*, ppl. a., 1847–] 1832 *Memoirs*, III, 323 His internal resources were too diffuse and unsystematized.

untake, v. [not in *O.E.D.*] 1802 *Journals*, V, 179 I had just taken my lodging – at Twickenham, Richmond proving too dear; & at Twickenham Miss Cambridge had recommended me to a friend of hers, who would just have suited me, in all ways. This I must untake as well & handsomely as I can.

unthin, v. [not in *O.E.D.*] 1799 *Journals*, IV, 279 He is better – but neither sleeps well, yet, nor unthins. Fattens is out of all sight or pretension.

veridically, adv. [*O.E.D. Veridically*, adv., 1836–] 1832 *Memoirs*, II, 179 And that not merely because, next to Shakespeare himself, Pope draws human characters the most veridically, perhaps, of any poetic delineator.

villaette, sb. [*O.E.D. Villaette*, 1862–] 1792 *Journals*, I, 184 Miss ord & myself set off for Sudbury, near Harrow, where her very elegant Relation, Mr Orde, has a villarette.

worsing, vbl. sb. [*O.E.D. Worsing*, vbl. sb., c. 1575 only] 1796 *Camilla*, IV, 6 'Well, my dear girl,' he cried, 'when are all these betterings and worsings to take place?'

J. N. WADDELL

NOTES

BIBLIOGRAPHY

INDEX

NOTES

ABBREVIATIONS

Barrett – The Barrett Collection of Burney
Papers, British Library (Egerton 3690–3708)
Berg – The Henry W. and Albert A. Berg
Collection, New York Public Library
*Complete Plays – The Complete Plays of Frances
Burney*, ed. Sabor, Cooke *et al*, 2 vols (1995)
Delany – *The Autobiography and
Correspondence of Mary Granville, Mrs
Delany: with Interesting Reminiscences of
King George the Third and Queen Charlotte*,
ed. Lady Llanover (1st series (vols 1–3) 1861,
2nd series (vols 4–6) 1862)
DL – *Diary and Letters of Madame d'Arblay
(1778–1840)*, ed. Austin Dobson, 6 vols
(1904–5)
Doody – Margaret Anne Doody, *Frances
Burney: The Life in the Works* (1988)
ED – *The Early Diary of Frances Burney,
1768–1778*, ed Annie Raine Ellis, 2 vols (1889)
EJL – *The Early Journals and Letters of Fanny
Burney 1768–1791*, ed. Lars E. Troide and
Stewart J. Cooke, 3 vols of a projected 12
published (1988, 1990, 1994)
Hemlow – Joyce Hemlow, *The History of
Fanny Burney* (1958)
JL – *The Journals and Letters of Fanny Burney
(Madame d'Arblay) 1791–1840*, ed. Joyce
Hemlow *et al*, 12 vols (1972–84)
Lonsdale – Roger Lonsdale, *Dr. Charles
Burney: A Literary Biography* (1965)
Mem – Madame d'Arblay (Fanny Burney),
Memoirs of Doctor Burney, 3 vols (1832)
Mem CB – *Memoirs of Dr. Charles Burney
1726–1769*, edited from autograph fragments
by Slava Kilma, Garry Bowers and Kerry S.
Grant (1988)
PRO – Public Record Office, London
*Thraliana – Thraliana: The Diary of Mrs.
Hester Lynch Thrale (later Mrs. Piozzi)*,
1776–1809, ed. Katharine C. Balderston, 2
vols (2nd edn, 1951)

PREFACE

1. DL 2, p.142
2. Sir Walter Scott to Matthew Weld
   Hartstonge, 18 July 1814, *The Letters of Sir
   Walter Scott*, ed. Sir H. Grierson (1932),
   vol. 3, p.465
3. JL 12, p.980
4. Roger Ingram (1948)
5. JL 12, p.761
6. Thomas Babington, Lord Macaulay,
   *Literary Essays contributed to the
   Edinburgh Review* (1913 edn), p.546
7. EJL 1, pp.1–2
8. Hester Thrale to Fanny Burney, 11 January
   1781, DL 1, p.460
9. EJL 1, p.235
10. DL 4, p.469
11. J.W. Croker, *Quarterly Review* (1833) xlix ,
    pp.97–125
12. Delany 2, p.318
13. DL 2, p.142
14. Mem 2, p.391
15. Hemlow, p.462
16. Lonsdale, p.449
17. Ibid, pp.440, 449
18. Mem 2, p.92
19. EJL 2, p.224
20. Doody, p.6
21. See *Burney Letters* (newsletter of the
    Burney Society), vol. 5, no. 1

CHAPTER 1: *A Low Race of Mortals*

1. *Thraliana* 1, p.368 & n
2. Ibid, p.399
3. Mem 3, p.411
4. *Thraliana* 1, p.50

5. 'Worcester Journal: Memoranda of the Burney Family, 1603–1845', p.8
6. Ibid
7. JL 11, p.189
8. *Monthly Review* xxx, p.306
9. Mem 1, p.5
10. Mem CB, p.36
11. Charles Burney to Fanny Burney d'Arblay, 29 October 1799, MS Osborn, quoted Lonsdale, p.400
12. Mem 1, p.25
13. Ibid, p.47
14. Doody, p.14
15. Mem CB, p.51
16. Charles Burney to Edmond Malone, 9–10 Nov 1806, Bodleian MS Malone 38 ff.133–4, quoted in Mem CB, p.15
17. Charles Burney to Dorothy Young, Mem 1, p.141 and *The Letters of Dr Charles Burney, Volume I: 1751–1784*, ed. Alvaro Ribeiro (1991)
18. See Hemlow 4 and n.2 & 3, p.492 n.A; Mem CB, pp.82–3 and n.3, 4 & 5
19. Information from the International Genealogical Index, parish records of St Vedast's Church in the Guildhall Library, and George Gordon, *The Churches of London*, vol. 2 (1839)
20. In October 1739; see Donovan Dawe, *Organists of the City of London, 1666–1850* (1983), p.12
21. Mem CB, p.83 n5; see also Percy A. Scholes, *The Great Doctor Burney*, vol. 1 (1948), p.52
22. Mem 1, p.63
23. Ibid
24. Ibid, p.80
25. Ibid, pp.79–80
26. JL 11, p.98
27. EJL 2, p.147
28. EJL 1, p.18
29. See ibid, pp.28–31
30. Mem 1, p.81
31. Doody, p.16
32. Mem 3, p.429
33. Mem CB, p.95
34. JL 11, p.190
35. Mem CB, pp.100–1
36. Charles Burney to Charles Burney junior, 20 December 1799, MS Berg, quoted in Lonsdale, p.38
37. To Mrs Burney, c.30 September 1751, *The Letters of Dr. Charles Burney*, op. cit., vol. 1, p.2
38. See Lonsdale, *Oxford Book of Eighteenth-Century Women Poets*, p.190
39. DL 2, p.138
40. Mem CB, p.115
41. Ibid
42. Mem 1, p.96
43. Ibid, p.97
44. Ibid, pp.97–8
45. Mem CB, p.115
46. Ibid
47. EJL 1, p.14
48. Mem CB, p.133n
49. Mem 1, p.96
50. Ibid, pp.128–9
51. Richard Tames, *Soho Past* (1994), p.12
52. Mem 1, p.134
53. Mem CB, p.133 n8
54. Ibid, p.136
55. DL 1, p.5
56. Mem 2, p.168
57. Ibid
58. JL 6, p.778
59. Mem CB, p.142
60. Kathryn Kris, 'A 70-Year Follow-up of a Childhood Learning Disability: The Case of Fanny Burney', *Psychoanalytic Study of the Child* 38 (1983), p.639
61. Mem CB, p.142
62. Macaulay, *Literary Essays*, op. cit., p.548
63. Mem 2, p.124
64. Ibid, p.123
65. Macaulay, *Literary Essays*, op. cit., p.548
66. Mem CB, p.144
67. Mem 1, p.143
68. ED 1, p.xlv
69. JL 4, p.254
70. Mem CB, p.145
71. JL 4, p.254
72. Mem 1, p.152
73. *The Letters of Dr. Charles Burney*, op. cit., vol. 1, p.30
74. Mem 1, p.139
75. JL 11, p.118
76. Mem 1, p.140
77. Ibid, pp.143–4
78. Elizabeth Rowe, *Friendship in Death in*

Twenty letters from the Dead to the Living (1733 edn), Letter 3

79. Mem CB, p.147
80. JL 11, pp.98–9
81. Mem CB, p.143
82. Mem 2, pp.170–1
83. Ibid, p.168

CHAPTER 2: *A Romantick Girl*

1. EJL 1, p.225
2. Ibid, p.314
3. Mem 1, p.167
4. Mem CB, p.62
5. Ibid, Appendix A
6. Ibid, p.150n
7. Ibid, p.150
8. Ibid, p.158
9. Ibid, p.156
10. Mem 1, pp.169–70
11. *Evelina*, p.89
12. Mem 1, pp.158–9
13. Ibid, p.51
14. Unattributed quote in A. MacNaughten, 'The Recluse of Chessington Hall', *Country Life*, vol. 142 (9 March 1967), pp.534–7
15. Mem 1, pp.49–50
16. Macaulay, *Literary Essays*, op. cit., p.555
17. Ibid
18. See T.H. White, *The Age of Scandal* (1962 edn), p.144
19. Samuel Crisp, *Virginia: A Tragedy* (1754), 'Advertisement'
20. Macaulay, *Literary Essays*, op. cit., pp.556–7
21. ED 2, Appendix 4, p.327
22. Macaulay, *Literary Essays*, op. cit., p.557
23. Before 1746 it was part of the Chessington Manor estate known as 'Fream', *The Victoria History of the County of Surrey*, ed. Malden, vol. 3 (1911), p.265
24. Mem 1, p.210
25. Mem 2, pp.185–6
26. Mem 1, p.181
27. Mem CB, p.160
28. Mem 1, p.209
29. Lease taken out on 16 January 1793, Surrey History Centre, ref. 210. For a view of the modern council flats on the site, see 'Virtual Chessington, Hook and Maldon Rushett' on the internet at http:/

ds.dial.pipex.com/sean/chessington/ index.htm
30. MS Berg
31. See Hemlow, pp.18–22
32. James Fordyce, *Sermons to Young Women*, fifth edn (1776), p.106
33. Ibid, p.17
34. Ibid, p.21
35. Ibid, pp.191, 272
36. Mem, 2, p.170
37. EJL 1, p.37
38. Ibid, p.99
39. *The Wanderer*, p.7
40. Mem 2, p.124
41. Ibid
42. Ibid, p.125
43. JL 11, p.347
44. e.g. EJL 1, p.36
45. e.g. Susan Elizabeth Burney MS journal, quoted in Mem CB, p.171, n1
46. DL 1, p.9
47. Mem 2, p.125
48. EJL 3, p.238
49. EJL 1, p.157
50. EJL 3, p.238
51. Mem 1, p.190
52. Mem CB, p.174
53. Ibid
54. Ibid, p.177
55. Quoted in JL 12, p.780
56. Stephen Allen to Charles Burney junior, 21 November 1832, MS Osborn, quoted Mem CB, p.182
57. Mem CB, p.174
58. Stephen Allen to Charles Burney junior, 21 November 1832, op. cit.
59. Mem 1, p.189
60. Ibid, p.190
61. Ibid
62. Ibid, pp.191–2
63. Ibid, p.191
64. Ibid, pp.193–4
65. Mem CB, p.177
66. Mem 1, p.196
67. Ibid, p.197
68. Ibid, pp.197–8
69. EJL 1, p.6
70. Mem CB, pp.174, 176
71. Elizabeth Allen Burney to Fanny Burney, 13 October 1767, MS Berg, quoted in EJL 1, p.50

72. EJL 1, p.315
73. *The Wanderer*, p.8
74. Mem 2, p.125
75. *The Wanderer*, p.8
76. Mem 2, p.125
77. DL 1, p.13
78. Ibid, p.12
79. EJL 1, p.70
80. See *The Wanderer*, p.8
81. EJL 1, p.2
82. Ibid, p.3
83. Ibid, p.36
84. Ibid, p.66
85. Ibid, p.43
86. Ibid, p.152
87. J.N. Waddell, 'Fanny Burney's Contribution to English Vocabulary', *Neuphilologische Mitteilungen*, 81, p.260
88. EJL 2, p.194
89. R. Brimley Johnson, *Fanny Burney and the Burneys* (1926), pp.119, 307
90. *Evelina*, p.394
91. *Notes and Queries*, vol. 225, pp.27–32
92. In *Neuphilologische Mitteilungen*, op. cit.
93. See JL 1, p.8: of some unwelcome French travellers at an inn during the French Revolution: 'we now were touched to shake off a part of the John Bullism that had encrusted us, & to ask them to our sitting Room, to drink Tea.'

CHAPTER 3: *Female Caution*

1. EJL 1, p.46
2. Ibid, pp.15, 10
3. White, *The Age of Scandal*, op. cit., p.142; *Early Diary of Frances Burney*, grangerised edition in the National Portrait Gallery, vol. 1, pt 2; vol. 2, pt 1
4. EJL 1, p.105
5. *Cecilia*, p.106
6. EJL 1, p.106
7. *Cecilia*, pp.127, 128
8. See Julia Epstein, *The Iron Pen* (1989) and Barbara Zonitch, *Familiar Violence* (1997) in particular.
9. EJL 1, p.83
10. Ibid, p.72
11. Mem CB, p.178; and *Thraliana* 1, p.137
12. EJL 1, p.79
13. Mem 1, p.216

14. Ibid, pp.216–17
15. *Dr. Burney's Musical Tours in Europe*, ed. Percy A. Scholes, vol. 1 (1959), p.306
16. See Lonsdale, pp.105–9
17. Mem CB, p.100
18. EJL 2, p.153
19. EJL 1, pp.329–30
20. EJL 2, p.239
21. Remarked on by Henry Thrale, EJL 3, p.137
22. EJL 2, p.15
23. Fordyce, *Sermons to Young Women*, op. cit., p.96
24. 'Cadenus and Vanessa', *The Poems of Jonathan Swift*, ed. H. Williams, vol. 2 (1937)
25. *Evelina*, p.29
26. Ibid, p.30
27. *Complete Plays* 1, p.77
28. Ibid, pp.204–5
29. EJL 3, p.153
30. JL 1, p.43
31. EJL 1, p.250
32. DL 1, p.357
33. EJL 3, p.396
34. Susan Elizabeth Burney journal, February 1791, MS Berg
35. EJL 3, p.439
36. Ibid, p.441
37. *Complete Plays* 1, p.275
38. EJL 2, p.17
39. EJL 1, p.35
40. EJL 3, p.87
41. EJL 2, p.222
42. EJL 1, p.17
43. Ibid, p.229
44. EJL 2, p.123
45. Ibid, pp.125–8
46. Ibid, pp.146–7
47. Ibid, p.147
48. See Lonsdale, p.156. The pamphlet, by 'Joel Collier' (a pseudonym), was called 'Musical Travels Through England' (1774)
49. Mem 1, p.260
50. Ibid, p.288
51. Ibid, p.269
52. Quoted in *Survey of London*, vol. 20, p.107
53. EJL 2, p.177
54. Ibid, p.226
55. See plate facing p.302 in *The Letters of Dr Charles Burney*, vol. 1, op. cit. For

photographs of the first-floor mantel-shelf and ground-floor fireplace taken before the demolition of the house in 1913, see plates 96b and c in *Survey of London*, vol. xx (pp.107–8), which also contains plans of the ground and first floors and drawings of the stair-posts.

56. Ibid, p.177
57. Ibid, p.60
58. Ibid, pp.62–3
59. Ibid, p.75
60. Ibid, p.76
61. Ibid, pp.98–9
62. Ibid, p.154
63. Ibid, p.156
64. EJL 1, p.235
65. EJL 2, p.186
66. Quoted in Evelyn Farr, *The World of Fanny Burney* (1993), p.79
67. Maria Rishton to Fanny Burney, 24 September 1776, MS Berg
68. Charlotte Ann Burney to Fanny Burney, 4 July (1778?), MS Egerton, quoted in Doody, p.28
69. *The Wanderer*, p.542
70. Ibid, p.543
71. *Thraliana* 1, pp.522–3

CHAPTER 4: *An Accidental Author*

1. Mem 3, p.235
2. EJL 1, p.320
3. *Evelina*, pp.27–8
4. Mem 2, p.126
5. MS Barrett
6. *The Wanderer*, p.8
7. Mem 2, p.126
8. Ibid
9. Ibid
10. Hemlow, p.62
11. EJL 2, p.199
12. EJL 3, p.116
13. *The Letters of Samuel Johnson with Mrs Thrale's Genuine Letters to Him*, ed. R.W. Chapman, vol. 2 (1952), p.226
14. Eliza Draper to Mary Bruce Strange, quoted in *Notes and Queries* 187 (1944), pp.30–1
15. *The Letters of Samuel Johnson*, op. cit., vol. 2, p.226
16. For this and other information in this

paragraph see Ralph S. Walker, 'Charles Burney's Theft of Books at Cambridge', *Transactions of the Cambridge Bibliographical Society* iii, pp.313–26
17. British Library Add. MS 39929
18. MS Osborn, quoted in Walker, op. cit.
19. Walker, op. cit., p.324
20. Charles Burney junior to Charles Parr Burney, 17 October 1804, MS Osborn
21. Fanny Burney d'Arblay to Charles Parr Burney, 26 February 1818, JL 10, p.795
22. DL 4, p.32
23. JL 7, p.472
24. *Thraliana* 1, p.360
25. EJL 2, p.213
26. Ibid, p.232
27. *Cecilia*, p.930
28. *Evelina*, p.38
29. EJL 3, p.90
30. *Evelina*, pp.199–200
31. Ibid, p.102
32. Ibid, p.321
33. Ibid, p.401
34. Ibid, p.309
35. White, *The Age of Scandal*, op. cit., pp.77–8
36. *Evelina*, p.166
37. See EJL 2, p.215
38. See for example Susan Fraiman, 'Getting Waylaid in *Evelina*', in *Unbecoming Women: British Women Writers and the Novel of Development* (1993), and Doody, pp.54–60
39. EJL 2, pp.215, 216
40. Ibid, p.215
41. Ibid
42. 'Introduction to His Paintings', D.H. Lawrence, *Selected Essays* (1950), p.308
43. For the history of the Burney connection with Gregg's Coffee House see EJL 3, Appendix 1
44. Mem 2, pp.132–3
45. EJL 3, p.4
46. Mem 2, p.132
47. EJL 3, p.5
48. Ibid
49. Marcel Proust, *By Way of Sainte-Beuve*, trans. Sylvia Townsend Warner (1958), p.79
50. EJL 3, p.5
51. *Evelina*, p.180

52. EJL 3, p.6
53. Ibid
54. Ibid, p.9
55. *London Review* vii, February 1778
56. *Monthly Review* lviii, April 1778
57. EJL 3, p.13
58. Ibid, pp.19–20
59. Ibid, p.17
60. *Thraliana* 1, p.331
61. MS Berg and EJL 2, Appendix 2, pp.293–4
62. EJL 3, p.21
63. *Complete Plays* 1, p.20
64. EJL 3, p.28
65. Ibid, p.26
66. Mem 2, p.169
67. EJL 3, p.55
68. Ibid, p.31

CHAPTER 5: *Entrance into the World*

1. Arthur Murphy, 'An Essay on the Life and Genius of Samuel Johnson, LL.D.', *Johnsonian Miscellanies*, ed. G.B. Hill, vol. 1, pp.423–4
2. *Autobiography, Letters and Literary Remains of Mrs Piozzi*, ed. A. Hayward, vol. 1 (1861), p.257
3. *Boswell's Life of Johnson*, ed. G.B. Hill and L. Powell, vol. 1 (1934), p.92
4. *Thraliana* 1, p.423
5. Ibid, p.137
6. Ibid
7. Ibid
8. Hester Thrale to Samuel Johnson, 18 October 1777, *The Letters of Samuel Johnson*, op. cit., vol. 2, p.225
9. Charles Burney to Hester Thrale, John Rylands Library Eng. MS 545.1
10. *Thraliana* 1, p.360n
11. EJL 3, p.41
12. Ibid, p.37
13. MS Berg, quoted in EJL 3, p.32n
14. EJL 3, p.41
15. Mem 2, p.143
16. 'The common story of Dr Burney her father having brought home her own first work and recommended it to her perusal', *The Journal of Sir Walter Scott*, ed. W.E.K. Anderson (1972), p.241
17. Mem 2, p.122
18. Ibid, p.141
19. Ibid
20. Ibid, p.142
21. Fanny Burney to Susanna Burney, 5 July 1778, EJL 3, pp.34–5
22. EJL 3, p.238
23. Ibid, p.35
24. Ibid, p.61
25. 19 January 1779, ibid, p.238
26. Mem 2, p.149
27. EJL 3, p.36
28. Ibid, p.58
29. Ibid, p.36
30. Ibid, pp.51–2
31. Ibid, p.45
32. Ibid, p.56
33. *Thraliana* 1, p.329
34. Ibid
35. EJL 3, p.58
36. Ibid, p.66
37. Ibid, p.62
38. Ibid, p.70
39. Ibid, p.73
40. Ibid, p.74
41. Ibid, p.75–6
42. Ibid, p.77
43. Ibid
44. Mem 2, p.166
45. EJL 3, p.79
46. Ibid, p.80
47. Ibid, p.82
48. Ibid, pp.115–16
49. Ibid, p.116
50. Ibid, p.117
51. Ibid, p.118

CHAPTER 6: *Downright Scribler*

1. EJL 3, p.123
2. Ibid, pp.101–2
3. Ibid, p.87
4. Ibid, p.89
5. Ibid, p.95
6. cf Mrs Thrale's comments in *Thraliana* 1 (p.415 and n) about Johnson's melancholia and his fits of abjection before her, and her remark that 'the Fetters & Padlocks will tell Posterity the Truth'. See also Chapter 23, 'The Padlock', of John Wain's *Samuel Johnson* (1974), and the discussion of Johnson's possible masochistic tendencies by

K.C. Balderston in *The Age of Johnson* (1949), pp.3–14

7. Quoted in Wain, op. cit., p.293
8. EJL 3, p.103
9. Ibid, p.172
10. Ibid, p.436
11. Ibid, p.151
12. Ibid, pp.89–90
13. Ibid, p.141
14. *The Poems of John Bampfylde*, ed. Lonsdale (1988)
15. EJL 3, p.224
16. Ibid, p.192
17. Ibid, p.211
18. Ibid, p.205
19. Ibid, p.202
20. Ibid, p.201
21. Ibid, p.91
22. Ibid, p.246
23. Ibid, p.235
24. Ibid
25. Ibid, p.110
26. *Thraliana* 1, p.381
27. EJL 3, p.153
28. *Thraliana* 1, p.329n
29. EJL 3, p.145
30. *Complete Plays* 1, pp.12–13n
31. Ibid, p.3
32. Ibid, p.45
33. Ibid, p.10
34. Ibid, p.101
35. EJL 3, p.187
36. Ibid, p.189
37. Ibid, p.212
38. *Thraliana* 1, p.381
39. Ibid
40. EJL 3, p.347
41. Ibid, p.350
42. See annotation to ALS Berg, Diary MSS 1, p.999
43. EJL 3, p.353
44. *The Letters of Dr. Charles Burney*, op. cit., vol. 1, p.279
45. EJL 3, p.347
46. Ibid
47. *Thraliana* 1, p.401
48. EJL 3, p.352
49. Ibid
50. Ibid, p.239
51. Ibid, p.353
52. Ibid
53. Ibid, p.390
54. See *The London Stage 1660–1800*, ed. Arthur H. Scouten (1960–8), vol. 5, p.458
55. EJL 3, p.349
56. *Thraliana* 1, p.368
57. EJL 3, p.86
58. Mem 2, p.172
59. *Thraliana* 1, p.400
60. Ibid, p.413
61. EJL 3, p.424
62. Ibid, p.384
63. Ibid, p.410
64. EJL 1, p.302
65. DL 2, p.128
66. EJL 3, p.405
67. Ibid, pp.362–3
68. Ibid, pp.430–1
69. *The Letters of Samuel Johnson*, op. cit., vol. 2, p.318

CHAPTER 7: Cecilia

1. DL 1, p.315
2. Ibid
3. Ibid, p.332
4. Fanny Burney to Queeney Thrale, 12 July 1798, Lansdowne MSS, quoted in James L. Clifford, *Hester Lynch Piozzi (Mrs Thrale)* (1941), p.178n
5. DL 1, p.325
6. *Thraliana* 1, p.439
7. Samuel Johnson to Queeney Thrale, 19 May 1780, *The Queeney Letters*, ed. Lansdowne (1934), p.20
8. *Thraliana* 1, p.443
9. Ibid, p.437 & n
10. Quoted in Constance Hill, *The House in St Martin's Street: Being Chronicles of the Burney Family* (1907), pp.257–8
11. Quoted in ibid, pp.258–9
12. Quoted in ibid, p.269
13. Quoted in ibid, p.264
14. *London Gazette*, 11 January 1780
15. G.E. Manwaring, *My Friend the Admiral: The Life, Letters and Journals of Rear-Admiral James Burney, FRS, The Companion of Captain Cook and Friend of Charles Lamb* (1931), p.144
16. See Christopher Lloyd, *St Vincent and Camperdown* (1963)
17. ED 2, p.141n

18. See, for example, the exhaustive household accounts of Parson Woodforde for this decade
19. DL 1, p.466
20. *Burford Papers*, ed. W.H. Hutton (1905), p.76
21. Richard Hough, *Captain James Cook: A Biography* (1994), p.335
22. *Burford Papers*, op. cit., p.76
23. Quoted in Constance Hill, *Good Company in Old Westminster and the Temple*, p.13
24. This was the singer Pacchierotti's view, as reported in ED 1, p.lxxiv
25. Quoted in Hemlow, p.146
26. See Terry Castle, 'Sister-Sister' (review of *Jane Austen's Letters*, ed. D. Le Faye), *London Review of Books*, vol. 17, no. 15 (3 August 1995), and David Nokes's article 'Cassandra's Partner' in *Times Literary Supplement* (15 September 1995). The widespread misinterpretation of Castle's article, fuelled by the sensational cover-line 'Was Jane Austen Gay?', provoked this restatement of her argument in the following issue ('Letters', *London Review of Books*, vol. 17, no. 16, 24 August 1995): 'The culture at large [of the eighteenth and early nineteenth centuries] reinforced – far more than our own culture does today – same-sex intimacy of all sorts. To point to a 'homoerotic' dimension in the Austen/Cassandra relationship is in one sense simply to state a truth about the lives of many English women in the early nineteenth century: that their closest affectional ties were with female relations and friends rather than with men.'
27. Exhaustively documented in Doody; see also Julia Epstein, *The Iron Pen*, op. cit., Barbara Zonitch, *Familiar Violence*, op. cit. and J.M.S. Tompkins, *The Popular Novel in England 1770–1800*
28. DL 2, p.55
29. DL 1, p.459
30. Fanny Burney to Susan Burney, quoted in Hill, *The House in St Martin's Street*, op. cit., p.318
31. *Burford Papers*, op. cit., p.59
32. MS Berg, quoted in Hemlow, p.153
33. *Burford Papers*, op. cit., p.82
34. Ibid
35. Ibid, p.76
36. Ibid, p.74
37. MS Berg, quoted in Hemlow, p.142
38. Hemlow, p.143
39. Ibid, p.147
40. Hester Thrale to Fanny Burney, 31 July 1782, MS Berg
41. *Cecilia*, p.831
42. DL 2, p.81
43. St John's College, Oxford, MS 279, quoted in Claire Tomalin, *Jane Austen: A Life* (1997), p.121
44. *Thraliana* 1, p.536
45. *Cecilia*, p.80
46. Ibid, p.96
47. Ibid, pp.743–4
48. Ibid, p.724
49. Ibid, p.723
50. Ibid, p.851
51. Ibid, p.944
52. See DL 2, pp.73, 78n
53. Ibid, p.88
54. *Burford Papers*, op. cit., p.63
55. DL 2, p.72
56. Ibid, p.92
57. *Burford Papers*, op. cit., p.81

CHAPTER 8: *Change and Decay*

1. See Wain, op. cit., p.355
2. Clifford, op. cit., p.209
3. *Thraliana* 1, p.531
4. DL 2, p.96
5. Ibid, p.122
6. Ibid, p.105
7. Ibid, p.114
8. *Thraliana* 1, p.452
9. Ibid, p.546
10. *Burford Papers*, op. cit., p.63
11. *Thraliana* 1, p.550
12. DL 2, p.230
13. *The Queeney Letters*, op. cit., pp.76, 70
14. *A Later Pepys: The Correspondence of Sir William Weller Pepys*, ed. A.C.C. Gaussen, vol. 1 (1904), p.408
15. *The Queeney Letters*, op. cit., p.86
16. DL 2, p.258
17. Fanny Burney to Queeney Thrale, 12 July 1798, Lansdowne MS, quoted in Clifford, op. cit., p.225n

18. Ibid
19. DL 2, p.283
20. Ibid, p.271
21. Ibid, p.239
22. Ibid, p.279
23. Ibid, p.216
24. Hannah More, *Poems*, p.75
25. Quoted in May Alden Hopkins, *Hannah More* (1947), p.105
26. DL 2, p.234
27. Hannah More, *Poems*, p.87
28. DL 2, p.229
29. Ibid, p.173
30. Ibid, pp.187–8
31. MS Berg, quoted in Hemlow, p.191
32. See Doody, p.152
33. DL 2, pp.78–9
34. Fanny Burney to Susan Burney Phillips, 30 December 1783, MS Berg, quoted in Doody, pp.154–5
35. Ibid
36. MS Berg, quoted in Hemlow, p.192
37. MS Berg, quoted in Hemlow, p.191
38. DL 2, p.245
39. MS Berg, quoted in Hemlow, p.192
40. Fanny Burney to Susan Burney Phillips, 24 May 1784, MS Berg, quoted in Doody, p.157
41. Manwaring, op. cit., p.178
42. Charles Burney to Charles Burney junior, 31 May 1808, ALS Osborn, quoted in JL 1, p.119n
43. Quoted in Lloyd, op. cit., pp.100–1
44. See JL 1, p.119n
45. EJL 1, p.152
46. See Manwaring, op. cit., p.172, and PRO Adm. 1, vol. 1504
47. PRO Adm. 1, vols. 1539, 1541
48. Susan Burney Phillips to Charlotte Burney Francis, 4 March 1786, MS Berg
49. Charles Burney to Thomas Twining, 31 July 1784, ALS Berg, quoted in Hemlow, p.194
50. Nikolaus Pevsner, *The Buildings of England: Surrey*, 2nd edn, p.389
51. Charles Burney to Twining, 31 July 1784, op. cit.
52. DL 2, p.265
53. Ibid, p.225
54. Ibid, p.263
55. JL 1, p.198

56. Quoted in R. Brimley Johnson, *Mrs Delany at Court and Among the Wits* (1925), p.xxviii
57. Quoted in ibid, p. xxix
58. Quoted as epigraph to ibid
59. Ibid, p.xiv
60. Amanda Vickery, *The Gentleman's Daughter: Women's Lives in Georgian England* (1998)
61. DL 2, p.315
62. Ibid, p.319
63. Ibid, p.337
64. Ibid, p.320
65. Ibid, pp.352–3
66. Epstein, op. cit., p.29
67. DL 2, p.352
68. *The Annual Register* lxii, pp.709–10
69. DL 2, p.358
70. Ibid, p.359
71. See Delany 3, p.355 and Lonsdale, p.320n
72. DL 2, p.363
73. Ibid, p.364
74. Ibid, p.365
75. Ibid, p.370
76. Delany 6, p.366
77. DL 2, p.371
78. Fanny Burney to Esther Burney, June 1786, MS Berg, quoted in Lonsdale, p.323
79. Lonsdale, p.324
80. Macaulay, *Literary Essays*, op. cit., p.571
81. Ibid, p.567
82. Ibid, p.570
83. Diary MS, 1788–9, MS Berg
84. DL 2, p.380
85. Ibid, pp.371–2
86. Ibid, p.380
87. Ibid, p.381
88. Ibid, p.382

CHAPTER 9: *Retrograde Motion*

1. Quoted in Aileen Ribiero, *The Art of Dress*, p.62
2. They did this for the entertainment of Mrs Siddons; see *Thraliana* 2, p.821 n4
3. DL 4, p.276
4. DL 2, p.339
5. DL 3, p.20
6. Remark attributed to George III in his illness, Jane Aiken Hodge, *Passion and Principle*, p.20

7. DL 2, p.389
8. DL 3, p.132
9. DL 2, pp.441–2
10. DL 3, p.9
11. Ibid, p.21
12. Fanny Burney to Susan Burney Phillips, (20?) June 1787, MS Berg, quoted in Doody, p.177
13. DL 3, p.148
14. Ibid, p.22
15. Ibid, pp.161–2
16. DL 2, pp.473–4
17. Ibid, p.400
18. DL 3, p.9
19. Ibid, p.15
20. Ibid, p.43
21. See J.T. Smith, *Nollekens and his Times* (1834)
22. Macaulay, *Literary Essays*, op. cit., p.546
23. *Camilla*, Dedication
24. DL 3, p.330
25. DL 2, p.330
26. Ibid, pp.337, 329
27. Ibid, p.336
28. Ibid
29. DL 3, p.373
30. DL 4, p.312
31. DL 3, p.6
32. Quoted in Hemlow, p.214
33. See rate books and *Survey of London*, vol. xx
34. MS Barrett, Maria Rishton to Fanny Burney d'Arblay, 24 December 1796
35. Barrett, Egerton 3692, f.43
36. JL 1, p.203 n50
37. EJL 1, p.183 n4
38. *The Letters of Sarah Harriet Burney*, ed. Lorna J. Clark (1997), p.60, n10
39. Susan Burney Phillips to Fanny Burney, 19 July–9 September 1787, MS Osborn
40. Charles Burney with Sarah Harriet Burney to Charles Burney junior, December 1807, quoted in *The Letters of Sarah Harriet Burney*, op. cit., p.60 n10
41. See her tombstone inscription, quoted in W.K. Ferminger, 'Madame D'Arblay and Calcutta', *Bengal Past and Present* vol. 9 (1914), pp.244–9
42. JL 11, p.195
43. Barrett, Egerton 3692, f.43, Susan Burney Phillips journals
44. H. Morris, *The Life of Charles Grant*

(1904), p.156
45. DL 3, p.417
46. Ibid, p.440
47. DL 4, p.48
48. Ibid, p.120
49. Ibid, p.122
50. Ibid, p.120
51. Ibid, p.131
52. Ibid, p.136
53. Ibid, p.129
54. Ibid, p.118
55. Ibid, p.169
56. Ibid, p.188
57. Ibid, p.158
58. Quoted in Ida Macalpine and Robert Hunter, *George III and the Mad-Business* (1991 edn), p.77
59. DL 4, p.242
60. Ibid, pp.243–4
61. Ibid, p.245
62. Ibid, pp.289–90
63. Ibid, pp.295–6
64. Ibid, p.302
65. Ibid, p.330
66. Ibid, p.292
67. Fanny Burney Diary, August 1789, MS Berg, quoted in Hemlow, p.211
68. DL 4, p.83
69. Fanny Burney Diary, May 1790, MS Berg, quoted in Hemlow, p.212
70. DL 4, p.392
71. Charles Burney to Charles Burney junior, 21 July 1790, quoted in Hemlow, p.215
72. DL 4, p.437
73. Ibid, p.451
74. Ibid, p.437
75. *Thraliana* 2, p.821
76. Ibid
77. DL 4, p.436
78. Ibid, p.413
79. Ibid, pp.478–9
80. *Complete Plays* 2, p.55
81. MS Berg, quoted in Hemlow, p.221
82. *Frances Burney: The Life in the Works* (1988), Chapter 5
83. *Complete Plays* 2, p.83
84. MS Berg, quoted in Doody, p.195
85. *Elberta, Complete Plays* 2, p.244; *Hubert de Vere*, ibid, p.114
86. JL 1, p.74
87. Ibid, p.4

CHAPTER 10: *Taking Sides*

1. JL 1, p.15
2. Susan Burney Phillips, journal, December 1791, MS Berg, quoted in JL 1, p.16n
3. JL 1, p.18
4. Ibid, p.16n
5. Ibid, p.18
6. Mem 3, p.149
7. JL 1, p.196
8. Susan Burney Phillips to Fanny Burney, October 1792, DL 5, p.116
9. *The Times*, 12 December 1792
10. DL 5, p.139
11. For résumés of Monsieur d'Arblay's military career see introduction to JL 2, which quotes a document in the Berg Collection drawn up in 1793, and Georges Six, *Dictionnaire biographique des généraux et amiraux français de la révolution et de l'empire* (1934), vol. 2
12. 'Je ne vois point d'espérance de tranquillité dans ma malheureuse Patrie pendant mes Jours. Le Peuple est tellement *vitié* par l'impunité du crime – par les desordres de tout espéce – par l'habitude de voir couler le sang.' Susan Burney Phillips, Diary, MSS v.4672–5, 16 December 1792, MS Berg, quoted in JL 2, p.3n
13. JL 2, p.3
14. Ibid, pp.5–6
15. ' "*Est-ce-vrai*" cries M. de Narbonne, que vous conserve encore quelque amitié, M. Lock, pour ceux qui ont la honte et le malheur d'être né françois [sic]?" ' Ibid, pp.8–9.
16. Ibid, p.8
17. Ibid, p.10
18. JL 1, p.247
19. JL 2, p.13 n5
20. Ibid, p.15
21. Ibid, Appendix II, p.190
22. 'Je n'ai jamais eu une envie veritable d' écrire, de parler, d'entendre La Langue françoise [sic] jusqu'ici.' Ibid, p.189.
23. Ibid, p.14
24. Ibid, p.190
25. Ibid, p.188
26. Ibid, pp.17–18
27. Ibid, p.14
28. Ibid, p.21
29. Ibid, p.22
30. JL 1, p.47
31. Ibid, p.49
32. The traveller, Moravian and later bookseller; see ED 1, pp.304–5 and JL 1, p.90n
33. JL 2, p.25
34. Ibid, p.26
35. Ibid, p.29
36. Ibid, p.26
37. 'Le cri est partout, ' "*Elle n'est ni Emigree, ni banni – – c'est M. de Narbonne qui la séduit de son Mari et de ses Enfans!*" – – C'est vainement que je parle du moeurs de son pais; on ne me réponde jamais que "*Elle est Femme, elle est Mère!*" ' Ibid, p.31.
38. 'Rien n'egale sa bienfaisance, son humanité, son obligeance, et le besoin qu'elle a de l'exercer.' Ibid
39. 'a ma femme, a ma soeur'. Ibid, p.32
40. Quoted in Linda Kelly, *Juniper Hall* (1991), p.17
41. JL 2, p.204
42. Ibid, pp.41–2
43. Ibid, p.41n
44. Susan Burney Phillips to Fanny Burney, 4 April 1793, MS Berg, quoted in JL 2, p.42n
45. JL 2, p.50
46. Ibid, p.65
47. 'ce n'est pas – actuellement – vôtre nom?' Ibid, p.62
48. Ibid, p.68
49. Ibid, p.70
50. Mem 3, p.180
51. JL 2, p.80
52. Ibid, p.81
53. Ibid, p.75
54. Ibid, p.52
55. 'brusque . . . Je me jette par ci – par la, – par de tous parts – dans l'instant!' Ibid, p.103
56. Ibid, p.102
57. Ibid, pp.138–9
58. JL 1, p.75
59. Quoted in Manwaring, op. cit., p.186
60. JL 2, p.129
61. Ibid, pp.129–30
62. Ibid, p.130
63. Ibid, p.136
64. Ibid, p.148
65. Ibid, pp.157–8n
66. Ibid, pp.140–1

CHAPTER 11: *The Cabbage-Eaters*

1. Maria Rishton to Susan Burney Phillips, 14 August 1793, MS Berg
2. JL 3, p.8
3. Ibid, p.2
4. Ibid, p.45
5. See family tree of the Piochard d'Arblays, in JL 6
6. JL 3, p.14
7. Ibid, pp.24–32
8. *Brief Reflections Relative to the Emigrant French Clergy*, p.24
9. Ibid, p.iv
10. Hannah More to Horace Walpole, 18 August 1792, *Horace Walpole's Correspondence* (ed. Lewis), vol. 31, p.370
11. JL 3, p.48
12. Ibid, p.49
13. Ibid, p.36 n2
14. Ibid, p.92
15. Ibid, p.93
16. Ibid, p.103
17. Ibid, p.99
18. Ibid, n9
19. Sarah Siddons to Hester Thrale Piozzi, 25 March 1795, John Rylands Library Eng. MS 582.5, quoted in W. Wright Roberts, 'Charles and Fanny Burney in the Light of the New Thrale Correspondence in the John Rylands Library', *Bulletin of the John Rylands Library*, vol 16, no. 1 (January 1932)
20. *Morning Herald*, 23 March 1795
21. See JL 3, Appendix A
22. For the history of the revisions to these plays over the next three decades, see *Complete Plays* 2
23. JL 3, p.117
24. *Camilla*, p.253
25. JL 3, p.177
26. Ibid, p.157
27. Hemlow, p.255
28. *Camilla*, pp.375, 484
29. Ibid, p.9
30. Ibid, p.238
31. Ibid, pp.13–14
32. Ibid, p.745
33. JL 3, p.137
34. *Camilla*, p.875
35. Epstein, op. cit., p.135
36. JL 3, p.130
37. Ibid, p.140
38. Ibid, Appendix B
39. *Analytical Review*, August 1796
40. JL 3, Appendix B
41. Ibid, p.222
42. Ibid, p.206
43. Jane Austen, *Northanger Abbey*, Chapter 5
44. *Camilla*, p.178
45. Ibid, p.255
46. Ibid, p.756
47. Though, as Pat Rogers has pointed out, Mrs Thrale used the phrase too, in her travel sketches and verse; see Pat Rogers, 'Sposi in Surrey', *Times Literary Supplement*, 23 August 1996
48. Ibid
49. Ibid
50. *Jane Austen's Letters*, ed. D. Le Faye (1995), p.26
51. JL 3, p.79
52. Ibid, pp.204–5
53. Charles Burney to Fanny Burney d'Arblay, September 1796, MS Berg, quoted in JL 3, p.201n
54. Susan Burney Phillips to Fanny Burney d'Arblay, 11–15 September 1796, MS Berg, quoted in JL 3, p.200n
55. JL 3, p.264n
56. Charles Burney to Fanny Burney d'Arblay, September 1796, MS Berg, quoted in JL 3, p.201n
57. Charles Burney to C.I. Latrobe, 14 November 1796, quoted in Lonsdale, p.383; and Charles Burney to Thomas Twining, 6 December 1796, quoted in Hemlow, p.278
58. JL 3, p.218
59. Ibid, p.212
60. Ibid, p.217
61. Charles Burney to Thomas Twining, 6 December 1796, op. cit.
62. JL 3, p.284
63. Ibid, p.243
64. Ibid, pp.223, 207.
65. Plan of the interior of Camilla Cottage by Monsieur d'Arblay, MS Berg. See plates section
66. JL 3, p.203
67. JL 4, p.51
68. Ibid, p.39
69. JL 3, p.336

70. *Complete Plays* 1, pp.171, 179
71. Ibid, p.188
72. JL 4, p.119
73. Ibid
74. Quoted in Hemlow, p.282
75. Sarah Harriet Burney to Anna Grosvenor, 28 May 1835, *The Letters of Sarah Harriet Burney*, op. cit., p.400
76. JL 4, p.275
77. Ibid, p.286
78. Ibid, pp.345, 347
79. Charles Burney junior to Charles Burney, 8 January 1800, MS Barrett, quoted in JL 4, p.381n
80. Charles Burney junior to Charles Burney, 6 January 1800, MS Barrett, quoted in JL 4, p.381n
81. JL 4, p.386
82. Ibid, p.382

CHAPTER 12: *Winds and Waves*

1. JL 4, p.387
2. Ibid, p.386
3. Mem 3, p.295
4. JL 4, p.410
5. Ibid, p.384
6. Ibid
7. Ibid
8. Ibid, p.411
9. 'Scrapbook', Charles Burney junior to Fanny Burney d'Arblay, 30 October 1799, MS Berg
10. Quoted in Hemlow, p.275
11. *Morning Chronicle*, 29 January 1800
12. JL 4, p.394
13. Ibid, p.395
14. Ibid
15. JL 5, p.7
16. Ibid, p.1
17. Ibid, p.87
18. Ibid, p.95
19. Ibid, p.96
20. Ibid, Introduction
21. *Complete Plays* 1, p.245
22. Ibid, p.283
23. JL 4, pp.394–5
24. *The Stage and Television Today*, 11 November 1993, quoted in *Complete Plays* 1, p.291
25. *Complete Plays* 1, p.379

26. Ibid, p.380
27. Ibid, p.312
28. Ibid, p.296
29. Ibid, p.351
30. JL 5, p.188.
31. Mem 3, p.311
32. JL 5, p.232
33. Ibid, p.290
34. Ibid, p.307
35. Ibid, p.313
36. JL 6, p.797
37. JL 5, p.355
38. Ibid, p.343
39. Ibid, p.355
40. Ibid, p.378
41. Ibid, p.322
42. Ibid, p.407
43. Ibid
44. *An Englishman in Paris, 1803: The Journal of Bertie Greatheed*, ed. Bury and Barry (1953), p.147
45. JL 5, p.446
46. Ibid, p.327
47. JL 6, p.528
48. Ibid, p.801
49. Ibid, p.550
50. Ibid, p.551
51. Quoted in Hemlow, p.354
52. *The Wanderer*, p.4
53. JL 6, p.585
54. Ibid, p.600
55. See O.H. and S.D. Wangensteen in *The Rise of Surgery* (1978), and Roy Porter and Anthony R. Moore in 'Preanesthetic Mastectomy: A Patient's Experience', *Surgery* 83 (February 1978), pp.200–5. The possibly benign nature of Fanny Burney d'Arblay's tumour was also suggested to me independently by Dr Annie Bartlett, for whose professional opinion I am grateful
56. 'A Mastectomy' [of 30 September 1811], JL 6, pp.596–616
57. Ibid, p.613
58. See Porter and Moore, 'Preanesthetic Mastectomy: A Patient's Experience', op. cit.

CHAPTER 13: *The Wanderer*

1. JL 6, p.706
2. Ibid, p.715
3. Joseph A. Grau, *Fanny Burney: An*

Annotated Bibliography (1981), p.82, Maria Edgeworth to Sophy Ruxton, 16 May 1813

4. JL 7, p.507
5. Mem 3, p.402
6. John Rylands Library Eng. MS, Clement Francis to Hester Thrale Piozzi, 3 September 1814, quoted in JL 7, p.11n
7. JL 7, p.12
8. Roberts, op. cit., p.21
9. *Extracts from the Journals and Correspondence of Miss Berry from the year 1783 to 1852*, ed. Lady Theresa Lewis (1866), vol. 2, p.508
10. Roberts, op. cit., p.21
11. JL 4, p.302
12. Quoted in Hemlow, p.333
13. JL 7, p.34
14. T.J. Hogg, *Life of Percy Bysshe Shelley* (1906)
15. *The Life and Letters of Thomas Campbell*, ed. Beattie, vol. 2 (1850), p.225
16. JL 7, p.171
17. Ibid, pp.181–2
18. Dedication to *The Wanderer*, pp.9–10
19. *British Critic* 1 (April 1814), p.374
20. *Jane Austen's Letters*, op. cit., p.227
21. JL 7, p.195
22. Ibid, p.33n
23. Ibid, p.338
24. Ibid, p.339n
25. *The Letters of Sarah Harriet Burney*, op. cit., p.172
26. JL 7, p.259
27. Mem 3, p.426
28. JL 7, p.323
29. Ibid, p.352
30. *The Wanderer*, p.8
31. Jane Austen, *Northanger Abbey* (1972 edn), p.58
32. *The Wanderer*, p.7
33. Ibid, p.128
34. In a letter from Mrs Thrale to Dr Johnson of 28 April 1780, *The Letters of Samuel Johnson*, op. cit., vol. 2, p.350
35. *The Wanderer*, p.325
36. Ibid, p.289
37. Ibid, p.873
38. DL 1, p.400
39. *The Wanderer*, pp.175, 177
40. Macaulay, *Literary Essays*, op. cit., p.586
41. Reviews in *The Anti-Jacobin* 46, pp.347–51, and *European Magazine*, November 1814
42. *Quarterly Review* 11 (April 1814), p.124
43. Sir Walter Scott to Matthew Weld Hartstonge, 18 July 1814, *The Letters of Sir Walter Scott*, op. cit., vol. 3, p.465
44. Lord Byron to Lady Melbourne, 30 March 1814, see Grau, op. cit., p.66
45. William Weller Pepys to Hannah More, 22 June 1814, quoted in Grau, op. cit., p.89
46. *The Wanderer*, p.676
47. Ibid, p.354
48. Hemlow, p.339
49. George Saintsbury, *The English Novel*; see Grau, op. cit., p.139
50. Alexander d'Arblay, 'Observations on the last work of the Author of Evelina intitled "the Wanderer" '; '87 miscellaneous holographs', MS Berg
51. JL 7, p.274
52. Ibid, p.387
53. Ibid, p.396
54. Ibid, p.401
55. Ibid, p.468
56. JL 8, p.340
57. Ibid, p.352
58. Ibid, pp.355–6
59. *An Englishman in Paris, 1803*, op. cit., pp.38, 75
60. Ibid, p.75
61. JL 8, p.142
62. Ibid, p.356
63. 'Ma chère amie, tout est perdu! – je ne puis entrer dans aucun detail. de grace partez – le plutôt sera le mieux.' Ibid, p.58
64. Ibid, p.379
65. Ibid, p.389
66. Ibid, p.70
67. Ibid, p.108
68. Ibid, p.104
69. Ibid, pp.199–200
70. Ibid, p.419
71. Ibid, pp.183–4
72. Ibid
73. Ibid, p.169
74. Ibid, p.213
75. Ibid, p.431
76. Ibid, p.433
77. See Henri-Marie Ghislain, *Souvenirs* (1840), vol. 1
78. JL 8, p.439
79. Ibid, p.443
80. Ibid, p.441

81. Ibid, p.215
82. Ibid, p.445
83. Ibid, p.223
84. Ibid, p.446
85. Ibid, p.238
86. Ibid, p.273
87. Ibid, p.447
88. Ibid, p.450
89. Ibid, p.461
90. Ibid, p.530
91. Ibid, p.329
92. Ibid, p.114
93. Ibid, p.233
94. Alexander d'Arblay, '87 miscellaneous holographs', MS Berg, op. cit., folder 1
95. *The Wanderer*, p.230
96. JL 8, pp.285, 284
97. Printed, as is the 'Waterloo Journal', in JL 8
98. JL 8, p.543
99. Ibid, p.504
100. Ibid, pp.505–6
101. Ibid, p.506
102. Ibid, p.522
103. Ibid, p.535
104. Ibid, p.536
105. 'M. de Talleyrand m'a oublié: mais on n' oublie pas M. de Talleyrand.'
106. JL 8, p.539

CHAPTER 14: *Keeping Life Alive*

1. JL 9, p.2
2. Hemlow, p.384
3. Hayward, op. cit., vol. 2, p.339
4. JL 11, p.206
5. *Thraliana* 2, p.760n
6. Hemlow, p.387
7. JL 9, p.77
8. Hemlow, p.388
9. JL 9, p.76
10. Hemlow, p.389
11. JL 10, pp.485, 537
12. 'Tout le monde dira à Alex qui est sa mere, mais – qu'il n'oublie pas qui a été son pere! C'est pour cela que je lui ai consacré et fait faire se Portrait.' JL 11, p.14
13. I am indebted to Dr Scott Ashley for this suggestion
14. JL 10, p.607
15. Ibid
16. Ibid, p.686

17. John Jones, *The Mysteries of Opium Reveal'd*, quoted in Alethea Hayter, *Opium and the Romantic Imagination*, p.24
18. JL 10, p.699
19. Ibid, pp.701–3
20. See her later account in JL 11, p.552
21. E. Le Fevre to F. Leverton Harris, 27 January 1912, MS letter, grangerised edition of Madame d'Arblay's *Diary and Letters*, National Portrait Gallery
22. Diary, MS Berg
23. JL 11, p.542
24. JL 12, p.593
25. 'La mer, ma chere Fanny, est entre nous, mais bientôt je l'espere nous serons reunis, et d'ailleurs rien ne sera jamais entre nos coeurs; j'en jure par le mien.' Monsieur d'Arblay to Fanny Burney d'Arblay, 16 June 1817, JL 9, p.436
26. JL 9, p.392
27. Text of memorial printed in Mem 3, p.436
28. 'Report from the Committee on petition of Trustees of the British Museum relating to the Collection of the late Dr Burney', House of Commons, 17 April 1818
29. DL 6, p.347
30. See editorial notes by Warren Derry in JL 10, p.587
31. JL 10, p.850
32. Ibid, p.779
33. In the Berg Collection
34. JL 10, p.781
35. Ibid, p.879
36. Ibid, p.880
37. 'Je ne sais si ce sera le dernier mot – mais, ce sera la derniere pensée – Notre Reunion!' Ibid, p.907
38. Ibid, p.908
39. Ibid, pp.908–9
40. JL 2, pp.41–2
41. JL 11, p.39
42. Ibid, p.29
43. Ibid, p.36n
44. Ibid, p.15
45. Ibid, p.81
46. Ibid, p.170
47. JL 12, p.725
48. JL 11, p.192
49. Ibid, p.190
50. Ibid, p.191
51. Ibid, p.186

52. Ibid
53. Ibid, p.191
54. Details of this incident are in a letter from Charlotte Burney Francis Broome to Charlotte Barrett, 29 July 1817, MS Berg
55. Now in the Berg Collection
56. JL 11, p.18
57. Ibid, p.513
58. Quoted in Richard Holmes, *Shelley: The Pursuit*, p.340
59. Alexander d'Arblay, '87 miscellaneous holographs', MS Berg, op. cit.
60. JL 11, p.262
61. Ibid, p.314
62. Ibid, p.324
63. Ibid, p.315
64. Marianne Francis to Charlotte Barrett, MS Berg, quoted in JL 12, p.672n
65. JL 11, p.547
66. JL 12, p.836
67. Julia Barrett to Charlotte Burney Francis Broome, 31 October–1 November 1826, MS Barrett, Egerton 3700A, quoted in JL 12, p.672n
68. JL 12, p.361n
69. MS Berg, quoted in ibid, p.681n
70. MS Barrett, quoted in Hemlow, p.443
71. Quoted in R. Ellis Roberts, *Samuel Rogers and his Circle* (1910), p.172
72. *The Journal of Sir Walter Scott*, op. cit., entry for 18 November 1826
73. See JL 12, pp.630–1.
74. *The Journal of Sir Walter Scott*, op. cit., p.241
75. JL 12, p.700
76. Ibid, p.702
77. Ibid, p.700
78. Ibid, p.764
79. Ibid, p.766
80. Grau, op. cit., p.66
81. Ibid, p.139
82. Mem 1, p.ix
83. Mem 3, p.434
84. Macaulay, *Literary Essays*, op. cit., p.546
85. Mem 1, pp.67–8
86. Macaulay, *Literary Essays*, op. cit., p.593
87. JL 12, p.763
88. See Mem 3, p.361; Lonsdale, p.451
89. Grau, op. cit., p.139
90. For an account of their contentious relationship see E.S. de Beer, 'Macaulay and Croker', *Review of English Studies* vol.

10, no. 40, pp.389–97.
91. JL 12, p.840n
92. P. Cunningham, *Handbook of London* (1850), p.219
93. JL 12, p.842
94. MS Berg
95. *The Letters of Sarah Harriet Burney*, op. cit., p.392
96. MS Barrett, Egerton 3701A
97. JL 12, p.863
98. Ibid, p.864
99. For what little is known of her background, see ibid, p.864n
100. MS Barrett, Egerton 3702A
101. JL 12, p.873
102. MS Berg
103. MS Berg, quoted in JL 12, p.886n
104. MS Barrett, Egerton 3702A
105. Cornelia Cambridge to Charlotte Barrett, 21–3 January 1837, MS Barrett, Egerton 3705
106. JL 12, p.917
107. Quoted in Hemlow, p.483
108. DL 6, p.415
109. JL 12, p.954
110. Ibid, p.935
111. MS Barrett, quoted in Hemlow, p.482
112. JL 12, p.921
113. Ibid, pp.951, 950
114. Ibid, p.980
115. Hemlow, p.491

POST MORTEM

1. Henry Crabb Robinson, *Diaries*, 23 May 1842, quoted in *The Letters of Sarah Harriet Burney*, op. cit., p.459
2. Anonymous review in the *Athenaeum*, April 1842
3. *The Letters of Sarah Harriet Burney*, op. cit., p.463
4. Mem 2, p.143
5. Anna Laetitia Barbauld, *The British Novelists* vol. 38 (1810)

APPENDIX

1. DL 3, p.414
2. *The History of the Trial of Warren Hastings Esquire, late Governor-General of Bengal, Before the High Court of Parliament in Westminster-Hall*, 1796

BIBLIOGRAPHY

Works by Fanny Burney

Evelina; or The History of a Young Lady's Entrance into the World (1778), ed. with an introduction and notes by Margaret Anne Doody (Penguin Classics, 1994)

Cecilia; or Memoirs of an Heiress (1782), ed. Peter Sabor and Margaret Anne Doody (Oxford World's Classics, 1988)

Brief Reflections relative to the Emigrant French Clergy; earnestly submitted to the humane consideration of the Ladies of Great Britain (1793)

Camilla; or A Picture of Youth (1796), ed. Edward A. Bloom and Lillian D. Bloom (Oxford World's Classics, 1983)

The Wanderer; or Female Difficulties (1814), ed. Margaret Anne Doody, Robert L. Mack and Peter Sabor (Oxford World's Classics, 1991)

Memoirs of Doctor Burney, arranged from his own manuscripts, from family papers and from personal recollections by his daughter, Madame d'Arblay, 3 vols (1832)

Diary and Letters of Madame d'Arblay, edited by her Niece, 6 vols (1842–6)

The Early Diary of Frances Burney, 1768–1778, ed. Annie Raine Ellis, 2 vols (1889)

The Journals and Letters of Fanny Burney (Madame d'Arblay) 1791–1840, ed. Joyce Hemlow *et al*, 12 vols (1972–1984)

A Busy Day, ed. Tara Ghoshal Wallace (New Brunswick, 1984)

The Early Journals and Letters of Fanny Burney, 1768–1779, ed. Lars E. Troide and Stewart J. Cooke, 3 vols (1988–94)

The Complete Plays of Frances Burney, 2 vols, ed. Peter Sabor, Stewart J. Cooke *et al* (1995)

The Witlings, ed. Clayton J. Delery (Michigan, 1995)

Select Bibliography

(Unless otherwise stated, the following are first editions, published in London)

A to Z of Georgian London, introductory notes by Ralph Hyde (London, 1982)

Ackerman, R., *Microcosm of London* (1904)

Aiken, Jane, *Passion and Principle: The Lives and Loves of Regency Women* (London, 1996)

Anderson, W.E.K. (ed.), *The Journal of Sir Walter Scott* (1972)

Austen, Jane, *Northanger Abbey* (1818)

Balderston, K.C. (ed.), *Thraliana: The Diary of Mrs. Hester Lynch Thrale (later Mrs. Piozzi), 1776–1809*, 2 vols (1942)

Balderston, K.C., *The Age of Johnson* (1949)

Barbauld, Anna Laetitia, *The British Novelists* (1810)

Barrow, John (ed.), *Captain Cook's Voyages of Discovery* (1906)

Beaglehole, J.C., *The Life of Captain James Cook* (1974)

Beattie, William, *The Life and Letters of Thomas Campbell*, 3 vols (1850)

Blake, Robert, *Disraeli* (1966)

Blodgett, Harriet, *Centuries of Female Days: Englishwomen's Private Diaries* (Gloucester, 1989)

Boaden, James, *Memoirs of Mrs Siddons* (1827)

Brayley, Edward Wedlake, *A Topographical History of Surrey* (1872)

Brewer, John, *The Pleasures of the Imagination: English Culture in the Eighteenth Century* (London, 1997)

Broughton, V.D. (ed.), *Court and Private Life in the Time of Queen Charlotte: Being the Journals of Mrs Papendiek, Assistant Keeper of the Wardrobe and Reader to Her Majesty*, 2 vols (1887)

Burney, Charles, *The Cunning-Man*, translated from Jean Jacques Rousseau, *Le Devin du village* (1766)

Burney, Charles [and Burney, Esther Sleepe], *An essay towards a history of the principal comets that have appeared since 1742*, prefaced by a letter upon comets by M. de Maupertuis, trans. E. Burney (Glasgow, 1770)

Burney, Charles, *A General History of Music from the Earliest Ages to the Present Period*, 4 vols (1776–89)

Burney, James, *A Plan of Defence against Invasion* (1797)

Burney, James, *A chronological history of the discoveries in the South sea or Pacific ocean*, 5 vols (1803–17)

Burney, James, *An Essay by way of a Lecture, on the Game of Whist* (1821)

Burney, James (ed. Beverley Hooper), *With Captain James Cook in the Antarctic and Pacific: The private journal of James Burney Second Lieutenant of the Adventure on Cook's Second Voyage 1772–1773* (Canberra, 1975)

Burney, Sarah Harriet, *Clarentine* (1796)

Bury, J.T. and Barry, J.C. (eds), *An Englishman in Paris, 1803: The Journal of Bertie Greatheed* (1953)

Chapman, R.W. (ed.), *The Letters of Samuel Johnson with Mrs Thrale's Genuine Letters to Him*, 3 vols (Oxford, 1952)

Chisholm, Kate, *Fanny Burney: Her Life* (London, 1998)

Clark, Lorna J. (ed.), *The Letters of Sarah Harriet Burney* (Athens, Georgia, 1997)

Clarke, Isabel C., *Six Portraits* (1935)

Clayden, P.W., *Rogers and his Contemporaries* (1889)

Clifford, James, *Hester Lynch Piozzi* (2nd edn, Oxford, 1987)

Cobban, Alfred, *A History of Modern France*, 2 vols (1957–61)

Collier, Joel, *Musical Travels Through England* (1774)

Copeland, Edward and McMaster, Juliet, *The Cambridge Companion to Jane Austen* (Cambridge, 1997)

Corbin, Alain, *The Lure of the Sea: The Discovery of the Seaside 1750–1840* (1995)

Crisp, Samuel, *Virginia: A Tragedy* (London, 1754)

Crown, Patricia, *Drawings by E.F. Burney in the Huntington Collection* (San Marino, Cal., 1982)

Cunningham, P., *A Handbook of London* (1850)

Dawe, Donovan, *Organists of the City of London 1666–1850* (1983)

Day, James Wentworth, *King's Lynn and Sandringham through the Ages* (East Anglian Magazine Ltd, 1977)

Delany, Mary (ed. Lady Llanover), *The Autobiography and Correspondence of Mary Granville, Mrs Delany: with Interesting Reminiscences of King George the Third and Queen Charlotte*, 6 vols (1861–2)

Dobson, Austin, *Fanny Burney (Madame d'Arblay)* (1903)

Doody, Margaret Anne, *Frances Burney: The Life in the Works* (New Brunswick, 1988)

Edwards, Averyl, *Fanny Burney, 1752–1840: A Biography* (1948)

Epstein, Julia, *The Iron Pen: Frances Burney and the Politics of Women's Writing* (Wisconsin, 1989)

Farr, Evelyn, *The World of Fanny Burney* (1993)

Fordyce, James, *Sermons to Young Women*, 2 vols (1755)

Fraiman, Susan, *Unbecoming Women: British Women Writers and the Novel of Development* (New York, 1993)

Gandy, Michael, *Catholic Family History: A Bibliography of General Sources* (1996)

Gaussen, A.C.C. (ed.), *A Later Pepys: The Correspondence of Sir William Weller Pepys* (1904)

Gérin, Winifred E., *The Young Fanny Burney* (1961)

Gordon, George and Britton, John, *The Churches of London*, 2 vols (1838–9)

Grau, J.A., *Fanny Burney, An Annotated Bibliography* (New York, 1981)

Greville, Robert Fulke (ed. F.M. Bladon), *The Diaries of Colonel the Hon. Robert Fulke Greville, Equerry to His Majesty King George III* (1930)

Grierson, Sir H. (ed.), *The Letters of Sir Walter Scott*, 3 vols (1932)

Hahn, Emily, *A Degree of Prudery: A Biography of Fanny Burney* (1961)

Harting, Johanna H., *History of the Sardinian Chapel* (1905)

Hayter, Alethea, *Opium and the Romantic Imagination* (1968)

Hayward, A. (ed.), *Autobiography, Letters and Literary Remains of Mrs Piozzi (Thrale)*, 2 vols (1861)

Hedley, Olwyn, *Queen Charlotte* (1975)

Hemlow, Joyce, *The History of Fanny Burney* (1958)

Hemlow, Joyce, with Jeanne M. Burgess and Althea Douglas, *A Catalogue of the Burney Family Correspondence, 1749–1878* (New York, 1971)

Henry, D., *An Historical Account of the Curiosities of London and Westminster* (1767)

Hibbert, Christopher, *George III: A Personal History* (1998)

Highfill Jr, Philip H., Burnim, Kalman A. and Langhans, Edward A., *A Biographical Dictionary of Actors, Actresses, Musicians, Dancers, Managers & Other Stage Personnel in London, 1660–1800*, 16 vols (Carbondale, Illinois, 1973–93)

Hill, Constance, *Juniper Hall* (1904)

Hill, Constance, *The House in St Martin's Street: Being Chronicles of the Burney Family* (1907)

Hill, Constance, *Fanny Burney at the Court of Queen Charlotte* (1914)

Hill, Constance, *Good Company in old Westminster and the Temple, founded on the early reflections of A. Lefroy* (1925)

Hill, George Birkbeck (ed.), *Johnsonian Miscellanies*, 2 vols (1897, reprinted 1966)

Hill, George Birkbeck (ed.), revised and enlarged by Powell, L.F., *Boswell's Life of Johnson, Together with Boswell's Journal of a Tour to the Hebrides and Johnson's Diary of a Journey into North Wales*, 6 vols (1934)

Hogg, T.J., *Life of Percy Bysshe Shelley* (1906 edn)

Hole, Robert (ed.), *Selected Writings of Hannah More* (1996)

Holmes, Richard, *Shelley: The Pursuit* (1974)

Hough, Richard, *Captain James Cook: A Biography* (1994)

Hutton, W.H. (ed.), *Burford Papers: Being Letters of Samuel Crisp to his Sister at Burford, and other Studies of a Century (1745–1845)* (1905)

Hyde, Mary, *The Thrales of Streatham Park* (Cambridge, Mass. and London, 1977)

Johnson, R.B., *The Women Novelists* (1918)

Johnson, R.B., *Mrs Delany at Court and Among the Wits* (1925)

Johnson, R.B. (ed.), *The Letters of Hannah More* (1925)

Johnson, R.B. (ed.), *Fanny Burney and the Burneys* (1926)

Kelly, Linda, *Juniper Hall: An English Refuge from the French Revolution* (1991)

Kelly, Linda, *Richard Brinsley Sheridan: A Life* (1997)

Keyes, Jean, *A History of Women's Hairstyles 1500–1965* (1968)

Kilpatrick, Sarah, *Fanny Burney* (Newton Abbot, 1980)

Klima, Slava, Bowers, Gary and Grant, Kerry S. (eds), *Memoirs of Dr. Charles Burney 1726–1769*, edited from autograph fragments (Lincoln, Nebraska, 1988)

Lamb, Charles (ed. Jonathan Bate), *Elia and The Last Essays of Elia* (Oxford, 1987)

Lansdowne, Marquis of (ed.), *The Queeney Letters: Being letters addressed to Hester Maria Thrale by Doctor Johnson, Fanny Burney and Mrs Thrale-Piozzi* (1934)

Le Faye, Deirdre (ed.), *Jane Austen's Letters* (Oxford, 1995)

Lewis, Lady Theresa (ed.), *Extracts from the Journals and Correspondence of Miss Berry from the year 1783 to 1852*, 2 vols (1866)

Lewis, W.S. et al, *The Yale Edition of Horace Walpole's Correspondence*, 48 vols (1937–83)

Lillywhite, B., *London Coffee Houses* (1963)

Lloyd, Christopher, *St Vincent and Camperdown* (1963)

London County Council, *Survey of London: Vol XX, Trafalgar Square and Neighbourhood* (1940)

Lonsdale, Roger, *Dr. Charles Burney: A Literary Biography* (1965)

Lonsdale, Roger (ed.), *The Oxford Book of Eighteenth-Century Women Poets* (Oxford, 1989)

Macalpine, Ida and Hunter, Richard, *George III and the Mad-Business* (1969)

Macaulay, Thomas Babington, Lord, *Literary Essays contributed to the Edinburgh Review* (Oxford, 1913)

McIntyre, Ian, *Garrick* (1999)

Maldon, H.E. (ed.), *The Victoria History of the County of Surrey* (1911)

Manwaring, G.E., *My Friend the Admiral: The Life, Letters and Journals of Rear-Admiral James Burney FRS* (1931)

Masefield, Muriel, *The Story of Fanny Burney* (Cambridge, 1927)

Mitchell, R.J. and Leys, M.D.R., *A History of London Life* (1958)

More, Hannah, *Poems* (1816, reprinted with an introduction by Caroline Franklin, 1996)

Morris, H., *The Life of Charles Grant, sometime member of Parliament . . . and director of the East India Company* (1904)

Nairn, Ian and Pevsner, Nikolaus, *The Buildings of England: Surrey*, (2nd edn, 1971)

Nichols, John, *Literary Anecdotes of the Eighteenth Century*, 9 vols (1812–15)

Nichols, John, *Illustrations of the Literary History of the Eighteenth Century*, 8 vols (1817–58)

Pearson, Jacqueline, *Women's Reading in Britain 1750–1834: A Dangerous Recreation* (Cambridge, 1999)

Piozzi, Hester Lynch (Thrale), *Anecdotes of the late Samuel Johnson, LL.D, during the last twenty years of his life* (1786)

Plumb, J.H., *England in the Eighteenth Century* (1950)

Porter, Roy, *English Society in the Eighteenth Century* (1990)

[Raper, Frances], *Laura Valcheret: a tale for adolescence* (1814)

Ribeiro, Aileen, *The Art of Dress* (Yale, 1995)

Ribeiro, Alvaro, S.J., *The Letters of Dr Charles Burney 1751–1784* (Oxford, 1991)

Ribeiro, Alvaro, S.J. and Basker, James G. (eds), *Tradition in Transition: Women Writers, Marginal Texts, and the Eighteenth-Century Canon* (Oxford, 1996)

Richards, Paul, *King's Lynn* (Chichester, 1990)

Roberts, R. Ellis, *Samuel Rogers and his Circle* (1910)

Rogers, Pat, *Samuel Johnson* (Oxford, 1993)

Rolt, M.S. (ed.), *A great-niece's journals: Extracts from the journals of F.A. Burney (Mrs Wood) from 1830 to 1842* (1926)

Rowe, Elizabeth, *Friendship in Death in Twenty Letters from the Dead to the Living to which are added Letters Moral and Entertaining* (1733)

Rudé, George, *Paris and London in the Eighteenth Century* (1970)

Sadler, Thomas (ed.), *Diary, Reminiscences and Correspondence of Henry Crabb Robinson*, 3 vols (1869)

Sahlins, Marshall, *Islands of History* (Chicago, 1985)

Scholes, Percy A., *The Great Dr Burney: His Life, his Travels, his Works, his Family and his Friends*, 2 vols (Oxford, 1948)

Scholes, Percy A., *Dr. Burney's Musical Tours in Europe*, 2 vols (1959)

Scouten, Arthur H. *et al* (eds), *The London Stage 1660–1800*, 5 parts in 11 vols (Illinois, 1960–8)

Seeley, L.B. (ed.), *Fanny Burney and her Friends* (5th edn, London, 1908)

Sermoneta, Duchess of, *The Locks of Norbury: The Story of a Remarkable Family in the Eighteenth and Nineteenth Centuries* (1940)

Sheppard, Ronald, *Micklam: The Story of a Parish* (Mickleham, 1991)
Simons, Judy, *Fanny Burney* (1987)
Smith, J.T., *Nollekens and his Times* (1834)
Spencer, Jane, *The Rise of the Woman Novelist* (Oxford, 1986)
Staël-Holstein, Baronne de (Madame de Staël), *Lettres à Narbonne*, ed. G. Solovieff (Paris, 1960)
Stone, Lawrence, *The Family, Sex and Marriage in England 1500–1800* (1977)
Stow, John, *A Survey of London written in the year 1598* (Stroud, 1997)
Straub, Kristina, *Divided Fictions: Fanny Burney and Feminine Strategy* (Lexington, Kentucky, 1987)
Swinnerton, Frank, *A Galaxy of Fathers* (1966)
Tames, Richard, *Soho Past* (1994)
Tomalin, Claire, *The Life and Death of Mary Wollstonecraft* (1974)
Tomalin, Claire, *Jane Austen: A Life* (1997)
Tomkins, J.M.S., *The Popular Novel in England 1770–1800* (1932)
Trevor-Roper, P., *The World Through Blunted Sight* (1970)
Turner, Cheryl, *Living by the Pen: Women Writers in the Eighteenth Century* (1992)
Vickery, Amanda, *The Gentleman's Daughter: Women's Lives in Georgian England* (Yale, 1998)
Wain, John, *Samuel Johnson* (1974)
Watkins, John, *Characteristic Anecdotes of Men of Learning and Genius* (1808)
Weiner, Margery, *The French Exiles 1789–1815* (1940)
White, T.H., *The Age of Scandal* (1950)
Williams, H. (ed.), *The Poems of Jonathan Swift*, 2 vols (1937)
Winton, M., *Vintage King's Lynn* (Hendon Publishing, 1976)
Wollstonecraft, Mary, *A Vindication of the Rights of Woman* (1792)
Woolf, Virginia, *The Common Reader*, 2nd series (1986)
Zonitch, Barbara, *Familiar Violence: Gender and Social Upheaval in the Novels of Frances Burney* (Newark, 1997)

Essays, Articles and Monographs

Benkovitz, Miriam, 'Dr Burney's Memoirs', *Review of English Studies*, vol. 10, no. 39 (1959), pp.257–68
Bloom, Lillian D. and Edward A., 'Fanny Burney's Novels: The Retreat from Wonder', *Novel: A Forum on Fiction* 12 (1979), pp.215–35
Broadley, A.M., 'The Rariora of Tea and the Tea Gardens', *Country Life* (14 June 1913), pp.875–8
Copeland, Edward W., 'Money in the Novels of Fanny Burney', *Studies in the Novel* 8 (1976), pp.24–37
de Beer, E.S., 'Macaulay and Croker: The Review of Croker's Boswell', *Review of English Studies*, vol. 10, no. 40 (1959), pp.388–97
Firminger, Walter K., 'Madame D'Arblay and Calcutta', *Bengal Past and Present* vol. 9 (1914), pp.244–9

Gandy, Michael, 'Catholics in Westminster: The Return of Papists of 1767',
Westminster History Review 2 (1998), pp.19–22

Greenfield, Susan C., ' "Oh Dear Resemblance of Thy Murdered Mother": Female
Authorship in *Evelina*', *Eighteenth-Century Fiction* 3 (1991), pp.301–20

Hemlow, Joyce, 'Fanny Burney and the Courtesy Books', *PMLA* 65 (1950),
pp.732–61

Hemlow, Joyce, 'Fanny Burney, Playwright', *University of Toronto Quarterly* xix
(1950), pp.70–89

Kris, Kathryn, 'A 70-Year Follow-up of a Childhood Learning Disability: The Case
of Fanny Burney', *Psychoanalytic Study of the Child* 38 (1983), pp.637–53

MacNaghten, Angus, 'The Recluse of Chessington Hall', *Country Life* (9 March
1967)

Morley, Edith J., 'Sarah Harriet Burney', *Modern Philology* 39 (November 1941),
pp.123–58

Pearson, Jacqueline, ' "Crushing the Convent and the Dread Bastille . . .": The
Anglo-Saxons, Revolution and Gender in Women's Plays of the 1790s',
Appropriations of Anglo-Saxon History, ed. Donald Scragg (Cambridge, 1999)

Porter, Roy and Moore, Antony R., 'Preanesthetic Mastectomy: A Patient's
Experience', *Surgery* 83 (February 1978), pp.200–5

René-Martin, Linda, 'A Burney Among the Jews: At Prayer in Early
Nineteenth-Century Brighton', *Jewish Quarterly* no. 174 (1999), pp.38–40

Ribeiro, Alvaro, S.J., ' "The Chit-Chat Way": The Letters of Mrs Thrale and Dr
Burney', *Tradition in Transition*, ed. A. Ribeiro and J. Basker (Oxford, 1996)

Roberts, W. Wright, 'Charles and Fanny Burney in the Light of the New Thrale
Correspondence in the John Rylands Library', *Bulletin of the John Rylands
Library*, vol. 16, no. 1 (January 1932)

Rogers, Pat, 'Sposi in Surrey', *Times Literary Supplement* (23 August 1996)

Waddell, J.N., 'Additions to OED from the writings of Fanny Burney', *Notes and
Queries* 225 (1980), pp.27–32

Waddell, J.N., 'Fanny Burney's Contribution to English Vocabulary',
Neuphilologische Mitteilungen 81 (1980), pp.260–3

Womersley, David, 'Fanny's First Plays', *Times Literary Supplement* (16 February
1996), p.27

INDEX